# THE ROUTLEDGE HANDBOOK OF LAW AND THE ANTHROPOCENE

*The Routledge Handbook of Law and the Anthropocene* provides a critical survey into the function of law and governance during a time when humans have the power to impact the Earth system.

The Anthropocene is a "crisis of the earth system." This book addresses its implications for law and legal thinking in the twenty-first century. Unpacking the challenges of the Anthropocene for advocates of ecological law and politics, this handbook pursues a range of approaches to the scientific fact of anthropocentrism, with contributions from lawyers, philosophers, geographers, and environmental and political scientists. Rather than adopting a hubristic normativity, the contributors engage methods, concepts, and legal instruments in a way that underscores the importance of humility and an expansive ethical worldview. Contributors to this volume are leading scholars and future leaders in the field. Rather than upholding orthodoxy, the handbook also problematizes received wisdom and is grounded in the conviction that the ideas we have inherited from the Holocene must all be open to question.

Engaging such issues as the Capitalocene, Gaia theory, the rights of nature, posthumanism, the commons, geoengineering, and civil disobedience, this handbook will be of enormous interest to academics, students, and others with interests in ecological law and the current environmental crisis.

**Peter D. Burdon** is Associate Professor at Adelaide Law School, University of Adelaide, Australia.

**James Martel** is Professor of Political Science at San Francisco State University, USA.

"This book opens up along a new horizon of what Anthropocene might mean for human juridical responsibility. Exceptionally interdisciplinary, this is a tapestry of perspectives that eschews romanticisation and remains critical throughout, reaching back to the indigenous roots of first laws and extending to new takes on geoengineering. This is a truly planetary book and perhaps its main lesson is this: that human exceptionalism must and can be translated into human responsibilisation with regards to our planet. If you want to find the tools to do this, read this book."

**Andreas Philippopoulos-Mihalopoulos**, *The Westminster Law & Theory Lab, London*

"Burdon and Martel have brought us an exciting and diverse collection of interdisciplinary essays that address today's most urgent and critical questions. The authors marshal a strikingly wide range of conceptual resources, inspiring us to reimagine the human and the rules by which we live. It is abounding in creativity when we most need it!"

**Hasana Sharp**, *McGill University, Canada*

# THE ROUTLEDGE HANDBOOK OF LAW AND THE ANTHROPOCENE

*Edited by*
*Peter D. Burdon and James Martel*

Routledge
Taylor & Francis Group
a GlassHouse Book

Designed cover image: © Getty Images /studio023

First published 2023
by Routledge
4 Park Square, Milton Park, Abingdon, Oxon OX14 4RN

and by Routledge
605 Third Avenue, New York, NY 10158

*Routledge is an imprint of the Taylor & Francis Group, an informa business*

A Glasshouse book



*British Library Cataloguing-in-Publication Data*
A catalogue record for this book is available from the British Library

ISBN: 978-0-367-43978-1 (hbk)
ISBN: 978-1-032-48249-1 (pbk)
ISBN: 978-1-003-38808-1 (ebk)

DOI: 10.4324/9781003388081

Typeset in Bembo
by Deanta Global Publishing Services, Chennai, India

# CONTENTS

# CONTRIBUTORS

Sam Adelman – School of Law, University of Warwick, UK.

Afshin Akhtar-Khavari – School of Law, Queensland University of Technology, Australia.

Ira Allen – Departments of English and Politics & International Affairs, Northern Arizona University, USA.

Kirsten Anker – Faculty of Law, McGill University, Canada.

Mark Antaki – Faculty of Law, McGill University, Canada.

Kathleen Birrell – La Trobe Law School, Latrobe University, Australia.

Klaus Bosselmann – Faculty of Law, University of Auckland, New Zealand.

Kerryn Brent – Adelaide Law School, University of Adelaide, Australia.

Peter Burdon – Adelaide Law School, University of Adelaide, Australia.

Rom Coles – Independent activist and scholar.

Erin Daly – Delaware Law School, Widener University, USA.

Felix Dube – Faculty of Law, North-West University, South Africa.

Kate Galloway – Griffith Law School, Griffith University, Australia.

Geoffrey Garver – Leadership for the Ecozoic Initiative, McGill University, Canada.

Paul Govind – Macquarie Law School, Macquarie University, Australia.

Nicole Graham – Sydney Law School, University of Sydney, Australia.

Anna Grear – School of Law and Politics, Cardiff University, UK.

Lia Haro – Independent activist and scholar.

Lachlan Hoy – School of Law, Queensland University of Technology, Australia.

Anatoli Ignatov – Sustainable Development Department, Appalachian State University, USA.

Rakhyun E. Kim – Copernicus Institute of Sustainable Development, Utrecht University, Netherlands.

Louis J. Kotzé – Faculty of Law, North-West University, South Africa

Michelle Lim – Singapore Management University, Yong Pung How School of law, Singapore.

Dina Lupin – School of Law, University of Southampton, UK.

Daniel Matthews – School of Law, University of Warwick, UK.

James Martel – Department of Political Science, San Francisco State University, USA.

Renisa Mawani – Department of Sociology, University of British Columbia, Canada.

Karen Morrow – Hillary Rodham Clinton School of Law, Swansea University, UK.

Emily Ray – Faculty of Political Science, Sonoma State University, USA.

Benjamin J. Richardson – Faculty of Law, University of Tasmania, Australia.

Han Somsen – Tilburg Law School, Tilburg University, Netherlands.

Prue Taylor – School of Architecture and Planning, University of Auckland, New Zealand.

Sally Wheeler – College of Law, Australian National University, Australia.

# INTERROGATING THE ANTHROPOCENE

*Peter Burdon and James Martel*

Research handbooks contain large chapters of exceptionally focused research. The aim is to find a balance that will serve a novice who is approaching a research area for the first time and a specialist who is seeking to expand the parameters of their knowledge. At best, a handbook should provoke a reader and encourage them to re-think long held assumptions or dogma that has become entrenched in a discipline.

To encourage these outcomes, we employed several strategies. First, the contributors to this handbook are inter-disciplinary scholars who go beyond juxtaposing disciplines and seek integration and interaction (Klein 2010). For example, Earth Systems Science is put into conversation with a conceptual block from law, history, philosophy, and other sciences such as ecology. The impact is to create something new – a theoretical innovation – where the original elements maintain some of their original integrity (Harvey 2000). Alongside inter-disciplinary scholarship, another dominant theme in this handbook is critique. By critique we don't mean trashing but a generative process whereby a scholar brings to the surface the underlying assumptions or presuppositions of a concept/discipline that is not apparent in its everyday self-description. Critique, as Ben Golder (2021) notes, has a unique role to play in times of crisis because it can open ways of thinking that have been disguised by a certain curation of facts.

Another strategy involved the kinds of authors we approached to contribute to this handbook. The first were leading experts whose inclusion required no justification. The second are authors who have never previously published on the Anthropocene but whose work we respect for its creativity and ability to transcend disciplinary countries. We also wanted people who would view our subject with fresh eyes and write in a way that was unencumbered by the weight of tradition and specialization: people, in other words, who would approach this work without the same assumptions and prejudices that build up around any scholarly activity. In taking this approach we are consciously upholding and affirming the idea of amateurism in scholarship. This claim is ripe for misrepresentation so let us be clear. In presenting this view we are not affirming a lack of rigor or shallow analysis. Rather we are affirming Edward Said's vision of a scholar who is

> moved not by profit or reward but by love for and unquenchable interest in the larger picture, in making connections across lines and barriers, in refusing to be died down to a speciality, in caring for ideas and values despite the restrictions of a profession.
>
> *(1996, 76)*

For Said, this role has an edge to it, and he argues that it cannot be done without

> a sense of being someone whose place it is publicly to raise embarrassing questions, to confront orthodoxy and dogma (rather than to produce them), to be someone who cannot easily be co-opted by governments or corporations, and whose *raison d'etre* is to represent all those people and issues that are routinely forgotten or swept under the rug.
>
> *(1996, 11)*

We all know people who fit this description. But as Said alludes, there are pressures that get in the way of fulfilling this function. One that Said unpacks is the pull toward specialization, which he describes as a gradual narrowing of knowledge and scope of concern. It may also result in self-censorship unless one is certified by the proper authorities, knows the lingua franca or a discipline, and can cite the right authorities (1996, 77). Expertise of this kind is not necessarily a bad thing, but Said argues that when such competence "involves losing sight of anything outside one's immediate field … and the sacrifice of one's general culture to a set of authorities and canonical ideas" then, Said argues, "competence of that sort is not worth the price paid for it" (1996, 76).

Usefully, Said draws a distinction between "expertise" and "knowledge" and affirms writing that is "fuelled by care and affection rather than by profit and selfish, narrow specialisation" (1996, 82). To be an amateur in this sense is to be someone who "considers that to be a thinking and concerned member of society, one is entitled to raise moral issues at the heart of even the most technical and professionalized activity" (1996, 83). The Anthropocene fits that description, and we hold out Said's description of the amateur as a disposition that encourages us to expand our methodological approach and think from as many different perspectives as possible.

While a great variety of issues can certainly benefit from Said's approach, we cannot think of a subject that needs it more urgently than the question of the environmental crisis and the Anthropocene. Indeed, we are using the word "crisis" with some reservation insofar as that word suggests a dire moment that will come and go, but we may well be facing a permanent alteration in the global condition. The nature of the crisis is so acute that it offers both the grave danger that existing ways of thinking (the very ways that helped to get us where we are today) will only be reinforced and doubled down upon, as well as a chance to radically re-think everything, every assumption, every understanding of systems, both human and non-human, that we thought we knew and understood – and hence controlled – so well. In this case, even those experts who have warned us for decades about the coming crisis that is now upon us need to have their conceptions be supplemented with new kinds of thinking. Recognizing that in effect the climate crisis trumps most other political and social issues in that the very context in which those issues occur is itself under threat, people who have not thought all that much about the environment are now suddenly highly motivated to do so. This handbook tries to capture that new attention as well as new thoughts that are generated by previous scholars who are more familiar with questions of environmentalism but for whom the scope of their work must also out of necessity expand and change.

Part I, "First Laws," deals with various modes of engaging with the Anthropocene through the lens of Indigenous and non-Western practices. In their essay "The Problem with Sustainable Development in the Anthropocene Epoch," Louis J. Kotzé, Sam Adelman, and Felix Dube argue against the notion of sustainable development by showing its own contribution to producing the Anthropocene. They do so through the lens of Ubuntu, which offers an entirely different approach to thinking about the human relationship to the environment (as well as to one another). In "The Sovereign Order of Tiŋa," Anatoli Ignatov looks to another African-based practice of Tiŋa in order to challenge European (and Eurocentric) notions of sovereignty to show a model of what he calls an "African ecology-based sovereignty," as a way to engage in and enhance Earth jurisprudence. In "The Superfactual Anthropocene and Encounters with Indigenous Law," Kirsten Anker and Mark Antaki argue against a romanticized version of Indigenous approaches to ecology, arguing that Indigenous legal practices offer concrete and – from the perspective of Western legal practices – radical possibilities that are critical for engaging in the Anthropocene in ways that do not merely replicate the problem.

Part II, "Subjects of the Anthropocene" deals with questions of legal and personal subjectivity and the way that they intersect with, and sometimes resist, the kinds of categories that come out of Western modes of political and legal thought which have contributed so much to producing and exacerbating the Anthropocene. In "the Anthropocene Archie," Kathleen Birrell explores the ways that the material world is itself subject to the kinds of hierarchies and isolations that come from Western thought more generally. Even as the law has extended the concept of "rights" to include rivers and other natural objects, such an extension does not preclude but rather reinforces the way that rights and the larger schema of Western subjectivity only adds to the determinations that have led to the Anthropocene in the first place.

In "We Earthbound People," Dan Matthews argues that constituent power, the modes by which people form and act within a community, must be rethought in ways that recognize forms of mutuality and collective purpose that go beyond the confines of the nation state and other forms of political divisiveness. Matthews asks how we can think about our ongoing project of "demogenesis" (the self-creation of a people) in new and powerful ways. In "Chastened Humanism in a Necrotic Anthropocene," Ira Allen argues that, rather than abandon the insights of humanism (some of which he readily admits have led to the current environmental catastrophe), we need to turn to a more "chastened" form of the above, neither denying that we have a form of agency in the world nor thinking that such agency is a ticket for complete mastery and domination of the world around us and of one another.

Part III, "Landscapes of Hope and Despair" focuses on those spaces in the environment whose condition is governed by regimes of law and governance. To this end, Paul Govind and Michelle Lim examine the way property law breaks up the living world into discrete units, each with an individual owner with decision-making authority. Property rights, they argue, build a culture of separation, hierarchy, and subordination, and are inappropriate for responding to the advent of the Anthropocene. With a particular focus on biodiversity, they argue instead for an ethic of human responsibility which is place-based and responsive to the more-than-human world.

Following this, we turn to two papers that foreground the ocean in discussions of the Anthropocene. In "The Law of the Sea: Ocean, Ships, and the Anthropocene," Renisa Mawani emphasizes the importance of Grotius's writings on the law of the sea in establishing patterns of colonialism, dispossession, extraction, and violence that continue to this day. Prue Taylor picks up on this extractive view of the ocean and argues that international governance regimes have thus far failed to account for ocean acidification by mandating reductions in carbon emissions. In response, Taylor calls for the emergency closure of all oceans outside of national jurisdictions as a method for protecting Earth's largest ecological system and to buy humanity time to fully confront the existential crisis ushered in by the Anthropocene.

The final chapter in this part takes us from the land and sea to outer space. While the Anthropocene challenges writers to think in terms of an Earth system, Emily Ray is interested in the anthropogenic forces beyond our own planet. Of particular concern is the way the political and economic logic that gave rise to the Anthropocene on Earth has been exported through modes of resource extraction, transportation, advertising, and the exertion of sovereignty over planets. As Ray contends, these developments require urgent democratic input and critical evaluation as part of our response to the Anthropocene.

Part IV is concerned with the development of ecological and Earth systems law. This has been the most significant legal response to the Anthropocene, and authors were challenged to consider the extent to which concepts derived from the ecological sciences remain relevant in the context of an Earth system. Rakhyun E. Kim argues that for international environmental law to stay relevant when the Earth system crosses irreversible tipping points, it needs to shift away from its traditional focus on restoring the past and play an active role in making planetary futures. This includes rethinking of notions of stewardship whereby humans consciously attempt to regulate the Earth system in a non-hubristic way. Following this, Klaus Bosselmann and Geoffrey Garver both interrogate the concept of ecological integrity and defend its relevance in the Anthropocene. In "Collapse or Sustainability" Bosselmann argues that ecological integrity ought to provide a normative re-orientation of states and function as a Grundnorm that states can follow in developing law and policy. In similar terms, Garver reorientates ecological integrity so that it is inclusive of human impact and supportive of mutually enhancing human–Earth relations.

In Part V, "Dignity and Human Rights," the question of legal rights is explored as being either an aid or a hindrance to larger issues of dealing with dislocation and disruption of the Anthropocene. In "The Anthropocene and Human Rights," Karen Morrow argues that there are resources within the current practice of international human rights law that can be drawn upon to better address collective human needs in the face of a changing world. While these practices do not tend to be dominant in international legal practices, Morrow offers examples of these types of supports and shows why we should expand upon them as a basis for future – and better – practices. In "Dignity in the Anthropocene," Erin Daly and Dina Lupin argue that one of the key consequences of the Anthropocene is a clearer focus on the collective agency of human actors. They argue that the concept of dignity is a way to enhance the collective in the face of legal forms that have tended to emphasize individual actors at the expense of the collective.

Many of the themes explored thus far grapple with a fundamental tension – the complexity and increasing unpredictability of the Earth system and the need for human beings to accept our responsibility in regulating parts of nature. In Part VI, "Regulating Nature and the Rule of Law," Han Somsen confronts this through the prism of the rule of law. For Somsen, the notion of "regulating nature" should be reconceptualized as "nature regulates" and "nature rules supreme." This view places emphasis on the autonomous sources of regulation that emerge from the Earth system and challenges pronouncements of human supremacy that are fundamental to the rule of law. Kerryn Brent, by contrast, pushes the importance of human regulation to its logical end through an analysis of solar geoengineering. While often relegated to a "boo word," Brent considers the conditions under which geoengineering can form part of our response to the Anthropocene. Acknowledging that there can be no pure answer, Brent engages in risk–tradeoff analysis to underline the importance of decision makers engaging with solar engineering in an open and democratic way that accounts for value judgements and alternative notions of risk. To close out this part, Romand Coles and Lia Haro draw inspiration from smart energy grids to propose a new form of grassroots regulation. Their concept of a "smart political energy grid" offers insight into how environmental politics might function in a way that is dynamic and highly responsive to a range of actors including industry, civil society, and government.

In Part VII, "Imagination and Utopia," the authors there think about how to envision ourselves living beyond and through the Anthropocene. What stories should we tell ourselves, and how can we think about a world in which human beings have so much power and so much responsibility? In "Imagined Utopias," Benjamin J. Richardson focuses on both literary and actual acts of imagination that help us to think our way forward in the face of the Anthropocene. He argues that even dystopian imaginations can help us to think about what we want and don't want as we move into this new and challenging era. In "Myth in the Anthropocene," Peter Burdon and James Martel examine certain myths, some classical and some contemporary, as ways to get our minds around the enormity of what we are facing and how we might take some lessons from these narratives to help us make our way in a world that is unprecedented even as many of its conditions have been predicted in the past. In "The Nomos of Creativity in the Anthropocene," Afshin Akhtar-Khavari and Lachlan Hoy argue that in our imagining about the Anthropocene, we must not rely exclusively on human perspectives. They argue for a new consideration based on the nomos but more in the spirit of Whitehead than Schmitt. Here, the non-human must be taken in as part of how a nomos can be constructed and encountered by human actors. in "Learning Ecological Law," Kate Galloway and Nicole Graham argue that legal education, even as it bears some responsibility for perpetuating models of legal subjectivity that are responsible for the contemporary and ongoing crisis, have resources that can work towards changing the way that we think about our individual and collective forms of responsibility and thus can be an important part of how we change the way we think and act in the face of the Anthropocene.

Finally, our postscript is a conversation between two inter-disciplinary scholars – Sally Wheeler and Anna Grear. Given the emphasis this handbook has on deep notions of relationships, we brought these scholars together to engage in topics ranging from the corporate form to emerging notions of materiality. The chapter also serves as a model for the kinds of deep, honest, and respectful engagements we hope that this handbook will generate.

Before closing, as editors we note that the handbook was written and assembled during the Covid-19 pandemic. Like many people, the virus touched us personally and caused us to say goodbye to family, friends, and colleagues before their time. The handbook is dedicated to those people and was completed out of a sense of fidelity to our common struggle. We also thank Shani Burdon for her invaluable assistance formatting footnotes and the authors for their patience, goodwill, and creativity in bringing this handbook together.

Peter Burdon & James Martel

*– Adelaide/Berkeley, July 2022.*

## References

Golder, B. 2021, 'From the Crisis of Critique to the Critique of Crisis', *University of Colorado Law Review*, 92(4), 1065–1078.

Harvey, D. 2000. *Reinventing Geography*. New Left Review. https://newleftreview.org/issues/ii4/articles/david-harvey-reinventing-geography

Klein, J. 2010. 'A Taxonomy of Interdisciplinarity', in R. Frodeman et al. (eds.), *The Oxford Handbook of Interdisciplinarity*, 15–30. Oxford University Press.

Said, E. 1996. *Representations of the Intellectual*. Vintage.

# PART I

# First Laws

# 1

# THE PROBLEM WITH SUSTAINABLE DEVELOPMENT IN THE ANTHROPOCENE EPOCH

## Reimagining International Environmental Law's Mantra Principle Through Ubuntu

*Louis J. Kotzé*, Sam Adelman**, and Felix Dube****

An alternative (and somewhat less subtle) title for this chapter, whose inspiration we draw from Springer (2016), could have been *Fuck Sustainable Development*. That would have left no doubt whatsoever as to where we stand in relation to one of environmental law's oldest and most foundational principles. Our message would have been unequivocally blunt, requiring little further contemplation or the need to justify our position. Such a title might have made a powerful point but would also have inevitably closed down the uncomfortable debate, which is now more urgent than ever before, addressing the exigencies of the Anthropocene, which Biermann and Kalfagianni (2020) say is a debate that must confront the delusions and panaceas that sustainable development creates and perpetuates. Given that the Anthropocene is itself not an uncontroversial notion, some caution that while it helpfully illuminates Anthropos' assumed telluric force and geological power, it also tends to unfairly universalize "the human" impact on Earth's system (Hornborg 2019; Grear 2015). Returning to our title, perhaps its provocativeness might also have stifled a conversation about the need to urgently replace the predatory paradigm of sustainable development with alternative epistemologies of care and humility that are better able to reframe and pursue the well-being of the entire living order in an equal and just way.

---

* Research Professor, North-West University South Africa; Senior Professorial Fellow in Earth System Law, University of Lincoln, United Kingdom. Research for this paper was supported by the South African National Research Foundation (NRF) under grant agreement number 118746. All opinions expressed here, and conclusions arrived at, are those of the authors and cannot be attributed to the NRF.

** Reader, University of Warwick, United Kingdom; Research Associate, North-West University, South Africa; Research Associate, Nelson Mandela University, South Africa. Research for this paper was undertaken as a British Academy/Leverhulme Senior Research Fellow 2020–2021.

*** Postdoctoral fellow, North-West University, South Africa.

DOI: 10.4324/9781003388081-2

A central argument in this chapter is that sustainable development has become so deeply embedded in international environmental law that it has become a quasi-constitutional principle. Sustainable development came of age in 1987, when the world acknowledged that it stood on the edge of an ecological precipice due to the "limits to growth" (Meadows et al. 1972). These initial motivations that generated the notion of sustainable development were positive in that its proponents sought to achieve social justice through development that is sustainable. They understood the increasing severity of the environment-development contradiction arising from the biophysical limits to endless growth, leading to multiple conflicts over dwindling natural resources. However, sustainable development as it is currently understood is different from its original conception. It has changed from being a "discourse of resistance, fusing radical environmental consciousness with a critical rethinking of a failed development enterprise" that focused on "scarcity and limits, affluence and poverty, global inequality, and the environmental viability of westernization," to one that helps to legitimize the "grand universal project of neoliberal globalization" (Carruthers 2001, 93). As we argue in this chapter, sustainable development was bedeviled from the outset by the contradiction between endless economic growth and environmental protection. Its acceptance by developed Western countries was contingent upon a greener form of capitalism, but it was not inevitable that they should be neoliberal. The fact that sustainable development has largely conformed to neoliberal orthodoxies (especially market fundamentalism) reflects the context in which it emerged in the last quarter of the twentieth century. Action on climate change and biodiversity loss, for example, reflects the belated understanding that markets tend to drive rather than prevent environmental degradation (Naess 2016). In this regard, the link between ecological modernization, sustainable development, green capitalism, and neoliberalism is important, as discussed by Adelman (2018).

Neoliberalism is an equally contested overarching paradigm within which the notion of sustainable development is ensconced (Kumi, Arhin, and Yeboah 2014). "It is potentially quite dangerous to simply stick our heads in the sand and collectively ignore a phenomenon that has had such devastating and debilitating effects on our shared world" (Springer 2016, 285). It is important, we believe, to demonstrate how popular but dangerous ideas such as sustainable development are complicit in perpetrating inequality and injustice. We instead need to recognize and reveal easily ignored and cunningly veiled realities that are perpetuated by paradigms such as sustainable development. Not unlike Earth's stratigraphy, these realities provide evidence of progressively invasive patterns of human mastery on Earth that have now become very evident in the Anthropocene and that lie buried beneath and within centuries-old layers of corporate greed, political opportunism, appropriation, slavery, colonialism, imperialism, patriarchy, ecocide, and (some privileged) humans' systemically entrenched entitlement that feeds off an increasingly vulnerable living order (Fineman and Grear 2013).

Our contention in this chapter is that sustainable development is not a socio-ecologically friendly concept and legal principle that can support the well-being of the entire living order in the Anthropocene epoch. It has instead contributed, and continues to exacerbate, the conditions that are responsible for creating the Anthropocene and its deepening socio-ecological crisis. We develop our argument first by briefly taking stock of sustainable development's history and legacy. We do so through the lens of the Covid-19 pandemic, which reemphasizes the extent of global inequality and injustice that are characteristic of the Anthropocene epoch, and that paradigms like sustainable development entrench and exacerbate. Second, we reflect on the ubiquitous influence of sustainable development on institutions concerned with human development through a focus on international environmental law. While our discussion is largely confined to international environmental law for the sake of brevity, we examine the principle's tenacious constitutional law-like grip on international environmental law and governance efforts that generally seem to benefit only a few at the expense of billions of vulnerable people and rapidly declining Earth system integrity. Third, with the aim of reimagining an alternative to sustainable development, we argue for the need to be open to other ways of seeing, being, and knowing that can replace hubristic epistemologies of dominance and mastery with alternative epistemologies of humility and care that international environmental law (among many other social institutions) must embrace in order to promote ecological sustainability. To that end, we employ the African notion of *Ubuntu*. We will argue that as an environmental ethic, *Ubuntu* promotes ideas of care, custodianship, and stewardship, and the kind of thinking that also underpins the rights of nature in Andean and Maori cosmovisions. To this end, *Ubuntu* is an African onto-epistemology that might stand alongside other Indigenous worldviews to provide alternative ways of seeing, being, and knowing to those we have become used to under the destructive reign of sustainable development.

## Welcome to the Anthropocene: Sustainable Development and Covid-19

In many ways, the Covid-19 pandemic illustrates the deeply uneven geological epoch we live in. Still to be officially formalized, this epoch is referred to as the Anthropocene, in which the privileged human (*Anthropos*) exercises decisive telluric force on an increasingly vulnerable living order. The pandemic highlights the broad and deep anthropogenic civilizational and existential crisis of the Anthropocene that has been created and is still perpetuated by social institutions such as law, where sustainable development continues to play a highly negative role that cannot be resolved by returning to pre-pandemic normality (which was in fact profoundly unjust and abnormal).

The pandemic is linked to unsustainable neoliberal models of development that drive biodiversity loss and facilitate zoonotic transmission of viruses (Adelman and Paliwala 2022). The pandemic also emphasizes the rapaciousness of a global economy that intensifies the vulnerability of the human and more-than-human world, notably to the extent that global economic development has become an existential transnational threat whose consequences will likely be dwarfed by the impacts of climatic harms (Barbier and Burgess 2020). The pandemic has clearly exposed the underlying precariousness and vulnerability of socio-economically disadvantaged communities that are driven by the ideological imperatives of neoliberal development, which is the hegemonic model of development around the world (Adelman and Paliwala 2022). It has done so by laying bare the divergent levels of resilience and capacities to find safety, security, and protection against disease and loss of livelihoods that sustainable development is supposed to eradicate.

We should, however, also take care not to overemphasize the similarities between Covid-19 and climate change. Grundmann (2021, e737) argues that the differences between them outweigh the similarities. The most significant difference is the timescales of responses to these emergencies and the scale of financial resources thrown at the pandemic in contrast to climate change. One of the main similarities is uncertainty in scientific knowledge, which is intrinsic to climate science but perhaps less so in virology and immunology. Denialism and conspiracy theories are common to both threats. In both cases, there is an irreconcilable tension between the economic orthodoxies about growth and profit and protecting human life. A less substantial similarity is the role of social institutions such as the United Nations Framework Convention on Climate Change in climate governance and that of the World Health Organization in dealing with the pandemic. But as we argue, the greatest similarity between these transboundary threats is the disproportionate vulnerability of the poor, particularly in the Global South (see Zang et al. (2021) show the close correlation between vulnerability arising from Covid-19 and climate change. The hierarchies and exclusions of race, gender, and socio-economic class are apparent during Covid-19 (Krieger 2020). This correlation reveals the stark differences that exist with respect to the abilities of people to be resilient, as well as the different levels of risk faced by the socially distanced rich in gated communities and the inhabitants of favelas forced to choose between eating and dying (United Nations 2015). Few will disagree that the least vulnerable benefiting the most from neoliberal development are usually those that are more resilient and better protected from the interlinked impacts of global disruptors such as climate change and pandemics.

Vaccine nationalism further exposes the hollowness of the empty rhetoric of the ever-elusive "global partnership for sustainable development" in the 2030 Agenda for Sustainable Development and the 17 Sustainable Development Goals (SDGs) and the 169 targets in it. The rhetoric of North-South cooperation and solidarity in the Agenda is not accompanied by the provision of financial resources, with the result that poor developing countries with weak adaptive capacities and public health systems are forced into a renewed cycle of indebtedness in order to deal with a global health crisis (Leal Filho et al. 2020). In this way, the predatory neoliberal global economic order is kept alive and well.

The immediacy and urgency of the Covid-19 pandemic, especially when considered in the larger context of other disruptors such as climate change, underscores the imperative to embark on a different future trajectory to promote the well-being of the entire living order in the Anthropocene. It is difficult to envisage how sustainable development can steer us onto such a trajectory. Sustainable development is deeply implicated in the myriad social (and specifically *legal*) systems, institutions, processes, and practices that have created the problems it is ostensibly designed to solve, as we shall see below. Paradoxically, given its radical pretensions, sustainable development's entwinement with neoliberalism has turned it into a deeply conservative and even reactionary ideology that protects elite vested interests. It is an anthropocentric epistemology of dominance over vulnerable entities rather than an epistemology of humility and care for the entire living order.

## Sustainable Development and International Environmental Law

The form in which a new concept emerges and the extent to which it is adopted and popularized is closely linked to expertise and ideological, financial, and political power. Powerful actors are able to frame issues, set the parameters of legitimacy, and confine what is acceptable within mainstream limits (Barnett and Duvall 2005). This is also the case with the concept of sustainable development. It is noticeable how few, if any, of the myriad definitions of sustainable development – and certainly not the SDGs – promote the radical transformation required to deal with exigencies of the Anthropocene such as climate change, biodiversity loss, and the Sixth Mass Extinction (Kotzé et al. 2022). How and why has sustainable development become a problem instead of a solution?

The Brundtland Commission's 1987 report laid the foundations for sustainable development to unfold in lockstep with neoliberalism. Sustainable development was essentially popularized through the Brundtland Report to accommodate industrial capitalism in a "green" eco-modernist way for at least two reasons. First, sustainable development could not be allowed to impede profits yielded by the exploitation of natural resources. Second, it was assumed that technological solutions to environmental destruction and climate change would be delivered by the sort of market fundamentalism promoted by neoliberal dogma and the techno-fetishism hyped by ecological modernization (Harvey 2003). The report has had far-reaching impacts on social institutions such as international environmental law during the past quarter century, as we shall see below. The Commission's impossible brief was to square the circle of growth as a precondition for development and environmental protection:

> The Brundtland definition of sustainable development possessed a conceptual ambiguity that made it palatable to the widest possible audience. It was broad enough to capture the energy of this environmental reawakening and to resonate with the increasingly international nature of popular thinking about environmental problems. Its central concern for equity with present and future generations retained sufficient idealism to garnish the support of ecological purists and advocates for distributive justice. Yet its vague, contradictory stance on ecological limits and economic processes weakened that very threat, leaving just enough wiggle room so that pro-growth economists, business leaders, and governments could also comfortably embrace the concept.
>
> *(Carruthers 2001, 99)*

The Commission defined sustainable development as "development that meets the needs of present generations without compromising the ability of future generations to meet their own needs" (World Commission on Environment and Development 1987, 43). This definition has become dominant but not consensual. One study published 15 years ago estimated that there were more than 140 "alternative and variously-modified" definitions of sustainable development (Johnston et al. 2007, 60), many of which are mutually exclusive (Redclift 2007, 66), with the inevitable result that it has become a term that is "increasingly regarded either as internally self-contradictory (an oxymoron) or, at best, plagued by ambiguous or distorted definitions" (Johnston et al. 2007, 60). It is precisely sustainable development's malleability that renders it so attractive and so easily appropriable despite the fact that its normative power is fundamentally at odds with its failure to protect the environment (Adelman 2018). It is endlessly remolded to legitimize environmental degradation in which it is complicit, to popularize government policies that prioritize growth over environmental protection in the weakest possible understanding of the term (Hopwood, Mellor, and O'Brien 2005), and to greenwash corporate social responsibility reports (De Freitas Netto et al. 2020).

After the World Conference on Environment and Development in 1987, sustainable development rapidly gained widespread support and was quickly insinuated into the operation of many social institutions to the extent that its arch proponent, Jeffrey Sachs celebrates the past 30 years as "the age of sustainable development" (Sachs 2015). More importantly for present purposes, sustainable development has deeply penetrated legal and policy domains, especially international environmental law, with sustainable development having since become a cornerstone of international environmental law, *if not its core principle* (Lang 1995). It is not unreasonable to maintain that the trajectories of sustainable development and international environmental law have overlapped to the extent that they have virtually had a common history since 1987. The links between development, environmental protection, and international environmental law were already tentatively drawn at the 1972 Stockholm Conference on the Human Environment and became progressively more explicit at consecutive global environmental conferences (Kotzé and French 2018).

As the first global environmental conference, Stockholm provided the context for ensuing deliberations and the framing of subsequent global environmental norms. As the name of this conference indicates, this context was thoroughly anthropocentric, and as we now know, one of the perverse consequences of an anthropocentric principle such as sustainable development is that it actually undermines human interests. It should be noted (in passing, however), that the solution is not to replace anthropocentrism with a combination of bio- and ecocentrism, thereby replacing the nature-society dualism with another one; the problem is centric thinking (Philippopoulos-Mihalopoulos 2015). Sustainable development is also mentioned in 12 of the 27 principles in the Rio Declaration on Environment and Development that was adopted at the Earth Summit in 1992 and that established the United Nations Framework Convention on Climate Change (UNFCCC). In these early days of ecological modernization and green capitalism, nature was treated as a reservoir of resources and services ripe for commodification (Spaargaren, Mol, and Buttel 2000). The underlying assumption of these environmental conferences was therefore that the environment exists to satisfy human needs and must therefore be *sustainably developed* for their benefit, health, well-being, and prosperity despite incontrovertible evidence of the mutual dependency of the well-being of the entire living order on planetary integrity (Kotzé 2018, 46). In this context, sustainable development has managed to facilitate a partial and selective greening of capitalism. It acknowledged limits to growth but displayed faith that markets and ecological modernization could provide ways of overcoming the absolute biophysical limits described by Earth system science. Brand and Wissen argue that, like

> "sustainable development" twenty years ago, Green Economy has become the norm for what is politically possible and plausible; at the same time, as in the case of sustainable development, it works to either obscure alternatives or make them seem unviable and irrational.
>
> *(Brand and Wissen 2015, 37)*

Intimately related to the foregoing, a core problem in international environmental law-making is the requirement that multilateral environmental agreements should be adopted by consensus. First, this tends to result in compromises around lowest common denominators and militates against the radical social and legal transformations required to deal with global disruptors such as climate change. Second, multilateral environmental agreements (MEAs), such as the Paris Climate Agreement and other quasi-legal political instruments such as the SDGs, reflect the power imbalances between developed and developing countries that often deprive the latter of ownership of their own development through the imposition of ideologies such as sustainable development. Aid, loans, capacity-building, technology transfer, and so forth, are turned into conditionalities that require compliance with the neoliberal orthodoxies of the International Monetary Fund and the World Bank. It remains the case that:

> [T]he World Bank and other institutions, far from disseminating recipes for development that will benefit all sectors of society, are constructing a legitimizing ideology that conceals the contradictions of capitalism as a global system, translates its structural requisites into a universal programme, and re-presents it as a remedy for the very human ills it generates.
>
> *(Cammack 2002, 160)*

In view of its embeddedness in international environmental law, one might argue that sustainable development has even assumed an international constitutional law-like character. Given the nature of the climate and environmental emergencies confronting us, the UNFCCC and the Paris Climate Agreement may be viewed as international "constitutional moments" similar to the adoption of the United Nations Charter in 1945 (Kotzé 2019a). Considering the failure of the climate regime to date, we should be wary of overestimating their global constitutional significance (Bodansky 2009), but the Conferences of the Parties to the UNFCCC and other multilateral environmental agreements nonetheless function as quasi-constitutional assemblies and deliberative fora for states to generate international legal frameworks, norms, rules, principles, governance institutions, and conflict resolution structures, and to agree on guiding "constitutional" principles of international environmental law that reflect, as legal principles generally do, the essence of environmental law, "its way of being and appearing, its physiognomy, its soul or spirit" (Alpa 1994, 2). And even if these complex regimes consisting of agreements and institutions fail to achieve their goals, they inevitably lead to facts on the ground that determine how environmental policies are to be conducted. This is so because MEAs delimit possibilities and the scope of what is regarded as legitimate. As COP 26 in Glasgow demonstrated, the Paris Climate Agreement is a constitution-like document that contains principles and procedural rules that must be adhered to. But this does not mean that actions undertaken within such a global constitutional arrangement necessarily solve environmental problems. Indeed, the main fallback position following the failure in Glasgow was to re-emphasize the *hope* that the ratcheting mechanism in the Agreement will eventually reconcile at some future point in time the disparity between the targets in Article 2 and the promises in the nationally determined constitutions of state parties.

Sustainable development in its Brundtland guise has been fully absorbed through these global constitutional-like processes into international environmental law, and it has even shaped (or *constituted*) the content, form, and objectives of many, if not most, multilateral environmental agreements (Guruswamy 2010, 231; Kotzé 2016). It has become so integral to the international environmental law endeavor that some scholars are convinced of the existence of a new body of law called "international sustainable development law" (Segger 2004). Whether or not one concurs with Cordonier-Segger, sustainable development appears to function as the foundational "constitutional" principle (or Kelsenian *Grundnorm*) of international environmental law, as international environmental law's raison d'etre, guiding objective, and of more concern, as its (sometimes) well-meaning, but persistently and deeply flawed, core ethical orientation (Guruswamy 2010, 233). International environmental lawyers have, therefore, at least to some extent, also been complicit in entrenching a socio-ecologically destructive understanding of sustainable development in a body of law whose overarching goal should be to advance environmental protection in pursuit of ecological sustainability rather than economic development (Kotzé 2019, 437–445). The SDGs, adopted by the UN General Assembly three months before the UNFCCC negotiated the Paris Climate Agreement in December 2015, are the political institutionalization of sustainable development. Unlike the Paris Climate Agreement, which is binding but unenforceable, the SDGs are neither binding nor enforceable. However, their influence on political action and social mobilization is patchy at best. The SDGs are intimately linked with international environmental law to the extent that many of the objectives of international environmental law overlap with and find expression in the goals, while international environmental law must help achieve (although it could also inhibit) the implementation of the SDGs, and of course, vice versa (French and Kotzé 2018).

The architects of the SDGs never ventured beyond the confines of weak anthropocentric sustainable development and therefore dogmatically reinforce the neoliberal human development agenda that has shaped international environmental law for half a century (Kotzé 2018, 49). If the aim of the SDGs was genuine ecological sustainability, their drafters would not have aimed so low. Lack of normative ambition clearly remains a significant defect of international environmental law and its associated political programs such as the SDGs (Kotzé 2019b). Moreover, the appearance of cross-cultural agreement about the SDGs says more about global power structures and hegemonic ideas of neoliberal development and neoliberal than what is actually required to reimagine well-being for the entire living order. In the absence of finance and explicit ecological metrics against which its targets and goals can be measured, the SDGs seem to be more concerned with appearance than reality. Apparent international consensus between industry and society, between countries, between the rich and the poor, between the privileged and the exploited, is more important than a viable planet (Hornborg 2009).

Part of the problem with the SDGs is that they are (similar to their central pillar of sustainable development), open-ended, contested, or vague, and have no baselines or poor yardsticks by which they can be measured. For example, although the aim of ending poverty seems unexceptionable, it is based upon the World Bank's definition of the extreme poor as those living on less than $1.90 a day – a problematic monetary measure that excludes broader measures of human and environmental well-being (World Bank n.d. accessed on 17 November 2021). Indicators are problematic and are widely critiqued as "reductionist analytical tools and their use risks oversimplification, particularly in highly complex and contested contexts" (Mair et al. 2018, 43). Randers et al. describe the difficulties involved in measuring SDGs against sustainability baselines and their compatibility with the planetary boundaries' framework. This arises in part from the tension between the three overtly "environmental" goals (SDGs 13, 14, and 15) and the other 14 "socio-economic" goals (Randers et al. 2019). The "environmental goals" fail, partly, because capitalism can be greened but never become environmentally friendly. The SDGs also contain many vague, hortatory aims; specific targets are commonly not linked to baselines by which ecological sustainability can be measured. An example is Goal 7.3, which says "By 2030, double the global rate of improvement in energy efficiency." Another is the aim of Goal 13 on climate change, to "[T]ake urgent action to combat climate change and its impacts," which is so vague as to be almost meaningless, as are its three accompanying targets. One of the subsidiary aims, "of mobilizing jointly $100 billion annually by 2020" is measurable but has not been realized since the commitment was made by developed countries at COP 15 in Copenhagen in 2006 and was yet again missed at COP 26.

The prioritization of non-environment goals is also a result of political-business cycle dynamics: short-term economic growth and ill-conceived ideas of development that trump the pursuit of longer-term planetary integrity while creating a vicious cycle that subordinates planetary integrity. And this goes to the heart of concerns related to the ontological design and ethical orientation of the SDGs which are fully "constituted," shaped, and steered by sustainable development: their focus is seen to remain on "growth and use of resources … and [it] departs from an individual, not collective, point of view"; while the goals remain

> underpinned by strong (Western) modernist notions of development: sovereignty of humans over their environment (anthropocentricism), individualism, competition, freedom (rights rather than duties), self-interest, belief in the market leading to collective welfare, private property (protected by legal systems), rewards based on merit, materialism, quantification of value, and instrumentalization of labor.
>
> *(Van Norren 2020, 453)*

The conclusion of a recent mid-term assessment of the literature investigating the ecological steering effects of the SDGs is that, on balance, the SDGs are not fully geared towards steering, and actually capable of facilitating, the pursuit of planetary integrity in any meaningful way (Kotzé et al. 2022). Another study supports this view, namely, that "environmental destruction [has not been] avoided with the Sustainable Development Goals" (Zeng et al. 2020).

In sum, the history of sustainable development's embeddedness and constitutional tenacity in international environmental law and quasi-legal development visions such as the SDGs suggests that we should not expect it to promote or ensure planetary integrity. In reality, "[U]nder the paradigm of sustainable development, current international [environmental] law has been unable to shape a real or equitable answer to the global ecological crisis" (Manzano et al. 2016, 382).

## *Ubuntu* as an Alternative Way of Seeing, Being, and Knowing

We have argued that the idea and the *reality* of sustainable development are at odds with the exigencies of the Anthropocene, which are amplified by the Covid-19 pandemic. Many critics argue that sustainable development should be reinterpreted, but in our view, the concept is unsalvageable because its intrinsically contradictory nature produces promises that are unattainable (Redclift 2007). Myriad attempts to reconceptualize it have borne little fruit, partially because its conceptual components – "the environment," "environmental protection," and its peculiar deployment of the core idea of "sustainability" – are continually at risk of becoming irrelevant as a result of the erosion of species boundaries, advances in climate and environmental science, and technological innovation (Kim 2021). We urgently need new principles to inform social institutions, including for international environmental law, that can better guide human behavior in the Anthropocene to promote the well-being of the entire living order in an equitable and just way while preserving planetary integrity.

A precondition for reframing and reimagining our current regulatory regimes is openness to alternative ways of seeing, being, and knowing that produce epistemologies of care and humility instead of hubristic epistemologies of dominance and mastery such as sustainable development (Adelman 2015). Epistemologies of care and humility are predicated upon a "relational sense of solidarity that recognizes that the subjugation and suffering of one is in fact indicative of the oppression of all" (Springer 2016, 289). We need conceptual frameworks commensurate with the scale and urgency of the demands of the socio-ecological crisis of the Anthropocene – the "radical new openings" that Redclift (2007, 71) calls for that can steer us away from the ecological destruction that sustainable development facilitates.

In the remainder of this chapter, we tentatively outline the possibilities offered by the African notion of *Ubuntu* as one example of such an epistemology of care and humility. Whereas other Indigenous cosmovisions such as *buen vivir* and *Kaitiakitanga* have led to legal changes (Ranta 2020; Johnson 2013), Indigenous African onto-epistemologies such as *Ubuntu* are relatively underdeveloped despite the adoption of the concept by South Africa's Constitutional Court and its lower courts. Acknowledging parallels between South Africa and the incorporation of Andean cosmovisions into the legal systems of Bolivia, Colombia, and Ecuador, reflected in a growing number of innovative, heterogeneous decisions on the rights of nature (Álvez-Marín et al. 2021), we believe that there is a kernel of *Ubuntu* that can be productively used to protect nature.

> *Ubuntu* can be used as an onto-epistemological principle through which the well-being of the entire living order can be reimagined; therefore, as an alternative to sustainable development, it has the potential to "infuse humans with a consciousness of wholeness and interdependence, on each other and their natural surroundings, including a spiritual level of being."
>
> *(Van Norren 2020, 440)*

*Ubuntu* is a sub-Saharan onto-epistemology and ethical framework. It has gained purchase as a constitutional value, a practice, and a philosophy in the region, particularly in South Africa (Terreblanche 2018, 169). *Ubuntu* has been defined in various ways, for example, as:

> A collection of values and practices that people of Africa or of African origin view as making people authentic human beings. While the nuances of these values and practices vary across different ethnic groups, they all point to one thing – an authentic individual human being is part of a larger and more significant relational, communal, societal, environmental and spiritual world.
>
> *(Mugumbate and Chereni 2020, v)*

The meaning of *Ubuntu* is related to its etymology in South African Nguni languages such as isiZulu and essentially refers to "human nature; humanness, good disposition of heart" (Bryant 1905, 455). A person who does not live by *Ubuntu* "has no humanness of heart, no feeling for another" (Bryant 1905, 455). Reflecting on its essence of relationality, Van Norren explains that *Ubuntu* means "the continuous motion of the enfoldment of the universe ... Abstract Ubu, brought to life by the life force Ntu," also understood as "'I am because we are' (a person is a person through other persons)" (Van Norren 2020). Grear argues that relationality illuminates the "agentic entanglement [of humans] with a planetary field of radically distributed, multiplicitous agentic forces" (Grear 2020, 358). *Ubuntu* is rooted in relationality, caring, and sharing in which humanness is derived from membership of a community of beings, where "the humanity of an individual is only complete if it re-affirms that of others" (Chibvongodze 2016, 157). *Ubuntu* is an ontology that "stresses the value of compassion and relatedness, and 'life as mutual aid'"; it "does not know the word development" and instead stresses the idea of "humaneness" in all human and non-human relations (Van Norren 2020, 439). This is a core element in a philosophy about "how we ought to relate to the other – what our moral obligation is towards the other (both human and non-human)" (Le Grange 2015, 304). *Ubuntu*, therefore, views humans as an essential part of the non-human world, that who we are is inextricably linked to others. Our identity emerges from positive relationships with others, including non-humans, and not in opposition to or isolation from them; in essence "our deepest moral obligation is to become more fully human and to achieve this requires one to enter more deeply into community with others" (Le Grange 2015, 304).

Although the concept appears to be anthropocentric, Chibvongodze convincingly shows this is not the case: "the epitomisation of *Ubuntu* centres on the consolidation of the human, natural and spiritual tripartite" (Chibvongodze 2016, 157). In this sense, *Ubuntu* aligns with *ukama* (relatedness), a Shona word implying relationship and an understanding of reality in terms of interdependence (Horsthemke 2015).

> *Ubuntu* is about *beingness* and the interconnectedness of humanity and the environment. It provides an alternative framework of looking at the issue of ethical conduct and values, which is principally derived from the experiences of people in sub-Saharan Africa. From *Ubuntu* metaphysics, we derive an ontology that is communitarian and an ontological essence of "liveliness" or vitality.
>
> *(Etieyibo 2017, 650)*

In the environmental context, *Ubuntu* has been deployed, if only still conceptually, to counter neoliberalism's tendency to undermine community agency and to promote environmental protection (Terreblanche 2018, 181). Terblanché-Greeff contends that *Ubuntu* can be used to develop a relational alternative to sustainable development consistent with degrowth theories (Terblanché-Greeff 2019). It has been invoked to introduce an Indigenous African perspective into the discourse on environmental protection against the backdrop of colonialism (Van Breda 2019, 438). Van Breda argues that *Ubuntu* includes a commitment to save Earth from the greed of humanity through "ecological or ecospiritual social work" (Van Breda 2019, 438). In a similar vein, Terreblanche contends that *Ubuntu* is a living ethics that "embodies an ecological ethics that could inspire socialist imaginaries in the battle against climate change" (Terreblanche 2018, 168), while Kelbessa argues that environmental policies in Africa can benefit by applying the principles of *Ubuntu* to climate change and environmental destruction (Kelbessa 2014). The underlying assumption of these scholars is that the essential elements of *Ubuntu* (humility, relationality, humaneness, compassion for others; and concern for their well-being) can be used to promote environmental protection.

Although *Ubuntu* emerged in precolonial times in Southern Africa as a maxim governing human behavior and a reproach against inhumane conduct, it became a *legal principle* and a constitutional value in post-apartheid South Africa when it was invoked in the name of reconciliation and healing of a deeply divided society. The interim 1993 South African Constitution (Act 200 of 1993), which paved the way for the final constitution – the Constitution of the Republic of South Africa, 1996 – contained a post-amble that called for *Ubuntu* rather than vengeance for colonial and apartheid excesses during the transition to democracy. The Constitutional Court has since elevated *Ubuntu* to a constitutional value despite the fact that it is not explicitly mentioned as a constitutional value in the final constitution. The Constitutional Court regards *Ubuntu* as an Indigenous value that should form part of South African constitutional law in order to create an inclusive jurisprudence that recognizes the value of Indigenous maxims and norms in adjudication, as was held in *S v Makwanyane* (para 306). It was, for example, used by the Constitutional Court to proscribe the death penalty in 1995 in *S v Makwanyane*. The apex court held that the death penalty is incompatible with a democratic country that prides itself in respecting human rights and dignity. Today, South African courts invoke *Ubuntu* in cases ranging from constitutional law to contract law (Himonga, Taylor, and Pope 2013, 369; Hutchison 2019; Du Plessis 2019).

While no South African court has yet relied on *Ubuntu* to adjudicate an environment-related dispute, we believe it is only a matter of time before this happens. Courts will be able to draw on a series of precedents in which *Ubuntu* has been recognized, albeit in the broader context of social justice (*Everfresh Market Virginia (Pty) Ltd v Shoprite Checkers (Pty) Ltd*, para 71). Relying on *Ubuntu* in an environmental context could offer courts an opportunity to appreciate that human conduct that imperils the livelihoods of others, such as building coal-fired powerplants close to poor informal settlements, places the survival of such communities in peril by endangering the foundations of life on which their survival depends. As an Indigenous way of seeing, being, and knowing, *Ubuntu* stands in direct contrast to sustainable development's anthropocentric, top-down, techno-managerial framing of socio-ecological breakdown and unrelatedness, individual autonomy, and human mastery that reproduce hierarchy while ignoring the insights of Indigenous onto-epistemologies about relationality and the vulnerability of our deeply intertwined relationships with other vulnerable humans and the non-human world (see Fineman and Grear 2013). *Ubuntu* promotes humility and care for others, and views humans not as independent, self-sufficient individuals but instead as part of the larger community of life that supports them. *Ubuntu's* incorporation into South African law and jurisprudence suggests that seemingly impenetrable epistemic, ontological, and regulatory closures of law might be more receptive to the type of urgent legal (and possibly even deep constitutional) change needed in the Anthropocene.

## Conclusion

Since the publication of *Our Common Future* in 1987, sustainable development has become the hegemonic conception of development (Heydon 2019). "[I]t has prompted so many business, government, academic, and nongovernmental publications and gatherings that it has been dubbed 'the mantra that launched a thousand conferences'" (Carruthers 2001, 93). Like the idea of development, it has spawned an industry that is promoted through the vested interests of scholars, lobbyists, politicians, and development economists. As Upton Sinclair acidly observed,

"[I]t is difficult to get a man to understand something when his salary depends on his not understanding it" (Sinclair 1935, 243).

To the extent that it conceals predatory and destructive development practices and the dire state of planetary integrity and the well-being of the living order in the Anthropocene, sustainable development reinforces hierarchical relationships between the powerful and other vulnerable humans and with the vulnerable non-human world. It is falsely presented as the solution to the "ineffectiveness of our laws and institutions to curb the environmental burden of modern civilization" (Richardson 2011, 3). The core problem with sustainable development is that it deepens the problems it pretends to solve because it is oxymoronic: endless compound growth on a finite planet cannot be ecologically sustainable (Adelman 2018). Sustainable development's intrinsic contradiction, therefore, makes it incapable of mediating irreconcilable tensions between economic growth and extractive development on the one hand and ecological sustainability on the other.

These tensions have been laid bare in the Anthropocene, a crisis of hierarchy characterized by climatic harms and the Covid-19 pandemic, among other disruptors (Grear 2015). The pandemic demonstrates that orthodoxies seemingly settled in stone can be overturned in a few months to confront a crisis that demands different ways of seeing, being, and living. Climate change is a larger crisis that will endure long into the future. It cannot be solved through sustainable development, which epitomizes Einstein's observation that insanity is repeatedly doing the same thing but expecting different results. We know what the problem is, what we need to do, and we have the means to do it. The problem is the collective failure of political will to bring about radical structural transformation. Finding new, different, and better ways of being human by learning from non-Eurocentric onto-epistemologies such as *Ubuntu* may enable us to better address the Anthropocene's socio-ecological crisis, from which humanity might just still recover, before it becomes a catastrophe from which there is no way back.

## References


Adelman, Sam. 2015. "Epistemologies of Mastery." In *Research Handbook on Human Rights and the Environment*, edited by A. Grear, and L. J. Kotzé, 9–27. Cheltenham: Edward Elgar.

Adelman, Sam. 2018. "The Sustainable Development Goals: Anthropocentrism and Neoliberalism." In *Sustainable Development Goals: Law, Theory and Implementation*, edited by Duncan French, and Louis Kotzé, 15–40. Cheltenham: Edward Elgar.

Adelman, Sam, and Abdul Paliwala. 2022. "Shifting the Frame from Law in Development and Ending Injustice." In *Beyond Law and Development: Resistance, Empowerment and Social Injustice*, edited by Sam Adelman, and Abdul Paliwala, 19–39. London: Routledge.

Alpa, Guido. 1994. "Principles of Law." *Annual Survey of International and Comparative Law* 1(1):1–37.

Álvez-Marín, Amaya, Camila Bañales-Seguel, Rodrigo Castillo, Claudia Acuña-Molina, and Pablo Torres. 2021. "Legal Personhood of Latin American Rivers: Time to Shift Constitutional Paradigms?" *Journal of Human Rights and the Environment* 12(2):147–176. doi: 10.4337/jhre.2021.02.01.

Barbier, Edward B., and Joanne C. Burgess. 2020. "Sustainability and Development after Covid-19." *World Development* 135:105082. doi: 10.1016/j.worlddev.2020.105082.

Barnett, Michael, and Raymond Duvall, eds. 2005. *Power in Global Governance*. Cambridge: Cambridge University Press.

Biermann, Frank, and Agni Kalfagianni. 2020. "Planetary Justice: A Research Framework." *Earth System Governance* 6:100049. doi: 10.1016/j.esg.2020.100049.

Bodansky, Daniel. 2009. "Is There an International Environmental Constitution?" *Indiana Journal of Global Legal Studies* 16(2):565–584. doi: 10.2979/gls.2009.16.2.565; https://www.repository.law.indiana.edu/ijgls/vol16/iss2/8.

Brand, Ulrich, and Markus Wissen. 2015. "Strategies of a Green Economy, Contours of a Green Capitalism." In *Handbook of the International Political Economy of Production*, edited by Kees van der Pijl, 508–523. Cheltenham: Edward Elgar Publishing.

Bryant, Alfred T. 1905. *A Zulu-English Dictionary*. Cape Town: Juta.

Cammack, Paul. 2002. "Neoliberalism, the World Bank, and the New Politics of Development." In *Development Theory and Practice: Critical Perspectives*, edited by Uma Khothari, and Martin Minogue, 157–178. London: Palgrave.

Carruthers, David. 2001. "From Opposition to Orthodoxy: The Remaking of Sustainable Development." *Journal of Third World Studies* 18(2):93–112. doi: https://www.jstor.org/stable/45193956.

Chibvongodze, Danford T. 2016. "*Ubuntu* Is Not Only About the Human! An Analysis of the Role of African Philosophy and Ethics in Environment Management." *Journal of Human Ecology* 53(2):157–166. doi: 10.1080/09709274.2016.11906968.

De Freitas Netto, Sebastião Vieira, Marcos Felipe Falcão Sobral, Ana Regina Bezerra Ribeiro, and Gleibson Robert da Luz Soares. 2020. "Concepts and Forms of Greenwashing: A Systematic Review." *Environmental Sciences Europe* 32(1):1–12. doi: 10.1186/s12302-020-0300-3.

Etieyibo, E. 2017. "*Ubuntu* and the Environment." In *The Palgrave Handbook of African Philosophy*, edited by A. Afolayan, and T. Folala, 633–657. New York: Palgrave Macmillan.

Fineman, Martha Albertson, and Anna Grear, eds. 2013. *Vulnerability: Reflections on a New Ethical Foundation for Law and Politics*. London: Routledge.

French, Duncan, and Louis J. Kotzé. 2018. "Introduction." In *Sustainable Development Goals*, edited by Duncan French, and Louis J. Kotzé, 1–12. Cheltenham: Edward Elgar.

Grear, Anna. 2015. "Deconstructing Anthropos: A Critical Legal Reflection on 'Anthropocentric' Law and Anthropocene 'Humanity'." *Law and Critique* 26(3):225–249. doi: 10.1007/s10978-015-9161-0.

Grear, Anna. 2020. "Legal Imaginaries and the Anthropocene: 'Of' and 'For'." *Law and Critique* 31(3):351–366. doi: 10.1007/s10978-020-09275-7.

Grundmann, Reiner. 2021. "Covid and Climate: Similarities and Differences." *Wiley Interdisciplinary Reviews: Climate Change* 12(6):e737:1–7. doi: 10.1002/wcc.737.

Guruswamy, Lakshman. 2010. "Energy Justice and Sustainable Development." *Colorado Journal of International Environmental Law and Policy* 21(2):231–276. doi: https://scholar.law.colorado.edu/articles/231.

Harvey, David. 2003. "The Fetish of Technology: Causes and Consequences." *Macalester International* 13(1):3–30. doi: http://digitalcommons.macalester.edu/macintl/vol13/iss1/7.

Heydon, James. 2019. *Sustainable Development as Environmental Harm: Rights, Regulation, and Injustice in the Canadian Oil Sands*. 1st ed. New York: Routledge.

Himonga, Chuma, Max Taylor, and Anne Pope. 2013. "Reflections on Judicial Views of Ubuntu." *Potchefstroom Electronic Law Journal* 16(5):369–427. doi: 10.4314/pelj.v16i5.8.

Hopwood, Bill, Mary Mellor, and Geoff O'Brien. 2005. "Sustainable Development: Mapping Different Approaches." *Sustainable Development* 13(1):38–52. doi: 10.1002/sd.244.

Hornborg, Alf. 2009. "Zero-Sum World: Challenges in Conceptualizing Environmental Load Displacement and Ecologically Unequal Exchange in the World-System." *International Journal of Comparative Sociology* 50(3–4):237–262. doi: 10.1177/0020715209105141.

Hornborg, Alf. 2019. "Colonialism in the Anthropocene: The Political Ecology of the Money-Energy-Technology Complex." *Journal of Human Rights and the Environment* 10(1):7–21. doi: 10.4337/jhre.2019.01.01.

Horsthemke, Kai. 2015. *Animals and African Ethics*. New York: Palgrave Macmillan.

Hutchison, Dale. 2019. "From Bona Fides to Ubuntu: The Quest for Fairness in the South African Law of Contract." *Acta Juridica* 1:99–126.

Johnson, Jay T. 2013. "Kaitiakitanga: Telling the Stories of Environmental Guardianship." In *A Deeper Sense of Place: Stories and Journeys of Indigenous-Academic Collaboration*, edited by Jay T. Johnson, and Soren C. Larsen, 127–138. Corvallis: Oregon State University Press.

Johnston, Paul, Mark Everard, David Santillo, and Karl-Henrik Robert. 2007. "Reclaiming the Definition of Sustainability." *Environmental Science and Pollution Research International* 14(1):60–66. doi: 10.1065/espr2007.01.375.

Kelbessa, Workineh. 2014. "Can African Environmental Ethics Contribute to Environmental Policy in Africa?" *Environmental Ethics* 36(1):31–61. doi: 10.5840/enviroethics20143614.

Kim, Rakhyun E. 2021. "Taming Gaia 2.0: Earth System Law in the Ruptured Anthropocene." *The Anthropocene Review* 9(3): 1–14.

Kotze, Louis. 2019. "International Environmental Law and the Anthropocene's Energy Dilemma." *Environmental and Planning Law Journal* 36(5):437–458.

Kotzé, Louis J. 2016. *Global Environmental Constitutionalism in the Anthropocene*. Oxford: Hart Publishing.

Kotzé, Louis J. 2018. "The Sustainable Development Goals: An Existential Critique Alongside Three New-Millennial Analytical Paradigms." In *Sustainable Development Goals*, edited by Duncan French, and Louis J Kotzé, 49–65. Cheltenham: Edward Elgar.

Kotzé, Louis J. 2019a. "A Global Environmental Constitution for the Anthropocene?" *Transnational Environmental Law* 8(1):11–33. doi: 10.1017/S2047102518000274.

Kotzé, Louis J. 2019b. "International Environmental Law's Lack of Normative Ambition: An Opportunity for the Global Pact for the Environment?" *Journal for European Environmental and Planning Law* 16(3):213–236. doi: 10.1163/18760104-01603002.

Kotzé, Louis J., and Duncan French. 2018. "The Anthropocentric Ontology of International Environmental Law and the Sustainable Development Goals: Towards an Ecocentric Rule of Law in the Anthropocene." *Global Journal of Comparative Law* 7(1):5–36. doi: 10.1163/2211906X-00701002.

Kotzé, Louis J. et al. 2022. "Planetary Integrity." In *The Sustainable Development Goals as Transformative Force? The SDG Scientific Mid-Term Assessment*, edited by Frank Biermann, Thomas Hickmann, and Carole-Anne Sénit. Cambridge: Cambridge University Press.

Krieger, Nancy. 2020. "Enough: Covid-19, Structural Racism, Police Brutality, Plutocracy, Climate Change - and Time for Health Justice, Democratic Governance, and an Equitable, Sustainable Future." *American Journal of Public Health* 110(11):1620–1623.

Kumi, Emmanuel, Albert Arhin, and Thomas Yeboah. 2014. "Can Post-2015. Sustainable Development Goals Survive Neoliberalism? A Critical Examination of the Sustainable Development–Neoliberalism Nexus in Developing Countries." *Environment, Development and Sustainability* 16(3):539–554. doi: 10.1007/s10668-013-9492-7.

Lang, Winfried. 1995. *Sustainable Development and International Law*. London: Graham and Trotman Ltd.

Le Grange, Lesley. 2015. "Ubuntu/Botho as Ecophilosophy and Ecosophy." *Journal of Human Ecology* 49(3):301–308. doi: 10.1080/09709274.2015.11906849.

Leal Filho, Walter, Luciana Londero Brandli, Amanda Lange Salvia, Lez Rayman-Bacchus, and Johannes Platje. 2020. "Covid-19 and the Un Sustainable Development Goals: Threat to Solidarity or an Opportunity?" *Sustainability* 12(5343):1–14. doi: 10.3390/su12135343.

Mair, Simon, Aled Jones, Jonathan Ward, Ian Christie, Angela Druckman, and Fergus Lyon. 2018. "A Critical Review of the Role of Indicators in Implementing the Sustainable Development Goals." In *Handbook of Sustainability Science and Research*, edited by Leal Walter Fihlo, 41–56. Cham: Springer.

Manzano, I. Jordi Jaria, Antonio Cardesa-Salzmann, Antoni Pigrau, and Susana Borràs. 2016. "Measuring Environmental Injustice: How Ecological Debt Defines a Radical Change in the International Legal System." *Journal of Political Ecology* 23(1):381–393. doi: 10.2458/v23i1.20225.

Meadows, Donella H., Dennis L. Meadows, Jørgen Randers, and William W. Behrens. 1972. *The Limits to Growth: A Report for the Club of Rome's Project on the Predicament of Mankind*. New York: Universe Books.

Mugumbate, Jacob Rugare, and Admire Chereni. 2020. "Now, the Theory of Ubuntu Has Its Space in Social Work." *African Journal of Social Work* 10(1):v–xvii.

Naess, Petter. 2016. "The Illusion of Green Capitalism." In *Crisis System: A Critical Realist and Environmental Critique of Economics and the Ecology*, edited by Petter Naess, and Leigh Price. London: Routledge.

Philippopoulos-Mihalopoulos, Andreas. 2015. "Actors or Spectators? Vulnerability and Critical Environmental Law." In *Thought, Law, Rights and Action in the Age of Environmental Crisis*, edited by Anna Grear, and Evadne Grant, 46–75. Cheltenham: Edward Elgar.

Du Plessis, Hanri Magdalena. 2019. "Legal Pluralism, Ubuntu and the Use of Open Norms in the South African Common Law of Contract." *Potchefstroom Electronic Law Journal* 22(1):1–37. doi: 10.17159/1727-3781/2019/v22i0a6456.

Randers, Jorgen, Johan Rockström, Per-Espen Stoknes, Ulrich Goluke, David Collste, Sarah E. Cornell, and Jonathan Donges. 2019. "Achieving the 17 Sustainable Development Goals within 9 Planetary Boundaries." *Global Sustainability* 2:1–11. doi: 10.1017/sus.2019.22.

Ranta, Eija. 2020. "Buen Vivir as Transformative Alternative to Capitalist Coloniality." In *The Routledge Handbook of Transformative Global Studies*, edited by Hamed S. A. Hosseini, James Goodman, Sarah C. Motta, and Barry K. Gills, 419–430. London: Routledge.

Redclift, Michael R. 2007. "Sustainable Development (1987-2005) - an Oxymoron Comes of Age." *Horizontes Antropológicos* 12:65–84. doi: 10.1002/sd.281.

Richardson, Benjamin J. 2011. "A Damp Squib: Environmental Law from a Human Evolutionary Perspective." *Osgoode Hall Law School Comparative Research in Law and Political Economy Research Paper Series*:1–42. doi: 10.2139/ssrn.1760043.

Sachs, Jeffery. 2015. *The Age of Sustainable Development*. New York: Columbia University Press.

Segger, Marie-Claire Cordonier. 2004. "Significant Developments in Sustainable Development Law and Governance: A Proposal." *Natural Resources Forum* 28(1):61–74. doi: 10.1111/j.0165-0203.2004.00072.x.

Sinclair, Upton. 1935. *I. Candidate for Governor: And How I Got Licked*. Berkeley: University of California Press.

Spaargaren, G., A. P. J. Mol, and F. H. Buttel. 2000. *Environment and Global Modernity*. London: SAGE Publications.

Springer, Simon. 2016. "Fuck Neoliberalism." *ACME: An International Journal for Critical Geographies* 15(2):285–292.

Terblanché-Greeff, Aïda C. 2019. "Ubuntu and Environmental Ethics: The West Can Learn from Africa When Faced with Climate Change." In *African Environmental Ethics*, edited by Munamato Chemhuru, 93–109. Cham: Springer.

Terreblanche, Christelle. 2018. "Ubuntu and the Struggle for an African Eco-socialist Alternative." In *The Climate Crisis: South African and Global Democratic Eco-socialist Alternatives*, edited by Vishwas Satgar, 168–189. Johannesburg: Wits University Press.

United Nations. 2015. *Transforming Our World: The 2030 Agenda for Sustainable Development*. Department of Economic and Social Affairs (un.org).

Van Breda, Adrian D. 2019. "Developing the Notion of Ubuntu as African Theory for Social Work Practice." *Social Work* 55(6):438–450.

Van Norren, Dorine E. 2020. "The Sustainable Development Goals Viewed through Gross National Happiness, Ubuntu, and Buen Vivir." *International Environmental Agreements: Politics, Law and Economics* 20(3):431–458. doi: 10.1007/s10784-020-09487-3.

World Bank. n.d. "Poverty." accessed 30 October 2021 https://www.worldbank.org/en/topic/poverty.

World Commission on Environment and Development. 1987. *Our Common Future*. Oxford University Press, Oxford.

Zang, Sheryl M., Ivy Benjenk, Suellen Breakey, Eleonor Pusey-Reid, and Patrice K. Nicholas. 2021. "The Intersection of Climate Change with the Era of Covid-19." *Public Health Nursing* 38(2):321–335. doi: 10.1111/phn.12866.

Zeng, Yiwen, Sean Maxwell, Rebecca K. Runting, Oscar Venter, James E. M. Watson, and L. Roman Carrasco. 2020. "Environmental Destruction Not Avoided with the Sustainable Development Goals." *Nature Sustainability* 3(10):795–798. doi: 10.1038/s41893-020-0555-0.

# 2

# THE SOVEREIGN ORDER OF *TIŊA*

## Enduring Traditions of Earth Jurisprudence in Africa

*Anatoli Ignatov*

In *Wild Law*, Cormac Cullinan cautions proponents of Wild Law not to rush to re-invent legal philosophies without acknowledging the multiple schools of Indigenous thought that have inspired the emerging discourses of earth jurisprudence and "rights of nature":

> it appears that certain cultures did manage to evolve laws and other means of regulating human conduct that enabled them to live successfully over very long periods of time as part of a wider community of living and non-living beings ... To me this suggests that they probably know things that we don't and which would be helpful for us to know ... We would be foolish indeed not to consult the fantastic library of different techniques of human governance that have succeeded over thousands of years.
>
> *(Cullinan 2011, 88–89)*

This chapter takes Cullinan's call seriously. It seeks to highlight an existing, albeit marginalized and contested, tradition of earth-centered jurisprudence in West Africa and to situate it within this "library of different techniques of human governance" (89) that has drawn on the earth as the source of law.

In particular, I explore the African concept of *Tiŋa* ("earth" in Gurene) as a shifting source of jurisprudential orientation for eco-political authority and sovereignty in northern Ghana that coexists with multiple other sources of law, authority, and legitimacy. This concept, which is widespread across many West African societies – e.g. the Gurensi, Boosi, Tallensi, Dagara, Kusasi, and Kasena, to name a few – reveals legal ideas and norms as woven into the continuous negotiation of mutually reciprocal relationships between people and the environment. It consists of a distinct repertoire of socio-cultural and embodied practices of aligning human laws and techniques of governance with the ecological cycles, agencies, and emergent properties of the earth, whereby the latter is granted various degrees of subjectivity and moral personhood. Despite its lack of visibility within official state and juridical discourses in Africa, the normative order of *Tiŋa* has developed innovative and adaptive forms of cohabitation with processes of institutionalization of colonial, state, and chiefly power, which historically have sought to integrate, negate, or mediate such pre-existing practices of law and governance (Niang 2018, 21–27).

 DOI: 10.4324/9781003388081-3

From the perspective of jurists, lawyers, and professional legal scholars, Ghana is characterized by a plural legal system where customary and statutory systems overlap. According to Kasanga and Kotey (2001, 13), around 80 to 90% of all the land in Ghana is held under a multiplicity of customary claims and land tenure interests. The ownership of land is expressed in terms of rights which form a hierarchy of interests in the land. At the top of this hierarchy is the allodial or paramount title followed by the sub-allodial title. The allodial title is the highest customary title to land in Ghana, which is vested in inanimate objects such as a stool or skin or social relationships such as clans or families and established through discovery and first settlement and, sometimes, conquest (Woodman 1996). There are a number of lesser rights that are derived from the allodial title such as the customary freehold (usufruct), leasehold, tenancy, license, and pledge. In the North, these hierarchies of land interests are commonly enshrined in contesting oral histories of founding ancestors' social compacts with the land.

What is missing from such common rights-based and secularized accounts of the constitution of Ghana's plural legal order is a recognition of the spiritual and ecological grounds of that order, which entangle it into the permanent jurisdiction of the earth. Insofar as this legal and normative order is collectively authored, its sources of authority and legitimacy are multiple, diverse, and more-than-human. They include land spirits and dead ancestors that exercise considerable influence over the configuration of prevailing patterns of legal action and thought within specific ecologies of life. In his writings on Gurensi land law, elder Christopher Azaare shows how land governance is articulated in a collective subscription to a principle of intergenerational trust that is woven into people's ancestral charter with the land:

> land is communal and sacred. Neither the tindaana nor any one individual could sell out land. The reason for the prohibition is that land belongs to the ancestors who live underneath the Earth. These ancestors still have vested interest in the preservation of the land which they have left behind for the living descendants ... one is bound to face fierce resistance in one's attempt to cut down sacred sites (where the ancestors reside) or taking soil from it ... if in his time any landed property of the family is sold or by any other means it ceases to belong to the family, his spirit after death would be perpetually troubled by those of his predecessors for having permitted the land of his ancestors to go into the possession of others.
>
> *(Azaare 2020, 25–26)*

The terms of the ancestral trust articulated by Azaare generate codes on social action – e.g. injunctions on the consumption of natural resources and commercialization of land relations; ethical obligations towards future generations; taboos and totemic responsibilities, etc. – that govern people's engagement with other groups of people and the environment. These codes are associated with the exercise of eco-political authority by clan elders, chiefs, and earth priests who have jurisdiction over human relations with sacred groves, animals, trees, and other nonhumans. The spiritual world, whose active agencies and vital forces permeate the earth and communicate to traditional rulers what the earth requires from them, is regarded as the primary lawgiver. From Azaare's view, human jurisprudence and the authority of chiefs and earth priests are derived from the broader and invisible "great jurisprudence" of the ancestral land spirits. Sovereignty and law are thus enacted in a variety of foundations and registers, which are "at once ecological, spatial, historical, ritual, and economic, all operating in conjunction rather than separately" (Niang 2018, 100). This integrated understanding of law in terms of multiple, overlapping human and nonhuman sources of norms and authority that reveals the spiritual domain as an active zone of politico-legal governance becomes regularly excised from official pronouncements of African states, jurists, and legislators. The latter tend to rely on imported Western categories that treat the realm of politics/law and the realm of ritual/religion as two distinct spheres of social action. Among the societies of northern Ghana and southern Burkina Faso, such distinctions are difficult to sustain (Azaare 2020; Niang 2018; MacGaffey 2013). In contrast to Christian or Judaic traditions of legal thought that might also view the source of law as spiritual, these societies do not embrace abstract and dualistic conceptualizations of a transcendent, spiritual world that is perceived to be distinct from material nature. They reject transcendentalist modes of thought by "making the visible world continuous with the invisible world" (Nkrumah 1964, 12). Within these African traditions of earth jurisprudence, the spiritual anchoring of law is also immanent and material.

Drawing on diverse scholarship on African customary law and environmental ethics, as well as on my ethnographic research in Ghana, I situate this earth-based order of *Tiŋa* within the fluidity and dynamic transformation of Indigenous notions of ancestral trusteeship of land within Ghana's plural land system. I aim to build on the evolving literature on earth jurisprudence in Africa (e.g. Cullinan 2011; Damtie 2012; Thiong'o 2012). First, the chapter introduces the basic principles of customary land law in Ghana, including the Indigenous concept of land as a form of ancestral trust and attribution of political sovereignty. It also clarifies the attendant notions of multigenerational ethical community and ecological stewardship grounded in such marginalized strands of African jurisprudential thought. Second, it explores how the tensions between customary and formal land regimes have been shaped by the growing commercialization of land and advancement of English jurisprudential categories, many of which are not easily translatable into the changing corpus of customary practice. I challenge discourses that erase Indigenous ecology-based sovereignty and reproduce the fiction that sovereignty is a singular, exclusively human authority linked to a state or other forms of centralized power. I view conflicts among chiefs and earth priests over who owns the land as conflicts over the inauguration of law and political authority. The very substance of what authorizes human legal order is at stake and I render visible coexisting sources of law and legitimacy that may provide us with new intellectual resources for recrafting legal and governance systems in the Anthropocene. This is a model for how alternate networks of legal, political, ecological, and spiritual practices can hold sway and reassert earth jurisprudence under conditions of mounting pressures by Eurocentric, state-based, and anthropocentric forms of sovereignty.

## Ghana's Legal Pluralism: A Constitutional View

Ghana's land tenure system is complex and pluralistic, "consisting of customary law tenures, common-law tenures and various combinations of both" (Woodman 1966, 476). Indigenous law, which is the basis of land law in Ghana, has experienced significant changes in response to British colonialism, the advance of Christianity, and various processes of political, social, and economic development. The customary system has been modified by the statutory enactments of courts and legislation, with common-law interests and English equitable principles superimposed onto it (Kasanga and Kotey 2001, 27–28; Woodman 1996, v).

Article 11 (2) of the 1992 Constitution of the Republic of Ghana defines the term "common law" as "the rules of law generally known as the common law, the rules generally known as the doctrines of equity and the rules of customary law including those determined by the Superior Court of Judicature." For the purposes of the same Article 11 (3), "customary law" means "the rules of law which by custom are applicable to particular communities in Ghana" and is recognized as one of the sources of Ghanaian law (Republic of Ghana 1992, 10). Article 267 (1) vests all customary lands in the appropriate stool, skin, or family "on behalf of, and in trust for the subjects of the stool in accordance with customary law and usage" (ibid., 161). The Constitution of Ghana recognizes this concept of trusteeship in landholding in Article 36(8), which emphasizes that stool and skin lands must be managed in accordance with the fiduciary obligations of traditional authorities:

> the state shall recognise that ownership and possession of land carry a social obligation to serve the larger community and, in particular, the state shall recognise that the managers of public, stool, skin and family lands are fiduciaries charged with the obligation to discharge their functions for the benefit respectively of the people of Ghana of the stool, skin or family concerned, and are accountable as fiduciaries in this regard.
>
> *(ibid., 38)*

In the south of Ghana, customary land is defined as *stool land* in reference to the carved wooden stool which serves as a political symbol of the authority of the chieftaincy and a shrine of the spirits of the ancestors. In the north of Ghana, customary land is defined as *skin land* in reference to the animal skins that chiefs sit on or the skins that *tindaanas* (earth priests) wear. In the Volta Region and Greater Accra, customary land is known as *family land* because it is family heads who exercise the fiduciary management of such lands, holding them in trust for the people. The Constitution, however, does not make specific provisions on how these types of customary land should be managed in accordance with the fiduciary duties of traditional authorities.

## Principles of Indigenous Land Law in Ghana: Sovereignty, Trusteeship, and Ancestral Ownership

In large parts of Ghana, the principal source of land law remains custom. The closest analogy to custom in Western jurisprudence is common law, with the important distinction that in customary jurisprudence the law-making function cannot be entirely identified with the courts. Traditional courts "declared, applied and even made law over the years, but they were essentially regarded as providing a forum for applying well-established norms of the community rather than as specialized organs for the recording, systematizing and shaping the growth of the law" (Asante 1975, xviii). According to Kasanga and Kotey (2001, iii–iv), "customary land tenure systems and management mechanisms remain strong, dynamic and evolutionary" and "in spite of the state law and despite their inherent weaknesses" these systems and mechanisms "still reign supreme in the North, and remain very strong in the South." In the context of Ghana's legal and institutional pluralism, it becomes essential to gain a deeper understanding of how this dynamism of custom has shaped the shifting meanings of traditional conceptions of property and political office-holding arrangements that are imbued with the idea of trusteeship. It is also important to gain insight into how such Indigenous political arrangements have developed mechanisms to hold off the predations of state forms of law and authority. One of the most preeminent concepts in the customary property system is the view of land as an ancestral trust committed to the living and unborn generations for the benefit of the whole community. This is anchored in forms of sovereign oversight that have important features in common across the north and south of Ghana.

### *Land Ownership as Attribute of Political Sovereignty*

Indigenous systems of land ownership in Ghana fall into two broad categories depending on the structure of the political organization of the society in question. The first refers to most centralized states such as Ashanti, Akyem, and Fanti, in which land belongs to the state and is thus the property of the whole community represented by the stool. The king exercises paramountcy over the lands of the state and the power of ratifying and confirming what his subjects grant, which is a form of sovereign oversight that does not carry with it the ownership of any particular land (Asante 1965, 850). Even within such systems that are commonly characterized as highly centralized, sovereignty itself is not incompatible with sub-systems of law and rule. In contrast to Akan states, Asante (1975) observes that a number of political systems that are common among the Ewes, Ga Adangbe, and many northern societies are not characterized by such a degree of centralization. However, his analysis resists the Eurocentric bias of Western jurists and anthropologists who have tended to equate law and political order with notions of Austinian sovereignty and hierarchy of courts and have viewed chiefless societies that do not exhibit such attributes as lawless. In Asante's view, the traditional legal process of less centralized polities has placed the administration of land law in family and clan heads who hold land in trust for family and clan members.

Another common aspect of customary jurisprudence in the North is the institution of the tindaana, a religious intermediary between the earth spirits and the living, who has been responsible for land allocation and administration. Asante also notes that successive constitutions of Ghana have dispelled any lingering doubts that such systems constitute law by recognizing customary law as one of the key sources of law of the Republic (Asante 1975, xvii–xx).[1]

Despite this heterogeneity of customary legal and political systems, Asante identifies a set of features in common that are universal throughout Ghana, such as the group involvement in land ownership, the emphasis on corporate interest in property, and the priority of conciliation in dispute settlement mechanisms (ibid., xx). Everywhere in Ghana, concepts of sovereign oversight and ownership of land are also bound up with a notion of custom as ancestral prescriptions, to which I turn next.

## *Ancestral Ownership*

Throughout Ghana, customary law reflects Indigenous cosmovisions and spiritual precepts that situate the sovereign oversight of land within the realm of ancestral jurisdiction. The idea of trusteeship, which underlies the traditional concept of property, proceeds from the fundamental premise that "basic property belonged to the ancestors and that the living were but temporary possessors, whose use of property was conditional upon strict compliance with time-honored ancestral prescriptions" (Asante 1975, 22). As Azaare (2020) states in the introduction of this chapter, land among many northern societies is seen as the property of the earth gods and ancestors, who still have a vested interest in the preservation and management of the land which they have left behind for their living descendants. Likewise, "the Gas attributed ownership of land to sacred lagoons, while the Ashantis regarded it as a supernatural female force – the inexhaustible source of sustenance and the provider of man's most basic needs. She was 'helpful if propitiated and harmful if ignored.'" (ACLP 2009, 4; Busia 1951, 40; Asante 1965, 852). Land was and continues to be viewed as the sanctuary and abode for the spirits of the dead ancestors that holds deep emotive and spiritual significance in community life in both the north and south of Ghana. Asante explains that this involvement with the ancestors proceeds from a metaphysical principle that asserts a continuity of experience under which past, present, and future are seen as a unified whole. The principle is given expression by the living's fidelity to the ancestors:

> Concepts of land ownership were thus bound up with the cult of ancestral worship ... predicated on the belief that the departed ancestors superintend the earthly affairs

> of their living descendants, protecting them from disaster and generally ensuring their welfare, but demanding in return strict compliance with time-honored ethical prescriptions ... In effect land was an ancestral trust committed to the living for the benefit of themselves and generations yet unborn.
>
> *(Asante 1965, 852)*

For generations, family lands have been seen as an ancestral heritage. The ancestors, who have been looking after the well-being of their descendants, are always ready to intervene to ward off any undeserved disasters that might threaten the living (Asante 1975, 21).

Because property is conceived as an ancestral trust, traditional and political authorities – chiefs, tindaanas, heads of families, and clans– are expected to act as "trustees" who administer the property in the primary interest of the group (ibid., 24). For Asante, "the eternal corporation of the past, present and future was the state, embodied by the stool" (Asante 1965, 852; See ACLP 2009, 5). Akan chiefs hold lands and other stool property in trust for the Asamanfo and for the well-being of stool subjects (Busia 1951). For Danquah (1928, 200), to deny this notion of stool ownership means to forfeit political membership in the nation to which one claims to belong. In other words, stool lands are defined both as lands that belong to the whole community and the area of political jurisdiction of the Akan state (Bentsi-Enchill 1964, 29). In the North, where the animal skins on which chiefs sit serve the same purpose as the stool in the south to express an Indigenous concept of corporation, this fusion of political sovereignty and ancestral ownership emerges under the term "skin property" (ibid., 30). In contrast to anthropocentric models of governance in the West, which treat materiality as a passive or inert conduit for human agency, here material objects such as skins and stools function as the lynchpin of political authority systems. The role of materiality is elevated: it is not the chief or tindaana but the seat of the traditional ruler that bestows power and authority.

In all political systems in Ghana, the Indigenous order of norms conceives of custom and morality as ancestral prescriptions. The universal concept of ancestral trust enjoins land trustees to uphold the honor of the ancestors. This promotion of the prosperity of the kingroup ensures the security of unborn generations, safeguarding them against poverty or deprivation (Asante 1975, 23). It is an active regulatory force that imposes an obligation to use and manage resources within an individual's possession for the well-being of the group and prohibits any abuse of natural resources that might affect the security of posterity. It advances the social or group interest in accordance with ancestral prescriptions and promotes the equitable distribution of community resources (ibid., 23, 82). The principle of trusteeship thus excludes an absolutist conception of individual or family ownership as it qualifies subordinate land interests such as the usufruct and private leasehold by impressing them with a "distinct social obligation," which does "not admit of the unfettered right to use and dispose of property" (ibid., 13, 24).

Although the Indigenous legal process has been characterized by a lack of effective mechanisms for enforcement of the fiduciary duties of chiefs, tindaanas, and family heads, the notion of "ultimate accountability to the ancestral spirits" has served in the past as the most common and operative deterrent to breach of trust (ibid., 25). Across Ghana, a series of taboos govern such breach of trust; ancestral sanctions can take place either immediately in this life in response to the breach of a norm or may be deferred to punish future generations. This ever-present possibility of deferred punishment decouples the kind of cause and effect that might limit belief in the efficacy of these rules. The vitality and legitimacy of fiduciary institutions thus have been profoundly interdependent with people's continued adherence to Indigenous cosmovisions, including the view of custom as ancestral moral prescriptions.

## *Eco-community and Moral Obligations to the Future Generations*

This notion of trans-generational obligation grounded in the principle of ancestral trusteeship reveals such strands of African jurisprudential thought as profoundly ecological. Ghanaian philosopher Kwasi Wiredu observes that the traditional African conception of world order views it as "inhabited by extra-human beings superior to humans in power" and legal authority (1994, 31). This means that there is "no question of trying to control or dominate this whole scheme of things and beings. One may seek to overcome specific problems deriving from specific components of this one system of reality, and one may also utilize other resources of the system in support of human life" (45–46). This latter activity, however, is always subject to the consideration that land "belongs not to individuals but to whole clans and individuals only have rights of use that they are obligated to exercise considerately so as not to render nugatory the similar rights of future members of the clan" (46). Wiredu characterizes this duty to preserve the environment for posterity as a "two-sided conception of stewardship":

> Of all the duties owed to the ancestors none is more imperious than that of husbanding the resources of the land so as to leave it in good shape for posterity. In this moral scheme the rights of the unborn play such a cardinal role that any traditional African would be nonplussed by the debate in Western philosophy as to the existence of such rights. In the upshot there is a two-sided concept of stewardship in the management of the environment involving obligations to both ancestors and descendants which motivates environmental carefulness.
>
> *(46)*

The present generation has a dual ethical responsibility to past and future generations. Since the ancestors made sure that the environment was able to sustain community lifeways, the living owe them a debt of gratitude, which not only entails respecting their legacy of environmental preservation but also a duty to ensure that their descendants are equally provided for. Here Behrens concurs with Wiredu that African traditions of thought offer important and underappreciated correctives to Western extractivist and utilitarian views of the environment:

> Firstly, the land … is a resource that is shared across generations. As such, we are not entitled to treat the environment as we like. We are required to preserve it for the use of those who will follow us … The second important notion is that the "ethical community" (as Bujo calls it) extends across generations … Not only are we interdependent with other natural entities, but there is an interdependence temporally as well between succeeding generations of people. This temporal interdependence similarly entails an obligation to promote the good of those whose well-being is tied up with ours.
>
> *(Behrens 2017, 201)*

For Behrens, these notions of land and community as interdependent relationships among multiple generations constitute the strength of African approaches. They address key theoretical concerns about moral obligations to the future that have dominated debates within Euro-American environmental ethics. In particular, the communitarian focus of African thought resists a conceptualization of the rights of future persons in the individualistic terms of dominant liberal discourses of rights: "Since our obligation is one owed by our generation as a whole to future generations, as wholes, exactly which future people come into existence is of little relevance" (Behrens 2012, 188).

It is important to note that this view of generational rights as group or communal rights does not fit neatly into the conceptual framework of human-centered law as we know it. First, these rights originate from the extra-human jurisprudence of the ancestors, within which the environment is conceived not only as a shared "resource" but also as a web of interdependent and reciprocating spiritual agencies that are in constant dialogue with humans. Second, here community is not just a multigenerational collective of humans but "a fluid habitation of interactive forces, beings, elements, and animate and inanimate matters of the environment" (Eze 2017, 625). Drawing on Bantu cosmology, Eze describes it as an "eco-community," in which human subjectivity is expressed in interaction with other beings:

> The sacredness of nature is because all elements have vital force ... everything on Earth – rivers, mountains, trees, plants, seas, the sun, moon, stars, et cetera – has embedded force and spirit. The environment is not just inconsequential, it is part of life and constitutive of humanity. This ontological holism with nature defines the terms of the relationship between the human person and his/her environment ... One's subjectivity is fully expressed only in dialogue with other beings within the eco-community.
>
> *(Eze 2017, 627)*

This concept of African eco-community resonates with Thomas Berry's observation that "the universe is a communion of subjects, not a collection of objects" and "the devastation of the planet can be seen as a direct consequence of the loss of this capacity for human presence to and reciprocity with the nonhuman world" (Berry 2006, 17–18; Thiong'o 2012, 173). To be human is a quality of interrelatedness with other humans, animals, plants, biological and non-biological life, spirits, and vital forces that make up such eco-communities (Eze 2017, 629).

African subjectivity finds its expression in its association not only with other people but also the nonhuman world and such associations include diverse relations of totemic responsibility. Biodiversity and regeneration of ecosystems are stimulated through a series of taboos that govern the proper ethical relations between Indigenous clans and their totems. As Azaare (2020, 111) observes, cutting or gathering wood for fuel in Gurensi sacred groves is either prohibited or restricted to certain species of trees and times of the year. Hunting of the animals living there – "the children of the *tingane*" – is also forbidden and offenders face strong punishments. In northern Ghana, such taboos extend beyond the confines of sacred groves and organize relations of extended families and clans with totemic animals, plants, and objects. Some such relations involve the return of the ancestors into trees, animals, and objects such as pythons, spiders, domestic dogs, foot rings, anklets, bracelets, or even articles of the regalia of chiefs and tindaanas. In Zoko-Kadare and Zoko-Tarongo, for instance, the killing and hunting of crocodiles are tabooed: when someone dies he or she turns into a crocodile. Other totems concern long-term family relationships with animals that saved an ancestor. These are relations of co-dependency and alliance-building forged through the recognition that the bio-cultural survivability of species is intertwined. Taboos and totemic obligations are also closely connected to the exercise of eco-political jurisdiction by traditional leaders; they are important attributes of leadership for all land trustees, enacting a collective obligation to adhere to the norms of ancestral governance (Azaare 2020).

## The Erosion of the Trusteeship Principle

This African view of land as a multigenerational trust offers a window into an Indigenous cosmovision that does not merely treat community as a collection of autonomous individuals who act as stewards of the environment because they are concerned with the needs of their own species. Rather, ancestral jurisprudence positions them as belonging to a diverse eco-community, in which subjectivity and agency are distributed among multiple generations of related humans, plants, animals, and inanimate things. In the 1970s Asante sounded a warning that there had been a "progressive erosion of the trusteeship idea" by the impact of British rule and ideas, new economic conditions, and the reception of Christianity, secularizing customary institutions and undermining the concept of ancestral ownership (1975, xiv, 83). New economic developments have "opened up to customary fiduciaries unprecedented opportunities for self-aggrandizement at the expense of the beneficiaries of their "trust," while the courts have shown themselves incredibly inept in fashioning effective substitutes for the old traditional restraints" (ibid., 83–84).

Contemporary scholarly updates of Asante's analysis testify to a recent intensification of such trends across Ghana which might further obscure these traditions of earth jurisprudence. Kasanga and Kotey speak of "a breakdown in the 'trusteeship principle'" and observe that "many customary law managers no longer act as if they are holding a fiduciary position and, in fact, behave as if they own community land on a personal basis" (2001, 28). Like Asante, they raise the question of accountability of land trustees in a rapidly monetizing economy characterized by the rise of commercial agriculture and the loss of traditional religion, especially in peri-urban areas of Ghana (22). In a study of customary land regulation by chiefs in peri-urban Kumasi, Ubink and Quan concur that during the conception of the Land Administration Project in Ghana "there was no wide and open discussion of the role of chiefs in the administration of stool land –including the tendency of chiefs to behave like private landlords – or of the possible checks and balances the state could place on stool land administration" (2008, 206). In the north of Ghana, a study by Yaro documents how "chiefs and clan heads are reinventing tradition in parallel with neoliberal modernization's forces that leads to disenfranchisement of their citizens of landed property" (2012, 351–352). These processes of reinvention of trusteeship have been identified as a driver of the contemporary proliferation of land disputes and litigation and the rising rates of landlessness and displacement. They have been further complicated by the stress exerted on local ecologies by the acceleration of climate change, biodiversity loss, and desertification in the Anthropocene. Rivers and streams that have historically served to demarcate the boundaries between the jurisdictions of earth spirits and tindaanas have been drying up, fueling competing claims to trusteeship of community lands. Totemic ancestors such as lions, monkeys, and crocodiles have been disappearing from the ancestral groves (*tingana*) that have served as their places of refuge from the impacts of urban and extractive development. These contemporary transformations highlight the immanence of the Indigenous order of trusteeship, anchored in the continuity between the spiritual and the material.

## The Fluid Order of *Tiŋa*: The Reinvention of Trusteeship in the Upper East Region

The challenges presented by the complexity of Ghana's plural land tenure systems and the changing power relations between land trustees become particularly evident in the Upper East region. Whereas chiefs occupy the customary office in most of Ghana, in the Upper East the offices of customary authorities are split between earth priests, chiefs, and clan/family heads. Transactions in land had rarely been the business of chiefs until the colonial period when, by appointing and in many places "inventing" chiefs, the colonial administration delegated land control to them, which they retained after Independence (Lund 2008). But in practice, land administration by earth priests continued, remaining invisible to the law until 1979 when the Constitution divested the state of its trusteeship over most lands in the Northern and Upper regions.[2] This legal development produced new conditions for the reinterpretation of customary law and ancestrally prescribed principles of trusteeship, intensifying the contestations over land ownership among tindaanas, chiefs, and family heads (Lund 2008).

## *The Normative Order of Tiŋa*

*Tiŋa*, the Gurene term for "land," refers simultaneously to (1) land, ground, earth, the physical world, and (2) country, town, and settlement (Dakubu, Arintono, and Nsoh 2007, 170). *Tiŋa* is the whole community, be it trees, stones, humans, or spirits; it is the ground on which we are sitting and "in which we bury" (Interview with Chris Azaare, 15 August 2012). During one of our conversations with a tindaana and his elders, Azaare summarizes the elders' definition of *tiŋa* as a "womb of the ancestors:" "*tiŋa* is like a womb. A woman has the womb and the *tiŋa* gives birth. And if you die, it means that you are nourishing the earth. That's why the *tiŋa* is the earth" (Interview with tindaana and elders, 14 December 2012).

According to Niang (2018), our understanding of *Tenga* (the equivalent term among the Mossi of Burkina Faso and other Voltaic societies) should not be confined to its designation as a geographical location, an ethnic grouping of "society" at large or a female deity. Rather, *it is a dynamic normative order that the African postcolonial state was internally built against.* It "consists of distinct social practices, a framework of interdependent relationships, a certain ecological homogeneity and a particular disposition against rigid hierarchy. It refers to an ecocultural field of identities, values, and subjectivities invested in social equilibrium" (ibid., 27). As a counter-discourse of state-making processes:

> agency, within the realm of *Tenga* was not just a matter of reaction to a threat of extinction but rather the means of preservation of preexisting forms and structures, therefore denoting a constant tension between invention and convention ... the agents of *Tenga* invested meaning ... in their practice of resistance through a serious of rituals and cultural practices that had to be constantly reworked in order to respond to anxieties generated by state power.
>
> *(ibid., 28)*

In this context of enlisting ritual as a form of resistance to state power, the contemporary tensions between political rulers (chiefs) and spiritual authorities (tindaanas) over overlapping jurisdictional prerogatives reveal the order of *Tenga* as a key site of political action. As we have seen, the Indigenous concept of land as an ancestral trust means that it is the dead –the ancestors (*yaabaduuma*) and the earth gods (*tingana*) –who are recognized as the "owners" of the land. *Tindaama* (earth priests) and *Yizuukɛɛma* (clan elders), and in a few exceptional cases *Naduma* (chiefs), are land trustees and hold custody of the *tingane*, i.e. the shrine containing the community spirits. But it is the "skin," the shrine itself that serves as the locus of land ownership and not the individual person of the tindaana or the chief:

> In our Gurune tradition, what we are sitting on we call Tingɔnŋɔ (land). The land also has its legs (entourage) in the forms of trees and stones ... The land therefore belongs to our ancestors, those yet unborn and those living today ... Our environment includes our trees, our stones, our rivers, our shrines, and we the human beings ... Anything that we want to do on land we have to seek the consent of the dead and also the shrines before you can do any development on the land.
>
> *(Interview with Chief and Traditional Council, 4 July 2018)*

The chief's view of land as an intergenerational asset presents an integrated concept of the social, natural, and spiritual worlds; human society negotiates with and seeks the consent of nature's spiritual agencies, rather than act as its conqueror. According to Millar, it is in the ownership, management, and use of land that the people of Bolgatanga and Bongo best express their cosmovisions and the notion that "land is the sanctuary for the gods seems to be the most active factor regulating its use" (1999, 131, 144). In the chief's statement above, the Gurene cosmovision indicates "a hierarchy in divine beings, spiritual beings (especially the ancestors), natural forces (such as climate, diseases, floods), soil, vegetation, animals, man, and woman. These hierarchies … give rise to several rituals in which the elders, priests, and soothsayers play prominent roles and prescribe the way problem-solving can take place" (ibid., 133–134). Such sacrifices and customary rites serve as binding mechanisms for the ancestral regulation of land. Sacrifices are made on a seasonal basis to encourage the ancestors to plead with God on behalf of the living before the growing season and after harvest. The performance of funerary rites is an essential condition for the inheritance of land: "there is the need to perform the funeral to bid your relative a farewell to the ancestral world and performing the funeral means he is gone forever and will reach the ancestors … The funerals are also performed to inherit the properties of your deceased relative. If the funeral is not performed you cannot inherit, it is a taboo … it means the deceased is still existing with you in spirit" (Interview with Chief and Traditional Council, 4 July 2018).

This view of land law as ancestral prescriptions and taboos is enshrined in various sayings and proverbs. For example, a chief recalls a common saying in his town: "We have an ancestral saying, 'the living does not uproot that which the ancestors have planted' (i.e. it is not proper for the current generation to reclaim land that their ancestors gave to another)" (ibid.). Another saying, according to a tindaana is "I proffered you to the *Tingane*" and he explains its meaning with a story:

> I once gave a piece of land to a man. This man fought and challenged me when I gave the land to the Polytechnic to build. Then I proffered him to the *Tingane*, saying if I unjustly hate you and want to illegitimately take the land from you, let's give ourselves a year for the *Tingane* to proffer. That is the taboo, the meaning is that if you want to talk about land, you should be truthful because the *Tingane* detests deceit.
>
> *(Tindaana at the Meeting of Upper East Tindaama Council, 6 July 2018)*

The notion of accountability to the land spirits, explains the chief, traditionally serves as the most common deterrent to breach of such taboos: "The procedure of accountability is death. If you the chief does not perform your role well, the gods or ancestors can kill you, if you the Tindaana does not perform your role very well, the Tingama will kill you" (Interview with Chief and Traditional Council, 4 July 2018). A tindaana agrees that the accountability for deceit in disputes is death: "Everybody knows that you can't cheat land. For anything you can cheat, but you can't cheat land, when you cheat land they bring you here [i.e. tindaana's house], and usually the result is that the person who cheated will die" (Interview with tindaana and elders, 12 July 2017).

In Millar's view, these ancestral regulations prescribe that access to production resources should be "negotiated and rarely traded-off for money" (1999, 136). This prescription is constantly reaffirmed by chiefs, elders, and tindaanas who insist that "we do not sell land here." The recent upsurge of leases, however, and the growing role of money in the formalities for allocation of land have put this taboo under pressure and have intensified the debate about whether land can be sold. Part of the disagreement arises due to the local term – "purchase" or "sale" (*tiŋa da'a*) – for this arrangement even though land is not sold outright in this area:

> When the ancestors first occupied the land ... the land was shared within the group. So if someone from Yikene comes and needs the land to farm because their land is becoming infertile, I as Tindaana take them to the bush where the land is fertile so that they farm. We do not sell the land but lease it out.
>
> *(Interview with tindaana and elders, 20 July 2017)*

In contrast to the tindaana's assurance that land cannot be sold, a chief suggests that custom is no longer respected by many people who have resorted to selling land as a way of addressing poverty. Such trends toward commercialization of land have been exacerbated by climate change, and especially by recent changes in land suitability and availability associated with greater rainfall variability, higher aridity, and diminishing livelihood opportunities provided by rain-fed agriculture. For the chief, due to the monetization of the allocation process, these practices amount to a *de facto* sale of land, even if legally land in Ghana cannot be alienated permanently:

> Land is not for sale, our ancestors never sold the land. If anybody wanted to develop the land for any purpose, it was free for that fellow to develop, if anyone wanted to farm, it was given free to that fellow to farm. But today we are witnessing a different trend of events. In one way or the other, we sell land with the pretense that it is being leased and because of its nature of taboo we hide behind leasing of land.
>
> *(Interview with Chief and Traditional Council, 4 July 2018)*

While these trends of commercialization of land are often shunned by both chiefs and tindaanas in public pronouncements, they have also intensified competition over who has the authority to endorse land transfers, resolve disputes and lay claim to the ground rent which accrues constitutionally to the allodial title holder. Terms such as allodial title and leasehold have become regularly incorporated into the definitions of customary prerogatives of the two offices.

These struggles between chiefs and earth priests can be also understood as contestations over competing constructions of land, jurisdiction, and space (Lund 2013). For chiefs, land is usually conceptualized as a political territory that they administer and hold in custody for their subjects:

> The chief is the sole custodian of the land. If the Naba owns you as a person, how can he not own the land? With regards to farming, we have the person tendering the land to feed the family but the overall land is the chief's.
>
> *(Interview with Chief and Traditional Council, 4 July 2018)*

Land is regarded as a domain of chiefs' administrative jurisdiction governed via taxation, litigation, and provision of infrastructure and development:

> If there is any infrastructural development by the government, they will have to consult the chief and sub chiefs. They will in turn contact the subject in ownership of the land to plead with him so that he allows the infrastructural development.
>
> *(ibid.)*

From this perspective, the naba controls the land by exercising his authority over the people and facilitating the release of land for development purposes (ACLP 2011, 275). This form of customary land control by chiefs is contested, however, by the Bolgatanga tindaanas:

> They call us Tiŋa-daana (land owner) ... The Tindaana is the allodial owner of the land. His duty is to take care of the land and ensure that if there is anything effecting or likely to affect the progress and peace of the land, he attends to it ... Everything on the land belongs to the Tindaana. Any person in need of land to settle acquires the land from the Tindaana. It has come that we now lease land. It is the Tindaana who endorses the land documents. Like the developments that has come, the Tindaana gives out land for such infrastructural development.
>
> *(Interview with tindaana and elders, 20 July 2017)*

While chiefs emphasize a concept of trusteeship as an attribute of political sovereignty, tindaanas stress their position as trustees of ancestral heritage on behalf of the community by virtue of their privileged role as intermediaries with the land spirits:

> One of my roles is that if there is drought during the planting season, the clan heads come to me, the Tindaana. They will tell me they want to leave the land because there is no rain. When we know that *Tingane* and the subsequent form of appeasement, we offer them the sacrifice so that our cry will reach God in order that we have our rain ... This is work related to the land, not the chieftaincy.
>
> *(Discussion with tindaana and elders, 26 July 2018)*

For tindaanas, land embodies a reciprocal social contract with the ancestors and the earth's spiritual agencies that must be continually renewed through rituals, sacrifices, and rites: "It is the Tindaana whose sacrificial role ensures the increase of the human race, not the chief. He Tindaana, makes sacrifices for the fruit of the womb" (tindaana at the Meeting of the Upper East Tindaama Council, 6 July 2018). In such statements, a recurrent theme is that the tindaana not only owns the land, but by virtue of his trusteeship, he is the only one who knows and is known by the land spirits because he is a descendant of the first settler of a community who "met the land."

Tindaanas and elders tend to view the above custodianship as an expression of the complementary roles that tindaanas and chiefs have traditionally played in social life, placing tindaanas in charge of spiritual issues, including land management, and chiefs in charge of conflict resolution in their role as community leaders. An account of the complementarity of the offices is provided by a traditional leader who doubles his roles as a chief and tindaana:

> I am a Tindaana but in my land, the one who serves as the Tindaana doubles as chief. However, the roles assigned to each are not same. A Tindaana is one who first settled on the land. In that case, anyone who comes to settle on the land later must see the first settler to be allotted a piece. You, as Tindaana, tell the new settler what the land abhors (taboos of the land). In the event that a calamity befalls the land, it is the Tindaana that is called, as and when necessary, he gives the boundaries of the land as given by the earth spirits. The role of the Tindaana is that he makes sacrifices to the Tingama (earth spirits) ... If there is shedding of the blood, it is the Tindaana who collects it. As population increases, it got to a point, there was need to have chiefs ... there was an urgent need to have somebody represent the Tindaana, he summons all the people and

> select from the lot, one of them or his child to be leader or chief ... They both play complementary roles. It is the Tindaanas who relegate the governance to the chiefs so it will only be deceitful for chiefs coming from the category of those appointed as chiefs by the Tindaana to claim ownership of the land today.
>
> *(Tindaana at the Meeting of the Upper East Tindaama Council, 6 July 2018)*

According to the above statement, the two offices are complementary but they are not equal. It is the tindaanas who "relegate the governance to the chiefs" and appoint them to serve as their representatives. Here the spiritual world is considered to be the primary lawgiver that regulates the performance of all other traditional forms of authority. Chieftaincy is responsible for administrative leadership but, as Millar (1999, 135–136) also shows, the power position of the chief is mitigated by parallel earth-based institutions that have spiritual roles to perform. They regulate the legitimacy and the powers of the chief and ensure morality and accountability in a chief's performance. The regulation of chiefs by the spirits becomes visible when chiefs establish and renew the terms of their alliance with the tindaanas through various rituals which inaugurate royal political office (Niang 2018).

## Conclusion: Ambiguities of Translation in the Anthropocene

The contemporary revival of tindaanas in Ghana highlights both the dangers and possibilities of translating African legal terms into Western counterparts, presenting opportunities for either the revitalization of the normative order of *Tiŋa* or its further marginalization within legal pluralism's overlapping registers of sovereignty. Lund observes that the "mindless translation of certain Indigenous property concepts into the language of ownership tends to strengthen exclusivity, benefiting the primary right holder at the expense of others" (2008, 15). For instance, indentures by tindaanas with the provision that the person should annually give them foodstuffs and animals to sacrifice to the land spirits have now become translated into the terminology of ground rent. Another example is provided by the difficulty to translate tindaanas' "first comer" claims into Western jurisprudential conceptions of acquisition of title by occupation that enable claimants to reduce property into ownership or possession. Although first settlement or occupation is an important basis of title in Ghana, it does not provide the customary justification of the Indigenous concept of property, which is impressed with the idea of trusteeship. The notion of land as an intergenerational trust entitles the living to be only temporary beneficiaries of a heritage that is destined to be passed onto the unborn and thus excludes an absolutist conception of family and individual property. Like occupation, the concept of trusteeship, rooted in ancestral jurisdiction, serves as a check on "exaggeration of the role of individual investment" and labor in creating property rights. This view of land as ancestral trust presupposes a social order, which invests the individual with a right to use community land, and not his or her labor (Asante 1975, 11–16). Land is also linked to a concept of a corporate subject of Indigenous law conceived as a multigenerational entity separate and distinct from the individuals who make it up – i.e. skin or stool – which includes not only the living but also the dead, the unborn, and the reciprocating environment (Bentsi-Enchill 1964, 23–32).

This ambiguity of translation reveals the contemporary conflicts over land ownership in Ghana not merely as contestations over land as a resource but also as contestations over the very grounds of collective identities, law, and authority. As sacrifice is converted into ground rent and trusteeship becomes individualized, the sovereign order of *Tiŋa* faces new pressures that aim to depoliticize it and relegate it to the realm of "traditional religion" or "precolonial past." As a system of checks on the centralizing tendencies of power, however, this order continues to endure, adapt and find innovative ways of cohabitation with such processes. It continues to motivate African communities to refuse human-centered hierarchies of governance by expressing primary allegiance to the law of ancestors, which carries an obligation to preserve the environment for posterity. The vitality of the eco-communitarian ethos imbued into the system of trusteeship, the adaptability of its non-hierarchical model of governance centered around the complementarity of political offices, and the multi-directionality of moral obligations to the past, present, and future generations provide this system with viable and time-tested resources to resist the growing rival basis of neoliberal forms of ownership. What is more, these resources are not confined to Ghana. They show a model for how the Anthropocene can be resisted worldwide through resurgent networks of earth-based sovereign orders that can multiply even if the dominant structures of government remain the same. The revival of tindaanas in Ghana is a manifestation of a growing transnational movement of custodian communities that is currently taking place in Ethiopia, Kenya, Uganda, South Africa, and Benin and is connecting with counterparts in South America (Chennells, Nadal, and The Gaia Foundation 2015, 24–25). The movement seeks to advance the national and international legal recognition of sacred natural sites and customary earth-based governance systems. By shaping a number of resolutions and recommendations by the African Commission, the International Union for Conservation of Nature and the World Wilderness Congress, this growing web of custodians aims to develop legal "precedents that contribute to building a body of African jurisprudence" (ibid., 25). Propelled by such networks, the order of *Tiŋa* provides us with an alternative multigenerational model of thought that allows us to reconceptualize law from an earth-centered perspective and treat future generations of humans and nonhumans as morally considerable eco-communities.

## Notes

1 Paradoxically, such recognition of northern customary legal systems may have simultaneously deepened and impeded processes of state-making and capital accumulation in Ghana. On the one hand, by calling these diverse assemblages of legal practices, material objects, and social relations "law," radical ecology-based alternatives such as the custodianship of tindaanas are brought to visibility and allowed to be practiced openly without triggering some kind of sovereign reaction (since they might otherwise be read as a rival for legal and political authority). Here these constitutional provisions may be also read as an acknowledgement of the historical inability of British colonial administrations and the Ghanaian nation state to exercise effective or unitary jurisdiction via forms of sovereign control and law imported from European jurisprudence (i.e. an admission of the *de facto* primacy of Indigenous legal orders that have developed various adaptations to coexist with state-making processes). These provisions may also act as a counterweight to longstanding representations of Northern societies as marginal to socio-political change in Ghana. The latter treat the plurality of stateless political systems in the North not as coeval, alternative forms of political organization, but as anachronistic structures lagging behind within an evolutionary continuum of state formation exemplified by centralized Akan states in the South (Allman and Parker 2005, 12–13). On the other hand, these shifts in state recognition can be situated within a history of colonial and Eurocentric anthropological constructions of African custom as a holistic, monolithic and ethnically bounded body of laws and knowledge practices that can be codified, stored and passed onto succeeding generations. By calling these practices "customary law" and systematizing this dynamic and diverse multiplicity of land relations into juridical discourse, state recognition might inadvertently depoliticize these relations and evacuate them from their lived negotiability.

2 Upon independence, the State Property and Contract Act of 1960 executed the transfer of property from the Crown to the Republic of Ghana by ascertaining that lands in northern Ghana – in contrast to the rest of the country – were vested in the government (i.e. "in the President in trust for and on behalf of the people of Ghana") (Bening 1995, 250). According to Lund (2008, 52–53), the 1979 shift in the status of recognition of ownership of northern Ghanaian lands was enabled by the

convergence of three key developments: first, an active campaign by hitherto marginalized northern elites "for the divestiture in order to put the North on par with the rest of the country;" second, the neoliberal promotion of modernized agriculture with the assistance of the World Bank, which viewed state ownership of land as incompatible with such market-driven investments; and, third, attempts by Acheampong's administration to ward off political opposition by forging alliances with influential groups in the North.

## References

Allman, Jean, and John Parker. 2005. *Tongnaab: The History of a West African God*. Bloomington: Indiana University Press.

Asante, S.K.B. 1965. "Interests in Land in the Customary Law of Ghana – A New Appraisal." *The Yale Law Journal* 74(5 April): 848–885.

Asante, S.K.B. 1975. *Property Law and Social Goals in Ghana 1844–1966*. Accra: Ghana Universities Press.

Azaare, Christopher. 2020. "Tindaanaship and Tindaanas in Traditional Gurensi (Frafra) Communities: Land Use and Practices." Africa's Local Intellectuals Series 90, no. 4.

Behrens, Gary Kevin. 2012. "Moral Obligations Towards Future Generations in African Thought." *Journal of Global Ethics* 8(2–3): 179–191.

Behrens, Kevin. 2017. "The Imperative of Developing African Eco-philosophy." In *Themes, Issues and Problems in African Philosophy*, edited by Isaac E. Ukpokolo, 191–204. Cham: Palgrave.

Bening, R.B. 1995. "Land Policy and Administration in Northern Ghana 1898–1976." *Transactions of the Historical Society of Ghana* 16(2 January): 227–266.

Bentsi-Enchill, Kwamena. 1964. *Ghana Land Law: An Exposition, Analysis and Critique*. Lagos: African Universities Press.

Berry, Thomas. 2006. *Evening Thoughts: Reflecting on Earth as Sacred Community*, edited by Mary Evelyn Tucker. San Francisco: Sierra Club Books & University of California Press.

Busia, K.A. 1951. *The Position of the Chief in the Modern Political System of Ashanti*. London: Oxford University Press.

Chennells, Roger, Carine Nadal, and The Gaia Foundation. 2015. "Submission to the African Commission: A Call for Legal Recognition of Sacred Natural Sites and Territories, and their Customary Governance Systems." The Gaia Foundation.

Cullinan, Cormac. 2011. *Wild Law: A Manifesto for Earth Justice*, 2nd ed. White River Junction: Chelsea Green Publishing.

Dakubu, Kropp, Awinkene Arintono, and Avea Nsoh. 2007. *Gurenɛ—English Dictionary*. Legon: Linguistics Department, University of Ghana.

Damtie, Melesse. 2012. "Anthropocentric and Ecocentric Versions of the Ethiopian Legal Regime." In *Exploring Wild Law: The Philosophy of Earth Jurisprudence*, edited by Peter Burdon, 159–172. Kent Town: Wakefield Press.

Danquah, J.B. 1928. *Gold Coast: Akan Law and Customs and the Akim Abuakwa Constitution*. London: George Routledge and Sons.

Eze, Michael Onyebuchi. 2017. "Humanitatis-Eco (Eco-humanism): An African Environmental Theory." In *The Palgrave Handbook of African Philosophy*, edited by Adeshina Afolayan and Toyin Falola, 621–632. New York: Palgrave.

Kasanga, Kasim, and Nii Ashie Kotey. 2001. *Land Management in Ghana: Building on Tradition and Modernity*. London: IIED.

Lund, Christian. 2008. *Local Politics and the Dynamics of Property in Africa*. Cambridge: Cambridge University Press.

Lund, Christian. 2013. "The Past and Space: On Arguments in African Land Control." *Africa* 83(1): 14–35.

Macgaffey, Wyatt. 2013. *Chiefs, Priests, and Praise-Singers: History, Politics, and Land Ownership in Northern Ghana*. Charlottesville: University of Virginia Press.

Millar, David. 1999. "Traditional African Worldviews from a Cosmovision Perspective." In *Food for Thought: Ancient Visions and New Experiments of Rural People*, edited by Bertus Haverkort and Wim Hiemstra. London: Zed Books.

Niang, Amy. 2018. *The Postcolonial African State in Transition: Stateness and Modes of Sovereignty*. London: Rowman and Littlefield International.

Nkrumah, Kwame. 1964. *Consciencism: Philosophy and Ideology for De-colonization*. Monthly Review Press.

The Project Secretariat of the ACLP. 2009. "Literature Review Report on Customary Law on Land in Ghana." *National House of Chiefs/Law Reform Commission.*

The Project Secretariat of the ACLP. 2011. "Report on the Pilot Phase of Ascertainment and Codification of Customary Law on Land and Family in Ghana." National House of Chiefs/Law Reform Commission.

Republic of Ghana. 1992. *Constitution of the Republic of Ghana.* Accra: Ghana Publishing Company.

Thiong'o, Ng'ang'a. 2012. "Earth Jurisprudence in the African Context." In *Exploring Wild Law: The Philosophy of Earth Jurisprudence*, edited by Peter Burdon, 173–182. Kent Town: Wakefield Press.

Ubink, Janine M., and Julian F. Quan. 2008. "How to Combine Tradition and Modernity? Regulating Customary Land Management in Ghana." *Land Use Policy* 25(2): 198–213.

Wiredu, Kwasi. 1994. "Philosophy, Humankind and the Environment." In *Philosophy, Humanity and Ecology: Philosophy of Nature and Environmental Ethics*, edited by H. Odera Oruka, 30–48. Nairobi: African Centre for Technology Studies.

Woodman, Gordon. 1966–1967. "The Scheme of Subordinate Tenures of Land in Ghana." *The American Journal of Comparative Law* 15(3).

Woodman, G.R. 1996. *Customary Land Law in Ghanaian Courts.* Accra: Ghana University Press.

Yaro, J.A. 2012. "Re-inventing Traditional Land Tenure in the Era of Land Commoditization: Some Consequences in Periurban Northern Ghana." *Geografiska Annaler: Series B, Human Geography* 94(4): 351–352.

# 3

# THE SUPER-FACTUAL ANTHROPOCENE AND ENCOUNTERS WITH INDIGENOUS LAW

*Kirsten Anker and Mark Antaki*

The contributors to this volume have been asked to think through what the Anthropocene might signify for law. The "Anthropocene" names the human as central to the definition of a geological era or a new state of Earth's geophysical systems and thereby announces something radically altered in the history of the earth. As the report from the Intergovernmental Panel on Climate Change (IPCC) states, "human influence has become the principal agent of change" *at the planetary level* with rapid and destabilizing consequences: climate change, ocean acidification, disruption to the nitrogen and phosphorous cycles, rising sea levels, and species extinction putting life on Earth as we know it at risk (Masson-Delmotte et al. 2019). With the Anthropocene, one might say, the biggest "fact" about the world is now the "feat" of humans. No longer can one (pretend to) live culture (or civilization) and nature separately. No longer can human history and earth history be told separately. If antisemitism, imperialism, and totalitarianism led Hannah Arendt to conclude that "human dignity needs a new guarantee which can be found only in a new political principle, in a new law on earth" (1973, ix), the Anthropocene, one might say, tells of the need for a new law on earth – but one that is also *of* the earth.

On the one hand, the entanglement of nature and culture (or their reconfiguration) appears to point in the direction of a "new" natural law or earth law (Holder 2000, Murray 2014) and may explain the appeal, for some, of Indigenous (legal) orders in which the nature–culture dichotomy does not obtain (Neidjie 1989, Descola 2005, Helender-Renvall 2010, Lyons 2010, Nadasdy 2021). In other words, it can be said, the Anthropocene invites or requires human beings to think and act (and feel) in ways that Indigenous traditions may have the resources for. What better place to look than so-called "chthonic legal traditions" (Glenn 2014) or Indigenous "grounded normativity" (Coulthard and Simpson 2016) for a law of the earth! *Of* the earth – like the laws of war are laws that govern war – but also in the sense that it somehow issues *from* the earth or is attentive to its demands, its patterns, its ways.

On the other hand, not so fast, some may say. If life on Earth as we know it is at risk, it is because the Anthropocene is a veritable rupture, tipping us into a "no-analogue" state (Crutzen and Steffan 2003, Glassberg 2014, Hamilton 2016). "Old" normal situations and the norms obtained within them are no longer helpful in a situation that is anything but normal (Schmitt

DOI: 10.4324/9781003388081-4

2007, Stacey 2018). "No-analogue" suggests that analogies, patterns, and the presence of the past cannot help us (Hourdequin 2015). If Indigenous traditions look attractive or even necessary in terms of the blurring, side-stepping, overcoming, or absence of a distinction between nature and culture, "no-analogue" suggests, at least for some, that earth-bound law is not useful to deal with the current predicament and the need to, somehow, get to a new normal. We are entering an age beyond human experience, write the editors of *The Anthropocene and the Global Environmental Crisis*, "and no cultural learning or transmission [can] prepare us for the kind of environmental/geological changes that loom" (Hamilton et al. 2015, 5). If the Anthropocene means it is urgent to think humanity and earth together, the emphasis on rupture means it is urgent that we do so in *new* ways somehow appropriate to a predicament that is utterly unprecedented. Indeed, the Anthropocene may hearken to the "supernatural," if not in the precise way Arendt stated that the "atomic bomb" generated a "horror of an energy that came from the universe and is supernatural in the truest sense of the word" (Arendt 2007, 158). For some, the Anthropocene might be so supernatural and so urgent that going down the rabbit hole of Indigenous law is spending time that we don't have. For the past can no longer guide the future and the earth is no longer what it once was. "Chthonic law" can no longer be of help in a time when the uprooting of human beings from the earth has defined and transformed the earth itself.

Although the above two paragraphs seem to pull in opposite directions – towards and away from Indigenous (legal) orders – when the problem becomes how to rethink the nature–culture dichotomy in a time of rupture, their combination seems to us to reduce Indigenous orders to what a very specific but all too abstract species-level "we" think we need from "them" but which they are now "too late" to be able to offer us. We worry that these frames and their combination may betray a tendency to romanticize and lump different peoples and ways of being together into one reductive vision of the "Ecological Indian," a concern one of us has already written about (Anker 2020, 105). The "Ecological Indian" is one too easily known "in advance" – de-politicized and de-juridified – given "our" own needs and lacks, fantasies and projections.

If the first frame captures the "draw" of Indigenous traditions, its risk can be summed up as follows: just the "ecology" please, but hold the Indian, especially the political Indian. And, by the way, by "ecology" I mean what *I* mean by "ecology." The risks of the first frame lead to the second frame, which appears to have already conclusively delimited and decided the matter of what is relevant to any future action, just as the potential contribution of Indigenous peoples to devising that action is already foreseen and rejected. These frames risk "playing out a colonial trope," obviating the need for (the lived and contingent texture of) encounters, with both traditional ecological knowledge and, especially, with the (legal) orders tied to this knowledge (Anker 2020, 105). In both frames, then, there is potentially a "we" that does not have to contend with Indigenous law as law, on its own terms, with Indigenous peoples as peoples, as polities with jurisdiction (ways of speaking law) that do not simply reveal epistemologies or ontologies that can be borrowed and deployed. What is to be avoided, it seems to us, is the summing up ways of being, lifeworlds, and legal orders in such a way that a quick judgment can be pronounced on their usefulness. Indeed, part of the challenge posed by the Anthropocene may be that of how (not) to say "we" (Nancy 2000, 72, Antaki 2016, 54).

This quick judgment may arise because certain constructions of the Anthropocene make it difficult to occupy anything but a "paranoid" position (borrowing from Sedgwick 1997) from which to diagnose problematic realities and take a vigilant stand against the challenges of the future, leaving no time or energy for other – for instance, "reparative" – work or readings. But knowledge is performative as well as cognitive, and a given "truth" about what humans have wrought upon the planet need not dictate what we do with it and how we feel from it. For the moment, there is one thing we can affirm, and that we explore below: the Anthropocene should not mean that "we" now know, in advance, that we have no time for (encounters with) Indigenous legal orders, that they've been left (or pushed) behind, this time not only by the "feat" of some humans (those enacting settler-colonialism) but by the scientific "fact" of the Anthropocene. This text comes out of our own ongoing encounters with Indigenous law – for instance, through our colleagues Aaron Mills, Kerry Sloan, John Borrows, Gabriel Doreen, and Wanda Gabriel, through local elders and community members who teach in our classes, and through a range of different texts, conventional and otherwise. It is through these encounters that we are enabled to suggest a different frame than the ones above. The question of "repair" – ethically, etymologically – is at once a question of fixing a problem and making or returning to a specific place or home. And repair, in both these senses, one may say, is *the problem* posed by the Anthropocene.

We've emphasized here the importance of openness to encounter and hinted at some of what may close it off. In our next section, we dwell more on the closure to encounter, trying to show how a particular vision of ontology that culture/nature gets folded into is related to the paranoid reading of the Anthropocene and the "negative" "we" that it generates. In our last section, we try to introduce the texture of encounter into the picture and begin to draw attention to what happens when law is a part of it.

## Facing the Human, Losing the Indigenous

Because of its newness, the Anthropocene requires a radical re-framing that enables an understanding of the role of humans in planetary history. But some refuse the contributions to re-framing that "Indigeneity" might bring because they seem to know in advance that it has nothing to offer. What does that refusal look like? How exactly is the "human" of the Anthropocene faced, and the Indigenous lost? What stands in the way of encounter? We offer one example of the push and pull of Indigeneity in the work of Australian economist and philosopher Clive Hamilton whose compelling wake-up calls, in a series of popular books (2001, 2004, 2010, 2013, 2017), both take the Anthropocene seriously and try to figure out why "we" have such a hard time responding to it adequately. In Hamilton's oeuvre, the overwhelming fact of the Anthropocene works in a number of ways that are both familiar and troubling. First, the Anthropocene is, initially, a fact about human impacts on, and relationships to, nature. Indigenous ways of thinking, being, and doing are then judged based on whether their configuration of human–nature meets this factual challenge. These ways are framed in terms of ontology (not law, ethics, or politics), and their (being called to) judgment takes place at a high level of abstraction. Second, as a ruptural event, the Anthropocene sets up a number of dichotomies – old and new, local and planetary, supernatural and natural, and, ultimately, us and them, that situate Indigenous people in a time and on a scale that seem irrelevant to the Anthropocene, a colonial othering in which "they" are either too late, too local, or – given contemporary demographics – too "like us" to be of any help. Finally, the urgency of our predicament makes the Anthropocene an anxiety-producing super-fact, one that "factually" comes before all other considerations. Urgency leaves no time for being open to the uncertainties of encounter; paradoxically, perhaps, it echoes the "time is money" concern of capitalist efficiency. And anxiety gives us only what Arendt calls "negative solidarity," (1968, 83) that is, a solidarity tied to a horrible collective fate, potential or actual. It is "us" against the immense power of Gaia unleashed.

The fact about "we humans" of or in the Anthropocene is that we are entangled in the non-human world and yet unique in our outsized ability to be world makers or world destroyers. As Hamilton argues in *Defiant Earth: The Fate of Humans in the Anthropocene*, while science and technology, agriculture, industrialization, and population growth may have led to the domination of "nature", the new "Earth system" that recent science reveals is an entity that is "less predictable, more dangerous and, crucially, less subject to human control" (2017, 45). Both humans and Earth have become "super agents" – humans for bending the arc of Earth history, and Earth for coming back at us with overpowering might. The antinomy of human–Earth power leads Hamilton to reject approaches to human–Earth relations which, he claims, give too little credence to one or the other of these super agents. Ecomodernists, for instance, assume humans are "essentially benign" (66) in their optimism regarding engineered approaches to addressing climate change and overestimate our ability to tame Earth in this way. Eco-philosophers (like Thomas Berry) and post-humanists (like Jane Bennett and Donna Harraway) who draw from "pre-modern ontologies" – notice the language – in which humans and nature are entangled or indistinct, either advocate centering the *eco* instead of the *anthropos* or see agency as distributed throughout networks of humans and non-humans. According to Hamilton, this is "a move that repudiates our distinctiveness as world makers at the very moment our unique world-transforming power reaches a climax" (56). He proposes instead a "new anthropocentrism": one that accepts the factual – or one might say super-factual – rather than a normative case for the unique significance of humans for planet Earth.

As Hamilton's work before *Defiant Earth* shows, a second significant aspect of the human in the Anthropocene is that "we" are not sufficiently moved to act in the face of existential risk. In *Growth Fetish* (2004), Hamilton points to economic growth and overconsumption as the main driver of environmental depletion and asks why, when growth has failed to correct social ills like inequality, insecurity, and unemployment – and is even antithetical to well-being – so many people are still wedded to it. In *Requiem for a Species: Why We Resist the Truth About Climate Change* (2010), he suggests that the inability to face up to "what climate science is telling us" exists because there are powerful forces lined up against our collective ability to act rationally in our own best interests – unreasoning optimism, greed, materialism, our alienation from nature and our hubris in thinking we can master it (for example, through geo-engineered solutions to the climate crisis that he critiques in *Earth Masters* (2013)). There appears to be an invitation to shift underlying paradigms according to which humans live on the earth, one that would recognize the link between ontology – what it means to be (human) – and the work of ethics, politics, and law. Hamilton's texts would appear to raise the following question: how to conceive of the "fact" of the Anthropocene so as to enable certain feats, and move humans towards undertaking them?

Like many others, Hamilton recognizes that Indigenous peoples (seem to) have something to contribute to this paradigm shift. Specifically, the Anthropocene and its entangled relations point to the need to review "the hard Cartesian division between subject and object, and the separation of humans from nature" (2017, 89), and decades of ethnographic research in and with Indigenous communities provides examples of alternative accounts of human/non-human relationships. Hamilton offers the work of French anthropologist Philippe Descola in his book *Nature and Culture* as a key example of such accounts, with his four archetypal ontologies that configure subject and object, interiority and exteriority in different ways: naturalism (as in the West, the world is made up of the same substance but beings have radically different internal lives), animism (common in the Americas where many human and non-human beings are known as having similar interiorities – culture, kinship, agency – but are made up of very different stuff), totemism (as among Australian Indigenous peoples, in which there is continuity between both interiority and physicality, across a very wide array of beings) and analogism (a sort of radical system of difference, in which each being has a uniquely constituted interior and physical existence) (Descola 2013, 122). *Nature and Culture* has been critiqued for its schematic essentialization of vastly different societies and for its "armchairish" quality (Fitzgerald 2013).

Hamilton's rendering is more exaggerated still: indeed, no single Indigenous person or society is mentioned, or its ontology discussed.

Such a schematic grasp of "Indigenous ontologies" might make any outright rejection of the relevance of "Indigeneity" obviously premature. Nevertheless, Hamilton's claim that Indigenous traditions are helpless in the face of our "new" predicament is structurally axiomatic: their "pre-modern ontologies" are disconnected from the problems created by modernity and defined out of participation in the modern world. For a start, any ontology that minimizes the distinctions between humans and non-humans is said to miss the mark because it is precisely what Descola qualifies as this "tiny quantum" of difference that has "shift[ed] the Earth's geological arc" (2017, 103). Second, it is not our relationship with the natural world *per se* that is characteristic of the Anthropocene but the world-ruining capacities of our exceptional technological achievements – and fossil fuels in particular. The world outside of the laboratory – the "fields" of law, politics, economics, and technology that are relevant to the production of emissions – Hamilton suggests (mysteriously) is organized other than entirely around the subject–object split (108). Finally, as local knowledges tied to cultural perspectives, Indigenous ontologies do not approach the problem at the appropriate level, which is that of the "implacable logic of Earth system science" (78), a blunt truth beyond any cultural system (79). We can easily see here that the potential contribution of Indigenous peoples is reduced to the question of the entanglement of nature and culture or human and non-human, and that the relevance of the related subject/object division to the drivers of emissions is likewise readily dismissed. However, one only has to point to the pervasive structure of property relationships as control by persons over things and its role in irresponsible resource exploitation, markets, and capital accumulation to start to see the links between emissions and the subject–object division.

There is one further reason why, according to Hamilton, it is implausible to seek a way out of the problems of modernity through animist or other "pre-modern" ontologies. It is that one of Descola's ontologies – Western naturalism – has become dominant and continues to eradicate the others. Because of this, Hamilton asserts, "at the risk of speaking on their behalf," that Indigenous peoples pursue at most a dialogue of their traditional ways with the modern world as a political strategy, or, for the vast majority living in urban contexts, "seek to adopt Western ways as quickly as they can" (107). Hamilton worries that turning to Indigenous peoples for solutions to the Anthropocene fetishizes them and places an impossible burden on their shoulders (106). Similarly, Indigenous peoples – and others outside the "North" who are not historically responsible for emissions and who may bear more of the burden of changes in the climate – are included in the super-agent human, not because there is no moral accounting to pursue with respect to colonization and globalization, but because the scale of the Earth system does not see divisions between humans. The rupture is a rupture in the history of humanity as a whole that we all have to live with (71).

This account of Indigenous ontologies having lost out (and the acceptance of this loss by Indigenous peoples), that their worlds revolve around "our" Western naturalist one, does not ring true. It does not make sense of the growing sensibilities towards reconciliation or decolonization in places like Canada, Australia, New Zealand, and the United States that center the need for the maintenance (or initiation) of lawful relations between state law and Indigenous law (Dorsett and McVeigh 2012, Chapter 6; Tully 2018), nor the movements for the nurturing or revitalization of Indigenous law, science, and governance (Borrows 2002; Zuni Cruz 2009; Asch et al. 2018; Cajete 2020). Some of that work does not pitch urban against pre-modern, for instance, but asks about the extent to which any law is "rooted in earth" or coherent with the "earthway," to take up the language of our colleague Aaron Mills, to which we return below.

We agree with Peter Reason that Hamilton's embrace of human entanglement in Earth systems is only partial and that his "embedded or new anthropocentrism" draws him into dichotomous either/or reasoning (Reason 2019). The colorful image of a "defiant" Earth pitches two superpowers against one other and certainly does not suggest a place of deep participation in earth's processes. Indeed, the opposite of a "defiant" Earth might well be a "compliant" one. If we saw entanglement as a more general and pervasive question, we might be open to learning from Indigenous peoples about how human–earth relationships are linked to ways of practicing law, ethics, and politics within community, and sidestep the defiant–compliant binary of a hot war between super agents. Indeed, we might understand that some of the traits of Enlightenment discourse (such as freedom) that became by turns "turbo-charged" (in Hamilton's words: 2017, 110), irresponsibly used and selectively promoted in modernity, may have emerged in their modern form(s) by way of conversations between colonists and Indigenous peoples (Graeber and Wengrow 2021). Rather than see Indigenous peoples as fated to "adopt Western ways," we could perhaps think of a *métissage* that not only happened to "them" as they became more like "us" but something that happened to "us" as we also became more like "them" (29–36). Hamilton urges us to think our way out of the Anthropocene from within modernity in order to move beyond it; such thinking is also thinking with Indigenous peoples.

The references to Indigenous ontologies – via Descola and his skeletal schema – are, as mentioned, devoid of actual encounters; there is neither interpersonal contact nor engagement with Indigenous authors. In this top-down exegesis, not only do the multiplicity of the world's ontologies get over-simplified, but they are also presented as severed from, or even irrelevant to, politics. However, without moving beyond caricatural ontology to ethics, politics, or law, "new anthropocentrism" is nothing more than a re-statement of the challenge of the Anthropocene, and of what humans have done to Earth. For instance, it is not clear why it is so important to center human super-agency and distinctiveness when the point is likely not to do more with it (the path of eco-modernism) but less. Hamilton struggles with how a "narrative of fiasco" and of being too late, a narrative we are drawn to not because it is desirable but because we are compelled to accept it, can move human beings and ground social movements. He suggests that despite its negative focus on human failure, the truth-telling function of the story of what we have become gives us the foundation to unite in a shared position as a geological force (2017, 145).

We think that the ontology of entanglement, the experience of lived encounters, the grounds for becoming a collective "us" and the motivation to act are all connected. If "the question of how to live with Earth could ultimately be resolved only after we had developed the power to destroy life on it" (124–125), it seems that, despite how much we might now also turn our attention to how to use our "supernatural powers" responsibly, we are joined in what Hannah Arendt termed "negative solidarity." In an essay first published in 1957, Arendt wrote that technology in the post-World War II era had brought the world together in a kind of solidarity. But this was *negative* solidarity because it was based on fear of the atomic bomb. According to Arendt, this "factual" solidarity "does not in the least guarantee a common future" (1968, 83); it speaks of a common fate without a common past or ways of doing things as a "we." What if an ontology of entanglement drew us to notice ways in which we have (always already?) been entangled? What if we were all already relatives? What if relational ontology were to be understood not as a fact but a practice, a feat, the kind of feat demanded by the Anthropocene? Can negative solidarity lead to other forms of solidarity?

Knowledge of our raw super-factual power as world-destroying beings does not seem to fit us with the ability to respond – to be moved – as world-participating beings. The super-fact of the Anthropocene can too easily overwhelm us; leading to, returning to Sedgwick's terms, paranoia – and possibly paralysis, at least with respect to an openness to encounter and the uncertainty that comes with it. Entanglement might provide a way to move from or link negative solidarity to positive solidarity, to move from, in Colin Scott's language, negative to positive reciprocity (1996). Negative reciprocity happens when people act as if they have no relatives or try to take as much as they can without giving anything in return (Lacourse 1987, 292). With positive reciprocity, benefits are given and received (either mutually or as general reciprocity). Receiving something as a gift generates gratitude, and mobilizes us to give, in return but not only (Kimmerer 2013). What is sometimes called "justice" is returned to its roots in grace (Meyer 2010, 27).

We have dwelt on Hamilton's work here because it exemplifies some tendencies that trouble us. The Anthropocene names "the human" as both embedded in natural processes and possessed of super-agency that "we" seem to lack the motivation to curb. In this frame, Indigenous knowledge can be declined as irrelevant only if certain slights of hand are performed. First, the problem of the Anthropocene comes to be defined as one that is greater than the human relationship to nature or the subject/object problem – notably because of its supernatural quality – while Indigenous ontologies are reduced to that feature. Lack of engagement with Indigenous people themselves enables that narrow view, but also treats "ontologies" as legible facts and not as practice of relationship in themselves. In turn, the overwhelming super-fact of the Anthropocene makes potential engagement seem like an indulgence: its planetary scale that highlights the super-subjectivity of humans precludes the relevance of ontologies at what appear to be smaller scales, its ruptural quality drives a wedge between modern and pre-modern even as it is said that the solution must come from within the paradigm that created the problem, and its urgency all but condemns us to reproducing a colonial (mis)encounter.

Let's begin again by trying to sidestep the two framings above rather than exemplify them. We do so by attending to the passage between, or entanglement of, ontology and law, to the constitution of a "we" and to hearing and being moved to act. Here are two stories that struck us, that led us to emphasize the contingent, textured quality of encounter.

## Naming, Hearing, Moving

Sometime in early 2000, Nobel Laureate Paul Crutzen stood up in the middle of a meeting of the International Geosphere-Biosphere Program in Mexico after listening uncomfortably to speaker after speaker using the term Holocene, the relatively stable period of Earth history since the last ice age (Davison 2019). The atmospheric chemist recalls "I suddenly thought this was wrong. The world has changed too much. So I said: 'No, we are in the Anthropocene.' I just made up the word on the spur of the moment" (Pearce 2007, 21). Although he was not the first to use related terms – Italian geologist Antonio Stoppani spoke in 1873 about humans as a "new telluric force" on the earth ushering in the "anthropozoic era" (Crutzen 2002, 23) while Russian geologist Alexei Pavlov coined the term "anthropogene" for the impact of humans on the geological record in 1922 (Rull 2017, 156), and biologist Eugene F. Stoermer referred informally to the "Anthropocene" from the 1980s (Trischler 2016, 310) – Crutzen's Mexico speech led to a collaboration with Stoermer and others, and catalyzed both a popular adoption of the term across academia and beyond, and a movement among Earth scientists to have it formally recognized by the International Commission on Stratigraphy as an official geological epoch (application for recognition still pending) (Rull 2017, 157).

Here's another story about a moment of insight into rupture, into urgency, and into agency. Sometime in 2004, Ktunaxa elder and elected Chief Chris Luke Snr. was in a community meeting about the Jumbo Glacier ski resort planned for the *Qat'muk* area in Ktunaxa territory. The Ktunaxa Nation was involved in a long process of consultation with the provincial government of British Columbia over the resort and community members were concerned about the impact of the project on grizzly bears and the hunting of bears for ceremonial purposes. When someone stated that the bears had no voice in the process, Luke recalls that he felt disgruntled, so he stood up and said, "How can you say they have no voice? The grizzly bear has songs, a dance, and ceremonies. But they need our voice and our support so that their place won't be eroded. We can't allow the development in that area" (cited in Carroll 2020, 41). Although he did not initially follow up on the realization that the bears needed human voices and support, in 2009 he found himself in a hospital following a heart attack and was visited in a vision by the Grizzly Bear Spirit, *Kławła Tukłułakʔis* (42). This visit convinced Luke that *Qat'muk* – the site of the project – was the home territory of *Kławła Tukłułakʔis* (his childhood memories were unspecific about the Grizzly Bear Spirit's home to the north of his community) (45) and eventually brought him to the conviction that he had to oppose the project altogether lest the Spirit be driven from its home (Ktunaxa Nation 2010). When the provincial Minister of Forests, Lands, and Natural Resource Operations decided to proceed with the project, the Ktunaxa Nation contested the decision in court and lost (*Ktunaxa v BC* 2017).

The juxtaposition of these stories allows us to make some observations and ask some questions about "law" that may turn out to be as revelatory about "ontology" as certain explicit discussions thereof. In the first story, one can imagine the rupture of the Anthropocene – the loss (or disrepair?) of our Holocene home – being experienced viscerally and all of a sudden by Crutzen, such that old ways of speaking seem wrong. In the second, the Ktunaxa are faced with a potential rupture to be caused by the proposed development, the loss of a home for *Kławła Tukłułakʔis*, the loss of the "thread of connection" between the Spirit and the people (Carroll 2020, 35). Like Crutzen, Luke is similarly compelled by something that comes to him in the moment to "take a stand." Both men experience a moment of insight that leads them to abruptly re-frame existing conversations so as to articulate the actual or anticipated rupture they identify. Accordingly, they both interpellate human beings as agents of disrepair and potential agents in repair, provided human beings learn to listen and give voice – to their geological significance, to the Grizzly Bear Spirit, with whom the Ktunaxa share dances, songs, and voices. Both moments of re-framing seek to move other humans and generate a kind of consensus (Antaki and LeGuerrier 2018) around how to act collectively in the face of a crisis with irreversible consequences.

However, both re-framings fall eventually on deaf ears because they are not immediately (re)cognizable; the collectives initially mobilized experience a limit in the capacity of others to listen to them, perhaps even to hear them in the first place, and thus to be moved by what they have to say. For Crutzen and other Earth scientists, there has been an unfathomably meager response by politicians and civil society to the very clear alarm bells they are ringing – to the point that a strike-like moratorium on climate research has been suggested until action is taken to reduce emissions (Glavovic et al. 2021). The struggle is thus not only within the scientific community with respect to naming a new geological era but also in having the "science" be heard and translated into law or policy. For the Ktunaxa Nation, the Court heard the voice of the Grizzly Bear Spirit as Luke's individual belief under a constitutional claim of freedom of religion; the majority of judges declined to accept that the scope of protection for religious beliefs could include a property-type right over the site as an object of a belief, as they characterized the Ktunaxa Nation's claim. In contrast, the minority opinion allowed for the significance of a connection between belief and its object, particularly for Indigenous religions where land is "itself … sacred" (*Ktunaxa v BC* 2017, [127]). However, the claim was discounted by them as amounting to a veto right which would constitute an unacceptable "restraint on public ownership," including on the interests of another Aboriginal group that supported the project

([150]). In the end, both judicial opinions treat the matter as one of internalized belief, not of law, collective politics, or of fact (of rupture, of urgency, of the voice of *Kławła Tukłułak?is*).

Alternatively, the other basis of the claim by the Ktunaxa plaintiffs – the adequacy of consultation under s.35 of the Constitution Act 1982 – was more explicitly about collective politics. S.35 "recognizes and affirms the existing Aboriginal and treaty rights of the Aboriginal peoples of Canada" and case law has interpreted it to include a "duty to consult" where rights are potentially impacted (*Haida Nation* 2004). However, in this claim, Luke's "revelation" was read by the Court not as the voice of the bears but as a sudden change of position with respect to consultation – a *new* claim by the Ktunaxa with respect to the area being the home of the Grizzly Bear Spirit that was "designed to require a particular accommodation" ([39]) – with the implication that it was either not a claim based on "traditional practice" of the kind protected by s.35 rights or did not represent good faith engagement in consultations, or both (Kislowicz and Luk 2019, Hickling 2020).

If the stories have something important in common, their differences can also serve to draw out the ways in which a frame of entanglement between humans and nature is and can be linked to law. Crutzen's "revelation," one might say, is a scientific moment of (the construction of) "fact" to which "law" and "policy" must respond, but which, it seems, remains outside of them. The revelation does not seem to be directly about law, even though it has major ramifications for it. In contrast, law is embedded in Luke's revelation from the beginning. His revelation is tied to what we may call the "standing" (Stone 1972) of the grizzly bears – both within the Ktunaxa legal order and in a contested process with an outside political body – and the question of lawful relations – both with the grizzly bears and with Canadian law. In some legal traditions, it is difficult to speak as if there are separate domains of law and fact, because the substance of law is not conceived as a context-independent rule that can be applied to a concrete situation (on the cultural specificities of the law/fact distinction, see Geertz 1983, Chapter 8). This non-separation of law and fact may well characterize the casuistry of the common law to some degree, but it is much more radical in Indigenous legal orders, especially, on the one hand, in the absence of any centralized authority which can "apply" the law, and, on the other hand, in light of a preference for non-propositional expressions of law. Indeed, what are sometimes characterized as "sources" of Indigenous law – stories, ceremonies, teachings from elders, dreams, and direct experience with a complex of ecological and social relations over one's lifetime (Borrows 2010) – our colleague Aaron Mills casts rather as *re*sources or a repertoire to guide decision-making (2019, 140–141). Luke's "revelation" and subsequent actions thus speak to a legal order in which "law" can be understood as reasoned decisions about how to act, and not a set of rules.

Second, the non-separation of law and fact (entangled with the "standing" of the grizzly bears) reveals a lifeworld, from which Ktunaxa law emerges, characterized by interdependence, in which "the entire web of life is connected to the Ktunaxa people in a reciprocal relationship of honour and respect" (Gahr 2013, 9). This "web of interconnections" encompasses not only relations with plant and animal species that confound the nature–culture binary (namely, bears are relatives and have social structures and cultural practices just as humans do), but also connections with supernatural beings and forces, as well as ceremony and ritual (Morigeau 2020). The legal grammar thus sidesteps the person-thing distinction in favor of "all are my relations" (Littlebear 2009; Antaki and Popovici 2022). This web of interconnections is of ontological and epistemological significance and "provides a way of understanding the world but also a way of coming to a better – and so, to some extent, a new – understanding of the world" (Carroll 2020, 33). If Crutzen's story provides the factual evidence that invites or requires humanity to enter into a "natural contract" with a newly recognized or emergent Earth where the realities of the parties' mutual entanglement must be negotiated (see Serres 1990), Luke's story shows how a "we" that includes humans and non-humans might *always already* be pre-supposed by Indigenous legal orders. These orders are embedded in relationships of interdependence and mutual aid – between and beyond humans – and are indeed shaped by those relationships and the responsibilities they engender. Reciprocity is not a "rule" but a kind of pervasive logic or ontology that Mills explicitly articulates as a form of constitutionalism, one he calls "rooted" because it borrows its patterned thinking from place-based ecological relationships (2016, 2019). Mills writes specifically about Anishinaabe law, but the themes of reciprocity, interdependence, and relational decision-making are echoed in many other Indigenous legal orders (Kuokkanen 2006, Black 2010, Salmond 2017).

Third, this ontology is not just about relations with non-humans but is deeply about human relationships as well. One might say it is about "being with" in the broadest sense. Luke's story not only reveals that his community includes both humans and non-humans, it also shows how humans are *with one another* in the solidarity engendered by mutual aid – and reveals the layered process of coming to decisions informed by Ktunaxa law. We rely here on the account carefully pieced together by religious studies scholar Michael Carroll (2020) from Luke's autobiography published in 2003, his affidavits for the case, and some media interviews, and read them through the lens of rooted constitutionalism that we evoked above. When he was a child, Luke attended Grizzly Bear ceremonies; his elder male relatives were leaders and helpers in those ceremonies and most of the Ktunaxa people in his community were in the Grizzly Bear clan (44); he heard Creation stories that linked the Grizzly Bear Spirit with land to the north of his community. Luke seems to have grown up in a context where dreams and visionary experiences are a source of guidance in life, and he writes about some of these in his autobiography (43). As numerous Indigenous authors have attested, these kinds of experiences are often discussed with others in order to discern their message or significance (Kovach 2021, 83; Rowe 2014, 12–13; Battiste 2010, 39). Indeed, Luke confirms in his affidavit that his choice to be the spokesperson for the Grizzly Bear Spirit following his vision was made "in consultation with other Ktunaxa persons, including knowledge holders and leaders, and with their affirmation" (Carroll 2020, 43). Whatever the nature of *Kȼawȼa Tukȼuȼakʔis*, its voice is not a unilateral command, even though it appears to give rise in Luke to a strongly felt compulsion; the vision acts as a prompt to engage in collective political discussions that generate consensus.

The point that we think this account suggests is that "traditional ecological knowledge" is legal from the beginning and inseparable from the legality of Indigenous orders. The Ecological Indian – that is, the Indigenous ontologies that entangle nature and culture – brings with it the "Indians" themselves and all their kin and invites us to rethink the very grammar of law and of relation. For instance, it invites us to return to the etymology of ecology and its roots in a human household. The attraction of Indigenous orders, then, ends up being less about "nature" and more about what it is to live law generally and how to say or not say "we." They open up the possibility of reflection on solidarity or "being with" that does not reproduce colonial law by imagining and freezing native peoples at a moment of contact. Moving beyond the Ecological Indian means, too, recognizing the constitutive roles of encounter with Indigenous peoples for "modernity" itself.

What we have seen above should help begin to resist the tendency to reduce Indigenous orders or traditions to what they have to say about the blurring of nature–culture and to sever this from what they have to say about human–human relations. It should hopefully also help resist the temptation to "raid" Indigenous law for what we think we need from it, a temptation bolstered by instrumental accounts of law that treat law simply as a tool or instrument to get what a pre-existing "we" want (White 1985) in response to "facts" out there. If the Anthropocene is a kind of uprooting or un-homing or disrepair, both of these tendencies are also "uprootings" – of human–human from human–nature, of law from fact or community – that some might link to the problems of the Anthropocene, how it arose to begin with, and why "we" have trouble responding to it. If the Anthropocene would be seized as a problem of "lawful relations" (Dorsett and McVeigh 2012) and not simply one of ontology or super-facts, there might well be more room for repair, for reparative readings, and reparative relations.

## References

Anker, K. (2020) 'Ecological jurisprudence and Indigenous relational ontologies: Beyond the "Ecological Indian"?' In K. Anker, P. D. Burdon, G. Garver, M. Maloney and C. Sbert (eds.), *From Environmental to Ecological Law*. Routledge, London. 104–118

Antaki, M. (2016) 'Declining accusation'. In G. Pavlich and M. P. Unger (eds.), *Accusation: Creating Criminals*. UBC Press, Vancouver. 44–69.

Antaki, M. and LeGuerrier, C. (2018) 'Monument, portrait, tableau: Making sense of and with Jacques-Louis David's Tennis Court Oath'. In S. Huygebaert et al. (eds.), *Sensing the Nation's Law: Historical Inquiries into the Aesthetics of Democratic Legitimacy*. Springer, Cham. 11–43.

Antaki, M. and Popovici, A. (2022) 'Interrupting the legal person: On techniques and grammars of law?' In A. Sarat, G. Pavlich and R. Mailey (eds.), *Interrupting the Legal Person (Studies in Law, Politics, and Society, Vol. 87B)*. Emerald Publishing Limited, Bingley. 101–117.

Arendt, H. (1968) *Men in Dark Times*. Harcourt, Brace & Co., New York.

Arendt, H. (1973) *The Origins of Totalitarianism*, 2nd edition. Harcourt, Brace, Yovanovich, New York.

Arendt, H. (2007) *The Promise of Politics*, reprint edition. Schocken, New York.

Asch, M., Borrows, J. and Tully, J. (eds.) (2018) *Resurgence and Reconciliation: Indigenous-Settler Relations and Earth Teachings*. University of Toronto Press, Toronto.

Battiste, M. (2010) 'Indigenous knowledge and Indigenous peoples' education'. In S. M. Subramanian and B. Pisupati (eds.), *Traditional Knowledge in Policy and Practice: Approaches to Development and Human Well-Being*. United Nations University Press, Tokyo. 31–51.

Black, C. F. (2010) *The Land Is the Source of the Law: A Dialogic Encounter with Indigenous Jurisprudence*. Routledge, London.

Borrows, J. (2002) *Recovering Canada: The Resurgence of Indigenous Law*. University of Toronto Press, Toronto.

Borrows, J. (2010) *Canada's Indigenous Constitution*. University of Toronto Press, Toronto.

Cajete, G. (2020) 'Indigenous science, climate change, and Indigenous community building: A framework of foundational perspectives for Indigenous community resilience and revitalization'. *Sustainability*, 12(22), 1–11.

Carroll, M. (2020) 'What evicting the Grizzly Bear Spirit does (and doesn't tell us) about Indigenous 'religion' and Indigenous rights'. *Religious Studies*, 49(1), 32–41.

Coulthard, G. and Simpson, L. B. (2016) 'Grounded normativity/place-based solidarity'. *American Quarterly*, 68(2), 249–255.

Crutzen, P. (2002) 'Geology of mankind'. *Nature*, 415(6867), 23.

Crutzen, P. and Steffen, W. (2003) 'How long have we been in the Anthropocene era?' *Climate Change*, 61(3), 251–257.

Davison, N. (2019) 'The Anthropocene epoch: Have we entered a new phase of planetary history?' *The Guardian*, 30 May <https://www.theguardian.com/environment/2019/may/30/anthropocene-epoch-have-we-entered-a-new-phase-of-planetary-history>, accessed 13 June 2022.

Descola, P. (2005) *Beyond Nature and Culture*. University of Chicago Press, Chicago.

Dorsett, S. and McVeigh, S. (2012) *Jurisdiction*. Routledge, Milton Park, Oxon.

Fitzgerald, D. (2013) 'Philippe Descola's *Beyond Nature and Culture*'. *Somatosphere*. http://somatosphere.net/2013/philippe-descolas-beyond-nature-and-culture.html/, accessed 13 June 2022.

Gahr, T. (2013) 'The Origins of Culture: An Ethnographic Exploration of the Ktunaxa Creation Stories'. MA thesis. Royal Roads University at Victoria.

Geertz, C. (1983) *Local Knowledge: Further Essays in Interpretive Anthropology*. Basic Books, New York.

Glassberg, D. (2014) 'Place, memory and climate change'. *The Public Historian*, 36(3), 17–30.

Glavovic, B., Smith, T. and White, I. (2021) 'The tragedy of climate change science'. *Climate and Development*, 14(9), 1–5.

Glenn, P. (2014) *Legal Traditions of the World: Sustainable Diversity in Law*. Oxford University Press, Oxford.

Graeber, D. and Wengrow, D. (2021) *The Dawn of Everything: A New History of Humanity*, Signal, Toronto.

*Haida Nation v British Columbia (Minister of Forests)* 2004 SCC 73.
Hamilton, C. (2001) *Running from the Storm: The Development of Climate Change Policy in Australia.* University of New South Wales Press, Sydney.
Hamilton, C. (2004) *Growth Fetish.* Pluto Press, London.
Hamilton, C. (2010) *Requiem for a Species: Why We Resist the Truth About Climate Change.* Earthscan, London.
Hamilton, C. (2013) *Earthmasters: The Dawn of the Age of Climate Engineering.* Yale University Press, New Haven.
Hamilton, C. (2016) 'The Anthropocene as rupture'. *The Anthropocene Review*, 3(2), 93–106.
Hamilton, C. (2017) *Defiant Earth: The Fate of Humans in the Anthropocene.* Polity, Cambridge.
Hamilton, C., Gemenne, F. and Bonneuil, C. (eds.) (2015) *The Anthropocene and the Global Environmental Crisis: Rethinking Modernity in a New Epoch.* Routledge, Abingdon, Oxon.
Helender-Renvall, E. (2010) 'Animism, personhood and the nature of reality: Sami perspectives'. *Polar Record*, 46(236), 44–56.
Hickling, J. (2020) 'Ktunaxa Nation v British Columbia: Sacred sites and saving graces'. *Oxford Journal of Law and Religion*, 9(1), 193–207.
Holder, J. (2000) 'New age: Rediscovering natural law'. *Current Legal Problems*, 53(1), 151–179.
Hourdequin, M. (2015) 'Ecological restoration, continuity and change: Negotiating history and meaning in layered landscapes'. In M. Hourdequin and D. G. Havlick (eds.), *Restoring Layered Landscapes: History, Ecology, and Culture.* Oxford University Press, Oxford. 13–33.
Kimmerer, R. W. (2013) *Braiding Sweetgrass: Indigenous Wisdom, Scientific Knowledge and the Teaching of Plants.* Milkweed Editions, Minneapolis.
Kislowicz, H. and Luk, S. (2019) 'Recontextualizing *Ktunaxa Nation v. British Columbia*: Crown land, history and Indigenous religious freedom'. *Supreme Court Law Review (2d)*, 88, 205–229.
Kovach, M. (2021) *Indigenous Methodologies: Characteristics, Conversations, and Contexts*, 2nd edition. Toronto University Press, Toronto.
*Ktunaxa Nation v. British Columbia (Forest, Lands and Natural Resource Operations)* 2017 SCC 54.
Ktunaxa Nation (2010) 'Qat'muk declaration'. http://www.ktunaxa.org/who-we-are/qatmuk-declaration/, accessed 2 June 2022.
Kuokkanen, R. (2006) 'The logic of the gift: Reclaiming Indigenous peoples' philosophies'. In T. Botz-Bornstein and J. Hengelbrock (eds.), *Re-Ethnisizing the Minds: Cultural Revival in Contemporary Thought.* Rodopi, Amsterdam. 231–271.
Lacourse, J. (1987) 'Reciprocité positive et reciprocité negative : De Marcel Mauss à René Girard'. *Cahiers Internationaux de Sociologie*, 83, 291–305.
Littlebear, L. (2009) *Naturalizing Indigenous Knowledges: Synthesis Paper.* University of Saskatchewan, Aboriginal Education Research Centre, Saskatoon, and First Nations and Adult Higher Education Consortium Calgary. http://neatoeco.com/iwiseconference.org/wp-content/uploads/2015/08/NaturalizingIndigenousKnowledge_LeroyLittlebear.pdf, accessed 13 June 2022.
Lyons, S. R. (2010) *X-Marks: Native Signatures of Assent.* University of Minnesota Press, Minneapolis.
Masson-Delmotte, V. et al. (2019) *Global Warming of 1.5°C: An IPCC Special Report* (Intergovernmental Panel on Climate Change). https://www.ipcc.ch/sr15/chapter/chapter-1/, accessed 26 February 2022.
Meyer, L. (2010) *Justice as Mercy.* University of Michigan Press, Ann Arbor.
Mills, A. (2016) 'The lifeworlds of law: On revitilizing Indigenous legal orders today'. *McGill Law Journal*, 61(4), 847–884.
Mills, A. (2019) 'Miinigowiziwin: All that has been given for living well together one vision of Anishinaabe constitutionalism'. PhD thesis, University of Victoria.
Morigeau, C. (2020) 'Ktunaxa traditional knowledge: Building Ktunaxa capacity for the future'. MA thesis, Royal Roads University at Victoria.
Murray, J. (2014) 'Earth jurisprudence, wild law, emergent law: The emerging field of ecology and Law—Part 1'. *Liverpool Law Review*, 35(3), 215–231.
Nadasdy, P. (2021) 'How many worlds are there? Ontology, practice and indeterminacy'. *American Ethnologist*, 48(4), 357–369.
Nancy, J.-L. (2000) *Being Singular Plural.* Stanford University Press, Stanford.
Neidjie, B. (1989) *Story About Feeling.* Magabala Books, Broome.
Pearce, F. (2007) *With Speed and Violence: Why Scientists Fear Tipping Points.* Beacon Press, Boston.
Reason, P. (2019) 'Review of *Defiant Earth* by Clive Hamilton'. https://thomasberry.org/review-of-defiant-earth-by-clive-hamilton, accessed 7 June 2022.

Rowe, G. (2014) 'Implementing Indigenous ways of knowing into research: Insights into the critical role of dreams as catalysts for knowledge development'. *Journal of Indigenous Social Development*, 3(2), 1–17.

Rull, V. (2017) 'The "Anthropocene": Neglects, misconceptions, and possible futures'. *European Molecular Biology Reports*, 18(7), 1056–1060.

Salmond, A. (2017) *Tears of Rangi: Experiments Across Worlds*. Auckland University Press, Auckland.

Schmitt, C. (2007) *The Concept of the Political*, expanded edition. University of Chicago Press, Chicago.

Scott, C. (1996) 'Science for the West, myth for the rest: The case of James Bay Cree knowledge construction'. In L. Nader (ed.), *Naked Science: Academic Enquiries into Boundaries, Power and Knowledge*. Routledge, New York. 69–86.

Sedgwick, E. (1997) 'Paranoid reading and reparative reading; Or, you're so paranoid you probably think this introduction is about you'. In E. Sedgwick (ed.), *Novel Gazing: Queer Readings in Fiction*. Duke University Press, Durham. 1–37.

Serres, M. (1990) *Le contrat naturel*. Éditions F. Bourin, Paris.

Stacey, J. (2018) *The Constitution of the Environmental Emergency*. Hart Publishing, Oxford.

Stone, C. (1972) 'Should trees have standing?' *Southern California Law Review*, 45, 450–501.

Trischler, H. (2016) 'The Anthropocene: A challenge for the history of science, technology, and the environment'. *N.T.M.* 24(3), 309–335.

Tully, J. (2018) 'Reconciliation here on earth'. In M. Asch, J. Borrows and J. Tully (eds.), *Resurgence and Reconciliation: Indigenous-Settler Relations and Earth Teachings*. University of Toronto Press, Toronto. 83–129.

White, J. B. (1985) 'Law as rhetoric, rhetoric as law: The arts of cultural and communal life'. *University of Chicago Law Review*, 52(3), 684–702.

Zuni-Cruz, C. (2009) 'Law of the land – Recognition and resurgence in Indigenous law and justice systems'. In B. J. Richardson, S. Imai and K. McNeil (eds.), *Indigenous Peoples and the Law: Comparative and Critical Perspectives*. Hart Publishing, London. 315–335.

# PART II

# Subjects of the Anthropocene

# 4

# THE ANTHROPOCENE ARCHIVE

## Human and Inhuman Subjects and Sediments

*Kathleen Birrell*

The Anthropocene, as both a scientific thesis and a critical provocation, prompts a reckoning with the epistemological archive of modern law. While this law does not literally "fossilize," its archive can be imagined as comprising both geologic and epistemic sediment (Pottage 2019, 155). Our apprehension of human planetary impact as evidenced in climatic change and ecological degradation elevates a Promethean humanity, to the extent that it is considered a "geomorphic force" (Yusoff 2013; Crutzen 2002; Crutzen and Stoermer 2000). While this scalar recalibration accommodates the "tectonic plates of humanity" (Serres 1995, 16), the Anthropocene also draws attention to our coincident and differential vulnerability. We bear witness to the devastating agency of our species, while also acknowledging the brevity of humanity within a vast planetary chronology (Macfarlane 2019, 15). The concept of the Anthropocene returns us yet again to the question of the human and to the ways in which subjectivity is constructed and rendered meaningful. The figure of the *anthropos* – the foundational and universalized humanity distilled in the (male) sovereign subject (Grear 2015, 226) – is simultaneously expanded and contracted by the constitutive tensions of the Anthropocene. The epistemic sediment within which this subject is steeped reflects the temporal discipline and ontological categorization of matter central to modernity, in accordance with which the human and the inhuman are demarcated (Povinelli 2016; Yusoff 2018; Latour 1993; 2017; 2018; Bennett 2010), and the appropriative and extractive impulses of empire are made manifest in the rights-bearing subject of modern law. This chapter examines the distillation of the relationship between modern law and matter in the legal subject, and explores encounters with more expansive renderings of human and inhuman subjectivity.

The very idea of the human, delimited by an "exclusionary logic" (Mignolo 2018, 155–157), is articulated most explicitly in the legal register of rights. The "proper" rights-bearing subject embodies the arrogations of empire and its appropriative narrative (Bhandar 2018, 4–5; Yusoff 2018, 65–68). In its most constrained form, Pottage suggests that the modern "figure of appropriation" might be construed as the "index fossil" for the Anthropocene, evidenced in the territorial demarcations and cartographic impositions of empire and its "geojurisprudence" (Pottage 2019, 168; Schmitt 1996, 328). This jurisprudence turns upon the ontological privileging of the (racialized) human as a proprietorial subject, as distinct from the inhuman as an appropriable object. As a constitutive constraint upon legal recognition, within which the legal subject remains enclosed (Povinelli et al. 2017, 175–176), this distinction animates and delimits contemporary renderings of legal subjectivity, including the relatively recent attribution of

DOI: 10.4324/9781003388081-6

legal personhood and rights to "nature" (Stone 1972; Cullinan 2011; Burdon 2015; Clark et al. 2018). Exploring the centrality of this ontological demarcation to historical and contemporary iterations of the modern subject, alongside Derrida's reading of such normative distinctions as fundamental questions of genre (1992a), this chapter imagines epistemic encounters between different renderings of subjectivity: the sedimented subject of the modern legal archive, the fossilized subject of geologic and social strata, the proper subject of legal recognition, and the sympoietic subjectivities of communal life.

This intervention emerges from an expansive scholarly archive on the relationship between human and inhuman forces, and the co-constitution of subjectivity and materiality. This archive draws upon Foucault's comprehensive engagement with the power relations of social stratification, and the integral relationship between subjectivity and its "social and material milieu" (Yusoff 2017, 107). In an interview following the release of *The Archaeology of Knowledge*, Foucault elaborates on his earlier discussion of the "death of the subject":

> In the rumbling that shakes us today, perhaps we have to recognize the birth of a world where the subject is not one but split, not sovereign but dependent, not an absolute origin but a function ceaselessly modified.
>
> *(Foucault 1989, 67)*

This reflection eschews the presumed autonomy and originary authority of the sovereign subject – "the Subject in capital letters" – in an acknowledgment of constitutive relationality, mutual dependency, and originary plurality (ibid.). The broader scholarship from which my own reading draws is embedded in Foucault's conceptualization of "geopower," elaborated and extended in the work of others, as a material force that contours political subjectivity (Grosz 2011; Yusoff et al. 2012; Yusoff 2017; Grosz et al., 2017). For Deleuze and Guattari, a fossilized substratum subtends social relations and forms of subjectivity emerge from the social "order of things," by which material "flows" are captured (Yusoff 2017, 110–111; Deleuze and Guattari 1987, 40–41; Yusoff 2018). Povinelli further explores this ontological demarcation as an expression of "geontopower," which delimits biopower and distinguishes life and nonlife (2016). While the geological process of sedimentation is conventionally understood as one of intensification and solidification, however, a Foucauldian reading of historical strata reveals both constitutive constraint and discursive dynamism (Yusoff 2017, 108). This dynamism reflects the relationship between geologic forces and social practices, which defines modes of subjectivity (Yusoff 2017; Deleuze and Guattari 1987; Foucault 1989).

Extending this dynamic rendering of sedimented subjectivity, I explore ways in which the Anthropocene reveals our "mineralogical dimension," challenging the categories and conceits underpinning conventional geological regimes of subjectification and their juridification (Yusoff 2013, 780; Yusoff 2018, 66–67; Yusoff and Thomas 2018). Tracing the emergence of earth jurisprudence and its ontological premises and consequent constraints, and a recent critical turn toward obligations (Birrell and Matthews 2020; Burdon 2020; Matthews 2019; Matthews and Veitch 2018), I contend that this schematic elevation of inhumanity to the juridical equivalent of its human other, in the attribution of legal personhood and associated rights to rivers and other inhuman entities, reinforces the prohibitive enclosure of subjectivity. That is, returning to Povinelli, it reinforces the construction of an ontological boundary, in accordance with which existence is defined and enclosed (Povinelli et al. 2017, 171). Understanding human life not as a putatively universal force effecting an "empire of impacts" (Yusoff 2013, 781), but rather as a community of bodies continuous with a mineralogical substrate and microbial symbionts, instead requires a radical reframing of subjectivity, both human and inhuman, within

Western intellectual traditions. The ethical relationality of Indigenous legal orders is central to this reframing, articulated in the work of Donald (2009) among others, and made explicit in the work of Todd on the sharing of territory with and obligations owed to inhuman communities (2018, 66–73). While the modern legal subject is animated by the fiction of an apparently closed autopoiesis, this chapter concludes with an exploration of the implications and challenges of its inherent sympoiesis – the mutuality of "making-with" (Haraway 2016, 58; Grear 2020, 361; Margulis 1991), by which it is iteratively constituted and sustained.

## The Sedimented Subject

The normative articulation of the "anthropozoic era," first proposed in 1873 (Crutzen 2002, 23; Crutzen and Stoermer 2000, 17; Zalasiewicz et al. 2010, 2228, citing Stoppani 1873), is complected by its epistemological contingency. In naming a new geological epoch, formally effected by the placement of a "golden spike" or Global Boundary Stratotype Section and Point (Waters et al. 2018), researchers appointed to the Anthropocene Working Group are tasked with identifying and locating material (stratigraphic) evidence of hominid impact: "In the end, it will be the rocks that have the final say" (Subramanian 2019). This singular focus is at variance with the contested reception of the Anthropocene thesis in the social sciences and the humanities, emerging from the multispecies and new materialist turns, and its re-articulation in posthumanist scholarship that explores and embraces the mutuality of human and inhuman flourishing (Bauer and Bahn 2018, 3; Bennett 2010; Braidotti 2013; Frost 2016). Indeed, for Povinelli, posthuman critique is now yielding to "post-life critique," as scholars interrogate the presumed ontological distinction between the lively and the inert – in Bennett's words, "the quarantines of matter and life" (2010, vii) – and, moreover, the historical abjuration of multiple ontologies (Povinelli 2016, 14). The Anthropocene specifically yet uncritically pivots around the appropriative yet abstracted *anthropos*, which is defined in opposition to its "others," human and inhuman (Grear 2015, 237, 241). I am concerned with the centrality of this categorical distinction to the conceptualization and operation of the rights-bearing subject of modern law, with its hierarchies and "ideological closures" (Grear 2015, 230; see also 226–227, 246), and the constitutive tensions within this epistemological sediment, as revealed by the Anthropocene. While the ontological constraints of the *Anthropos* are embedded within the Anthropocene concept, the implicit tensions of the former are made explicit in the latter.

Principal among the "legitimate fictions" of modern law (Derrida 1992b, 183; Derrida 2002, 240 citing Montaigne 1962, 1203; Montaigne 1933, 970) is the sovereign rights-bearing subject. This subject is reflected in the fictitious autonomous body of biology: returning to Povinelli, "even within the natural sciences the closed, self-organized body is at best a working fiction" (Povinelli 2016, 53; Haraway 2016, 33). The idea of the human – the *anthropos* (Greek) or *humanus* (Latin) – and its definitional exclusions and institutional apparatus (Mignolo 2018, 156) reflect the categorical enclosures of life and nonlife. The "geontological conditions" (Yusoff 2017, 118) enabling the emergence of this social subject might be perceived by observing the historical relationship between epistemic sediment and geologic strata. In this part of the discussion, I would like to examine the epistemic sediment from which the rights-bearing subject emerges, imagined as a trace fossil of the Anthropocene, and epitomized in the "figure of appropriation" (Pottage 2019, 171). In geological terms, a trace fossil or ichnofossil is a behavioral rather than skeletal remnant of a past organism, such as a foot or burrow print, by which aspects of the relationship between life and nonlife might be discerned (Pottage 2019, 153–154). In paleoecology, trace fossils are identified and classified according to the behavior rather than the organism that created them, using a "Linnean nomenclature": for example, "fugichnia are escape burrows, agrichnia are farming burrows, and domichnia are dwelling burrows" (Bottjer 2016, 129). This linguistic separation of an organism from its behavioral trace in classificatory cascades might be usefully applied to the behavioral (and linguistic) traces evident within the archive of modern law. Returning to Pottage, the behavioral and discursive traces in accordance with which we now define and contemplate the Anthropocene and its modes of subjectivity might be similarly observed and classified:

> Discourses of the Anthropocene themselves have a geology, and any analysis of the Anthropocene is made from within a layering of epistemic sediments, which condition what is seen and how it is analysed.
>
> *(Pottage 2019, 157)*

Despite his assertion that "law does not fossilize," Pottage here draws together geologic and social strata in a discussion of the epistemic sediment that informs our apprehension of the Anthropocene and its geojurisprudence. Reading Koselleck, he extends a historiographical transposition of geological strata and sediment: whereas geological strata are commonly considered static and impermeable, historical sediment is dynamic and iterative (Pottage 2019, 155–156; Koselleck 2018). Pottage draws attention to the normative structures of repetition inherent within law and its discursive sediments or "fossils" (Pottage 2019, 156–157). Engaging with Schmitt's schema of "appropriation/distribution/production," as articulated in *The Nomos of the Earth,* Pottage argues that appropriation might be imagined as a "jurisprudential sediment" and, furthermore, as the index fossil or "*leitfossil*" for the Anthropocene, which is rehearsed and reactivated in discourses of the Anthropocene (Pottage 2019, 167; 174; Schmitt 1996). In this way, the epistemic layering of the Anthropocene is imagined to be dynamic, enlivened by a discursive process of repetition and reinvention (ibid., 157). In my reading, the "figure of appropriation," construed as an index fossil for the Anthropocene, is indicative of the epistemic sediment and discursive trace fossils of modern law, observable in the ontological distinctions and dynamics that contour the rights-bearing subject.

The epistemic limit defining the distinction between life and nonlife, and ensuing modes of subjectification, might be usefully explored by a brief excursion into the troubling question of genre (Derrida 1992a). For Derrida, the "law of genre" is prohibitive, establishing a limit or boundary that is nonetheless defined by a "law of overflowing, of *excess*" (ibid., 228). In the context of a broader discussion of the constitutive transgression of genres, and with prescient relevance to the temporal and material transgressions that define the Anthropocene, Derrida instances the normative distinction between "*phusis*" ("nature," biology) and "*technē, thesis, nomos*" (broadly construed as artifice, postulate, law) (ibid., 224–225; Motha 2021). The "enigma" of genre, he argues, is the necessary subversion of its enclosure; the law of genre is "a principle of contamination, a law of impurity, a parasitical economy" (Derrida 1992a, 227). This constitutive transgression is exemplified in the confluence of biological and geological fossil records and attendant modes of subjectivity, to which the Anthropocene draws our attention (Yusoff 2013, 780). The "technofossil," a term now adopted by the Anthropocene Working Group, illustrates this confluence, in which human and inhuman agency are rendered indistinguishable components of the "technosphere" (Pottage 2019, 154). The technofossil is an expansion of the geologic "trace fossil," its linguistic recourse to *technē* rather than *physis* emphasizing its (catastrophic) artificiality (ibid., 154). Nonetheless, it is the very articulation of the Anthropocene – as a geologic epoch precipitated by the excesses of human habitation and consumption – that illuminates the constitutive transgression of *technē* and *physis*. In the "figure of the technofossil," the contamination of genre is writ large – reading Pottage's illustrative list, human and inhuman agency and behavior are collapsed in fossilized "plastics, plastiglomerates, purified metals and minerals, Plutonium-239, and so on" (ibid.). The material refuse of human industrial processes and consumptive practices reveals the intimate relationship between biological and geological strata and the material and discursive movement between them. Considering the example of the "geosociality" of oil, Yusoff describes the ways in which the manifold flows and forms of oil connect "biology, geology and culture" in a dissolution of clear boundaries between the living and the inert (Yusoff 2017, 118, citing LeMenager 2014, 6–7). The extent to which this relationality is perceptible or "articulable," however, is epistemologically contingent (Yusoff 2017, 115–116, citing Deleuze 2006, 44). The Anthropocene thesis, itself an "epistemological claim," (Yusoff 2017, 116) alongside the revelation of the technofossil, themselves enact the constitutive transgressions that disrupt the ontological distinction between subjectivity and matter.

## The Fossilized Subject

Explorations of the material and spatial forces subtending human and inhuman subjectivity, and the consequent rupture of this distinction, have been also grounded in a Foucauldian discussion of geopower. Grosz locates Foucault's early thinking on geopower in his "Questions on Geography" (Foucault 1980; Grosz et al. 2017, 134), an interview in which Foucault is pressed to elaborate on the spatial and geopolitical dimensions of his broader analyses of power and knowledge. This notion of geopower is distinguished from biopower, where the latter is described as a mode of extrinsic and institutionalized bodily control (Grosz et al. 2017, 134). In contrast, geopower subtends biopower and is the condition for human and inhuman agency and activity (ibid., 135). For Grosz, the autonomy and agency attributed to human life and its apparently linear temporal trajectory are now confronted by the apprehension of a constitutive "geological context," from which life and identity emerge and are perpetually transformed by the dynamism of the earth and its forces: "life must look outside itself to attain the possibility of continuing itself and knowing itself" (ibid., 132). Accordingly, the inhuman should not be understood as the "opposite or overcoming" of the human; rather, the inhuman both "supplements and subtends biopolitics" (ibid., 135). The presumed binary relationship between the human and the inhuman, which is fundamental to the construction of the modern legal and political subject, is not dissolved but disrupted in the revelation of geopower: life is (re)mineralized and the force of nonlife acknowledged (ibid., 136–137; Yusoff 2013).

Following this (Foucauldian) conceptualization of strata, Yusoff has developed a further reading of geopower, in accordance with which the material strata of "geologic forces" subtend "geosocial forces," and their expression in forms of subjectivity (Yusoff 2017, 109; 125). Drawing upon Grosz, Yusoff argues that geologic strata are immanent in and constitutive of power relations, forming "a material and affective infrastructure" for the embodiment of subjectivity and social bonds (2017, 109; Grosz 2012, 975). Power is here understood as the capture or "stabilization and stratification of force" (Yusoff 2017, 115) in a cycle of co-constitution. This infrastructure is illuminated by the Anthropocene, where the latter reveals the organization of geologic material and its subsequent "capture" and institutionalization in social strata (Yusoff 2017, 111; Deleuze and Guattari 1987, 40). The geologic authorship of the Anthropocene epoch, articulated in the putative "final say" of the fossil record, can be understood as the material evidence of geopower: that is, the confluence and co-constitution of categories of strata as geological, biological, and social (Yusoff 2017, 111). These strata are epistemologically contingent (Yusoff 2017, 116; Deleuze 2006, 44), and are challenged by the Anthropocene. Given geology is both retrospective and anticipatory, the Anthropocene references an "*anticipatory geologic* moment … what we are ceasing to be" (Yusoff 2017, 123). It simultaneously marks the historical confluence of geologic and social strata, as evidenced in the fossil record and sedimented social infrastructures and subjective modes, while also anticipating the possibility of revolutionary "lines of flight" (Guattari 2016; Yusoff 2017, 112). Indeed, the relationality to which the Anthropocene draws our attention precipitates this revolution: the possibility that the relationships between social organization and material flows, made manifest in the extractive economies of capitalism and its modes of subjectivity, might be disrupted or de-stratified, and the earth cognized as more than "standing reserves or inert strata" (Yusoff 2017, 113).

This reading of the mutual constitution of social and geologic strata is further extended in Povinelli's discussion of "geontopower" which, she argues, governs the ontological distinction between Life (*zoe* or *bios*) and Nonlife (*geos*) (2016). Explicitly contrasting liberal renderings of "nonlife (*geos*) and being (ontology)," Povinelli describes this nomenclature as an effort to create a "critical language" with which to articulate the ontological enclosures that govern modes of subjectivity and attendant relations of power (ibid., 5). She describes geontopower as a mode of late liberal governance that exceeds and subtends a Foucauldian biopower, encapsulated in the modern subject as a geontological construction (ibid., 16; Povinelli et al. 2017). In an interview with Povinelli, Yusoff and Coleman draw attention to the ways in which geontology provides an intellectual framework with which to scrutinize the presumed demarcations between the biological, meteorological, and geological that are patently disrupted by the Anthropocene, as well as the epistemological sediment from which these emerge (Povinelli et al. 2017, 172). The attribution of "self-oriented sovereignty" to molecular life (Povinelli 2016, 39; Barad 2003) is contrasted with a "bootstrapping-less" nonlife (Povinelli et al. 2017, 172), the latter variously prefigured as inert, subdued, idealized and fetishized, in an idea or ideal of "nature" as object: standing reserve, resource commodity, sublime wilderness. Forms of political subjectivity are consequently constrained by this "geontological imaginary," in accordance with which modes of existence are confined and enclosed by their ontological categorization (Povinelli et al. 2017, 175–176).

The collapse of "natural" and human history effected by the Anthropocene (Chakrabarty 2009, 201) fundamentally disrupts this ontological distinction, and the construction and privileged positioning of the human of its central thesis. For Povinelli, the Anthropocene instead reveals the integral primacy of Nonlife, in which a fleeting Life is enfolded: "Life is merely a moment in the greater dynamic unfolding of Nonlife" (2016, 176). Nonetheless, in her words, "[t]he sovereign people of geontopower" submit themselves to and govern in accordance with the "sovereign ... division of Life and Nonlife" (ibid., 35). Indeed, in an insightful discussion of contemporary political ontology, McGee reflects upon Schmitt's definition of the sovereign as "he who decides" (Schmitt 2005, 5), and contends that the sovereign is instead "that which divides the exception from the common," the originary division being that of "Human" from "Nature" (McGee 2017, 62). The very notion of Nature, as an idealization of inert materiality, denies the entanglement of human and inhuman agency (ibid., 75–76). This ontological demarcation is reflected in the relationship between modern law and matter, made explicit in the sovereign human subject of modern law and in the legal register of rights.

## The Proper Subject

For Mignolo, in the context of the sixteenth-century Christian reframing of Greek cosmology, the idea of the human subject is pure invention: "Human was a fictional noun pretending to be its ontological representation" (2018, 155). He draws upon an established postcolonial framing of the constitutive binaries of colonial subjectivity, in accordance with which the "model" human subject is delineated: "white and nonwhite, progress and stagnation, developed and underdeveloped, First and Second/Third World" – and, significantly for my purposes, the concomitant construction of "the idea of *nature*" (ibid., 155; 153). The juridical rendering of this binary construction turns upon appropriation, as effected by the "proper legal subject" of modern law, which is exemplified in historical accounts of the appropriations of empire and the construction of "racial regimes of ownership," made manifest in property law (Bhandar 2018, 4). This "mythic settling of the world" (Fitzpatrick 1992, 83; Bhandar 2018, 4), in which the proprietorial subject is privileged, establishes and entrenches a relationship between the human and the inhuman that is premised upon *dominium rerum:* "private power over material reality" (Fonseca 2017, 129; Vitoria 1991, 248). Its narrative enables a political economy of dispossession, defining land and waters in terms of (human) territorial occupation, use, cultivation, and wasteland (Bhandar 2018, 47; Fonseca 2017, 142). In this context, reading with Fitzpatrick, "[t]he appropriated and the yet to-be-appropriated share in the same universal order of things" (1992, 64; Foucault 1970, 56-7).

In Bhandar's critical account of the mutual construction of property law and racialized subjects, she locates legal subjectivity within the relational matrix of colonial dispossession. The binary opposition between cultivation and wasteland, established in the jurisprudence of Locke and subsequently Blackstone, is drawn from the earlier economic enmeshing of land and people consistent with an "ideology of improvement" (Bhandar 2018, 39; 47–48). This ideology defines the parameters of "proper human subjectivity" (ibid., 58), in accordance with which the (racialized, gendered) rights-bearing human subject is circumscribed by (his) proprietorial relationship to the inhuman. The categorization of matter intrinsic to property law and its consequent regimes of subjectification is also made manifest in the proprietorial categories and conceits of geology. In a critical examination of the constitutive relationships between race, materiality, and geology, Yusoff contends that the appropriative "grammar of geology" enables the discursive and visceral construction of the racially categorized inhuman, as an extractable and fungible commodity (Yusoff 2018, 70–71). Her analysis traces the ways in which geology, as both a "colonial geo-logics" and an extractive praxis, underpins the idea of white liberal subjectivity; in short, geology is simultaneously "a mode of accumulation … and of dispossession" (ibid., 2–3; 59). In a broadly Hegelian analysis, her argument suggests that modes of subjectivity exist in a dialectical relationship with modes of subjugation, such that the appropriative human subject is defined by (his) oppositional yet constitutive relationship with (his) inhuman property. This analysis returns us to the "figure of appropriation" drawn out earlier, the index fossil for the Anthropocene, in accordance with which land claimed as "radical title" is rendered property, to which rights are attributed and distributed (Pottage 2019, 171; Schmitt 1996, 328). The appropriative subject to which these rights accrue is explicitly reflected in the modern rights-bearing subject. The privileging of this subject, in the language and discourse of rights, is pivotal to contemporary political claims.

In an increasingly climate-constrained world, rights language is now deployed in the pursuit of legal protections for human rights to land, shelter, food, clean water, and air, as well as rights for the inhuman in an emergent earth jurisprudence, normatively individuated yet simultaneously depoliticized as a proper noun, "Nature" (Latour 2017, 225). The apparent expansion of the ontological limits of the human subject to the erstwhile inhuman object, in the attribution of legal personhood and associated rights, exemplifies the rehearsal and reactivation of the appropriative subject, embedded within the epistemological archive of modern law. The earth jurisprudence movement has emerged as a contemporary manifestation of a longer jurisprudential and philosophical history, which draws upon several philosophical threads: the theological, ascetic and transcendental traditions of John Muir and Henry David Thoreau, the "deep ecology" of Aldo Leopold and Thomas Berry, and the attribution of legal personhood to the inhuman, famously inaugurated by Christopher Stone, who queried whether trees should be afforded legal standing (Berry 1999; Stone 1972; Burdon 2011; O'Donnell et al. 2020, 5). Adopting elements of each of these threads, various modes of legal recognition have been granted to inhuman entities throughout the world, most emphatically to rivers (O'Donnell et al. 2020; Clark et al. 2018). The centrality of Indigenous perspectives to the development of this jurisprudence is contested, variously embraced as an opportunity for the emergence of a "pluralist ecological jurisprudence" that aspires to more explicitly acknowledge Indigenous advocacy and jurisprudences (O'Donnell et al. 2020), and elsewhere countered as a diminution or denial of extant ancestral rights and obligations (Marshall 2020). As a strategy for collective action and agitation, and in the pursuit of Indigenous agency and partnership, the reach and momentum of the rights for nature movement to date are undeniably impressive. Some legal scholars have described this movement as the emergence of a "new normative order," which self-consciously departs from a modernist anthropocentrism and embraces the ecocentrism of a "fully realized" ecological jurisprudence (Clark et al. 2018, 791–792). Others have been more circumspect, such as Escobar's description of it as a "transition discourse," which he attributes to a broader turn away from anthropocentrism (2011, 138).

Despite this strategic force, the ecological integrity imagined and even fetishized in the ecocentrism that informs earth or ecological jurisprudence fails to adequately acknowledge the complexity and contestation surrounding the concept of "nature" and its historical subsumption within and discipline by modernity (De Lucia 2017, 190; Arias-Maldonado 2015, 28). The binary between anthropocentrism and ecocentrism has been briskly dismissed – for Philippopoulos-Mihalopoulos, "[t]here is no more room for such antiquated debates" (2017, 150); for De Lucia, ecocentric approaches remain "thickly embedded *within* modernity" and the limitations of the "subject-object grammar" of an anthropocentric rights frame (2017, 189). While purporting to acknowledge the now well-established refutation of the conventional nature-culture binary, this jurisprudence is yet to grapple with the ways in which the interpellation of the inhuman as a rights-bearing subject reinforces the ontological enclosures of (human) legal subjectivity, reinscribing the very enlightenment dualisms it proposes and purports to overturn (Rawson and Mansfield 2018, 100). Indeed, advocates of this jurisprudence retain a commitment to legal modes of recognition and abstracted forms of subjectivity that are freighted with the epistemological and ontological constraints of modernity, which compromise the more radical philosophical and political projects to which earth or ecological jurisprudence might otherwise aspire. I will briefly draw out the key elements of this constraint, before finally turning to the possibilities of an emergent discourse of obligations and an exploration of more expansive renderings of subjectivity.

The existential limits of recognition in occidental legal traditions, particularly in "settler" nation states, are well established (Simpson 2011, 2017; Coulthard 2014; Bhandar 2007; Birrell 2016). Recognition in this context is not dialectic but proprietorial, limited to recognition of that which is prescribed or "proper" to itself (Nancy 1993, 10; Bhandar 2007, 142; Birrell 2016, 91). That is, recognition of the subject before this law is limited to recognition of a prescribed subjectivity, within "an ontological 'economy of the same'" (Bhandar 2007, 142, citing Derrida 2001, 317). The legal subject is construed as difference that is *proper* to law – indeed, as its *property*. Recognition of the rights-bearing subject, human or inhuman, is accordingly delimited. This limit is reflected in Golder's astute analysis of the relationship between form and content in rights discourse. For Golder, the *content* of the rights-bearing subject is disciplined by its *form*: the epistemological frame within which the subject is enclosed – the disembodied, abstracted, proprietorial, rational, sovereign subject (Grear 2015, 237) – hinders its reworking and re-articulation in new contexts (Golder 2015). More pithily: "form here sets the limits of intelligibility for substance" (Golder 2014, 112). This form is iteratively (re)produced, the epistemological sediment from which it emerges reactivated with each claim. In the context of earth or ecological jurisprudence, the river or tree cannot be normatively construed as "pre-political and before the law" (Golder 2015, 111). Rather, the ontological limits that define the form of the *human* legal subject are perversely applied to the *inhuman*, which is only then recognized as the rights-bearing legal subject. Rights may yet be redeemed (Golder 2014) – rights language may be expanded in new contexts and adopted strategically, the iterative performance of rights claims contouring emergent subject forms (Golder 2015, 111). Despite this ambivalence, however, the sedimented rights form constrains the liberatory aspirations of contemporary rights discourse. Within normative formulations of liberal legal subjectivity, the rights-bearing subject remains the *property* of modern law, reinforcing the limits of the anthropocentric "figure of appropriation" and largely foreclosing alternative political possibilities.

## The Sympoietic Subject

The ontological enclosure rehearsed in liberal rights discourse, by which legal subjectivity is defined and rendered capable of recognition, is profoundly challenged by the perspectival shifts of the Anthropocene. While the "golden spike" by which geology marks the Anthropocene epoch can be interpreted as a triumphal marker of historical and future appropriation and dispossession, it also marks an acknowledgment of our mutually constitutive relationship with the animate ground beneath us. Exploring the histories of subterranean landscapes and imaginaries, Macfarlane describes this intimacy:

> We tend to imagine stone as inert matter, obdurate in its fixity. But here in the rift it feels instead like a liquid paused briefly in its flow. Seen in deep time, stone folds as strata, rock absorbs, transforms, levitates from seabed to summit. … We are part mineral beings too – our teeth are reefs, our bones are stones – and there is a geology of the body as well as of the land.
>
> *(2019, 37)*

Bodies emerge from stone, Macfarlane reminds us, the mineralogical conversion of calcium to bone evident in our skeletal architecture (ibid.). Our apparent vulnerability to the impacts of climatic change prompts a scalar recalibration to accommodate the planetary, while our differential experience of vulnerability across space and time deepens our entrenchment within localized mineralogical substrates. Yet further, the continuum between the human and the inhuman, made explicit in a global pandemic, reveals the extent to which our bodies are part of a larger microbial community (Birrell and Lindgren 2021; Philippopoulos-Mihalopoulos 2020). Acknowledging this relationality, the historical demarcation between the human and the inhuman that defines the rights-bearing subject and contours its claims has become increasingly strained, exemplified in the diminution of the inhuman within the confines of liberal legal subjectivity. In this context, recent critical legal scholarship has proposed a tempering of "rights talk" and the acknowledgment of a subtending discourse of obligation, which precedes and exceeds rights (McGee 2017, 117; Matthews 2019; Birrell and Matthews 2020; Burdon 2020).

This turn toward obligation engages with the tension between different modes of contemporary climate activism, alternately galvanized by the pursuit of individuated rights and associated protections, and the formation of a transnational movement valorizing emplaced community and connection (Klein 2014, 337; 292). In an insightful reflection upon this latter embrace of local "connection," McGee draws out the distinction between these modes of activism, suggesting that the connection to place described by Klein is best understood as a "bond of dependence characterized less by powers, privileges, and rights than by liabilities, burdens, and duties" (McGee 2017, 122). The appropriative impulse of right is here inverted by the communal bonds or "ligaments" inherent to law, where law and obligation are etymologically derivative of *ligando* (binding) (ibid., 124) or *ligare* (to bind, bond or weave) (Matthews 2019, 12–14; DeLoughrey 2019, 192). The land appropriations that define Schmitt's rendering of an "extractive *nomos*," as the legal architecture of spatial ordering upon which radical title is grounded, are similarly inverted: reading Latour, McGee contends that it is instead "the land that seizes and holds us" (McGee 2017, 124; 122; Latour 2017, 230). Accordingly, attachment to place is generated less by the political enclosures of nativist allegiance (McGee 2017, 123), and more by the mutual bonds and dependencies of communal life. Drawing upon the work of Simone Weil, Matthews extends McGee's analysis in a discussion of the "*existential* register of obligation," which is concerned not with the institutionalized and codified obligations of modern law but with the reciprocal claims that bind us in community, and thereby assume priority over rights (Matthews 2019, 14; Weil 2001; Weil 2005). Matthews describes this as a shift from the "*aesthetics*" or *form* of rights, towards the "*aesthesis*" of obligations, made manifest in affective social relations (2019).

Without reverting to the essentialism and fetishism that so often accompany non-Indigenous engagements with Indigenous political ecologies, this critical conversation might be further extended by a reading of interspecies obligations in Paulatuuq (arctic Canada) and amiskwaciwâskahikan (Edmonton, Alberta, Canada) legal orders, as elaborated by Métis scholar Zoe Todd. The ontological enclosures of modernity, by which the individuated rights-bearing subject is defined, are challenged by Indigenous accounts of inhuman agency and interspecies relationality (Todd 2018; Povinelli 2016, 30–56). This challenge – or, in Todd's terms, "refraction" (2018) of colonial imaginaries and legal orders – is not necessarily a resort to animism, which frequently galvanizes land claims (Povinelli 2016, 34–35), but is a more complex affirmation of the relational bonds between the inhuman and the inhuman that organize social and political life. Ancestral "fish stories" in Paulatuuq communities present a counter-narrative to continued colonial impositions and dominant economic and scientific imperatives, depicting fish as "political actors, more-than-human beings, and kin," to whom "reciprocal responsibilities" are owed (Todd 2018, 72). Even as fish are harvested for human consumption in these communities, human obligations owed to one another are calibrated by reference to obligations and duties owed to fish (ibid., 67). This extends to the sharing of territory between humans and fish and, moreover, to a commitment to the habitation of spaces through time in accordance with an ethic of care, reciprocity, and even tenderness (ibid., 74; Donald 2009).

Already replete with stories, the places described here do not vacantly await human narrative inscription but are instead "lively landscapes" (Van Dooren 2014, 79; Cronon 1992, 1368), perpetually engaged in the sympoiesis of human and inhuman formation. Reading Haraway alongside Todd, the fictitious sovereign subject of *autopoiesis*, as described by Haraway and made manifest in the colonial privileging of the appropriative subject, is revealed to be dependent upon and generatively extended by the *sympoiesis* or "making-with" of biotic and abiotic reciprocity and obligation (Grear 2020, 360–361; Haraway 2016, 58). Sympoiesis is a term that describes contingent, porous, dynamic entities, which are not singular but relational (Haraway 2016, 60; Grear 2020, 361). Human bodies are sympoietic organisms, comprised of an array of microbial communities engaged in bonds of dependency that exceed the mutual benefit of "host + symbiont" exchange, to create an entity described as a holobiont (Gilbert 2017; Haraway 2016, 59–60; Margulis 1991). This lively relationality persists amidst the ontological rigidity of dominant political and legal forms: indeed, for Haraway, "[s]ympoiesis enfolds autopoiesis" (2016, 58). The fleshy relationality Todd is concerned to elevate in the politics of Indigenous "survivance" (Todd 2018; Vizenor 2008) might be understood as an expression of the inherent sympoiesis of human and inhuman "becoming" (Haraway 2016, 64), affirming Inuvialuit legal orders that acknowledge the agency of their "fishy interlocutors" and, moreover, of the waters they share, as integral to the formation of human political and legal subjectivities (Todd 2018, 62).

## Conclusion

The very notion of the human as the geologic force of the Anthropocene makes explicit the constitutive relationship between geologic and biologic modes of subjectivity. Yet, the ontological bifurcations of modernity – the "self-oriented sovereignty" of life, defined earlier in opposition to a "boot-strappingless" nonlife (Povinelli 2016, 39; Povinelli et al., 2017, 172) – presume and enforce the detachment of human subjectivity from its inhuman sympoiesis. This chapter has traced the ways in which this demarcation, which has historically defined the human through the hermeneutics of material encounter, is distilled in the rights-bearing subject of modern law. Considering the geologic and epistemic sediment subtending this legal archive, and indeed our apprehension of the Anthropocene, I have examined the ontological enclosures governing modes of subjectivity and their legal recognition. The material flows of extractive economies are reflected in the appropriative subject of modernity, imagined as the trace fossil of the Anthropocene, and made explicit in the legal register of rights. The extension of the rights form to the inhuman, in the attribution of rights to "nature" in earth jurisprudence, reactivates and reinforces this ontological enclosure. For Latour, the collapse of this demarcation, prompted by the constitutive tensions of the Anthropocene, presents us with an existential conundrum: "Some are readying themselves to live as Earthbound in the Anthropocene; others decided to remain as Humans in the Holocene" (Latour 2013, 63; Haraway 2016, 41). A turn toward the reciprocal bonds of obligation inflects the normative legal rendering of subjectivity, which might be informed and galvanized by encounters with the refractive politics of Indigenous legal orders. Addressing the question of subjectivity, as a part of the vertiginous experience of the Anthropocene in which the human is simultaneously elevated and diminished, challenges us to "stay with the trouble" (Haraway 2016) aroused by encounters and negotiations between both sedimented and sympoietic subjectivities.

## References

Arias-Maldonado, Manuel. 2015. *Environment and Society: Socionatural Relations in the Anthropocene*. Cham: Springer.

Barad, Karen. 2003. "Posthumanist Performativity: Toward an Understanding of How Matter Comes to Matter." *Signs: Journal of Women in Culture and Society* 28(3): 801–831.

Bauer, Andrew M. and Mona Bahn. 2018. *Climate Without Nature: A Critical Anthropology of the Anthropocene*. Cambridge: Cambridge University Press.

Bennett, Jane. 2010. *Vibrant Matter: A Political Ecology of Things*. Durham: Duke University Press.

Berry, Thomas. 1999. *The Great Work: Our Way into the Future*. New York: Harmony/Bell Tower.

Bhandar, Brenna. 2007. "Re-covering the Limits of Recognition: The Politics of Difference and Decolonisation in John Borrows's Recovering Canada: The Resurgence of Indigenous Law." *Australian Feminist Law Journal* 27(1): 125.

Bhandar, Brenna. 2018. *The Colonial Lives of Property: Law, Land, and Racial Regimes of Ownership*. Durham: Duke University Press.

Birrell, Kathleen. 2016. *Indigeneity: Before and Beyond the Law*. Abingdon, Oxon, and New York: Routledge.

Birrell, Kathleen and Daniel Matthews. 2020. "Re-storying Laws for the Anthropocene: Rights, Obligations and the Meeting of Laws." *Law and Critique* 31(3): 275–292.

Birrell, Kathleen and Tim Lindgren. 2021. "Anthropocenic Pandemic: Laws of Exposure and Encounter". *Critical Legal Thinking* (4 Jan 2021) at https://criticallegalthinking.com/2021/01/04/anthropocenic-pandemic-laws-of-exposure-encounter/ accessed 3 May 2021.

Bottjer, David J. 2016. *Paleoecology: Past, Present, and Future.* Chichester, West Sussex: Wiley.

Braidotti, Rosi. 2013. *The Posthuman.* Cambridge and Maiden: Polity Press.

Burdon, Peter. 2011. "The Jurisprudence of Thomas Berry." *Worldviews: Global Religions, Culture, and Ecology* 15(2): 151–167.

Burdon, Peter D. 2015. *Earth Jurisprudence: Private Property and the Environment.* Abingdon: Routledge.

Burdon, Peter. 2020. "Obligations in the Anthropocene." *Law and Critique* 31(3): 309–328.

Chakrabarty, Dipesh. 2009. "The Climate of History: Four Theses." *Critical Inquiry* 35(2 Winter): 197–222.

Clark, Cristy, Nia Emmanouil, John Page and Alessandro Pelizzon. 2018. "Can You Hear the Rivers Sing? Legal Personhood, Ontology, and the Nitty Gritty of Governance." *Ecology Law Quarterly* 45(4): 787–844.

Coulthard, Glen Sean. 2014. *Red Skin White Masks: Rejecting the Colonial Politics of Recognition.* Minneapolis and London: University of Minnesota Press.

Cronon, William. 1992. "A Place for Stories: Nature, History, and Narrative." *Journal of American History* 78(4) (March): 1347–1376.

Crutzen, Paul J. 2002. "Geology of Mankind." *Nature* 415(1 January): 23.

Crutzen, Paul J. and Eugene F. Stoermer. 2000. "The Anthropocene." *Global Change Newsletter* 41(1 May): 17.

Cullinan, Cormac. 2011. *Wild Law: Governing People for Earth*, 2nd ed. Claremont: Siber Inc.

De Lucia, Vito. 2017. "Beyond Anthropocentrism and Ecocentrism: A Biopolitical Reading of Environmental Law." *Journal of Human Rights and the Environment* 8(2): 181–202.

Deleuze, Gilles. 2006. *Foucault.* Translated by Seßn Hand. London: Bloomsbury.

Deleuze, Gilles and Félix Guattari. 1987. *A Thousand Plateaus: Capitalism and Schizophrenia.* Translated and Foreword by Brian Massumi. London and Minneapolis: University of Minnesota Press.

DeLoughrey, Elizabeth. 2019. *Allegories of the Anthropocene.* Durham: Duke University Press.

Derrida, Jacques. 1992a. "The Law of Genre." In *Acts of Literature*, by Jacques Derrida (Derek Attridge, Ed.), 221–252. New York: Routledge.

Derrida, Jacques. 1992b. "Before the Law." In *Acts of Literature*, by Jacques Derrida (Derek Attridge Ed.), 181–220. New York: Routledge.

Derrida, Jacques. 2001. "From Restricted to General Economy: A Hegelianism without Reserve" in *Writing and Difference*, by Jacques Derrida. Translated by Alan Bass. London: Routledge.

Derrida, Jacques. 2002. "Force of Law: The 'Mystical Foundation of Authority'." In *Acts of Religion*, by Jacques Derrida. Translated by Mary Quaintance. Edited and with an introduction by Gil Anidjar, 228–298. New York and London: Routledge.

Donald, Dwayne. 2009. "Forts, Curriculum and Indigenous Métissage: Imagining Decolonization of Aboriginal-Canadian Relations in Educational Contexts." *First Nations Perspectives* 2(1): 1–24.

Escobar, Arturo. 2011. "Sustainability: Design for the Pluriverse." *Development* 54(2): 137–140.

Fitzpatrick, Peter. 1992. *The Mythology of Modern Law.* London and New York: Routledge.

Fonseca, Manuel Jiménez. 2017. "Jus Gentium and the Transformation of Latin American Nature: One More Reading of Vitoria?" In *International Law and Empire: Historical Explorations*, by Martii Koskenniemi, Walter Rech and Manuel Jiménez Fonseca (Eds.), 123–148. Oxford: Oxford University Press.

Foucault, Michel. 1970. *The Order of Things: An Archeology of the Human Sciences.* London: Tavistock.

Foucault, Michel. 1980. "Questions on Geography." In *Power/Knowledge: Selected Interviews and Other Writings, 1972–1977*, by Colin Gordon (Ed.). Interviewed by the editors of the journal *Hérodote.* New York, 173-182.

Foucault, Michel. 1989. *Foucault Live: Collected Interviews, 1961–1984.* New York: Semiotext(e).

Frost, Samantha. 2016. *Biocultural Creatures: Towards a New Theory of the Human.* Durham, London: Duke University Press.

Gilbert, Scott F. 2017. "Holobiont by Birth: Multilineage Individuals as the Concretion of Cooperative Processes." In *Arts of Living on a Damaged Planet: Ghosts and Monsters of the Anthropocene*, by Anna Tsing, Heather Swanson, Elaine Gan and Nils Bubandt (Eds.). Minneapolis, Minnesota; London, England: University of Minnesota Press, 73–89.

Golder, Ben. 2014 "Beyond Redemption? Problematising the Critique of Human Rights in Contemporary International Legal Thought." *London Review of International Law* 2(1): 77–114.

Golder, Ben. 2015. *Foucault and the Politics of Rights.* California: Stanford University Press: Stanford.

Grear, Anna. 2015. "Deconstructing Anthropos: A Critical Legal Reflection on 'Anthropocentric' Law and Anthropocene 'Humanity'." *Law and Critique* 26(3): 225–249.

Grear, Anna. 2020. "Legal Imaginaries and the Anthropocene: 'Of' and 'For'." *Law and Critique* 31(3): 351–366.
Grosz, Elizabeth A. 2011. *Becoming Undone: Darwinian Reflections on Life, Politics and Art.* Durham: Duke University Press.
Grosz, Elizabeth. 2012. "Geopower: A Panel on Elizabeth Grosz's 'Chaos, Territory, Art: Deleuze and the Framing of the Earth'." *Environment and Planning D: Society and Space* 30(6): 971–988.
Grosz, Elizabeth, Kathryn Yusoff and Nigel Clark. 2017. "An Interview with Elizabeth Grosz: Geopower, Inhumanism and the Biopolitical." *Theory, Culture and Society* 34(2–3): 129–146.
Guattari, Félix. 2016. *Lines of Flight: For Another World of Possibilities.* London: Bloomsbury.
Haraway, Donna J. 2016. *Staying with the Trouble: Making Kin in the Chthulucene.* Durham: Duke University Press.
Klein, Naomi. 2014. *This Changes Everything: Capitalism vs. the Climate.* Penguin Random House.
Koselleck, Reinhart. 2018. *Sediments of Time: On Possible Histories.* Ed. and Trans. Sean Franzel and Stefan-Ludwig Hoffman. Stanford: Stanford University Press.
Latour, Bruno. 1993. *We Have Never Been Modern.* Translated by Catherine Porter. Cambridge: Harvard University Press.
Latour, Bruno. 2013. "War and Peace in an Age of Ecological Conflicts." Lecture for the Peter Wall Institute, Vancouver, BC, Canada, 23 September 2013, 51–63, 63 at http://www.bruno-latour.fr/node/521 accessed 3 February 2023.
Latour, Bruno. 2017. *Facing Gaia: Eight Lectures on the New Climatic Regime.* Translated by Catherine Porter. Cambridge and Medford: Polity Press.
LeMenager, Stephanie. 2014. *Living Oil.* Oxford: Oxford University Press.
Macfarlane, Robert. 2019. *Underland: A Deep Time Journey.* Great Britain: Hamish Hamilton.
Margulis, Lynn. 1991. "Symbiogenesis and Symbionticism." In *Symbiosis as a Source of Evolutionary Innovation: Speciation and Morphogenesis*, by Lyn Margulis and R. Fester (Eds.), 1–14. Cambridge: MIT Press.
Marshall, Virginia. 2020. "Removing the Veil from the 'Rights of Nature': The Dichotomy between First Nations Customary Rights and Environmental Legal Personhood." *Australian Feminist Law Journal.* https://doi.org/10.1080/13200968.2019.1802154.
Matthews, Daniel. 2019. "Legal Aesthetics in the Anthropocene: From the Rights of Nature to the Aesthesis of Obligation." *Law, Culture and the Humanities.* https://doi.org/10.1177/1743872119871830.
Matthews, Daniel and Scott Veitch (Eds.). 2018. *Law, Obligation, Community.* Abingdon: Routledge.
McGee, Kyle. 2017. *Heathen Earth: Trumpism and Political Ecology.* Goleta: Punctum Books.
Mignolo, Walter D. 2018. "The Invention of the Human and the Three Pillars of the Colonial Matrix of Power: Racism, Sexism, and Nature." In *On Decoloniality: Concepts, Analytics, Praxis*, by Walter D. Mignolo and Catherine E. Walsh (Eds.), 153–176. Durham and London: Duke University Press.
Montaigne, Michel de. 1933. *The Essayes of Montaigne.* Translated by John Florio. New York: Modern Library.
Montaigne, Michel de. 1962. *Essais 3, Ch 13. "De l'Expérience".* Paris: Biblioteque de la Pléade.
Motha, Stewart. 2021. "'The End Begins': Law (*Nomos*) and Nature (*Physis*) as Genre." *Law, Culture and the Humanities.* https://doi.org/10.1177/17438721211030139.
Nancy, Jean-Luc. 1993. "Identity and Trembling." In *The Birth to Presence*, by Jean-Luc Nancy. Translated by Brian Holmes and Others. 9–35, Stanford: Stanford University Press.
O'Donnell, Erin, Anne Poelina, Alessandro Pelizzon and Cristy Clark. 2020. "Stop Burying the Lede: The Essential Role of Indigenous Law(s) in Creating Rights of Nature." *Transnational Environmental Law.* https://doi.org/10.1017/S2047102520000242.
Philippopoulos-Mihalopoulos, Andreas. 2017. "Critical Environmental Law as Method in the Anthropocene". In Andreas Philippopoulos-Mihalopoulos and Victoria Brooks (Eds.), *Research Methods in Environmental Law*, 131–155. Northampton, MA: Edward Elgar Pub.
Philippopoulos-Mihalopoulos, Andreas. 2020. "Life and Language in the Virocene". *Critical Legal Thinking* (20 Nov 2020) at https://criticallegalthinking.com/2020/11/20/life-and-language-in-the-virocene/ accessed 3 May 2021.
Pottage, Alain. 2019. "Holocene Jurisprudence." *Journal of Human Rights and the Environment* 10(2): 153–175.
Povinelli, Elizabeth A. 2016. *Geontologies: A Requiem to Late Liberalism.* Durham: Duke University Press.
Povinelli, Elizabeth A., Mathew Coleman and Kathryn Yusoff. 2017. "An Interview with Elizabeth Povinelli: Geontopower, Biopolitics and the Anthropocene." *Theory, Culture and Society* 34(2–3): 169–185.
Rawson, Ariel and Becky Mansfield. 2018. "Producing Juridical Knowledge: 'Rights of Nature' or the Naturalization of Rights?" *Environment and Planning E: Nature and Space* 1 (1–2): 99–119.

Schmitt, Carl. 1996. "Appropriation/Distribution/Production: An Attempt to Determine from Nomos the Basic Questions of Every Social and Economic Order." In *The Nomos of the Earth*, by Carl Schmitt (Ed.), 324–335. London: Telos.

Schmitt, Carl. 2005. *Political Theology: Four Chapters on the Concept of Sovereignty*. Translated by George Schwab. Chicago: University of Chicago Press.

Serres, Michel. 1995. *The Natural Contract*. Ann Arbor: University of Michigan Press.

Simpson, Leanne Betasamosake. 2011. *Dancing on our Turtle's Back: Stories of Nishnaabeg Re-creation, Resurgence and a New Emergence*. Winnipeg, Manitoba: ARP Books.

Simpson, Leanne Betasamosake 2017. *As We Have Always Done: Indigenous Freedom Through Radical Resistance*. Minneapolis: University of Minnesota Press.

Stone, Christopher D. 1972. "Should Trees Have Standing? Towards Legal Rights for Natural Objects." *Southern California Law Review* 45: 450-501.

Stoppani, Antonio. 1873. *Corsa di Geologia*. Milan.

Subramanian, Meera. 2019. "Humans versus Earth: The Quest to Define the Anthropocene." *Nature* (6 August 2019) at https://www.nature.com/articles/d41586-019-02381-2#correction-0, accessed 3 February 2023.

Todd, Zoe. 2018. "Refracting the State Through Human-Fish Relations: Fishing, Indigenous Legal Orders and Colonialism in North/Western Canada." *Decolonization: Indigeneity, Education and Society* 7(1): 60–75.

Van Dooren, Thom. 2014. *Flight Ways: Life and Loss at the Edge of Extinction*. New York: Columbia University Press.

Vitoria, Francisco de. 1991. "On the Latin American Indians." In *Vitoria: Political Writings*, by Anthony Pagden and Jeremy Lawrence (Eds.), 231–292. Cambridge: Cambridge University Press.

Vizenor, Gerald. 2008. *Survivance: Narratives of Native Presence*. Lincoln: University of Nebraska Press.

Waters, Colin N., Jan Zalasiewicz, Colin Summerhayes, Ian J. Fairchild, Neil L. Rose, Neil J. Loader, William Shotyk et al. 2018. "Global Boundary Stratotype Section and Point (GSSP) for the Anthropocene Series: Where and How to Look for Potential Candidates." *Earth-Science Reviews* 178(March): 379–429.

Weil, Simone. 2001. *The Need for Roots: Prelude of a Declaration of Duties Towards Mankind*. Abingdon: Routledge.

Weil, Simone. 2005. "Draft for a Statement of Human Obligations." In *Simone Weil: An Anthology*, by Sian Miles (Ed.), 221–230. London: Penguin.

Yusoff, Kathryn. 2013. "Geologic Life: Prehistory, Climate, Futures in the Anthropocene." *Environment and Planning. Part D: Society and Space* 31(5): 779–795.

Yusoff, Kathryn. 2017. "Geosocial Strata. " *Theory, Culture and Society* 34(2/3): 105–127.

Yusoff, Kathryn. 2018. *A Billion Black Anthropocenes or None*. Minneapolis: University of Minnesota Press.

Yusoff, Kathryn, Elizabeth A. Grosz, Arun Saldanha and Catherine Nash. 2012. "Geopower: A Panel on Elizabeth Grosz's Chaos, Territory, Art: Deleuze and the Framing of the Earth." *Environment and Planning. Part D: Society and Space* 30(6): 971–988.

Yusoff, Kathryn and Mary Thomas. 2018. "The Anthropocene." In *The Edinburgh Companion to Animal Studies*, by Lynn Turner, Undine Sellbach and Ron Broglio (Eds.), 52–64. Edinburgh: Edinburgh University Press.

Zalasiewicz, Jan, Mark Williams, Will Steffen and Paul Crutzen. 2010. "The New World of the Anthropocene." *Environmental Science and Technology* 44(7): 2228–2231.

# 5

# WE, EARTHBOUND PEOPLE

## Constituent Power in Entangled Times

*Daniel Matthews*

### Introduction

Constituent power refers to the capacity to make and un-make a constituted order. Vested in the "nation" or "people," constituent power both *precedes* and *exceeds* formal, constituted powers,[1] and is usually evoked in moments of crisis when extant institutions have shown themselves to be inadequate, corrupt or otherwise in need of radical revision. As a creature of Enlightenment political thought and practice, constituent power is predicated on a belief in the unique capacity of human collaboration and institutionalization, made in an effort to rise above those "natural attachments" that bind the human in various forms of servitude and indignity and, on the basis of a supposedly universal rationality, create a social world that is the product of and answers to expressly *human* needs and aspirations alone. In a recent effort to recapture this heritage, the popular will has been described as the "organised effort to rise above, from below, the shackles created by mutual dependence" (Somek and Wilkinson 2020, 974).

Such a characterization of political power feels strangely incongruous in the context of the Anthropocene, which is marked by ecological and geological entanglements which cross national borders and traverse distinctions between human and more-than-human agencies. The Anthropocene underscores that "mutual dependence" is the *sine qua non* of our continued habitation of the planet. Modern social life has shown itself capable of disturbing the earth system's basic functioning and the constitutive relations between human collectives and a range of putatively "natural" forces are raising new ontological, ethical, and legal challenges. In this context can "the people" or "nation" continue to play a defining role in structuring the prevailing sense and direction of the political? Is it not the elaboration of "alternative figurations or *conceptual personae*" (Braidotti 2019, 34) which can attend to the complex interweaving of human and inhuman relations that is needed as we grapple with the challenges associated with the "new climatic regime" (Latour 2017)?

In lieu of leaving the language and history of constituent power entirely behind us, in this chapter, I examine how constituent power might be reimagined in light of the Anthropocene and its various entailments. As Bruno Latour has argued, we live today in a renewed period of "demogenesis" (or the creation of peoples) in which social and political movements that once took place *within* more or less clearly defined nations are today raising the question of peoplehood itself (Latour 2018, 353–361). In this sense, the axiomatic claim of constituent power

DOI: 10.4324/9781003388081-7

– that "the people" legitimate the constituted order – is, if anything, proliferating rather than waning. To suggest that legal and political theory can entirely avoid these inherited categories *and* retain some meaningful connection to the lived realities and aspirations of extant political communities and movements strikes me as being hollowly aspirational. Moreover, constituent power evokes values of autonomy, self-determination, democratic participation, majoritarianism, and equality which should be promoted and defended as increasingly potent forms of authoritarianism take hold around the world, and the values of civic life continue to be undermined by the expansion market rationalities (Brown 2015). The most pressing question is not whether "nationhood" or "the people" can finally be superseded by some new avatar of legitimacy, but whether these concepts can be rendered in such a way that allows us to meaningfully sense, represent and address the political challenges associated with our new climatic conditions? How might we understand the unfolding articulation of "demogenesis" in ways that think with and through the Anthropocene and the bio-geo-socio-ecological entanglements which it has brought into view?

## An Ecological Supplement

In its classic formulation, the assertion of a people or a nation's capacity to constitute a new political order is understood as an expression of *autonomy*. Heteronomous powers – whether natural, divine, or colonial – are neutered by a felicitous declaration of a people's capacity for self-rule. This invariably constitutes a rupture with the old and, taking shape in a form of collective action, makes the political world anew. While I don't wish to oppose the values and aspirations of autonomy or collective self-determination, these long-standing tropes, which so often bolster theories of constituent power, tend to obscure prior forms of *dependence* and *relationality* which are the condition of possibility for any claim to political "independence." The challenge of theorizing constituent power in light of our current ecological entanglements lies in resituating aspirations for political autonomy *within* a broader network of "natural" dependencies that the Anthropocene problematic has inserted into the heart of legal and political discourse. This need not entail the "naturalization" of our political thinking, in which power is ceded to imperatives that lay beyond our control. But nor should it involve the renewal of Enlightenment traditions which reassert forms of human exceptionalism that remain largely oblivious to the network of nonhuman forces and relations on which existing forms of associative life rely.

Judith Butler's (2015) work on constituent power and the politics of assembly opens some productive possibilities in this context. Butler insists on an *a priori* plurality that conditions political action in order to explore the ways in which acting and speaking in the name of the people are as much enactments of *dependence* as they are assertions of *independence*. For Butler human life is always in negotiation with forms of "unchosen cohabitation" (2015, 99–122) which generate pre-contractual and non-consensual ethical obligations. Drawing on Hannah Arendt, Butler insists that the "already-entangledness" of human sociality is the very condition of political action and freedom. As Arendt suggests at the close of *Eichmann in Jerusalem* (2006), it was Eichmann's belief that he possessed the "right to determine who should and who should not inhabit the world" (2006, 279) that both justified his execution and marked his irrevocable ex-communication from the sphere of politics, properly understood.[2] The possibility of political action is predicated on "an obligation to live with those who already exist" (Butler 2015, 111). And an effort to deny the unchosen conditions of our earthly cohabitation amounts to a denial of the very possibility of politics; as Arendt put it, political action "corresponds to the human condition of plurality, to the fact that men, not Man, live on the earth and inhabit the world" (Arendt 1998, 7).

Examining the assemblies in Tahrir Square in 2011 and the Occupy Wall Street Movement of the same year, Butler assesses the meaning and significance of the forms of plurality that precede claims to peoplehood by focusing on the strategy of inserting bodies in public space in mass assemblies and occupations. Butler argues that this kind of political manifestation foregrounds the bodily needs of subjects (for care, space, food, and shelter) and poses questions of equality, precarity, publicity, and relationality in the context of resistance to neoliberal governance. The simple acts of sleeping, cooking, eating, or studying in public make the infrastructure that facilitates a people's appearance as a political actor possible, illustrating that the forms of relationality and dependence which constitute human collectives are essential to political freedom and action. In this way, Butler highlights the environmental conditions which are essential to the sustenance of human life, suggesting that she "seeks to offer an ecological supplement to Arendt's anthropocentricism" (ibid., 113). This "ecological supplement" aims to evoke a "broader sense of life, one that includes organic life, living and sustaining environments and social networks that affirm and support interdependency" (ibid., 214).

If the classic theories of constituent power cultivate a myth of human exceptionalism whereby certain "natural attachments" are overcome, following Butler we can see that any such claims can only ever be made in negotiation with a set of interdependencies on which human life relies. Nonetheless, the "ecological supplement" that Butler points to in this context is notably thin. While she regularly gestures towards the environmental context within which political action is always already enfolded, Butler invariably returns to an anthropic register in which social and ethical questions predominate. As Cary Wolfe (2012, 17–21) has argued, Butler's attention to the "precariousness" and the variable "grieveability" of life remains largely blind to nonhuman animal life, largely because Butler's theory of community depends on a theory of mutual recognition. Further, Butler's account of differential precarity is largely concerned with *economic* questions of the distribution of harms and benefits, which ignores the forms of differential *ecological* precarity that are becoming increasingly pressing in the new climatic regime. As we repeatedly see with each new extreme weather event or environmental disaster, communities are inured and exposed to ecological threats in multifarious ways. And though this differential precarity often mirrors uneven economic distribution, with the poor disproportionality affected by climatic change and extreme weather, this is not always straightforwardly the case (Beck 2016).

Despite these limitations, Butler opens a space for thinking more thoroughly about how the ecological forces and relations central to the climate crisis might be incorporated within an account of constituent power and peoplehood. Indeed, the provocative evocation of an "ecological supplement to Arendt's anthropocentricism" urges us to return to Arendt's work on political action and constituent power through an ecological or Anthropocenic lens. As Jacques Derrida famously elaborated, a "supplement" can refer to an addition from the outside, which allows that which is being supplemented to sustain or complete itself, but so too does it indicate a more "dangerous" and disruptive displacement that draws attention to the fragility and incompleteness of that which requires supplementation (Derrida 1997, 141–143). This dual sense of supplementarity, referring both to the capacity to "add to" and "replace," can put prevailing structures of thought and conceptual distinctions radically in question. Though there is no space here to explore this point in the depth it deserves, Butler's passing reference to an "ecological supplement" to Arendt's political theory should not be overlooked. Indeed, the entire architecture of Arendt's profoundly influential thought takes on new valences, uncertainties, and possibilities when ecological themes are foregrounded in her work.

In the next section, we will briefly engage with two of Arendt's most important categories – *the social* and *action* – in order to illustrate this. Arendt is a highly creative thinker of peoplehood, constituent power, and constitutional form (Arendt 1958; Arendt 1973; Arendt 2005). Her seminal reading of the French and American revolutions, her defense of "council democracy," and her forceful critique of sovereignty have been widely debated.[3] Rather than engage with this material directly, by drawing out how contemporary ecological thought might supplement Arendt's conception of the *social* and *action*, we are able to critically engage some of the presuppositions that inform Arendt's republicanism: questioning the extent to which political freedom can be meaningfully severed from social and natural necessity, and examining how the scope of political action might be radically extended.

The approach I take in what follows involves both reading *with* and *against* Arendt. I aim to extend the meaning and applicability of some of her key concepts (particularly, *the social* and *action*) into nonhuman worlds and agencies, while also being sensitive to the fact that Arendt was herself aware of the need to grapple with these very challenges and possibilities. Arendt's recuperation of classical distinctions between freedom and necessity; public and private, is hedged by a sensitivity to many of the themes that have animated debates about the Anthropocene (Belcher and Schmidt 2020). For instance, Arendt foregrounds the "earth-bound" nature of human life (Arendt 1998, 3; cf. Latour 2017) and understands the novelty of twentieth-century techno-scientific developments, like nuclear fission, space travel, and automation (Arendt 1998, 148–149), to lie in the capacity of human agency to act *into nature*, rather than simply act *on nature* (ibid., 231). As Arendt comments, her effort to trace the history of the classic distinctions that underpin social thought takes place "at the very moment it was overcome by the advent of a new and yet unknown age" (ibid., 6). It is as if Arendt could see the frailty of her own conceptual architecture in the face of the techno-socio-ecological transformations, which have come to be understood as key aspects of the Anthropocene problematic. These transformations evermore tightly entangle human agency within natural systems and processes, underscoring both the inescapabilty of our "earthbound" condition and the need to render these earthly entanglements politically meaningful. By pushing some of Arendt's key concepts beyond the anthropic confines that she erects for them, I aim to indicate ways in which some of the challenges provoked by the Anthropocene might be accommodated within constitutional thought, without abandoning entirely our inherited, and enduringly important, notions of constituent power and peoplehood.

## From the Social to the Socio-Ecological

In Arendt's well-known formulation, "the rise of the social" (Arendt 1998, 38–49), refers to the weakening of classic distinctions between public/private and freedom/necessity. Modern associative life is understood and managed through a set of dispositions, knowledges, and techniques which tend to "normalize" behavior, encouraging uniformity at the expense of spontaneity, and purposively excluding the possibility of meaningful political action (ibid., 40). The social is associated with the generalization of statistical knowledge and associated forms of administration and bureaucracy (ibid., 43–44), akin to the disciplinary techniques famously elaborated by Foucault (2003). Perhaps the most important factor in giving rise to "the social," however, is the massive expansion of commodity exchange through the nineteenth and twentieth centuries (Benhabib 2000, 25). When production and exchange are no longer tied to the household (*oikos*), nor even to the "marketplace" – a physical locale, dedicated to commercial life – but permeate all aspects of the human collective existence, life's "necessities," the fact of earning a wage, putting food on the table, providing shelter, and so on take on a new public importance. As Arendt suggests: "society is the form in which the fact of mutual dependence for the sake of life and nothing else assumes public significance and where the activities connected with sheer survival are permitted to appear in public" (Arendt 1998, 46). If in the political domain, the uniquely human capacities of *action* and *freedom* are towards what the *vita activia* is orientated, the social is only concerned with meeting the biological needs of "a specimen of the animal species man-kind" (ibid., 46).

By bringing these biological and economic "necessities" into the public sphere, the once categorical delimitation between the household (*oikos*), a space in which private, familial needs are met, and the *polis*, where human freedom can be enacted, breaks down. The social is neither properly *political*, nor properly *private*, its emergence allows for "housekeeping, its activities, problems and organisational devices" (ibid., 38) to dominate the public domain. Today, public life is almost exclusively understood through the dictates of the economy (*oikonomia*), a mode of knowledge and organization once confined to the *oikos*, which the ancients conceived as a space of "privation" (ibid., 38) that was the necessary *precondition* for political life. In terms that the modern obsession with "political-economy" finds almost unthinkable, it was once only *beyond* the imperatives of *oikonomia*, that politics proper could take place.

Under the conditions of modern "social life" *labor* dominates, with *work* – by which Arendt means the craftsmanship which creates artifacts that endure across time (ibid., 136–174) – increasingly displaced by a kind of "creaturely life" (Santner 2006) of mere labor and consumption:

> The spare time of *animal laborans* is never spent in anything but consumption, and the more time left to him, the greedier and more craving his appetites. That these appetites become more sophisticated, so that consumption is no longer restricted to the necessities but, on the contrary, mainly concentrates on the superfluities of life, does not change the character of this society, but harbours the grave danger that eventually no object of the world will be safe from consumption and annihilation through consumption.
>
> *(Arendt 1998, 133)*

Here Arendt alludes to the rise of "false necessities" within modern consumer society. The effort required to sustain the biological necessities of life has been largely replaced by the seeming "necessities" of a larger house, a promotion at work, a second car, an annual holiday, and so forth. These all become "must haves" for the aspirational laborer, each being readily consumed, with future desires chained to wholly predictable, quasi-natural cycles of "advancement." In many post-industrial economies, labor itself has become increasingly unmoored from the "necessities" of production, with vast numbers of white-collar, administrative, and managerial jobs largely divorced from the labor power that produces surplus value (Graeber 2018). As Arendt herself notes, service sector employment often loses its connection to the vivifying dimensions of labor which attune us to the "elemental happiness of being alive" (Arendt 1998, 108) that comes from a proper balance of painful exhaustion and pleasurable regeneration (ibid., 134). Perhaps consumer society speaks less of the public valorization of necessity and labor *per se* but instead cultivates a *simulacrum of necessity* and an *ersatz labor*.

These points can be extended if we supplement Arendt's *economic* rendering of the social with attention to *ecological* relations, referring to the complex interactions between biotic and abiotic elements which constitute the planet's "critical zone" (Brantley et al. 2007). For Arendt, labor and necessity are tied to the biological processes of the body and the natural patterns of metabolism which allow for an individual life to sustain itself (ibid., 79–93). From an *ecological, planetary* perspective, the expansion of "consumer society" speaks less of *consumption* than it does of unchecked *waste production*. The purchase, short-term use, and ready disposal of vast quantitates of so many "superfluities," is precisely what fails to be consumed at an ecological or planetary scale. This unconsumed excess litters the earth with such vast amounts of waste that the planet's own metabolic systems are manifestly failing to process it. Arendt gestures to this when she suggests:

> The social realm, where the life process has established its own public domain, *has let loose an unnatural growth*, so to speak, of the natural; and it is against this growth, not merely against society but against a constantly growing social realm, that the private and the intimate, on the one hand, and the political (in the narrower sense of the word), on the other, have provided incapable of defending themselves.
>
> *(ibid., 47, my emphasis)*

We can think of the Anthropocene itself in these very terms: a shift in the earth's systemic functioning, brought on by specifically socio-genic forces (Hornberg and Malm 2014), is knowable because "unnatural growths" within the planetary strata are now visible. "Fossil energy, rock phosphate, and other raw materials" (Lenton and Latour 2018) essential to the perpetuation of today's consumer economy are extracted from the earth at a speed that far outstrips the planet's capacity to integrate them in its biogeochemical processes and conveyors. This leaves readable traces in the earth, atmosphere, and oceans – un-metabolized remnants of our global "consumer society" – which stratigraphers treat as material evidence of a move beyond the climatic conditions of the Holocene.

As our perception of "consumption" shifts from a *biological* (individual) metabolism to an *ecological* (planetary) scale, our conception of "necessity" changes with it. By focusing on the short-term, metabolic necessities which sustain biological life, the "elemental" and "earthly" conditions of human existence – and our necessary dependence on "autotropic" (Lenton and Latour 2018), planetary processes and forces – are largely backgrounded in *The Human Condition*. Arendt describes natural cycles and processes as taking shape in an "unceasing, indefatigable cycle in which the whole household of nature swings perpetually" (Arendt 1998, 97). By binding ourselves to these natural cycles, our society of laborers is chained to an animal-like, "dire necessity" (ibid., 48) which forecloses the possibility of human freedom. But this eternal, unchanging view of nature, rhythms to which *animal laborans* is apparently fettered, is challenged by today's ecological mutation. In this context, it is our dependency on once reliable, but now wholly uncertain, processes – the carbon and nitrogen cycles, freshwater systems and aquifers, ocean conveyors, biodiversity, and so on – that has been put in question. The Anthropocene shows, then, that our "laboring society" has disrupted the supposedly eternal patterns of nature; *animal laborans* is no longer merely subject to natural imperatives but is actively – if irresponsibly – shaping the earth's systemic functioning, assuming the capacity to divert planetary history.

What, then, does an ecological supplement to Arendt's conception of the social reveal and disrupt? Through the cultivation of the "false necessities" which define consumer society, the rise of the social plays an important role in obscuring the ecological, geological, and planetary dependencies which allow human life to sustain itself. At the very moment the forces of production and consumption which define the social are reaching ever deeper into the natural world, disrupting the apparently "indefatigable cycles" which sustain planetary life, the imperatives of economically defined "necessities" inure us to this fact. This speaks to one of the central contradictions of modern ideology: the connection between the natural and human worlds was arguably over-represented in premodern societies when the material connection between them was largely tenuous, but as the interaction between natural and anthropic registers becomes inescapable, this connection is "under- and mis-represented" (Viñuales 2020, 17). The rise of the social is instrumental, then, in facilitating the human reach into *geo-history*, while also constructing a worldview in which ecological interdependencies are backgrounded in favor of the "false necessities" associated with consumerism. Rather than follow Arendt in attributing the alienation from the "world" (of material things, created through work) to capital accumulation and expropriation, or the alienation from the "earth" (understood in naturalistic terms) to modern scientific knowledge (Arendt 1998, 248–273), what I want to emphasize here is that the material and ideological imperatives of "the social" are implicated in the simultaneous disruption of, and alienation from, our ecological and geological conditions.

By attending to the ecological forces and relations which subtend Arendt's thinking, it becomes increasingly impossible to approach the social in purely economic, administrative, or bureaucratic terms. This requires an elaboration of "socio-ecological" formations which can attend to the entanglements between patterns of production and consumption – along with the ideologies which sustain them – and the processes and systems which constitute the earth system. If this is the case, then the normative dimensions of Arendt's project, which aim to reclaim the uniqueness of the political sphere from the dictatorship of "social needs," appears entirely misplaced in relation to the challenges associated with the climate crisis. In light of the Anthropocene thesis, it makes little sense to define the political in opposition to the "mutual dependencies" which sustain social life because such dependencies are increasingly felt in *ecological* rather than purely *economic* terms. Drawing out the implications of an "ecological supplement" to Arendt forces us to reassess the opposition, on which Arendt insists, between *political freedom* and *social* (and *natural*) *necessity*. Any effort to define the unique capacities for human collective action and natality *in opposition to* the necessities of (eco-)social life, manifestly fails to grapple with the exigencies of the climate crisis and the modes of political thought and action needed if we are to integrate the ecological demands of the present into the fabric of our political thought and praxis.

## Extending the Scope of Action

For Arendt, action is the dimension of the *vita activa* that is proper to the political. Seyla Benhabib refers to the *agonal* (or revelatory), and *narrational* (or constructivist) dimensions of action (2000, 125–6) in a way that helps unpack its meaning and significance. In its *agonal* mode, action reveals the singularity of each human actor: it is through our speech and our deeds (speech being a species of action) that our distinctness as unexchangeable beings in the world is able to appear (Arendt 1998, 176); and, for Arendt, it is this co-appearance of singular beings in public which constitutes the *polis*. As Benhabib's allusion to the "agonistic" suggests, the singularity that action reveals is only possible by virtue of the plurality within which action is situated. As intimated above, Arendt insists that action can only take place *within* an a priori web of "unchosen" human relations. In this sense, action speaks to the "singular plural" (Nancy 2000) nature of political life: independent agents can only come to presence if predicated on a prior network of dependencies. Arendt connects this capacity for singular beings to appear in public and act freely, to *natality*; that is, the potential to begin or initiate newness in the world (Arendt 1998, 177). Natality "always appears in the guise of a miracle" (ibid., 178), in that it can establish the "infinitely improbable" as a reality (Arendt 1960, 46). The web of relations, within which action takes place, makes action unpredictable because action is always in negotiation with the actions of others: "it is because of this already existing web of human relationships, with its innumerable, conflicting wills and intentions, that action almost never achieves its purpose" (Arendt 1998, 184). In this way, action can only be understood as taking place within chains of *reaction*, where every intervention provokes subsequent transformations, either in the form of accommodation or resistance (ibid., 190). Arendt claims that the capacity for *action*, *freedom*, and *natality*, is uniquely human (ibid., 178); a life without speech and action, "is literally dead to the world; it has ceased to be a human life because it is no longer lived among men" (ibid., 176).

In a moment we can put Arendt's human exceptionalism in question, but first, let's briefly introduce the *narrational* dimensions to action. Arendt claims that action "'produces' stories with or without intention as naturally as fabrication produces tangible things" (ibid., 184). The scare quotes attached to "production" are imperative because for Arendt *action* must be distinguished from *work*, which is the domain of production proper. Action engenders stories that can never be known or "modelled" in advance (ibid., 192). The "stories" that action engenders have the peculiar quality of revealing a singular *agent, actor*, or *hero*, but these stories emerge entirely without an *author*:

> Although everybody started his life by inserting himself into the human world through action and speech, nobody is the author or producer of his own life story. In other words, the stories, the results of action and speech, reveal an agent but this agent is not an author or producer. Somebody began it and is its subject in the twofold sense of the word, namely its actor and sufferer, but nobody is its author.
>
> *(ibid., 184)*

The "story" to which Arendt alludes here is the result of the agonistic relations – actions and reactions – that takes place within a web of human relationships. There is no author here because each actor is never entirely in command of the results of their actions. Words and deeds performed in public create waves of action through a network of relationships which are variously accommodated or resisted by other actors in turn. The resulting "narrative" is never of one's own devising; action is an irreducibly *collective practice* that engenders a story that can only ever be co-authored with fellow actors, who might well fall outside our ken. There is, then, an important ambivalence within action: it reveals the *personal singularity* of the "who" that acts, but in the same stroke it engenders a story that is wholly *impersonal* because it can never be "possessed" (Weil 2005; Esposito 2015, 152) by any singularity in isolation.

There is no providence, no model, no "invisible hand" or "world spirit" (Arendt 1998, 185) that stands outside the web of relations endowed with the capacity to guide the course of events. Nonetheless, action is capable of *retrospective* reconstruction. This is the preserve of the "storyteller" who is able to reconstruct events and "make" a story that can endure across generations, shaping the beliefs, values, and outlook of political actors: "action reveals itself fully only to the storyteller, that is to the backward glance of the historian, who indeed always knows better what it was all about than the participants" (ibid., 192). Within the agonistic play of action and reaction, each actor is engaged in a process of which they themselves are never fully cognizant. In this way, action gives rise to what we might call "pre-representational stories" that can only subsequently be narrated and re-presented by a storyteller: "the light that illuminates processes of action, and therefore all historical processes, appears only at their end, frequently when all the participants are dead" (ibid., 192).

Where Arendt sees action as an irreducibly *human* capacity, contemporary ecology extends the scope of action to include nonhuman – both biotic and abiotic – actors within the "web of relations" which gives rise to natality and freedom. Arendt herself makes passing reference to a form of natality and action taking place within nonhuman forces, claiming that without some generalized form of natality, "*no* earth would ever arise out of cosmic occurrences, that no life would develop out of inorganic processes, and that *no* man would ever develop out of the evolution of animal life" (1960, 44). But these are described as being "automatic" occurrences – taking shape in "unceasing, indefatigable cycles" (Arendt 1998, 97) – and are therefore different from the "miraculous" change that can come about through anthropic action and freedom (Arendt 1960, 45).

Today's ecological science, in the form of Gaia theory, Earth System Science, and studies of the "critical zone," offers a radically different view of these apparently "automatic" processes of nature. By "extending the domain of freedom" (Latour and Lenton 2019) these new approaches emphasize the emergent, self-regulation of all living things in a way that departs from modernist categories of "Nature" which have "always situated life forms *inside* a larger frame" (ibid., 664). Whether by reference to providence, natural selection, or the bio- or eco-sphere, these earlier accounts consider "life" to be *subject to* these superordinate systems; the larger frame establishes forms of command and control which determine the rules to which all elements must submit. For instance, the novelty within the Gaia theory, developed by Lovelock and Margulis, is that there is no superordinate order to which lifeforms are subject: "there is *no other order*, and certainly *no order superior* to what those intertwined agents have been producing through their entanglements" (ibid., 664). Gaia presents an account of life in which *immanent relations* alone constitute our earthly reality. There are no "automatic processes" in the sense that Arendt evokes of an "unceasing cycle," there are instead *autonomous* systems, forces, and relations which have the extraordinary capacity to self-regulate:

> The novelty introduced in the notion of the Earth by the joint efforts of Lovelock and Margulis consists in granting *historicity and agency to all life forms*, that is, in attributing to the life forms themselves the task of creating the conditions for lasting in time and expanding in space. It is in this sense that they can be said to obey their own laws.
>
> *(ibid., 664)*

Rather than think of organisms living *on* the Earth or *in* an environment, Gaian agents actively create the conditions for their own survival, they create, to evoke an Arendtian vernacular, their own "stories" from within the agonistic play of action and reaction.

Crucial to this view is the innovation introduced by Margulis (1998), who jettisons an understanding of "environment" as a background *in which* an organism resides and *to which* it adapts. The "outside" (environment) is also "inside" (organism), with each actant *always in relation*. We cannot start with the organism and work out how it fits with its environment; nor vice versa. It is from within these interactions between organism and environment that the "laws" which allow for continuance in time and expansion in space are able to emerge. This emergent form of self-regulation can be described in terms that Arendt's reserves for the purely anthropic sphere of *action*. As Latour puts it – here glossing Lovelock's account of how each lifeform's struggle for survival is implicated in an open-ended network of biotic and abiotic relations –

> what is true for an actor taken as the starting point of the analysis is *equally true for all of the actor's neighbours*. If A modifies B, C, D, and X to benefit A's own survival, it is just as true that B, C, D, and X modify A in return.
>
> *(Latour 2017, 99)*

It is this play of action and reaction, where "providence is blurred, pixelated and final fades away" (ibid., 100), that guarantees that no "author" can ever stand above and beyond the sphere of action, that no superordinate order which commands obedience to each element in the system. Action, in the Gaian and Arendtian modes alike, is always immanent to a play of forces that takes place *between* actors who have a shared *interest* (an "*inter-est*") that binds them together in a collective practice (Arendt 1998, 182).

Gaia theory, alongside other insights from contemporary ecology, insists that the quality of emergent self-rule and natality are constituted through waves of action-reaction that extend throughout all lifeforms, dependent on "sympoietic" (Haraway 2016) relations with a range of fellow actors who are all co-authors of the conditions which sustain life. We must conclude, then, that "*both sides* of the ancient dichotomy between necessity and freedom" have been irredeemably broken (Lenton and Latour 2019, 679). Freedom – understood in the explicitly Arendtian terms of *action* and *natality* – is found throughout the web of life. Gaia is not a domain of necessity, of indefatigable cycles and automatic processes, but instead a vast, complex network of actors which have "in some extraordinary ways, made their own laws, to the point of generating over eons multiple, heterogeneous, intricate, and fragile ways of lasting longer in time and extending further in space" (ibid., 679). In the same breath, human agency is shot through with forms of *necessity* and *dependency*, which Arendt sees as anathema to the true potential of political life: "more freedom in the domain of necessity is fully matched by more necessity in the domain of freedom" (ibid., 679).

## We, Earthbound People

What do these reflections say about our theorization of constituent power in the context of the Anthropocene? First and foremost, peoplehood cannot be understood to emerge out of a pure claim to freedom and action, shorn of necessity and the imperatives of ecological entanglement. In the context of our present ecological and climatic mutation, the postulation of a political freedom "rising above" socio-ecological necessities, is deeply problematic. The climate crisis makes the question of elemental needs and dependencies – for fresh water, clean air, biodiversity, and stability within a range of biogeochemical processes and conveyors – some of our chief political concerns. The ontological distinctions on which Arendt relies, between human action and natural necessity, is confronted by both contemporary ecology and the Anthropocene thesis itself which shows, in ways that perhaps Arendt herself dimly foresaw, that human freedom is today acting ever deeper into the biogeochemical functioning of the earth. If freedom extends into the realm of putative necessity, necessity likewise relocates itself within the sphere of human freedom, bringing into view non-negotiable obligations to sustain the conditions of habitability within the planet's critical zone. If, as we indicated above, constituent power is most commonly associated with a claim of *self-governance*, contemporary ecology repopulates the natural world with a number of neighboring systems and processes that are themselves authors of related, though distinct, forms of *autonomy*. This view allows us to sense the disruptions that human governance projects – invariably made in the name of a people or nation – are causing within the self-regulating systems within which they have been inserted. As Jorge Viñuales comments:

> To us … human self-regulation still appears modern, reasonable, even desirable. We may not even realise how rebellious and unsettling our self-regulation is, in its unintended effects, with respect to the wider and deeper sense of self-regulation performed by life on biogeochemical cycles. Dramatically, whether we realise it or not, our rebellion cannot succeed; it would be a secession to nowhere.
>
> *(Viñuales 2020, 32)*

The only way forward, for Viñuales, is to develop forms of "alignment" where autonomy, security, prosperity, and so on are understood to only be meaningful if resituated *between* and *amongst* the earth's self-regulating processes. Endorsing such a view rearticulates the nature of constituent power within a *normatively plural* scenography that the modern political ethos, to which Arendt remains "reluctantly" bound (Benhabib 2000), is entirely unable to countenance.

In these different ways, the Anthropocene necessitates a radical redescription of constituent power that draws in and binds together human and inhuman agencies, needs, and interdependencies. On this point, we can turn to Emmanuel-Joseph Sieyès, the inaugural theorist of constituent power, who undertook a similar task of redescription and accounting in an effort to reimagine the nature of political community shorn of feudal hierarchies and privileges in late eighteenth-century France. For Arendt, Sieyès's conception of constituent power ultimately remains caught within a transcendent political imaginary, in which "The Nation" is endowed with the same kind of absolute, abstract, and unitary sovereign power that was previously the preserve of the monarch (Arendt 1973, 161–165). But as Lucia Rubinelli's important historical contextualization of his thought has shown, Sieyès was at pains to avoid the rhetoric of "sovereignty" (Rubinelli 2019; Rubinelli 2020, 33–74), developing instead a *relational* approach in which political power is never reducible to either element of the constituent-constituted dialectic.[4] Indeed, the very opening of *What is the Third Estate?* illustrates that Sieyès's chief ambition was to *assemble*, not presuppose, the nation. He knew that the nation had to be *composed* in a form that was sensitive to the immanent relations which constituted the new economic, social, and cultural order of the moment.

Sieyès achieves this feat by explicit reference to what Arendt would call *the social*: that is the "private activities" (Sieyès 1963, 53) that constitute socio-economic life. From this elliptical but nonetheless incisive tracing of socio-economic relations, emerges a "complete nation" (Sieyès 1963, 56), with the bonds of mutual dependence between peasants and artisans, merchants and service providers shown to be the very thing that generates a new actor capable of founding a new legal and political order. Within the old regime, of course, "the nation" – qua Third Estate – was *nothing*, it formed no part of the political imagination of the privileged orders, but through Sieyès's powerful redescription, what was once *nothing* becomes *everything*:

> Who is bold enough to maintain that the Third Estate does not contain within itself everything needful to constitute a complete nation? It is like a strong and robust man within one arm still in chains. If the privileged order were removed, the nation would not be something less but something more. What then is the Third Estate? All; but an "all" fettered and oppressed
>
> *(Sieyès 1963, 57)*

If the nation cannot be *presupposed* but must be *assembled*, the overriding concern becomes the quality of the composition (Latour 2010): have the constituent elements been put together well or badly, is this composition faithful to social realities, are the bonds that tie economic classes fragile or enduring? Here Sieyès, from our historical vantage, is almost certainly left wanting; his redescription of the Third Estate too quickly obscures his own bourgeois class interests and collapses hierarchical class distinctions into an apparently egalitarian conception of nationhood (Sewell 1994). Nonetheless, as a strategy of redescription and of tracing the socio-economic relations which constitute a nation, Sieyès's pamphlet remains instructive.

In the context of today's ecological mutation, it is precisely this kind of *redescription* and *reassembly* of a people or a nation, properly sensitive to its socio-ecological conditions, that is needed. This must involve tracing the ligaments of mutual dependency between situated human actors and the various inhuman forces and relations that constitute the continued habitability of our planet. The *salus populi* depends on clean air, potable water, productive soil, and a host of nonhuman animal life necessary for protein and pollination, not to mention a range of larger scale conveyors and systems that animate the earth system, providing the meteorological conditions within which extant nations and peoples persist. Might constituent power be redescribed in these terms? As emerging out of a singular constellation of bonds that tie human actors to these inhuman forces, intersecting, disrupting, or aligning with inhuman forms of self-regulation as well as a shared aspiration for autonomy, self-governance, and security held by neighboring peoples? This redescription of a people's presence could bring to light both alliances and enmities that are at present hidden by our too-speedy equation of peoplehood with an already delimited human population, or else an increasingly fragile fiction of unity and belonging tied to national identity.

This may seem a daunting task, but as Henrik Enroth has rightly argued this work is already underway in a range of political, scientific, legal, and activist responses to the Anthropocene (Enroth 2020). The enormous upsurge of writing on this topic over the last decade or so constitutes, what Enroth calls, new "declarations of dependence" which seek to draw up "specific lists of dependencies by specific terrestrial agents" (Enroth 2020, 18). Such a radical redescription of the agencies that constitute a given place puts in question any "we" presupposed by existing theories of constituent power, calling on all putative political communities to engage in a kind of accounting exercise that attends to the socio-ecological dependencies out of which any claim to "peoplehood" can emerge. To think of such practices in terms of a "declaration" – in the tradition of the Enlightenment revolutions – underscores that a new community *is brought into being* by these recent publications and other activities on the Anthropocene, Gaia, and the critical zone. In keeping with the rhetorical structure of the declaration, these emergent *communities of dependence*, could not have existed *before* these "declarations" had been made (Enroth 10, cf. Derrida 1986); indeed, such an entangled, "earthbound community," is almost entirely occluded by those communities of *independence* – existing nations, states, and peoples – which continue to structure so much of our political thought and practice.

We can discern the kind of shift in perspective to which Enroth points within contemporary climate activism. As Naomi Klein makes clear in her survey of what she calls "Blockadia" (Klein 2014, 293–336) – a network of highly localized movements that resist fossil fuel extraction – diverse assemblies come together and form temporary alliances on the basis of shared socio-ecological needs. As the slogans suggest – "water is life," "you can't eat money" (ibid., 303) – it is the elemental, necessities of life that are at stake in such movements, necessities that are being undermined by extractive industries. The Standing Rock protests, which sought to resist the construction of the Dakota Access Pipeline in 2016, speak to this altered sense of political agency that emerges within a diverse network of human and inhuman relations. As Kyle McGee comments:

> The Standing Rock public managed to translate a dispute framed originally as a Native American sovereignty question into a more complicated nesting of issues such as ecological and human health, religious freedom, freedom of speech, freedom from state repression, racial equality and ethnic dignity, and so on, through broad enrolment of allies interested in both the outcome and the means utilised to quash the pipelines opponents.
>
> *(McGee 2016, 119)*

The formation of unlikely alliances – "coalitions that brought together vegan activists who think that eating meat is murder with cattle farmers whose homes are decorated with deer heads" (Klein 2014, 302) – is testament to the fact that the ligaments that tie the "public" need not be reduced to some shared "essence" of belonging. What this points to instead is a political "sympoiesis" or *making-with* (Haraway 2016) where the multifarious bonds that connect a people to a place, in socio-ecological terms, are understood to take on a broader political significance.

These movements help illustrate the kind of shift that the Anthropocene prompts on the question of "demogenesis" (Latour 2018). By tracing the ligaments that assemble a people within a socio-ecological web of relations, we might reassert the "dialectic of determinacy and indeterminacy, of closure and openness" (Loughlin 2014, 228) within the modern state form and ponder how well-existing constituted powers represent or align with "constituent power" reimagined as an earthbound assemblage of human and inhuman actors. We might question, too, the putative *telos* of constituent power as taking shape within a liberal form of limited government: new forms of representation, of personhood, and of fundamental rights and obligations come into view if constituent power is extending and complexified through this work of reassembly and redescription. Sadly, most constitutional theory remains inured to these challenges, finding solace instead in the recuperation of Enlightenment traditions of collective political action and forms of belonging, which supposedly "rise above" these ecological entanglements (Somek and Wilkinson 2020).

By extending Butler's evocation of an "ecological supplement" to Arendt, this chapter has tried to establish some points of connection between our current socio-ecological challenges and some of the presuppositions which inform theories of constituent power. This does not entail the supersession of our inherited legal and political concepts entirely but instead calls for a recuperation of the creative energy which informed the early theorists of peoplehood and nationhood, underscoring that changed socio-economic and socio-ecological realities alike, require the composition of new actors that can bring about the kind of legal and political transformation that the present crisis demands.

If the approach outlined here puts into question some of the conceptual distinctions which animate Arendt's thinking, it also reaffirms the importance of two themes that are central to her account of the political: *storytelling* and *action*. It is, Arendt tells us, only the "backward glance" (1998, 192) of the storyteller who can really capture the nature of action. But the storyteller's gaze is never entirely shorn of a prospective dimension. As Sieyès's redescription of the Third Estate as an "entire nation" so clearly shows, stories of how a people come to be, inevitably shape the futures that they make and the work needed to bring about the "newness" to which politics, at its best, is always orientated. The radical redescription of peoplehood argued for in this chapter not only urges us to retell the story of a people via their mutual and situated dependencies to nonhuman forces and relations but also underscores the unique capacity for action and engagement within a newly expanded political sphere. The effort to resituate human agency within a complex field of self-regulating forces and agencies is not an argument *against* long-standing, and rightly cherished, aspirations for human autonomy and the possibility of collective action but it does seek to relocate that human agency within a socio-ecological context to which prevailing theories of constituent power remain largely blind. With these important caveats, which draw attention to the socio-ecological forces within which constituent power remains irredeemably bound and out of whose networks of action-reaction it ultimately springs, Arendt's celebration of the "miraculous" power of human action has an enduring resonance: "no less than the continued existence of mankind on earth may depend this time upon man's gift to 'perform miracles,' that is bring about the infinitely improbable and establish it as reality" (Arendt 1960, 46).

## Notes

1 This understanding of constituent power is not shared by all. For many liberal theorists, constituent power is entirely exhausted in the constituted order and only arises in an interstitial moment following the complete breakdown of the constitution; see, for instance, Rawls (2005, 231) or Dyzenhaus (2007),

both referred to in Muldoon (2016). For an alternative approach which develops a theory of "open constituent power," which does not presuppose that a constituted order needs to be the actualized, or even desired, outcome of an expression of "constituent power," see Wall (2012).

2 Arendt fails to see the contradiction in calling for Eichmann's execution whilst affirming forms of "unchosen cohabitation" as a prerequisite for political thought and action.

3 Some recent and indicative references include: Arato and Cohen (2009); Martel (2010); Muldoon (2016); and Lukkari (2020).

4 As Rubinelli argues (ibid., 22–23), Schmitt's influential reading of Sieyès, in which constituent power is elided with the capacity to decide on the state of exception, held by a representative "sovereign dictator," has unfairly colored the reception of Sieyès's thought, which was adamantly opposed to sovereigntist thinking, monarchical and popular alike. The constituted order will always be threatened by the re-emergence of the popular will, which can overthrow the constituted regime. In this way, a superordinate, legitimating power is always held in reserve by the nation. But constituent power is itself only part of the picture: it refers to a power-potential, *potentia*, not *potestas* (Negri 1999, 31–33), tasked with the limited remit of founding a new order with common laws and a representative assembly. If constituent power is an inchoate capacity that has substance but lacks form (Wall 2012, 45–53), constituted powers are never plenary *in stricto sensu*. In this way Sieyès understands constituent power in *relational* rather than *absolutist* terms, with neither the constituted nor constituent element capable of meaningfully claiming the mantel of "sovereignty."

## References


Arato, Andrew and Cohen, Jean. 2009. 'Banishing the Sovereign? Internal and External Sovereignty in Arendt'. *Constellations* 16(2), 307–330.

Arendt, Hannah. 1958. *The Origins of Totalitarianism*. New York: Meridian Books.

Arendt, Hannah. 1960. 'Freedom and Politics: A Lecture'. *Chicago Review* 14(1) (Spring), 28–46.

Arendt, Hannah. 1973. *On Revolution*. London: Penguin Books.

Arendt, Hannah. 1998. *The Human Condition*. Chicago: University of Chicago Press.

Arendt, Hannah. 2005. *The Promise of Politics*. Jerome Kohn (ed.). New York: Schocken Books.

Arendt, Hannah. 2006. *Eichmann in Jerusalem: A Report on the Banality of Evil*. London: Penguin Books.

Beck, Ullrich. 2016. *The Metamorphosis of the World*. Cambridge: Polity.

Belcher, Oliver and Schmidt, Jeremy J. 2020. 'Being Earthbound: Arendt, Process and Alienation in the Anthropocene'. *Environment and Planning. Part D: Society and Space* 39(1), 103–120.

Benhabib, Sayla. 2000. *The Reluctant Modernism of Hannah Arendt*. London: Rowman & Littlefield Publishers.

Braidotti, Rosi. 2019. 'A Theoretical Framework for the Posthumanities'. *Theory, Culture and Society* 36(6), 31–61.

Brantely, Susan L., Goldhaber, Martin B., and Ragnarsdottir, K. Vala. 2007. 'Crossing Disciplines and Scales to Understand the Critical Zone'. *Elements* 3(5), 307–314.

Brown, Wendy. 2015. *Undoing the Demos: Neoliberalism's Stealth Revolution*. New York: Zone Books.

Butler, Judith. 2015. *Towards a Performative Theory of Assembly*. Cambridge: Harvard University Press.

Derrida, Jacques. 1986. 'Declarations of Independence 1'. *New Political Science* 7(1), 7–15.

Derrida, Jacques. 1997. *Of Grammatology*. Trans. Gayatri Chakravorty Spivak. Baltimore: The Johns Hopkins University Press.

Dyzenhaus, David. 2007. *The Paradox of Constitutionalism*. Martin Loughlin and Neil Walker (eds.). Oxford: Oxford University Press.

Enroth, Henrik. 2020. 'Declarations of Dependence: On the Constitution of the Anthropocene'. *Theory, Culture and Society* 38(7–8), 189–210.

Esposito, Roberto. 2015. *Categories of the Impolitical*. New York: Fordham University Press.

Foucault, Michel. 2003. *Society Must Be Defended Society Must Be Defended: Lectures at the Collège de France 1975–1976*. London: Picador.

Graeber, David. 2018. *Bullshit Jobs: A Theory*. London: Penguin.

Haraway, Donna. 2016. *Staying with the Trouble: Making Kin in the Chthulucene*. Durham: Duke University Press.

Hornberg, Alf and Malm, Andreas. 2014. 'A Geology of Mankind? A Critique of the Anthropocene Narrative'. *The Anthropocene Review* 1(1), 62–69.

Klein, Naomi. 2014. *This Changes Everything: Capitalism VS the Planet*. London: Penguin.

Latour, Bruno. 2010. 'An Attempt at a "Compositionist Manifesto"'. *New Literary History* 41, 471–490.
Latour, Bruno. 2017. *Facing Gaia: Eight Lectures on the New Climatic Regime*. Cambridge: Polity.
Latour, Bruno and Lenton, Timothy. 2019. 'Extending the Domain of Freedom, or Why Gaia Is so Hard to Understand'. *Critical Inquiry* 45(Spring), 659–680.
Latour, Bruno, Milstein, Denise, Marrero-Guiliamón, Isaac and Rodríguez-Giralt, Israel. 2018. 'Down to Earth Social Movements: An Interview with Bruno Latour'. *Social Movement Studies* 17(3), 353–361.
Lenton, Timothy and Latour, Bruno. 2018. 'Gaia 2.0'. *Science* 361(6407), 1066–1068.
Loughlin, Martin. 2014. 'The Concept of Constituent Power'. *European Journal of Political Philosophy* 13(2), 218–237.
Lukkari, Hanna. 2020. 'Hannah Arendt and the Glimmering Paradox of Constituent Power'. In Matilda Arividsson, Brännström Leila, and Panu Minkkinen (eds.), *Constituent Power: Law, Popular Rule and Politics*. Edinburgh: Edinburgh University Press, 97–113.
Margulis, Lynn. 1998. *Symbiotic Planet: A New Look at Evolution*. New York: Basic Books.
Martel, James. 2010. 'Can There Be Politics Without Sovereignty? Arendt, Derrida and the Question of Sovereign Inevitability'. *Law, Culture and the Humanities* 6(2), 153–166.
McGee, Kyle. 2016. *Heathen Earth: Trumpism and Political Ecology*. New York: Punctum Books.
Muldoon, James. 2016. 'Arendt's Revolutionary Constitutionalism: Between Constituent Power and Constitutional Form'. *Constellations* 23(4), 596–607.
Nancy, Jean-Luc. 2000. *Being Singular Plural*. Stanford: Stanford University Press.
Negri, Antonio. 1999. *Insurgencies: Constituent Power and the Modern State*. Minneapolis: Minnesota University Press.
Rawls, John. 2005. *Political Liberalism*. New York: Columbia University Press.
Rubinelli, Lucia. 2019. 'How to Think Beyond Sovereignty: On Sieyès and Constituent Power'. *European Journal of Political Theory* 18(1), 47–67.
Rubinelli, Lucia. 2020. *Constituent Power: A History*. Cambridge: Cambridge University Press.
Santner, Eric. *On Creaturely Life: Rilke, Benjamin, Sebald*. Chicago: Chicago University Press.
Sewell, William. 1994. *A Rhetoric of Bourgeois Revolution: The Abbé Sieyès and 'What is the Third Estate'*. Durham: Duke University Press.
Sieyès, Emmanuel-Joseph. 1963. *What Is the Third Estate? [1789]*. Trans. M. Blondel, ed. S. E. Finer. London: Frederick A. Praeger.
Somek, Alexander and Wilkinson, Michael. 2020. 'Unpopular Sovereignty?' *The Modern Law Review* 83(5), 955–978.
Viñuales, J. E. 2020. 'Two Layers of Self-Regulation'. *Transnational Legal Theory* 11(1–2), 16–32.
Wall, Illan Rua. 2012. *Constituent Power and Human Rights: Without Model or Warranty*. Abingdon: Routledge.
Weil, Simone. 2005. 'Human Personality'. In Sian Miles (ed.), *Simone Weil: An Anthology*. London: Penguin, 69–98.
Wolfe, Cary. 2012. *Before the Law: Humans and Other Animals in a Biopolitical Frame*. Chicago: Chicago University Press.

# 6
# CHASTENED HUMANISM AND/OR NECROTIC ANTHROPOCENE
## Transcendence toward Less

*Ira Allen*

I live at a wildland-residential interface in the US mountain west and, as human-driven global heating continues to dry out these high ponderosa forests and diminish year-over-year snowpack, I fully expect my home to burn. This essay, urging "chastened humanism" as a frame for making sense of and living with and perhaps beyond the world-consuming catastrophes we humans are building, is written by the light and in the shadow of that anticipated future blaze.

How should we be and think we are, we pods of anthro, in relation to this era that a small group of us has determined bears our name? What rhetorical, ethical, and epistemic stances *ought* we to take toward our time, toward the enframing age we at once produce and find ourselves constrained by? Since Paul Crutzen and Eugene Stormer's coining of the term "Anthropocene" in 2000, and as consensus grows that the age has been well enough named, our little piece of this era has been going, to put it mildly, very badly. We're dying out there. In Australia's 2019–20 bushfires alone, nearly 3 billion vertebrate animals were killed or displaced (Commonwealth 2020, 5). Today, somewhere in the neighborhood of 8 billion human animals occupy the globe – 3.6 billion, nearly half, face inadequate access to water at least one month of each year, a number that only grows (World Meteorological Organization 2021, 5). We are burning and parched, flooded out, and starving.

Ordinarily, this is not too troubling for more comfortable denizens of the rich countries. But these days, as an aghast *New York Times* roundup put it in the summer of 2021, "Climate Change Comes for Rich Countries" (New York Times 2021). By contrast with the tut-tutting complacence about the "Inequality of Climate Change" that reigned, say, a decade earlier (Lowrey 2013), another *Times* headline from July 2021 laments, "'No One Is Safe': How the Heat Wave Battered the Wealthy World" (Sengupta 2021). *The New York Times* is nearly as good a barometer of the moods of a global majority-shareholder class as are stock markets, so that's a significant shift in framing. Meanwhile, we all participate in annihilating our nonhuman kin, an untold and untellable devastation that redounds against humans both morally and existentially. And we haven't gotten to the bad parts yet.

Before getting to the bad parts, be assured that this essay is not all darkness and difficulty. Despair requires no advocate. Rather, I urge a rhetorical hermeneutic for living well enough through and with realistic climate despair. The chastened humanism developed here comprises three entwining tendencies, potentially useful attitudes toward interpretive action: (1) epistemic humility on the

 DOI: 10.4324/9781003388081-8

basis of human species membership, (2) a corresponding moral humility, and (3) a commitment to something like transcendence all the same. The transcendence specific to chastened humanism is transcendence toward less, an overcoming of the apparent ecological law that all biota expand or construct available resource niches as fully as they can. For anything like a decent future to be viable, humans – an exceptionally adaptive species-metabolizer of resources – will have to stop ourselves short of consumption-unto-death. We will have to transcend ecological law to consume less than we *could* consume and to *become* thereby other than we at present are.

Chastened humanism, as a rhetorical hermeneutic, cannot help but respond to the late-twentieth and early-twenty-first century emergence of posthumanism. That set of interpretive and prescriptive strategies aimed to "deprivilege" the human agent (a deprivileging accomplished, of course, in a sense-making apparatus very particular to humans).[1] As a rhetorical hermeneutic, chastened humanism is an approach to interpretive invention, to the worldmaking we humans do *as audiences*. Its claims are smaller than those of posthumanism, and at once more hopeful. This humanism is chastened, in part, by recognizing the impossibility of simply leaving behind ways we have been shaped by traditions – including bad old Enlightenment humanism – by the mere disavowing of those traditions. If we are to become other than we have been by consuming less than we can metabolize, it will be by negotiating, not simply declaring null and void, the constraints that have made us the more or less specific species that we are. One way of thinking about this is in audiential terms.

To recognize ourselves as audiences is to grasp immediately the complexity of taking ourselves to know anything definitively, to urge anything decisively. We receive more than we can make sense of, and our sense-making itself is shaped by how prior moments of receiving happen to have shaped us. The constrainedness of our sense-making capacities calls for what Steven Mailloux (2017, 1989) has termed rhetorical hermeneutics. In Mailloux's sense, these are conceptual tools for and practices of navigating the demands of multiplicities, where "in a vast array of different cultural spheres, questions about who we are involve questions about how we interpret ourselves, how others interpret us, and how we interpret ourselves through how others interpret us" (Mailloux 2017, 9). Rhetorical hermeneutics is, above all else, *chastened attitudes* toward interpretation, ways of approaching our own apprehending of the world that foreground complexity and reflexivity in the service of something like humility. Our capacity for apprehension falls short of the world's demand. We cannot consume every datum and produce an infinite knowledge. As audiences, we are at once partial and ourselves inscribed in what we come to hear and see and feel – and so, to think and urge and do.

Chastened humanism is an orientation toward a complexly dying world that fosters political possibility by entwining humility with transcendence. As a hermeneutic for interpretively inventing well enough with the difficulty and darkness and sheer unfathomable *complexity* of our necrotic Anthropocene, chastened humanism's three braided strands are rhetorical. They orient toward the possibility of negotiating constraints and the impossibility of not being audiences. Posthumanism, decentering human agency, and all the rest (ethical aspirations notwithstanding) end up laying conceptual foundations that serve, in effect, as denial of both specifically human limitations and the monumentally human effectivity currently destroying the world's carrying capacity for our species and most others. Chastened humanism, by contrast, starts from a particular kind of human *in*capacity. We cannot help but know the world through species lenses and particularist traditions. We cannot help but be audiences in a very particular sense. Humans are rhetorical animals (though surely not the only rhetorical animals) with an unusual ability – at present – to construct our own ecological niche, but likely no special grasp of the character of being *qua* being. As a specific sort of audience, we can know that we miss a great deal about how things are, but so knowing does not allow us to stop being the partial audiences that we are.

Seen from this vantage point, the epistemic pretensions of posthumanism – the overweeningness of its claims to novel knowledge[2] – are of a piece with that desperate commitment to infinite expansion of species boundaries that is capitalist "growth." We can always know more, know better, know it all. There is no end to the material we can extract, the calories we can metabolize, in service of our knowing, our making, our profitably posthuman practices. But in the rotting lifeworlds of a necrotic Anthropocene, what we need more than anything is the reflexive, self-conscious, humbler aspiration of degrowth, what Kate Soper terms the "alternative hedonism" of post-growth living (Soper 2020, *passim*). We need to come to love and enjoy, more than we could perhaps suppose possible, living with less, knowing less, *becoming* less. Chastened humanism is a hermeneutic for agential audiences in a world at once too complex to comprehend and very much of our making, a world that can become simpler and worse or simpler and better. It is a way, perhaps, of transcending the firm law that dictates that humans, like other biota, must fill our ecological niche via an ever-expanding maximum metabolization of resources.

We are, we anthropos, audiences for our own actions and for other audiences' apprehensions of our actions. We come interpretingly into being, and may yet come into being quite otherwise. The "chastening" of chastened humanism – its epistemic and moral humility – opens the way for transcendence toward less. Pragmatically speaking, chastened humanism cashes out in the humbled but also outrageously radical aspiration of escaping our own deadening and deadly trajectory of (delusionally) infinite economic growth. Capitalism's wager is that there is no limit to the extent to which humans can fill and expand our ecological niche, our metabolization of resources to reproduce and further complexify social worlds. A chastened humanism turns us toward Soper's alternative hedonism, or toward the degrowth advocated by Timothée Parrique, among others, a degrowth now endorsed by the IPCC as one route for the transformation of unsustainable human lifeways.[3] Chastened humanism opens a psychic pathway for transcendence toward less novel complexity and more lively flourishing.

All this is not to say that degrowth and chastened humanism will enable us to fix a world system that the wealthier portion of anthropos has broken badly enough to call our own. Rather, committing to transcendence means deciding to believe we *can* do better than automatically continue the deadly building out of our ecological niche as fully as possible. We can shrug off the bonds of an apparently iron law of expansion, that expansion fostered beyond all reason and rhyme by humans' own iterative, self-reflexive complexity-orientation in our metabolization of resources – like any other species, but with the historical accident of greater effectivity. We can intentionally become not other to *what we are*, as in transhumanist dreams, but otherwise to *how we are*. At stake is a chastened sort of transcending. We can, as Jayna Brown puts the point in her evocative reading of Sun Ra's cosmic poetry, hit upon something even more than "the possibility of imagining the human differently" (Brown 2021, 173).[4] We can, in transcendent fusion with a cosmos that exceeds us, discover not "a new genre of the human but a new genre of *existence*, an entirely new mode of being" (173). We can outgrow the old humanist and the new posthumanist visions of transcendence toward more. We may do so by transcending toward less: joyfully, fantastically less.

I write these words from a sunny front deck, blown by a firewind both beautiful and terrible, a wind to which the fiercely churning giant ponderosas and I alike are subject. I do not escape human specificity through such an interpretation, nor even by submitting to the sublimity of that wind. Dropping the arch-critical posture of posthumanism, we change how we become not by disavowing what we cannot help but be, but by inhabiting species constraints differently. Chastened humanism invites me to dwell, reflexively, with such moments – that I may become someone who enjoys a great deal less consumption overall, maybe a more placid mind in and as this turbulent body. And indeed, is there not something about self-reflexively, iteratively, and other-directedly attuning with an alien world that could be called a common human yen? Brown names this "a desire, a utopian urge, a radical longing, to merge with the cosmos, to diffuse into the marvelous particles we understand so little about" (178). There exist attitudes that can help us transcend endlessly increasing caloric spend, the encroachment and expansion and complexification that characterize our species-being *now*, toward something simpler and far more intensely relational.

I am talking about what it might take for humans to live less awfully together toward and into unfolding catastrophic times than, left to our own too-belated and so reactionary impulses, we are likely to do. Having ushered in a geological age that's necrotic, with earth systems breaking down at all levels (like cell death this accumulates, driving feedback loops that further damage the whole), the search for expansively complex ways out (concretene [Robson 2021]! billionaires in space, but with more William Shatner! solar geoengineering![5] lab-grown meat! fully automated luxury communism![6]) drives thinkers and doers from across the ideological spectrum. Perhaps those efforts will pay off in time for the majority-shareholder class to live ever more feudally opulent lives uninterrupted, as in the dark vision articulated by Jodi Dean (2020), but the hard constraint on any future contiguous with the present is that there's a lot of misery locked in for the rest of us, humans and all our relations alike – and very little action underway to forestall the worst.[7]

Precisely those of us most capable of action have been, on the whole, least able or willing to recognize our problem as one of the universal, or generally global, scale of our local effectivities. William T. Vollman addresses the inheritors of our mess to explain our species-rulers' unthinkable idiocy: "As we contaminated our homes, warmed our atmosphere and acidified our seas, whatever would happen next stayed comfortably unthinkable, or at least potentially acceptable, back in the days when I was alive" (Vollman 2018, 511). Perhaps – so the old humanist posit, with one cluster of roots in Greek tragedy – if we can see the suffering to come, we shall find a way of coming to be differently now. Or, at least, of making meaning of our failures to do so.

## As Matters Stand …

Humans are currently expanding our ecological niche with extraordinary effectivity, out-competing all other charismatic life for access to metabolic resources. And it's going terribly. The current global warming of 1.2°C above pre-industrial levels already produces catastrophes the world over, catastrophes that will be manyfold worse within a short space of time. Even in rich countries! As an exceptional late 2021 *Guardian* article has it, "The Climate Disaster Is Here" and though we are "tumbling down a painful, worsening rocky slope rather than about to suddenly hit a sheer cliff edge … the world's governments are currently failing to avert a grim fate" (Milman, Witherspoon, Liu, and Chang 2021). Meanwhile, a leaked early draft of IPCC working group III's 6th assessment report explained in matter-of-fact tones: "Global emissions in 2030 as projected on a continuation of current policies exceed current national pledges" (Leaked 2021, 11–24).[8] In other words, most of our public narratives about global heating – which are structured as though national pledges were on track to being achieved – are nonsense at their core. This is no surprise.

At no point have any of the major carbon-emitting countries implemented policies that would result in the 1.5°C hotter-than-pre-industrial world imagined in the Paris climate agreement, nor even in the 2°C hotter world grudgingly assumed by that agreement. Matters are still worse, however: "Current pledges are not consistent with long-term emission pathways that would *likely* limit global warming to 2°C during the 21st century" (Leaked 2021, 11–25). We are not on track to stay within the bounds of our worst best-case scenario, itself nearly twice as bad as emissions-driven current global heating. To get on the worst best-case track, global carbon emissions would need to somehow peak by 2025, shortly after this essay appears in print. The very notion seems fanciful.

Moreover, to report on "what is" is to say little of significant further global heating feedback loops. Associated with albedo loss from glacial and sea-ice melt, the release of methane trapped in permafrost, or changes in earth's core climate gradients, such as the polar jet stream and Atlantic Meridional Overturning Circulation (Caesar et al. 2021), these blow our rosier dark projections out of the water. Nor does this speak to the related but distinct global biodiversity loss that Elizabeth Kolbert chillingly termed *The Sixth Extinction*. In Kolbert's most recent work, *Under a White Sky*, she notes in passing that "extinction rates are now hundreds – perhaps thousands – of times higher than the so-called background rates that applied over most of geologic time" (Kolbert 2021, 74). And it's not just vertebrates. "Even among insects, a class long thought to be extinction-resistant, numbers are plunging. Whole ecosystems are threatened, and the losses have started to feed on themselves" (74). *We* did that, and not just the "we" of the wealthy countries. And we did it before even starting to cook ourselves and our nonhuman kin in a carbon-saturated atmosphere and ocean system. Most of the great making-die to date isn't even about heating due to human carbon spend: it's about the land- and sea-use patterns our emissions enable, fruits of an extraordinary and ever-expanding capacity for resource metabolization. All of this should be understood as a broadly human construction of a global species-niche, though of course, an expansion accomplished at extraordinary cost to most of humanity itself.

By dint of interactions between historically very particular forms of human activity and extra-human physical regularities, between 1970 and 2016 the population of human animals doubled and managed to force an average 68% drop across the populations of all nonhuman vertebrates: killing mammals, birds, amphibians, reptiles, and fish by indiscriminate billions upon billions upon billions (WWF 2020, 6). Our mechanism of action for this wholesale devastation was primarily environmental use patterns, not carbon emissions. From clear-cutting rainforests to deep-sea trawling, capitalism's requirement of infinite expansion has led us toward both brute-force and clever-ingenuity methods for reconstructing the partial ecological niches our species occupied somewhat more placidly for millennia. Climate change due to our "release" of carbon by burning fossil fuels has certainly contributed to our casual massacre of most of the earth's non-domesticated biomass, but the unsurvivable heating, sea-level rise and acidification, and destructive weather intensification of anthropogenic climate change have barely even come into play yet.

We remain today in something of a grace period with respect to the effects of carbon emissions, and so continue to increase our aggregate redistribution of carbon molecules in ways we know with certainty are damaging. Crutzen and Stormer date an Anthropocene's origin to the late-eighteenth century because "this is the period when data retrieved from glacial ice cores show the beginning of a growth in the atmospheric concentrations of several 'greenhouse gases', in particular CO2 and CH4," and because that also "coincides with James Watt's invention of the steam engine in 1784" (Crutzen and Stormer 2000, 17–18). An Anthropocene, all this highlights, is both an indiscriminate slaughter machinery and a Carbonocene, an age of exceptional human access to inhuman power predicated on the global rearrangement of carbon molecules. Our rearrangement of carbon adds to the mass deaths we produce by other means, tilting global ecosystems toward the necrotic. We have formed a new geological age from the dying out of most living beings on earth. The age of humans threatens, too, our own species' survival – as warned in the IPCC report released in August 2021, days before a US military withdrawal from Afghanistan captured all media reporting for the better part of a month.[9]

Our era, the time *we here now* share, is characterized by humans' ever-still-increasing accumulation of carbon in the atmosphere. It is *our* carbon that warms the skies, acidifies the seas – and still, "we" are not all equally to blame. Indeed, wide swathes of the human species live already in eschatological times, after the end of worlds. "For a large share of humanity," Achille Mbembe argues of those living in the ravaged zones of colonialism's wake,

> the end of the world has already occurred. The question is no longer to know how to live life while awaiting it; instead it is to know how living will be possible the day after the end, that is to say, how to live with loss, with separation.
>
> *(Mbembe 2019, 29)*

An Anthropocene is without doubt unevenly distributed, even for anthropos, in time and place. And yet even for those most immiserated, a new end *also* approaches. We share, *New York Times* readers and *subaltern humanity* alike, a looming, shimmering zone of impossibility, a loss-to-come that can hardly be confronted. We share a horizon of climate genocides.

Necropolitics designates the theory and practice that make genocidality a logic, rather than the end of logic. Mbembe's term articulates our collective agency in the making-die of others as worldmaking that maintains and extends the structures of a world of domin ance-through-resource-metabolization. Within the sociopolitical terrain designated by our realistic fears of "the end of the world" there exists already "a subaltern category of humanity, a *genus of subaltern humanity*, which, as a superfluous and almost excessive part for which capital has no use, seems destined for zoning and expulsion" (178). Subaltern humanity's present and future entwine with our species' casual eradication of nonhuman life. Making-die as the making of a world is the basis of climate genocide as the accidental-on-purpose product of political decisions. For instance, as croplands throughout Central America are devastated by global heating's most immediately, barely begun sequelae, can anyone be surprised that the Biden administration militarizes the southern US border as zealously as did the Trump administration – and does nearly as little to reduce carbon emissions or mitigate catastrophic land- and sea-use patterns? The majority-shareholder class certainly supposes that not all can be saved.

Necropolitics is the order of a human world organized by decisions about who *cannot* be saved. Such decisions beget their own "whys" and, in such begetting, rob all humanity of transcendent moral possibility. As Mbembe puts it, "the norm now is to *live* by the sword. Including in democracies, political struggle increasingly consists in a struggle to know who can develop the most repressive measures faced with the enemy threat" (31). This formulation, apt enough for last century's "late" capitalism, is even more trenchant in regard to looming climate genocides. Our species has already committed or *been* committed wholesale to organizing the deaths not only of subaltern humanity but of most living creatures on earth. Today, humanity's dominant modes of life constitute a causing-to-die of most of all that crawls or flies or swims or slithers or runs. And yet, even as we reckon with consequences of that fact, the complex machinery of our interimbricated global society is such that there is no one *actually able* to shut off the great carbon pump of modernity. There is no switchman to stop the seemingly ineluctable processes whereby we transform the carbon of the earth into the greenhouse gases of the sky and the acid of the sea. Things are going badly indeed.

Not for nothing, then, does William T. Vollman begin his two-volume opus *Carbon Ideologies* by declaring,

> Someday, perhaps not long from now, the inhabitants of a hotter, more dangerous and biologically diminished planet than the one on which I lived may wonder what you and I were thinking, or whether we thought at all. This book is for them.
>
> *(Vollman 2018, 3)*

There is, it seems, little we can do. As Vollman dourly puts the point, "Now that we are all gone, someone from the future is turning this book's brittle yellow pages. Unimpressed with what I have written so far, he wishes to know why I didn't do more" (12). Because, he continues,

> when I was alive there were elephants and honeybees; in the Persian Gulf people survived the summers without protective suits; the Arctic permafrost had only begun to sizzle out methane; San Francisco towered above water, and there were still even Marshall Islands; Japan was barely radioactive, Africa not entirely desertified.
>
> *(12–13)*

Vollman concedes, "Well, in the end I did nothing just the same, and the same went for most everyone I knew. This book may help you in the hot dark future to understand why" (13). And yet, are we really so stuck as that? Can we aim for nothing better than explaining ourselves to a future that may not come?

## A Dark Optimism …

The perspective offered by chastened humanism is optimistic, albeit darkly so. Our Anthropocene is indeed necrotic, characterized by cell death at many levels. Its organization-toward-death is necropolitical, the exhaustive reconstruction of the political animal as the animal-who-makes-die. The human capacity for resource metabolization has grown monstrous, destroying ever more worlds to make ever fewer. So what, then? We may or may not be able to revivify the world around us, in ways that allow once more for its exceeding and containing of us. It is certainly worth trying, and not all ways of trying will have equally good chances.

A realistic optimism is dark because it sets out from honesty about catastrophe. If the world in its totality is organismic, our species has destroyed enough of the elements that make up that great living alien but anthropos-encompassing and, above all, *active* totality – what Isabelle Stengers and Bruno Latour each in their different ways think of as *Gaia*[10] – to produce cascading deadly consequences within most domains of life-sustaining systematicity. Two twin names for the corpse-piling disaster of the human age that is most particularly our own are "climate catastrophe" and, more apparently neutral but if anything at once more immediately threatening and more psychically devastating, "biodiversity loss."

The best, indeed the transcendent, hope for the human species is that we will pursue leveling strategies that allow us to collectively pull up short our stipulated – guaranteed necrotic – future of infinite expansion. Climate catastrophe and biodiversity loss trace the outline of a necropolitical world in which "humanity is in the process of leaving behind the grand divisions between the human, the animal, and the machine so typical of the discourse on modernity and on humanism" (Mbembe 2019, 179). Our best chance of throwing off a future in which "it is deemed enough to liberate the enslaved's mimetic potential," where "the newly emancipated slaves expend themselves in wanting to become the masters they will never be" (179), is to commit ourselves to becoming less than we *can* be, to leaving vast swathes and dimensions of the human ecological niche undeveloped, unbuilt-out. The close of this essay is devoted to laying out a chastened humanism I believe can aid in such revolutionary modesty. I draw there primarily from Giambattista Vico's orations on humanistic education. First, though, I examine a little what it might mean for humans to transcend a kind of "natural" ecological law toward a juridical ecological law that expresses chastened humanism. Ideationally and logistically, we need to and can develop a degrowth rooted in alternative hedonisms, a way of valuing and litigating and *enjoying* transcendence toward less.

A world that, for millennia, more or less sustained complexifying life and reproduction for most of the species comprising it is circling the drain. Faced with the holocaustal consequences of our extractive energy regime and an economic system that can only be maintained through infinite expansion, the challenge for humanity today is to *become less than all that we can be.* We must, to avoid the very worst, stop expanding the boundaries of our ecological niche. We must learn to construct differently, to collectively consume less energy than is available to us for propagation. In doing so, paradoxically, we would transcend what we take to be a core ecological law: that biota construct their ecological niches to the fullest extent possible, wherever not interrupted by competition from other biota.

## Ecological Law as Immanence, Ecological Law as Transcendence

An "ecological niche" is a conceptual chunk of material world. We living beings who derive sustenance and substance from a mattering multiplicity are occupants and constructors of niches. We inhabit, expand, and refashion chunks of metabolic world. In the standard formulation, "Ecological theory states that each species has a unique niche, which encompasses its habitat and its use of resources in the presence of competition and other biotic interactions" (Slagsvold and Wiebe 2007, 19). It is the "other biotic interactions" that, as examined in recent decades by everyone from zoologists and biologists to evolutionary psychologists and bioarchaeologists, have driven niche theory from the static to the dynamic. Where ecological niches were in early iterations hypostasized, supposed at least temporarily static, their actively constructed character has come increasingly to the fore. An ecological niche, as a conceptual chunk of the world, is never *only* a being but always *also* a becoming. Not because we humans will it so but because, as far as we can tell, such is the character of reality.

Species do not only occupy niches of resource metabolization; they construct these niches, expand them. And they do so at varying rates. The greater the *gradient* of effectivity with which a species constructs its niche – reorganizes its ability to metabolize resources as compared to proximate biota – the worse for all biota concerned. The ecological law of niche construction, though immanent to all biota, has in *Homo sapiens*' ever-increasing ability to metabolize resources produced "growing capacities for advanced cognition and demographic and geographic expansion, along with an exponential increase in the scope and impact of human niche constructing activities that have culminated in fundamental changes to planetary ecosystems" (Boivin et al. 2016, 6388). Humanity's challenge, if we will transcend ecological law to forestall our worst necrotic tendencies, is to become in and as world *less* than the earth environment and our own capacities would yet allow.

This essay thus also concerns a subtending question for the blossoming discourse around ecological law and the Anthropocene. Specifically, and in line with Peter Burdon's (2020) argument for de-emphasizing the search for a non-anthropocentric theory in the articulation of ecological law, I am asking what theory of the human animal's place in the world might suit sufficiently radical rethinking of planetary legal and moral structures. What view of humanity's place in the world is appropriate for an Anthropocene? How can we understand the *meaning* of our species-effectivity in ways that engage the demands of an Anthropocene, demands on and beyond collective (human) capacities for intentional action? In suggesting *chastened humanism* as one answer to that question, I sidestep the self-thwarting dilemma raised by an academic focus on "posthumanism" as god-term for ethico-political thought. Chastened humanism is not a salvatory term, but rather one for living with painful hard constraints, and yet it names a style of thinking that refuses the dread tyranny of what apparently is, on behalf of the least worst futures that may be discoverable through human agency. In essence, this is an essay about transcending through limitation: about wishing to transcend rotten conditions of our own helpless making, and about how self-limiting frames of mind may add an element of realistic hope to such wishing.

Translated from *res* to *res publica*, the phrase "ecological law" offers a sort of constraint-negotiating transcendence. Beyond the limitations of liberal *environmental law* and its strictly human world of ultimate aims – which presuppose the continuity of a legal landscape even in times of radical rupture, and yet has already failed to secure such continuity[11] – *ecological law* has been proposed as an "umbrella term" that "imagines law as if nature matters" (Burdon 2020, 33). It injects a notion of the *mattering* and *worth* of the nonhuman world into the heart of all legal theory, and so requires literal regrounding of juridical regimes. As the term for a transcending legal framework, something to be made by humans but not restricted to characteristic human concerns, ecological law at once challenges and requires anthropocentrism. Burdon's thinking of this has become increasingly restless with an early focus on "getting beyond" anthropocentrism. In light of the systemic world picture of harmful human effectivity suggested by an Anthropocene, he argues, "Our challenge is not to construct a non-anthropocentric ethics but to come to terms with our new-found power and think about how we might act with humility and responsibility as geological agents" (45). We must transcend the desire to transcend our humanity, must fall back into a descriptive anthropocentrism that, appropriately humbled,[12] allows us to take effective responsibility for a disaster that is broadly *our own*. At stake for a juridical ecological law that transcends ontic ecological law is the question of how to rein in human niche construction.

Degrowth is one name for the aim of reining in a human, and specifically capitalist, tendency toward ecological niche construction that would be infinitizing-toward-death.[13] The transcendence of liberal environmental law by ecological law entails something like degrowth in the economic domain. After all, as Tim Jackson puts it, "The legitimacy of the social contract forged in the crucible of capitalism is fatally dependent on a false promise: that there will always be more and more for everyone" (2021, 151). The demand levied by the twin catastrophes of runaway climate change and global biodiversity loss is for us to recognize that humanity *can* metabolize more resources than there *are*. There may be enough for everyone, but there cannot be always more. Our challenge is to learn to want something other than more, to come to desire less. This, in turn, requires that richer societies at large – and the wealthy, globally – "accept a less expansionary, more reproductive material style of living" (Soper 2020, 6). For such acceptance, we need conceptual and juridical frameworks that are chastened but transcending. The alternative hedonism Soper urges would include joys that are "less dependent on innovation and continuous replacement of goods" and more predicated on "leisure time along with the cultural and recreational provisions with which to enjoy it" (6). This would be a wholesale transformation in both productive and consumptive relations, especially for richer societies and persons. Chastened humanism offers a conceptual framework for such transformation. Ecological law aims to institutionalize a juridical framework for it.

Most articulations of ecological law orient toward a sort of negotiated species-mutuality, toward juridical frameworks that establish not merely the claims *of* but also claims *on* human resource metabolization. Human legal constructs should be built with meaningful regard to a nonhuman world filled with effective and moral agents, and such building requires a more-than-(typically?)-human view of what sorts of things and processes can and ought to matter. As

Kirsten Anker et al. put it, ecological law aims to foster "a legal future that is staked neither on the management of natural resources for the short-term gain of some, nor on the false choice between human interests and the environment, but on a negotiated terrain of mutual flourishing" (2021, 7). At such moments, and there are many of them,[14] theorists of ecological law name, and hope by so naming (though not by naming alone) to help bring into being, a domain of legal reality at once newly unconstrained and newly binding. As against the settled verities of environmental law, which helplessly align with necropolitics, ecological law aims at newly emergent possibility. Addressed to human audiences in our character as agents, ecological law offers us a framework for self-transcending: toward less. This symbolic transcendence of a drive to construct our biota's niche for the metabolization of ever more resources, together with the alternative hedonisms that *desiring less* entails, may be conceptually sustained by something like a chastened humanism.

## Chastened Humanism

"The Anthropocene" is a term of chagrin. Even where carried upon triumphal undertones – as it often is[15] – it operates to name the incalculable damage our species has done to every other living thing on the only planet we inhabit, and may well have done to our own ability to inhabit this planet in any way approximating flourishing. Against that backdrop, *chastened humanism* (a) accepts that human activity is necessarily accomplished along lines of moderate species-specificity and (b) laments that humans have radically reconstructed our ecological niche, with nihilating effects on planetary biological diversity and at the level of experience for most living beings, while (c) betting all the same on our collective capacity to do something different, something better, on purpose. This orientation cashes out in epistemic humility, a corresponding moral humility, and an aspirational transcendence toward less. Would such a chastened humanism be enough to change the devastating course of the sixth extinction we have set in motion, or enough to help humans transcend the ecological law establishing us, too, as a species blindly determined to fill and exceed its niche by metabolizing all the calories that can be extracted from this earth? Probably not. But, having done so much damage already, we would be fools to bet against ourselves now.

The sense of what it means to hope darkly for transcendence toward less from "the human," I feel in closing through Giambattista Vico's orations on humanistic education. In that series of six inaugural addresses delivered between 1699 and 1707, Vico establishes a vision of human transcendence that is supposed to result from rhetorical education. Let's be clear, though: there's a reason the old humanists have been so pilloried these decades past. We find humility and transcendence in Vico, yes, but also an endlessly self-reinforcing system of binaries that places mind above matter, human above animal, man above woman, and European above everyone else, and that anchors all this in a highly particularistic concept of the divine.[16] Hard pass on all that. Rather than read Vico straight, then, I excavate here a relationship between epistemic humility, moral humility, and transcending aspirations that subtends his inaugural orations. In this, I take as axiomatic that any rhetorical humanism *should* be chastened from the start. There is no thinking of rhetorical appeals that is itself not also a rhetorical appeal, an agential bid for the attention and adherence of some audience.[17] To recognize our knowing as the knowing of and for audiences, the knowing of rhetorical hermeneutics, is to accept a partiality, a contingency, not only in what we take to be the case but equally in what we take to be the good. Humans (though clearly not only humans) are creatures of history, formed of sedimented and sedimenting narratives. Apprehending that, as rhetoric must, should induce a rightsizing of epistemic claims and sensibilities.

We know *not* that we know nothing (who could know *that*?!), but that whatever "knowing" we do is contingent on language, culture, and audiential species constraints of all sorts. So knowing means that we must, as Mailloux (2017) argues, account for the historicity of our interpretive inventions. Epistemic humility is not disavowal of that which has shaped us, nor an avowal exactly, but negotiation of it as material-conceptual constraint. Part of such negotiation is responsibility for our contingent and partial choices of what to attend to. In this spirit Vico closes the final oration of *On Humanistic Education* with a nod to tradition: "This is the advice which I am not ashamed to have given, because, though I be not wise, I have followed those who are" (1993, 140). A chastened humanism is epistemically humbled in recognizing itself as the rhetorical recipient of history, of a multiplicity of prior narratives from among which it hopes to have chosen well. Meanwhile, for Vico, we are simply incapable of transcendent, infinitizing knowledge, even as we are in some sense "born to" it: "Nature has unhappily established that we, by the impetuousness of our mind, fall into error and are brought around to that truth which we are born to reach by a direct path only by a tortuous one" (111). We know but partially, and even our frameworks for degrowth and ecological law – transcendent though they would be – must be continually renegotiated, not only with regard to other biota's characteristic forms of life and Gaia's unfolding in an era of planetary upheaval but also with regard to our own "impetuousness" and our knowing's having been shaped by others.

Vichian epistemic humility accepts the constrainedness of our capacities for knowing, we creatures of history. Vico starts from the position that "innumerable and almost infinite proofs of human frailty and misery are available everywhere" (38). The course of humanistic education is "tortuous" and seems roundabout only because of our "impetuousness," our desire to immediately and wholly consume everything, without yet knowing our own limitations and real capacities. Epistemic humility in humanistic education becomes a historically conditioned form of slowing ourselves down, taking in less at once and less altogether. Here, that bad old mind-matter split warrants a distinction between receptivity and consumption. In Vico's fifth oration, the "truth we are born to reach" is that "nations have been most celebrated in glory for battles and have obtained the greatest political power when they have excelled in letters" (110). The consuming fires of the former must give way to the placid wisdom of the latter, he argues. Vico's humanistic education orients toward a life of the mind that – literally, materially – would consume less, metabolize fewer resources than other forms of life. Epistemic humility, then, begins in apprehending our own physical partiality and continues in negotiating rather than hoping simply to set aside historical traditions. It ends in fostering forms of life that, like Soper's alternative hedonism, flourish in receptivity rather than consumption.

And yet, all this is no stilling of general activity. "Why then are the wise idle?" asks Vico. Why else, but "so that when it becomes necessary they may find themselves thoroughly prepared" (112). Prepared for what? Why, war of course, for

> arms and letters not only do not conflict with one another in ways that will lead the one to rout and destroy the other, but actually they agree so that letters may make known the glory of the military and celebrate the dignity of the military order.
>
> *(113)*

In such formulations, it seems as though Vico would be hard-pressed to get us to moral humility.[18] Indeed, his orations are just *filled* with grand claims. In his first inaugural address, for instance, the Royal Professor of Eloquence exhorts his students at the University of Naples, "You are born and fashioned to learn to perfection, in a short time and in a fitting manner, the arts and sciences in their fullness! What, therefore, remains? Your will!" (52). Here is the overweeningness of Enlightenment humanism in full flourish. But, and this is crucial, here also is a suggestion of something more, which is to say, something less. After all, Vico's students are to learn not mastery of but receptivity to the world, not riches and glory but "this oath – to bear all mortal conditions and to be unperturbed by those which are not possible to escape" (69). The perfection of humanistic education to which these students must turn their desire begins with epistemic humility and proceeds through moral humility, a slowing down of niche construction. This latter entails audiential, receptive relations with the material world.

The overweeningness characteristic of old humanism may deserve censure, but let us also take responsibility for our own. Recognizing that the tendency to maximize consumption is more ours than Vico's should spur some moral humility. Desiring to become otherwise, on behalf of a world that codifies human obligations to nonhumans, is a goad toward transcendence. On this point, take Vico's second inaugural oration, "On Virtue and Wisdom." Here, the end of humanistic education is development of the Godly soul, of a "divine reason" which alone can legitimate citizenship in the city of god. At first blush, it's not a good look. Here, "man alone … is the most important among all creatures" (56). It is "man," and let's leave the *sic* out because it would be ubiquitous, "for whom nature has produced such abundance of useful and pleasurable things, to whom all lands and seas are open for exploration and conquest" (56). Humans are awfully important, and *should* build out our ecological niche to consume all resources we can come to have encountered! Vico lays out a vision of wisdom as a Christian virtue to be developed through intensive engagement with the liberal arts, anchoring that vision in human supremacism or secondness only to a divine. So far, so blah blah blah.

But also, so far, so us. Recall: it is not *simply* capitalist extractivism that produces a necrotic Anthropocene, but also and as much the massive increase in human population allowed by a few technological accidents surrounding the reorganization of carbon. Sure, human history includes plenty of less intensive land- and sea-use patterns.[19] But a generally human *present* does not, at least as a matter of overarching species-organizational social structures. To accept species membership as a constraining characteristic is to acknowledge that we cannot simply *become the good guys* by fantastically identifying with human societies that have devoted less energy to maximizing their ability to metabolize resources. What are we to do, asks Vico, with a world that is ours for the conquering? We are *not* to conquer it. It is the fool who "is always seeking excitement, never in touch with himself. He is always searching for new surroundings, new responsibilities, new ways of life, initiating new hopes even to the time of death. He is forever fleeing from himself" (66). Vico's humanistic education aims at a kind of self-knowledge in tune with limits, an attunement to "divine reason, which is present through the universe and all its parts" (67) and which allows us to "concern [ourselves] only when needed with the fragile and the troublesome" (69). We who live in the shadow of climate genocides to come would do well to better know ourselves, to feelingly apprehend the foolishness of our endless maximizing of resource metabolization. We will continue constructing our ecological niche – but degrowth and alternative hedonism require from many of us *less* concern for luxuries and even lifespans, for the "fragile and the troublesome." Developing our agential capacities to escape the prison of necropolitics requires frameworks that make it both plausible and desirable to wager on collective transcendence, not toward more but toward less.

Chastened humanism suggests transcendence through moral humility, and here again, there is something important to take from Vico. The address "On Virtue and Wisdom" is directed against "the joys of the fool (which cannot truly be called joys but rather renewals of pain)" (64). Vico exhorts his listeners to abjure those joys, fleshly conveniences, for the city of God. There, "Man's privilege of citizenship is not by birth, nor by one's legitimate children, nor is it a reward earned in the fields of battle or at sea, but only by the possession of wisdom" (66–67). Humans are the inheritors of a "very great community" founded upon the "law" of "divine reason, which … permeates all things and protects and sustains the world. This divine reason is in God, and it is called Divine Wisdom" (67). Helping students to seek it is the work of a liberal arts *studium*. But the contents of the city of God remain obscure. The "purpose of human life and the highest of our aspirations is to know the certain and do the right, to contemplate God by the former and to imitate him by the latter" (68–69). In transcending toward but never wholly reaching this aspiration, we escape a prison, find freedom from "opinions, falsity, and error" (70). We outwit the guards, which "are the senses, … keenest in childhood but dulled by old age and throughout life severely impaired by perverse passions" (70). How? By humanistic education devoted to the life of the mind, the study of letters. We unify ourselves with God in virtue, with the "perfect reason by which God acts upon all things and the wise understands all things" (69). Should we be fools, failing at properly motivated studies of the liberal arts and so at achieving virtue, well: "The dark dungeon is our body" itself (70).

On the one hand, the critique of humanism is all right there! It takes nothing but to read Vico straight. And yet, on the other hand, isn't a secularized version of this *just what we need*? Is not the urge toward transcendence through understanding of the physical world and deprivileging of acquired comforts precisely that which degrowth and a (juridical) ecological law would require of us? The notion of transcendence on behalf of an epistemically and morally uncertain – and yet terribly urgent – good at stake in Vico's orations is just the sort of goad we need to become less than we can be together. Seen thus, some of Vico's formulations are perhaps not so alien after all. In the fourth oration, "On Education for the Common Good," he speaks of a "natural nationalism" that exceeds even the law of peoples. A "necessity binds you together," Vico tells his charges, who "feel something of which none of you is aware" (95). What is that something? A "kind of necessity" and "degree of love" that come of our helpless descent from "the motherland [that] has given us birth" (96). Is it such a stretch to say, for us today, that this motherland could be Gaia herself? Would not ecological law, degrowth, and all the rest attend upon our transcendent, self-limiting love of her?

Let me return to the epistemic humility that anchors chastened humanism. These orations by Vico address a being who, in its being, tends to be wrong in species-specific ways. Indeed, Vico at times takes turns we might miss if we were too ready to rehearse the standard critiques of humanism. Back in "On Virtue and Wisdom," he follows the Aristotelian and Ciceronian lines in distinguishing between "two powers like a pair of horses" within the human spirit. We are prepared for the good one to be male- and reason-identified, the bad one to be female- and sense-identified. Instead, both operate "in that part of the spirit which is distinct from reason altogether" (62). Working in the idiom available to him, Vico offers up a horse that "is male and thus rebellious, spirited, and impetuous" and another that is "female and thus pliable, languid, and idle" (62). So far, so misogynist. But that's not all there is to see here. Neither horse can be trusted, for "how many enemies that were hidden come out from those two horses as if each had been a Trojan horse!" (62). Much of the rest of the oration, for all its "the body is the prison of the mind" vibe, is given over to amplification of the ways in which we are, indeed, routinely fooled by our own dispositions. We are fallible in ways that register the particular organization of our species constitution. Our takes *are* subject to materially patterned and repetitive errors, our passions routinely captured by the felt good of the moment and all-indifferent to any fuller or longer sense of obligation. Which is more identified with a Gaian "divine reason" and which with the fool: seeking patiently to understand the world organism we are destroying with an Anthropocene we do not ourselves yet understand, or doubling down on the techno-promise of capitalist expansion, sure that if we all can consume precisely what we want whenever we want we will along the way know all that we could ever need to know?

Chastened humanism – by contrast with "posthumanism," which has served here as something of a foil – lets us approach our necrotic Anthropocene without averting our gaze from the horror of what we are nor despairing at it. Chastened humanism is a pathway, surely not the only one, toward a realistically dark optimism in the face of interlocking, self-incurred catastrophes. At stake is yet another transcendence, the transcendence of an immanent law that novel juridical frameworks would hope to make possible. If we will pay what's due, to one another and to the nonhuman persons who make up a world, we must break the law that says every biota constructs its niche to maximize resource metabolization. If such a law holds, our clever species growth in niche-constructing capacities all but assures necropolitical futures. Hope in the face of a necrotic Anthropocene requires realistic belief in human agency: for transcending (immanent) ecological law in the construction of (juridical) ecological law. This means voluntarily restricting exhaustion of the resources afforded us, developing degrowth mindsets and systems to guide new ways of inhabiting a niche. Chastened humanism gives grounds, if not exactly for full-throated hope, then for living hopefully with a planet whose time, sadly, is all ours.

Chastened humanism, once more, comprises three tendencies: (1) epistemic humility on the basis of species membership, (2) a corresponding moral humility, and (3) a commitment to something like transcendence all the same. I practice epistemic humility in recognizing species constraints on my own pursuit of knowledge and historical constraints on my interpretive invention. What I can say or take myself to know meets hard limits that are in one or another way the products of my being, as it happens, human.[20] This admission of the simultaneously very specific and not wholly transcendible limitations associated with species membership should prompt in me a corresponding moral humility. If I cannot take myself to know with any great certainty how the world *is* – for reasons of my being human, thus not readily amenable by one or another sort of cultural learning – then I can hardly suppose myself to have an excellent grasp on how the world *ought to be*.[21] And yet, the one who notes her epistemic limitations and thus draws conclusions about the foreshortened grasping of her moral intuitions immediately suggests, in the moment of sharing that observation in any fashion, that others might do well to also so note. We want more from our discourse about the world than mere description, and we cannot help so desiring. We need, if we are to somehow transcend that great ecological law that binds us to metabolizing as much as we can, to become other to ourselves, to become *less* than we can be.

So, what does or can "transcendence" mean in the context of an Anthropocene? It must mean *less* than is possible: efflorescently, flourishingly less. If this essay is correct – that chastened humanism can help in transcending the ecological law that dooms humans to fill their niche as fully as possible by continually reconstructing it to encompass ever more, such that we doom perhaps ourselves and certainly many other species and without question assure billions and billions of individual sensate beings of dramatically increased death and suffering – what would such transcendence be *toward*? For what might we realistically hope, we who are doomed to humanity's epistemic limitations and foreshortened moral horizons? Nothing less, and nothing more, than what Jayna Brown terms "new genres of *existence*, entirely different modes of material being and becoming" (2021, 9). What genre of existence could be more novel than the transcending of an ecological law immanent to all biota – toward degrowth, toward less metabolization of resources than would be possible for a human species?

## Notes

1 As I have written elsewhere (Allen 2020), posthumanist critiques habitually get at something important. Their positive project is less suasive.

2 Simone Bignall and Rosi Braidotti, for instance, describe the "posthuman convergence" as "an epistemological framework for supporting the elaboration of alternative values and new codes of interrelation that extend beyond human influence and cognizance" (2019, 2). Well and good, but the point remains *extension* of the domain of human influence and cognizance. Posthumanism theorizes through questions like "How can human thought adequately conceive nonhuman temporality and spatiality?" and "What is a posthuman system of language, or of perception and sensibility?" (4). Are these not the orienting questions of Enlightenment humanism's own overweening desire for certainty?

3 Parrique has done yeoman's work compiling references to degrowth in the wildly undermediated 6th report of IPCC Working Group II on "Impacts, Adaptation, and Vulnerability." As he notes, that body discusses degrowth in 2022 for the first time ever (Parrique 2022). Chastened humanism aligns, too, with the epistemic and moral stance outlined by Brand et al. (2021).

4 My thanks to Timothy Oleksiak for putting me on to this wonderful text.

5 "Solar geoengineering would not just be cheap, relatively speaking; it would also be speedy. ... But if a fleet of SAILs looks like a quick, cut-rate solution, that's primarily because it isn't a solution. What the technology addresses are warming's symptoms, not its cause. For this reason, geoengineering has been compared to treating a heroin habit with methadone, though perhaps a more apt comparison would be to treating a heroin habit with amphetamines" (Kolbert 2021, 180).

6 Bastani (2019) develops a "left" refusal of limits to growth (not without its appeal, but premised on ever-expanding extractive regimes).

7 For one image of the worst, see Wallace-Wells (2019). UN Secretary-General António Guterres memorably described IPCC Working Group II's 6th Assessment Report as "an atlas of [far more than merely] human suffering and a damning indictment of failed climate leadership" (2022).

8 References are to page and line number in the leaked draft. WG III's report saw final public release in April 2022, with the "Summary for Policymakers" predictably tilted toward denial by representatives of national governments, fossil fuel concerns, and so on.

9 See esp. IPCC 2021. See also the Global Assessment Report on Biodiversity and Ecosystem Services, 2019. Perhaps it is sheer dismal coincidence that a Russian invasion of Ukraine preceded by mere days the release of IPCC Working Group II's 6th report in February 2022, and thus that almost no global media attention was devoted to this unprecedented call for transformative change at all levels of society.

10 See Stengers (2015, *passim*). In *Facing Gaia*, Latour urges us to become "the people of Gaia" (2017, 214), a people capable of confronting the "New Climate Regime" of a richly agential world, which "is astonishing in that it imposes a terrible and totally unforeseen solidarity between the victims and the responsible parties" (216). Under that regime, "the fact that all the collectives from now on ... share the certainty that they fear nothing but 'being crushed by the falling sky' gives a totally different idea of universal solidarity" (216).

11 Lynda Collins puts the point well: "Environmental law has proven wholly inadequate when assessed against the crucial parameter of sustainability (i.e., the capacity of societies to survive and thrive over the coming decades and centuries)" (2021, 3).

12 Being humbled is what, if anything can, rescues chastened humanism from the sorts of critiques with which Rorty's frank ethnocentrism, originally articulated as "anti-anti-ethnocentrism" (1986), has rightly met over the years.

13 For a primer on degrowth as a justitial economic system oriented in substance toward redistribution and away from delusions of infinite economic growth, see Hickel (2021). For a fuller picture, see Parrique's impressive dissertation, "The Political Economy of Degrowth," which identifies degrowth as "our best shot to uncancel the future" (2019, 5).

14 See especially the climate justice work of Bronwyn Lay, rooted in the philosophical grounding of her *Juris Materiarum* (2016). See also Garver (2020).

15 Eileen Crist (2016) argues that "this name is neither a useful conceptual move nor an empirical no-brainer, but instead a reflection and reinforcement of the anthropocentric actionable worldview that generated 'the Anthropocene' – with all its looming emergencies – in the first place" (14). I take Crist's critique of "Anthropocene" to be apt, but selling new terms for a thing in order to allow humans to negotiate ourselves hardly escapes the critique. Too, a lot of assertions in this discourse on the discourse – Crist's arch "anthropos meaning 'man' and always implying 'not-animal'" (16), for instance – go

unwarranted. For a duly chastened humanism, anthropos *of course* means "animal"; it's just one animal that happens to be making life impossible for most of the rest.

16 Posthumanist theorizing treats this system of binaries as something to be overcome simply by having the right thoughts, perhaps adding a few good disciplinary practices. Given the ideational entanglement with materiality that is not only capitalism but *any* structured lifeworld, they make the same error that Marx discerned in Feuerbach and the philosophers. This essay detoured through an emerging juridical concept of ecological law because chastened humanism acknowledges real material constraints to be negotiated and recognizes such negotiation as a collective action problem. Law is one site for such negotiation.

17 These arguments are extended in Allen (2014) and Allen (2018). See also esp. Mailloux (1989) and, well, most rhetorical theory.

18 For a rich reading of the chastenedness of Vichian ethics, see Struever (1992), esp. 216–224.

19 See Graeber and Wengrow (2021) for a fascinating survey.

20 This doesn't oblige anyone to spend energy defining or caring what humans *are*, and thus getting invested in who's in and who's out.

21 Such a view traces at least back to the famous MacGuffin of early rhetorician Gorgias, *On What Is Not, or On Nature*. As the standard gloss goes, "(a) nothing is; (b) even if it is, it is incomprehensible to man; (c) even if it is comprehensible, it is incommunicable to the next man" (MacDowell 2005, 11).

## References


Allen, Ira. 2014. "Rhetorical Humanism vs. Object Oriented Ontology: The Ethics of Archimedean Points and Levers." *SubStance* 43(3): 67–87.

Allen, Ira. 2018. *The Ethical Fantasy of Rhetorical Theory*. Pittsburgh: University of Pittsburgh Press.

Allen, Ira. 2020. "Response to Cooper." *College Composition and Communication* 71(3): 517–523.

Anker, Kirsten, Peter D. Burdon, Geoffrey Garver, Michelle Maloney, and Carla Sbert. 2021. *From Environmental to Ecological Law*. New York: Routledge.

Bastani, Aaron. 2019. *Fully Automated Luxury Communism*. London: Verso.

Bignall, Simone, and Rosi Braidotti. 2019. "Posthuman Systems." In Rosi Braidotti and Simone Bignall (Eds.), *Posthuman Ecologies: Complexity and Process after Deleuze*, 1-16. London: Rowman & Littlefield.

Boivin, Nicole L., Melinda A. Zeder, Dorian Q. Fuller, Alison Crowther, Greger Larson, Jon M. Erlandson, Tim Denham, and M. D. Petraglia. 2016. "Ecological Consequences of Human Niche Construction: Examining Long-Term Anthropogenic Shaping of Global Species Distributions." *PNAS* 113(23): 6388–6396.

Brand, Ulrich, Barbara Muraca, Éric Pineault, Marlyne Sahakian, Anke Schaffartzik, Andreas Novy, Christoph Streissler, et al. 2021. "From Planetary to Societal Boundaries: an Argument for Collectively Defined Self-Limitation." *Sustainability: Science, Practice, and Policy* 17(1): 264–291.

Brown, Jayna. 2021. *Black Utopias: Speculative Life and the Music of Other Worlds*. Durham: Duke University Press.

Burdon, Peter. 2020. "Ecological Law in the Anthropocene." *Transnational Legal Theory* 11(1–2): 33–46.

Caesar, L., G. D. McCarthy, D. J. R. Thornalley, N. Cahill, and S. Rahmstorf. 2021. "Current Atlantic Meridional Overturning Circulation Weakest in Last Millennium." *Nature Geoscience* 14(3): 118–120.

Collins, Lynda. 2021. *The Ecological Constitution: Reframing Environmental Law*. New York: Routledge.

Commonwealth of Australia. 2020. *Royal Commission into National Natural Disaster Arrangements*. https://naturaldisaster.royalcommission.gov.au/publications/royal-commission-national-natural-disaster-arrangements-report.

Crist, Eileen. 2016. "On the Poverty of Our Nomenclature." In Jason W. Moore (Ed.), *Anthropocene or Capitalocene? Nature, History, and the Crisis of Capitalism*. Oakland: PM Press.

Crutzen, Paul, and Eugene F. Stoermer. 2000. "The 'Anthropocene'." *International Biosphere-Geosphere Programme Global Change Newsletter* 41: 17–18.

Dean, Jodi. 2020. "Communism or Neo-feudalism?" *New Political Science* 42(1): 1–17.

Garver, Geoffrey. 2020. *Ecological Law and the Planetary Crisis: A Legal Guide for Harmony on Earth*. London: Routledge.

Gorgias. 2005 [1982]. *Encomium of Helen*. Introduction, Notes, and Trans. D. M. MacDowell. London: Bristol Classical Press.

Graeber, David, and David Wengrow. 2021. *The Dawn of Everything: A New History of Humanity*. New York: Farrar, Straus, & Giroux.

Guterres, António. "António Guterres (UN Secretary-General) to the Press Conference Launch of IPCC Report." *United Nations*, February 28, 2022. https://media.un.org/en/asset/k1x/k1xcijxjhp.
Hickel, Jason. 2021. "What Does Degrowth Mean? A Few Points of Clarification." *Globalizations* 18(7): 1105–1111.
Jackson, Tim. 2021. *Post Growth: Life after Capitalism*. Cambridge: Polity.
Kolbert, Elizabeth. 2021. *Under a White Sky: The Nature of the Future*. New York: Crown.
Latour, Bruno. 2017. *Facing Gaia: Eight Lectures on the New Climatic Regime*. Trans. Catherin Porter. Cambridge: Polity.
Lay, Bronwyn. 2016. *Juris Materiarum: Empires of Earth, Soil, and Dirt*. New York: Atropos Press.
Leaked IPCC Report. 2021. "Summary for Policymakers Draft 2." *Scientist Rebellion*, August 20, 2021. https://scientistrebellion.com/we-leaked-the-upcoming-ipcc-report/.
Lowrey, Annie. 2013. "The Inequality of Climate Change." *New York Times*, November 12, 2013. https://economix.blogs.nytimes.com/2013/11/12/the-inequality-of-climate-change/.
Mailloux, Steven. 1989. *Rhetorical Power*. Ithaca: Cornell University Press.
Mailloux, Steven. 2017. *Rhetoric's Pragmatism: Essays in Rhetorical Hermeneutics*. University Park: Pennsylvania State University Press.
Mbembe, Achille. 2019. *Necropolitics*. Durham: Duke University Press.
Milman, Oliver, Andrew Witherspoon, Rita Liu, and Alvin Chang. 2021. "The Climate Disaster Is Here." *Guardian*, October 14, 2021. https://www.theguardian.com/environment/ng-interactive/2021/oct/14/climate-change-happening-now-stats-graphs-maps-cop26.
*New York Times*. 2021. "CLIMATE FWD: Climate Change Comes for Rich Countries." *New York Times*, July 21, 2021 https://www.nytimes.com/2021/07/21/climate/nyt-climate-newsletter-wildfires-disasters.html.
Parrique, Timothée. 2019. "The Political Economy of Degrowth." PhD dissertation. Université Clermont Auvergne and Stockholm University, December 16, 2019. https://tel.archives-ouvertes.fr/tel-02499463/document.
Parrique, Timothée. 2022. "Degrowth in the IPCC AR6 WGII." March 5, 2022. https://timotheeparrique.com/degrowth-in-the-ipcc-ar6-wgii/.
Robson, Steve. 2021. "The 'Secret Sauce' Made in Manchester That Could Change an Industry – and the Planet." *Manchester Evening News*, October 13, 2021. https://www.manchestereveningnews.co.uk/news/greater-manchester-news/secret-sauce-made-manchester-could-21835256.
Rorty, Richard. 1986. "On Ethnocentrism: A Reply to Clifford Geertz." *Michigan Quarterly Review* 25(3): 525–534.
Sengupta, Somini. 2021. "'No One Is Safe': How the Heat Wave Has Battered the Wealthy World." *New York Times*, July 17, 2021. https://www.nytimes.com/2021/07/17/climate/heatwave-weather-hot.html.
Slagsvold, Tore, and Karen L. Wiebe. 2007. "Learning the Ecological Niche." *Proceedings of the Royal Society: Biological Sciences* 274(1606): 19–23.
Soper, Kate. 2020. *Post-growth Living*. London: Verso.
Stengers, Isabelle. 2015. *In Catastrophic Times: Resisting the Coming Barbarism*. Open Humanities Press.
Struever, Nancy S. 1992. *Theory as Practice: Ethical Inquiry in the Renaissance*. Chicago: University of Chicago Press.
Vico, Giambattista. 1993. *On Humanistic Education (Six Inaugural Orations, 1699-1707)*. Trans. Giorgio A. Pinton and Arthur W. Shippee. Ithaca: Cornell University Press.
Vollman, William T. 2018. *No Immediate Danger: Volume One of Carbon Ideologies*. New York: Viking.
Wallace-Wells, David. 2019. *The Uninhabitable Earth: Life after Warming*. New York: Tim Duggan Books.
World Meteorological Organization. 2021. *2021 State of Climate Services – Water*. https://public.wmo.int/en/resources/library/2021-state-of-climate-services-water.
WWF. 2020. *Living Planet Report 2020 – Bending the Curve of Biodiversity Loss*. R.E.A. Almond, M. Grooten, and T. Petersen (Eds.). Gland: WWF.

# PART III

# Landscapes of Hope and Despair

# 7

# BIODIVERSITY

## The Neglected Lens for Reimagining Property, Responsibility, and Law for the Anthropocene

*Paul J. Govind and Michelle Lim*

The Anthropocene reveals the embeddedness of humanity with nature. Embeddedness represents a radical departure from the idea of separation and subordination that has framed the relationship between humanity and nature in Western culture (Adelman 2021; Haraway 2015). In contrast, Indigenous laws and ontologies have decentered human authority for millennia. Such cosmologies see humans as but one of the millions of species that inhabit this planet (Bawaka Country et al. 2015, Martuwarra et al. 2020).

A (relatively) small group of humans have played and continue to play a unique role in precipitating the Anthropocene (Burdon 2020, 321; see Yussof 2015). Meanwhile, humans are the only species capable of leading a response to the impacts of the Anthropocene at the planetary scale (Adelman 2021(b), 51). This ontological reality is reflected in Philippopoulos-Mihalopoulos' concept of the *middle* (Philippopoulos-Mihalopoulos 2012; Haraway 2008).

The middle refers to the space humanity occupies as a unique species within nature. Meanwhile, the philosophy of the middle is clearly detached from the idea of hierarchy (Philippopoulos-Mihalopoulos 2012). The middle operates in distinct contrast to the idea of the *center*, which privileges certain perspectives, interests, and benefits by making them a central point through which all meaning is formed, and trade-offs resolved. We argue that the unprecedented global social-ecological shifts brought about by the Anthropocene mean that humanity must embrace its role as a unique part of nature rather than superior and separate to nature (Crutzen 2002; see Biermann and Lövbrad 2019).

When taken together, the aspects of uniqueness and embeddedness place an onus on humanity to adopt an ethical framework of responsibility (see Govind 2021; Burdon 2020) Coyne 2021). This necessitates a shift in the basis of our ethics. It calls for a moving away from the enlightenment views that preach that morality and ethics are based upon freedom (Grear 2015; Grear 2020 Adelman 2015; Adelman 2019). The pursuit of freedom directs our ethical compass and underlies our laws. In Western legal systems, this pursuit is conveyed through the proliferation of rights. Law, including international law, still exists and operates in the era of rights, and any perceived opposition to freedom is fiercely resisted (Kotzé and French 2021, 1, 4; Coyne 2018). Legal systems have been very reluctant to impose anything that could be perceived as a restriction on individual liberties.

DOI: 10.4324/9781003388081-10

To play an effective role in managing the human and nature assemblage in the Anthropocene, the exercise of rights must be counterbalanced by an ethic of human responsibility (Morrow 2017, 270; see Fasso and Kirk 2021, 165). Morrow highlights the emergence of responsibility to counteract rights (Morrow 2017). She proposes that while the notion of (individual) human responsibilities has limited reach in the rights-centric legal framework, especially in the state-orientated human rights canon. Thus, invoking responsibility in the environmental context would place a limit on the pursuit of rights, responding to the unique position of humans as ecosystem actors in respect of other humans and other life forms (Morrow 2017, 270).

This chapter traces the distance between ethics and law in the Anthropocene (see Voight 2005, 126; Adelman 2021, 75). As the primary agent of planetary change (Adelman 2021(b), 51), humans have a special capacity and responsibility to allow multi-species assemblages to thrive in the Anthropocene. The power that humanity yields must therefore be guided by responsibility. Climate and biodiversity are the two most important planetary boundaries (Steffen et al. 2015). By examining the two key international law instruments focused on these key planetary boundaries we provide a means for reconsidering law in the Anthropocene more broadly. The central question of the chapter, therefore, is how the ethical underpinnings of international climate and biodiversity law need to shift to provide an ethic of responsibility in the Anthropocene.

We demonstrate below how responsibility needs to emerge as the ethical framework to guide the legal response to the Anthropocene. In doing so, we explore how rights, in the absence of corresponding responsibilities, have given rise to the instrumentalization of nature and, by extension, its unparalleled destruction. We introduce the concept of Nature's Contribution to People (NCP) and describe how NCP presents an understanding of the relationship between humans and nature that challenges the hegemony of rights as the principal ethical framework. NCP and relational values highlight how biodiversity law can initiate a shift toward an ethical framework of responsibility by departing from instrumental views of nature. This value change and the relationship to ethics are then analyzed in the context of the international legal regimes regulating climate change and biodiversity loss. We conclude by challenging the appropriateness of climate law as the proxy legal response to the Anthropocene.

## The Anthropocene and the Emergence of an Ethic of Responsibility

### *Rights and an Instrumental Value of Nature*

Rights form the ethical framework of Western legal systems (Adelman 2021, 78). Similarly, environmental laws are constructed with rights as the central concern (Coyle and Morrow 2004 5–6; Andreas Philippopoulos-Mihalopoulos 2017, 141; Boulot and Sterlin 2021). Much of environmental law is aimed at curtailing the excesses of property and balancing individual rights and interests of enjoying particular environments against the proprietary rights of developers. Sustainable development for example is a principle that promotes the primacy of human development within limits that are designed to protect the interest of future generations of humanity (Wapner 2014, 37). The principle offers no guidance on how to stay within planetary boundaries (Robinson 2014, 15; Kim and Bosselmann 2013; Richardson 2017, 7).

This throws up two interrelated issues relevant to the Anthropocene: 1) how rights formed the basis for artificial distinctions between humanity and nature; and 2) how rights have driven a series of discrete legal responses that manage relationships with nature independently and without overarching values and coherence. The notion of rights continues to resonate most powerfully with the concept of property – especially *dephysical* property (Graham 2010; Bartlett and Graham 2016).

Dephysical property separates the value ascribed to property rights from the material and physical qualities of the property holding itself, we see this, for example, in Western land law. Dephysicalization converts the relationship between humanity and land into a "bundle of rights." It is an exercise in abstraction, "to conceptually separate land from ecological networks beyond human significance, and to conceptually and physically disconnect people from place (and the significance they imbued in it over generations and centuries)" (Graham forthcoming, 281). The residual effect of humanity's relationship with nature is that property rights have little to do with the materiality of land itself. This is problematic for more-than-human species with which we share land.

The operation of dephysical property rights has provided an ethical basis for establishing and maintaining a hierarchy between humanity and nature. Rights and property are both strongly invested in the individual (Hamilton, Gemenne, and Bounneuil 2015, 8). Effectively, both operate to proclaim the sanctity and freedom of the individual against unwarranted interference by others, including authority. Property is first and foremost a social and political expression of individuality rather than a legal one. Through the support of law, the notion of dephysical property rights has, or at least is perceived to have, an elevated reverence. This is because property rights are closely attached to freedom and the related idea of choice (Babie 2012; Waldron 1988). Both are central to the prevailing Western political philosophy of liberalism (Adelman 2021, 70; Voight 2005, 112). The primacy of choice is reflected in the default position adopted by Western legal systems that the exercise of property rights is an expression of freedom (Adelman 2021, 70).

Western law has facilitated the expansion and protection of property rights (Adelman 2021, 74). The inviolability of rights allowed an expansion of property interests that was unrestrained or limited in any way by a countervailing ethic of responsibility. This situation developed over centuries and created two consequences that would drive the Anthropocene. The realization of rights became a measure of humanity's capacity to survive and flourish in the face of challenges thrown down by a "hostile" nature. (Merchant; De Lucia 2013, 168) The conquest and conversion of nature into property were equated with humanity's flourishing. The notion of property rights operates to both progress and protect this flourishing through the utilization of nature and the resources it provides (Bartel and Graham 2016; Davies 2020).

Property has the power to privilege some and separate and subordinate others. The concentration of property rights and their professed benefits are concentrated in a small sector of humanity at the apex of a hierarchy that separates and subordinates nature (Adelmam 2015, 10). The prevalence of rights as the ethical framework of Western legal systems directs attention to how nature and more-than-human species are valued (see Humphreys and Otomo 2016, 802). As outlined above, rights-based ethics has facilitated an instrumental value of nature that is central to driving the planet toward the Anthropocene epoch and its devastating consequences A view of nature that prefers an instrumental value is premised upon the separation and subordination that is the result of hierarchy and is antithetical to the ontological reality of embeddedness of humans with and within nature.

Rights-based ethics have ultimately operated to separate and detach humanity and nature (Govind 2021). As mentioned, dephysicalized property rights separate the value of property from the physical, material qualities of the relevant land and space to which it applies (Graham 2010; Bartel and Graham 2016; Davies 2020). The value of property is reflected in the rights of an owner to sell land and make a profit. The detachment of value from the materiality of land is dangerous for the natural environment and more-than-human species that inhabit the land. It relegates the health of the land to how it might influence the value of property from the perspective of the property rights holder. Dephysical property rights, provide a basis for the instrumental view of land and by extension the instrumentalization of nature and biodiversity.

The benefits that accrue are exclusively enjoyed by humanity, meaning that these laws have a strong anthropocentric orientation (Dalby 2016, 34). This has allowed the interests of humanity to receive primacy in any values, decisions, and, indeed, laws that managed the relationship with nature (Swyngedouw 2015, 241).

## *Responsibility and Multiple Values of Nature*

In contrast to dominant views of individual rights discussed above, the ethic of responsibility emerges from a recognition of the power humanity has displayed when exercising its rights (Jonas 1985; Haraway 2008). Implicit in this finding is that the use of power has been irresponsible and has resulted in the transgression of planetary boundaries, which has driven the Anthropocene epoch (see Govind 2021; Burdon 2020;). The Anthropocene creates a break with the past from which point humanity cannot deny its impact on the Earth and all its inhabitants. Correspondingly, humans need to assume responsibility for what has happened and what will happen in the future. This section demonstrates why law must embrace responsibility as a counterbalance to rights and in particular the proliferation of dephysical property rights that has served to cement the distance between humanity and nature and the instrumental view of nature.

Fineman highlights that what binds humanity and nature is a shared vulnerability of individuals embedded in nature (Fineman 2008, 11–12). The unpredictable and often violent environmental impacts resulting from the transgression of planetary limits have placed humanity in an unprecedented state of vulnerability. Human embeddedness in the impacts of the Anthropocene shatters the myth that humanity and nature are separated in a hierarchy. Responsibility changes the central focus of our inquiry and changes our values and behavior. We value something differently when we understand it to have worth outside of what it can do for us. An ethic of responsibility means that we understand our uniqueness but do not frame that uniqueness as a reason for separation and superiority. If we believe that we must act responsibly it indicates that there is something wrong with the destruction that we have caused and our capacity to do so again (see Jonas 1985).

An ethical frame of responsibility departs from an instrumental view of nature (Govind 2021). Adelman's explanation of planetary environmental ethics resonates strongly with responsibility as it highlights similar aspects of the ontological basis of embeddedness, situated knowledge, neo-materialism, and intergenerational and interspecies obligations (Adelman 2021). The residual message is the need to depart from the abstraction and separation that has fired current ethical frames.

In the context of the Anthropocene and planetary survival, it could be argued that responsibility is motivated by our own existential vulnerability and selfish reasons for self-preservation and survival. Our survival and that of the planet are undeniably linked. In that sense there is a dependency on redressing planetary change – however, responsibility goes further (see Frisso and Kirk 2021, 165–166). It is not only a question of being more aware of the context within which we exist – the core of responsibility is that we have caused suffering to others through our ability to engineer change (Jonas 1985).

An ethical frame of responsibility requires us to push our concerns aside to aid others, especially where we are responsible for their vulnerability (Coyne 2021, 145–146; see Coyne 2018; see Dinneen 2017). If we can re-orientate our laws away from anthropocentrism to not only include the interests of other species but place them on an equal footing while recognizing vulnerability to harm regardless of species (see Jonas; Coyne 2021, 145–146) – this would be truly transformative. This speaks to a recognition of value that goes beyond simply taking care of other species because they ultimately perform a function that serves us – it is about putting ourselves aside when necessary. The next section argues that the ethic of responsibility is promoted through the concept of NCP, which challenges prevailing instrumental views of nature and promotes a relational understanding of the relationship between humanity and nature that helps to promote an ethic of responsibility. In the next section, we explore how ecosystem services support an instrumental view of nature that benefits the prevailing rights-based ethical framework.

## From Ecosystem Services to Nature's Contribution of People

It is well-established that biodiversity and human well-being are closely intertwined (Millennium Ecosystem Assessment 2005). For more than a decade, the ecosystem services approach (popularized by the Millennium Ecosystem Assessment) has been the dominant framing of human-environment relationships (Norgaard 2010, 1219). The complexity of these relationships is becoming increasingly apparent (Ricketts et al. 2016). This has led a growing body of scholarship which highlights the limitations of the ecosystem services approach to adequately encapsulate the diverse ways in which humans and nature interact (Diaz et al. 2018; Gunton et al. 2017; Norgaard 2010). This section commences with a discussion of these limitations. We argue that NCP provides a useful framing for challenging anthropocentric views of nature and facilitating the emergence of an ethic of responsibility for the Anthropocene.

### *Limitations of the Ecosystem Services Approach*

The Millennium Ecosystem Assessment brought the ecosystem services approach into the mainstream. The Millennium Ecosystem Assessment itself emphasized the importance of a broad set of values (including those that stem from cultural relationships). Nevertheless, it was the natural science and economics focus that received the most attention. At the same time, a key theme of the Assessment was the allocation of monetary value to ecosystem flows (Diaz et al. 2018, 217).

The end result was a broad understanding of ecosystem services as being represented as a stock-flow model which views nature as a fixed stock of capital that sustains a limited flow of ecosystem services (Norgaard 2010, 1219). The narrow valuation of nature within a stock-flow approach is insufficient to represent the diverse interests and attitudes of multiple stakeholders to ecosystems or the myriad of human motives for conservation (Gunton et al. 2017, 249).

Failing to account for all aspects of coupled human-environment systems runs the risk of being blindsided by unintended consequences (Norgaard 2010). This ultimately results in misguided policy- and law-making. A key critique of the ecosystem services approach is that instead of drawing on ecology, and other knowledge systems to provide comprehensive advice for governance, a market-based ideology became the key focus (Norgaard 2010, 1225) A further issue is that by defining our world as a collection of service commodities, owners of capital are the ultimate beneficiaries of marketization and legislation aimed at maximizing these services (Gunton et al. 2017, 252).

In a similar vein, ecosystem services have been critiqued for focusing on optimizing the economy while putting aside larger questions of how we create substantial institutional change to reduce anthropogenic pressures in an equitable manner, particularly in the face of significant global environmental change (Norgaard 2010, 1220). At the time of its conceptualization, there was a sense, perhaps a hope, even among those who intrinsically value nature, that regardless of how abhorrent the concept of defining nature and its relationships to people through a dollar value, speaking the language of the economy through market metaphors was a necessary evil to awaken the public (Norgaard 2010).

## *Re-Framing Human-Environment Relationships: The Conceptual Framework of the Intergovernmental Science-Policy Platform for Biodiversity and Ecosystem Services (IPBES) and Nature's Contribution To People*

IPBES is the intergovernmental body that assesses the state of biodiversity and the contributions of biodiversity to human well-being. IPBES co-produces this knowledge with and in response to requests from decision-makers (Intergovernmental Science-Policy Platform for Biodiversity and Ecosystem Services (IPBES)).

IPBES aims to provide policymakers with the tools and methods to protect and sustainably use biodiversity. The IPBES Conceptual Framework, which underpins all activities of the platform, was developed through a two-year co-production process that involved experts from a range of disciplines and knowledge systems as well as over 100 governments and non-governmental organizations (Diaz et al. 2015a). The conceptual framework aims to inspire integrated thinking which considers the full cycle of interactions across the complex systems of nature, nature's contributions to people (see Diaz et al. 2015a, 2015b), and good quality of life, as well as anthropogenic assets and direct and indirect drivers (Diaz et al. 2015b).

NCP is a central component of the conceptual framework of IPBES. NCP has framed understandings of nature represents an evolution in thinking from "services" to "contributions." The key differences between NCP and Ecosystem Services are that NCP:

- Emphasizes the central and pervasive role of culture in shaping all interactions between humans and nature. NCP is viewed as being co-produced by humans and nature and is viewed through a range of cultural lenses;
- Elevates Indigenous and local knowledge in understanding human-environment relationships while operationalizing and implementing these understandings (Diaz et al. 2018, 270, 271).

NCP draws on multiple worldviews and knowledge systems and facilitates a much more comprehensive and socially legitimate approach than its predecessor (Diaz et al. 2018). This suggests the possibility for the requisite shift, at the policy level, to a greater ethic of responsibility. There has, however, yet to be significant attention paid to how law interacts with NCP (Lim 2019; Lim 2021).

## *NCP and a Framework of Ethical Responsibility*

The values espoused and promoted by NCP resonate strongly with the ethical responsibility required in the Anthropocene. The relevance of NCP goes beyond the regulation of the biodiverse (i.e. biosphere integrity) planetary boundary. The underpinning values of this conceptual framework are also useful to integrate stewardship across planetary boundaries. This is in large part due to the diverse worldviews that help compose NCP. NCP framing aims to broaden how nature is valued away from the intrinsic/instrumental binary. This shift ultimately involves ethical questions. As explained above, NCP embraces relational values (Ellis et al. 2019).

Pascual et al. (2017) explain that relational values are derived from our relationships with nature and our responsibilities towards it. The connection between relationship and responsibility emerges for recognition of humanity's ontological position to nature. It is reminiscent of how ethical responsibility in the Anthropocene is linked to the embeddedness of humanity within nature. Relational values reflect Indigenous framings of nature which are imbued by values such as "connectivity, responsibility, reciprocity and mutuality – where humans are connected as part of the whole 'ecosystem.'" (Hemming 2019). As mentioned earlier in the chapter, relational values are in contrast with the disconnected subject that mediates the relationship with nature through the maintenance of dephysicalized property rights. Relational values can therefore divert the focus away from the liberal, autonomous individual as the subject of ethical concern that is at the core of Western law and introduce a diversity of legal perspectives (Seck 2019).

The association of liberalism, the rights-based discourse, and property suggests that relational values would, by contrast, gravitate more toward an ethic of responsibility. Relational values, therefore, resonate more powerfully with the Anthropocene paradigm than instrumental or intrinsic values. Both instrumental and intrinsic values propagate the separation of humanity from nature. Instrumental value undermines the recognition of nature as part of life support systems while intrinsic value also appears incongruent with the Anthropocene lens because it projects an image of nature that is free from human involvement.

Relational values are crucial to embeddedness because they place humanity in nature. As described earlier in the chapter, the Anthropocene serves to reiterate the embeddedness of humanity and nature by sweeping away epistemic fallacies of separation and dichotomy. It accepts and recognizes that humanity and nature share relations of need and reciprocity which give rise to value. The nature relationship is viewed as symbiotic – it is permissible for humans to rely on nature, but the relationship is reciprocal. The sentiment of separation that underlies both instrumental and intrinsic value is therefore absent.

It must be noted that neither recognition of the Anthropocene nor relational value and any link between them is a normative outcome in and of itself. Both intellectual pursuits prompt discussions on how the relationship between humanity and nature should be managed, thus pointing to the need for ethical considerations. We maintain that the relevance of relational value strengthens the case for responsibility to be the central ethical response to the Anthropocene. By promoting NCP as core to its work, IPBES has effectively translated the ethical position discussed above into a framework for discourse at the science-policy interface. There is potential for NCPs to inform conceptualizations of human-nature relationships across environmental law. This could facilitate fundamental changes in the ethical orientation of environmental law in ways that endorse deeper relationships of responsibility to nature.

## Understandings of Nature – Climate vs Biodiversity Law

Climate law has emerged as the centerpiece in legal responses to the Anthropocene (Verschuuren 2021, 246). This situation risks obscuring the importance of other planetary boundaries. Once a problem is framed in a particular way, it will necessarily influence the contours of the response and how that response is to be evaluated as effective and successful. An evaluation of success that is too closely linked to climate change risks being unduly narrow and will fail to provide the appropriate scope to understand the challenges of the Anthropocene.

The connection between biodiversity, IPBES, and NCPs means that affording the biosphere integrity planetary boundary, a greater profile as representative of the Anthropocene will pressure the primacy of climate change law and the rights-based ethic it perpetuates. In this section, we critically analyze the limitations of climate law in reorienting ethics toward responsibility. We argue that comparisons across climate and biodiversity law reveal the former's anthropocentricism.

We argue that a biodiversity lens based upon NCP could challenge prevailing conceptions of the instrumental views of nature sustained in climate law. To illustrate this and interrogate the capacity of climate law to drive the ethical change necessary to respond to the Anthropocene, we contrast how climate law and biodiversity law conceptualize and frame the relationship between humanity and nature through ecosystem services. We compare the limited ecosystem service framing that exists in relation to climate law against NCP. The relationship between climate change and biodiversity is framed in a way that gives overarching emphasis to the instrumental value of biodiversity as a climate tool – underlining that climate law is anthropocentric in orientation.

## *The International Climate Law Regime*

### Biodiversity in the Service of Climate Change Adaptation

The orientation of mitigation and adaptation under climate law has, to date, been predominantly, if not exclusively, anthropocentric (Hordequin 2021). Collectively, the climate law treaties, the United Nations Framework Convention on Climate Change (UNFCCC) and the Paris Agreement, do not recognize either the intrinsic or relational values of nature. By contrast, climate law displays an instrumental view of nature. Laws are dedicated to the promotion of human interests and nature is included to secure these ends.

Recognition of ecosystems in the Paris Agreement perpetuates instrumentalism (Article 2.1). As a result, all references to ecosystems have a distinct anthropocentric orientation and are "guided by the neoliberal, human-focused economic development priorities of a small, privileged subset of the human population rather than socio-ecological concerns related to the entire vulnerable living order" (Kotzé, du Toit, and French 2021).

The singular reference to biodiversity in the entire climate law regime appears in the Paris Agreement through a preambular provision:

> Noting the importance of ensuring the integrity of all ecosystems, including oceans, and the protection of biodiversity, recognized by some cultures as Mother Earth, and noting the importance for some of the concept of "climate justice," when taking action to address climate change.
>
> *(emphasis added)*

The language is soft, requiring nations to "note" the protection of biodiversity. It is ambiguous as to whether the "protection of biodiversity" is an exclusive consideration or recognized as part of "the integrity of ecosystems." At no point under either the climate law regime is the connection between extinction and climate change made clear.

In climate law, the relationship between humanity and the "service" of nature is most prominent in the context of adaptation. Here, the effectiveness of adaptation interventions is evaluated in relation to anthropocentric interests. Nature is proclaimed to be valuable in terms of helping humanity build adaptive capacity and reduce vulnerability to climate change. The separation of humanity and nature is very much tipped in the favor of the latter. At the same time, while adaptation is characterized as a localized response within climate law, the consequences must be seen in the broader contours of planetary boundaries. Both humanity and nature are vulnerable to climate change, and the adaptive capacity of natural planetary processes must not be compromised because of human intervention. Any role that nature might play in adaptation interventions should reflect the embeddedness of humanity and nature under the Anthropocene paradigm. Such interventions can carry immense power and must be exercised with responsibility.

### The UNFCCC

References to ecosystems under the UNFCCC suggest that biodiversity protection occurs for the purpose of ecosystem integrity. "Adverse impacts" under the UNFCCC means "changes in physical environment or biota resulting from climate change which have significant deleterious effects on the composition, resilience, or productivity of natural and managed ecosystems"

(UNFCCC, Article 1). In other words, changes to biodiversity are interpreted through the impact on ecosystems. The residual message is that biodiversity and ecosystems are so fundamentally linked that the ecosystem is assumed to include biodiversity within its scope. As discussed below, this characterization resonates throughout the operative provisions of the Paris Agreement and the rest of the climate regime more broadly.

The value of ecosystems is framed in terms of their service to adaptation. However, the effectiveness of adaptation law is not assessed or evaluated in terms of protecting nature. The UNFCCC includes natural ecosystems in its definition of "adverse effects of climate change." However, "adverse" is limited to the "significant deleterious effects" of climate change on the "composition, resilience, or productivity" of natural ecosystems – presenting an instrumental value of ecosystems.

The UNFCCC states that adaptation of ecosystems to climate change is to occur naturally – presumably free of human intervention (UNFCCC, Article 2):

> Such a level should be achieved within a time frame sufficient to allow ecosystems to adapt naturally to climate change, to ensure that food production is not threatened and to enable economic development to proceed in a sustainable manner.

**Paris Agreement**

The framing of the UNFCCC has carried over to the Paris Agreement where the objectives under Article 2 frame adaptation as a distinctly anthropocentric pursuit. Adaptation is to be performed in the context of sustainable development and is conditioned on ensuring that adaptation does not threaten food production (Paris Agreement, Article 2). Consequently, any benefits that nature might derive from the application of laws is an incidental or residual effect. Such an outcome is perpetuated by mainstreaming adaptation into sustainable development – a process that permeates Article 7 of the Paris Agreement which is specifically devoted to adaptation. Article 7.1 underlines that the formulation of adaptation in international climate law is premised upon contributing to sustainable development (Paris Agreement, Article 7.1).

Through Article 7, ecosystems are included as a consideration that is to be taken into account (see Paris Agreement, Articles 7.2, 7.5, and 7.9(c)) as part of adaptation generally. Article 7.2 adds that "parties recognize" that adaptation "makes a contribution to the long-term global response to climate change to protect people, livelihoods and ecosystems." (Paris Agreement, Article 7.2). It is a soft provision in that it only confirms the recognition of ecosystems. The inclusion of ecosystems follows the protection of people and livelihoods suggesting a commonality between the three that hints toward anthropocentric interests. This is sustained under Article 7.5 which states that various aspects of adaptation practice, including "communities and ecosystems," "should be" considered "with a view to integrating adaptation into relevant socio-economic policies" where appropriate (Paris Agreement, Article 7.5).

Subsidiary bodies under the UNFCCC structure endorse an ecosystem services frame. In 2013, the Subsidiary Body for Scientific and Technological Advice (SBSTA) once described the impact of climate change on ecosystems as affecting the functions and the "many benefits and services they provide to people" and that loss of services presents a barrier to the achievement of the Millennium Development Goals (Subsidiary Body for Scientific and Technological Advice 2011, 3). Ecosystem and biodiversity loss are framed and understood insofar as it diminishes the instrumental value it provides in terms of development goals. This is inherently and explicitly anthropocentric in its focus and understanding of loss.

The UNFCCC claims that biodiversity is one of the priority areas under the Nairobi Work Programme (NWP) (in the first part of its 48th session, held in Bonn from 30 April to 10

May 2018). In 2018 and 2019 reports by the Subsidiary Body on Scientific, Technical and Technological Advice (SBSTTA) on the NWP fail to mention biodiversity. It appears that biodiversity is represented through ecosystem-based adaptation – a specific manifestation of ecosystem services:

> Ecosystem-based adaptation (EbA) and ecosystem-based disaster risk reduction (Eco-DRR) are types of nature-based solutions (NbS) and are common terms encompassing the use of biodiversity and ecosystems to address societal adaptation to global change. There is widespread momentum for implementation of EbA, Eco-DRR, and NbS since recent years
>
> *(Subsidiary Body for Scientific and Technological Advice 2011, 4)*

While ecosystem-based adaptation carries the additional benefit (in theory) of preserving local biodiversity, this might not be a particularly accurate way of detecting the scale, complexity, or rate of loss.

The instrumentalism of ecosystems in serving anthropocentric adaptation confirms the feeling of separation and detachment from nature that goes against relational values and the ethic of responsibility. The climate law regime as currently composed is antithetical to leading changes in the ethical orientation toward responsibility in response to the ontological challenges of the Anthropocene. The anthropocentric focus of climate law means it is inherently limited in terms of facilitating an ethical shift and this in turn limits the depth of transformative response required to respond to the Anthropocene. The central role of climate law in the Anthropocene response means that this value will likely proliferate through other legal systems – a trend that will be investigated in relation to biodiversity law below.

## *The Prevalence of Ecosystem Services*

Reinforcing relationships of an ethic of responsibility across climate and biodiversity law is crucial to any credible legal response to the Anthropocene. We argue that an examination of the relationship between climate law and biodiversity law reveals the anthropocentric nature of climate law.

Under climate law, especially the Paris Agreement, there is a very strong instrumental quality to the integration of biodiversity and nature generally. The relationship is framed in a way that the benefits accrued are primarily helping achieve the anthropocentric objectives of climate law. Within climate law, biodiversity protection is promoted as important to the maintenance and upkeep of ecosystem services that assist in climate mitigation, adaptation, loss, and damage.

Our critique of ecosystem services in law aims at its increasing use as the "key metric for the measurement of the usefulness of biodiversity, and the central framework for the achievement of human well-being." (De Lucia 2018, 112). While not opposed to the ecosystem approach and services in principle, we maintain that this trend is extending too far and will result in a blinkered approach that evaluates the success of ecosystem approaches and services (and by extension climate change interventions) with no regard for the intrinsic values of biodiversity and the more-than-human species that constitute ecosystems. Apart from operating primarily for human benefit, an ecosystem services framing commodifies biodiversity values. It can result in the fragmentation of land where species are marginalized if their presence does not align with the overarching rationale and benefit of the ecosystem service that becomes the primary function of land use. It thereby affirms the primacy of the Western, liberal, dephysicalized property framework.

The ecosystem services framing results in a stronger utilitarian and instrumental understanding of nature as the "guiding element of environmental policy" (De Lucia 2018, 113). The emphasis on what is effectively instrumental value leads to poor, defective understandings of biodiversity loss, as it does not necessarily translate biodiversity loss into the functioning of an ecosystem service. We contend that law promotes and facilitates ecosystem services in ways that push them further away from any eco-centric origin or starting point.

The frame of ecosystem services is a limited way of regulating biodiversity loss and extinction. In the following subsection, we demonstrate how climate law maintains the separation and detachment of humanity and nature, rather than embracing embeddedness. It also underlines the anthropocentric orientation of climate change law and casts doubts over its efficacy of climate change law as the flagship in a legal response to the Anthropocene.

### *The International Biodiversity Law Regime*

The *Convention on Biological Diversity* (CBD) does not include climate change in its text. Subsequent plans produced under the CBD such as the Kunming-Montreal Global Biodiversity Framework (GBF) and its predecessor the Aichi Targets, highlight that climate change heightens the vulnerability of ecosystems.

The GBF, concluded at the 15th Conference of the Parties of the CBD in Montreal in December 2022, includes 23 targets that countries should strive to meet by 2030. Target 8 specifically addresses the need to 'Minimize the impact of climate change and ocean acidification on biodiversity'. This new global target on climate-biodiversity links recognizes that climate action can in some circumstances be harmful to biodiversity. Interestingly, nature-based solutions are identified as one of the key ways to minimize climate impacts.

The text of Target 8 frames biodiversity use in a climate-centric way. This suggests on the one hand that state parties are keen to develop synergies and consistencies across the climate and biodiversity regimes. However, what we also see is a creeping of the instrumentalization of nature, characteristic of climate law, into the biodiversity law regime. It is critical therefore that if Target 8 of the GBF is understood in the broader context of the other 23 targets – especially targets that emphasize the critical role of Indigenous peoples and local communities (see in particular Targets 1, 21 and 22). Failing to do so risks unwarranted elevation of the instrumental values of nature.

## Conclusions: Legal Frameworks for the Anthropocene Need to Be Far More Holistic

The legal response to the planetary changes of the Anthropocene is not moving in the direction of endorsing ethical responsibility. This is due in large part to the dominance of climate change law as central to the legal response. Comparative analysis of the two most important planetary boundaries and the international law regimes that regulate them exposes the anthropocentric nature of climate law and the limited role that biodiversity law has played to date to challenge this position in the context of law's burgeoning response to the challenges presented by the Anthropocene.

To date, ecosystem services have been at the core of approaches in the climate regime which relate to the regulation of nature. However, ecosystem services only value certain types and functions of biodiversity. Similarly, the joint IPBES-IPCC report reiterates that in the twenty-first century, climate change is likely to become a key driver of biodiversity loss. Scenarios show that meeting the Sustainable Development Goals and the CBD's 2050 Vision for Biodiversity depends on considering climate change impacts in the definition of future goals and objectives. Unsustainable consumption and production are key causes of climate change and biodiversity loss. The report calls for shifting individual and societal values away from materialism and beyond dominant worldviews which equates continuous economic growth with human well-being.

Can the integrity of the ecosystem and its ability to adapt and recover be the focus of law, independent of evaluating the effectiveness, through its ability to continue as an ecosystem service to humanity? Probably not. This demonstrates that anthropocentric, instrumental interests prevail because trade-offs are resolved in favor of the measures that serve human interests. These inherent limitations mean that ecosystem services are a poor framework for understanding and regulating biodiversity loss.

We must be wary that climate law, while vital, is limited in the way it can trigger a shift away from the values that were formed in the Holocene and have driven change toward the Anthropocene epoch (see Bleby et al. 2021, 42). When considering the relationship between humanity and nature as we have in this chapter, the operation of climate law facilitates and perpetuates division, separation, and subordination between humanity and nature. The existing climate law regime takes a far too service-based approach to ecosystems. We must ensure that we do not replicate the hierarchical, anthropocentric, and commodification characteristics of the climate law regime. Instead, we need to move to a responsible, place-based orientation of law in the Anthropocene.

## Bibliography

### *Books:*

Coyne, Lewis. 2021. *Life, Technology and the Horizons of Responsibility*. Bloomsbury Academic.
Graham, Nicole. 2010. *Lawscape: Property, Environment, Law*. Routledge.
Jonas, Hans. 1985. *The Imperative of Responsibility: In Search of an Ethics for the Technological Age*. University of Chicago Press.
Merchant, Carolyn. 2015. *Autonomous Nature: Problems of Prediction and Control from Ancient Times to the Scientific Revolution*. Routledge.
Merleau-Ponty, Maurice. 1996. *Phenomenology of Perception*. Motilal Banarsidass Publications.
Plumwood, Val. 2002. *Feminism and the Mastery of Nature*. Routledge.

### *Book Chapters:*

Adelman, Sam. 2015. "Epistemologies of Mastery." In *Research Handbook on Human Rights and the Environment*, edited by Anna Grear and Louis J Kotzé, 9–27. Edward Elgar.
Adelman, Sam. 2019. "Sovereignty or sustainability in the Anthropocene." In *Human Rights and the Environment Legality, Indivisibility, Dignity and Geography*, edited by Erin Daly and James R. May Edward Elgar.
Adelman, Sam. 2021. "Planetary Boundaries, Planetary Ethics and Climate Justice in the Anthropocene." In *Research Handbook on Law, Governance and Planetary Boundaries*, edited by Louis J. Kotzé and Duncan French, 65–83. Edward Elgar.
Albertson Fineman, Martha. 2008. "The Vulnerable Subject: Anchoring Equality in the Human Condition" *Yale Journal of Law and Feminism* 20: 1–24.
Biermann, Frank and Eva Lövbrad. 2019. "Encountering the Anthropocene: Setting the Scene." In *Anthropocene Encounters: New Directions in Green Political Thinking*, edited by Frank Biermann, 1–22. Cambridge University Press.
Bleby, Alice, Cameron Holley and Ben Milligan. 2021. "Exploring the Planetary Boundaries and Environmental Law: Historical Development, Interactions and Synergies." In *Research Handbook on Law, Governance and Planetary Boundaries*, edited by Louis J. Kotzé and Duncan French, 21–44. Edward Elgar.
Coyle, Sean and Karen Morrow. 2004. *The Philosophical Foundations of Environmental Law: Property, Rights and Nature*: Hart Publishing.

De Lucia, Vito. 2017. "Critical Environmental Law and the Double Register of the Anthropocene: A Biopolitical Reading." In *Environmental Law and Governance for the Anthropocene*, edited by Louis J. Kotzé, 97–116. Bloomsbury.

Frisso, Giovanna and Elizabeth A. Kirk. 2021. "Changing Role of Law-Making in Responding to Planetary Boundaries?" In *Research Handbook on Law, Governance and Planetary Boundaries*, edited by Louis J. Kotzé and Duncan French, 147–166. Edward Elgar.

Graham, Nicole. forthcoming. "Dephysicalised Property and Shadow Lands." In *Handbook on Space, Place and Law*, edited by Robyn Bartel and Jennifer Carter, 281–291. Edward Elgar.

Grear, Anna. 2017. "Anthropocene, Capitalocene, Chthulucene: Re-encountering Environmental Law and Its 'Subject' with Haraway and New Materialism." In *Environmental Law and Governance in the Anthropocene*, edited by Louis J. Kotzé, 77–96. Bloomsbury/Hart Publishing.

Grear, Anna. 2020b. "Resisting Anthropocene Neoliberalism: Towards New Materialist Commoning?" In *The Great Awakening: New Modes of Life Amidst Capitalist Ruins*, edited by Anna Grear and David Bollier, 317–356. Punctum Press.

Hemming, Steve et al. 2019. "Ngarrindjeri Vision for the Ecological Character Description of the Coorong and Lower Lakes." In *Natural History of the Coorong, Lower Lakes and Murray Mouth Region*, edited by Luke Mosley, 494. Royal Society South Australia.

Humphreys, Stephen and Yoriko Otomo. 2016. "Theorizing International Environmental Law." In *The Oxford Handbook of the Theory of International Law*, edited by Anne Orford and Florian Hoffman, 798–819. Oxford University Press.

Kim, Rakhyun E, Klaus Bosselmann. 2013. "International Environmental Law in the Anthropocene: Towards a Purposive System of Multilateral Environmental Agreements." *Transnational Environmental Law* 2: 285–309.

Kim, R. E. and H. van Asselt. 2016. "Global Governance: Problem Shifting in the Anthropocene and the Limits of International Law." In *Research Handbook on International Law and Natural Resources*, edited by Elise Morgera and K. Kulovesi, 473. Edward Elgar.

Kotzé, Louis J. and Duncan French. 2021. "Staying Within the Planet's 'Safe Operating Space'? Law and the Planetary Boundaries." In *Research Handbook on Law, Governance and Planetary Boundaries*, edited by Louis Kotzé and Duncan French, 1–19. Edward Elgar.

Kotzé, Louis J, Louise Du Toit and Duncan French. 2021. "Friend or foe? International environmental law and its structural complicity in the Anthropocene's climate injustices." *Oñati Socio-Legal Series* 11(1): 180–206.

Lange, Bettina. 2017. "How to Think about 'Nature-Society' Relations in Environmental Law 'in Action'." In *Research Methods in Environmental Law – A Handbook*, edited by Andreas Philippopoulos-MIhalopoulos and Victoria Brooks, 29–50. Edward Elgar.

Morrow, Karen. 2017. "Of Human Responsibility: Considering the Human/Environment Relationship and Ecosystems in the Anthropocene." In *Environmental Law for the Anthropocene*, edited by Louis J. Kotzé, 269–287. Bloomsbury/Hart Publishing.

Philippopoulos-MIhalopoulos, Andreas. 2015. "Epistemologies of Doubt." In *Research Handbook on Human Rights and the Environment*, edited by Anna Grear and Louis J. Kotzé, 28–45. Edward Elgar.

Philippopoulos-MIhalopoulos, Andreas. 2017. "Critical Environmental Law as Method in the Anthropocene." In *Research Methods in Environmental Law – A Handbook*, edited by Andreas Philippopoulos-MIhalopoulos and Victoria Brooks, 131–156. Edward Elgar.

Richardson, Benjamin J. 2017. "Doing Time – The Temporalities of Environmental Law." In *Environmental Law for the Anthropocene*, edited by Louis J. Kotzé, 55–74. Bloomsbury/Hart Publishing.

Swyngedouw, Erik. 2015. "Depoliticized Environments and the Promises of the Anthropocene." In *The International Handbook of Political Ecology*, edited by Raymond L. Bryant, 131–145. Edward Elgar.

Taylor, Prue. 2010. "'The Imperative of Responsibility' in a Legal Context: Reconciling Responsibilities and Rights." In *Democracy, Ecological Integrity and International Law*, edited by J. Ronald Engel, Laura Westra and Klaus Bosselmann, 198–225. Cambridge Scholars Publishing.

Verschuuren, Jonathan. 2021. "Climate Change." In *Research Handbook on Law, Governance and Planetary Boundaries*, edited by Louis Kotzé and Duncan French, 246–260. Edward Elgar.

## Journal Articles:

Adelman, Sam. 2021b. "A Legal Paradigm Shift Towards Climate Justice in the Anthropocene." *Oñati Socio-Legal Series* 11(1): 44–68.

Anderies, John, Stephen R. Carpenter, Will Steffen and Johan Rockström. 2013. "The Topology of Non-linear Global Carbon Dynamics: From Tipping Points to Planetary Boundaries." *Environmental Research Letters* 8: 04408.

Babie, Paul. 2012. "How Property Law Shapes Our Landscapes." *Monash University Law Review* 38(2): 1–24.

Bartel, Robyn and Nicole Graham. 2016. "Property and Place Attachment: A Legal Geographical Analysis of Biodiversity Law Reform in New South Wales." *Geographical Research* 54(3): 267.

Baskin, Jeremy. 2015. "Paradigm Dressed as Epoch: The Ideology of the Anthropocene." *Environmental Values* 24(1): 9–29.

Bennett, Elena M., Wolfgang Cramer, Alpina Begossi, Georgina Cundill, Sandra Díaz, Benis N. Egoh, Ilse R. Geijzendorffer et al. 2015. "Linking Biodiversity, Ecosystem Services, and Human Well-Being: Three Challenges for Designing Research for Sustainability." *Current Opinion in Environmental Sustainability* 14: 76–85.

Bonneuil, Christophe (Editor), Francois Gemenne (Editor), Clive Hamilton (Editor), The Anthropocene and the Global environmental crisis: rethinking modernity in a new epoch (Routledge, 2015).

Boulot, Emille and Joshua Sterlin 2021. "Steps Towards a Legal Ontological Turn: Proposals for Law's Place beyond the Human" *Transnational Environmental Law* 11(1): 13–38.

Brondizio, Eduardo S. and Francois-Michel Le Tourneau. 2016. "Environmental Governance for All." *Science* 352(6291): 1272–1273.

Burdon, Peter D. 2020. "Obligations in the Anthropocene." *Law and Critique* 31(3): 309–328.

Country, Bawaka, Sarah Wright, Sandie Suchet-Pearson, Kate Lloyd, Laklak Burarrwanga, Ritjilili Ganambarr, Merrkiyawuy Ganambarr-Stubbs, Banbapuy Ganambarr and Djawundil Maymuru. 2015. "Working with and Learning from Country: Decentring Human Authority." *Cultural Geographies* 22(2): 269–283.

Coyne, Lewis. 2018. "Responsibility in Practice: Hans Jonas as Environmental Political Theorist." *Ethics, Policy and Environment* 21(2): 229–245.

Crutzen, Paul J. 2002. "Geology of Mankind" *Nature* 415 (23): 23.

Dalby, Simon. 2016. "Framing the Anthropocene: The Good, the Bad and the Ugly." *The Anthropocene Review* 3(1): 33–51.

Dalby, Simon. 2017. "Anthropocene Formations: Environmental Security, Geopolitics and Disaster." *Theory, Culture and Society* 34(2–3): 233–252.

Davies, Margaret. 2020. "Can Property Be Justified in an Entangled World?" *Globalizations* 17(7): 1104–1117.

De Lucia, Vito. 2013. "Towards an Ecological Philosophy of Law: A Comparative Discussion." *Journal of Human Rights and the Environment* 4(2): 167–190.

De Lucia, Vito. 2018. "A critical interrogation of the relation between the ecosystem approach and ecosystem services." *Review of International and Comparative Environmental Law* 27: 104–114.

De Lucia, Vito. 2020. "Rethinking the Encounter Between Law and Nature in the Anthropocene: From Biopolitical Sovereignty to Wonder." *Law and Critique* 31(3): 329–349.

Díaz, Sandra, Sebsebe Demissew, Carlos Joly, W. Mark Lonsdale, Anne Larigauderie. 2015a. "A Rosetta Stone for Nature's Benefits to People" *PLoS Biology* 13(1): e1002040, 1-8.

Díaz, Sandra, Sebsebe Demissew, Julia Carabias, Carlos Joly, Mark Lonsdale, Neville Ash, Anne Larigauderie et al. 2015b. "The IPBES Conceptual Framework—Connecting Nature and People." *Current Opinion in Environmental Sustainability* 14: 1–16.

Díaz, Sandra, Unai Pascual, Marie Stenseke, Berta Martín-López, Robert T. Watson, Zsolt Molnár, Rosemary Hill et al. 2018. "Assessing Nature's Contributions to People." *Science* 359(6373): 270–272.

Dinneen, Nathan. 2014. "Hans Jonas's Noble 'Heuristics of Fear': Neither the Good Lie nor the Terrible Truth." *Cosmos and History: The Journal of Natural and Social Philosophy* 10(2):1–22.

Dinneen, Nathen. 2017. "Ecological scenario planning and the question of the best regime in the political theory of Hans Jonas" *Environmental Politics* 26(5): 938–955.

Dryzek, John S. 2014. "Institutions for the Anthropocene: Governance in a Changing Earth System." *British Journal of Political Science* 46(4): 937–956.

Ellis, Erle C., Unai Pascual and Ole Mertz. 2019. "Ecosystem Services and Nature's Contribution to People: Negotiating Diverse Values and Trade-Offs in Land Systems." *Current Opinion in Environmental Sustainability* 38: 86–94.

Folke, Carl, Stephen Polasky, Johan Rockström, Victor Galaz, Frances Westley, Michèle Lamont, Martin Scheffer, Henrik Österblom, Stephen R Carpenter, F. Stuart Chapin III et al. 2021. "Our Future in the Anthropocene Biosphere." *Ambio* 50(4): 834–869.

Govind, Paul J. 2021. "Extinction in the Anthropocene and Moving Toward an Ethic of Responsibility." *Griffith Law Review* 29(4): 1–27.

Grear, Anna. 2015. "Deconstructing Anthropos: A Critical Legal Reflection on 'Anthropocentric' Law and Anthropocene 'Humanity'." *Law and Critique* 26(3): 225–249.

Grear, Anna. 2020. "Legal Imaginaries and the Anthropocene: 'Of' and 'For'." *Law and Critique* 31(3): 351–366.

Gunton, Richard M., Eline N. van Asperen, Andrew Basden, David Bookless, Yoseph Araya, David R. Hanson, Mark A. Goddard, George Otieno and Gareth O. Jones. 2017. "Beyond Ecosystem Services: Valuing the Invaluable." *Trends in Ecology and Evolution* 32(4): 249–257.

Hamilton, Clive. 2016. "The Anthropocene as Rupture." *The Anthropocene Review* 3(2): 93–106.

Haraway, Donna. 2008. *When Species Meet*: University of Minnesota Press.

Haraway, Donna. 2015. "Anthropocene, Capitalocene, Plantationocene, Chthulucene: Making Kin" *Environmental Humanities* 6(1): 159–165

Hourdequin, Marion. 2021. "Ethics, Adaptation and the Anthropocene." *Ethics, Policy and Environment* 24(1): 60–74.

Jianguo, Liu et al. 2015. "Systems Integration for Global Sustainability." *Science* 347: 1258832-1–1258832-9.

Lim, Michelle. 2019. "How Do We Address Unprecedented Biodiversity Decline? — the IPBES Global Assessment and the Opportunities for Australian Law and Policy." *Australian Environment Review* 34(6): 103–109.

Lim, Michelle. 2021. "Biodiversity 2050: Can the Convention on Biological Diversity Deliver a World Living in Harmony with Nature?" *Yearbook of International Environmental Law* 30(1): 1–23.

Liu, Jianguo, Vanessa Hull, Mateus Batistella, Ruth DeFries, Thomas Dietz, Feng Fu, Thomas W. Hertel et al. 2013. "Framing Sustainability in a Telecoupled World." *Ecology and Society* 18(2).

Mace, Georgia M., Belinda Reyers, Rob Alkemade, Reinette Biggs, F. Stuart Chapin III, Sarah E. Cornell, Sandra Díaz, Simon Jennings, Paul Leadley, Peter J. Mumby, Andy Purvis et al. 2014. "Approaches to Defining a Planetary Boundary for Biodiversity." *Global Environmental Change* 28: 289–297.

Martuwarra River of Life, Anne Poelina, Donna Bagnall, Michelle Lim. 2020. "Recognizing the Martuwarra's First Law Right to Life as a Living Ancestral Being." *Transnational Environmental Law* 9(3): 541–568.

Matthews, Daniel. 2019. "Law and Aesthetics in the Anthropocene: From the Rights of Nature to the Aesthesis of Obligations." *Law, Culture and the Humanities*: 1–21.

Norgaard, Richard B. 2010. "Ecosystem Services: From Eye-Opening Metaphor to Complexity Blinder." *Ecological Economics* 69(6): 1219–1227.

Palomo, Ignacio, María R. Felipe-Lucia, Elena M. Bennett, Berta Martín-López and Unai Pascual. 2016. "Disentangling the Pathways and Effects of Ecosystem Service co-Production." *Advances in Ecological Research* 54: 245–283.

Pascual, Unai, William M. Adams, Sandra Diaz, Sharachandra Lele, Georgina M. Mace and Esther Turnout. 2021. "Biodiversity and the Challenge of Pluralism." *Nature Sustainability* 4(7): 567–572.

Pascual, Unai, Patricia Balvanera, Sandra Díaz, György Pataki, Eva Roth, Marie Stenseke, Rovert T. Watson, Esra Basask Dessane, Mine Islar, Eszter Kelemen et al. 2017. "Valuing Nature's Contributions to People: The IPBES Approach." *Current Opinion in Environmental Sustainability* 26–27: 7–16.

Pottage, Alain. 2019. "Holocene Jurisprudence." *Journal or Human Rights and the Environment* 10(2): 153–175.

Ricketts, Taylor H., Keri B. Watson, Insu Koh, Alicia M. Ellis, Charles C. Nicholson, Stephen Posner, Leif L. Richardson, and Laura J. Sonter. 2016. "Disaggregating the Evidence Linking Biodiversity and Ecosystem Services." *Nature Communications* 7(1): 1–8.

Robinson, Nicholas A. 2014. "Fundamental Principles of Law for the Anthropocene." *Environmental Policy and Law* 44(1–2): 13–27.

Rockström, Johan, Will Steffen, Kevin Noone, Åsa Persson, F. Stuart Chapin III, Eric F. Lambin, Timothy M. Lenton et al. 2009. "Planetary Boundaries: Exploring the Safe Operating Space for Humanity." *Ecology and Society* 14(2).

Rockström, Johan, Will Steffen, Kevin Noone, Åsa Persson, F. Stuart Chapin III, Eric F. Lambin, Timothy M. Lenton et al. 2009. "A Safe Operating Space for Humanity." *Nature* 461(7263): 472–475.

Seck, Sara J. 2019. "Relational Law and the Reimagining of Tools for Environmental and Climate Justice." *Canadian Journal of Women and the Law* 31(1): 151.

Steffen, Will, Katherine Richardson, Johan Rockström, Sarah E. Cornell, Ingo Fetzer, Elena M. Bennett, Reinette Biggs, Stephen R. Carpenter, Wim de Vries, Cynthia A. de Wit et al. 2015. "Planetary Boundaries: Guiding Human Development on a Changing Planet." *Science* 347: 1259855.

Voigt, Christina. 2005. "From Climate Change to Sustainability: An Essay on Sustainable Development, Legal and Ethical Choices." *Worldviews: Global Religions, Culture, and Ecology* 9(1): 112–137.

Waldron, Jeremy. 1988. *The Right to Private Property* Oxford University Press.

Wapner, Paul. 2014. "The Changing Nature of Nature: Environmental Politics in the Anthropocene." *Global Environmental Politics* 14(4): 36–54.

Yussof, Kathryn. 2015. "Geologic Subjects: Nonhuman Origins, Geomorphic Aesthetics and the Art of Becoming Inhuman." *Cultural Geographies* 22(3): 383–407.

## Legal Instruments:

Aichi Biodiversity Targets for 2020 in the Tenth Meeting of the Conference of Parties to the Convention on Biological Diversity (18–29 October 2010 – Nagoya Aichi Prefecture, Japan) COP 10 Decision X/2, 2010.

Convention on Biological Diversity (adopted on 5 June 1992, entered into force 29 December 1993). 1760. UNTS 79.

Intergovernmental Science-Policy Platform on Biodiversity and Ecosystem Services (IPBES), Summary for Policymakers of the Global Assessment Report on Biodiversity and Ecosystem Services for the Intergovernmental Science-Policy Platform on Biodiversity and Ecosystem Services (IPBES, 29 May 2019) IPBES/7/10/Add.1, 4.

*Kunming-Montreal Global Biodiversity Framework*, UN Doc CBD/COP/15/L.25 (18 December 2022)

Open Ended Working Group on the Post 2020 Global Biodiversity Framework, First Draft of the Post 2020 Global Biodiversity Framework Third meeting Online, 23 August–3 September 2021 CBD/WG2020/3/3 5 July 2021.

Paris Agreement (adopted on 13 December 2015, entered into force 4 November 2016) Registration No. 54113 55 ILM 740.

United Nations Framework Convention on Climate Change (adopted on 9 May 1992, entered into force 21 March 1994) 1771 UNTS 107, 31 ILM 849.

2050 Vision: The Strategic Plan for Biodiversity 2011–2020 and the Aichi Biodiversity Targets, Doc UNEP/BD/COP/DEC/X/2 (2010), Annex, para 11.

# 8

# THE LAW OF THE SEA

## Oceans, Ships, and the Anthropocene

*Renisa Mawani*

In an era that scientists have termed the Anthropocene, oceans have become a critical index of human-induced climate change (Alaimo, 2020; DeLoughrey, 2017). The world's oceans make up 70 percent of the planet and absorb 30 percent of its carbon dioxide. They moderate rising temperatures to keep the planet cool. But oceans have long been sites of anthropogenic change. They have featured prominently in European struggles over imperial dominance, served as stages for racial and colonial violence, and have continued to be vital to the expansion of western militarism and global capitalism (Khalili, 2020; Campling and Colas, 2021). The world's oceans have long been the dumping grounds for human detritus, including garbage, plastics, and radioactive waste (Alaimo, 2020, 318).

Ships are deeply implicated in oceanic change and planetary destruction. Although their effects are not often visible on the undulating surfaces of the seas, their movements continue to pollute waters, damage marine ecologies, and produce species extinction while physically transforming the biochemical composition of ocean waters. Today, ships carry 90 percent of global trade. They generate carbon dioxide emissions and other pollutants that continue to acidify the world's oceans, albeit not equally or evenly (Harrould-Kolieb, 2008, 2). In the early seventeenth century, under the auspices of the "free seas" and in defense of Dutch maritime imperialism and colonialism, Hugo Grotius (1868/2006) viewed oceans and winds as eternal, unalterable, and unchanging forces of nature. "Consider the ocean, which God has encircled the different lands, and which is navigable from boundary to boundary," Grotius wrote,

> consider the breath of the winds in their regular courses and in their special deviations, blowing not always from one and the same region but from every region at one time or another: are these things not sufficient indications that nature has granted every nation access to every other nation?
>
> *(Grotius, 1868/2006, 303)*

But anthropogenic climate change has dramatically altered the oceans. In the Indian Ocean world, which was a focus of Grotius's writings, ocean waters are warming faster than those of other regions. Rising temperatures are disrupting weather patterns, increasing sea levels, and endangering islands and coastal states (Ghosh, 2016; Hofmeyr & Lavery, 2020). If the "most visible sign of planetary change is sea-level rising," as Elizabeth DeLoughrey (2019, 134) argues,

DOI: 10.4324/9781003388081-11

then oceans, ships, and maritime histories must be centered in ongoing discussions of climate catastrophe. What does the Anthropocene look like from the sea, I ask in this chapter, from the tracks of moving European ships that have been critical to colonial extraction, imperial violence, and the making of a western international legal order?

Origin stories of the Anthropocene remain highly contested. Paul Crutzen and Eugene Stoermer (2000) first introduced the concept to argue that human activity had driven the earth out of the Holocene into a new geological era marked by anthropogenic change. Initially, Crutzen (2000) dated the Anthropocene to James Watt's invention of the steam engine in 1784. However, he later revised his thinking to align more closely with the periodization proposed by the Anthropocene Working Group. Since 2009, the Working Group has sought to develop "a formal definition of the chronostratigraphic Anthropocene," one that is "associated with the Great Acceleration of the mid-twentieth century" (Zalasiewicz et al., 2021, 2). According to many climate scientists, the 1950s onward marks a surge in human activity that has left measurable effects on the planet (Zalasiewicz, J. et al., 2021). But a twentieth-century focus is historically limited and politically troubling. As critics point out, it requires a willful forgetting of European colonialism, including the terrorizing violence directed at Indigenous peoples, enslaved Africans, and other colonized peoples, and against local ecologies of the so-called new world (Davis and Todd, 2017; Yusoff, 2019). The stakes are high. "How can we account for the planetary upheavals" of our time, Anne McClintock (2020) asks,

> unless we illuminate the long arc of their beginnings in the military geographies of European imperialism – the foundational violences of slavery, genocides of Indigenous peoples, and the centuries of ecocides and onslaughts of the environment that shaped – and are now undoing – the world?

Dating the Anthropocene to the "Great Acceleration" obscures the extractive and exploitative histories to which McClintock (2020) and others draw attention (see also Davis and Todd, 2017; Lewis and Maslin, 2015; Moore, 2017; Yusoff, 2019). More importantly for my purposes here, a twentieth-century focus erases the significance of the world's oceans, not only as sites of planetary crisis but as spaces of inter-imperial contest over the emergence of a European international legal order. The international law of the sea, I argue – to which the movement of ships has been crucial – is inseparable from and deeply implicated in planetary destruction. In Grotius's (1868/2006, 303) account of European maritime commerce, ships were supposedly ordained by the laws of nature as evidenced in "the breath of the winds." Today, his arguments continue to inform the UN Convention on the Law of the Sea (1982).

In this chapter, I argue that the world's oceans, and the European ships that crossed them, must be made better visible in contemporary discussions of climate catastrophe. To emphasize their historical and contemporary importance, I revisit Grotius's writings on the freedom of the sea and situate his thinking within wider concerns of a planet in crisis. The Anthropocene, as many have argued, is always already colonial, both as a discourse (Simpson, 2020) and as a long process of dispossession, extraction, and violence directed at Indigenous, enslaved, and colonized peoples (Davis and Todd, 2017; McClintock, 2020; Verges, 2017; Yusoff, 2019). What Grotius's writings point to is how an international law of the sea authorized European colonialism and imperialism under the auspices of maritime commerce and freedom of navigation, while also producing an extractive view of nature that has devastated human, more-than-human life, and the planet. A critical rereading of *Mare Liberum* (1609/2004) and the twelfth chapter of the *Commentary on the Law of Prize and Booty* (1869/2006) from which it was drawn, I suggest, points to a legal history and geography of climate catastrophe that demands further attention.

For geographers Simon Lewis and Mark Maslin (2015), the devastating effects of European conquest and colonization in the so-called new world is perceptible from the early seventeenth century. In 1492 there were approximately 54 to 61 million Indigenous peoples in the Americas, they observe. By 1650, because of European colonization – the violent dispossession of Indigenous peoples from their lands and waterways, mass killings, and the introduction and spread of European diseases – this number plunged to 6 million (cited in Davis and Todd, 2017, 766). The genocide of Indigenous peoples, Lewis and Maslin (2015, 175) suggest, can be detected in a "dip in atmospheric CO2" which they term the "Orbis spike." They call the atmospheric changes that mark 1610 "as the beginning of the Anthropocene the 'Orbis hypothesis.'" It bears noting that the publication of *Mare Liberum* in 1609 coincides with their periodization of the Anthropocene in 1610. Whereas Lewis and Maslin (2015) focus on the Atlantic and the Americas, Grotius's concerns centered on Southeast Asia and the Indian Ocean, a region that opens additional, albeit neglected genealogies of anthropogenic change (Chatterjee, 2020; Ghosh, 2016). Ultimately, a maritime view of climate catastrophe may connect these seemingly disparate geographies and histories of a planet in crisis.

Though largely discounted by scientists, efforts to date the Anthropocene in the early seventeenth century and in European imperial and colonial violence have generated critical and lively discussions. Scholars have drawn on Lewis and Maslin's (2015) claims to emphasize the destructive role of European colonial expansion in the long arc of climate catastrophe and to stress the overlaps and entanglements between violence directed at human beings and violence directed at the planet (Davis and Todd, 2017; Yusoff, 2019). As crucial as these insights are in shifting attention to the planetary and world-altering effects of European imperialism and colonialism, they miss a crucial connective force, one that joined the so-called old world and the new: ships. To begin, European vessels that crossed the Indian, Atlantic, and Pacific Oceans were the vehicles that made conquest and colonization possible. Though often overlooked in discussions of settler colonialism the oceangoing ship, as both a legal and technological form, was instrumental to the mobility of European settlers, the genocide of Indigenous peoples, and the forced transport of West African captives (Hasty and Peters, 2012; Mawani, 2016, 2022a; Rediker, 2008). European ships carried flora and fauna that destroyed local ecologies. Yet, oceangoing ships rarely draw comment in contemporary discussions of climate catastrophe except in the case of accidents at sea. Their movements, past and present, and especially their role as legal forms that have been central to the making of a western international legal order, raise important questions on the uneven effects and unequal responsibilities for a planet in crisis. By taking a longer maritime perspective that centers the European ship as an imperial, legal, and technological form in the colonization of the planet, I argue that the international law of the sea emerges - not as a response - but as a condition of possibility for climate catastrophe (on the problem of international law see also de Repentigny, 2020; Ranganathan, 2020; Vidas, 2011).

## Ships and the Free Sea

At the heart of Grotius's *Mare Liberum* lies a Portuguese carrack, the *Santa Catarina*. Its 1603 capture has been well-documented and is routinely referenced by legal scholars and international lawyers. However, the Dutch seizure of the vessel bears repeating for two reasons. First, to underscore the significance of European ships to the legal concept of the "free sea" and second, to highlight the importance of the Indian Ocean in the emergence of a European international legal order. The "incontrovertible doctrine" of the free sea, which was Grotius's response to the *Santa Catarina*, inaugurated an expansion in maritime traffic, resource extraction, and exploitation that has led to a flourishing of maritime global capitalism which has had a material effect on oceans and the planet (Anand, 1977, 207). Yet curiously, we do not often hear of ships as legal forms that are implicated in the climate crisis, except in the case of oil spills and marine accidents. For Grotius (1886/2006) ships did not leave a legal, political, or material imprint: "a ship sailing over the sea no more leaves behind itself a legal right than it leaves a permanent track." But oceangoing vessels have left an environmental mark through collisions, wrecks, pollution, and disruptions to marine life. What insights might we gather on the Anthropocene and the unequal responsibilities of planetary crisis under a Western international legal order when we follow the moving ship and make it visible? What kinds of histories do the well-traveled routes European ships both conceal and reveal?

On 25 February 1603, three Dutch vessels surrounded and captured the *Santa Catarina* in the Straits of Singapore. The carrack, with its racially polyglot crew, left the Portuguese-controlled island of Macao and was on course to Portuguese-controlled Goa. Acting in his own right as commander of the Dutch fleet, Jakob van Heemskerk attacked and seized the carrack (Borschberg, 2002, 34). Apparently, he was not ordered to do so, either by the ship's owners or by the newly established Dutch East India Company (VOC). Rather, van Heemskerk acted opportunistically and on his own legal authority. In the end, his decision proved both profitable and monumental. The *Santa Catarina* was carrying a high-value cargo including gold, ceramics, silks, and cotton. Together, the collection of treasures was worth a substantial prize of approximately three million Dutch guilders (van Ittersum, 2006a, 1). Amsterdam's Admiralty Court was tasked with deciding whether van Heemskerk's seizure of the *Santa Catarina* was legitimate or illegitimate, whether it was privateering or piracy. After hearing the case and situating the capture of the carrack within a longer history of Portuguese attacks against Dutch ships in the Indian Ocean region, the court concluded that van Heemskerk acted in self-defense and his actions were legally justified.

Grotius, a talented lawyer in his early 20s at the time, was commissioned by the Directors of the VOC to consider the implications of van Heemskerk's actions. Though the case was decided on 9 September 1604 (van Ittersum, 2006a, iii), the Dutch capture of the *Santa Catarina* raised a wider set of questions regarding the legal status of the high seas and the rights of the Dutch to engage in trade and colonization in the Indian Ocean world. In writing his rejoinder, Grotius drew on the notarized testimonies of Dutch seafarers and merchants and on van Heemskerk's account, which included his justifications for privateering (van Ittersum, 2006a, iv, 4). From these recollections, Grotius wrote *De Rebus Indicis* (*On the Affairs of the Indies*), more commonly known as *De Jure Praedae* (*Commentary on the Law of Prize and Booty*). The full text was not discovered until 1864 and remained unpublished until 1868 (Armitage, 2004, xiii). However, a version of the twelfth chapter of the longer monograph was published anonymously in 1609 as *Mare Liberum* or "Free Sea." Grotius wrote this pithy text between September 1604 and November 1606 and completed it two years after the Admiralty Court had reached its decision (van Ittersum, 2009). Despite being a short excerpt from a much longer work, Grotius's arguments on the freedom of the sea, in which he vigorously defended Dutch imperialism, would have far-reaching consequences. Grotius's writings sanctioned Dutch colonialism and imperialism, increased maritime traffic, and authorized an extractive view of the sea as an expendable and exploitable resource (Anand, 1977).

It is now commonplace to mention Grotius and *Mare Liberum* in discussions of international law. Yet by most accounts, the *Santa Catarina* and the Indian Ocean appear as historical backdrops rather than as significant sites and sources of an international legal order. The Dutch Admiralty Court rendered its decision on van Heemskerk's attack in Amsterdam. Importantly, however, the capture of the carrack took place in the Straits of Singapore. The law of the sea and the emergence of an international legal order, as this case suggests, may have reverberated across European cities and courtrooms, and informed international treaties. However, it bears remembering that the "free sea" that formed the basis of an international legal order emerged and developed from contests over ships at sea (Benton and Ford, 2016, 121). Although the legal status of oceans have, since the time of *Mare Liberum*, been debated, revised, and expanded in negotiations over international agreements, the *Santa Catarina* reminds us that the juridical and maritime claims of European empires unfolded on the decks of ships, in the actions of their captains and commanders, and in struggles over jurisdiction in the Indian Ocean world (Anand, 1982; Mawani and Hussin, 2014; Mawani and Prange, 2021).

Grotius was well aware of the legal significance that ships carried in imperial contests over maritime trade in Southeast Asia. After all, his arguments in *Mare Liberum* were guided by the affidavits of seafarers, including van Heemskerk's own testimony (van Ittersum, 2006). International lawyer, Charles Henry Alexandrowicz (1967) suggests that in formulating his arguments on the freedom of the sea, Grotius must have been attuned to the maritime practices of Asian seafarers. As legal histories from the rich polyglot world of the Indian Ocean reveal, Grotius was not the first to discuss the freedom of the sea. For Arab and Chinese seafarers, Alexandrowicz (1967, 229) explains, "the high sea had been, since time immemorial, considered a free international highway." Thus, the free sea, he concludes, was a longstanding convention that preceded European encroachment in the Indian Ocean world. It is evident in Asian maritime customs, in Islamic seaborne practices, and was even written into the Quran (Anand, 1982, 10; Khalilieh, 2019, 32). *Mare clausum*, or closed sea, Alexandrowicz (1967, 44) notes, was far more prevalent in seventeenth-century European legal and political thought. Grotius, he suggests, must have been familiar with Asian maritime legalities, even if he never referenced them directly. The extent to which Grotius was influenced by Asian seafarers and their seaborne practices remains an ongoing point of historiographical dispute (Borschberg, 2009, 51).

In making his arguments on the legal status of the high seas, Grotius drew explicitly on the writings of Roman and Greek jurists and poets (Jones, 2011). He drew from their claims on the circumscribed space of the Mediterranean Sea and projected them onto the vast Indian Ocean arena. Roman jurisdiction over the seas, Grotius (1868/2006, 329) observed, was not about possession but protection: "the Roman people were authorized to distribute fleets for the protection of sailors and to punish pirates captured at sea." Elsewhere in Europe, *mare clausum* or closed sea was a common guiding principle, albeit one that was not applied on the open ocean. The Venetians made sovereign claims to the Adriatic Sea, the Genoese over the Ligurian Sea, and the Danish extended their sovereignty into the Baltic (Muldoon, 2016, 17). These efforts to control the seas were not specific to continental Europe. In the late sixteenth century, James Muldoon (2016, 17) explains, "James VI (1567–1625) of Scotland and I (1603–25) of England attempted to claim jurisdiction over the seas around Britain, especially over the herring fisheries where there was a strong Dutch presence." For Grotius, a ship did not leave its legal mark on an ever-changing ocean and thus could not extend an empire's legal right to possession. However, he acknowledged that moving ships, which he suggested were sources of legal authority, could expand jurisdictional claims to the sea through regular passage (Benton, 2009, 109; Mawani, 2018, 48–49).

The legal status of ships has been described in different ways but always in relation to oceans. "Ships played a dual role as sources of order in the oceans," Lauren Benton (2009, 112) argues, "they were islands of law with their own regulations and judicial personnel, and they were representatives of municipal legal authorities – vectors of law thrusting into ocean space." For others, ships at sea signal a jurisdictional plurality that cannot be fully captured in terrestrial metaphors of islands or territories. In *The Nationality of Ships*, international lawyer and judge Herman Meyers (1967) details the multiple legalities that were ascribed to vessels in Anglo legal systems. In state practices, international treaties, and legal scholarship, he claims, a ship became a legal entity in three interrelated ways. First, a ship was viewed as moveable property. Second, a vessel was "a collective noun for designating particular persons who have an interest in that moveable property" (Meyers, 1967, 8). Finally, the term "ship" was commonly used to reference the authority of a vessel's flag state. In the second two definitions, Meyers (1967, 8) notes, "a ship is written about as if it were a person," a sovereign representative of its state and/ or sponsors. The law of the sea, he implies, was shaped by the movement of ships: "the whole law of the sea is a law regulating the use of the sea," he writes. "The majority of those who make use of the sea … [are] people who use the sea through the medium of a ship" (Meyers, 1967, 12). Contrary to Grotius's insistence that ships did not leave a trace, the personhood of ships became an imperial, gendered, and racial expression of European masculinity and sovereignty at sea (Mawani, 2018, 2022b). Interestingly, the frontispiece to the 1633 edition of *Mare Liberum* pictures a Dutch vessel with Grotius's name inscribed on its sails.

Grotius's writings on the free sea were concerned with the movement of Dutch ships and thus with a particular scale of technology and legality which developed and expanded with the rise of British and then American imperial power. Under Anglo maritime customs, ships were viewed as sentient beings animated by distinct personalities and temperaments (Mawani, 2018). The personhood that sailors and seafarers ascribed to ships created new forms of maritime law. In the nineteenth century, under US admiralty law, ships were ascribed a legal personality that granted vessels specific rights and responsibilities (Lind, 2009–2010; Mawani, 2022b). Through their transoceanic movements, vessels extended Anglo-imperial jurisdiction along the high seas. But as legal persons, they were rendered juridically distinct from their owners and operators (Mawani, 2018, 2022b). As moving ships projected jurisdictional claims to oceans through their regular movements, their designation as legal persons vindicated owners and sponsors of legal responsibility for accidents, wrecks, and crimes at sea. Ships became legal entities that were granted freedom of navigation, through the "breath of winds" (Grotius, 1868/2006, 303) and were ascribed legal autonomy and responsibility through legal personhood.

Grotius composed his arguments on the freedom of the sea on the presumed elemental differences between land and water. This physical and material distinction informed and shaped his legal thinking in important ways (Mawani, 2018, 43). If land was solid and could be appropriated, improved through human labor, and possessed, Grotius (1868/2006, 315) viewed oceans as *res communis*, belonging to no one and held in common to all (Benton and Straumann, 2010, 27). Given their vast, fluid, and ever-changing properties, the seas could not be improved or occupied. The elemental properties of the seas, Grotius claimed, made them resistant to containment and capture but open for trade, commerce, and extraction. In elaborating this argument, Grotius insisted that the sea shared a greater likeness to air than to land: "the element of the sea is common to all, to wit, so infinite that it cannot be possessed and applied to all uses, whether we respect navigation or fishing" (Grotius, 1609/2008, 25). The material qualities of air and sea, he suggested, made them accessible to all humanity. However, Grotius was explicitly concerned with defending Dutch imperialism and with securing the rights of a white male propertied subject (Stelder, 2021). Beginning with the elemental, Grotius's writing laid the groundwork for a European international legal order that while profoundly unequal, was thought to be established on the seemingly natural and incommensurable distinctions between land and sea (Armitage, 2004, xix). Although Grotius later refined his arguments in recognition of coastal waters, the moving ship continues to reinforce divisions between land and sea in important ways (Siegert, 2015, 70). For the VOC, it was the capture of the *Santa Catarina* and the presumed rights of the Hollanders to access the Indian Ocean as a right of nature, that necessitated a law of the sea that was distinct from the law of land. Today, the land-sea distinction that featured so prominently in Grotius's arguments continues to be challenged and undermined by anthropogenic climate change. Coastal areas in the Indian Ocean and the Caribbean – regions that have been central to histories of European colonial conquest and imperial expansion – face the greatest threats of erosion and "oceanic submersion" due to warming waters and rising sea levels (DeLoughrey, 2017, 22; Hofmeyr and Lavery, 2020).

Some commentators read *Mare Liberum* as "an argument for the right of free travel across the seas" for all of humankind (Muldoon, 2016, 15). But as critics point out, in justifying van Heemskerk's seizure of the *Santa Catarina*, Grotius was concerned with advancing Dutch navigation, trade, and colonization in the Indian Ocean region (Anand, 1982; van Ittersum, 2010). Therefore, conquest and colonization were central to his conceptions of the free sea. As Martine van Ittersum (2016, 99) puts it, Grotius was "the godfather of Dutch imperialism." His writings created two juridical and political orders: one for Europe and another for Asia (van Ittersum, 2010, 386). Recall that Grotius's initial title of the *Commentary on the Law of Prize and Booty* was *De Rebus Indicis* (*On the Affairs of the Indies*). When read with the subtitle of *Mare Liberum – A Disputation Concerning the Right Which the Hollanders Ought to Have to the Indian Merchandise for Trading* – it is clear that Grotius was drawing on the elements to support the supposedly natural rights of the Dutch to trade, and ultimately to colonize Southeast Asia. While Grotius recognized the presence of Indigenous sovereigns, and may or may not have been influenced by Asian seafarers, he did not advocate for the rights of Indigenous or Asian rulers to advance maritime commerce or trade in their own interests (Mawani, 2018, 61).

Grotius may not be the progenitor of the free sea. But what makes the timing of his writings so significant, as several scholars have noted, is that *Mare Liberum* sanctioned an imperial system of commerce, trade, and colonization that would set the foundation for a modern law of the sea (de Repentigny, 2020, 185; Gumplova, 2021;Muldoon, 2016, 17). It is precisely this "freedom" – that was extended only to Europe through arguments on the right to maritime trade, and which authorized imperial powers to expand their jurisdiction through the movement of ships, that is overlooked in contemporary discussions of the Anthropocene. Grotius's *Mare Liberum*, as I read it, instantiated a concept of the free sea that centered on the moving ship as a juridical form and which continues to carry influence into the present day. The freedom of the sea has shifted from a freedom enjoyed by European imperial powers to a freedom enjoyed by powerful states to assert legal control over oceans through the competing interests of maritime protection, trade, and an expanding global capitalism (Campling and Colas, 2021; Ranganathan, 2019).

Although Grotius was concerned with Dutch and Portuguese inter-imperial rivalries over trade and colonization in the Indian Ocean, his writings on the free sea must be read as a world-making project that has had far-reaching implications. Drawing from Roman law, Grotius characterized oceans as abundant and inexhaustible reservoirs of natural resources. As I discuss further below, these claims have reinforced an extractive view of nature which continues to hold significant legal, political, and ecological implications today (de Repentigny, 2020;Vidas, 2011). My rereading of Grotius thus far underscores the importance of an oceanic reorientation to contemporary discussions of the Anthropocene, one that implicates ships as imperial technologies and juridical forms that sanctioned European trade, introduced new patterns and intensities of colonial and racial violence, while laying the groundwork for an international legal order (see also Anand, 1977; Ranganathan, 2019, 576;Vidas, 2011). In the following section, I develop this argument by exploring the freedom of the sea and climate catastrophe through Grotius's writings on Dutch and English disputes over the North Atlantic herring trade.

## Inexhaustible Oceans

Grotius's arguments on the free sea might be read as two interconnected legal histories. The first, as I have discussed thus far, extends across the surface of the ocean and centers on the routes of European ships and the freedom of navigation enjoyed by their captains and sponsors. The second descends below the water line and follows the movements of fish. In *The Sovereignty of the Sea*, Thomas Wemyss Fulton (1911, 347) remarks on these intersecting legal histories. Grotius, he writes, may have placed "navigation and fishing in the sea on the same footing," however, "he looked upon interference with the freedom of fishing as a greater offence than an interference with navigation." In Grotius's writings, the navigation of ships clearly overlapped with the right to fish. However, the two carried very different implications for property, propriety, and possession (van Ittersum, 2006b, 250). Recall that for Grotius, commerce, trade, and imperial expansion were rights bestowed to European powers under the authority of natural law. "Our purpose is shortly and clearly to demonstrate," Grotius (1609/2008, 10) declared on the opening page of *Mare Liberum*, "that it is lawful for the Hollanders … to sail to the Indians as they do and entertain traffic with them." But while "the sea is common property," the "fish become the property of the persons who catch them" (Grotius, 1868/2006, 323). To emphasize this point Grotius repeated Plautus: "'That which my net and hooks have gotten is principally mine'" (Plautus, cited in Grotius, 1609/2004, 26). If the sea was free and common to all (Europeans), the fish beneath its surface were the property of those who caught them.

In his introduction to *The Free Sea*, David Armitage (2004) argues that Grotius's wide-ranging arguments on the freedom of the sea "ensured that *Mare Liberum* would be understood as a general statement of the right to freedom of trade and navigation." Given the capaciousness of Grotius's claims, he writes, the text "sparked a wider and more enduring controversy regarding the foundations of international relations, the limits of national sovereignty, and the relationship between sovereignty (*imperium*) and possession (*dominium*) that would guarantee its lasting fame and notoriety" (Armitage, 2004, xv). While *Mare Liberum* was intended to be a direct response to the *Santa Catarina* and to Dutch-Portuguese imperial struggles in the Indian Ocean region, several of Grotius's contemporaries read his claims through ongoing political and legal disputes between the Dutch and English over herring in the North Atlantic. In *Mare Liberum*, Grotius never mentioned the North Atlantic directly. However, he did reference fish as property. Thus, English and Scottish jurists feared that his conceptualization of the "free sea" would be used to further justify Dutch encroachment in the herring fisheries (Reiser, 2020).

Initially, *Mare Liberum* was published anonymously. Grotius anticipated that the text might receive critical responses, most likely from Spanish readers (van Ittersum, 2006b, 244), as the "new world" featured prominently in his thinking. To begin, Grotius was well aware of Spain's ongoing efforts to conquer the Americas. He was also an admirer of the School of Salamanca and was particularly inspired by the Dominican theologian, Francisco de Vitoria (Armitage, 200, xv). Grotius anticipated that his critique of the Pope and his denunciation of the Papal Bull "Inter Caetera," which sought to divide the world into East and West, granting authority and influence to Portugal and Spain respectively, might draw censure. "[T]he Pope is not a temporal lord of the whole world," Grotius charged, "it is sufficiently understood that he is not lord of the sea" (Grotius, 1609/2004, 38). Given that his writings were focused on Portuguese encroachment in the Indian Ocean, what Grotius may not have anticipated were the critical rejoinders he would receive from English and Scottish thinkers. The most fulsome and famous reply to *Mare Liberum* was penned by the English scholar John Selden. His book *Mare Clausum*, or closed sea, was a direct rejoinder to Grotius's claims that the sea was free. For Selden, King James I held the requisite authority to restrict the commercial waters surrounding Britain, granting access only to his subjects and to those who were issued royal licenses (Muldoon, 2016, 21). English monarchs, Selden claimed, already held jurisdiction over the English Channel and the waters surrounding the British Isles, making "the North Atlantic … a British 'Mare Nostrum'" (Muldoon, 2016, 22).

The legal struggle between *Mare Liberum* and *Mare Clausum* has been commonly referenced as the "Battle of the Books" (Anand, 1977, 207). But some have questioned whether the open and closed seas were in fact conflicting positions. In the case of Britain, as Armitage (2000, 105) observes, the oscillation between the open and closed seas has long been a cornerstone of British imperial power. Britannia sought to "rule the waves," as the famous eighteenth-century ballad makes clear, while at the same time insisting on the freedom of the sea to further their own interests, objectives, and advantages over maritime control (Mawani, 2018). Notably, these tensions between *mare liberum* and *mare clausum* continue to inform maritime legal boundaries, as evidenced historically in the distinctions between territorial waters and the high seas, and more recently in the creation of Exclusive Economic Zones (EEZ).

Grotius did not respond to Selden's *Mare Clausum*. However, he did write an impassioned reply to William Welwod who also penned a critical response to *Mare Liberum*. In 1590, Welwod, a Scottish legal scholar and Professor at St. Andrews University published *The Sea-Law of Scotland, Shortly Gathered and Plainly Dressit for the Reddy Use of All Sea-Fairingmen*. In this brief text – totaling 29 pages which he dedicated to James VI of Scotland – Welwod described Scotland's law of the sea through the movement of ships and the duties of their masters (van Ittersum, 2006b, 244). In 1613, after being forced to resign from St. Andrews and following his move to England, Welwod published a revised and much longer volume, the *Abridgement of All Sea-Lawes*. Chapter 27 of this text was a direct refutation of *Mare Liberum*. There, Welwod insisted that European sovereigns could assert ownership over the sea and its resources, including fish. Technological developments, such as navigation instruments, he claimed, expanded human sovereignty and control over the sea. "There were plenty of 'eminent and visible marks above water'," Welwod wrote, "which, along with human inventions like the compass, [which] helped sailors to determine their position at sea and establish maritime boundaries" (cited in van Ittersum, 2006b, 247).

Significantly, Welwod also took exception to Grotius's assertions of the sea as inexhaustible. The inherent freedom to fish, he charged, was informed by the assumptions that fish were an abundant and unlimited resource. Dutch-English conflicts proved these claims to be unfounded. The herring fisheries had once been sustainable, Welwod claimed. By the early sixteenth century, however, fish stores were declining and the effects were visible in the demise of other species including whales, seals, and birds (Bolster, 2012, 34). It was Dutch encroachment in the North Atlantic herring fisheries, Welwod insisted, that was responsible for the depleting fish: "whereas aforetime the white fishes daily abounded even into all the shores on the eastern coast of Scotland," he observed,

> now forsooth by the near and daily approaching of the buss-fishers the shoals of fishes are broken and so far scattered away from our shores and coasts that no fish now can be found worthy of any pains and travails, to the impoverishing of all the sort of our home fishers and to the great damage of all the nation
>
> *(Welwod, 1613/2008, 74)*

For Welwod, the diminishing herring population was a consequence of the annual intrusion of Dutch herring busses (van Ittersum, 2006b, 249).

In *Mare Liberum*, Grotius may not have remarked directly on the herring or the North Atlantic fisheries. But in his response to Welwod, which remained unpublished during his lifetime, Grotius discussed the fisheries at length (van Ittersum, 2006b). As several scholars have noted, the herring trade was the "backbone of the Dutch economy in the sixteenth and early seventeenth centuries," and was likely not far from Grotius's concerns (van Ittersum, 2006b, 241). As Alison Reiser (2020) argues, Grotius's immediate focus may have been Dutch-Portuguese conflicts in the Indian Ocean region, but herring featured prominently in his conception of the free sea. "Grotius crafted a new, secular law of nations based upon the natural properties of the seas and its herring," she writes. "Exhaustion of the great shoal was impossible" for Grotius, "its return to its ancient haunts in the North Sea reflected rhythms and patterns that were the voice of God speaking through nature" (Reiser, 2020, 203). To be sure, herring created the conditions for European rivalries that were fought at sea through ships and firepower. In Reiser's (2020, 201) reading of *Mare Liberum*, herring "with its particular habits and biological properties ... coproduced the freedom of the seas."

The legal histories of navigation and fishing that Grotius composed were dependent on specific imaginaries of nature. In advancing the argument that commerce and trade were fundamental rights accessible to all European nations, Grotius, like his early seventeenth-century counterparts, advanced conceptions of nature as exploitable, extractable, and inexhaustible (Porras, 2014). Importantly, his emphasis on the elemental differences between land, sea, and air, and their physical and legal incommensurabilities also shaped his views on abundance and scarcity. Whereas land-based resources were limited, Grotius claimed, the sea by comparison was boundless and abundant. The "forest will soon be without game and the river without fishes, which is not so in the sea," he wrote (Grotius, 1609/2008, 47). These historical imaginaries of nature as endless, exploitable, and free for European extraction and consumption, have held devastating effects, producing a planet in crisis (Mirzoeff, 2014, 219). Grotius's arguments on unlimited and extractible oceans, whether real or strategic, established the basis for an international legal order that is deeply implicated in anthropogenic climate change, I am suggesting here, and in the exploitation and destruction of marine resources which has resulted in various forms of species extinction (Telesca, 2020).

Grotius spent a considerable amount of time ruminating on the elemental properties of land, sea, and air. By contrast, he spent comparably less time reflecting on the vibrancy of ocean ecologies and their more-than-human inhabitants. Although Grotius argued, in his response to Welwod, that fish were abundant in the North Atlantic, they appear in his writings as objects of proprietary control. Fish were to be caught and commoditized as property (Porras, 2014). Selden and Welwod both objected to Grotius's conceptualization. The changing migratory patterns of herring, for example, offered one important reason why coastal states and island nations might lawfully extend their sovereignty into the sea. Grotius acknowledged the rights of nations over a narrow band of coastal waters, an argument that later gained traction. In the eighteenth century, the Dutch international lawyer, Cornelius van Bynkershoek, suggested that the jurisdiction of coastal states should extend three miles into the water, the length of a cannon shot (Muldoon, 2016, 14). By the mid-twentieth century, countries in the global south began disputing the territorial lines inaugurated by *Mare Liberum*, which they rightly argued were imposed in the interests of European imperialism and maritime global capitalism. More recently, with changing technologies, the freedom of navigation that extended along the ocean's surface has been recast into a vertical depth that has facilitated new forms of resource extraction along the ocean floor (Ranganathan, 2019). Thus, "the freedom to navigate across the oceans and to trade with distant peoples," a claim that Grotius made in the early seventeenth century, has in the twentieth century become "the freedom to descend into the oceans and to claim animate and inanimate resources" (Esmeir, 2017, 86).

From the mid-twentieth century onwards, the era that scientists have termed the "Great Acceleration," concerns about overfishing and the protection of marine resources have encouraged new legal claims to the world's oceans. The migratory patterns of fish may not have informed Grotius's writings but they became vital to discussions regarding the law of the sea. The destruction of marine ecologies has pushed fish further and further outside of coastal waters generating new international legal agreements (de Repentigny, 2020, 187). Growing fears of ecological destruction have also inaugurated new maritime lines and boundaries. In the 1940s, the US issued two Truman Proclamations. The first extended jurisdiction over the continental shelf and the second established zones where fisheries would be subject to US regulations (Ranganathan, 2019, 575). In 1952, in response to the changing migratory patterns of fish, Latin American countries including Chile, Peru, and Ecuador, along with countries in Asia and Africa disputed the "vertical freedom in the sea" and instead called for international support to extend their sovereign claims further outward (Esmeir, 2017, 87). Exclusive Economic Zones (EEZs), which cover 200 nautical miles into the sea, were written into the United Nations Convention of the Law of the Sea (1982).

Today, nearly half of the world's oceans – which Grotius insisted were common to all – fall within the jurisdiction of nation-states. Eighty-three countries, most of them small island states, have more ocean than land under their territorial control (Bellamy Foster et al., 2019). Although efforts to limit the law of the sea through the extension of EEZs might be viewed as an anti-colonial response by coastal states, mainly in the global south, to the European imperial exploitation of oceans and marine resources, these initiatives have opened additional prospects for imperial and territorial expansion through what Surabhi Ranganathan (2019) has called an "ocean floor grab." The Truman Proclamations and EEZs, Elizabeth DeLoughrey (2017, 32) observes, are "the most significant, and yet largely unremarked, twentieth-century remapping of the globe." They "created a scramble for the oceans, catalyzing EEZ declarations by nations all over the world and a UN Convention on the Law of the Sea that effectively remapped 70 percent of the planet." The legal status of the sea may have changed since Grotius's *Mare Liberum*, however, power and control over oceans and maritime resources remain in the hands of imperial nations (Bellamy Foster et al., 2019).

The ideological foundations of the free sea, Davor Vidas (2011, 910) argues, facilitated the Industrial Revolution and encouraged levels of development that continue to have "ever-greater human impacts on the Earth System." This claim, as important as it is, reinforces the "Great Acceleration" origin story of the Anthropocene. The free sea inaugurated by Grotius, I suggest in this chapter, did much more than establish an ideological foundation for nineteenth- and twentieth-century industrialization and ecological crisis. By authorizing the movements of European ships across the so-called free sea, *Mare Liberum* set the foundations for a European international legal order that created new patterns of inter-imperial competition and initiated a global imaginary in which oceans and marine resources became exploitable and extractable commodities. For R.P. Anand (1977, 207–208), Grotius's free sea opened "safe navigation to new markets in the wake of the Industrial Revolution in Europe," and granted western countries the "unlimited freedom to exploit the living resources of the oceans without consideration for the interests of other countries," particularly coastal states in the Indian Ocean region. Following the ship as a juridical form brings the significance of oceans into sharper focus while also implicating international law in the destruction of the planet.

## Oceans Speak Back

In advancing his arguments on the freedom of the sea, Grotius emphasized the elemental and material composition of oceans and drew on their aqueous properties to develop and reinforce his legal arguments. Although he reiterated the vast, formlessness, and perpetual change of the seas, in *Mare Liberum* they featured as a passive backdrop rather than a force and fury to be reckoned with. Interestingly, in the *Commentary on the Law of Prize and Booty*, Grotius (1868/2006, 331) began to personify the ocean as a living entity:

> The subject of our discussion is the Ocean, which was described in olden times as immense, infinite, the father of created things, and bounded only by the heavens; the Ocean, whose never-failing waters fed not only upon the springs and rivers and seas, according to the ancient belief, but upon the clouds, also, and in certain measure upon the stars themselves; in fine, that Ocean which encompasses the terrestrial home of mankind with the ebb and flow of its tides, and which cannot be held nor enclosed, being itself the possessor rather than the possessed.

In this passage, Grotius capitalizes "the Ocean," describes it as "the father of created things," and perhaps most significantly, as "the possessor rather than the possessed." His argument appears to make a clear departure from seventeenth-century thinking, in which nature was portrayed "as [an] enemy to be subdued" (Mirzoeff, 2014, 217). Perhaps Grotius was influenced by Dutch and Asian mariners who made their lives and livelihoods at sea. Oceans could not be easily subdued, as sailors were well aware. They troubled Europe's aspirations to conquer nature and to establish a global capitalist system (see Campling and Colas, 2021). Through extreme weather events, warming waters, rising sea levels, and species extinction, oceans continue to speak back in ways that illuminate the uneven effects of climate catastrophe and with an intensity that can no longer be ignored.

The effects of anthropogenic climate change have unsettled the land/sea divide that figured so prominently in *Mare Liberum* and in the making of a European international legal order. As I point out earlier in this chapter, many of the areas that, today, are at greatest risk of being submerged by rising water levels are located along the Indian Ocean and in the Caribbean Sea, "old world" and "new world" regions that were central to European conquest. Whereas Indian Ocean slavery, trade, and commerce established juridical regimes that authorized forms of racial exploitation and colonial conceptions of sovereignty (Anand, 1982), the Caribbean, or "new world," was the site of Indigenous genocide, transatlantic slavery, indentured labor, and the devastation of human and more-than-human ecologies (Lewis and Maslin, 2015; Wynter, 2003; Yusoff, 2019). Oceangoing ships, despite their absence in discussions of the Anthropocene, as I argue throughout, legally connected these geographical regions, their long histories of colonial and imperial violence and struggles against European hegemony over land and water.

In their field-defining essay, "On the Importance of a Date, or, Decolonizing the Anthropocene," Heather Davis and Zoe Todd (2017) remind us of the political and ethical stakes in periodizing planetary crisis. "The stories we tell about the origins of the Anthropocene," they write, "implicate how we understand the relations we have with our surrounds." When and how we identify "its start date [will] have implications not just for how we understand the world," but for the "material consequences that affect bodies and land" (Davis and Todd, 2017, 767). Where we begin discussions of the Anthropocene – whether on land or sea – is equally important to the stories we tell and to how we account for the uneven effects and responsibilities of climate catastrophe. Scientists and scholars who seek to periodize the Anthropocene in 1610, 1784, 1800, or 1950, Elizabeth DeLoughrey (2019, 8) argues, rarely think of these dates in relation to one another. Extending her argument further, we might rethink the origin stories of the Anthropocene – European conquest, genocide, slavery, militarization, extraction, steam, industrialization, and acceleration – as key historical moments in a longer arc of planetary destruction that can be visibly connected through maritime movements and struggles over imperial control.

Today, ships remain responsible for the destruction of the planet. Oceangoing vessels have altered the seas through carbon emissions and other pollutants. By following fish further and further into the high seas, fishing vessels have dramatically impacted the migratory patterns of marine species (Telesca, 2020). When the ship – as an imperial, legal, and technological form – is centered in origin stories of climate catastrophe, alternative histories of climate catastrophe become visible. The moving ship serves as a potent reminder that the international law of the sea that Grotius formalized in *Mare Liberum* remains deeply implicated in the destruction of the planet.

## Acknowledgments

Many thanks to Peter Burdon and James Martel for inviting me to contribute to this volume. I am especially grateful to Antoinette Burton, Sam Frost, James Martel, Surabhi Ranganathan, and Mikki Stelder for the care with which they read earlier drafts and for pushing me to clarify and refine my arguments.

## References

Alaimo, S. (2020) 'Afterword: Adequate Imaginaries for Anthropocene Seas', in I. Braverman and E.R. Johnson (eds.), *Blue Legalities: The Life and Laws of the Sea*. Durham: Duke University Press, pp. 311–325.

Alexandrowicz, C.H. (1967) *An Introduction to the History of the Law of Nations in the East Indies (16th, 17th, and 18th Centuries)*. Oxford: Clarendon Scholarship.

Anand, R.P. (1977) 'Winds of Change in the Law of the Sea', *International Studies*, 16(2), pp. 207–226.

Anand, R.P. (1982) *Origin and Development of the Law of the Sea*. Leiden: Brill.

Armitage, D. (2000) *The Ideological Origins of the British Empire*. Cambridge: Cambridge University Press.

Armitage, D. (2004) 'Introduction', in D. Armitage (ed.), *The Free Sea, Hugo Grotius*. Indianapolis: Liberty Fund, pp. xi–xx.

Bellamy Foster, J., Holleman, H., and Clark, B. (2019) 'Imperialism in the Anthropocene', *Monthly Review*, July 2019, pp. 70–88. doi:10.14452/MR-071-03-2019-07_5.

Benton, L. (2009) *A Search for Sovereignty: Law and Geography in European Empires, 1400–1900*. Cambridge: Cambridge University Press.

Benton, L. and Ford, L. (2016) *The Rage for Order: The British Empire and the Origins of International Law*. Cambridge: Harvard University Press.

Benton, L. and Straumann, B. (2010) 'Acquiring Empire by Law: From Roman Doctrine to Early Modern Practice', *Law and History Review*, 28(1), pp. 1–38.

Bolster, W.J. (2012) *The Mortal Sea: Fishing the Atlantic in the Age of Sail*. Cambridge: Harvard, Belknap Press.

Borschberg, P. (2002) 'The Seizure of the Sta. Catarina Revisited: The Portuguese Empire in Asia, VOC Politics and the Origins of the Dutch-Johor Alliance (1602-c.1616)', *Journal of Southeast Asian Studies*, 33(1), pp. 31–62.

Borschberg, P. (2009) 'Grotius, Intra-Asian Trade and the Portuguese Estado Da India Problems', in H.W. Blom (ed.), *Property, Piracy and Punishment: Hugo Grotius on War and Booty in De Jure Praedae – Concepts and Contexts*. Leiden: Brill, pp. 31–60.

Campling, L. and Colas, A. (2021) *Capitalism and the Sea: The Maritime Factor in the Making of the Modern World*. New York: Verso.

Chatterjee, E. (2020) 'The Asian Anthropocene: Electricity and Fossil Developmentalism', *The Journal of Asian Studies*, 79(1), pp. 3–24.

Crutzen, P.J. (2000) 'Geology of Mankind', *Nature*, 415(6867), p. 23. doi:10.1038/415023a.

Crutzen, P.J. (2006) 'The Anthropocene', in E. Ehlers and T. Krafft (ed.), *Earth System Science in the Anthropocene*. Berlin: Springer, pp. 13–18.

Crutzen, P.J. and Stoermer, E.F. (2000) 'The Anthropocene', *IGBP Newsletter*, 41(May), pp. 17–18. doi:10.1007/978-3-030-82202-6_2.

Davis, H. and Todd, Z. (2017) 'On the Importance of a Date, or, Decolonizing the Anthropocene', *ACME: An International Journal for Critical Geographers*, 16(4), pp. 761–780.

De Repentigny, P.C. (2020) 'To the Anthropocene and Beyond: The Responsibility of Law in Decimating and Protecting Marine Life', *Transnational Legal Theory*, 11(1–2), pp. 180–196.

DeLoughrey, E.M. (2017) 'Submarine Futures of the Anthropocene', *Comparative Literature*, 69(1), pp. 32–44.

DeLoughrey, E.M. (2019) *Allegories of the Anthropocene*. Durham: Duke University Press.

Esmeir, S. (2017) 'Bandung: Reflections on the Sea, the World, and Colonialism', in L. Eslava, M. Fakhri, and V. Nesiah (eds.), *Bandung, Global History, and International Law*. Cambridge: Cambridge University Press, pp. 81–94.

Fulton, T.W. (1911) *The Sovereignty of the Sea*. Edinburgh: W. Blackwood.

Ghosh, A. (2016) *The Great Derangement: Climate Change and the Unthinkable*. Chicago: University of Chicago Press.

Grotius, H. (2004) 'The Free Sea', in D. Armitage (ed.), *The Free Sea, Hugo Grotius*. pp. 2–62, Indianapolis: Liberty Fund.

Grotius, H. (2006) *Commentary on the Law of Prize and Booty*. Indianapolis: Liberty Fund.

Gumplova, P. (2021) 'Rights of Conquest, Discovery and Occupation, and the Freedom of the Seas: A Genealogy of Natural Resource Injustice', *Isonomía – Revista de Teoría y Filosofía del Derecho*, 54, pp. 1–36.

Harrould-Kolieb, E. (2008) *Shipping Impacts on Climate Change: A Source with Solutions*. Available at https://www.cleanshipping.org/download/Oceana_Shipping_Report1.pdf (Accessed: 1 March 2021).

Hasty, W. and Peters, K. (2012) 'The Ship in Geography and the Geography of Ships', *Geography Compass*, 6(11), pp. 660–676.

Hofmeyr, I. and Lavery, C. (2020) 'Exploring the Indian Ocean as a Rich Archive of History – Above and Below the Waterline', *The Conversation*, 7 June 2020. Available at: https://theconversation.com/exploring-the-indian-ocean-as-a-rich-archive-of-history-above-and-below-the-water-line-133817 (Accessed: 3 March 2021).

Jones, S. (2011) 'The Poetic Ocean in *Mare Liberum*', in O. Ben-Dor (ed.), *Law and Art: Justice, Ethics and Aesthetics*. Oxon: Routledge, pp. 188–203.

Khalili, L. (2020) *Sinews of War and Trade: Shipping and Capitalism in the Arabian Peninsula*. New York: Verso Books.

Khalilieh, H. (2019) *Islamic Law of the Sea: Freedom of Navigation and Passage Rights in Islamic Thought*. Cambridge: Cambridge University Press.

Lewis, S.L. and Maslin, M.A. (2015) 'Defining the Anthropocene', *Nature*, 519(7542), pp. 171–180.

Mawani, R. (2016) 'Law, Settler Colonialism, and the "Forgotten Space" of Maritime Worlds', *Annual Review of Law and Social Science*, 12(1), pp. 107–131.

Mawani, R. (2018) *Across Oceans of Law: The Komagata Maru and Jurisdiction in the Time of Empire*. Durham: Duke University Press.

Mawani, R. (2022a) 'Oceans as Method: Law, Violence, and Climate Catastrophe', *The Funambulist*, 39, pp. 16–18.

Mawani, R. (2022b) 'The Ship, the Slave, the Legal Person', *Studies in Law, Politics, and Society*, 87B, pp. 19–42 (forthcoming).

Mawani, R. and Hussin, I. (2014) 'The Travels of Law: Indian Ocean Itineraries: Introduction', *Law and History Review*, 32(4), pp. 733–747.

Mawani, R. and Prange, S. (2021) 'Unruly Oceans: Law, Violence, and Sovereignty at Sea', *TWAILR*. Available at: https://twailr.com/unruly-oceans-law-violence-and-sovereignty-at-sea/ (Accessed: 12 April 2021).

McClintock, A. (2020) 'Monster: A Fugue in Fire and Ice', *e-Flux Architecture*. Available at: https://www.e-flux.com/architecture/oceans/331865/monster-a-fugue-in-fire-and-ice/ (Accessed: 12 March 2021).

Meyers, H. (1967) *The Nationality of Ships*. The Hague: Martinus Nijhoff.

Mirzoeff, N. (2014) 'Visualizing the Anthropocene', *Public Culture*, 26(2), pp. 213–232.

Moore, J.W. (2017) 'The Capitalocene, Part I: On the Nature and Origins of Our Ecological Crisis', *Journal of Peasant Studies*, 44(3), pp. 594–630.

Muldoon, J. (2016) 'Who Owns the Sea?' in B. Klein (ed.), *Fictions of the Sea: Critical Perspectives on the Ocean in British Literature and Culture*. London: Routledge, pp. 13–27.

Porras, I. (2014) 'Appropriating Nature: Commerce, Property, and the Commodification of Nature in the Law of Nations', *Leiden Journal of International Law*, 27(3), pp. 641–660.

Ranganathan, S. (2019) 'Ocean Floor Grab: International Law and the Making of an Extractive Imaginary', *European Journal of International Law*, 30(2), pp. 573–600.

Ranganathan, S. (2020) 'Visualizing Clime and Loss: The Law of the Sea', *Visualizing Climate and Loss*. Available at: https://histecon.fas.harvard.edu/climate-loss/lawofthesea/lawofthesea.html (Accessed: 3 June 2021).

Rediker, M.2008) *The Slave Ship: A Human History*. New York: Penguin Books.

Reiser, A. (2020) 'Clupea Liberum: Hugo Grotius, Free Seas, and the Political Biology of Herring', in I. Braverman and E.R. Johnson (eds.), *Blue Legalities: The Life and Laws of the Sea*. Durham: Duke University Press, pp. 201–218.
Siegert, B. (2015) *Cultural Techniques: Grids, Filters, Doors, and other Articulations of the Real*. Trans. G. Winthrop-Young. New York: Fordham University Press.
Simpson, M. (2020) 'The Anthropocene as Colonial Discourse', *Environment and Planning. Part D*, 38(1), pp. 50–71.
Stelder, M. (2021) 'The Colonial Difference in Hugo Grotius: Rational Man, Slavery, and Indigenous Dispossession', *Postcolonial Studies*, 25(4), pp. 1–20.
Telesca, J. (2020) *Red Gold: The Managed Extinction of the Giant Bluefin Tuna*. Minneapolis: University of Minnesota Press.
van Ittersum, M. (2009) 'Preparing Mare Liberum for the Press: Hugo Grotius' Rewriting of Chapter 12 of de Iure Praedae in November-December 1608', in H. Blom (ed.), *Property, Piracy and Punishment: Hugo Grotius on War and Booty in De Iure Praedae*. Leiden: Brill, pp. 246–280.
van Ittersum, M.J. (2006a) *Profit and Principle: Hugo Grotius, Natural Rights Theories and the Rise of Dutch Power in the East Indies, 1595–1615*. Leiden: Brill.
van Ittersum, M.J. (2006b) 'Mare Liberum versus the Propriety of the Seas? The Debate between Hugo Grotius (1583–1645) and William Welwod (1552–1624) and Its Impact on Anglo-Scotto-Dutch Fishery Disputes in the Second Decade of the Seventeenth Century', *Edinburgh Law Review*, 10(2), pp. 239–276.
van Ittersum, M.J. (2010) 'The Long Goodbye: Hugo Grotius's Justification of Dutch Expansion Overseas, 1615–1645', *History of European Ideas*, 36(4), pp. 386–411.
van Ittersum, M.J. (2016) 'Hugo Grotius: The Making of a Founding Father of International Law', in A. Orford and F. Hoffman (eds.), *The Oxford Handbook of the Theory of International Law*. doi:10.1093/law/9780198701958.003.0005.
Verges, F. (2017) 'Racial Capitalocene', in G.T. Johnson and A. Lubin (eds.), *Futures of Black Radicalism*. New York: Verso.
Vidas, D. (2011) 'The Anthropocene and the International Law of the Sea', *Philosophical Transactions of the Royal Society*, 369(1938), pp. 909–925.
Welwod, W. (2008) 'Of the Community and Propriety of the Seas', in D. Armitage (ed.), *The Free Sea, Hugo Grotius*. Indianapolis: Liberty Fund.
Wynter, S. (2003) 'Unsettling the Coloniality of Being/Power/Truth? Freedom: Towards the Human, After Man, Its Overrepresentation: An Argument', *CR: The New Centennial Review*, 3(3), pp. 257–337.
Yusoff, K. (2019). *A Billion Black Anthropocenes or None*. Minneapolis: University of Minnesota Press.
Zalasiewicz, J., C.N. Wters, E.C. Ellis, M.J. Head, D. Vidas, W. Steffen, J.A. Thomas, E. Horn, C.P., Summerhayes, R. Leinfelder, J.R. McNeill, A. Glauszka, M. Williams, A.D. Barnosky, D. de B. Richter, P.L. Gibbard, J. Syvitski, C. Jeandel, A. Caerretam A.B. Cundy, I.J. Fairchild, N.L. Rose, J.A. Ivar do Sul, W. Shotyk, S. Turner, M. Wagreich, J. Zinke (2021) 'The Anthropocene: Comparing Its Meaning in Geology (Chronostriatigrapy) with Conceptual Approaches Arising in Other Disciplines', *Earth's Future*, 9(3), pp. 1–25.

# 9

# OCEAN ACIDIFICATION AND THE ANTHROPOCENE

## An Emergency Response

*Prue Taylor*

Social science literature on the Anthropocene and Earth system science often uses climate change as the poster child. The purpose of this chapter is to expose its lesser-known "evil twin" – ocean acidification – and to reconsider human responses to this and other existential risks of our making. It begins by providing an overview of the current science, which is evolving rapidly. Ocean acidification is primarily caused by the interaction between anthropogenic $Co_2$ emissions in the atmosphere and seawater. Acidification is a significant compounding threat to already weakened ocean ecological integrity. However, it has also become a cause of positive (climate) feedback loops. These feedback loops threaten to drive further climate change beyond the 1.5–2.0°C temperature targets of the Paris Agreement.

Despite this "reality," a survey of current governance and legal regimes in this chapter reveals an alarming systems failure. The $CO_2$ emissions reduction levels required under the international climate regime do not account for acidification of the ocean and associated positive climate feedbacks. Emissions reduction levels are determined solely by the global atmospheric temperature targets. Furthermore, the ocean is still conceived of as an available "sink" for $CO_2$ emissions in efforts to offset continuing emissions from source. This is so despite the fact that rising acidification levels signal that a limit has already been reached or exceeded. In short, our climate change regime fails to integrate the critical role of the ocean in maintaining an Earth system conducive to supporting life, as we currently know it. In addition, no other governance or legal regime has emerged or adapted to address ocean acidification. Proposed solutions predominantly treat the matter as another governance and regulatory "gap" to be filled by an existing or new multilateral environmental instrument.

It is against this scientific and legal background that this chapter then uses the framing of the Anthropocene (and the Earth system science that underpins it) to reconsider how humanity might respond in ways that go far beyond palliative care for the "environment" (e.g. pollution control via mitigation and adaptive management) and directly address humanity's relationship with the whole Earth system. In taking this approach, this chapter does not attempt to develop a legal response to ocean acidification consistent with an emerging juridical framework and set of objectives for *Lex Anthropocenae* (Anthropocene law) or Earth system law. It does, however, provide a brief overview of these valuable developments. Rather, this chapter proposes that the endeavor of Anthropocene law may become the vessel

 DOI: 10.4324/9781003388081-12

of human hubris if it is not preceded by much deeper human reflection, action, and observation. Accordingly, a question is posed: does the Anthropocene and Earth system science now require humanity to first "stop the harm" by stepping back in radical ways to give ocean ecological systems the opportunity to recover and (possibly) maintain their integrity? This should not be confused with re-wilding or active human efforts of ecosystem restoration or marine protection and conservation. It is much more fundamental. It is an emergency closure of the ocean requiring humanity to "get out of the way" or "give space to nature" so that complex ocean evolutionary and biogeochemical processes can continue with significantly reduced anthropogenic stressors. Are we brave enough to consider this action as part of what is needed to live in the Anthropocene?

Before proceeding, it is important to clarify how this chapter understands and uses the Anthropocene concept. While in many respects a contested concept, it also reflects an emerging view that planet Earth has entered a new geological epoch. The point of departure is the argument made by Hamilton and Grinevald: this new epoch is not one characterized by progressive degrading human impacts on the surrounding environment. The Anthropocene responds to the observations of Earth system science; the Earth is a whole complex system that humanity is now disrupting in sudden, dangerous, and irreversible ways (Hamilton and Grinevald 2015). Some have referred to the paradigm-changing observations of Earth system science as the second Copernican revolution (Angus 2016). In Hamilton and Grinevald's view, properly understood, the Anthropocene describes a "radical rupture" with all previous ideas of human and planetary evolution. It stands as a rebuke and challenge to our current "serious underestimation and mischaracterization of the kind of human response necessary to slow its onset or ameliorate its impacts" (Hamilton and Grinevald 2015, 67).

In addition to the above understanding of the Anthropocene, this chapter also proceeds on the basis that we are now in a "planetary emergency." In a recent article on climate change tipping points, Rockström et al. argue that Earth system tipping points (abrupt and irreversible changes in the climate system and biosphere) are dangerously close to happening now and at temperature thresholds much lower than previously anticipated (i.e. at 1.0 to 2.0°C) (Rockström et al. 2019). The risks of tipping points are extremely high; they can trigger abrupt carbon dioxide release into the atmosphere, amplifying climate change and significantly reducing remaining emissions budgets. They can also trigger irreversible global cascades or interrelated Earth system tipping points. The authors outline examples of this global cascade beginning to occur now, driven by Arctic sea-ice melt, and argue further that the situation is urgent as our intervention time is now at zero because our reaction time is still set at around 30 years – i.e. the 2050 net zero target under the Paris Agreement (Rockström et al. 2019, 594). They conclude: "we are in a state of planetary emergency: both the risk and urgency of the situation are acute" (Rockström et al. 2019, 595) and argue that we need a change of approach – an emergency response – an essential argument of planetary emergency which has recently been reinforced by evidence that the global average temperature is already at 1.2°C, with a one in five chance of reaching 1.5°C by 2025 (WMO 2020 State of the Global Climate Report 2021, 2).

The author acknowledges that in some later writing on the Anthropocene, Hamilton suggests we may already have gone beyond a point at which any human responses could potentially "slow or ameliorate" its impacts (Hamilton 2017). Whereas Rockström et al. argue that we may have lost control of whether tipping points happen, but emergency responses *could* (not *will*) slow the rate at which damage accumulates and therefore lessen the risks (Rockström et al. 2019, 595). Either way, we need at least to begin by acknowledging a present state of planetary emergency. This state demands that we think and act in radically different ways. Emergency responses adopted now create the potential for a positive impact on the Earth system's trajectory.

## The Evolving Science: More than a Threat to Ocean Ecosystems – An Emerging Threat to the Climate System

Ocean acidification has been referred to as the "evil twin" of climate change (Cooke and Kim 2018, 67). This is because, like climate change, it is an adverse repercussion of excessive atmospheric $CO_2$ emissions. While related to climate change in this way, it is important to distinguish ocean acidification as a unique issue. Ocean acidification hides in plain sight because it is often incorrectly treated as a consequence of a changing climate. This is problematic because it shifts focus to managing or adapting to acidification as an impact of climate change on ocean life, and away from directly addressing the root cause of acidification being excessive anthropogenic $CO_2$ emissions. Emerging science suggests that acidification is more than a threat to ocean ecosystems; it can drive further climate change through positive (climate) feedback loops, disrupting the Earth system. These concerns have motivated increasing calls for ocean acidification to be used as an additional threshold for determining emissions reduction levels (Steinacher, Joos, and Stocker 2013, 200). If used in addition to global atmospheric temperatures, global emissions reductions would need to increase in magnitude.

The acidification process is relatively simple. When $CO_2$ dissolves at the ocean's surface, it forms carbonic acid which reduces pH levels, acidifying the ocean (IPCC 2019, 218). The ocean rapidly absorbs approximately one-third of anthropogenic $CO_2$, which has resulted in a 26 percent increase in ocean acidity since pre-industrial times (IPCC 2019, 83). The Intergovernmental Panel on Climate Change (IPCC) has stated that acidification will continue to worsen under most emissions scenarios (specifically, emissions scenarios ranging between RPC 2.6 and 8.5) and that it is irreversible on human time scales (IPCC 2019, 452, 76). The most recent WMO 2020 Climate Report identifies a steady increase in ocean acidification, with current $CO_2$ emissions at nearly 415 parts per million (ppm) and rising (WMO 2020 State of the Climate Report 2021, 6).

There are numerous negative consequences that arise from ocean acidification, which can cascade to reduce resilience across all ocean ecosystems and flow on to affect human systems (IPCC 2019, 624). To date, the direct ecological effects receive the most attention in ocean science and governance contexts. These include coral reef degradation, reduced calcification, increased bioerosion, and the expansion of hypoxic zones, among other wide-ranging impacts on ocean ecosystems and their inhabitants (IPCC 2019, 496, 498, 494). These consequences affect human communities in numerous ways including negatively impacting the seafood industry, reducing the nutritional value of seafood, and decreasing the resilience of low-lying coastal communities (IPCC 2019, 512, 383).

However, other potentially dire consequences of acidification are the positive feedback loops which can affect the climate system by driving further temperature increases.[1] To date, these aspects of acidification have received much less attention. There are multiple processes through which this occurs. First, acidification of the ocean reduces its ability to sequester $CO_2$ (Gehlen et al. 2011, 230–231). An important element of oceanic carbon sequestration is the transportation of carbon from the near-surface to the deep ocean (Gehlen et al. 2011, 233). This process is controlled by three "pumps" – the solubility pump, the carbonate pump, and the soft tissue pump – all of which are affected by the changes in the ocean's chemistry and environmental conditions caused by acidification (Gehlen et al. 2011, 233). Reducing the efficiency of these three pumps decreases the ability of the ocean to sequester $CO_2$ which could create significant positive feedback on climate change as levels of ocean acidification increase.

A second kind of positive feedback occurs through the reduction of atmospheric sulfur. Marine emissions of dimethylsulphide (DMS) are the largest natural source of atmospheric sulfur (Walsh 2013). As the ocean becomes more acidic, marine production of DMS is reduced (Six et al. 2013, 975). This is a problem because DMS reduces the amount of solar energy that reaches the Earth's surface, thus mitigating climate change. In the atmosphere, DMS reacts to form gaseous sulfuric acid which can increase cloud albedo (reflectivity) and longevity (Six et al. 2013, 975). Changes in rates of marine DMS emissions can therefore increase the amount of solar radiation reaching the Earth's surface, exacerbating climate change. Simulations have suggested a 50 percent decrease in DMS could result in a mean surface temperature net increase of 1.6°C (Gehlen et al. 2011, 244).

A third positive feedback results from oxygen denitrification and nitrous oxide production. Ocean acidification reduces $O_2$ levels, extending oxygen minimum zones (Gehlen et al. 2011, 240). In these zones, a process of denitrification creates nitrous oxide ($N_2O$), a potent greenhouse gas (Gehlen et al. 2011, 240). Most $N_2O$ produced in the ocean is released into the atmosphere, meaning that an increase in the marine production of $N_2O$ exacerbates climate change (Gehlen et al. 2011, 244). While simulation has not yet been undertaken, it has been postulated that oceanic $N_2O$ emissions could double as a result of ocean acidification (Gehlen et al. 2011, 244).

Another greenhouse gas affected by ocean acidification is ozone ($O_3$). Ocean acidification induces shifts in plankton communities, which reduces the marine production of iodocarbons (Hopkins, Nightingale, and Liss 2011, 222). A reduction in iodocarbons (together with other processes) inhibits the depletion of $O_3$ in the troposphere. This is problematic as tropospheric $O_3$ is another potent greenhouse gas (Hopkins, Nightingale, and Less 2011, 223).

A final kind of positive feedback on climate change is caused by the threat posed to vegetated coastal ecosystems, which play an important role in storing sequestered carbon. The combined processes of ocean warming and acidification can negatively impact upon these ecosystems. The projected loss of these habitats would both inhibit $CO_2$ uptake *and* release carbon previously stored, worsening climate change (IPCC 2019, 508).

Scientists are beginning to signal that using ocean acidification as a threshold to determine $CO_2$ emissions reduction requirements (in addition to the existing temperature targets) would result in more stringent obligations. The severity of acidification, along with the long-lasting damage it causes, demands that emissions are reduced both drastically and urgently (Pelejero, Calvo, and Hoegh-Guldberg 2010, 334). Gattuso et al. (2011, 301) note the acceptable limit of atmospheric $CO_2$ concentration to control ocean acidification is between 350 ppm and 450 ppm. This is significant because current concentrations now exceed 410 ppm and have been increasing by approximately 20 ppm per decade since 2000 (Lindsey 2020; IPCC 2018, 54). A 2013 study by Steinacher, Joos, and Stocker took an Earth system approach and determined that temperature-based targets for $CO_2$ emissions are insufficient to control other variables such as ocean acidification (Steinacher, Joos, and Stocker 2013, 197). Using targets associated with two indicators of ocean acidification, four scenarios were run with each yielding significantly lower emissions thresholds than corresponding temperature targets (Steinacher, Joos, and Stocker 2013, 199). This study was referenced in the IPCC's 2019 Special Report on the Ocean and Cryosphere to support the claim that pH-associated thresholds have implications for the modeling of emission-reducing scenarios (IPCC 2019, 542). These findings show that current reductions are insufficient, and using acidification as a threshold would require more drastic reductions.

Ocean acidification also limits the ability to use ocean processes and natural systems as a sink to "net out" emissions. There is no way to stop the ocean from absorbing $CO_2$, meaning it will continue to become more acidic until atmospheric concentrations reduce *and* pH levels stabilize to pre-industrial levels. This may take thousands of years to happen, so emissions must first and foremost be reduced at their source. Many policy responses to soaring $CO_2$ emissions include net targets that allow states to rely on short-term natural carbon sequestration to meet their obligations. This is apparent in numerous nationally determined contributions (NDCs) under the Paris Agreement. For example, a 2017 survey of NDCs found that 27 included blue-carbon mitigations, with countries including measures to enhance and protect marine ecosystems to enable oceanic carbon storage (Gallo, Victor, and Levin 2017, 835). While the role of ecosystems as carbon sinks is important, their use (through protection, restoration, and enhancement) should be treated as additional to urgent and substantial emissions reductions at source and not as a substitute for "real" emissions reductions (Skelton et al. 2020).[2]

Several technical responses to ocean acidification have been offered, including ocean fertilization and artificial ocean alkalinization. Ocean fertilization can artificially increase the ocean's primary production, subsequently increasing carbon uptake by phytoplankton (Cao and Caldeira 2010, 304). This approach has limited feasibility because while it would de-acidify the surface to some extent, it would lead to greater acidification of the deep ocean (Cao and Caldeira 2010, 310). Another potential geoengineering solution is artificial ocean alkalinization, which has been favored for its long duration of effectiveness (Burns and Corbett 2020, 154). Artificial alkalinization involves adding highly reactive lime or calcium hydroxide to the ocean surface, or injecting it into deep seawater currents, or manufacturing alkalinity at sea using marine energy sources (Burns and Corbett 2020, 154). Scientific understandings of this response are in their infancy, and there are risks such as the inhibition of photosynthesis in phytoplankton communities, making the ocean more alkaline than in pre-industrial times, and the introduction of toxic heavy metals (Burns and Corbett 2020, 155). Given the significant risks associated with these geoengineering approaches, they have largely been prevented through provisions in the UN Convention on Biological Diversity (CBD) and the 1996 Protocol to the London Convention (Fennel and VanderZwaag 2016).

Put simply, as atmospheric $CO_2$ emissions go up, ocean acidification increases. This harms already degraded ocean ecosystems, but science now tells us that it can also drive further climate change through feedbacks. Combined, this damage to the Earth's biogeochemical system is rapidly bringing us closer to critical and irreversible planetary tipping points. Acidification is the symptom. The root cause needs to be addressed by reductions in $CO_2$ emissions at source that are both more ambitious and urgent than those currently required by temperature targets under the Paris Agreement. These additional reductions need to account for both the harm to already seriously degraded ocean ecosystems[3] and the potential positive climate feedbacks. Using the ocean and other natural systems as a carbon sink and reservoir should not be a substitute for emissions reductions at source. In addition, we must address how to protect ocean ecosystems from the degradation already caused.

## The Current Law and the Governance Gap

Despite the emerging science, ocean acidification is notably absent from current environmental governance regimes. Existing ocean protections still emphasize direct human overexploitation, with minimal provision made for more diffuse or systemic threats such as acidification (Mendenhall 2019, 40). International legal frameworks currently fail to adequately address ocean-related climate change issues, with informal and fragmented connections between the ocean and climate regimes (IPCC 2019, 541; Makomere and Mbeva 2019). This has resulted in substantial governance gaps. There is no single unifying instrument relating to ocean acidification, and it does not fit neatly within any other existing regime (IPCC 2019, 542). Despite being characterized as a treaty creating a sound legal framework for ocean protection, the United

Nations Convention on the Law of the Sea (UNCLOS) does not specifically mention acidification (Harrison 2017, 304). The Paris Agreement also does not mention ocean acidification, and it receives little attention from United Nations Framework Convention on Climate Change (UNFCCC) discussions more generally (IPCC 2019, 542). Some potential controls on ocean acidification appear in marine pollution control instruments, such as the 1996 Protocol to the London Convention, the International Convention for the Prevention of Pollution from Ships (MARPOL), and the Global Programme of Action for the Protection of the Marine Environment from Land-Based Activities, but these are limited and largely ineffective (Fennel and VanderZwaag 2016, 352–353). MARPOL, for example, addresses $CO_2$ emissions from ships, but only in part, and potential measures to further limit emissions have been controversial (Fennel and VanderZwaag 2016, 352). The CBD highlights the need for taking adaptive measures to counter acidification, expressly mentioning it in Aichi Target 10 regarding the minimization of anthropogenic pressures on vulnerable ecosystems (Fennel and VanderZwaag 2016, 353).

Although general climate change mitigation and adaptation actions often apply to ocean acidification by implication, as the IPCC recently highlighted, acidification poses unique issues that need to be directly addressed (IPCC 2019, 542). For the reasons outlined below, this has not yet happened.

## Reasons for the Existence of the Governance Gap

A multitude of factors have been identified as contributing to the so-called governance gap. Some of the most prominent are: the technical distinction between ocean acidification and climate change; the risk of politicization; the nature of the issue; regime complexity; and a belief in miracles.

International environmental law has focused extensively on climate change issues, but as acidification is a distinct issue, it is not included within these regimes. This means that important regimes, such as the UNFCCC, do not view acidification as being within their jurisdiction (IPCC 2019, 542). Furthermore, climate change regimes often promote the idea of using the ocean as sinks and reservoirs of greenhouse gases, including $CO_2$ (Fennel and VanderZwaag 2016, 350). As seen above, rising acidification significantly limits the ability to use the ocean as a carbon sink, and this may be a reason for its limited inclusion within the climate change regime.

Second, intimately connecting ocean acidification with climate change policy has been warned against by some public perception studies. These studies have emphasized the risk of polarizing values-based attitudes (e.g. pro- versus anti-climate change) reducing the influence of scientific knowledge (Harrould-Kollieb 2019, 1226; Cooke and Kim 2018, 70–71; Capstick et al. 2016, 766). In the US, separating ocean acidification from climate change is thought to have led to domestic acidification policies successfully overcoming partisan politics (Harrould-Kollieb 2019, 1226).

Third, the nature of the acidification issue itself contributes to the governance gap. Ocean acidification is a complex problem that has not been researched as extensively as other environmental problems such as climate change. This means there is a deficit of knowledge and awareness regarding the extent and scope of acidification, and possible responses. Ocean acidification only provides minimal opportunities for natural systems to adapt and there is a lack of effective technological solutions (Baird, Simons, and Stephens 2009, 462). Unlike climate change, where there is the ability to mitigate and adapt, ocean acidification can only be addressed by reducing $CO_2$ emissions (Baird, Simons, and Stephens 2009, 462). The limited options to address acidification and the intensity of response required to reduce $CO_2$ emissions at source reduces political will to tackle the problem. It can appear to be too difficult to resolve, particularly given our current inability to halt emissions and associated increases in global atmospheric temperatures.

Fourth, the regime complexity of environmental governance must take a portion of the blame. International law's response to environmental issues typically develops in an issue-specific way which can lead to fragmented policy approaches (Baird, Simons, and Stephens 2009, 463; Harris 2019, 441). Due to this complexity, some commentators consider it unlikely a new regime to address acidification specifically will receive political support (Baird, Simons, and Stephens 2009, 471). This reality has led to suggestions that addressing ocean acidification must be done via reference to a variety of existing regimes (such as climate regimes, marine pollution regimes, and biodiversity conservation regimes) (Baird, Simons, and Stephens 2009, 463–470).

Finally, a great deal of general environmental political inaction is due to a lack of belief in the existence or seriousness of issues (Harris 2019, 442). This blissful ignorance enables political leaders to turn a blind eye to the realities of environmental degradation in the hope that it will all work itself out. As Harris states: "One is tempted to hope for a miracle that will magically make all of these impacts, and so many others, go away, or for these impacts to be a figment of the collective imagination" (Harris 2019, 443).

Ultimately, many factors are contributing to the existence of the governance gap. Despite this current reality, there are some signs of emerging attention being paid to the issue of acidification as a unique and significant cause for concern.

## Emerging Attention

Recent decades have seen a rapid expansion of scientific exploration on ocean acidification, with a 15-fold increase between 2004 and 2012 (Fennel and VanderZwaag 2016, 342). Concerns have also been raised through a range of international science and governance structures such as the IPCC, UNCLOS, the CBD, the United Nations Environment Programme, and the Intergovernmental Oceanographic Commission of UNESCO (IPCC 2019, 542). The UNFCCC COP25 (or Blue COP) decision document acknowledges the climate–ocean nexus and recognizes connections between climate change and oceans (COP 2019, paragraph 29). The most recent UN General Assembly resolution on the Oceans and the Law of the Sea expressed serious concern regarding climate change and acidification, stressing the urgent need for action (UNGA 2019, preamble).[4] Increasing attention is also evidenced by the growing discourse on the law and governance of acidification over the last decade.

Despite these signs, the international community of states has not responded. As of 2017, only 14 NDCs included any reference to acidification (Gallo et al. 2017) (these NDCs reference acidification as an additional stressor to ocean systems resulting from $CO_2$ emissions). Ocean acidification remains hidden in plain sight. It seems that we are in a similar place today with acidification as we were some 30 years ago with climate change. However, a big difference is this – we no longer have time for incremental responses. Yet, as will be seen below, the proposed responses are all predicated on an assumption that we do.

## Some Proposed Responses

Fennel and VanderZwaag have stated:

> One thing is clear about the future regulation of human activities that contribute to ocean acidification and the degradation of marine ecosystems. It will remain a work in progress for decades to come. Mitigation not adaptation must be the global mantra. The work has hardly begun.
>
> *(Fennel and VanderZwaag 2016, 356)*

A broad range of solutions have been offered in response to the governance gap. General consensus supports an increased focus on the marine–climate nexus, and aligning ocean and climate regimes across jurisdictions (Fidelman 2019, 279, 282; Makomere and Mbeva 2019; IPCC 2019, 542). Some have suggested the establishment of a novel mechanism for acidification. It has been argued that this is desirable due to the shortfalls of the current polycentric order of acidification governance and that acidification necessitates a clear and direct intervention (Kim 2012, 258). Despite these suggestions, the IPCC (2019, 542) has noted that this approach is not widely supported and requires political will that is currently scarce.

Other commentators have suggested adapting existing regimes to better accommodate ocean acidification. Telesetsky explores the use of UNCLOS as a potential mechanism for the regulation of ocean–climate relations. Although UNCLOS does not specifically mention climate change, according to Telesetsky the text's definition of marine pollution could be interpreted to strengthen states' strategies for climate mitigation and adaptation (Telesetsky 2019, 325–327).

Another suggestion is to bring acidification within the work of the UNFCCC. As a pragmatic solution, the IPCC (2019, 542) has recommended enhancing UNFCCC involvement in acidification governance and increasing the utilization of environmental multilateral agreements. For example, an argument has been made that ocean acidification is an anthropogenic interference with the "climate system" which is defined under the UNFCCC as the entire atmosphere, hydrosphere, biosphere, and geosphere and respective interactions between these spheres (UNFCCC 1992, article 1.3). Ocean acidification is caused by interactions between the atmosphere and hydrosphere, affects the hydrosphere and biosphere, and impacts interactions between the atmosphere, hydrosphere, and biosphere (Harrould-Kolieb 2019, 1127). It therefore falls within a broader understanding of the UNFCCC's purpose and requires states to take it into account under their general obligations to protect the climate system (Harrould-Kolieb 2019, 1127) or by making it a central aim of the Paris Agreement (Harrould-Kolieb 2019, 1132).

Fennel and VanderZwaag favor setting $CO_2$ emissions reduction targets under the Convention that would be sufficient to address both climate change and acidification, but note the need to address it systemically across other treaties such as the CBD (Fennel and VanderZwaag 2016, 355). Other scholars argue that because the majority of the UNFCCC focuses on climate *change*, this narrows interpretations of more general references to the climate *system* to issues of global warming (Harrould-Kolieb 2019, 1128). Kim (2012, 246) argues it is inappropriate to bring ocean acidification under the framework of the Convention because it is not an effect of climate *change*. Finally, others suggest that at least the marine ecosystem impacts of acidification are now being dealt with at a local and regional level (Campbell et al. 2016, 531). Overall, the importance of taking precautionary and ecosystem-based approaches in response to acidification has been emphasized, as has the need for multi-scalar governance (UNGA 2019, paragraph 213; IPCC 2019, 540).

The recent draft text of an agreement under UNCLOS on "conservation and sustainable use of marine biological diversity of areas beyond national jurisdiction" (BBNJ) mentions ocean acidification (released 27 November 2019, United Nations, 2019). A general principle of the BBNJ is an approach that improves ecosystem resilience in the face of adverse effects of climate change and acidification and restores ecosystem integrity (article 5(h)). An objective of the marine protection and conservation mechanisms is to rehabilitate and repair biodiversity and ecosystems to increase productivity and build resilience to stressors, including those related to climate change and ocean acidification (article 14(e)). Vulnerability to ocean acidification is also identified as a criterion for determining areas requiring protection (annex I). This approach uses marine protected areas (MPAs) as an adaptation response to the ecosystem and biodiversity threat of acidification but says absolutely nothing about the cause of acidification and neither does it address the serious issue of continuing to use the ocean as a carbon sink for anthropogenic emissions. Furthermore, meaningful references to climate change and acidification are reportedly being resisted by some negotiators (De Santo et al. 2019). The serious limitations of the BBNJ text from an Earth system perspective are further considered below.

## Ocean Acidification in the Anthropocene

From the perspective of current international governance and law, ocean acidification is another problem to be "fixed" when the science, political will, and regime complexities all pull in the right direction and overcome the vain hope that it might all go away or be sufficiently addressed under the climate change regime. On the basis of the above discussion of current science and governance responses, the favored solutions include: (a) new $CO_2$ emissions reductions that account for both atmospheric warming and acidification (at some future point in time, when political will allows); (b) use of marine protection mechanisms to manage the harm already occurring by allowing ocean ecosystems to progressively adapt through minimizing other stressors; and (c) maintaining restrictions on geoengineering responses.

From the perspective of the Anthropocene and Earth system science, ocean acidification is a further manifestation of dangerous and rapid human-caused disruption to the interconnected complex Earth system itself. A disruption, which together with others (rising global atmospheric temperatures and loss of biosphere integrity), may irreversibly push the Earth system into a new state – one that does not support the existence of life as we have known it. From this perspective, to continue creating law and governance premised on "managing" our way out via traditional reactive atmospheric pollution control and adaptive environmental protection measures would represent a "serious underestimation and mischaracterization of the kind of human response necessary" (Hamilton and Grinevald 2015, 67). In short, more human complacency and hubris. We would potentially be repeating the fallacies of the past – a past that has caused what is now being identified as a systemic "planetary emergency" by scientists (Rockström et al. 2019) and global governance leaders alike (UNEP 2021).[5]

In an effort to correctly understand the problems faced and the solutions now required, the biophysical and social sciences are beginning to respond in interdisciplinary ways. A recent article surveyed social science literature to determine how the "planetary boundaries framework" has been used to help identify and frame key governance challenges (Kim and Kotzé 2020). The planetary boundaries framework emerged in 2009 (updated in 2015) as a means to translate Earth system science into a boundary-setting tool for limiting negative human impact on the Earth system (Steffen et al. 2015). It uses a set of nine specific yet interrelated planetary boundaries for key Earth system processes. If crossed, as is currently the case for at least four boundaries – including the two most important: climate change and biosphere integrity – the chance of maintaining the whole Earth system in a state that supports life (and human wellbeing) as currently known diminishes as dangerous levels and tipping points are reached. Expressed positively, the boundaries collectively create a "safe operating space" for humanity provided they are not breached. Ocean acidification is one of the planetary boundaries identified. As of 2015, we were at the limit of the safe operating space for acidification. However, this was based on keeping $CO_2$ emissions at 350 ppm (Steffen et al. 2015). As previously noted, we are now at around 415 ppm and still rising.

The literature survey identifies and discusses four related problem framings, within which many critical questions are asked. For example, under the theme of "planetary boundaries as upper ecological limits" for human activity, commentators stress this says little to nothing about the structurally embedded drivers of ecological degradation (e.g. paradigms of limitless economic growth). Furthermore, a universalized "humanity" leaves issues such as anthropocentrism, global inequality, and intra/intergenerational justice unaddressed (Kim and Kotzé 2020). Using another example, under the theme "planetary boundaries as dynamic and interdependent" is the observation that integrated and coordinated international environmental institutions need to replace fragmented regulation if we are to prevent protecting one boundary at the expense of another. Ocean acidification is a case in point because the ocean is being used as a carbon sink and reservoir (Kim and Kotzé 2020, 4). The other two themes for problem framing are: "planetary boundaries as global in scale" (focusing on the Earth system and not variations of the human environment); and "planetary boundaries as political constructs" (reflecting issues around who decides what is safe and for whom). These problem framings, and the issues they raise, will be helpful in thinking through the detail of future governance and legal responses to acidification and other Earth system threats.

More specific to this chapter, Kim and Kotzé (2020) also survey the literature for solutions to the above problem framings. These solutions broadly relate to ideas around institutionalizing, coordinating, downscaling, and democratizing the planetary boundaries. On the specific matter of governance and law, they note an emerging consensus *against* new multilateral processes/institutions for various planetary boundaries and identify more support for "building on, improving and better coordinating existing multilateral environment treaty regimes" to bolster those legal boundaries to better respond to planetary boundaries (Kim and Kotzé 2020, 6). In this author's view, Kim and Kotzé correctly observe that the challenges presented by planetary boundaries (and the Anthropocene) go far beyond solutions based on strengthening existing institutions. These challenges "question some of the most fundamental ideas in contemporary law and governance" (Kim and Kotzé 2020, 6). These include its partnership with an exploitative human-centered economic growth paradigm and state sovereignty (in particular sovereignty over natural resources) but go deeper to include its normative foundations (Kotzé et al. 2020) and failure to identify the Earth system as a legal object protected by proactive and universally applicable norms (or legal purposes).

In response to these many failures, a number of innovative legal initiatives are emerging. The Common Home of Humanity (CHH) is one example. Deeply embedded in Earth system science, it conceptualizes the Earth system as a shared global ecological commons that can be characterized as a legal object in the form of the "intangible natural heritage" of all humanity. From this perspective, "legal boundaries must translate (as accurately as possible to our always incomplete knowledge) to the physical reality of a finite world … and thereby delimit acceptable levels of human activity" (Magalhães 2021) However, this alone is insufficient, as doing less harm needs to be accompanied by a legal obligation to achieve net positive ecological benefits or outcomes. This element of CHH has the potential to challenge and potentially disrupt some of the current economic drivers of incremental but cumulative ecosystem degradation.

Returning to the work of Kim and Kotzé, their own contribution is to propose the notion of Earth system law, which they define as a "new legal paradigm that can better respond to the Earth system's complex governance challenges and is better fit for purpose in the Anthropocene" (Kim and Kotzé 2020, 11). They go on to outline four key objectives for Earth system law that can be used to help reimagine very different legal responses and to critique current governance and law (Kim and Kotzé 2020, 11–12). Again, in the context of ocean acidification, this work is potentially very valuable and helpful. Ultimately, the immediate cause of acidification is $CO_2$ emissions (a by-product of current human civilization) and we urgently need a legal means to reduce atmospheric emissions levels at source, as part of radical economic, social, and ecological change. We also need to account for current levels of acidification. However, before embarking on such a task, this chapter proceeds on the basis that we must first take more radical emergency action.

Employing the Anthropocene concept as describing a *radical rupture* with all previous ideas of human and planetary evolution, one which calls into urgent question our comprehension of complex ecosystems and evaluation of the kind of human responses necessary, this author's proposal is that we use ocean acidification to think and act in a radically different way. Specifically, a form of emergency closure of the ocean. Given the current ocean governance regime, this proposal could initially focus on "areas beyond national jurisdiction" (ABNJ), being the high seas and the deep-sea bed, or "Area" (UNCLOS, parts VII and XI). It would require strong restrictions on all forms of harmful human activity in the ABNJ including fishing, mining, oil and gas exploration, bioprospecting, and discharge of pollutants. As the vast majority of world trade is currently by ship, shipping activities on the high seas would also need to comply with strict standards to avoid ecological harm.

This emergency ocean closure could have at least two important outcomes. First, it has the potential to enable a large swathe of the ocean to recover and maintain its already threatened ecological integrity, through the removal of a whole range of additional human stressors.[6] If implemented urgently and at scale (the ABNJ comprises two-thirds of ocean space and the ocean itself comprises 70 percent of the Earth's surface), there is the potential that this action *could* (not *will*) slow the rate at which damage accumulates and therefore lessen the risks of irreversible tipping points (Rockström et al. 2019, 595). Of course, emergency closure alone will not stop acidification. This depends on reducing emissions at source and the capacity of the ocean to re-establish pH levels over time. However, emergency closure of the ocean (within the ABNJ) could be maintained pending the development of a truly innovative governance and legal response to the multiple systemic threats to ocean ecosystems and the global climate system.

A second outcome of emergency closure is that it has the potential to reset or recalibrate humanity's relationship with the ocean itself, an integral part of the Earth system. Given its nature (immediate) and magnitude, closure has the potential to thrust humanity into a new and deeper relationship with the Earth system: a relationship based on humility and respect fostering observation and reflection rather than on the traditional paradigms of sustainable use, conservation, environmental protection, and ecosystem management. It also opens the potential for humanity (as a collective global community) to change our relationship with each other from competitors for ocean resources and defenders of national interest, to holders of collective ecological responsibilities.

This proposal should not be confused with concepts of re-wilding, some of which attempt to remove invasive species and humanity from ecological systems entirely. It accepts humanity as an integral part of ecological systems and acknowledges that it is impossible (on human time scales) to remove many pre-existing anthropogenic stressors (e.g. existing acidification levels, marine heatwaves, persistent organic pollutants, and micro-plastics). However, by removing as many other human stressors as possible (within the ABNJ), the ocean is given the opportunity and space to restore its ecological integrity. Furthermore, this proposal should not be confused with the concept of marine reserves or protected areas. The purpose and scale here are very different. It does not protect selected parts of the marine environment, based on current scientific knowledge of their ecosystem diversity and range of threats, or economic and political trade-offs (Heffernan 2018). There is no choice about what is and what is not worth protecting. The purpose is to radically disrupt current human activity to enable a key component of the Earth system (the ocean) to function as part of the whole, recognizing the magnitude of the harm already done to the Earth system, the high risk of irreversible outcomes (if we fail to make an urgent emergency response), and our responsibility for these harms and risks.

Implementation of this proposal will have many difficulties, the resolution of which will be critical to the achievement of its objectives. For example, as an emergency response, it requires all states to agree to suspend the exercise of existing freedoms of the high seas and the pursuit of deep-sea mining. Given the interconnectedness of all ocean spaces and systems, emergency closure would also need to reframe the issue of adjacent jurisdictions ("adjacency") around positive ecological responsibilities, for all relevant activities conducted within national jurisdiction. Emergency closure of the ABNJ would also have to address and respond to issues around any potential to drive further inequality between states.[7] More generally, what might begin as a political response will need to find formulation in law. As Westerlund cautions, ultimately legal responses are required, as that which is not illegal is protected by the law and failure to address this can exacerbate degradation (Westerlund 2008). Furthermore, the legal concepts used must resonate with culturally and spiritually rooted human values (Gaines 2014).[8]

Of course, a fundamental observation of Earth system science is the identification of one interdependent complex system – a global ecological commons supporting and shared by all life. In this context, singling out the ocean in this way is potentially artificial and contradictory if not accompanied by ambitious means to keep within *all* planetary boundaries, recognizing their interdependence, complexity, instability, and unpredictability (Kim and Kotzé 2020). However, for the reasons outlined below, the ocean is a critical place to *begin* confronting what the Anthropocene means, the implications for all life, and how humanity must govern itself. Dramatic change here may seed a very different understanding of what is required as we confront the reality of an Earth system as a global ecological commons on the verge of abrupt, irreversible, and destructive changes.

First, as previously outlined, the ocean is pivotal to the function of other parts of the Earth system. Put simply, it is the birthplace of life on Earth and its ecological integrity and processes are critical to sustaining that life. Despite our terrestrial obsession and blindness to the significance of the ocean and ocean ecosystems, humanity occupies "planet Ocean." What we do or do not achieve here will be defining. Second, scientific reports reveal the perilous state of the ocean from the cumulative impact of multiple anthropogenic stressors (IPBES 2019). The so-called "sixth mass species extinction" includes ocean life. Third, while much of the ocean is already suffering from cumulative human stressors, we currently stand on the threshold of a whole new era of ocean exploration and exploitation due to technological developments, perceived resource needs, and threats to peace and security. This creates a critical opportunity to decide to do things very differently now before we repeat the failures of the past. This includes the opportunity to act before vested interests and geopolitical tensions manifest further. Acting now prior to new exploitation beginning would be truly precautionary, fully acknowledging our responsibility for the past and the limits of our current knowledge. Finally, if humanity can comprehensively step back from the ocean in time, then its current restorative capacity *may* (not *will*) deliver remarkable positive results (Duarte et al. 2020).

To summarize, the above section has argued that before using Earth system governance and law as a framework to respond to the multiple complexities of ocean acidification, we should first employ the concept of the Anthropocene and a state of planetary emergency to formulate a deeper and more radical human response: one which requires us to step back from ongoing negative human interference with the vast ocean system, thereby shocking or disrupting the current human–nature relationship and potentially slowing down the accumulating harm and reducing the risks of tipping points.

The potential of triggering a radical shift in human action and perception is not just a "nice to have" outcome. In the view of this author, without it, we run the risk of Earth system science (and the planetary boundaries) being used as a more sophisticated, complex, and global version of "measuring and managing" ecosystems to maintain human use. Why might this be a risk? First, our entrenched habit of utilizing ecological systems as "resources," up to their assessed maximum capacity, is deeply embedded. In this context, we continue to avoid difficult issues around human population growth, inequality, and consumption. Ecological constraints could become another version of "environmental bottom lines," distracting from the urgent need to act now by enabling ecological systems (nature) to recover, to the fullest extent possible, from existing degradation.

Second, we continue to "other" the problem of destructive human impact on ecological systems in profound ways. Put simply, in our efforts to manage the *environment* (or ecosystems or potentially planetary boundaries), we deflect from the need to manage *ourselves* and address the very essence of what it means to be a human being, including our limitations and responsibilities, in the face of what is now a planetary emergency. The concerns expressed here go much deeper than the potential of ecocentric legal framings to address and mitigate. They call into question humanity's relationship with the Earth system at this exact juncture in planetary and human evolution, when tipping points are beginning to occur. What it means to be a human in an age of planetary emergency is different from what it means to be a human in an age of ecological constraints. Is it now time for a transformation in human existence to one that *makes space for* and *enables* the flourishing of ecological systems and humanity? If so, could we begin this transformation using emergency closure of the ocean (in response to acidification) as our starting point?

As noted above, ultimately, we may need to employ Earth system governance and law to develop a truly innovative response to the multiple systemic threats to ocean ecosystems and the global climate system. The point being made here is: before doing so (as a prerequisite), the Anthropocene requires us to challenge our ability to proceed even with the benefit of developments in Earth system science, governance, and law. Simply put, as a precondition, we must ask ourselves if living within the current limits of the Earth system in a state of planetary emergency requires us to step back to the greatest extent possible enabling the greatest planetary system – the ocean – to recover. As Kim and Kotzé acknowledge, their proposals for Earth system law rely on a fundamental assumption: the Earth system has not yet reached critical tipping points. They leave the matter of how we might respond, when we do, as an open question (Kim and Kotzé 2020, 13). The proposal made here is, first and foremost, a contribution to addressing that open question – it is a response to a planetary emergency.

This chapter now turns to briefly consider this proposal in the context of current developments in ocean governance.

## Current Ocean Governance and Law – Start by Stopping!

As previously explained, the draft BBNJ treaty is the international community's current effort to address threats to ecosystems within the ABNJ while also managing ongoing human use. Its treatment of acidification is extremely limited, with no reference to its cause nor to the significant risk that current levels of acidification (combined with other stressors) put the ocean at the threshold of an irreversible tipping point. There is no sense of a planetary emergency. Acidification is treated as a gradual background environmental stressor. For example, the BBNJ's narrow purpose of "conservation and sustainable use" results in a very limited suite of traditional management measures (e.g. marine protected areas, area-based management tools, and environmental impact assessments). This is seen as evidence that negotiations are not yet grappling with complex systemic threats to the ocean including climate change and ocean acidification (De Santo et al. 2019). Perhaps more concerning is the suggestion that negotiators are intentionally keeping these systemic threats off the table and minimizing their relevance within the rubric of "cumulative impacts" (De Santo et al. 2019). As we have seen, leaving the issue of acidification to the existing climate change regime is wrong at best, and disingenuous at worst.

As regards provisions for the creation of MPAs (a tool for adaptation), the BBNJ is, in part, an attempt to create a global mechanism for the establishment of MPAs within the ABNJ. They could be used as a means for ecosystems to adapt by building resilience to acidification. The international community has made a number of commitments including specific targets to protect various percentages of ocean space or marine ecosystems. However, thus far, even the most modest targets have been missed, including Aichi Target 11 calling for the protection of 10 percent of representative coastal and marine areas by 2020.[9] Again, the negotiations are on track to deliver very little. This is because there are no ambitious targets specified for MPAs and some of the core criteria for successful MPAs (e.g. comprehensive restrictions on all commercial activities) are absent.[10] In sum, the draft BBNJ may eke out a few pockets of ocean space for nature, where rates of ecosystem decline may reduce or ecosystems adapt. In the face of urgent, irreversible, and complex systemic threats to the entire ocean system such as ocean acidification, this is woefully inadequate.

Beyond the limited confines of BBNJ negotiations, scientists are painting a much clearer picture of just how unrealistic it is to proceed in this way. For example, a 2019 coalition of scientists and Greenpeace released a blueprint for protection of 30 percent of ocean space by 2030 through the creation of a planet-wide network of fully protected marine areas (Greenpeace 2019). A number of mapping exercises have followed, some of which take a more systemic approach to the interactions between human activities, biodiversity collapse, and issues such as climate change (e.g. Sala et al. 2021). In a related development, some 50 countries have joined a high-ambition coalition pledging to protect 30 percent of the Earth's land *and* ocean by 2030 (this is known as the High Ambition Coalition). Whether these pledges will become action under the CBD umbrella is highly uncertain. However, at face value, this coalition is an acknowledgment that climate change action now requires more than emissions reductions – it also requires protection and restoration of biodiversity. In a more radical proposal, Sala et al. (2018) argue the scientific and economic feasibility and merits of governing the whole of the high seas as an MPA free of all commercial fishing. In a related context, increasing concern about a new generation of deep seabed mining has resulted in growing calls for moratoriums both within the ABNJ and national jurisdictions (e.g. the WWF initiative). Thus far, there is no indication that developments such as these will penetrate the BBNJ negotiations before their intended conclusion in 2022.

As Vidas argues, given the reality of Earth system change, breached planetary boundaries, and the current inability of international governance and law to respond, we need to mount a fundamental challenge to the "normative and institutional structures of the law of the sea" – thereby challenging international law itself. Simply continuing as we are is comparable to collective suicide, conscious or otherwise (Vidas 2011, 921). Given the significant inadequacies of the draft BBNJ, this challenge could usefully begin by mobilizing civil society and experts to reject the BBNJ negotiations in their current form on the grounds that what is politically "achievable" is no longer acceptable because it is so deficient as to be profoundly dangerous.

Admittedly this is a modest starting point, but it has the potential to disrupt the prevailing culture that something is better than nothing (since the near collapse of the 2009 climate negotiations in Copenhagen) and *any* agreement is a good agreement. At the least, this modest disruption to our complacency would (if successful) hold open an opportunity to begin the task of conceptualizing and developing Earth system governance and law, commensurate with our planetary emergency. This disruption may also give support to initiatives attempting exactly this kind of transformation, as part of the Stockholm 50+ 2022 preparations.

## Conclusion

Thirty years ago, we were confronted with the peril of climate change. Today, we stand in a similar position confronted by its "evil twin." However, fundamental differences are in play. We have less time to respond, and we are facing a planetary emergency caused in part by our ongoing failure to address climate change. In these circumstances, it is critical that we take a clear-eyed look both at this reality and at ourselves. We need to learn fast so as not to repeat our failures. The proposal of emergency closure of the ocean may not be politically feasible. But, from the perspective of our current ecological reality, it is worth serious consideration. It would be a truly precautionary response that *may* (not *will*) create the opportunity for a change of trajectory – both for the future of the Earth system and our governance and legal responses.

## Notes

1 Positive feedbacks are processes that can accelerate climate change by driving temperature increases. On the other hand, negative feedback loops can potentially help reduce climate change.
2 There are considerable uncertainties around the use of ocean ecosystems and coastal and continental shelf sea sediment for carbon sequestration. Carbon would need to be removed over very long time scales and at large scales. Given the many uncertainties, reliance on blue carbon may be overstated and difficult to verify (Williamson et al. 2021). Therefore, the priority must be to significantly reduce emissions as rapidly as possible.
3 The IPBES Global Assessment Report on Biodiversity and Ecosystem Services reported that 66 percent of ocean ecosystems have already suffered degradation (IPBES 2019, 24). In the specific context of climate change, the compounding harms (in addition to acidification) are: marine heatwaves, deoxygenation, and sea-level rise.
4 See also UNFCCC SBSTA 2021 and International Alliance to Combat Ocean Acidification (www.oaalliance.org/about).
5 This UNEP report takes a systemic approach and uses the term "planetary emergency" multiple times. It argues that without significant change, including to economic systems, the UN sustainable development goals (SDGs) will not be attainable.
6 A recent report claims that only 3 percent of the world's *land* ecosystems retain ecological integrity, using a healthy proportion of original species and undisturbed habitat as measures of ecological intactness. Expert commentary suggests humanity needs to give nature significantly more space, but this should not displace restoration efforts (Carrington 2021).
7 Thuesen (for example) considers this in the context of closing the high seas to all fishing (Thuesen, parts 3 and 4).
8 A number of Indigenous cultures use concepts of closure (of space and/or species removal) for intertwined cultural and ecological purposes. In New Zealand, this is known as a "rāhui" (see https://maoridictionary.co.nz/word/6420).
9 COP Decision X/2, Strategic Plan for Biodiversity 2011–2020 (2010) and UN Global Biodiversity Outlook 5 (2020).
10 In contrast, a number of Pacific Island states have sought to legally protect the whole of their very large exclusive economic zones (EEZs), including Palau, Kiribati, and the Seychelles. More generally, despite UNCLOS's recognition of the "marine environment" as one integrated whole for the purposes of marine protection (UNCLOS, part XII, section 8), use of the "ecosystem-based approach" to marine governance may be blocked and not fully used in the BBNJ treaty (Vito 2019).

## References

Angus, Ian. 2016. *Facing the Anthropocene: Fossil Capitalism and the Crisis of the Earth System*. New York: Monthly Review Press.

Baird, Rachel, Meredith Simons, and Tim Stephens. 2009. "Ocean Acidification: A Litmus Test for International Law." *Carbon and Climate Law Review* 3(4): 459–71.

Burns, Will, and Charles R. Corbett. 2020. "Antacids for the Sea? Artificial Ocean Alkalinization and Climate Change." *One Earth* 3(2): 154–56.

Campbell, Lisa M., Noella J. Gray, Luke Fairbanks, Jennifer J. Silver, Rebecca L. Gruby, Bradford A. Dubik, and Xavier Basurto. 2016. "Global Oceans Governance: New and Emerging Issues." *Annual Review of Environment and Resources* 41(1): 517–43.

Cao, Long, and Ken Caldeira. 2010. "Can Ocean Iron Fertilization Mitigate Ocean Acidification?" *Climatic Change* 99(1–2): 303–11.

Capstick, Stuart B., Nick F. Pidgeon, Adam J. Corner, Elspeth M. Spence, and Paul N. Pearson. 2016. "Public Understanding in Great Britain of Ocean Acidification." *Nature Climate Change* 6(8): 763–67.

Carrington, Damian. 2021. "Just 3% of World's Ecosystems Remain Intact, Study Suggests." *The Guardian*, April 15, 2021.

CBD (United Nations Convention on Biological Diversity. 1992).

Conference of the Parties 25, 2019. "Chile Madrid Time for Action, COP FCCC/CP/2019/L.10."

Cooke, Sandra L., and Sojung C. Kim. 2018. "Public Understanding of Ocean Acidification in the United States." *Science Communication* 41(1): 66–89.

De Lucia, Vito. 2019. "The Ecosystem Approach and the Negotiations towards a New Agreement on Marine Biodiversity in Areas beyond National Jurisdiction." *Nordic Environmental Law Journal* 2: 7–25.

De Santo, E.M., Á. Ásgeirsdóttir, A. Barros-Platiau, F. Biermann, J. Dryzek, L.R. Gonçalves, R.E. Kim, et al. 2019. "Protecting Biodiversity in Areas beyond National Jurisdiction: An Earth System Governance Perspective." *Earth System Governance* 2: 100029.

Duarte, Carlos M., Susana Agusti, Edward Barbier, Gregory L. Britten, Juan Carlos Castilla, Jean-Pierre Gattuso, Robinson W. Fulweiler, et al. 2020. "Rebuilding Marine Life." *Nature* 580(7801): 39–51.

Fennel, Katja, and David VanderZwaag. 2016. "Ocean Acidification: Scientific Surges, Lagging Law and Policy Responses." In *Routledge Handbook of Maritime Regulation and Enforcement*, edited by Robin Warner and Stuart B. Kaye, 342–55. Oxford: Routledge.

Fidelman, Pedro. 2019. "Climate Change in the Coral Triangle: Enabling Institutional Adaptive Capacity." In *Climate Change and Ocean Governance: Politics and Policy for Threatened Seas*, edited by Paul G. Harris, 274–89. Cambridge: Cambridge University Press.

Gaines, Sanford. 2014. "Reimagining Environmental Law for the 21st Century." *Environmental Law Reporter* 44(3): 10188–215.

Gallo, Natalya D., David G. Victor, and Lisa A. Levin. 2017. "Ocean Commitments under the Paris Agreement." *Nature Climate Change* 7(11): 833–38.

Gattuso, Jean-Pierre, Jelle Bijma, Marion Gehlan, Ulf Riebesel, and Carol Turley. 2011. "Ocean Acidification: Knowns, Unknowns, and Perspectives." In *Ocean Acidification*, edited by Jean-Pierre Gattuso and Lina Hansson, 291–312. Oxford: Oxford University Press.

Gehlen, Marion, Nicolas Gruber, Reidun Gangstø, Laurent Bopp, and Andreas Oschiles. 2011. "Biogeochemical Consequences of Ocean Acidification and Feedbacks to the Earth System." In *Ocean Acidification*, edited by Jean-Pierre Gattuso and Lina Hansson, 230–48. Oxford: Oxford University Press.

Greenpeace. 2019. *30x30 A Blueprint for Ocean Protection*.

Hamilton, Clive. 2017. *Defiant Earth: The Fate of Humans in the Anthropocene*. Oxford: Polity Press.

Hamilton, Clive, and Jacques Grinevald. 2015. "Was the Anthropocene Anticipated?" *The Anthropocene Review* 2(1): 59–72.

Harris, Paul G. 2019. "Ocean Governance Amidst Climate Change." In *Climate Change and Ocean Governance: Politics and Policy for Threatened Seas*, edited by Paul G. Harris, 239–447. Cambridge: Cambridge University Press.

Harrison, James. 2017. *Saving the Oceans Through Law: The International Legal Framework for the Protection of the Marine Environment*. Oxford: Oxford University Press.

Harrould-Kolieb, Ellycia R. 2019. "(Re)Framing Ocean Acidification in the Context of the United Nations Framework Convention on Climate Change (UNFCCC) and Paris Agreement." *Climate Policy* 19(10): 1225–38.

Heffernan, Olive. 2018. "How to Save the High Seas." *Nature* 557(7704): 154–56.

Hopkins, Frances, Philip Nightingale, and Peter Liss. 2011. "Effects of Ocean Acidification on the Marine Source of Atmospherically Active Trace Gases." In *Ocean Acidification*, edited by Jean-Pierre Gattuso and Lina Hansson, 210–29. Oxford: Oxford University Press.

IPBES (Intergovernmental Science-Policy Platform on Biodiversity and Ecosystem Services). 2019. "Global Assessment Report on Biodiversity and Ecosystem Services."

IPCC (Intergovernmental Panel on Climate Change). 2018. "Special Report on Global Warming of 1.5°C."

IPCC (Intergovernmental Panel on Climate Change). 2019. "Special Report on the Ocean and Cryosphere in a Changing Climate."

Kim, Rakhyun E. 2012. "Is a New Multilateral Environmental Agreement on Ocean Acidification Necessary?" *Review of European Community and International Environmental Law* 21(3): 243–58.

Kim, Rakhyun E., and Louis J. Kotzé. 2020. "Planetary Boundaries at the Intersection of Earth System Law, Science and Governance: A State-of-the-Art Review." *Review of European, Comparative and International Environmental Law* 30(1): 1–13.

Kotzé, Louis, Louise du Toit, and Duncan French. 2020. "Friend or Foe? International Environmental Law and Its Structural Complicity in the Anthropocene's Climate Injustices." *Oñati Socio-Legal Series* 11(1): 180–206.

Lenton, Timothy M., Johan Rockström, Owen Gaffney, Stefan Rahmstorf, Katherine Richardson, Will Steffen, and Hans Joachim Schellnhuber. 2019. "Climate Tipping Points — Too Risky to Bet Against." *Nature* 575(7784): 592–95.

Lindsey, Rebecca. 2020. "Climate Change: Atmospheric Carbon Dioxide." NOAA Climate.gov, August 14, 2020.

Magalhães, Paulo. 2021. "Common Interest, Concern or Heritage?" In *Earth System Law: Standing on the Precipice of the Anthropocene*, edited by M. Hulbert et al. Abingdon: Routledge (in press).

Makomere, Reuben, and Kennedy Liti Mbeva. 2019. "Contested Multilateralism." In *Climate Change and Ocean Governance: Politics and Policy for Threatened Seas*, edited by Paul G. Harris, 255–73. Cambridge: Cambridge University Press.

Mendenhall, Elizabeth. 2019. "The Ocean Governance Regime." In *Climate Change and Ocean Governance: Politics and Policy for Threatened Seas*, edited by Paul G. Harris, 27–42. Cambridge: Cambridge University Press.

Pelejero, Carlos, Eva Calvo, and Ove Hoegh-Guldberg. 2010. "Paleo-perspectives on Ocean Acidification." *Trends in Ecology and Evolution* 25(6): 332–44.

Sala, Enric, Juan Mayorga, Darcy Bradley, Reniel B. Cabral, Trisha B. Atwood, Arnaud Auber, William Cheung, et al. 2021. "Protecting the Global Ocean for Biodiversity, Food and Climate." *Nature* 592(7854): 397–402.

Sala, Enric, Juan Mayorga, Christopher Costello, David Kroodsma, Maria L.D. Palomars, Daniel Pauly, U. Rashid Sumaila, and Dirk Zeller. 2018. "The Economics of Fishing the High Seas." *Science Advances* 4(6): eaat2504.

Six, Katharina D., Silvia Kloster, Tatiana Ilyina, Stephen D. Archer, Kai Zhang, and Ernst Maier-Reimer. 2013. "Global Warming Amplified by Reduced Sulphur Fluxes as a Result of Ocean Acidification." *Nature Climate Change* 3(11): 975–78.

Skelton, Alasdair, Alice Larkin, Andrew Ringsmuth, Caroline Greiser, David Fopp, Duncan McLaren, Doreen Stabinsky, et al. 2020. "10 Myths about Net Zero Targets and Carbon Offsetting, Busted." *Climate Home News*, December 11, 2020.

Steffen, W., K. Richardson, J. Rockstrom, S.E. Cornell, I. Fetzer, E.M. Bennett, R. Biggs, et al. 2015. "Planetary Boundaries: Guiding Human Development on a Changing Planet." *Science* 347(6223): 1259855.

Steinacher, Marco, Fortunat Joos, and Thomas F. Stocker. 2013. "Allowable Carbon Emissions Lowered by Multiple Climate Targets." *Nature* 499(7457): 197–201.

Telesetsky, Anastasia. 2019. "Managing Marine Resources." In *Climate Change and Ocean Governance: Politics and Policy for Threatened Seas*, edited by Paul G. Harris, 325–39. Cambridge: Cambridge University Press.

Thuesen, Gretchen. n.d. "Closing the High Seas: Potential Implications and Outcomes." *Closing High Seas Fisheries*, part 3. Sustainable Fisheries UW.org.

Thuesen, Gretchen. n.d. "Alternatives to Closing the High Seas to Fishing." *Closing High Seas Fisheries*, part 4. Sustainable Fisheries UW.org.

UNEP (United Nations Environment Programme). 2021. "Making Peace with Nature: A Scientific Blueprint to Tack the Climate, Biodiversity and Pollution Emergencies."

UNFCCC (United Nations Framework Convention on Climate Change, 1992).
United Nations Framework Convention on Climate Change Scientific Body for Scientific and Technological Advice, Ocean and Climate Change Dialogue to Consider How to Strengthen Adaptation and Mitigation Action, Informal Summary Report by the Chair of the Subsidiary Body for Scientific and Technological Advice. April 29, 2021.
United Nations General Assembly Resolution 74/19, UN doc A/RES/74/19 (2019).
United Nations. 2019. Revised Draft Text of an Agreement Under the United Nations Convention on the Law of the Sea on the Conservation and Sustainable Use of Marine Biological Diversity of Areas Beyond National Jurisdiction.
United Nations Global Biodiversity Outlook 5 (2020).
United Nations Convention on the Law of the Sea, 10 December 1982, 1993. U.N.T.S.
Vidas, Davor. 2011. "The Anthropocene and the International Law of the Sea." *Philosophical Transactions of the Royal Society, Series A: Mathematical, Physical and Engineering Sciences* 369(1938): 909–25.
Walsh, B. 2013. "Ocean Acidification Will Make Climate Change Worse." TIME.com.
Westerlund, Staffan. 2008. "Theory for Sustainable Development: For or Against." In *Sustainable Development in International and National Law*, edited by Hans-Christian Bugge and Christina Voigt, 49–66. Groningen: Europa Law Publishing.
Williamson, P., P.W. Boyd, D.P. Harrison, N. Reynard, and A. Mashayek. 2021. "Biologically-Based Negative Emissions in the Open Ocean and Coastal Seas." In *Negative Emission Technologies*, edited by M. Bui and N. Mac Dowell. London: Royal Society of Chemistry.
World Meteorological Organization. 2021. "WMO 2020 State of the Global Climate Report."

# 10

# OUTER SPACE IN THE ANTHROPOCENE

*Emily Ray*

The Anthropocene is ordinarily associated with terrestrial life and the conditions of climate change here on Earth. This chapter argues that those concerned about the Anthropocene are long overdue to reckon with outer space as another human environment. First, humans have long studied and impacted outer space, and all planetary life is dependent upon the complex relationships between Earth and other celestial bodies. While most basic education about climate change includes diagrams, videos, and descriptions of such processes, particularly the warming effect on the planet from, among other causes, trapped greenhouse gases in the atmosphere and loss of sunlight-deflecting ice on the polar caps, there exists a firm cultural partition between inner space and outer space, as though outer space exists wholly apart from life on Earth.

Exploring outer space is often approached as a new frontier and opportunity to expand civilization, but through economic and legal arrangements for sharing access to outer space and for the transformation of celestial materials into economically viable resources. Interest in outer space adventure and development is, in some part, driven by anxieties about the livability of this planet under the stress of the Anthropocene. Positions about outer space as part of a solution to climate change range from optimistically pointing to technological advancements that allow outer space development and colonization which can also be put to use improving conditions on Earth, to wholesale dismissal of pursuing life in outer space. Political science engagement with the Anthropocene and outer space is primarily concerned with militarization and securitization, rather than studying the political and economic efforts to extend civilization, and more specifically civilization as it is developed through neoliberal market society, into space. This chapter works to address this by reviewing the social scientific literature on outer space and the Anthropocene and the existing outer space policies that have shaped how space figures into current political and economic regimes. Finally, I look toward critical theory as a guide to thinking about outer space in the Anthropocene as already part of the broad human environment, but without reducing it to the wilderness sublime or to a stockpile of resources. Building from Marcuse, it is not necessary to pretend as though these technological advances do not exist, but it is necessary to think about how they fit into a qualitative shift in our social organization.

"The Anthropocene" is a loaded term full of warning and controversy about its scientific and political uses. The term "Anthropocene" was used in 1922 by a Soviet geologist, again in the 1980s by Eugene Stoermer, and in 2000 by Paul Crutzen (Angus 2016). The Anthropocene marks the time when the impact of human activities overtook the natural geological activity

 DOI: 10.4324/9781003388081-13

of the Earth. Scientists and social scientists debate about the start of the Earth-altering impact caused by organized human life. Angus presents evidence that the Great Acceleration after the Second World War, marked by intense use of petroleum-based energy, is the start of a new geological epoch of human dominance over Earth systems (Angus 2016). Chakrabarty speaks to "Anthropocene time" stating, "the Anthropocene debate thus entails a constant conceptual traffic between Earth history and world history" (Chakrabarty 2018, 6). He points out that "the term 'Anthropocene' was used from its very inception as a measure not of geological time but of the *extent* of human impact on the planet" (Chakrabarty 2018, 6–7). "The Anthropocene" is not the only name given to this epoch. Donna Haraway has given us the Cthulhucene, Jason Moore the Capitalocene, and Timothy Luke's *Anthropocene Alerts* reminds us that before the term was coined, we have been, more or less, discussing the Anthropocene since the mid-1800s. "Crutzen and his warning unfortunately turn up far more than a day late and dollar short. The world has been repeatedly warned for over 150 years to practically no avail" (Luke 2019, 207). While Crutzen's work on the Anthropocene is important, it is not the first warning about the impact of human activity, specifically technological and economic accelerations that produce sustained damage to Earth systems. What does the debate about naming the Anthropocene do toward addressing the multi-dimensional crisis of anthropogenic climate change?

> do Crutzen's Cassandra-like conceptualizations of the particularities in today's current climate change crisis leave him and other scientists in the role of taxonomic traffic cops, who are left letting the accelerating juggernaut of nearly out-of-control global economic development off with a warning about how fast the world is speeding into a cluster of irreversible ecological catastrophes?
>
> *(Luke 2019, 208)*

How does the conversation about the Anthropocene move beyond "taxonomic traffic policing" and toward robust politics? I continue this intervention to challenge the discourses of the Anthropocene to not just more squarely address itself to politics but to consider more widely the impact of anthropogenic forces beyond our own planet. The Anthropocene is a serious political concern beyond policy development and security matters. Some of the vital questions that emerge from understanding and addressing the Anthropocene are deeply political, such as questions of power relations, resource distribution, and the role of the state and non-state actors in producing the crises associated with such an epoch, and in creating the solutions. As the metaphorical climate change alarm sound across the globe in wildfires, floods, superstorms, and ocean acidification, public outer space agencies and private companies invested in spacefaring are making these assessments and decisions without democratic participation. In knitting together the Anthropocene and outer space through politics, perhaps the Anthropocene debates can move beyond alarm sounding.

The Anthropocene has a hard time reconciling itself to outer space. Critical geographer Fraser MacDonald lamented that his own field is inattentive to outer space and overdue to acknowledge that outer space is already integral to life on Earth (MacDonald 2007). Olson and Messeri identify an "inner environment" and "outer environment" and in reviewing geology, social science, and humanities literature find that the Anthropocene is often used to demarcate the inner "earthly" world of human life and ecosystems from the cosmological world of the outer environment, or outer space.

> Despite ways in which extraterrestrial science and technologies contribute to understandings of the environmental dynamics at enlarged spatial scales, the Anthropocene

> concept is being deployed in ways that privilege downward, inward, and spherically enclosed terra- and anthropocentric understandings of what counts as environment.
> *(Olson and Messeri 2015, 29)*

Outer space is relegated to peripheral relation to the inner, terrestrial world of the planet, with the "contemporary social scientific topologies ... marking outer space as a de-environmentalized technosite that produces alienating perspectives" (Olson and Messeri 2015, 35). The aim of their work is to "un-Earth" the Anthropocene, to expand the Anthropocene into a wider category of environments. This is a compelling project, yet these contributions and others exploring the Anthropocene and outer space provide anthropological, geographic, sociological, and economic insights, but very few from political theory.

Much of the literature addressing outer space and the Anthropocene concerns itself with spatial and temporal relations and different ways of viewing the home planet. According to Chakrabarty, we hold the Anthropocene in temporal tension between two lives, "a scientific life involving measurements and debates among qualified scientists, and a more popular life as a moral-political issue," and in this tension, the focus remained on the human impact, "and questions of geological time simply fell into the shadows" (Chakrabarty 2018, 9). The loss of geological time in the discussion poses a serious challenge to our ability to think about the scale of human activity played out in multiple temporalities. Shifting the vantage point from on Earth to above Earth could include cosmic time in the Anthropocene, but instead, it mostly reaffirms interest in terrestrial life. Instead of challenging the boundary between outer and inner space, the shift to studying the Earth from above has only affirmed a managerial approach to terrestrial bio- and ecosystem sustainability thanks to the new technologies that permit a whole earth vantage point. The infamous photographs of Earth taken from the Apollo 8 (1968) and Apollo 11 (1972) missions were primarily used by the environmentalist movement to draw attention to the fragility of planet Earth and our relative loneliness in the universe; there is only one home planet so we have to take care of it (Cosgrove 1994). The reception and use of these photographs did not more tightly bind the inner and outer environments but reinforced the use of the outer environment as a new vantage point to explore the inner one. Helmreich compares the representation of Earth through the Apollo "moonrise" photograph to that of Google Earth, which "thus shares with Spaceship Earth something of the quality of a fetish ... a shimmering image meant to be consumed, perhaps as an icon of nostalgia for an Earth we may be about to lose" (Helmreich 2011, 1219). Viewing Earth from outer space, particularly through space-rendered technologies like satellites, reinforces Earth as a manipulatable object (the countless configurations available through Google Earth layers) and outer space as a staging ground for techno-rational management of terrestrial systems.

Other scholarly work critically links capitalism to outer space development. Some authors join the social scientists who criticize Anthropocene literature for generalizing all of humanity by arguing that the "we" taking up the next space race is not humankind but *capitalistkind* (Shammas and Holen 2019). Dickens employs David Harvey to argue that outer space is used as a "spatial fix" to the crisis of resource availability that literally and figuratively fuels capitalism (Dickens 2009; Dickens and Omrod 2007). Outer space development feeds the commodity economy, and as Parker argues, public outer space organizations themselves are commoditized, evident when Russia sold space on its Proton Rocket for a Pizza Hut advertisement (Parker 2009; Smith 2015). The connections to capitalism are important but remain a fraction of the literature on the Anthropocene and outer space. Discussions about the Anthropocene and how humans should navigate it toward a better, sustainable world need to include outer space in the range of systems impacted by human activity on Earth, and in debates about energy resourcing and use. The Anthropocene addresses terrestrial life, but it does not account for our place just outside the upper limits of the atmosphere. Space enthusiasts, advocates, and expansionists are often pitted against a simplistic argument to just "focus here on Earth," which erroneously assumes that outer space has nothing to do with terrestrial life, and that outer space exploration and expansion will stop developing with enough insistence. Acknowledging the place of space in the Anthropocene and environmentalism is insufficient by itself. I argue that critical theory provides a key framework for exploring the dialectical tension between the promises of outer space as a way to support a qualitatively better life for humans and the potential for space-faring technologies and policies to further entrench human and more-than-human life in the neoliberal capitalist relations driving the climate crisis. First, I contextualize space exploration in the twenty-first century, then discuss the major policies and treaties that govern space exploration and development with emphasis on commercialization, and conclude by suggesting that one of the ways to take up the questions of outer space and the Anthropocene is through the analytic frames of critical theory.

## The Anthropogenic Stamp on Space

Humans have already breached the upper atmosphere with technological breakthroughs in rocketry, and humans have had a continuous presence in low earth orbit on the International Space Station since 31 October 2000. It is time to acknowledge that outer space is part of our natural environment and to think about our uses and habitation in it in discussions on climate change and the Anthropocene. Space development is already connected to the Great Acceleration through technological advances like nuclear weapons, long-range rockets and satellites, and electronic digital computers (Deudney 2020). Space expansionists, those who wish to extend human life into the cosmos, imagine that these various projects, cast in techno-optimistic arguments, will solve the crises on Earth, including climate change pressures. The argument runs that "solving the Earth's problems with space technology not only benefits the Earth but also helps establish the foundations for ambitious expansions far beyond the Earth" (Deudney 2020, 11). Deudney finds a direct connection between the enthusiasm to expand into space and the pressures of the Anthropocene:

> Space advocates also point to a large number of ways in which the Earth as a habitat for humanity is threatened, and they offer space projects as solutions to these problems. These contemporary habitability problems include ecological degradation and pollution, scarcity of resources and energy, overpopulation, and climate change.
>
> *(Deudney 2020, 11)*

As Angus, Hamilton, and Luke have noted, geo-engineers in particular are often excited about the prospects of the Anthropocene: An era that may for now be marked by the negative consequences of human world-changing activity but can also be marked by the innovative solutions to climate change that only human ingenuity can produce. Not only can we get ourselves out of this mess, but we can also make the world anew within a cleaner, greener capitalist economy governed by "various networks of scientific and technical experts [who] once again position themselves to administer from above and from afar any collective efforts to mitigate or adapt to rapid anthropogenic climate change" (Luke 2019, 207). Capitalists of all stripes but an especially eager bunch in Silicon Valley are eager to join the networks of experts to manage the crisis; a bureaucratic and private sector fusion that is all too familiar to observers of the climate crisis. We are already surveilled under their watchful eyes with SpaceX's fleet of satellites.

Space is not just "out there." Hamilton acknowledges as much when he notes that Earth systems are more than the sum of their parts, and these systems are animated by the forces of the sun and Moon (Hamilton 2017). Simply noting the influence of celestial bodies is an insufficient analysis of how important outer space is, not just to ecosystems, but to the politics of climate change. We already use low earth orbit and outer space as a great "landfill" of orbital debris. Space debris is largely generated by satellite explosions and collisions, and before 2007, "explosions from launch vehicle upper stages and spacecraft" (ARES | Orbital Debris Program Office | Frequently Asked Questions n.d.). The volume of space debris orbiting the Earth is staggering:

> More than 23,000 orbital debris larger than 10 cm are known to exist. The estimated population of particles between 1 and 10 cm in diameter is approximately 500,000. The number of particles larger than 1 mm exceeds 100 million. As of January 1, 2020, the amount of material orbiting the Earth exceeded 8,000 metric tons.
>
> *("ARES | Orbital Debris Program Office | Frequently Asked Questions" n.d.)*

The European Space Agency (ESA) puts the number of particles between 1 cm and 10 cm at closer to 900,000 (Kwong 2020). Space junk threatens operational satellites and spacecraft in orbit, and could congest flight paths out of low earth orbit on missions to the Moon, Mars, and near-Earth objects (NEOs). The ESA has partnered with a Swiss entrepreneurial firm, ClearSpace-1 to execute the "first space mission to remove an item of debris from orbit" scheduled for 2025. "The mission is being procured as a service contract with a startup-led commercial consortium, to help establish a new market for in-orbit servicing, as well as debris removal" (ESA Commissions World's First Space Debris Removal 2019). The problems of careless human activity in space are now an opportunity to create a new commercial sector for space garbage hauling. Outer space, like the sea, is often considered vast empty space that can absorb human waste. The ESA Director General compared the urgency to remove space debris as a danger similar to sailing on the high seas with all shipwrecks in history bobbing in the waves (ESA Commissions World's First Space Debris Removal 2019). Outer space is an inviting emptiness in which humans can test new technologies, dispose of old ones or let them lapse into junk, and try and make habitable planets beyond Earth. Commercializing and commoditizing environmental crises means addressing environmental issues through the marketplace, so that solution to pressing problems becomes a new market, and the new market will operate within the framework of global capitalism. NASA promotes NEO mining and has teamed up with SpaceX to send a manned mission to Mars to, in part, prepare for Mars colonization as the Earth becomes less habitable for humans and countless other species.

Advocacy for space colonization found great support in the 1970s and continues to be a serious but small topic of scholarly and popular conversation about the political and ethical dimensions of colonization, including the design of a virtual game to simulate Mars settlement and collective action problems (Brand 1977; Grove 2021; Janssen, Gharavi, and Yichao 2020; Sutch and Roberts 2019). The exploration effort is increasingly carried out under the auspices of empire-building. The Trump administration "proclaimed the goal of achieving 'space dominance,' a major departure from previous American military policies" and the National Space Council no longer considers space a public commons (Deudney 2020, 22). In the race to commodify all commons is a sub-race to do so while they are usable for space development.

> In a symbolic indicator of the fact that humanity is entering the Anthropocene far more decisively than that Space Age, many major American space facilities, located on coasts and islands, will soon be under water as sea level rises due to climate change.

(*Deudney 2020, 21*)

The development of space programs and technologies has been driven by military advancement as much as it has been driven by scientific exploration. Global military activities, particularly the US military, are a major contributor to pollution, resource use, and climate change (Crawford 2019), a tight link between the military and the Anthropocene. Given the coupling between military and space development, the space race and Anthropocene are inseparable from one another. The US has been a competitive actor in the space race well before Sputnik. MacDonald argues that the space race started in the late 1700s and through the mid-1800s when John Adams advocated for federal funding for observatories to boost American prestige and demonstrate the country's ability to compete with Europe on the Western world stage of astronomical studies, advances in sea navigation, and the ability to draw internationally renowned scientists to their state-of-the-art facilities. MacDonald recounts a public lecture given by scientist Ormsby MacKnight Mitchel in 1842 lamenting that the "Russian hordes" managed to have a modern observatory, but the US did not, despite the country's "freedom and intelligence" (A. MacDonald 2017, 55). The US's own efforts were largely driven by "grand amateurs" – individuals who personally funded significant astronomical facilities and establishments for their own personal use (A. MacDonald 2017, 78). State-funded outer space development has always depended on the "grand amateurs" like Elon Musk and Jeff Bezos, two of the world's wealthiest capitalists investing heavily in the outer space economy.

The history of modern outer space exploration is worthy of more rigorous treatment, but in following the lead of Musk and Bezos, I look specifically at the commercialization of space, rather than the suite of outer space development issues, including militarization, securitization, and space debris cleanup (Peoples 2010; McCormick 2013; Newman and Williamson 2018). The treaties discussed below address a range of issues, but my focal point is on those articles and statements related to commercialization. Celestial bodies, including NEOs, like asteroids and meteors, and bodies like the Moon, are believed to have commercial value, as "asteroid-mining proponents perceive the terrestrial incorporation of cosmic wealth as a kind of heavenly providential resource that would end the extraction-based degradation of Earth" (Olson 2013, 203). Olson argues that in accounting for the environmental history of NEOs we can see how outer space and its objects cross the boundaries, physically, politically, and metaphorically, into our terrestrial lives, particularly in an effort to render them, and by extension the Earth, manageable through technological innovation and risk calculation. These management efforts are not limited to assessing the risk of a NEO collision with the planet, they are also marshaled into the effort to make outer space profitable. The commercial possibilities of NEO mining include using these resources *in situ* for rocket fuel restocking for future Mars colonization flights and long space voyages (Grush 2018). Not only does this reveal new market possibilities in producing the transport vehicles, equipment, transit routes, and the financialization of risk, it allows for capital to bypass terrestrial ecological limits by looping outer space into its resource metabolism without confronting outer space as an environment protected by conservation efforts (Ray and Parson 2020).

## Brief Journey through Outer Space Regulation

Following WWII there was interest in space activity from the developments in German rocketry brought to the US with Nazi scientist Werner Von Braun and his team. The launch of Sputnik, alongside the growing tension between the US and USSR, drew concerns about the legality of overflights of satellites (Reynolds & Merges 1997, 4). In the 1958 Starfish Prime atomic bomb test, the US detonated a thermonuclear warhead in the upper atmosphere. NASA was established in the same year, one year after the USSR successfully launched Sputnik. Just prior to the historic launch in 1952, "a UN lawyer, Oscar Schachter, asked 'Who owns the universe?' He suggested that space and celestial bodies belong, like the high seas, to all mankind" ( Reynolds & Merges 1997, 6). Space law over the last several decades has tried to walk the line between ownership and commons, drawing on maritime and air law to guide the effort toward international treaties and agreements largely overseen by the UN. One of the first such treaties was the Limited Test Ban Treaty in 1963, with the US and USSR as the key signatories. The treaty prohibited nuclear testing in outer space, an important step in limiting the use of outer space for warfare. Not long after the test ban, the Outer Space Treaty (OST) was ratified in 1967. The OST continues to serve as a legal guidepost to sovereignty and use of outer space and celestial bodies, although it is increasingly challenged by developments in outer space commercialization. The first article states:

> The exploration and use of outer space, including the Moon and other celestial bodies, shall be carried out for the benefit and in the interest of all countries, irrespective of their degree of economic or scientific development, and shall be the province of all mankind.
>
> *(RES 2222 (XXI) 1996)*

Outer space exploration should not be exclusive to whichever countries and their citizens can marshal the capital and technology to become space-faring. The second article states: "Outer space, including the moon and other celestial bodies, is not subject to national appropriation by claims of sovereignty, by means of use or occupation, or by any other means" (RES 2222 (XXI) 1996). This passage implies that states cannot claim sovereign control over the Moon, asteroids, and similar, or "air" territory in outer space. The treaty is not clear about how private entities claim resources like minerals and water on these bodies.

The subsequent Moon Treaty brought these questions of resource access to the fore when it was drafted in 1979. The treaty sought to "prevent the moon from becoming an area of international conflict, bearing in mind the benefits which may be derived from the exploitation of the natural resources of the moon and other celestial bodies" (Reynolds & Merges 1997, 110). Article 11 states that the surface and subsurface of the Moon and its natural resources cannot become the property of any "state, international intergovernmental or non-governmental organization, national organization, or non-governmental entity or of any natural person" (Reynolds & Merges 1997, 105) but later states one of the purposes the international regime dedicated to cooperative outer space activities is to maintain "(a) the orderly and safe development of the natural resources of the moon; (b) the rational management of those resources; (c) The expansion of those opportunities in the use of those resources" (Reynolds & Merges 1997, 106):

> In a letter for November 13, 1979, Senator Richard Stone, also a member of the Senate Committee on Foreign Relations, urged Secretary Vance to reevaluate the US position on the draft moon treaty, which he describes as having "extremely dangerous potentialities" because it appeared to decrease "the ability of the United States to advance in yet unexplored fields" and to "greatly inhibit the actions and desires of U.S. corporations in space, negate the notion of free enterprise, and … place the United States in a position subservient to the Soviet Union".
>
> *(Reynolds & Merges 1997, 112)*

The hesitancy to ratify the treaty rested on concern for commercial development and economic competition with the USSR and drew out the desire to ensure a free market approach to outer space development, sending capitalism skyward as an extension of the economic forces of the Anthropocene. Neither the US, the USSR, nor China signed the treaty, and as such it carries little weight in international space law. In 2015, with support from Congressional Republicans, the 114th US Congress passed the US Commercial Space Launch Competitiveness Act, the purpose of which is to, "facilitate a pro-growth environment for the developing commercial space industry by encouraging private sector investment and creating more stable and predictable regulatory conditions" (McCarthy 2015). The law moved to remove unwarranted constraints from the commercial space industry, to facilitate commercial exploration for and recovery of space resources by US citizens, and to discourage government barriers to the development in the United States of economically viable industries for commercial exploration and space resource extraction. Section 51303 states:

> A United States citizen engaged in commercial recovery of an asteroid resource or a space resource under this chapter shall be entitled to any asteroid resource or space resource obtained, including to possess, own, transport, use, and sell the asteroid resource or space resource obtained in accordance with applicable law, including the international obligations of the United States.
>
> *(McCarthy 2015)*

This Act codifies in the law what the Moon Treaty failed to guarantee to signatories: The right to acquire property in outer space for private entities, and the right to commercial exploitation of outer space resources. This Act marks a pivot away from the OST and the pledge to consider outer space as a global commons that is non-exclusionary, and instead focuses legal protection on private commercial enterprise.

In 2020, President Trump and NASA Administrator James Bridenstine developed the Artemis Accords, which promises to land a man and a woman on the Moon, to explore Mars and other planets, and to encourage and tighten the relationship between the private and public sectors to develop space-faring technologies and space commerce. "The Signatories emphasize that the extraction and utilization of space resources, including any recovery from the surface or subsurface of the Moon, Mars, comets, or asteroids, should be executed in a manner that complies with the Outer Space Treaty and in support of safe and sustainable space activities" (James F. Bridenstine 2020). The Accords claim that this article does not run afoul of the Outer Space Treaty. Australia, Canada, Italy, Japan, Luxembourg, the United Arab Emirates, and the United Kingdom joined the US in signing this agreement. These signatories come as little surprise:

> JAXA, Japan's space agency, signed a memorandum of understanding with a private company, Tokyo-based iSpace Inc., to establish an industry for the mining, transport, and use of resources on the moon. Luxembourg has also joined the race, aiming no less than to lead Europe in the space-mining sector … Luxembourg has set aside V 200 million for space-mining operations, partnered with Deep Space Industries and Planetary Resources … in July 2017, Luxembourg adopted a law regulating the extraction of space resources which recognizes that space resources are capable of being owned by private companies. The United Arab Emirates (UAE) has also set the goal of asteroid mining and is preparing national space legislation that will regulate this activity.
>
> *(Tepper 2019, 3)*

Each successive treaty and accord produced by the US emphasizes commercial activity driven by free market principles. Interpreting these treaties is complicated by a fractured understanding of commons and common pool resources. Legal and economic definitions of commons vary and are often conflated, and each object in space, from satellites to celestial bodies, may be subject to different legal and economic regimes (Tepper 2019; Steer 2017). While outer space may not be considered part of the environment in the way "environment" is often invoked here on Earth, it is looped into the extractive industries operating in a neoliberal capitalist environment, which binds outer space to the terrestrial environment through the mass exploitation, or anticipated exploitation, of these spaces and objects as natural resources. Outer space objects are "naturalized" as resources, and space joins the environment but on the terms of capital. Perhaps with little resistance from environmentalists, outer space will be the next eco-managed environment monitored by engineering, mining, and geo-space experts with public contracts to ensure the efficient extraction, transport, and sale of outer space resources; a new market for a dying planet with state-of-the-art technologies that may make extraction gentler here on Earth as ice recedes, melts, and exposes new commercial opportunities.

## Managing Outer Space

Outer space commercialization extends beyond resources, a lesson learned from commoditizing the ocean. The seas have likewise been subject to centuries of exploration and commercial development and are increasingly subject to the forces of technological rationality as they are monitored, measured, quantified, probed by radar, manned and unmanned vehicles, used as a means of warfare through international naval powers, irradiated by atomic bomb tests, trawled, farmed, crosshatched with fishing nets, and home to a staggering volume of garbage, plastics, agricultural runoff, and biological waste. The sea and its contents, flows, and movements are mostly treated as technological managerial problems. Solutions include rendering the seas understandable and predictable for ocean-crossing commerce and military activity and developing new means of collecting waste and managing fisheries to protect lucrative markets. Even these management techniques and the uncertainty they attempt to conquer provide market opportunities. In their history of capitalism and its relationship with the sea, Campling and Colás describe this transformation:

> The Atlantic Ocean acts here as a real geophysical and logistical barrier in forcible population transfers, yet also creates multiple profit-making opportunities for insurers, traders, bankers, ship- and slaveowners, manufacture, commodity exchange and transport. With the advance of industrial capitalism, the oceans became increasingly commodified – its living and inanimate resources appropriated, extracted and processed in the realization of exchange-value.
>
> *(Campling and Colás 2021, 12)*

The risks become a new market, just as the rational management of the seas and outer space produces new economic opportunities. "The oceans (not unlike the exploitation of outer space) demand a high price for such subordination of natural forces to the further extension of commodity frontiers" (Campling and Colás 2021, 14). Akin to the commodification of transport on the oceans, Musk has made clear that SpaceX is in the business of building a transportation system similar to the Union Pacific Railroad (Patel 2016) while Bezos has redoubled his efforts to make Blue Origin competitive as a space transport company with payload routes to the Moon (Blue Moon n.d.). Companies like Global Aerospace, AXA XL, and Gallagher offer insurance for outer space activities and craft, and private investment in space companies set a new annual record in 2020 at $8.9 billion (Sheetz 2021). Extending the commodity frontiers is one way to redefine the boundaries of the planetary but doing so through the discursive and economic tools of neoliberalism.

Herbert Marcuse argued that human domination over nature could be a force for liberation as well as a force for domination. To argue for a "return to nature" or to scale back technology to a more primitive period of human life would not move us closer to a liberated existence.

> Nature is a part of history, an object of history; therefore, "liberation of nature" cannot mean returning to a pre-technological stage, but advancing to the use of the achievements of technological civilization for freeing man and nature from the destructive abuse of science and technology in the service of exploitation.
>
> *(Marcuse 1972, 60)*

This can be applied two-fold to outer space: First to include outer space as the nature that is part of history, to not exclude outer space as a realm that exists outside of politics and of what scholars call "second nature," or the environment as experienced through social construction; and second, to think about the technological advances that enable exploration of space as always containing the dual potential to be used toward domination or to be used toward liberation. However, the speed and type of manipulation of the natural environment primarily serve the interests of capital. This manipulation has contributed to an ever-widening gulf of material inequality around the globe, and it has accelerated anthropocentric climate change and its cascade of environmental catastrophes.

> On the one hand, our capacity to transform the natural environment has reached unprecedented heights and continues to soar ... There is, it seems, almost nothing that we cannot do to control our non-human environment and place it at the service to human life. Yet at the same time, these transformations of our ecologies are creating feedbacks that are increasingly difficult to control.
>
> *(Biro 2011, 5)*

The tension between controlling the natural environment for a society founded on liberation and controlling it for a society founded on domination allows for a more critical examination of outer space development than simply a cause for techno-optimists or a brusque dismissal by mainstream environmentalists. In an article exploring the militarization of space and critical theory, Peoples wrestles with the implications of rocketry technologies:

> Marcuse's approach is suggestive of a move from, to paraphrase one of his own works, technology to hauntology: current developments in space technology in the US in particular are haunted most immediately by the prospects for greater destructive capacity that they portend, but also by alternative visions for the use of space that they preclude.
>
> *(Peoples 2009, 106)*

The balance may be tipped toward the destructive capacities of our space-faring technologies, but they are not beyond recovery. To suggest there is a possibility to harness these technologies for the public good and liberation is not a techno-optimist argument. Techno-optimism is grounded in technocratic schemes of simply applying science and engineering to various social ills and, without fundamentally altering the way society is organized, executing technical projects to address symptoms associated with the great inequality wrought by iterations of capitalism.

The support behind commercializing outer space is rarely checked by an impulse to protect it as a natural environment worthy of respect as it exists. "Nature, if not left alone and protected as 'reservation,' is treated in an aggressively scientific way: it is there for the sake of domination; it is value-free matter, material" (Marcuse 1972, 61). The United Nations Committee on the Peaceful Uses of Outer Space uses "sustainability" to mean guaranteed long-term access to peaceful outer space activities, marginal in this concern is the integrity of celestial bodies (Committee on the Peaceful Uses of Outer Space 2020). Outer space, which has not yet reached the status of "nature" or "environment," is typically regarded as value-free matter wasted in the void of space. Outer space and celestial bodies are treated in an "aggressively scientific way" or are aggressively spiritualized in New Age attempts to make the stars reveal hidden truths about the meaning of life. In either iteration, outer space is excluded from consideration as nature which ought to be reconceived in a qualitatively different social organization, one in which "the development of scientific concepts may be grounded in an experience of nature as a totality of life to be protected and 'cultivated,' and technology would apply this science to the reconstruction of the environment of life" (Marcuse 1972, 61). Simply folding outer space into mainstream environmentalism is insufficient to realize the possibilities of a liberated nature, including the cosmos. "At the same time, however, the political function of ecology is easily 'neutralized' and serves the beautification of the Establishment" (Herbert Marcuse 1972, 61). Environmentalism must be part of the qualitative change Marcuse argues is necessary for an end to domination and the beginning of a liberated life.

As the brief overview of outer space policies demonstrates, the use of outer space for commercial and resource exploitation is a legal open question, as well as a political, economic, and ethical one. Yet outer space is still marginally included in the realm of environmental concerns that constitute the Anthropocene while it is more seriously considered as part of techno-optimistic solutions to the same. The legal frames around outer space development are increasingly hemmed in by a mandate to commercially develop the resources, bodies, and transportation routes available in and through outer space. These opportunities are often framed as hopeful developments in the face of climate change in the Anthropocene. In order to seriously consider the place of space in the questions of climate change disaster and livability on Earth, outer space needs to be reckoned with as an environment already looped into our terrestrial lives in critical ways and no longer seen as a blank new frontier onto which to project the same dominating forces on Earth responsible for our climate catastrophe. Luke's "world watchers" understand the strategic value of outer space, and outer space entrepreneurs continue to dazzle the public with displays of technological sophistication and a promise of a better world if you can afford a ticket off the planet or do not mind indentured servitude for the opportunity (McFall-Johnsen and Mosher 2020). There is still time to address these questions but dialectically, carefully, and with an eye toward the systems in which outer space exploration is currently conceived.

## References

"ARES | Orbital Debris Program Office | Frequently Asked Questions." n.d. Accessed July 13, 2020 https://orbitaldebris.jsc.nasa.gov/faq/#.

Angus, Ian. 2016. *Facing the Anthropocene*. New York: Monthly Review Press.

Biro, Andrew. 2011. *Critical Ecologies*. Toronto: Toronto University Press.

"Blue Moon." n.d. *Blue Origin*. Accessed May 26, 2021. https://www-dev.blueorigin.com/blue-moon.

Brand, Stewart. 1977. *Space Colonies*. Edited by Stewart Brand. London: Penguin Books.

Bridenstine, James F. *Artemis Accords*. Accessed January 31, 2023: https://www.nasa.gov/specials/artemis-accords/index.html

Campling, Liam, and Alejandro Colas. 2021. *Capitalism and the Sea*. London and New York: Verso Press.
Chakrabarty, Dipesh. 2018. "Anthropocene Time." *History and Theory* 57(1): 5–32. https://doi.org/10.1111/hith.12044.
Peoples, Columba. 2009. "Haunted Dreams: Critical Theory, Technology and the Militarization of Space." In *Securing Outer Space: International Relations Theory and the Politics of Space*, 1st ed., 91–115. London: Routledge.
Peoples, Columba. 2010. "The Growing 'Securitization' of Outer Space." *Space Policy* 26(4): 205–208. https://doi.org/10.1016/j.spacepol.2010.08.004.
Committee on the Peaceful Uses of Outer Space. 2020. "Revised Draft 'Space2030' Agenda and Implementation Plan." United Nations. https://www.unoosa.org/res/oosadoc/data/documents/2020/aac_105c_2l/aac_105c_2l_316_0_html/AC105_C2_L316E.pdf.
Cosgrove, Denis. 1994. "Contested Global Visions: One-World, Whole-Earth, and the Apollo Space Photographs." *Annals of the Association of American Geographers* 84(2): 270–294.
Crawford, Neta C. 2019. "Pentagon Fuel Use, Climate Change, and the Costs of War." *Watson Institute Brown University*, June. https://watson.brown.edu/costsofwar/files/cow/imce/papers/2019/Pentagon%20Fuel%20Use,%20Climate%20Change%20and%20the%20Costs%20of%20War%20Final.pdf.
Deudney, Daniel. 2020. *Dark Skies: Space Expansionism, Planetary Geopolitics, and the Ends of Humanity*. Oxford and New York: Oxford University Press.
Dickens, Peter. 2009. "The Cosmos as Capitalism's Outside." *The Sociological Review* 57(1): 66–82. https://doi.org/10.1111/j.1467-954X.2009.01817.x.
Dickens, Peter, and James S. Omrod. 2007. *Cosmic Society: Towards a Sociology of the Universe*. London: Routledge.
"ESA Commissions World's First Space Debris Removal." 2019. September 12, 2019. https://www.esa.int/Safety_Security/Clean_Space/ESA_commissions_world_s_first_space_debris_removal.
Grove, Nicole Sunday. 2021. "'Welcome to Mars': Space Colonization, Anticipatory Authoritarianism, and the Labour of Hope." *Globalizations*, January, 1–16. https://doi.org/10.1080/14747731.2020.1859764.
Grush, Loren. 2018. "Why Mining the Water on the Moon Could Open Up Space Exploration." *The Verge*, August 23, 2018. https://www.theverge.com/2018/8/23/17769034/nasa-moon-lunar-water-ice-mining-propellant-depots.
Hamilton, Clive. 2017. *Defiant Earth*. Cambridge: Polity Press.
Helmreich, Stefan. 2011. "From Spaceship Earth to Google Ocean: Planetary Icons, Indexes, and Infrastructures." *Social Research* 78(4): 1211–1242.
Janssen, Marco A., Lance Gharavi, and Michael Yichao. 2020. "Keeping Up Shared Infrastructure on a Port of Mars: An Experimental Study." *International Journal of the Commons* 14(1): 404–417. https://doi.org/10.5334/ijc.1017.
Kwong, Emily. 2020. "Space Junk: How Cluttered Is the Final Frontier?: Short Wave." *NPR.Org*, January 13, 2020 https://www.npr.org/2020/01/10/795246131/space-junk-how-cluttered-is-the-final-frontier.
Luke, Timothy W. 2019. *Anthropocene Alerts: Critical Theory of the Contemporary as Ecocritique*. New York: Telos Press.
MacDonald, Alexander. 2017. *The Long Space Age*. New Haven: Yale University Press.
MacDonald, Fraser. 2007. "Anti-*Astropolitik* — Outer Space and the Orbit of Geography." *Progress in Human Geography* 31(5): 592–615. https://doi.org/10.1177/0309132507081492.
Marcuse, Herbert. 1972. *Counterrevolution and Revolt*. Boston: Beacon Press.
McCarthy, Kevin. 2015. "Text - H.R.2262 - 114th Congress (2015-2016): U.S. Commercial Space Launch Competitiveness Act." Legislation. 2015/2016. November 25, 2015. https://www.congress.gov/bill/114th-congress/house-bill/2262/text.
McCormick, Patricia K. 2013. "Space Debris: Conjunction Opportunities and Opportunities for International Cooperation." *Science and Public Policy (SPP)* 40(6): 801–813. https://doi.org/10.1093/scipol/sct028.
McFall-Johnsen, Morgan, and Dave Mosher. n.d. "Elon Musk Says He Plans to Send 1 Million People to Mars by 2050 by Launching 3 Starship Rockets Every Day and Creating 'a Lot of Jobs' on the Red Planet." *Business Insider*. Accessed May 22, 2021. https://www.businessinsider.com/elon-musk-plans-1-million-people-to-mars-by-2050-2020-1.
Newman, Christopher J., and Mark Williamson. 2018. "Space Sustainability: Reframing the Debate." *Space Policy* 46(November): 30–37. https://doi.org/10.1016/j.spacepol.2018.03.001.
Olson, Valerie. 2013. "NEOEcology: The Solar System's Emerging Environmental History and Politics." In *New Natures: Joining Environmental History with Sciences and Technology Studies*, edited by Dolly Jørgensen, Finn Arne Jørgensen, and Sara B. Pritchard, 195–211. Pittsburgh: University of Pittsburgh Press.

Olson, Valerie, and Lisa Messeri. 2015. "Beyond the Anthropocene: Un-Earthing an Epoch." *Environment and Society* 6(1). https://doi.org/10.3167/ares.2015.060103.

Parker, Martin. 2009. "Capitalists in Space." *The Sociological Review* 57(1): 83–97. https://doi.org/10.1111/j.1467-954X.2009.01818.x.

Patel, Neel V. 2016. "Elon Musk Wants to Make SpaceX the Union Pacific Railroad to Mars." *Inverse*, September 27, 2016. https://www.inverse.com/article/21490-elon-musk-mars-spacex-union-pacific-railroad-mars.

Ray, Emily, and Sean Parson. 2020. "Star Power: Outer Space Mining and the Metabolic Rift." In *Limits to Terrestrial Extraction*, 1st ed., 54–73. London: Routledge.

"RES 2222 (XXI)." 1996. United Nations Office for Outer Space Affairs. https://www.unoosa.org/oosa/oosadoc/data/resolutions/1966/general_assembly_21st_session/res_2222_xxi.html.

Reynolds, Glenn H., and Robert P. Merges. 1997. *Outer Space: Problems of Law and Policy*, 2nd ed. Boulder, CO: Westview Press.

Shammas, Victor L., and Tomas B. Holen. 2019. "One Giant Leap for Capitalistkind: Private Enterprise in Outer Space." *Palgrave Communications* 5(1): 10. https://doi.org/10.1057/s41599-019-0218-9.

Sheetz, Michael. 2021. "Investment in Space Companies Put at Record $8.9 Billion in 2020 despite Covid." *CNBC*, January 25, 2021. https://www.cnbc.com/2021/01/25/investing-in-space-companies-hits-record-8point9-billion-in-2020-report.html.

Smith, Yvette. 2015. "The Star of the ISS." *Textile*. NASA. July 9, 2015. http://www.nasa.gov/star-of-the-iss.

Steer, Cassandra. 2017. "Global Commons, Cosmic Commons: Implications of Military and Security Uses of Outer Space." *Georgetown Journal of International Affairs* 18(1): 9–16. https://doi.org/10.1353/gia.2017.0003.

Sutch, Peter, and Peri Roberts. 2019. "Outer Space and Neo-colonial Injustice: Distributive Justice and the Continuous Scramble for Dominium." *International Journal of Social Economics* 46(11): 1291–1304. https://doi.org/10.1108/IJSE-03-2019-0152.

Tepper, Eytan. 2019. "Discourse on the Exploitation of Space Resources." *Space Policy* 59 (August). https://doi.org/10.1016/j.spacepol.2018.06.004.

# PART IV

# Ecological and Earth Systems Law

# 11

# TAMING GAIA 2.0

## Earth System Law in the Ruptured Anthropocene[1]

*Rakhyun E. Kim*

The Earth system is on the verge of crossing tipping points. Defined as "a critical threshold at which a tiny perturbation can qualitatively alter the state or development of a system" (Lenton et al. 2008, 1786), tipping points mark an abrupt change in the equilibrium state of Earth's various tipping elements. Among the most impending tipping points is in the West Antarctic ice sheet, which is predicted to disintegrate if current global warming trends continue (IPCC 2019). This transformational process will in turn interact with other tipping elements such as the thermohaline circulation and the Amazon rainforest, which could also transition into a new state (Nobre et al. 2016; Stouffer et al. 2006). The interactions between tipping points will likely generate a global tipping cascade (Lade et al. 2020; Rocha et al. 2018), posing catastrophic or even existential risks to humanity and other life forms (Bostrom and Ćirković 2008; Xu et al. 2020). Based on models and observations, Earth system scientists warn that "we might already have lost control of whether tipping happens" (Lenton et al. 2019, 595), and that the risk of irreversible transformation on a planetary scale could be imminent. This has led some critics to conclude that "[i]t's too late to negotiate with the Earth" (Hamilton 2015a, 39). Humanity is not simply standing on a precipice as many seem to argue (Ord 2020), but rather stumbling toward it. We may fall at any moment, which will mark an irreparable rupture in time (Hamilton 2015b).

Yet, taking the idea of rupture as a plausible hypothesis and discussing its governance implications have largely been avoided in academic literature. The situation might be comparable to how adaptation was considered taboo in early climate policy debates (Pielke et al. 2007). Understandably, we would want to remain hopeful that there is still time to save humanity from falling off the precipice; otherwise, we might have no reason to act now. But accepting that global tipping could be inevitable is not necessarily a matter of binary choice between environmental determinism and technological utopianism (Dalby 2016). Rather, it is about accepting what is likely inescapable and creating a habitable planet (Dryzek and Pickering 2019). It underscores the need for humanity to fully embrace the idea of planetary stewardship and become humble yet active stewards of the Earth system (Chapin et al. 2010; Steffen et al. 2011). What this new form of "environmentalism" will look like is yet unclear. We have only begun to reflect on the assumptions of today's environmental institutions in the search for a new teleology in what I call the ruptured Anthropocene that lies beyond the precipice.

In this article, I explore the implications of the concept of Anthropocene rupture for international environmental law in particular, which is here loosely understood as the system of norms,

DOI: 10.4324/9781003388081-15

rules, principles, and other institutions that work to protect the global environment from human impact (Kim and Mackey 2014). My thesis is that, for international environmental law to stay relevant in the ruptured Anthropocene, it would need to shift away from its traditional focus on restoring the planetary past, and instead play an active role in the making of planetary futures. When tipping occurs, the relatively stable conditions of the Holocene will likely become impossible to restore, especially through the conventional environmental approach of simply reducing the human footprint. The notion of environmental protection would then lose its relevance, and international environmental law will need a new purpose in the ruptured Anthropocene.

This new purpose, as I will argue, is to create a life-supporting Gaia 2.0 by nurturing the planetary stewardship capacity of human societies. Gaia 2.0 is a term Lenton and Latour (2018) introduced to denote a fundamentally new state of the Earth system. Whereas Gaia has so far "operated without foresight or planning on the part of organisms," the hypothesis is that humans are now capable of playing a significant role in the deliberate self-regulation of Gaia 2.0 (Lenton and Latour 2018, 1066). We may for example set goals and steer the course of "Spaceship Earth" toward a desirable future for all life forms. Gaia 2.0 is, in a way, a Gaia tamed by humanity. International environmental law would then need to provide an effective and legitimate framework for human societies to fully embrace the complexity of the Earth system, intimately connect with Gaia, and become responsible stewards of all earthlings (Folke et al. 2021).

Under various banners such as Lex Anthropocenae (Kotzé and French 2018), scholars have been sketching out the contours of next-generation international environmental law 2.0 for a profoundly changed, complex world of the Anthropocene (Brown Weiss 2020; Brunnée 2019; Gonzalez 2015; Kim and Bosselmann 2013; Kotzé 2017; Lim 2019; Robinson 2014; Scott 2013; Vidas et al. 2015; Viñuales 2018). In this article, I contribute to this burgeoning literature, and more broadly to the study of global environmental governance in the Anthropocene (Biermann 2021; Burch et al. 2019; Dryzek and Pickering 2019; Galaz 2014; Pattberg and Zelli 2016), by drawing on the concept of Earth system law that has emerged as a promising alternative legal imaginary (Kotzé and Kim 2019). As a nascent concept, however, Earth system law has not yet fully embraced the inevitability of global tipping. Instead, the discussion has been occupied with the limitations of current international environmental law for respecting planetary boundaries (Kotzé 2020) and how Earth system law could be more effective in that regard (Kim and Kotzé 2021). Noting this, the aim of this article is to explore the implications of the Anthropocene rupture, specifically, for Earth system law and governance.

Following this introduction, I begin with an overview of the key differences between the Holocene and the Anthropocene, which I further divide into two distinct periods: the early Anthropocene and the ruptured Anthropocene, separated by the moment when a global cascade of tipping points is triggered. Then I explain why international environmental law in its current form would lose its relevance in the ruptured Anthropocene, and argue that it will need to support an active form of planetary stewardship and become instrumental in taming Gaia 2.0. Finally, I refer to the concept of Earth system law and offer my perspective on how it might capture what is required of international environmental law 2.0 in the ruptured Anthropocene.

## The Ruptured Anthropocene

The concept of the Anthropocene is highly contested. There is a lack of consensus on when exactly this most recent geological epoch began with estimates ranging very widely from the first deliberate use of fire by hominids one to two million years ago and the onset of agriculture about 10,000 years ago, to the Great Acceleration in human activity that followed the Second World War (Lewis and Maslin 2015; Malhi 2017). Despite the disagreement, the core idea of the Anthropocene is widely shared: the Anthropocene denotes a period in geological time when Homo sapiens has become a geophysical force (Steffen et al. 2007). For the first time in planetary history, a single species has acquired the power to disturb the self-regulation of the Earth system. No doubt this demands we rethink our place and role in the community of life (Biermann and Lövbrand 2019).

With the Anthropocene understood in such a way, however, its implications for international environmental law have not been fundamentally different from those of the Holocene; that is, we must live within the limits of the planet Earth. Humanity would simply need to take more of the same measures as stipulated in existing international environmental agreements to prevent serious or irreversible damage, such as "dangerous anthropogenic interference with the climate system" (United Nations Framework Convention on Climate Change, Article 2). The only difference would be the sense of urgency and priority to implement these laws by, for example, recognizing that we are in a climate emergency. This has led legal scholars to call for bolstering existing "legal boundaries" to limit human impact on the environment within planetary boundaries (Chapron et al. 2017), which collectively define the Holocene basin of attraction (Rockström et al. 2009).

But fundamentally, planetary boundaries will lose much of their relevance and usefulness once we step over the edge of the cliff that lies somewhere beyond the boundaries, and start a deep dive into the Anthropocene's dark abyss (Biermann and Kim 2020; Kim and Kotzé 2020). This is not to suggest that our current environmental efforts to minimize our interference with the Earth system are completely meaningless. Even if we have lost the ability to avoid tipping points, we would not want to overshoot at high speed. However, it is important to recognize that, once we cross tipping points, the transformation of the Earth system will likely be irreversible, making a return to Holocene conditions an impossibility in the absence of active intervention on the part of humans (Steffen et al. 2018).

What I, therefore, take as the starting point for reimagining international environmental law is that the Anthropocene signifies the start of an entirely new, non-analog state of the Earth system, one that is fundamentally different from the Holocene (Steffen et al. 2004). At its core is the notion of regime shift or critical transition (Scheffer et al. 2012), in which the Earth system transitions from one epoch to another. We are familiar with examples of such ecosystem change at sub-global scales (Folke et al. 2004) with tundra turning to boreal forests or tropical forests turning to savannas (Biggs et al. 2018). The idea of the Anthropocene suggests that similar thresholds exist at the planetary scale, and the entire Earth system, as it has in the past, can and will go through a regime shift from one stable state to another, but this time due to human actions. Once the Earth system crosses a critical tipping point in the climate system, for example, it would enter a new basin of attraction and takes on new dynamics. Then the Earth system will never be the same again even if human societies manage to reduce the atmospheric greenhouse gas concentrations back to pre-industrial levels. The Earth system would need to be pushed even harder to the opposite extreme to be brought out of the new stable state (Steffen et al. 2018). When the West Antarctic ice sheet collapses, for example, it will not regrow to the present extent until temperatures are at least one degree Celsius below pre-industrial levels (Garbe et al. 2020).

This understanding of the Anthropocene as a rupture in planetary history (Hamilton 2015b) builds on the view of the Earth system as a complex adaptive system (Steffen et al. 2020). It is a system that exhibits nonlinear properties such as resilience but also threshold behavior if pushed too far. From this perspective, to say that the Earth system has entered the Anthropocene means that humans have pushed the planet beyond some of its critical tipping points and triggered global tipping cascades (as opposed to simply suggesting that humans have the ability to do so), and now the Earth system has started a one-way transition into a new stable state. This planetary regime shift may take place on geological timescales over millennia to complete due to feedback delays. Based on the current trajectory, scientists predict that a "Hothouse Earth" awaits at the end (Steffen et al. 2018), which will likely be hostile to life as we know it. Once the Earth system reaches that state, the resilience of the system will try to keep it in the new state. Simply reducing the human footprint would be insufficient or even counterproductive to move the Earth system out of the new basin of attraction.

From a governance perspective, it is then useful to differentiate the Anthropocene epoch into two distinct periods: before and after global tipping cascades are triggered. I call them the early Anthropocene and the ruptured Anthropocene, which are two different conceptualizations of the Anthropocene from stratigraphic and Earth system perspectives, respectively (Steffen et al. 2016). Table 11.1 provides an overview of their key differences, also in relation to the Holocene. From an Earth system perspective, the early Anthropocene is when the Earth system still remains in the Holocene basin of attraction, whereas the ruptured Anthropocene begins when the Earth system has entered a new basin of attraction. The precise moment when the Earth system would move into a new basin is difficult to predict. But for the purpose of informing governance responses, it is reasonable to assume that the ruptured Anthropocene begins when we can no longer avoid tipping points by just reducing the human footprint on the planet, but when humans must also actively intervene in the Earth system (e.g. MacMartin et al. 2018). In the rest

*Table 11.1* The Holocene, the early Anthropocene, and the ruptured Anthropocene

| | *Holocene* | *Anthropocene* | |
|---|---|---|---|
| | | *Early Anthropocene* | *Ruptured Anthropocene* |
| Human impact | Human impact is negligible on the functioning of the Earth system | Humans as a geophysical force pushed the Earth system to the edge of the Holocene basin of attraction | Humans trigger a global tipping cascade and cause the Earth system to move into a new basin of attraction |
| System state | The Earth system is within the Holocene envelope of natural variability | The Earth system is in an unstable transition state, but it remains in the Holocene basin of attraction | The Earth system is in a new basin of attraction, and it gravitates to the bottom (a new stable state) at an accelerating rate |
| Start date | 11,700 years ago due to natural causes | When humans started leaving stratigraphic signatures; contested but the mid-twentieth century is a strong candidate | When the Earth system crosses critical tipping points; uncertain but the early twenty-first century is a reasonable estimate |
| Evidence | Carbon dioxide concentrations in ice cores | Stratigraphic presence of radioactive elements from the first atomic bomb test | Early warning signals for critical transitions in various tipping elements |
| Governance response | Manage natural resources sustainably | Minimize human interference with the Earth system, and maintain or restore ecological integrity | Actively intervene in the Earth system to move it out of the hostile state and into a human-maintained basin of attraction |

of this article, I proceed with the assumption that we have reached that point of no return, given the combined commitments under the United Nations Framework Convention on Climate Change (2021) still fall far short of what is required to limit global warming below two degrees Celsius, which is expected to be the tipping point for the Greenland and West Antarctic ice sheets (Pattyn 2018).

## International Environmental Law in a State of Limbo

If we accept that humanity has in effect entered the ruptured Anthropocene, then it prompts us to revisit and scrutinize the foundations of international environmental law. This is necessary not only because the rupture implies the blurring of the human-nature dichotomy (Biermann 2021), but more importantly because the environment itself is undergoing profound transformations, as the Earth system tends toward a new, less habitable, basin of attraction. The biosphere is not simply disappearing into the technosphere, but a new "environment" is arriving, and this time, it will in all likelihood not be friendly to humans and many other forms of life. Modern environmentalism, therefore, has come to an end with the Anthropocene rupture in the sense that the environment no longer exists as an object for protection from humans. International environmental law, in its current form, would therefore soon lose relevance since it has been designed precisely with this objective in mind: to protect the environment from human activities.

Current international environmental law, just like domestic environmental law (Tarlock 1994), has been founded on the equilibrium paradigm in ecology (Kim and Mackey 2014). The assumption is that the basin of attraction in the Holocene is known to science, and if the Earth system was left by itself with little anthropogenic interference, we may reasonably predict the stable state in which the system would end up. This state is called Holocene stability, which is what international environmental law currently aims to restore. Generally speaking, international environmental law emerged and evolved over the past few decades with a view to regulating human activity to "let nature be" and maintain global environmental change within the Holocene envelope of natural variability. This claimed purpose of international environmental law found its expression in the notion of integrity, which was famously proposed by Leopold (1949) as a normative ideal on par with the beauty and stability of the biotic community. Today, all major soft law instruments of international environmental law such as the Rio Declaration on Environment and Development embrace global ecological integrity as a key virtue (Kim and Bosselmann 2015), as well as several multilateral environmental agreements including the Paris Agreement that notes in its preamble "the importance of ensuring the integrity of all ecosystems."

But what is the meaning of global ecological integrity in the ruptured Anthropocene where equilibrium no longer remains a valid assumption on a planetary scale? The integrity of Earth's ecosystem in the ruptured Anthropocene would not be the same as integrity as we know it. The Earth system after rupture acquires a different identity, and its new normal state will unlikely be forgiving to many life forms, including humans. The Earth system will continue to support life in the ruptured Anthropocene, but the life that would thrive in such conditions will be drastically different from today. Indeed the sixth mass extinction is accelerating, whereby more than three-quarters of species may disappear in a geologically short interval (Barnosky et al. 2011). Humans in particular will likely struggle to prosper in such changing conditions, and for those in vulnerable positions, even to survive (Lynas, 2020). Living in harmony with nature might eventually become an oxymoron as the "revenge of Gaia" intensifies (Lovelock 2006). And yet, this nonlinear transition from the early Anthropocene to the ruptured Anthropocene is irreversible, unless humans destabilize the new stable state. The notion of planetary integrity that has played a significant role in guiding international environmental law will therefore lose its utility as a reference point for the unattainable re-wilding campaign of international environmental law (Bridgewater et al. 2014).

So, international environmental law is currently in a state of limbo, or the "Anthropocene gap" (Galaz 2014). It remains nostalgic for the past, but the past conditions of the Holocene have become impossible to restore by reducing our ecological footprint. The Earth system has silently crossed irreversible tipping points (or it will do so soon), and humanity has no other option but to go forward in time into the (un)knowable unknown. Global environmental protection as currently understood as curtailing human interference with the Earth system will not remain suitable as the dominant paradigm during this one-way transition into a deep, likely hostile, basin of attraction. What it means to be an environmentalist when the Earth system was tending toward Holocene stability is fundamentally different from when the Earth system is undergoing a transformation in the ruptured Anthropocene. International environmental law will need a new raison d'être for "postapocalyptic" environmentalism.

## Taming Gaia 2.0

The idea of Anthropocene rupture is not about giving up and "try anything now" (Purdy 2015). Accepting that the Earth system will not go back to the Holocene state does not imply there is no urgency or reason for humans to act responsibly. For one, we may still have some control over the rate at which environmental risks cascade or damage accumulates (Hughes et al. 2013; Lenton et al. 2020; Rocha et al. 2018). This is especially so if we manage to maintain biodiversity for ecosystem resilience (Folke et al. 2021) or govern interacting tipping elements (Galaz et al. 2017; Sterner et al. 2019; Walker et al. 2009). But we must act fast. The Earth system will pick up momentum as it goes through transformation, and there is little we could do then to change its trajectory. The sooner we act, the more agency we would have over the future of Earth.

At a more fundamental level, however, what surviving in the ruptured Anthropocene demands is a paradigm shift from a passive to an active form of planetary stewardship. The idea that humans need to become active stewards of the Earth's life-support system implies that simply reducing human interference is not sufficient to maintain planetary life-supporting capacity, but we need to actively intervene where necessary. Metaphorically speaking, humanity needs to make Spaceship Earth maneuverable. If international environmental law in the early Anthropocene aimed to maintain Spaceship Earth on its previous trajectory (Kim and Bosselmann 2013), international environmental law 2.0 in the ruptured Anthropocene should help imagine a safe and just future for all, put the "derailed" spaceship back on a desirable trajectory, and monitor its course.

Gaia 2.0 as conceptualized by Lenton and Latour (2018) is a useful metaphor for thinking about the challenge of navigating Spaceship Earth through the ruptured Anthropocene. The basic premise of this concept is that, in the Anthropocene, humans have not only become a geophysical force, but we have become aware of the consequences of our actions on the planet. The emergence of self-awareness as a new feedback loop between humanity and Gaia theoretically allows for deliberate self-regulation. In other words, Gaia 2.0 refers to a hypothetical state of the Earth system where humans have not only acquired disruptive agency, but also some degree of curative agency for life on Earth. Gaia 2.0 is a Gaia tamed by humanity. I borrowed the notion of taming from Barabási (2005) in the context of "taming complexity," but also from the French novel Le Petit Prince by Antoine de Saint-Exupéry (1943). In the novel, the fox explains to the little prince that "apprivoiser" (taming) means "créer des liens" (establishing ties) and "deviens responsable pour toujours de ce que tu as apprivoisé" (becoming responsible forever for what you have tamed). It is in this sense that humanity may need to act somewhat like "the God species" (Lynas 2011). As I will illustrate below, however, the idea of playing God to survive on Earth raises uncomfortable questions. A key role for the new form of international environmental law would then be to regulate, or strengthen and limit, the exercise of our curative agency.

One could imagine geoengineering, as a potential interventionist tool, becoming a significant part of what international environmental law 2.0 would need to regulate. Here I am not resorting to geoengineering as a quick fix or cheaper alternative to costly climate mitigation measures (Caldeira et al. 2013). Geoengineering is neither quick nor cheap when unintended consequences and associated costs of externalities are fully taken into account (Barrett 2008; Zarnetske et al. 2021). But certain forms of geoengineering, such as ocean alkalinity enhancement (Burns and Corbett 2020), may become a necessary part of long-term survival strategies for creating the minimally required conditions for a habitable planet. Despite uncertainties and imperfections, geoengineering may become indispensable for terraforming Earth so it can continue to support life as we know it in the ruptured Anthropocene. International environmental law 2.0 would then need to provide the legal basis for humanity to make wise use of powerful but controversial tools such as geoengineering for the purpose of active planetary stewardship.

The idea of Gaia 2.0 is still hypothetical, and hence it needs to be considered with caution. The exercise of curative agency, despite its good intentions, will certainly lead to unintended consequences with social and environmental implications. In fact, it may no longer be useful to frame humans as "overwhelming the great forces of nature" (Steffen et al. 2007, 614). The ability to perturb a system may not require great force. Although humans have agency to disturb the Earth system and push it across tipping points, we will unlikely acquire the power to shape it precisely the way we want. We will need to approach the Earth system as a hypercomplex entity, whose behavior we will never entirely master and control. Gaia has always been powerful and will remain so.

While continuing to express humanity's humility in the light of powerful Gaia, international environmental law 2.0 would need to become a key instrument with which human societies negotiate and tame Gaia 2.0. Environmentalism in the ruptured Anthropocene will not stay in the reactive and passive form of environmentalism, curtailing our impact or interference with the environment as it has been doing and continues to do so, but must rather adopt a form of active planetary stewardship (Steffen et al. 2011). This means identifying, deliberating, and selecting interventions, and actively steering the Earth system toward a desirable future among many other plausible futures (Bai et al. 2016). We disturbed the system and now, whether we like it or not, we must take full responsibility by taking ownership and choosing our own future. Earth system governance scholarship has begun exploring the implications of such thinking (Burch et al. 2019), and international environmental law scholarship will need to join the debate (Stephens 2018; Vidas et al. 2014; Viñuales 2018).

## Earth System Law: A Legal Imaginary for Charting a Habitable Future

In recent years, a group of scholars in the Earth system governance community has proposed Earth system law as a new legal paradigm for the Anthropocene (Gellers 2021; Kotzé 2020; Kotzé and Kim 2019, 2021; Kim and Kotzé 2020; Mai and Boulot 2021). Although its meaning is still evolving, Kim and Kotzé (2020, 11) offer a tentative definition:

> Earth system law [is] an innovative legal imaginary that is rooted in the Anthropocene's planetary context and its perceived socio-ecological crisis. Earth system law is aligned with, and responsive to, the Earth system's functional, spatial, and temporal complexities; and the multiple Earth system science and social science-based governance challenges arising from a non-analog state in which the Earth system currently operates.

While it is neither exclusively confined to the international nor environmental domains, the Earth system law imaginary finds its origin in international environmental law scholarship. Conceived as forming the juridical dimension of Earth system governance, Earth system law is useful for the systematic interrogation of the role of international environmental law in the Anthropocene, particularly in relation to questions about complexity, inclusivity, interdependencies, and pathways for planetary justice (Kotz 2019).

Importantly, Earth system law, as currently conceptualized, acknowledges that the pursuit of environmental protection is unlikely to remain tenable as we move deeper into the Anthropocene (Lorimer 2015). Although primarily built on the assumptions of what I define as the early Anthropocene (Table 11.1), Earth system law does recognize the possibility and implications of the Anthropocene rupture. In particular, it is explicit in finding international environmental law ill-equipped "for navigating, and ultimately surviving, the unknown and unsafe space that lies far outside the planetary boundaries' upper limits" (Kim and Kotzé 2020, 13). In that sense, Earth system law acknowledges the arrow of time (or the irreversibility of the Anthropocene rupture) and seeks to address the normative void (or global environmental protection becoming an outdated concept). Earth system law is proactive rather than reactive, and future-oriented rather than past-dependent. It is founded on neither anthropocentric nor ecocentric ethics, the division of which has become irrelevant. Instead, Earth system law embraces the ethics of planetary stewardship (Schmidt et al. 2016).

However, the concept of Earth system law and its attendant scholarship have not yet fully embraced the idea of Anthropocene rupture. In that regard, there are at least four prominent challenges that Earth system law research will need to address in the coming years. Addressing these challenges will help to institute active planetary stewardship for taming Gaia 2.0 through the exercise of curative agency.

The first is the challenge of building reflexivity into the design of Earth system law. Stewarding the Earth system demands us to think about the consequences of our actions in "deep time" and plan on geological timescales (Shoshitaishvili 2020), but also to react quickly to abrupt changes and cascading risks (Galaz 2019). For example, we will need to align our thinking with very slow Earth system processes as well as pick up early warning signals for anticipating critical transitions and navigating these very transitions as they unfold (Scheffer et al. 2009, 2012). Therefore, Earth system law will need to strike a balance between stability and flexibility (which would constantly shift), while accepting change as the norm and institutionalizing reflexivity into law (Dryzek 2014). We may need a system of law that is fully modeled after the complex adaptive Earth system itself (Kim and Mackey 2014). The architecture of Earth system law would not only allow for institutional adaptation to incremental changes but also for switching to a new system state when the state of its regulatory objects undergoes transformation.

The second is the challenge of democratizing Earth system science. Earth system law needs to be informed by Earth system science, and yet Earth system science has been criticized for lacking democratic legitimacy. This is particularly concerning because Earth system science heavily depends on modeling as a key method (Steffen et al. 2020), where the assumptions that modelers bring to their models influence output. Therefore, it is important to consider who these scientists are and where they come from, especially those that participate in the drafting of authoritative scientific assessments that shape policy (Ho-Lem et al. 2011; Gay-Antaki and Liverman 2018). One issue under discussion is how to democratize planetary boundaries (Kim and Kotzé 2020), which are criticized as technocratic (Biermann and Kim 2020). Some argue that democratization in this context is achievable through a legitimate division of labor between experts, citizens, and policymakers (Pickering and Persson 2019). Yet, the non-governmental nature of such target-setting initiatives raises fundamental questions of the legitimacy and accountability of Earth system science. The recently formed Earth Commission is an example (Rockström et al. 2021), which faces the inherent challenge of representing diverse values in the targets they set for all. Earth system law will need to become instrumental in addressing such issues and ultimately improve the science–policy interface.

The third is the challenge of expanding the scope of planetary justice. At the core of Earth system law are fundamental questions of justice on a planetary scale (Biermann and Kalfagianni 2020). The politics of the ruptured Anthropocene will likely be "ugly" (Dalby 2016) or unsettling to say the least, and this will have myriad implications for justice at all levels and scales. Whichever trajectory humans choose for the future of our planet, certain groups and species will win while others will lose from new planetary risks (Berkhout 2014). Then it is the role of Earth system law to ensure that the costs and benefits are equitably shared. Importantly, the scope of planetary justice must reach beyond Holocene thinking, and address normative questions involving resource allocation not only between the rich and the poor (Kashwan et al. 2020) but also between the present and future generations, as well as between humans and non-humans (Dryzek and Pickering 2019). Earth system law should guarantee the marginalized, the unborn, and the non-human a voice and a seat at the table (Gellers 2021), and ensure their needs and interests are properly considered when choosing a future.

The fourth is the challenge of anticipatory governance. In the ruptured Anthropocene, the politics of the future will become increasingly potent. The imaginaries of the future will become powerful while the images of the irreversible past will lose relative importance. Then it becomes important to consider who is actively creating the imaginaries of the future, through what process, which imaginary becomes dominant, and why (Lövbrand et al. 2015; Oomen et al. 2021). The making of planetary futures does not and should not happen in a "cockpit" (Hajer et al. 2015), and global goal-setting becomes "the ultimate challenge of planetary stewardship" in the Anthropocene (Young et al. 2017, 53). A key role of Earth system law will be to regulate the power of "futuring" and ensure inclusivity in the process of social exploration and experimentation (Carpenter et al. 2019). This would require the strengthening of democratic institutions at all levels of governance. For example, the world's diverse regions should be able to maintain autonomy and make their own choices about their futures (Bennett et al. 2021), but these choices will need to be reconciled at the global level through deliberative governance (Dryzek et al. 2019).

## Conclusion

The Anthropocene is not simply pointing to the increasing scale and magnitude of human impact and the associated need for urgent action. As a rupture in planetary history, the Anthropocene requires a corresponding "state shift" in the way we think about the past and future. This includes a reconsideration of the assumptions on which international environmental law is founded, namely the restorability of Holocene stability. When the Earth system crosses critical tipping points and begins a forceful, nonlinear transformation into a new state, the notion of protecting the global environment from humans will lose its meaning.

Earth system law for the ruptured Anthropocene is therefore not merely a more stringent form of international environmental law of the early Anthropocene. The environment as we know it will soon end, and it will no longer exist as an object for protection from human activities. By embracing a new set of assumptions of the ruptured Anthropocene, Earth system law will have to be radically different in fundamental ways from international environmental law in its current form. What will become key is to regulate the exercise of our curative agency in taming Gaia 2.0 and maintaining its capacity to support life as we know it. In this regard, Earth system law will need to play an active role in steering Spaceship Earth toward a desirable future, while centrally concerned with questions of justice on a planetary scale.

With the overall aim to stimulate a debate, this article has raised more questions than providing answers. What exactly this new form of Earth system law will look like remains an open question. But I argue that Earth system law is critical in enabling a safe and just transition for a safe and just future, by creating a level playing field for the politics of the future. Its contents should be filled by as many human and non-human voices as possible. To that end, Earth system law scholarship will require interdisciplinary and transdisciplinary research efforts, not only by drawing on legal theories but also by actively engaging with Earth system scientists and Earth system governance scholars, as well as various stakeholders who can represent the marginalized, the unborn, and the non-human.

## Note

1 This chapter is a stylistic modification of the article originally published as "Taming Gaia 2.0: Earth system law in the ruptured Anthropocene," *The Anthropocen Review*: https://doi.org/10.1177/20530196211026721. The article is published under Creative Commons license 4.0. For details see https://creativecommons.org/licenses/by/4.0/.

## References

Bai, Xuemei, Sander van der Leeuw, Karen O'Brien, Frans Berkhout, Frank Biermann, Eduardo S. Brondizio, Christophe Cudennec, et al. 2016. "Plausible and Desirable Futures in the Anthropocene: A New Research Agenda." *Global Environmental Change* 39: 351–62.

Barabási, Albert-László. 2005. "Taming Complexity." *Nature Physics* 1(2): 68–70.

Barnosky, Anthony D., Nicholas Matzke, Susumu Tomiya, Guinevere O. U. Wogan, Brian Swartz, Tiago B. Quental, Charles Marshall, et al. 2011. "Has the Earth's Sixth Mass Extinction Already Arrived?" *Nature* 470(7336): 51–7.

Barrett, Scott. 2008. "The Incredible Economics of Geoengineering." *Environmental and Resource Economics* 39(1): 45–54.

Bennett, Elena M., Reinette Biggs, Garry D. Peterson, and Line J. Gordon. 2021. "Patchwork Earth: Navigating Pathways to Just, Thriving, and Sustainable Futures." *One Earth* 4: 172–76.

Berkhout, Frans. 2014. "Anthropocene Futures." *The Anthropocene Review* 1(2): 154–59.

Biermann, Frank. 2021. "The Future of 'Environmental' Policy in the Anthropocene: Time for a Paradigm Shift." *Environmental Politics* 30(1–2): 61–80.

Biermann, Frank, and Agni Kalfagianni. 2020. "Planetary Justice: A Research Framework." *Earth System Governance* 6: 100049.

Biermann, Frank, and Rakhyun E. Kim. 2020. "The Boundaries of the Planetary Boundary Framework: A Critical Appraisal of Approaches to Define a 'Safe Operating Space' for Humanity." *Annual Review of Environment and Resources* 45(1): 497–521.

Biermann, Frank, and Eva Lövbrand, eds. 2019. *Anthropocene Encounters: New Directions in Green Political Thinking*. Cambridge: Cambridge University Press.

Biggs, Reinette, Garry D. Peterson, and Juan C. Rocha. 2018. "The Regime Shifts Database: A Framework for Analyzing Regime Shifts in Social-Ecological Systems." *Ecology and Society* 23(3): 9.

Bostrom, Nick, and Milan M. Ćirković, eds. 2008. *Global Catastrophic Risks*. Oxford: Oxford University Press.

Bridgewater, Peter, Rakhyun E. Kim, and Klaus Bosselmann. 2014. "Ecological Integrity: A Relevant Concept for International Environmental Law in the Anthropocene?" *Yearbook of International Environmental Law* 25(1): 61–78.

Brunnée, Jutta. 2019. "The Rule of International (Environmental) Law and Complex Problems." In *The International Rule of Law: Rise or Decline?*, edited by Heike Krieger, Georg Nolte, and Andreas Zimmermann. 211–231, Oxford: Oxford University Press.

Burch, Sarah, Aarti Gupta, Cristina Y. A. Inoue, Agni Kalfagianni, Åsa Persson, Andrea K. Gerlak, Atsushi Ishii, et al. 2019. "New Directions in Earth System Governance Research." *Earth System Governance* 1: 100006.

Burns, Wil, and Charles R. Corbett. 2020. "Antacids for the Sea? Artificial Ocean Alkalinization and Climate Change." *One Earth* 3(2): 154–56.

Caldeira, Ken, Govindasamy Bala, and Long Cao. 2013. "The Science of Geoengineering." *Annual Review of Earth and Planetary Sciences* 41(1): 231–56.

Carpenter, Stephen R., Carl Folke, Marten Scheffer, and Frances R. Westley. 2019. "Dancing on the Volcano: Social Exploration in Times of Discontent." *Ecology and Society* 24(1): 23.

Chapin III, F. Stuart, Stephen R. Carpenter, Gary P. Kofinas, Carl Folke, Nick Abel, William C. Clark, Per Olsson, et al. 2010. "Ecosystem Stewardship: Sustainability Strategies for a Rapidly Changing Planet." *Trends in Ecology and Evolution* 25(4): 241–49.

Chapron, Guillaume, Yaffa Epstein, Arie Trouwborst, and José Vicente López-Bao. 2017. "Bolster Legal Boundaries to Stay within Planetary Boundaries." *Nature Ecology and Evolution* 1(3): 1–5.

Dalby, Simon. 2016. "Framing the Anthropocene: The Good, the Bad and the Ugly." *The Anthropocene Review* 3(1): 33–51.

de Saint-Exupéry, Antoine. 1943. *Le Petit Prince*. New York: Reynal & Hitchcock.

Dryzek, John S. 2014. "Institutions for the Anthropocene: Governance in a Changing Earth System." *British Journal of Political Science* 46(4): 937–56.

Dryzek, John S., Quinlan Bowman, Jonathan Kuyper, Jonathan Pickering, Jensen Sass, and Hayley Stevenson. 2019. *Deliberative Global Governance*. Cambridge: Cambridge University Press.

Dryzek, John S., and Jonathan Pickering. 2018. *The Politics of the Anthropocene*. Oxford: Oxford University Press.

Folke, Carl, Steve Carpenter, Brian Walker, Marten Scheffer, Thomas Elmqvist, Lance Gunderson, and C. S. Holling. 2004. "Regime Shifts, Resilience, and Biodiversity in Ecosystem Management." *Annual Review of Ecology, Evolution, and Systematics* 35(1): 557–81.

Folke, Carl, Stephen Polasky, Johan Rockström, Victor Galaz, Frances Westley, Michèle Lamont, Marten Scheffer, et al. 2021. "Our Future in the Anthropocene Biosphere." *Ambio – A Journal of the Human Environment* 50(4): 834–69.

Galaz, Victor. 2014. *Global Environmental Governance, Technology and Politics: The Anthropocene Gap*. Cheltenham: Edward Elgar.

Galaz, Victor. 2019. "Time and Politics in the Anthropocene: Too Fast, Too Slow?" In *Anthropocene Encounters: New Directions in Green Political Thinking*, edited by Frank Biermann and Eva Lövbrand. 109–127, Cambridge: Cambridge University Press.

Galaz, Victor, Jonas Tallberg, Arjen Boin, Claudia Ituarte Lima, Ellen Hey, Per Olsson, and Frances Westley. 2017. "Global Governance Dimensions of Globally Networked Risks: The State of the Art in Social Science Research." *Risk, Hazards and Crisis in Public Policy* 8(1): 4–27.

Garbe, Julius, Torsten Albrecht, Anders Levermann, Jonathan F. Donges, and Ricarda Winkelmann. 2020. "The Hysteresis of the Antarctic Ice Sheet." *Nature* 585(7826): 538–44.

Gay-Antaki, Miriam, and Diana Liverman. 2018. "Climate for Women in Climate Science: Women Scientists and the Intergovernmental Panel on Climate Change." *Proceedings of the National Academy of Sciences of the United States of America* 115(9): 2060–65.

Gellers, Joshua C. 2021. "Earth System Law and the Legal Status of Non-humans in the Anthropocene." *Earth System Governance* 7: 100083.

Gonzalez, Carmen G. 2015. "Bridging the North-South Divide: International Environmental Law in the Anthropocene." *Pace Environmental Law Review* 32(2): 407–34.

Hajer, Maarten, Måns Nilsson, Kate Raworth, Peter Bakker, Frans Berkhout, Yvo de Boer, Johan Rockström, Kathrin Ludwig, and Marcel Kok. 2015. "Beyond Cockpit-Ism: Four Insights to Enhance the Transformative Potential of the Sustainable Development Goals." *Sustainability* 7(2): 1651–60.

Hamilton, Clive. 2015a. "Human Destiny in the Anthropocene." In *The Anthropocene and the Global Environmental Crisis: Rethinking Modernity in a New Epoch*, edited by Clive Hamilton, Christophe Bonneuil, and François Gemenne. 32–43, London: Routledge.

Hamilton, Clive. 2015b. "The Anthropocene as Rupture." *The Anthropocene Review* 3(2): 93–106.

Ho-Lem, Claudia, Hisham Zerriffi, and Milind Kandlikar. 2011. "Who Participates in the Intergovernmental Panel on Climate Change and Why: A Quantitative Assessment of the National Representation of Authors in the Intergovernmental Panel on Climate Change." *Global Environmental Change* 21(4): 1308–17.

Hughes, Terry P., Stephen Carpenter, Johan Rockström, Marten Scheffer, and Brian Walker. 2013. "Multiscale Regime Shifts and Planetary Boundaries." *Trends in Ecology and Evolution* 28(7): 389–95.

IPCC. 2019. *IPCC Special Report on the Ocean and Cryosphere in a Changing Climate*. Cambridge, UK: Cambridge University Press.

Kashwan, Prakash, Frank Biermann, Aarti Gupta, and Chukwumerije Okereke. 2020. "Planetary Justice: Prioritizing the Poor in Earth System Governance." *Earth System Governance* 6: 100075.

Kim, Rakhyun E., and Klaus Bosselmann. 2013. "International Environmental Law in the Anthropocene: Towards a Purposive System of Multilateral Environmental Agreements." *Transnational Environmental Law* 2(2): 285–309.

Kim, Rakhyun E., and Klaus Bosselmann. 2015. "Operationalizing Sustainable Development: Ecological Integrity as a Grundnorm of International Law." *Review of European, Comparative and International Environmental Law* 24(2): 194–208.

Kim, Rakhyun E., and Louis J. Kotzé. 2020. "Planetary Boundaries at the Intersection of Earth System Law, Science and Governance: A State-of-the-Art Review." *Review of European, Comparative and International Environmental Law* 30(1): 3–15.

Kim, Rakhyun E., and Brendan Mackey. 2014. "International Environmental Law as a Complex Adaptive System." *International Environmental Agreements: Politics, Law and Economics* 14(1): 5–24.

Kotzé, Louis J., ed. 2017. *Environmental Law and Governance for the Anthropocene*. Oxford: Hart Publishing.

Kotzé, Louis J. 2019. "Earth System Law for the Anthropocene." *Sustainability* 11(23): 6796–13.

Kotzé, Louis J. 2020. "Earth System Law for the Anthropocene: Rethinking Environmental Law alongside the Earth System Metaphor." *Transnational Legal Theory* 11(1–2): 75–104.

Kotzé, Louis J., and Duncan French. 2018. "A Critique of the Global Pact for the Environment: A Stillborn Initiative or the Foundation for Lex Anthropocenae?" *International Environmental Agreements: Politics, Law and Economics* 18(6): 811–38.

Kotzé, Louis J., and Rakhyun E. Kim. 2019. "Earth System Law: The Juridical Dimensions of Earth System Governance." *Earth System Governance* 1: 100003.

Kotzé, Louis J., and Rakhyun E. Kim. 2020. "Exploring the Analytical, Normative and Transformative Dimensions of Earth System Law." *Environmental Policy and Law*: 50 457–470.

Lade, Steven J., Will Steffen, Wim Vries, Stephen R. Carpenter, Jonathan F. Donges, Dieter Gerten, Holger Hoff, Tim Newbold, Katherine Richardson, and Johan Rockström. 2020. "Human Impacts on Planetary Boundaries Amplified by Earth System Interactions." *Nature Sustainability* 3(2): 119–28.

Lenton, Timothy M., Hermann Held, Elmar Kriegler, Jim W. Hall, Wolfgang Lucht, Stefan Rahmstorf, and Hans Joachim Schellnhuber. 2008. "Tipping Elements in the Earth's Climate System." *Proceedings of the National Academy of Sciences of the United States of America* 105(6): 1786–93.

Lenton, Timothy M., and Bruno Latour. 2018. "Gaia 2.0." *Science* 361(6407): 1066–68.

Lenton, Timothy M., Johan Rockström, Owen Gaffney, Stefan Rahmstorf, Katherine Richardson, Will Steffen, and Hans Joachim Schellnhuber. 2020. "Climate Tipping Points — Too Risky to Bet Against." *Nature* 575(7784): 592–95.

Leopold, Aldo. 1949. *A Sand County Almanac*. Oxford: Oxford University Press.

Lewis, Simon L., and Mark A. Maslin. 2015. "Defining the Anthropocene." *Nature* 519(7542): 171–80.

Lim, Michelle, ed. 2019. *Charting Environmental Law Futures in the Anthropocene*. Singapore: Springer.

Lorimer, Jamie. 2015. *Wildlife in the Anthropocene: Conservation after Nature*. Minneapolis, MN: University of Minnesota Press.

Lövbrand, Eva, Silke Beck, Jason Chilvers, Tim Forsyth, Johan Hedrén, Mike Hulme, Rolf Lidskog, and Eleftheria Vasileiadou. 2015. "Who Speaks for the Future of Earth? How Critical Social Science Can Extend the Conversation on the Anthropocene." *Global Environmental Change* 32: 211–18.

Lovelock, James. 2006. *The Revenge of Gaia*. London: Penguin Books.

Lynas, Mark. 2011. *The God Species: Saving the Planet in the Age of Humans*. Washington, DC: National Geographic.

Lynas, Mark. 2020. *Our Final Warning: Six Degrees of Climate Emergency*. New York: HarperCollins.

MacMartin, Douglas G., Katharine L. Ricke, and David W. Keith. 2018. "Solar Geoengineering as Part of an Overall Strategy for Meeting the 1.5°C Paris Target." *Philosophical Transactions of the Royal Society, Series A: Mathematical, Physical and Engineering Sciences* 376(2119): 20160454–19.

Mai, Laura, and Emille Boulot. 2021. "Harnessing the Transformative Potential of Earth System Law: From Theory to Practice." *Earth System Governance* 7: 100103.

Malhi, Yadvinder. 2017. "The Concept of the Anthropocene." *Annual Review of Environment and Resources* 42(1): 77–104.

Nobre, Carlos A., Gilvan Sampaio, Laura S. Borma, Juan Carlos Castilla-Rubio, José S. Silva, and Manoel Cardoso. 2016. "Land-Use and Climate Change Risks in the Amazon and the Need of a Novel Sustainable Development Paradigm." *Proceedings of the National Academy of Sciences of the United States of America* 113(39): 10759–68.

Oomen, Jeroen, Jesse Hoffman, and Maarten A. Hajer. 2022. "Techniques of Futuring: On How Imagined Futures Become Socially Performative." *European Journal of Social Theory*: 25 252–270.

Ord, Toby. 2020. *The Precipice: Existential Risk and the Future of Humanity*. New York: Hachette Books.

Pattyn, Frank, Catherine Ritz, Edward Hanna, Xylar Asay-Davis, Rob DeConto, Gaël Durand, Lionel Favier, et al. 2018. "The Greenland and Antarctic Ice Sheets under 1.5°C Global Warming." *Nature Climate Change* 8(12): 1053–61.

Philipp, Pattberg, and Fariborz Zelli, eds. 2016. *Environmental Politics and Governance in the Anthropocene: Institutions and Legitimacy in a Complex World*. London: Routledge.

Pickering, Jonathan, and Åsa Persson. 2019. "Democratising Planetary Boundaries: Experts, Social Values and Deliberative Risk Evaluation in Earth System Governance." *Journal of Environmental Policy and Planning* 22(1): 59–71.

Pielke Jr., Roger, Gwyn Prins, Steve Rayner, and Daniel Sarewitz. 2007. "Climate Change 2007: Lifting the Taboo on Adaptation." *Nature* 445(7128): 597–98.

Purdy, Jedediah. 2015. *After Nature: A Politics for the Anthropocene*. Cambridge, MA: Harvard University Press.

Robinson, Nicholas A. 2014. "Fundamental Principles of Law for the Anthropocene?" *Environmental Policy and Law* 44(1–2): 13–27.

Rocha, Juan C., Garry Peterson, Örjan Bodin, and Simon Levin. 2018. "Cascading Regime Shifts within and across Scales." *Science* 362(6421): 1379–83.

Rockström, Johan, Joyeeta Gupta, Timothy M. Lenton, Dahe Qin, Steven J. Lade, Jesse F. Abrams, Lisa Jacobson, et al. 2021. "Identifying a Safe and Just Corridor for People and the Planet." *Earth's Future* 9(4): e2020EF001866.

Rockström, Johan, Will Steffen, Kevin Noone, Åsa Persson, F. Stuart Chapin, Eric F. Lambin, Timothy M. Lenton, et al. 2009. "A Safe Operating Space for Humanity." *Nature* 461(7263): 472–75.

Scheffer, Marten, Jordi Bascompte, William A. Brock, Victor Brovkin, Stephen R. Carpenter, Vasilis Dakos, Hermann Held, Egbert H. van Nes, Max Rietkerk, and George Sugihara. 2009. "Early-Warning Signals for Critical Transitions." *Nature* 461(7260): 53–9.

Scheffer, Marten, Stephen R. Carpenter, Timothy M. Lenton, Jordi Bascompte, William Brock, Vasilis Dakos, Johan van de Koppel, et al. 2012. "Anticipating Critical Transitions." *Science* 338(6105): 344–48.

Schmidt, Jeremy J., Peter G. Brown, and Christopher J. Orr. 2016. "Ethics in the Anthropocene: A Research Agenda." *The Anthropocene Review* 3(3): 188–200.

Scott, Karen N. 2013. "International Law in the Anthropocene: Responding to the Geoengineering Challenge." *Michigan Journal of International Law* 34(2): 309–58.

Shoshitaishvili, Boris. 2020. "Deep Time and Compressed Time in the Anthropocene: The New Timescape and the Value of Cosmic Storytelling." *The Anthropocene Review* 7(2): 125–37.

Steffen, Will, Paul J. Crutzen, and John R. McNeill. 2007. "The Anthropocene: Are Humans Now Overwhelming the Great Forces of Nature?" *Ambio – A Journal of the Human Environment* 36(8): 614–21.

Steffen, Will, Reinhold Leinfelder, Jan Zalasiewicz, Colin N. Waters, Mark Williams, Colin Summerhayes, Anthony D. Barnosky, et al. 2016. "Stratigraphic and Earth System Approaches to Defining the Anthropocene." *Earth's Future* 4(8): 324–45.

Steffen, Will, Åsa Persson, Lisa Deutsch, Jan Zalasiewicz, Mark Williams, Katherine Richardson, Carole Crumley, et al. 2011. "The Anthropocene: From Global Change to Planetary Stewardship." *Ambio – A Journal of the Human Environment* 40(7): 739–61.

Steffen, Will, Katherine Richardson, Johan Rockström, Hans Joachim Schellnhuber, Opha Pauline Dube, Sébastien Dutreuil, Timothy M. Lenton, and Jane Lubchenco. 2020. "The Emergence and Evolution of Earth System Science." *Nature Reviews Earth and Environment* 1(1): 1–10.

Steffen, Will, Johan Rockström, Katherine Richardson, Timothy M. Lenton, Carl Folke, Diana Liverman, Colin P. Summerhayes, et al. 2018. "Trajectories of the Earth System in the Anthropocene." *Proceedings of the National Academy of Sciences of the United States of America* 115(33): 8252–9.

Steffen, Will, Angelina Sanderson, Peter Tyson, Jill Jäger, Pamela A. Matson, Berrien Moore III, Frank Oldfield, et al. 2004. *Global Change and the Earth System: A Planet Under Pressure*. Berlin: Springer.

Stephens, Tim. 2018. "What Is the Point of International Environmental Law Scholarship in the Anthropocene?" In *Perspectives on Environmental Law Scholarship: Essays on Purpose, Shape and Direction*, edited by Ole W.. 121–139 Pedersen. Cambridge: Cambridge University Press.

Sterner, Thomas, Edward B. Barbier, Ian Bateman, Inge Bijgaart, Anne-Sophie Crépin, Ottmar Edenhofer, Carolyn Fischer, et al. 2019. "Policy Design for the Anthropocene." *Nature Sustainability* 2(1): 1–8.

Stouffer, R. J., J. Yin, J. M. Gregory, K. W. Dixon, M. J. Spelman, W. Hurlin, A. J. Weaver, et al. 2006. "Investigating the Causes of the Response of the Thermohaline Circulation to Past and Future Climate Changes." *Journal of Climate* 19(8): 1365–87.

Tarlock, A. Dan. 1994. "The Nonequilibrium Paradigm in Ecology and the Partial Unraveling of Environmental Law." *Loyola of Los Angeles International and Comparative Law Review* 27: 1121–44.

United Nations Framework Convention on Climate Change. 2021. *Nationally Determined Contributions under the Paris Agreement: Synthesis Report by the Secretariat.* FCCC/PA/CMA/2021/2. UNFCCC.

Vidas, Davor, Ole Kristian Fauchald, Øystein Jensen, and Morten Walløe Tvedt. 2015. "International Law for the Anthropocene? Shifting Perspectives in Regulation of the Oceans, Environment and Genetic Resources." *Anthropocene* 9: 1–13.

Vidas, Davor, Jan Zalasiewicz, and Mark Williams. 2014. "What Is the Anthropocene—and Why Is It Relevant for International Law?" *Yearbook of International Environmental Law* 25(1): 3–23.

Viñuales, Jorge E. 2018. "The Organisation of the Anthropocene: In Our Hands?" *Brill Research Perspectives in International Legal Theory and Practice* 1(1): 1–81.

Walker, Brian, Scott Barrett, Stephen Polasky, Victor Galaz, Carl Folke, Gustav Engström, Frank Ackerman, et al. 2009. "Looming Global-Scale Failures and Missing Institutions." *Science* 325(5946): 1345–46.

Weiss, Edith Brown. 2020. *Establishing Norms in a Kaleidoscopic World.* Leiden: Brill Nijhoff.

Xu, Chi, Timothy A. Kohler, Timothy M. Lenton, Jens-Christian Svenning, and Marten Scheffer. 2020. "Future of the Human Climate Niche." *Proceedings of the National Academy of Sciences of the United States of America* 117(21): 11350–55.

Young, Oran R., Arild Underdal, Norichika Kanie, and Rakhyun E. Kim. 2017. "Goal Setting in the Anthropocene: The Ultimate Challenge of Planetary Stewardship." In *Governing through Goals: Sustainable Development Goals as Governance Innovation*, edited by Norichika Kanie and Frank Biermann. 53–74 Cambridge, MA: The MIT Press.

Zarnetske, Phoebe L., Jessica Gurevitch, Janet Franklin, Peter M. Groffman, Cheryl S. Harrison, Jessica J. Hellmann, Forrest M. Hoffman, et al. 2021. "Potential Ecological Impacts of Climate Intervention by Reflecting Sunlight to Cool Earth." *Proceedings of the National Academy of Sciences of the United States of America* 118(15): e1921854118.

# 12

# COLLAPSE OR SUSTAINABILITY?

## Ecological Integrity as a Fundamental Norm of Law[1]

*Klaus Bosselmann*

The Anthropocene invites us to ask questions that have perhaps never been asked before. Does human predominance spell the demise of the human species? How much non-human life will vanish? Are people ("Anthropocene") or rather Western civilization the problem? Over the last few decades, we have been experiencing a multitude of accelerating crises, but are we even beginning to understand the underlying "logic of self-extermination" (Bosselmann 1995, 40–50)? None of these questions can be answered with any certainty, but ecophilosophers and eco-lawyers may be able to provide some clues. Cartesian dualist ontology – res cognita vs res extensa, mind vs body, rationality vs spirituality, humans vs nature, me vs you, etc. – has shaped Modernity with its hallmarks of progress, expansion, and wealth. What has worked for some, came at the expense of others, i.e. non-capitalists, non-Westerners, and non-humans. As a consequence, humanity and nature, or, in non-Cartesian terms, the Earth system, have reached a crisis point.

This handbook aims for exploring the perspective of ecological law in the Anthropocene. Most eco-lawyers agree that the Anthropocene corresponds with Western dominant thought shaped by anthropocentrism, dualism, and utilitarianism. What seems less clear is whether living in the Anthropocene requires a shift to non-dualist ecocentrism. For some, this prospect appears unrealistic arguing that human impacts on the Earth system are irreversible with no route back to a relative equilibrium that dominated the Holocene (Burdon 2019, 97). I agree with Peter Burdon that in the Anthropocene we "need to come to terms with our new-found power and think about how we might act with humility and responsibility as geological agents" (Burdon 2020, 45). But how might this be possible, I wonder, without a deep appreciation of the human-nature nexus that Western dominant thought so profoundly lacks? To start with, responsible geological agency needs a global – not Western – worldview. This requires conventional environmental ethics and law to learn from non-Western cultures and Indigenous traditions and, in this way, develop Earth-centered perspectives. Can ecological thinking bridge the gap between Western and non-Western concepts of caring for the Earth?

The answer, of course, depends on what is meant by "ecology." Understanding it merely as environmental biology or as science relevant to conservation management is certainly not good enough. Nor would any notions of ecosystem ecology be sufficient if they exclude humans. Ecologists study how living things interact with their environments, but most of them are in the scientific tradition of Cartesian dualism. Shallow ecology keeps humans separated from their environments.

DOI: 10.4324/9781003388081-16

Essentially though, ecology is the study of relationships and interconnectedness. More to the point, Barry Commoner's four laws of ecology are still valid in the Anthropocene (Commoner 1971). The laws are: (1) Everything is connected with everything else; (2) Everything must go somewhere; (3) Nature knows best; and (4) There is no such thing as a free lunch. This was 50 years ago. Seventy ago, Eugene Odum, "the father of modern ecology" (University of Georgia 2018), described the "fundamentals of ecology" (Odum [1953] 2021) as holistic, interdisciplinary, and critical for human survival. In the mid-1970s, Odum observed "The Emergence of Ecology as a New Integrative Discipline" (Odum 1977). Others have described shallow ecology as outdated Cartesian science and deep (Devall and Sessions 1985) or post-modern ecology (White 1997) as the epistemological framework for navigating the Anthropocene (Fellows 2019; Küpers 2020). In this way, ecological philosophy has guided the conceptualization of ecological law.[2]

In the Anthropocene, ecological law is our only hope for returning to (relative) ecological sustainability comparable to the living conditions of the Holocene. Peter Burdon reasons that the Anthropocene requires "a new kind of anthropocentrism" (Burdon 2019, 97–98)[3] and distinguishes between an inescapable human condition ("perceptual anthropocentrism") and the assumption of human superiority ("normative anthropocentrism") (Burdon 2020, 38–39). Such a distinction, also known as "weak" or "trivial" anthropocentrism vs "strong" anthropocentrism (Fox 1984, 196), helps to define the challenge of the Anthropocene: normative anthropocentrism has created it, so a shift to normative ecocentrism is needed if humans are to survive.

This is as valid in the Anthropocene as it has been since the beginnings of the Green movement. The German Greens Manifesto from 1983, for example, stated: "We must stop the violation of nature, so we can survive in it" (Dobson 2007, 58). Ecological policy was defined in this way:

> Based on the laws of nature and particularly the acceptance that in a finite system no infinite growth is possible, ecological policy means to recognize ourselves and our environment as part of nature. Human life, too, is embedded in the control loops of ecosystems: we interfere through our actions and this retroacts on us. We must not destroy the stability of ecosystems.
>
> *(Die Grünen 1980, 4)*

This is the counter model to anthropocentric, utilitarian environmental policies. Ecological policy is based on ecocentrism.

Ecocentrism does not view nature as "the other," nor is it nature-centered as opposed to human-centered. The "center" of ecocentrism is ecological interrelationships within nature as well as within the Earth system.[4] Humans have always altered their natural environments – and vice versa. What makes the Anthropocene different from the Holocene is the scale of human dominance now affecting the integrity of the entire Earth system. Unless we finally learn and develop policies and laws based on ecocentrism, the logic of self-extermination will run its course and the Earth system will eventually get rid of humans.

For this reason, it would be wrong to assume that ecological law is conceptually different from what has been described as Earth system law (Kotzé and Kim 2019, 7). The common ethical stance is ecocentrism and the aim is for maintaining and restoring the integrity of ecological systems (that humans are inevitably part of). Contrary to Louis Kotzé's and Rakhyun Kim's claim, ecological law does not aim for restoring "a particular moment in the past when there was little or no human interference" (Kotzé and Kim 2019, 7) but for the integrity of all ecological systems including the Earth system. Earth system law, therefore, while having its own parameters, is an expression of ecological law.

The following chapter aims for showing the importance of ecological integrity as an orientation and guide for decision-making in the Anthropocene. It does so, by highlighting the legacy from the Holocene, i.e. the constant struggle between the sustainability and collapse of socio-ecological systems. We can observe multiple forms of collapse, at local, national, or global levels, that may be triggered by specific events, yet follow a pattern: basically, the ability or non-ability to learn from experience.

## The Principle of Sustainability

Sustainability is best explained as the ability to avoid or withstand collapse. Examples of the ability to sustain ("sustain-ability") are health, love, and meaningful relationships, but also resilience, self-organization, and robustness. The term itself gives us further clues. The English term *sustainability* (lat. *sustinere* = endure, persevere) is a translation from the German term *Nachhaltigkeit* which in turn comes from *Nachhalt*, literally "holding on." The *Dictionary of the German Language* from 1809 defined *Nachhalt* as "what one holds on to when everything else does not hold any more." In other words, *Nachhalt* is what sustains you when everything else is falling apart. Ulrich Grober, in its seminal text on the cultural history of sustainability (Grober 2012), stresses that "sustainability" is the antonym and direct opposite of "collapse." When the authors of the famous 1972 Club of Rome Report *Limit to Growth* looked for a world model capable of supporting human life, they described it as "sustainable" and "without sudden and uncontrollable collapse" (Grober 2012, 117). The entire report is an effort to present sustainability as the antithesis of the growth model of modern society (Grober 2012, 155–161).

What then does sustainability mean? The cultural and epistemological history of sustainability shows that the core idea is to maintain the natural conditions that human life and flourishing depend on. So the precondition for all social and economic development is ecological sustainability. Preserving and restoring the integrity of ecological systems has to be the number one priority for any prospect of a sustainable, flourishing society – especially in the Anthropocene. The hierarchy is "ecology first, society second and economy third." Also known as "strong sustainability" (Bosselmann 2013), this hierarchical understanding is crucial for any successful policies aiming for long-term social and economic security (Bosselmann 2017).

The message of the increasingly popular planetary boundaries framework (Rockström et al. 2009) is similar. The framework is based on resilience theory where the complete Earth system is seen as a single adaptive ecological system (Folke et al. 2002). Trying to break down complexities of the Earth system into quantifiable sub-systems a group of 29 scientists has, so far, identified nine planetary boundaries that humanity must not overstep: (1) climate change; (2) stratospheric ozone depletion; (3) ocean acidification; (4) rate of biodiversity loss; (5) interference with the nitrogen and phosphorous cycles; (6) global freshwater use; (7) change in land use; (8) chemical pollution; and (9) atmospheric aerosol loading. Evidence indicates that the thresholds for three of these – climate change, biodiversity loss, and the nitrogen cycle – have already been crossed, and we are getting dangerously close to others (Rockström et al. 2009; Steffen et al. 2015). Respecting planetary boundaries would create "a safe operating space for humanity," which is only possible on the basis of ecological sustainability. The planetary boundaries framework makes the scientific case for strong sustainability: ecology first, society second, and economics third. To sustain ecological, social, and economic systems they must maintain their integrity.

In the following, I want to show that sustainability can be defined as a fundamental ethical and legal norm setting the *raison d'etre* for any decision society and governments must make with respect to social and economic development. The core idea is the preservation of the integrity of Earth's ecological system, an idea that has been expressed in a number of key international agreements albeit in a somewhat hidden manner. Earth system integrity includes not just "natural" systems, but also "human" systems such as social or economic, or financial systems. All systems possess a certain degree of integrity, i.e. the ability to maintain the functions of self-organization, while also responding to external changes. In this way, it is possible to perceive integrity as an overarching policy concern for ecological, energy, financial, economic, and political systems. I will conclude with a call for stewardship and trusteeship to guide political institutions, both nationally and internationally. In the end, nothing will save us but a strong sense of trusteeship for the Earth system.

## Ecological Integrity as a Fundamental Norm

The concept of ecological integrity is well known in international environmental law. No less than 27 international soft and hard law agreements contain specific references to it. The first of such agreements was the Convention on the Conservation of Antarctic Marine Living Resources adopted in 1980, which recognized in its preamble, the importance of "protecting the integrity of the ecosystem of the seas surrounding Antarctica." Another example is the preamble of 1992 Rio Declaration on Environment and Development which calls for "working towards international agreements which respect the interests of all and protect the integrity of the global environmental and developmental system." Principle 7 of the Rio Declaration postulates: "States shall cooperate in a spirit of global partnership to conserve, protect and restore the health and integrity of the Earth's ecosystem." This is repeated in key documents such as Agenda 21, the 2002 Johannesburg Declaration, and the 2012 Rio+20 outcome document The Future We Want calling for "holistic and integrated approaches to sustainable development to guide humanity for restoring the health and integrity of the Earth's ecosystem" (II. 40).

The Preamble of the 2015 Paris Climate Agreement notes "the importance of ensuring the integrity of all ecosystems, including oceans, and the protection of biodiversity, recognized by some cultures as Mother Earth" and refers to "environmental integrity" in several operating articles. Similarly, the Preamble of the 2017 Draft Global Pact for the Environment refers to the need for "respecting the balance and integrity of the Earth's ecosystem," and Article 2 defines the "Duty to take care of the environment" as contributing "to the conservation, protection and restoration of the integrity of the Earth's ecosystem." According to Article 18, the purpose of cooperation between states is "to conserve, protect and restore the integrity of the Earth's ecosystem and community of life."

Finally, the foundational 1987 Brundtland Report itself described the "integrity of the natural system" as the basic condition for "the survival of life on Earth" and in this way described the core idea behind sustainability as a prerequisite for development.[5]

Applying the usual standards for the recognition of concepts as international law, we can say that the repeated and consistent references to ecological integrity amount to an emerging fundamental goal or *grundnorm* of international environmental law (Kim and Bosselmann 2013; Kim and Bosselmann 2015; Bosselmann 2018). But even independently of any legal status under international or domestic law, the *grundnorm* quality of ecological integrity should be without dispute. Surely, no one would doubt the fundamental importance of keeping the Earth's life-supporting systems intact.

Yet, governments have consistently ignored their own commitments to conserve, protect, and restore the integrity of Earth's ecological systems. Governments and the United Nations continue to talk about it, but keep ignoring its fundamental importance.

It was a great mistake of environmental law scholars to not criticize this ideologically motivated behavior of states in clear enough, strong terms. In the main, legal scholarship has underestimated the importance of ecological integrity. One of the pioneers of environmental law, the late Staffan Westerlund, went so far as to say that the entire academic discipline of environmental law over the last 30 years has failed. Rather than looking at ecological sustainability from the perspective of law (resulting in "environmental protection"), we should have looked at the law from the perspective of ecological sustainability ("ecological integrity"). According to Westerlund, the central reference point of environmental law is not some undefined "environment" or "sustainable development," but sustainability with ecological integrity at its core (Westerlund 2008).

Douglas Fisher, one of Australasia's pioneers of environmental law, makes the same point: in his book "*Legal Reasoning in Environmental Law*," Fisher analyzed the methodology of politicians, administrators, and judges when dealing with environmental matters. They reach their decisions without a specific environmental "point of commencement" (as Fisher calls it). Rather, most politicians readily employ well-trodden assumptions about human well-being, economic prosperity, cost-benefit analysis, and environmental protection. The environment appears as an unknown entity, too abstract and not nearly as well defined as human rights or property rights. As a consequence, vague environmental interests are bound to lose against hard economic interests. The book concludes with a plea for "processes of legal reasoning which reflect the fundamental *grundnorms* of the system – the rule of law in general and sustainability in the context of environmental governance" (Fisher 2013, 433).

There is an obvious deficiency that environmental lawyers – in academia and in practice – have ignored for too long. Like most economists, most lawyers have overlooked the fundamentality of ecological systems. Their ecological blindness led them to assume that somehow "the economy" or "the law" or society can operate in a vacuum. Sanford Gaines' critique of environmental law and environmental law scholarship confirms this view. Gaines observes that "environmental law, which once expressed a social movement, has failed to keep pace with comprehensive ecological degradation" (Gaines 2014, 10188). He calls for "reimagining of environmental law" based on interdisciplinary approaches and suggests that "global sustainability must become a foundation of society. It can and must be part of the bedrock of nation states" (Gaines 2014, 10213).

Reimaging environmental law, 100 environmental law scholars adopted, in 2016, a manifesto entitled "From Environmental Law to Ecological Law" at the IUCN Academy of Environmental Law Colloquium in Oslo, Norway. The *Oslo Manifesto* has since been endorsed by numerous environmental lawyers and environmental law organizations and has also led to the establishment of the Ecological Law and Governance Association in late 2017 (Ecological Law and Governance Association 2016). ELGA is a global network of lawyers and environmental activists that coordinates initiatives for transforming law and governance.

One of these initiatives is the Earth Trusteeship Initiative (ETI), established on 10 December 2018 in the Peace Palace in The Hague. This date marked the 70th anniversary of the adoption of the Universal Declaration of Human Rights (Ecological Law and Governance Association 2016). With the support and endorsement of many human rights, environmental, and professional organizations, the ETI launched the Hague Principles for a Universal Declaration on Responsibilities for Human Rights and Earth Trusteeship (Earth Trusteeship, n.d.; Bosselmann and Taylor 2019).

The three "Hague Principles" re-conceptualize human rights and responsibilities. Any rights that human beings enjoy depend on the responsibilities that we have for each other and for Earth. We cannot live in dignity and well-being without accepting fundamental duties for each other and for preserving and restoring the integrity of the Earth system.

## *Socio-ecological Integrity*

Sociologist Immanuel Wallerstein, in his world system analysis (Wallestein 2011), makes the point that the natural world ("Earth systems") and the social world ("world systems") are ultimately inseparable. Many cultures have known this all along, and if they haven't, they were destined for failure. In the following, I want to explore how we can bring the two colliding worlds of society and ecology (Bosselmann 1995) back together again.

Dennis Meadows explains that "the world is a complex, interconnected, finite, ecological-social-psychological-economic system" (Gaines 2014, 10205). Each component can be viewed in terms of the sustainability-collapse dichotomy. The concept of "integrity" can help us to define more closely how to avert collapse or, at least, mitigate against it.

The rationale for the following is the notion that ecological integrity is partly a reflection of the integrity of societies inhabiting the ecological space. With a healthy, vibrant society chances are higher that we will see healthy vibrant nature. And vice versa, with a society lacking in integrity, loss of ecological integrity is not surprising. Can we expect to achieve ecological integrity if we have a financial and economic system that lacks integrity? But then, what is economic integrity? What might the implications for ecological integrity be for an economic system involving personal relations of trust and mutual aid, in contrast to a depersonalized system emphasizing "self-interest" (as expressed in Hobbes and Smith)? Moreover, to what extent do practical difficulties arise in achieving global *ecological* integrity without global *political* integrity?

## *Integrity and Collapse*

The aim here is to explore the interrelationships of systems at the conceptual level. This is only possible if we assume that systems – whether natural or cultural – share certain characteristics that allow a degree of comparability. For good measure, there is an important difference between ecological systems and human-made systems (such as social or economic systems). The self-organizing principles of ecosystems (following natural patterns) differ from the self-organizing principles of human systems (following cultural patterns). We may also say that ecological systems have no apparent objective, whereas human-made systems are made with purposes aiming for certain outcomes.

However, both types of systems have some basic characteristics in common such as structure, spatial and temporal boundaries, and interconnectivity of their elements as well as exchanges of matter and energy with other systems. We would consider a system "healthy" if it functions in a continuous, stable, flexible, and resilient manner. Likewise, we would consider an "unhealthy" system as chaotic, unstable, rigid, or disintegrating. We can also perceive a healthy system as possessing integrity. A system losing its integrity would then appear as shifty, declining, untrustworthy or corrupt until integrity is completely lost resulting in (gradual) disintegration or (sudden) collapse. Integrity and collapse, therefore, can be seen as opposite poles on a scale of descending characteristics.

It is certainly useful to keep the *terms* integrity and collapse open to their various resonances. Integrity thus signifies wholeness, soundness, completeness, resilience, health, and naturalness. Ecological integrity is a scientifically measurable aspect of the overarching concept of strong sustainability. It is a useful term because it provides not only the scientifically measurable aspect of ecological systems, but also moral resonances, such as something or someone one can rely on, and also honesty. Collapse, in contrast, is considered the opposite of ecological integrity and strong sustainability as mentioned. Joseph Tainter defines "collapse" as a significant, relatively quick reduction in complexity (Tainter 1998, 5). It is a loss of integrity beyond a system's threshold of resilience from which it can recover. Collapse occurs when integrity has eroded beyond a certain (often unhealthy) extent.

"Collapse" in the everyday sense has connotations of rapidity. A house of cards collapses quickly, as does a building. However, many collapses of systems, in relation to an individual human lifetime, are "slow collapses." Thus, the collapse of an empire can take many centuries. It is worth recognizing that collapse has often been part of the flow of history. Sometimes it has been judiciously avoided. However, often collapses of systems have proven difficult to manage. It is worth considering why, and what the implications for ecological integrity are.

### *Analyzing Socio-ecological Systems in Four Stages*

For the purpose of applying the concept of integrity to socio-ecological systems, we can identify four different phases or stages: status quo, collapse, pre-collapse, and post-collapse. For each system, we will first consider the current *status quo*, which leads to the default position in the absence of a norm of integrity: collapse. The possibilities for reform of law and governance pre-collapse will then be explored. That is, what might enhanced integrity in this aspect of the world system look like? Finally, consideration will be given to the implications for law and governance in a post-collapse scenario. This is no utopian (or dystopian) blueprint, merely an attempt to prompt a broader conversation and think in a concrete way about integrity.

The following analyses of five global systems – ecology, energy, finance, commerce, and politics – are tentative and not meant to be complete or even correct in detail. Their purpose is to demonstrate their feasibility, in principle, and show that socio-ecological systems can behave in certain ways measured by four stages – somewhere between integrity and collapse – and that they mutually condition each other. For example, financial systems of integrity are likely to keep economic systems within integrity (and vice versa) and both depend on the integrity of ecological systems. In this way, we may gain a more informed sense of what ecology essentially means, i.e. the science and wisdom of interconnectedness and mutual dependence.

## Ecological Integrity

### *Status Quo*

The twentieth century saw exponential increases in fossil fuel use (especially oil), global population, and levels of debt (money loaned into existence by banks). These three exponentials are surely interrelated. A plausible interpretation is that energy was driving economic growth, with the larger economy sustaining a larger population and an increase in debt (based on future hopes for growth) (Orlov 2013, 27). Growth in human population, energy use, and economic consumption has put increasing stress on ecosystems, as has been well documented (Heinberg 2007). With varying degrees of scale and intensity, we can observe processes that put the integrity of the Earth's ecological systems at risk.

### *Ecological Collapse*

No disaster or accident is required in order for environmental collapse to unfold – just more business as usual. Dennis Meadows holds that the actual form of any environmental collapse will be too complex for any model to predict. "Collapse will not be driven by a single, identifiable cause simultaneously acting in all countries," he observes. "It will come through a self-reinforcing complex of issues" – including climate change, resource constraints, and socioeconomic inequality (Mukerjee 2012).

### *Pre-collapse Reform to Promote Ecological Integrity*

Rockström's planetary boundary framework suggests "the need for novel and adaptive governance approaches at global, regional, and local scales" (Rockström 2009). The recent formation of the Global Commons Alliance with the launch of an Earth Commission marked a step in this direction. Trusteeship of the global commons is a key requirement for our time (Bosselmann 2015). There are other innovative ideas, of course, and they all point to the need of transforming law and governance. As the influential Millennium Ecosystem Assessment concluded: "The warning signs are there for all to see. The future lies in our hands" (Millenium Assessment 2006). It is now a question of whether societies and governments are able to undertake the required changes quickly enough.

Post-ecological Collapse Challenges and Opportunities: Local and Global

#### Local Ecological Collapse

One increasingly pertinent governance issue is that of "climate refugees," and other displaced populations due to changes in habitats. Shifts in large numbers of populations will present challenges. For example, Greece (currently with a population of around 11 million) might choose, or be forced, to implement a comprehensive transition to a steady-state economy, based on a stable population and calculated "standard of living" (Bosselmann et al. 2009). Under pressure to receive climate refugees, would Greece take them all, or refuse to compromise its plans for "ecological integrity"? Greece is under constant pressure to absorb increasing numbers of refugees from Syria, Afghanistan, and other collapsing countries, but would it really do so given the immediacy of collapsing economy and finance? Is it realistic that "ecological integrity" will prevail in such pressing circumstances? Most likely, concerns for ecological integrity have to be balanced against other essential requirements such as human rights.

#### Global Ecological Collapse

Global ecological collapse is a real prospect of the Anthropocene (Zalasiewicz et al. 2010). The process may take centuries or multiple planetary thresholds may be crossed relatively quickly, resulting in more rapid ecological decline – the data is not yet clear (Rockström 2009). The requisite extent of ecological collapse to be termed "global" would have to be extensive (though not necessarily complete). It is always possible to imagine various scenarios, at the ultimate end of which we are left without a home, having rendered Earth (our home planet) uninhabitable. However, such a scenario is not inevitable. It is worth remembering that, ultimately, the opposite of global ecological collapse is global ecological integrity.

## Economic Integrity

### *Status Quo*

What does the relationship between economic and ecological integrity entail? Gaines has expressed concern about "depersonalized economic relationships" (Gaines 2014, 10208). Does this perhaps point us to an alternative conception of economic relations, more congruent with the achievement of ecological integrity?

Most people in (over-)developed economies are dependent for survival on strangers halfway across the world, who provide most of their material needs. There is a high level of dependence on commercialized, impersonal systems. Global supply chains are long and distant. In an environment where most of one's needs are addressed by readily available, standardized product-service offerings, actual human relationships become a luxury, reserved for sex and fun (Orlov 2011, 165). People live in "communities," but they do not "need" each other for the essentials of life. Rather, impersonal "trade" currently occupies the dominant position in commercial relations between people (Orlov 2011, 99).

## *Economic Collapse*

It is possible that a financial collapse (that is, in the abstract realm of modern finance) could lead to a disruption of actual commercial activity. This may be minor, or could be severe enough to be termed a "collapse." In a commercial collapse, faith that "the market shall provide" is lost. Money is devalued and/or becomes scarce, commodities are hoarded, import and retail chains break down and widespread shortages of survival necessities become the norm.

## *Pre-collapse Reform to Promote Economic and Ecological Integrity*

Ecological economics (discussed above) provides a model which would enhance both resilience of commercial systems and ecological integrity. As one example, global commerce moves masses of freight, much of which could not be considered "essential" in terms of Maslow's hierarchy of needs. Efforts can be made to reduce long, energy-hungry supply chains, by relocalizing much food production. Governance policies could conceivably reverse, to an extent, the move to large industrial agribusinesses (which are addicted to fossil fuels and artificial inputs), and revert to smaller-scale family farming. There is no reason why food production should be relegated to the area of technology. People grew and gathered food with little or no technology for many thousands of years. F.H. King's fascinating 1911 book, *Farmers of Forty Centuries; Or, Permanent Agriculture in China, Korea, and Japan*, explains how these regions sustained enormous populations for millennia on tiny amounts of land, without mechanization, pesticides, or chemical fertilizers. Instead, they relied on sophisticated crop rotation, interplanting, and ecological relationships among farm plants, animals, and people. With such a model, for most of its history, China maintained the highest standard of living in the world – even England only really overtook it in the 1820s, well past the time of the Industrial Revolution (Graeber 2011). The example of Ancient China shows that while there may be dismay at the current lack of environmental consensus between states, a large, hierarchical state *can* be ecologically sustainable (at least, when based on sophisticated governance and organic farming). As J.M. Greer observes, "while Utopia is not an option, societies that are humane, cultured and sustainable are quite another matter. There have been plenty of them in the past; there can be many more in the future" (Greer 2009, 76).

Post-collapse Challenges and Opportunities for Economic and Ecological Integrity

### Gift Economy

An example of one model of commerce more congruent with ecological sustainability is the gift economy. Depersonalized modern commerce is a commercial model markedly different from other historical modes of economic activity. It is a curious point that in traditional societies, trade and theft formed a continuum (Orlov 2011, 88). These societies had "gift economies" (Mauss 1954). The norm in many traditional societies can be conceptualized as a "relationships pyramid" (like the food pyramid) (Orlov 2011, 85–86). Fitting at the bottom of the pyramid, most economic relations occurred between family, extended family, and one's tribe or community, in the form of a gift. In the middle layer of the pyramid would be classed friends and allies, with (still personal) economic acts in the form of barter and tribute (less frequently than gifts). Finally, in the smallest, top triangle would be placed strangers, with whom one occasionally engaged in (impersonal) trade. In modern commerce, therefore, we have flipped the "gift economy" upside down, with trade predominating and with gifts used mainly for ceremonial uses.

Of course, it is not suggested that reversion to a traditional "gift economy" would be a viable option. However, the anthropological record shows it has been present for long stretches of human prehistory and appears to have been ecologically sustainable. Perhaps it can throw the current system into sharper relief, prompting reflection on how to increase commercial resilience and integrity. For example, steps may be taken to rehumanize economic relations, by – if possible – dealing with people you actually know, and dealing with them face to face, avoiding the use of money and documents, while emphasizing trust, integrity, and verbal agreements (Orlov 2011, 99). Commercial resilience (and thus integrity) could be enhanced by giving preference to family, relations (even distant ones), then old friends and neighbors, then new friends and neighbors, while doing one's best to minimize dealings with distant strangers, including representatives of corporations. The transition from a framework where services are rendered by strangers to one where needs are served by friends and acquaintances will bring more and more activities back into the home: the kitchen, the basement workshop, the back yard and the home office (Orlov 2011, 165). Governance structures that promote, or at least permit, such developments will allow an increase in commercial resilience (and therefore, commercial integrity). Furthermore, commercial dealings based on trust will foster a different ethos in the community.

It is possible that in the Anthropocene, with a reduction in opportunities for individualistic economic activity, the family could reemerge as a fundamentally important economic unit. The "family as an economic unit" is a successful human cultural universal: a family is three generations (at a minimum), living together, pooling resources, and allocating them in the best interests of the whole. This, in turn, could strengthen communities, because a strong community is made up of strong families (Orlov 2011, 39). A real community is one in which people know each other and are willing to help each other. This may lead to increased prospects for alternative, autonomous governance. An autonomous community is a band of such families capable of self-governance (Orlov 2011, 42).

### Traditional "Credit" Economy

Another model of commerce emerges from historical research (from court cases) done by Craig Muldrew (Muldrew 1998). This has revealed that, in smaller towns in sixteenth- and seventeenth-century England, ordinary people such as the local butcher or baker would put things on "tab." In a typical village, the only people likely to pay in cash were passing travelers. Everyone was thus both creditor and debtor (with accounts settled around every 6 months). Such English villagers seem to have seen no contradiction between older systems of mutual aid and "the market." On the one hand, they believed strongly in the collective stewardship of fields, streams, and forests, and the need to help neighbors in difficulty. On the other, markets, too, were entirely founded on trust.

### "Commercial Integrity"

In such a context, "credit" did not denote interest-bearing bank debt (as it largely does for us today). The word credit comes from the same root as the words creed and credibility, referring to one's trustworthiness (Graeber 2011). This can perhaps provide a starting point to imagine a rehumanized commercial context. Commercial "integrity" would increasingly be based on one's own "integrity," in the moral sense of one's "honesty," keeping one's word and faithfully fulfilling one's obligations. This is a stark contrast to Adam Smith's vision of rational economic actors motivated by self-interest. In such a market economy, individuals are motivated by greed and fear. The pernicious nature of this kind of market is illustrated by the common view that friends and family shouldn't have business dealings with each other (Orlov 2013, 92). Such commercial relations may even be considered corrosive to the human spirit. If, in the Anthropocene, a community experiences "commercial collapse" in the form of seriously disrupted access to global supply chains, in addition to difficulties in making a transition, a new ethic of commercial autonomy and integrity may be a possibility. The community may revert from a Darwinian or Hobbesian "war of all against all" to a Kropotkin-like ethic of community cooperation (as expressed in *Mutual Aid: A Factor in Evolution*, 1902).

## Political Integrity

### *The Political Status Quo*

Governments are good at some things: protecting national borders, building infrastructure, and providing primary education and basic healthcare. But, in the current situation, states seem to be having great difficulty in agreeing to the fundamental importance of sustainability and ecological integrity (and implementing it through meaningful change). What can be holding states back? To take just one issue, that of "defense," from the perspective of the "realist" school of political philosophy. That is, a nation with an economy within the bounds of ecological integrity (a steady-state economy) would have difficulty securing its well-stewarded resources against a more powerful aggressor with a resource-hungry industrial-military growth economy. Ancient China was noted above as a "sustainable state," based on organic farming. China's arrangements were unable to compete with the industrialized West, leading to its "century of shame." Pre-Meiji Japan also discovered, in the nineteenth century, that the options were to either maintain its low-impact agrarian economy and be overrun by Western industrial-military powers or to rapidly industrialize and earn a place – by defeating Russia in 1904–1905 – at the conference table of nations. It is clear that *before* the industrial revolution – states were not inherently incapable of sustainability. The state system after the industrial revolution, with industrial-military technology, might have changed things. Consider, for example, the level of complexity proper to the current world military powers (such as China and the USA), if they were to transition their economies to maintain ecological integrity. It emerges, therefore, that political integrity is a practical issue that is worth considering in relation to the achievement of global ecological integrity.

### *Political Collapse*

States will remain the primary form of political organization for the foreseeable future (Rees 2013, 309). However, this is an attempt to think through the Anthropocene in terms of the big picture. (Heidegger, in 1966, said he thought it might take 300 years to think through the fundamental thrust of our present age) (Heidegger 1976). Perhaps, later in the Anthropocene, the nation state will be viewed as an ephemeral form of political organization. From an anthropological point of view, anarchic systems of governance have been the norm in human societies for most of human existence (Graeber 2011). If states continue with the current model over the longer term, the various possibilities of ecological, energy, financial, and commercial collapse may lead to a drastic reduction in political integrity. When this loss of integrity goes beyond a certain threshold point, the term political collapse becomes apt.

In the Anthropocene, the following extreme scenario could be imagined. A southern European nation finally decides that its farce with debts has gone on long enough. Its unorthodox economic measures cause a catastrophic loss of confidence in the tools of globalized finance, leading to a global financial crisis. This causes problems in commerce because cargo cannot be financed. With global supply chain disruption, a nation's business activity is drastically curtailed. This impacts tax revenues, which reduces the state's ability to govern and control some areas, particularly in areas distant from main centers.

In a scenario of "political collapse," faith that "the government will take care of you" is lost. For example, as officials attempt to mitigate widespread loss of access to commercial sources of survival necessities fail to make a difference, the political establishment loses legitimacy and relevance. Political collapse could be relatively swift (like a financial collapse), or it could be a much slower process, with legitimacy and control over areas gradually eroding over the long term.

## *Pre-collapse Reform to Promote Political and Ecological Integrity*

The conventional solution to the environmental crisis is to hope that politicians will eventually come through, in response to a dramatic shift in the consciousness of the people. The dream of a global economy, globally governed to remain within global ecological limits, would (if achieved) be preferable. It is looking increasingly likely, however, that reality will prove less tidy.

Doubts have been expressed about states voluntarily and collectively agreeing to transition to a model which respects planetary boundaries. However, *at present*, there is not an easily detectable, broad "shift in consciousness" nationally or globally. *If* such a shift happens, emerging from grassroots democracy, reform may be possible.

Others perceive insurmountable obstacles at the present time.[6] There are still calls for change. But one gets the sense that hopes for such "calls for change" are different from when they were made in the 1970s. Frustrated with official structures, some try to act for change outside these institutions. Of politicians, they may adhere to Solzhenitsyn's maxim of "Don't trust them, don't fear them, don't ask anything of them."

### The "Degrowth" Movement

The degrowth movement has rediscovered anarchy's charms. Anarchy can be defined from hierarchy (from the Greek "*an*," not/without, and "*archos*", ruler) (Orlov 2013, 133). With this concept, different forms and levels of governance can be viewed to fall somewhere on a continuum of anarchy to hierarchy. The degrowth movement has doubts about large-scale representative democracy, suspecting true democracy to only function in a smaller polis or community (Garver 2013, 210). The concept of autonomy is an important notion in the movement. Autonomy derives *auto* (self) and *nomos* (custom, law). A community seeking autonomy will attempt to become free from contingent global mechanisms (Candiago 2013, 223).

### The Polis

It has been suggested that the city-state, or smaller political communities, may be more sustainable in scale and a better form of political organization to achieve ecological integrity than larger scale nation-states (Ophuls 2011). The city-state has been one of the most successful political constructs in human history. The Ancient Greek *polis* and the free cities of medieval Europe were conducive to sophisticated culture and learning.[7]

Proposals advocating the city-state have been criticized by Sanford, who disavows the idea as elitist (Gaines 2014, 10205). This is a valid concern. However, as will be outlined, lower-level scales of governance may become the default choice, in some places, in the Anthropocene. It is also worth noting that many current nation-states have elitist elements. For example, it is not an unheard-of sentiment that justice systems in some states tend in practice to work in favor of the educated, the corporations, and the rich, and take unfair advantage of the uneducated, the private citizen, and the poor.

Peter Burdon is attracted to successful models of the Paris commune and Israeli Kibbutzim (Burdon 2013, 248). However, Burdon recognizes the issue of scale, with small communities being unequipped to deal with large-scale problems such as climate change. Like Burdon, Garver (2013) notes the problem of interdependencies (pollution having no borders), and sees the European principle of subsidiarity as a way to reconcile local and transnational. Along with the issue of scale is the practical issue that the current political arrangement is unlikely to voluntarily devolve into such small communities, or even to an artisanal set of intensely local polities, along the lines of the prosperous city states of medieval Europe.

### Dangers of Eco-fascism

In the Anthropocene, ecological challenges will probably result in stress for affected communities. In challenging times, there is the danger of people starting to think about "strong leadership." During the difficult times of the Roman republic, dictatorship was seen as a good form of governance in a bad situation. Similarly, even "sustainability thinkers" may at times feel a sense of frustration with the slow progress democracy is making in relation to pressing environmental challenges.[8] However, history shows that dictatorships can be problematic. Particularly, in attempting to achieve "ecological integrity and sustainability," without a broad change in community ethos, through education, any reforms will themselves be unsustainable. Therefore, any erosions of democracy must be rejected. Rather, the importance of education (stressed above) reemerges. A reminder is provided by the words of Thomas Jefferson: "I know of no safe repository of the ultimate power of society but people. And if we think them not enlightened enough, the remedy is not to take the power from them, but to inform them by education."

## *Post-collapse Challenges and Opportunities for Political and Ecological Integrity*

Ideas about local autonomy and anarchist thought about governance could not compete in the West in the twentieth century. Under "New Deal" arrangements, the working class gained the right to unionize, strike, and bargain collectively. Public education, government pensions, and health care were provided. This was all in exchange for submitting to the hierarchical control system of an industrial state (Orlov 2013, 126). Now, for various reasons, the industrial experiment is looking increasingly unattractive, and ideas about local autonomy are reemerging in sustainability thinking.

In a situation of "political collapse," when the centralized state does not "look after" people, smaller groups of people will have to revert to various forms of anarchic, autonomous self-governance. If the state loses coercive power, it can remain defunct as a ceremonial vestige (Orlov 2013, 162). In its stead will come a myriad of tiny polities, with smaller-scale economies. Those groups that have sufficient social cohesion, direct access to natural resources, and enough cultural wealth (especially in the form of face-to-face relationships and oral traditions) would manage to reconfigure in the absence of modern finance, commerce, and the state. While imaginable in a country like for example New Zealand with its relative cultural homogeneity, obviously, there are huge problems that would arise in such a scenario in other contexts.[9]

Sustainable governance voluntarily chosen by the state would make a smoother transition. But chances are that countries (outside or within the West) would experience loss of "political integrity" to some extent. The Anthropocene, as a geological epoch, is by definition a very long time frame. What will future governance look like in 300 years? If this question were asked by John Locke and Constantine, the latter would probably be more surprised than the former by the actual shape of governance 300 years after his time. While anarchic forms of governance seem implausible now, they may become a real option.

The link between political integrity and ecological integrity has been identified here and needs to be considered. The challenge may be, in Hegelian terms, to progress from the thesis of anarchic governance in human prehistory, through the antithesis of the modern nation state, and achieve a synthesis that is able to incorporate true local autonomy *and* deal with transnational pollution and ecological destruction arising from modern technology.

## Conclusion

This chapter sketched the dynamics of collapse and sustainability, how they panned out in history and how they may shape the future. It then focused on ecological integrity as a fundamental concern for any society aspiring for sustainability. We have seen how ecological integrity has, in fact, already informed contemporary international and domestic environmental law. This could lead us to conclude that preservation of ecological integrity constitutes, at least potentially, a fundamental norm or *grundnorm* that ought to guide law and governance. We can liken such a *grundnorm* to similar basic concepts such as the rule of law, freedom, justice, and equality that modern Western civilization prides itself on. Perceived in this way, our current global civilization is not doomed to collapse – provided it takes the preservation and restoration of Earth's ecological systems seriously. It will be a key challenge in the Anthropocene.

Given the fundamentality of ecological integrity for survival and prosperity, human-made systems need to be designed accordingly. At present they are not. It may be a matter of debate whether or not current developments within the global financial and commercial system are disastrous and life-threatening to humanity. Some would say, we are just experiencing yet another crisis thinking, for example, that Europe's and Greece's problems can be solved. Others see the European crisis as symptomatic of something more systemic. Certainly from an ecological perspective, economies are doomed to fail as long as they rely on growth. There is no infinite growth in a finite world. The alternative is ecological economics, i.e. the embedment of economics (*oikos* + *nomos*) in ecology (*oikos* + *logos*). Even if we take the growth problem out of the equation, the threat of ecological and economic collapse remains.

If our diagnosis of current socio-ecological systems revealed anything, it is the absence of ecologically sound design that keeps haunting them. Things on Earth are interconnected, and humans do not occupy a space separated from non-humans.

In the Anthropocene, we need to develop a deep sense of responsibility for the Earth as a whole. This is best expressed in the ethics of guardianship and trusteeship calling for new responsibilities. Humans and their institutions such as nation-states need to understand themselves as trustees – trustees of human well-being (human rights) and of the Earth system (Earth trusteeship) (Earth Trusteeship, n.d.; Bosselmann 2020).

## Notes

1 Some parts of this chapter are derived from Bosselmann (2017a).
2 See e.g. *2016 Oslo Manifesto* https://elgaworld.org/oslo-manifesto and *2017 Siena Declaration https://elgaworld.org/siena-declaration*
3 Citing Hamilton (2017, 43): "There is no going back to the Holocene."
4 This seems to be misunderstood by Kotzé and Kim (2019, 7) where the dichotomy between ecocentric and anthropocentric ethics is portrayed as an expression of "Cartesian dualism." While anthropocentrism undoubtedly reflects Cartesian dualism, ecocentrism aims for overcoming it.
5 Report of the World Commission on Environment and Development (n.d.): "Nature is bountiful, but it is also fragile and finely balanced. There are thresholds that cannot be crossed without endangering the basic integrity of the system. Today we are close to many of these thresholds; we must be ever mindful of the risk of endangering the survival of life on Earth."
6 See, for example, Burdon (2013, 252): "the capitalist class will never willingly surrender power."
7 It is noted, however, that Athens was still built on slave labour and – as Thucydides describes – eventually had its own little "empire," with many conniving great plans to dominate the whole Mediterranean.
8 Burdon (2013, 246) mentions (but rejects) the idea of a benevolent totalitarian regime. For a detailed discussion, see Zimmerman (1993).
9 For example, in a country with nuclear power plants, it is obviously desirable that the government maintains the ability to manage them. All of them have to be supplied with sufficient energy for many decades, or they will be in danger of melting down like Fukushima. Perhaps in the Anthropocene it is time to challenge the assumption that all nations with nuclear power will – for the timeframe required – be intact enough to manage them and handle any nuclear emergency.

## References

Bosselmann, Klaus. 1995. *When Two Worlds Collide: Society and Ecology*. Auckland: RSVP.

Bosselmann, Klaus. 2013. "The Concept of Sustainable Development." In *Environmental Law for a Sustainable Society*, edited by Klaus Bosselmann, David Grinlinton and Prue Taylor, 2nd ed., 104. Auckland: NZCEL Monograph Series 1.

Bosselmann, Klaus. 2015. *Earth Governance: Trusteeship of the Global Commons*. Cheltenham: Edward Elgar.

Bosselmann, Klaus. 2017a. "The Imperative of Ecological Integrity: Conceptualising a Fundamental Legal Norm for a New 'World System' in the Anthropocene." In *Environmental Law and Governance for the Anthropocene*, edited by Louis Kotzé, 241–265. Oxford: Hart Publishing.

Bosselmann, Klaus. 2017b. *The Principle of Sustainability: Transforming Law and Governance*, 2nd ed. London: Routledge.

Bosselmann, Klaus. 2018. "The Ever-Increasing Importance of Ecological Integrity in International and National Law." In *Ecological Integrity, Law and Governance*, edited by Laura Westra, Prue Taylor and Agnès Michelot, 225–232. London: Routledge.

Bosselmann, Klaus. 2020. "The Role of Trusteeship in Earth Governance." In *Ecological Integrity in Science and Law*, edited by Laura Westra, Klaus Bosselmann and Matteo Fermeglia, 218–232. Cham: Springer.

Bosselmann, Klaus and Prue Taylor. 2019. "Promoting Global Ethics: The Earth Trusteeship Initiative." In *The Crisis in Global Ethics and the Future of the Earth Charter* edited by Peter Burdon, Klaus Bosselmann and Kirsten Engel, 279–283. Cheltenham: Edward Elgar.

Burdon, Peter. 2013. "The Project of Earth Democracy." In *Confronting Economic and Ecological Collapse*, edited by Laura Westra, Prue Taylor and Agnès Michelot, 244–254. Abingdon: Routledge.

Burdon, Peter. 2019. "Rethinking Global Ethics in the Anthropocene." In *The Crisis of Global Ethics and the Future of Global Governance*, edited by Peter Burdon, Kirsten Engel and Klaus Bosselmann, 90–108. Cheltenham: Edward Elgar Publishing.

Burdon, Peter. 2020. "Ecological Law in the Anthropocene." *Transnational Legal Theory* 11(1–2): 33–46.

Candiago, Noémi. 2013. "The Virtuous Circle of Degrowth and Ecological Debt: A New Paradigm for Public International Law?" In *Confronting Economic and Ecological Collapse*, edited by Laura Westra, Prue Taylor and Agnès Michelot, 215–225. Abingdon: Routledge.

Commoner, Barry. 1971. *The Closing Circle*. New York: Alfred A. Knopf.

Devall, Bill and George Sessions. 1985. *Deep Ecology: Living as If Nature Mattered*. Salt Lake City, UT: Peregrine Smith.

Die Grünen, *Das Bundesprogramm*, 1980

Dobson, Andrew. 2007. *Green Political Thought*. Abingdon: Taylor and Franics.
Earth Trusteeship. n.d. "The Hague Principles for a Universal Declaration on Responsibilities for Human Rights and Earth Trusteeship." Accessed August 30, 2021. www.earthtrusteeship.world.
Ecological Law and Governance Association. 2016. "'Oslo Manifesto' for Ecological Law and Governance." Accessed August 30, 2021. https://elgaworld.org.
Ecological Law and Governance Association. n.d. "Our Misson, Our Vision." Accessed April 8, 2021. https://elgaworld.org.
Fellows, Andrew. 2019. *Gaia, Psyche and Deep Ecology*. London: Routledge.
Fisher, Douglas. 2013. *Legal Reasoning in Environmental Law: A Study of Structure, Form and Language*. Cheltenham: Edward Elgar.
Folke, Carl, Steve Carpenter, Thomas Elmqvist, Lance Gunderson, C. S. Holling and Brian Walker. 2002. "Resilience and Sustainable Development: Building Adaptive Capacity in a World of Transformations." *ISCU Series on Science for Sustainable Development* 3: 1–72.
Fox, Warwick. 1984. "Deep Ecology: A New Philosophy of Our Time?" *The Ecologist* 14: 194–200.
Gaines, Stanford E. 2014. "Reimagining Environmental Law for the 21st Century." *Environmental Law Reporter* 44(3): 10188.
Garver, Geoffrey. 2013. "Moving Forward with Planetary Boundaries and Degrowth." In *Confronting Economic and Ecological Collapse* edited by Laura Westra, Prue Taylor and Agnès Michelot, 203–214. Abingdon: Routledge.
Graeber, David. 2011. *Debt: The First Five Thousand Years*. New York: Melville House.
Greer, John Michael. 2009. *The Ecotechnic Future: Envisioning a Post-peak World*. Gabriola Island: New Society.
Grober, Ulrich. 2012. *Sustainability: A Cultural History*. Totnes: Green Books.
Hamilton, Clive. 2017. *Defiant Earth: The Fate of Humans in the Anthropocene*. Sydney: Allen and Unwin.
Heidegger, Martin. 1976. "Nur noch ein Gott Kann Uns Retten." (1976) 30(23) *Der Spiegel* 193–219. Trans. by William Richardson as 'Only a God Can Save Us' in Martin Heidegger, *Heidegger: The Man and the Thinker* (1981) (ed) Thomas Sheehan 45–67.
Heinberg, Richard. 2007. *Peak Everything: Waking up to the Century of Declines*. Gabriola Island: New Society.
Kim, Rakhyun E. and Klaus Bosselmann. 2013. "Towards a Purposive System of Multilateral Environmental Agreements." *Transnational Environmental Law* 2(2): 285–309.
Kim, Rakhyun E. and Klaus Bosselmann. 2015. "Operationalizing Sustainable Development: Ecological Integrity as a Grundnorm of International Law." *Review of European Community and International Environmental Law* 24(2): 194–208.
Kotzé, Louis and Rakhyun Kim. 2019. "Earth System Law: The Juridical Dimensions of Earth System Governance." *Earth System Governance* 1(100003): 1–11.
Küpers, Wendelin. 2020. "From the Anthropocene to and 'Ecocene'." *MDPI Open Access Journal* 12(9): 1–20.
Mauss, Marcel. 2011. *The Gift*, Reprint of 1954 Edition. London: Forgotten Books.
Mukerjee, Madhusree. 2012. "Apocalypse Soon: Has Civilization Passed the Environmental Point of No Return?" May 23, 2012. https://www.scientificamerican.com/article/apocalypse-soon-has-civilization-passed-the-environmental-point-of-no-return/.
Muldrew, Craig. 1998. *The Enemy of Obligation: The Culture of Credit and Social Relations in Early Modern England*. New York: Palgrave.
*News from the University of Georgia*, 9 January 2018. https://news.uga.edu/the-father-of-modern-ecology/.
Odum, Eugene. 1977. The Emergence of Ecology as New Integrative Discipline. *Science* 195(4284): 1289–1293.
Odum, Eugene. 2021. *The Fundamentals of Ecology*, 5th ed. (with Gary Barrett), 1953. Chichester: John Wiley & Sons.
Ophuls, William. 2011. *Plato's Revenge: Politics in the Age of Ecology*. Cambridge, MA: MIT Press.
Orlov, Dmitry. 2011. *Reinventing Collapse*. Gabriola Island: New Society.
Orlov, Dmitry. 2013. *The Five Stages of Collapse*. Gabriola Island: New Society.
Rees, William E. 2013. "Confronting Collapse: Human Cognition and the Challenge for Economics." In *Confronting Economic and Ecological Collapse*, edited by Laura Westra, Prue Taylor and Agnès Michelot, 288–314. Abingdon: Routledge.
Rockström, Johan, Will Steffen, Kevin Noone, Asa Persson, F. Stuart III Chapin, Eric Lambin, Timothy M. Lenton et al. 2009. "Planetary Boundaries: Exploring the Safe Operating Space for Humanity." *Ecology and Society* 14(2): 32.

Steffen, Will, Katherine Richardson, Johan Rockström, Sarah E. Cornell, Ingo Fetzer, Elena M. Bennett, Reinette Biggs, Stephen R. Carpenter, Wim de Vries et al. 2015. "Planetary Boundaries: Guiding Human Development on a Changing Planet." *Science* 347(6223): 1–10.
Tainter, Joseph. 1988. *The Collapse of Complex Societies*. Cambridge: Cambridge University Press.
Toynbee, Arnold J. 1934–61. *A Study of History*. Vol. I–XII. Oxford: Oxford University Press.
Urban, Mark. 2015. "Accelerating Extinction Risk from Climate Change." *Science* 348(6234): 571–573.
Wallerstein, Immanuel. 2011. *The Modern World-System*. Vol. I–IV. San Francisco, CA: University of California Press.
Westerlund, Staffan. 2008. "Theory for Sustainable Development Towards or Against?" In *Sustainable Development in International and National Law*, edited by Hans Christian Bugge and Christina Voigt, 48–65. Groningen: Europa Law Publishing.
White, Daniel. 1997. *Postmodern Ecology*. Albany, NY: Suny Press.
Zalasiewicz, Jan, Mark Williams, Will Steffen and Paul Crutzen. 2010. "The New World of the Anthropocene." *Environmental Science and Technology* 44(2): 2228–2231.
Zimmerman, Michael E. 1993. "Rethinking the Heidegger-Deep Ecology Relationship." *Environmental Ethics* 15(3): 195–224.

# 13

# MAKING ECOLOGICAL INTEGRITY HUMAN-INCLUSIVE IN THE ANTHROPOCENE

*Geoffrey Garver*

Preserving, restoring, and enhancing ecological integrity, or sometimes biological integrity or biosphere integrity, are at the core of many proposals to halt and reverse ecological destruction and degradation, which at the global scale aligns with the rise of the Anthropocene. In these proposals, ecological integrity carries considerable normative weight as a desirable policy or management goal or ultimate endpoint (Sbert 2020, 86–87). The moral force of ecological integrity comes through in Aldo Leopold's famous proposal that "a thing is right when it tends to preserve the integrity, stability, and beauty of the biotic community. It is wrong when it tends otherwise" (Leopold 1949, 224–225). More recently, a core normative objective of the Earth Charter is to "[p]rotect and restore the integrity of Earth's ecological systems, with special concern for biological integrity and the natural processes that sustain life" (Earth Charter 2000). Kim and Bosselmann (2013) give numerous other examples of international agreements or soft instruments of law or policy that include ecological integrity as an important, or even fundamental, normative objective.

Yet, ecological integrity often lacks clear meaning, especially in the context of the Anthropocene. The understanding of the Anthropocene in this chapter is not necessarily tied to the mid-twentieth century stratigraphical markers that the Anthropocene Working Group of the Subcommission on Quaternary Stratigraphy of the International Union of Geological Sciences formally associates the Anthropocene epoch within geology (Anthropocene Working Group 2019). Rather, this chapter adopts a more informal understanding of the Anthropocene, aligning it with

> the present geological time interval, in which many conditions and processes on Earth are profoundly altered by human impact [which] has intensified significantly since the onset of industrialization, taking us out of the Earth System state typical of the Holocene Epoch that post-dates the last glaciation.
>
> *(Anthropocene Working Group 2019)*

This informal alignment of the Anthropocene with the era of colonial expansion, industrialization, and globalization nonetheless places the focus of analysis of the meaning of ecological integrity on the Earth system as a whole. The Earth system is not merely the aggregation of sub-global ecosystems but also the integration of climatic, oceanic, and ecospheric systems (the


DOI: 10.4324/9781003388081-17

atmosphere, the lithosphere, the cryosphere, the hydrosphere, and the biosphere) that can only be fully appreciated at the planetary level (Hamilton 2019). Human impacts associated with the Anthropocene certainly manifest in widely diverse sub-global ecosystems. However, at the Earth system scale to which the Anthropocene concept necessarily applies, definitions of ecological integrity that imply the absence of human impacts are hopelessly elusive, given the long history and inevitable continuation of the global aggregation of human impacts on Earth's ecosystems.

Definitions of "ecological integrity" often refer to pristine nature virtually free of human impacts, as with one definition that aligns it with "wild nature that is virtually unchanged by human presence or activities" (Westra et al. 2000, 20). In some definitions, it also requires continuity in time, such that the conversion of a grassland to a forest or even a grassland with different species, even if entirely as a result of non-human forces, could be considered a loss of integrity, even if the system remains flourishing and life-enhancing (Rohwer and Marris 2021, 2–4). Adherence to historic trajectories is the approach in ecological restoration, where reference conditions tied to ecological integrity are typically limited to natural or historical ranges of variation that allow for very little human presence or impact (Higgs 2003, 124; Hobbs et al. 2014, 558; Rohwer and Marris 2021, 3).

Yet, the very concept of the Anthropocene indicates that human presence or activities dating as far back as paleolithic times have significantly, and in many cases irreversibly, altered ecosystems across the planet (Ellis and Ramankutty 2008; Minteer 2012; Foley et al. 2013; Balaguer et al. 2014; Ruddiman et al. 2014; Lewis and Maslin 2015; Garver 2021). Research indicates that in the contemporary era, so-called "anthropogenic biomes" that humans have deeply influenced, as opposed to relatively untouched "wildlands," cover more than 75% of Earth's ice-free terrestrial systems (Ellis and Ramankutty 2008). By a more recent reckoning, only about 2.8% of the Earth's land surface now has the same habitat, number of fauna species, and density of those species as existed prior to human impacts (Plumptre et al. 2021). Thus, the reference conditions for concepts such as "wild" or "pristine" nature in some definitions of ecological integrity seem hopelessly elusive (Rohwer and Marris 2021; Burdon 2020).

In light of this compelling research, defining ecological integrity at the global scale – what might be called Earth system integrity – with reference to pristine nature is particularly problematic. Normative proposals to pursue ecological integrity, defined with reference to pristine conditions free of human impacts, at the Earth system level imply a need to eliminate humans from Earth (Garver 2021, 153). In a purely ecocentric approach, the elimination of humanity from Earth may be entirely acceptable, but the normativity with which I propose to imbue ecological integrity does not include that as an acceptable or desired outcome. Aiming to protect and expand wilderness that approaches strict definitions of ecological integrity may be useful in some situations.[1] However, the more interesting and intriguing challenge is how to apply notions aligned with ecological integrity – wholeness, functional intactness, resilience, self-organization – to the vast parts of Earth, and to the Earth system as a whole, that cannot return to a human-free wilderness-like state as long as humans remain on the planet.

Ecological integrity can also be defined so vaguely as to be effectively meaningless. *The future we want*, the agreed final text of the Rio+20 conference on sustainable development that spurred the development of the United Nations' Sustainable Development Goals (SDGs), combines aspirations for vaguely defined, or undefined, ecological integrity with seemingly inconsistent, but more prominent, objectives promoting more of the kind of economic development that historically has driven ecological degradation and led to the Anthropocene. The SDGs, as a whole, leave no reasonable prospect for preserving, enhancing, or restoring ecological or biological integrity, however defined, particularly at the Earth system scale. For example, *The future we want* called for "holistic and integrated approaches to sustainable development which will guide humanity to live in harmony with nature and lead to efforts to restore the health and integrity of the Earth's ecosystems" (United Nations 2012). However, this goal is secondary to the paramount commitment to sustained economic growth, which *The future we want* calls for over 20 times. Sustained economic growth is also the core objective of SDG 8: Decent Work and Economic Growth. Historically, economic growth correlates very clearly and broadly with many forms of ecological degradation and destruction aligned with the Anthropocene, including global heating, anthropogenic additions of nutrients to ecosystems, and loss of terrestrial and marine biodiversity and species abundance (Bai et al. 2018). An ecological footprint analysis of the SDGs as a whole found not surprisingly that SDGs virtually certain to increase ecological footprint (and hence likely to undermine ecological integrity, however defined), such as SDG 8, but also goals related to poverty reduction, adequate food, and education, far outweighed goals that would likely lead to reduced ecological footprints (Wackernagel et al. 2017). Thus, references to ecological integrity in texts like *The future we want* and the SDGs are too compromised to have useful meaning and application.

What to do with these contrasting uses of the term ecological integrity in the context of the Anthropocene? Rohwer and Marris (2021, 2) contend that ecosystems are not "the kinds of things that have integrity [and] that the value of ecological integrity is, in many cases, an imperfect placeholder for the values of biodiversity, complexity, and important cultural attachments to particular historical ecosystem states." This critique resonates most strongly at the Earth system level. One proposal is simply to abandon ecological integrity as a useful term in the quest to divert humanity from the path to ecological catastrophe that the Anthropocene illuminates (Burdon 2020, 44–45; Rohwer and Marris 2021). However, I propose that abandoning the concept of ecological integrity be considered a last resort, even at the Earth system scale, because it would place a big question mark over the meaning of the Earth Charter and the numerous other texts that use the term. An alternative is to accept that the term is so widely used that it cannot easily be retired, and seek a useful understanding of ecological integrity that avoids the pitfalls of both overly strict and compromised definitions of it. This would be a way of harnessing the widespread use of the term toward a positive end (Kim and Bosselmann 2013). That ecological integrity is widely seen as elastic and not bound to a rigid definition (Higgs 2003, 122; Rohwer and Marris 2021, 2) may be helpful in that this definitional flexibility may help yield a better understanding of it, although it also likely indicates that the effort will be a difficult challenge. In this chapter, while remaining open to abandoning ecological integrity as too elusive to be useful in the Anthropocene, especially at the Earth system scale, I aim to accept the challenge and propose a human-inclusive understanding of ecological integrity that will help inform normative approaches for establishing a mutually enhancing human–Earth relationship (Berry 1999) in response to the rise of the Anthropocene.

## Two Axioms for Ecological Integrity in the Anthropocene

My proposal for understanding ecological integrity is grounded in two propositions taken to be axiomatic. First, ecological integrity requires that ecosystem structures and functions (including at the Earth system scale) maintain resilience and a capacity to support life broadly consistent with the ecosystem's past (deserts and ice caps come to mind), even if ecosystems continually change and evolve in response to human and non-human impacts. Although some reference to an evolutionary trajectory tied to natural or historical conditions inheres in common definitions of ecological integrity (Higgs 2003, 124), the term should also account for how ecosystems over time undergo "an unspooling series of changes on the landscape, driven by changes in climate, evolution, and accident" (Rohwer and Marris 2021, 4). The role of humans in this unspooling is of particular concern in the Anthropocene. From a systems perspective, this means that ecological integrity has scalar dimensions; it is not static in time, and it may mean different things at different spatial scales. For example, observations at the Earth system scale may mask the nature and degree of ecosystem change at local or regional scales (Brook et al. 2013, 400). In terms of temporality, the geologic timescales that are most relevant in defining the Anthropocene and in characterizing the Earth system complicate any understanding of ecological integrity at that scale (Kotze and Kim 2019). Further, the higher the spatial scale is toward the global level, the harder it is to exclude humans from the ecosystems, or the Earth system, being considered.

The second axiom, which follows from this, is that ecological integrity must be understood to allow for some degree of human presence in and use of ecosystems, which inevitably means that ecological integrity can exist even in systems that have endured human impacts on their structure and functioning. Ecology and Earth system science are not human-free disciplines. Because humans are part of and interdependent with Earth's ecosystems, and most certainly the Earth system as a whole, "ecological integrity must encompass not only the most pristine wild ecosystems but also dense human settlements and other areas in which humans or their impacts have significantly transformed the evolutionary trajectory of the per-human or an imagined human-free ecosystem" (Garver 2021, 154). This axiom rejects any categoric notion that human impact is always associated with ecosystem damage or harm or an undermining of ecological integrity (Balaguer 2014, 17). Conversely, the possibility the removal of humans from some ecosystems may undermine ecological integrity cannot be categorically excluded, and at the Earth system scale, the analysis in this chapter rejects elimination of humans as a normative goal. Again, questions of scale are important for considering when human impacts undermine or enhance ecological integrity.

These two axioms can support a functional, human-inclusive understanding of ecological integrity if they are linked to an overarching objective of working perpetually toward a mutually enhancing human–Earth relationship (Berry 1999). With this link to achieving a mutually enhancing human–Earth relationship, the understanding of ecological integrity that I propose might appear to be more akin to social-ecological integrity. Indeed, I propose to merge these terms. At the global scale, ecological integrity aligns with ecosphere or Earth system integrity, and it necessarily includes humans as a particularly significant component – the term Anthropocene underscores that fact (Sbert 2020, 87–88; Burdon 2020, 42). Because ecological integrity, at any scale, should not categorically exclude humans, it subsumes any separate notion of social-ecological integrity; they become one and the same. However, even at sub-global scales, terms like human–Earth relationship or social-ecological systems should not be read to connote a separation of humans from nature. Rather, they provide a signal that questions regarding the human role in and impact on the ecosystems in which they are embedded, as well as the relationship of humans and human communities with other components of those systems, are important and demand special attention. Thus, as the second axiom noted above indicates, regardless of scale, ecological integrity subsumes social-ecological integrity for ecosystems in which humans or their impacts play a significant role – which is the case for nearly all of them in the Anthropocene, and is certainly the case at the Earth system level.

Tying ecological integrity to mutual human–Earth enhancement provides a novel way to interpret the meaning of wholeness, which is typically considered a core element of ecological integrity (Rohwer and Marris 2021). If seen only as pertaining to the physical and biological composition of an ecosystem, wholeness is a challenging concept because flourishing, seemingly whole ecosystems can have some ecological niches unfilled, and well-functioning ecosystems can seem less than whole in that they typically lack clear boundaries or have elements, like migratory birds, that come and go (Rohwer and Marris 2021, 4–5). This concern decreases if the focus of wholeness is on the mutuality of the relationship between humans and the ecosystems in which they are embedded – or that they mostly leave alone. The broad focus of inquiry regarding wholeness becomes whether, given the immensity of the weight of human presence on Earth that the Anthropocene connotes, humans – by intervening or refraining from doing so – are enabling an ecosystem to be flourishing as well as possible (Perring et al. 2014, 3). The answer likely will often depend on whether humans are having an impact only to the extent necessary to meet true needs and not liberally undertaking anything that money, technology, or unfettered desires will allow (Sbert 2020). Thus, something like the energy-intensive extraction of gold for jewelry or other luxury purposes, especially in regions where regulation of the social and ecological impacts is weak, represents a human–Earth relationship that is not whole, and therefore almost certainly ecosystems lacking ecological integrity.

Sbert (2020) incorporates ecological integrity into the notion of ecological primacy, which she describes as one pillar, along with ecocentrism and ecological justice, of ecological law. This imbues ecological integrity with normativity, similar to the proposals for ecological integrity here. Acknowledging the problem by tying ecological integrity only to pristine nature free of human impacts, she combines Parks Canada's interpretation that "ecosystems have integrity when they have their native components (plants, animals and other organisms) and processes (such as growth and reproduction) intact" (Parks Canada Agency 2000) with the caveat that "ecosystems are inherently dynamic, and have a history of human intervention and even management" (Woodley 2010, 159). A similar broadening of human-free definitions with an insistence on continuing to include humans as members of Earth's life systems, and of the Earth system as a whole, is proposed here as appropriate for the Anthropocene.

## A Focus on Relationship

The foregoing underscores that what is most fundamental in considering ecological integrity in the Anthropocene is the integrity not only of human-inclusive ecosystems as a whole but also of the relationships and role of humans within ecosystems and the Earth system as a whole. At the Earth system scale, the planetary boundaries, which include biosphere integrity as an aspect of the boundary for biodiversity (Steffen et al. 2015), are important because they provide the outer contours of "safe operating space for humanity" (Rockström et al. 2009). Thus, even if they do not entirely align with ecological integrity (Burdon 2020) (which in this case needs to be distinguished from biosphere integrity), they represent an outer limit of even the possibility of human-inclusive ecological integrity at the Earth system scale, because crossing them signals a dangerous risk of human-driven ecological catastrophe. In this sense, the planetary boundaries provide a starting point for determining whether humans' relationships with each other and with all else, and the role humans play in Earth's communities of life, are consistent with ecological integrity at the Earth system scale. As well, ecological integrity can be compromised at sub-global scales even if all of the planetary boundaries are being met (Brook et al. 2013, 400).

From the starting point of contours like the planetary boundaries, the understanding of ecological integrity that I propose avoids perpetuation of the view, which echoes in classical thought, Judeo-Christian traditions, and the Enlightenment, of humans as separate from and superior to nature, and ordained to exercise dominion and control over it (Merchant 1980; Capra and Mattei 2015). The term Anthropocene itself certainly confirms something about the uniqueness of humans among species (Burdon 2020). Part of the danger that ecological warning signs in the Anthropocene (Woolley 2021, 64–65) highlights is that something is amiss with the dominant thinking about the human–Earth relationship underlying the profound anthropogenic ecological and geological change in the Anthropocene's Earth system.

Ideologies grounded in human separateness, superiority, and dominion over the rest of Earth's ecosystems support actions that critically impair the capacity for social-ecological integrity, and hence ecological and Earth system integrity. In the modern global economy, they encourage exploitation and market-driven profit-making, and money-centered investments and decisions that have profound impacts on people and ecosystems that are far away, out of sight, and out of mind (Garver 2019) – as well as on the Earth system as a whole.

Even pockets of wilderness, or artificially carved out parks and protected areas, in which ecological integrity according to human-free definitions is high lose broader value if, in line with human-nature dualism, they exist only in the broader context of an overall trend of ecological deterioration in the aggregate or at the Earth system scale. Indeed "[p]rotected areas necessarily seek to protect nature and biodiversity by abstracting them from their complex social contexts [and] the histories of particular protected areas are often simplified by omitting the role people have played in forging these landscapes" (West and Brockington 2006, 610). These isolated havens ("nature" areas) can serve as a tacit justification for not worrying about the ecological integrity of vast areas deemed already too greatly impacted by human activity (Hobbs et al. 2014) ("human" areas). The potential for human-inclusive ecological integrity increases with ideologies grounded in human membership in Earth's life communities (Brown, 2015) and relationships of humans with each other and with other members of the life communities based on reciprocity and respect (Brown and Garver 2009) – that is, with ideologies that reject human-nature dualism.

## How to Recognize Ecological Integrity

Definitions of ecological integrity tied to pristine ecosystems unaltered by human impacts led to some fairly concrete methodologies in ecology for establishing indicators and reference conditions that align with ecological integrity (Westra et al. 2000, 20; Wurtzebach and Schultz 2016, 448). Recognizing ecological integrity when it is defined in the human-inclusive manner proposed here, in a way that takes into its scalar dimension and is useful as a normative tool, may seem more complex and challenging. Yet, doing so is essential if a functional, coherent understanding of human-inclusive ecological integrity is sought.

> The most pristine ecosystems are part of higher-scale landscapes and ecosystems, and ultimately the entire ecosphere. ... The anthropogenic impacts or alterations in those larger landscapes and ecosystems at some point become significant, compromising ecological integrity (if defined with reference to pristine nature) at least to some degree.
>
> *(Garver 2021, 155)*

With the role of humans, the prevalence of human impacts in the Anthropocene and questions of scale acknowledged, "a rigorous yet practicable notion of ecological integrity must acknowledge and accept a conditional level of symbiosis between humans and non-human nature in order to be consistent with a mutually enhancing human-Earth relationship" (Garver 2021, 157). However, precise definitions are not necessarily essential at the crisis stage that the Anthropocene and planetary boundaries research, including climate research, indicate humanity currently is in. When the Earth's ecosystems, and the Earth system as a whole, are as off-kilter as they are now, being very clear that ecological integrity is being broadly and severely undermined is the key message. When ecological integrity is so clearly lacking on a broad scale, and at the Earth system scale, halting and reversing processes of ecosystem degradation and allowing regimes of ecosystem restoration, protection, and enhancement to ramp up is what is most urgent and important. Although the need for more clarity and definition cannot be ignored, it will take a while on this corrective course before humanity needs to start worrying deeply about precise definitions of human-inclusive ecological integrity. Even then, it may be helpful to approach this definition as a "wicked problem" characterized by "(1) interconnection and complexity of components, (2) uncertainty, (3) ambiguity of definition, (4) controversy, and (5) social constraints" (Geist and Galatowitsch 1999, 971). For such problems, community engagement and deliberation in the quest for solutions are likely as important as the solution itself, which in any event is likely to be an evolving one. In this context, the broad concepts of a mutually enhancing human–Earth relationship and the relative ecological stability of the Holocene (Steffen et al. 2015) can serve to center and frame the quest for greater clarity and precision in the meaning of ecological or Earth system integrity.

Beyond the urgency of the current moment, however, broad contours of the shifts in human relationships and the human role in Earth's communities of life are emerging. Here, I will highlight four ways to begin to determine whether ecological integrity exists or is possible with these changes in the relevant social-ecological systems. These four areas of inquiry relate most obviously to social-ecological systems at the local or landscape scale. It bears emphasis that even if Anthropocene-defining Earth system changes reflected in planetary boundaries and other similar research have implications beyond the mere aggregation of sub-global impacts, the diverse drivers and the wide array of consequences of Earth system change are all manifested at sub-global scales. Therefore, attention to ecological integrity (which, as I have argued already, aligns with social-ecological integrity) through these areas of inquiry at sub-global scales will resonate up to the Earth system level and to the root causes of the Anthropocene.

First, monocultures, broadly defined, impede ecological integrity and signal a need for social change if they become too extensive or dominant. Second, ecological and eco-cultural restoration provides lessons for recognizing when the integrity of social-ecological systems has been impaired and for returning those systems to a pathway to ecological integrity. The notion of reciprocal restoration is particularly useful. Third, the conditions in which different communities around the world have learned to provision themselves from common pool resources (that is, non-human components of ecosystems in which those communities are embedded) while maintaining the integrity of both the human communities and their supporting ecosystems (Ostrom 1990) may provide lessons for how to achieve ecological integrity more broadly. Fourth, novel ecosystems that have resulted from (often irreversible) human activities and that have adapted to be life-enhancing in novel ways may yield lessons for recognizing human-inclusive ecological integrity that is particularly well suited to the Anthropocene.

## Monocultures

In complex systems theory, anthropogenic monocultures are typically associated with "engineering resilience" by which the system is manipulated through technology and design to maintain a specific system state that is highly controlled, predictable, efficient, uniform, and constant – as with, for example, industrial pork production or car manufacturing (Gunderson and Holling 2002; Garver 2021, 173). Yet, this kind of resilience always leads to other kinds of system vulnerability (Gunderson and Holling 2002) – such as, in pork production, the perpetual need to develop new antibiotics, genetic manipulations, and other tweaks to keep the hogs healthy and maintain the desired uniform meat quality (Johnson 2006). Moreover, the vulnerabilities to which industrial and other monocultures give rise typically result from the sacrificing of systems complexity and other system features that are important for ecological integrity (Hummel et al. 2011). Indeed, engineering resilience stands in contrast to ecological or ecosystem resilience, "by which the system fends off disturbances that could alter its overall structure, function and behavior by developing a broad-based defense that relies predominantly on diversity, adaptiveness, far-from-equilibrium conditions and unpredictability" (Gunderson and Holling 2002; Garver 2021, 173).

Problematic monocultures do not only exist in industrial agriculture, manufacturing, and other industrial processes. Monocultural institutions and processes have also taken firm root, for example, in governance, in the form of the globally dominant state-centered model; valuation, in that the value of countless things, including ecosystems, is increasingly expressed in the single-unit form of money; spirituality, with monotheistic religions with roots in the Middle East having becoming prevalent throughout the world, often by displacing Indigenous cosmologies; language, in that a relatively few number of languages, such as Mandarin, Spanish, and English, are now dominant globally; and happiness, in that the globalization of markets has opened all corners of the world to advertising and other forms of salesmanship that frame happiness and well-being in market-driven ways. Commodification is a red flag of problems related to many of these forms of monoculturalism that undermines ecological integrity (Higgs 2003, 188–195).

As with industrial monocultures, the cost of all these monocultures is a loss of diversity, and often an erosion of local or regional traditions and customs that have evolved in connection to the ecologies of their place. In social-ecological systems, these monocultures, therefore, erode social-ecological resilience, and in particular features such as learning, innovation, and transformability that enable systems to adapt and evolve while maintaining their essential structure, functioning, and integrity in the face of change (Garver 2021, 173). As a result, monoculturalism in any form is virtually certain to signal a loss of ecological integrity and social-ecological integrity.

## *Reciprocal Restoration*

Ecological restoration and eco-cultural restoration involve translating broad objectives tied to ecological or social-ecological integrity into practicable approaches at various scales, taking into account as well historical information regarding the human–Earth relationship affecting the site of restoration (Garver 2021, 157–160). The applied science of ecological or eco-cultural restoration involves a "process of assisting the recovery of an ecosystem that has been degraded, damaged, or destroyed" (Society for Ecological Restoration International 2004), taking into account criteria such as ecological integrity, historical fidelity and community engagement (Higgs 2003).

Inherent in the proactive domains of ecological and eco-cultural restoration is the deliberate choice that is involved in pursuing "a vision of a better relationship between humans and the rest of the world" (Egan et al. 2011, 1). Because of this element of choice, ecological or eco-cultural restoration "is inherently (1) value-laden, (2) context driven, (3) prone to be immersed in disagreement and compromise, and (4) experiential" (Egan et al. 2011, 1–2). Thus, sound processes of informed community engagement and deliberation, with an emphasis on trustworthy knowledge holders, are needed to allay concerns that intentional human intervention in ecosystems is ill-advised based on humanity's often poor record in messing with Mother Nature (Minteer 2012, 857).

Although restoration ecology at times links ecological integrity to pristine human-free nature (Higgs 2003), ecological integrity in this context more commonly has a broader connotation that accounts for human presence in ecosystems. For example, Higgs (2003) describes integrity as "an all-encompassing term for the various features – resilience, elasticity, stress response, and so on – that allow an ecosystem to adjust to environmental change" (122). This notion of integrity inherently includes human-induced environmental change. Human-inclusive ecological integrity framed this way allows for

> a flexible range of options that include a human presence and that maintains (1) a basis for mutual flourishing of the human and non-human spheres of nature, (2) ties to historical conditions in which a mutually enhancing human-Earth relationship existed, (3) insistence on core notions of resilience and persistence in accordance with broad historical socio-ecological trajectories, and (4) recognition of embedded, resilient and communal connections of people and place.
>
> *(Garver 2021, 159)*

Reciprocal restoration, which is one approach to ecological and eco-cultural restoration, can be particularly helpful in working toward a human-inclusive understanding of ecological integrity. Reciprocal restoration is "the mutually reinforcing restoration of land and culture such that the repair of ecosystem services contributes to cultural revitalization and renewal of culture promotes restoration of ecological integrity" (Kimmerer 2011, 258). Thus, reciprocal restoration "resonates strongly with the notion of a mutually enhancing human–Earth relationship, and with the pairing of ecosystem services to humans with human services to ecosystems" (Garver 2021, 158–159). Traditional ecological knowledge, drawn from time-tested practices of ecologically sustainable human communities with a strong attachment to place, has a strong role to play in bringing lessons from reciprocal restoration to human-inclusive understandings of ecological integrity (Egan et al. 2011, 255):

> Reciprocal restoration … arises from a creative symbiosis between traditional ecological knowledge (TEK) and restoration science, which honors and uses the distinctive contributions of both intellectual traditions. Reciprocal restoration recognizes that it is not just the land that is broken, but our relationship to it. Reciprocal restoration encompasses repair of both ecosystem and cultural services while fostering renewed relationships of respect, responsibility, and reciprocity. All flourishing is mutual.
>
> *(Kimmerer 2011, 258)*

## *Governance of Common Pool Resources*

Human-inclusive ecological restoration, and especially reciprocal restoration, depends strongly on community engagement to be successful and to advance functional human-inclusive understandings of ecological integrity (Higgs 2003; Egan et al. 2011). Strong processes of dialogue and community building have helped some communities, including many Indigenous communities, to maintain sustainable, enduring use of at least some common pool resources (CPRs) in their supporting ecosystems for long periods of time (Ostrom 1990). Key features that Ostrom (1990, 90) found were typically necessary for social systems to maintain human provisioning from ecosystems of at least some human needs in perpetuity are:

- **Clearly defined boundaries.** Individuals or households who have rights to withdraw resource units from the CPR must be clearly defined, as must the boundaries of the CPR itself;

- **Congruence between appropriation and provision rules and local conditions.** Appropriation rules restricting time, place, technology, and/or quantity of resource units are related to local conditions and to provision rules requiring labor, material, and/or money;
- **Collective-choice arrangements.** Most individuals affected by the operational rules can participate in modifying the operational rules;
- **Monitoring.** Monitors, who actively audit CPR conditions and appropriator behavior, are accountable to the appropriators or are the appropriators;
- **Graduated sanctions.** Appropriators who violate operational rules are likely to be assessed graduated sanctions (depending on the seriousness and context of the offense) by other appropriators, by officials accountable to these appropriators, or by both;
- **Conflict-resolution mechanisms.** Appropriators and their officials have rapid access to low-cost local arenas to resolve conflicts among appropriators or between appropriators and officials;
- **Minimal recognition of rights to organize.** The rights of appropriators to devise their own institutions are not challenged by external government authorities;
- **Nested enterprises.** Appropriation, provision, monitoring, enforcement, conflict resolution, and governance activities are organized in multiple layers of nested enterprises.

The establishment of these community features, which rein in human demands on the supporting ecosystems, depends on a strong communal attachment to place and the local community, and to intergenerational continuity (Garver 2021). The existence of these community features likely indicates that human-inclusive ecological integrity exists, or at least is possible.

## *Novel Ecosystems*

If humans are integral parts of their supporting ecosystems and of the Earth system as a whole, then the central question about ecological integrity is not whether humans have had an impact on those ecosystems, but what kind of impact they have had. This implies acceptance that at least some ecosystems altered by human impacts can have ecological integrity if they have adapted in enduring ways that enhance life and flourishing. Reluctance to accept that novel ecosystems, which are a cogent indicator of the shift from the Holocene to the Anthropocene (Corlett 2015, 36), can have ecological integrity is a stark illustration that resistance to acknowledging human impacts in defining ecological integrity persist.

Novel ecosystems are "those that depart from historical precedents through rapid environmental (climate) and ecological change (species invasion)" (Egan et al. 2011a, 20). More broadly, they can include any ecosystem for which a return to even broadly defined historical reference conditions that incorporate human presence and impacts is deemed impracticable (Higgs et al. 2014; Balaguer et al. 2014, 12). Novel ecosystems can be further distinguished from hybrid ecosystems, which "retain characteristics of the historic system but whose composition or function now lies outside the historic range of variability" (Hobbs et al. 2009, 601). By contrast, novel ecosystems exhibit a more complete transformation, although historic, hybrid, and novel ecosystems fall along a continuum of a degree of human alteration, and the distinctions among them are somewhat arbitrary (Hobbs et al. 2009, 601). For example, national parks and other protected areas are artificial creations, with man-made boundaries, and sometimes their creation has involved the eviction of people that lived in or used the land in the parks prior to their establishment (Brockington and Igoe 2006, 433). The world's first national park, Yellowstone National Park in the United States, is a leading example. When Yellowstone was established, 27 Native American tribes who had lived on or made use of the park's territory were banished from the park (Poirier and Ostergren 2002; National Park Service 2021). Although the United

States government does sometimes establish historic baselines to implicitly include pre-colonial human presence in what are now protected areas (Ruhl 2011, 13–14; Wurtzebach and Schultz 2016, 448), determining the nature and degree of human alteration and the appropriate historical references in such a case is more complex than might appear at first blush.

In ecological and eco-cultural restoration circles, some posit that novel ecosystems have moved into territory for which human-inclusive ecological integrity, at least if cast as an objective for restoration tied to historical conditions, is no longer possible (Balaguer et al. 2014, 12). Resistance to accepting that novel ecosystems can have ecological integrity is due, among other reasons, to doubts over claims that they are already widespread and are a new and growing normal, that they have a proven capacity to retain valuable ecosystem functioning despite their novelty and that the impacts that make them novel are truly irreversible (Murcia et al. 2014, 549–550). For others, because "the development of ecosystems that differ significantly from those found historically is increasingly inevitable and likely to occur over large areas of the world" (Hobbs et al., 2009: 600), and because some novel ecosystems provide valuable ecosystem functions, restoration principles can still apply to them. For novel ecosystems, the goal is not to return an ecosystem to its historical range of variability (including any human alteration that inheres in that variability), but rather to guide it to "more highly valued" composition and function than exists in its disturbed state (Hobbs et al. 2009, 602). For example, where the introduction of non-native species is effectively irreversible, as with many non-native species in the Americas dating back to the Columbian Exchange, the focus would be on new forms of thriving rather than restoration through elimination of the non-native species.

For ecological integrity in the Anthropocene, novel ecosystems might push the understanding of human-inclusive ecological integrity toward a breaking point. This is perhaps most clear if the Earth system that the Anthropocene connotes is seen as a particularly clear example of a novel ecosystem. Certainly, ecological integrity loses meaning if an ecosystem can retain or regain ecological integrity regardless of the extent of anthropogenic alteration and novelty – that is, if anything goes. Concern also exists that if novel ecosystems fall too far out of the realm of the undesirable, breaking conventional taboos, "the 'novel ecosystem' label may provide a 'license to trash' or 'get out of jail' card for companies seeking to fast-track environmental permits or to avoid front-end investment in research, offsets, and restoration" (Murcia et al. 2014, 551). By contrast, including novel ecosystems in the realm of places where ecological integrity is possible gives credence to the notion that "[i]n the state space where traditional conservation and restoration outcomes are unlikely, a range of options exists that can still result in beneficial outcomes in terms of ecosystem services, biodiversity conservation and ecological integrity." (Hobbs et al. 2009, 604).

With this broader set of options, regaining or achieving human-inclusive ecological integrity can be undertaken in settings, such as urban areas, where it might otherwise be assumed not to apply (Hobbs et al. 2014, 2). In addition, several ways are possible for avoiding anything-goes outcomes that deprive ecological integrity of all meaning. For example, "novel ecosystems that result from self-assembly and persist without human intervention can reasonably be considered wild and are often beautiful" (Corlett 2015, 37), in which case ecological integrity should not be difficult to acknowledge. Likewise, the lack of ecological integrity should be clear in an asphalt parking lot that remains an asphalt parking lot. In the gray areas, the key is to contextualize novel ecosystems with the human–Earth relationship with which they are imbued, with wariness when reference to ecological integrity in novel ecosystems reflects human-nature dualism and not a mutually enhancing human–Earth relationship, as outlined earlier in this chapter. For example, companies seeking to avoid ensuring the integrity of ecosystems they impact or alter on the grounds that they are novel ecosystems will typically reflect approaches based on human superiority and dominion over nature, ideologies in which ecosystems are first and foremost seen as property.

Corlett summarizes well the overall context in which novel ecosystems in the Anthropocene can shed light on human-inclusive ecological integrity. He notes:

> two parallel realizations: that conservation can no longer focus only on preserving and restoring ecosystems of the past, because this will be impossible in many places, and that we can no longer treat natural systems as separate from human systems. While some authors see these changed perceptions as a threat, fearing that they will 'cultivate hopelessness in those dedicated to conservation' and 'undermine both conservation and restoration objectives', most seem prepared to accept the reality and focus on the inevitably novel future rather than the irretrievably lost past.
>
> (Corlett 2015, 38)

Scaling up to the Earth system level at which the Anthropocene concept resonates most fully, it is virtually beyond dispute that Earth is now a novel ecosystem. Further, with several planetary boundaries already crossed and trends toward Earth system restoration not yet established for most of them (depletion of stratospheric ozone being a possible exception, Garver 2021, 84–86), it is a novel ecosystem that lacks ecological integrity and will – to the extent sense can be made of ecological integrity at this scale – for a long time to come.

## Conclusion

Overcoming the ecological challenges of the Anthropocene will require humanity to decide not to do things that are economically, technologically, politically, and (for now) legally possible – many of which are being done today. From a normative perspective, a concept like ecological integrity is most useful if it serves as a helpful guide for humans to decide which of the myriad good and bad human choices available are wise and ecologically sound in the Anthropocene. Normative applications of the concept of ecological integrity inevitably involve some kind of social discourse. One element of ecological integrity in this discourse is its role as an enunciation of an ideal end state. I have proposed aligning the meaning of ecological integrity in the Anthropocene with an overarching objective of a mutually enhancing human–Earth relationship. Above all, this means ecological integrity is human-inclusive. It also means that ecological integrity cannot be applied only to islands of wild nature in a sea of human-led ecological decay.

Proponents of human-free definitions of ecological integrity tied to pristine wilderness may well resist alternative understandings that allow the term to apply to ecosystems altered by humans – at least past a point. It may well be that the term can only be stretched so far before it loses its meaning and usefulness in overcoming the enormous challenges that the Anthropocene poses for humanity and the rest of Earth's life communities. These concerns are particularly resonant at the Earth system scale at which the concept of the Anthropocene has its fullest expression. In this chapter, I have attempted to make the case for continuing, for now, to adapt the term to the circumstances of the Anthropocene. In doing so, I have backed away from any call for a precise new definition or set of criteria for determining whether ecological integrity or social integrity exists. Instead, I have proposed to focus for now on bringing those terms together, and I have attempted to paint the broad contours of what human-inclusive ecological integrity looks like. From here, I am happy to let the meaning of ecological integrity continually evolve through values-led applications of it (Artelle et al. 2018) and ongoing discourse, understanding that in light of Earth's arrival in the Anthropocene, achieving anything like ecological integrity at the Earth system scale is in the distant future if it can be achieved at all.

## Note

1 The artificial creation of wilderness in national parks in the United States and Canada through the forced removal of Indigenous peoples is certainly a model to be avoided. See Poirier and Ostergren 2002; Brockington and Igoe 2006, 433; and discussion of novel ecosystems in this chapter.

## References


Anthropocene Working Group. (2019) 'Working Group on the "Anthropocene", Results of Binding Vote by AWG, Released 21st May 2019', *Subcommission on Quaternary Stratigraphy*. Available at: http://quaternary.stratigraphy.org/working-groups/anthropocene/ (Accessed: 8 December 2021).

Artelle, K.A., Stephenson, J., Bragg, C., Housty, J.A., Housty, W.G., Kawharu, M., and Turner, N.J. (2018) 'Values-Led Management: The Guidance of Place-Based Values in Environmental Relationships of the past, Present, and Future', *Ecology and Society*, 23(3), p. 35.

Bai, X., van der Leeuw, S., O'Brien, K., Berkhout, F., Biermann, F., Brondizio, E.S., Cudennech, C., Dearing, J., Duraiappahj, A., Glaserk, M., Revkin, A., Steffen, W., and James Syvitskio, J. (2018) 'Plausible and Desirable Futures in the Anthropocene: A New Research Agenda', *Global Environmental Change*, 39, pp. 351–362.

Balaguer, L., Escudero, A., Martin-Duque, J.F., Mola, I., and Aronson, J. (2014) 'The Historical Reference in Restoration Ecology: Re-defining a Cornerstone Concept', *Biological Conservation*, 176, pp. 12–20.

Berry, T. (1999) *The Great Work: Our Way Into the Future*. New York: Three Rivers Press.

Brockington, D., and Igoe, J. (2006) 'Eviction for Conservation: A Global Overview', *Conservation and Society*, 4(3), pp. 424–470.

Brook, B.W., Ellis, E.C., Perring, M.P., Mackay, A.W., and Blomqvist, L. (2013) 'Does the Terrestrial Biosphere Have Planetary Tipping Points?', *Trends in Ecology and Evolution*, 28(7), pp. 396–401.

Brown, P.G. (2015) 'Ethics for Economics in the Anthropocene', in P.G. Brown, and P. Timmerman (eds.), *Ecological Economics for the Anthropocene*. pp. 66–88, New York: Columbia University Press.

Brown, P.G., and Garver, G. (2009) *Right Relationship: Buiilding a Whole Earth Economy*. San Francisco, CA: Berrett-Koehler.

Burdon, P.D. (2020) 'Ecological Law in the Anthropocene', *Transnational Legal Theory*, 11(1–2), pp. 33–46.

Capra, F., and Mattei, U. (2015) *The Ecology of Law: Toward a Legal System in Tune with Nature and Community*. San Francisco, CA: Berrett-Koehler.

Corlett, R.T. (2015) 'The Anthropocene Concept in Ecology and Conservation', *Trends in Ecology and Evolution*, 30(1), pp. 36–41.

Earth Charter. (2000) *Earth Charter*. Available at: https://earthcharter.org/read-the-earth-charter/ (Accessed: 8 December 2021).

Egan, D., Hjerpe, E.E., and Abrams, J. (eds.). (2011) *Human Dimensions of Ecological Restoration: Integrating Science, Nature and Culture*. Washington, DC: Island Press.

Egan, D., Hjerpe, E.E., and Abrams, J. (2011a) 'Why People Matter in Ecological Restoration', in D. Egan, E.E. Hjerpe, and J. Abrams (eds.), *Human Dimensions of Ecological Restoration: Integrating Science, Nature and Culture*. pp. 1–19, Washington, DC: Island Press.

Ellis, E.C., and Ramankutty, N. (2008) 'Putting People in the Map: Anthropogenic Biomes of the World', *Frontiers in Ecology and the Environment*, 6(8), pp. 439–447.

Foley, S.F., Gronenborn, D., Andreae, M.O., Kadereit, J.W., Esper, J., Scholz, D., Pöschl, U., Jacob, D.E., Schöne, B.R., Schreg, R., Vött, A., Jordan, D., Lelieveld, J., Weller, C.G., Alt, K.W., Gaudzinski-Windheuser, S., Bruhn, K.-C., Tost, H., Sirocko, F., and Crutzen, P. (2013) 'The Palaeoanthropocene – The Beginnings of Anthropogenic Environmental Change', *Anthropocene*, 3, pp. 83–88.

Garver, G. (2019) 'Confronting Remote Ownership Problems with Ecological Law', *Vermont Law Review*, 43(3), pp. 425–454.

Garver, G. (2021) *Ecological Law and the Planetary Crisis: A Legal Guide to Harmony on Earth*. New York: Routledge.

Geist, C., and Galatowitsch, S.M. (1999) 'Reciprocal Model for Meeting Ecological and Human Needs in Restoration Projects', *Conservation Biology*, 13(5), pp. 970–979.

Gunderson, L.H., and Holling, C.S. (eds.). (2002) *Panarchy: Understanding Transformations in Human and Natural Systems*. Washington, DC: Island Press.

Hamilton, C. (2019) 'The Anthropocene', in B. Fath (ed.), *Encyclopedia of Ecology, 2nd edition*. Amsterdam: Elsevier, pp. 239–246.

Higgs, E. (2003) *Nature by Design*. Cambridge, MA: The MIT Press.

Higgs, E., Falk, D. A., Guerrini, A., Hall, M., Harris, J., Hobbs, R.J., Jackson, S.T., Rhemtulla, J.M., and Throop, W. (2014) 'The Changing Role of History in Restoration Ecology', *Frontiers in Ecology and the Environment*, 12(9), pp. 499–506.

Hobbs, R.J., Higgs, E., Hall, C.M., Bridgewater, P., Chapin III, F.S., Ellis, E.C., Ewel, J.J., Hallett, L.M., Harris, J., Hulvey, K.B., Jackson, S.T., Kennedy, P.L., Kueffer, C., Lach, L., Lantz, T.C., Lugo, A.E., Mascaro, J., Murphy, S.D., Nelson, C.R., Perring, M.P., Richardson, D.M., seastedt, T.R., Standish, R.J., Starzomski, B.M., Suding, K.N., Tognetti, P.M., Yokob, L., and Yung, L. (2014) 'Managing the Whole Landscape: Historical, Hybrid, and Novel Ecosystems', *Frontiers in Ecology and the Environment*, 12(10), pp. 557–564.

Hobbs, R.J., Higgs, E., and Harris, J.A. (2009) 'Novel Ecosystems: Implications for Conservation and Restoration', *Trends in Ecology and Evolution*, 24(11), pp. 599–605.

Hummel, D., Jahn, T., and Schramm, E. (2011) 'Social-Ecological Analysis of Climate Induced Changes in Biodiversity – Outline of a Research Concept', *Biodiversität und Klima Forschungszentrum*, Knowledge Flow Paper No. 11. Available at: http://publikationen.ub.uni-frankfurt.de/frontdoor/index/index/docId/22258 (Accessed: 8 December 2021).

Johnson, D. (2006) 'Swine of the Times', *Harper's*, May issue. Available at: https://harpers.org/archive/2006/05/swine-of-the-times/# (Accessed: 21 April 2021).

Kim, R.E., and Bosselmann, K. (2013) 'International Environmental Law in the Anthropocene: Towards a Purposive System of Multilateral Environmental Agreements', *Transnational Environmental Law*, 2(2), pp. 285–309.

Kimmerer, R. (2011) 'Restoration and Reciprocity: The Contributions of Traditional Ecological Knowledge', in D. Egan, E.E. Hjerpe, and J. Abrams (eds.), *Human Dimensions of Ecological Restoration: Integrating Science, Nature and Culture*. pp. 257–276, Washington, DC: Island Press.

Kotze, L., and Kim., R. (2019) 'Earth System Law: The Juridical Dimensions of Earth System Governance', *Earth System Governance*, 1, p. 100003.

Leopold, A. (1949) *A Sand County Almanac*. New York: Oxford University Press.

Lewis, S.L., and Maslin, M.A. (2015) 'Defining the Anthropocene', *Nature*, 519(7542), pp. 171–180.

Merchant, C. (1980) *The Death of Nature: Women, Ecology and the Scientific Revolution*. San Francisco, CA: Harper & Row.

Minteer, B.A. (2012) 'Geoengineering and Ecological Ethics in the Anthropocene', *BioScience*, 62(10), pp. 857–858.

Murcia, C., Aronson, J., Kattan, G.H., Moreno-Mateos, D., Dixon, K., Simberloff, D. (2014) 'A Critique of the "Novel Ecosystem" Concept', *Trends in Ecology and Evolution*, 29(10), pp. 548–553.

National Park Service. (2021) *Historic Tribes*. Available at: https://www.nps.gov/yell/learn/historyculture/native-american-affairs.htm (Accessed: 23 April 2021).

Ostrom, E. (1990) *Governing the Commons: the Evolution of Institutions for Collective Action*. New York: Cambridge University Press.

Parks Canada Agency. (2000) *Unimpaired for Future Generations? Protecting Ecological Integrity within Canada's National Parks, Volume 1, A Call to Action. Report of the Panel on the Ecological Integrity of Canada's National Parks*. Ottawa: Government of Canada. Available at: https://publications.gc.ca/site/eng/9.661581/publication.html (Accessed: 8 December 2021).

Perring, M.P., Audet, P., and Lamb, D. (2014) 'Novel Ecosystems in Ecological Restoration and Rehabilitation: Innovative Planning or Lowering the Bar?', *Ecological Processes*, 3(8), pp. 1–4.

Plumptre, A.J., Baisero, D., Belote, R.T., Vázquez-Domínguez, E., Faurby, S., Jędrzejewski, W., Kiara, H., Kühl, H., Benítez-López, A., Luna-Aranguré, C., Voigt, M., Wich, S., Wint, W., Gallego-Zamorano, J., and Boyd, C. (2021) 'Where Might We Find Ecologically Intact Communities?', *Frontiers in Forests and Global Change*, 4, art 626635.

Poirier, R., and Ostergren, D. (2002) 'Evicting People from Nature: Indigenous Land Rights and National Parks in Australia, Russia and the United States', *Natural Resource Journal*, 42(2), pp. 331–351.

Rockström, J., Steffen, W., Noone, K., Persson, Å., Chapin, F.S., III, Lambin, E., Lenton, T.M., Scheffer, M., Folke, C., Schellnhuber, H., Nykvist, B., De Wit, C.A., Hughes, T., van der Leeuw, S., Rodhe, H., Sörlin, S., Snyder, P.K., Costanza, R., Svedin, U., Falkenmark, M., Karlberg, L., Corell, R.W., Fabry, V.J., Hansen, J., Walker, B., Liverman, D., Richardson, K., Crutzen, P., and Foley, J. (2009) 'Planetary Boundaries: Exploring the Safe Operating Space for Humanity', *Ecology and Society*, 14(2), p. 32. Available online at: http://www.ecologyandsociety.org/vol14/iss2/art32/.

Rohwer, Y., and Marris, E. (2021) 'Ecosystem Integrity Is Neither Real nor Valuable', *Conservation Science and Practice*, 3(411), pp. 1–11.

Ruddiman, R., Vavrus, S., Kutzbach, J., and He, F. (2014) 'Does Pre-industrial Warming Double the Anthropogenic Total?', *The Anthropocene Review*, 1(2), pp. 147–153.

Ruhl, J.B., and Salzman, J. (2011) 'Gaming the Past: the Theory and Practice of Historic Baselines in the Administrative State', *Vanderbilt Law Review*, 64(1), pp. 1–57.

Sbert, C. (2020) *The Lens of Ecological Law: A Look at Mining*. Northampton, MA: Edward Elgar.

Society for Ecological Restoration International (2004) *The SER International Primer on Ecological Restoration*. Tucson: Society for Ecological Restoration International Science & Policy Working Group. Available at: https://cdn.ymaws.com/www.ser.org/resource/resmgr/custompages/publications/ser_publications/ser_primer.pdf (Accessed: 8 December 2021).

Steffen, W., Richardson, K., Rockström, J., Cornell, S.E., Fetzer, I., Bennett, E.M., Biggs, R., Carpenter, S.R., de Vries, W., de Wit, C.A., Folke, C., Gerten, D., Heinke, J., Mace, G.M., Persson, L.M., Ramanathan, V., Reyers, B., and Sörlin, S. (2015) 'Planetary Boundaries: Guiding Human Development on a Changing Planet', *Science*, 347(6223). https://doi.org/10.1126/science.1259855.

United Nations. (2012) *The Future We Want*. New York: United Nations.

Wackernagel, M., Hanscom, L., and Lin, D. (2017) 'Making the Sustainable Development Goals Consistent with Sustainability', *Frontiers in Energy Research*, 5, art 8.

West, P., and Brockington, D. (2006) 'An Anthropological Perspective on Some Unexpected Consequences of Protected Areas', *Conservation Biology*, 20(3), pp. 609–616.

Westra, L., Miller, P., Karr, J.R., Rees, W.E., and Ulanowicz, R.E. (2000) 'Ecological Integrity and the Aims of the Global Integrity Project', in D. Pimentel, L. Westra, and R.F. Ness (eds.), *Ecological Integrity: Integrating Environment, Conservation, and Health*. Washington, DC: Island Press, pp. 19–41.

Woodley, S. (2010) 'Ecological Integrity and Canada's National Parks', *The George Wright Forum*, 27(2), pp. 151–160.

Woolley, O. (2021) 'Ecological Law in the Anthropocene', in K. Anker, P.D. Burdon, G. Garver, M. Maloney, and C. Sbert (eds.), *From Environmental to Ecological Law*. pp. 61–75, New York: Routledge.

Wurtzebach, Z., and Schultz, C. (2016) 'Measuring Ecological Integrity: History, Practical Applications, and Research Opportunities', *BioScience*, 66(6), pp. 446–457.

# PART V

# Dignity and Human Rights

# 14

# THE ANTHROPOCENE AND HUMAN RIGHTS

## A New Context and the Need to Revisit Collective Human Concerns

*Karen Morrow*

The Anthropocene, being hallmarked by global-scale anthropogenic impacts on the Earth system, infringing on planetary boundaries and in consequence impinging on the safe operating space for humanity, (Steffen et al. 2015) is itself intensely anthropocentric. This is manifest in various ways: it is caused by humans (albeit implicated to hugely differing degrees) (Chakrabarty 2018); often characterized in terms of its consequences for humans (Hamilton 2017); and can potentially, though only partially, be addressed by human actions (Lade et al. 2019). The planet-wide, past-rooted, present-manifesting, and future-shaping, species-wide nature of the Anthropocene certainly has massive ramifications for humanity. The Anthropocene is however disruptive and/or potentially destructive not only of the Anthropos, the human sphere, but also of aspects of the perivallon, which encapsulates the physical environment and the living flora and fauna that inhabit it (Weisman 2008). The Anthropocene is then unsettling to the living and non-living environment, planet-wide in its reach, and has species-level implications, including for human flourishing and survival.

The Anthropocene at base calls for understanding and acting on the fundamental importance of connection (Potts 2014) in the world we are fashioning: connection now and in the future between humans and the perivallon at all levels, including its most expansive, the biosphere; and connections between humans both now and reaching into the future. This chapter will focus on some under-interrogated aspects of inter-human connection in the Anthropocene and how we might address them. The implications of the Anthropocene, as an epochal change, operate at a global level (Litfin 2009) and thus ultimately apply to humanity as a species, in the here and now and, necessarily, to future generations. The implications of the systemic change that is already being wrought on the planet and the living legacy that we are shaping are such that adopting an expanded spatial and temporal perspective on how we regard humanity can no longer be regarded as optional; it is imperative. Engaging with the interests of future generations, what we could term the temporal dimension of the collective interest, though not without its challenges, is a well-developed area of scholarly debate (Brown Weiss 1990), if not of substantive legal provision. The necessary element of future focus also implicitly invokes the less-developed notion of collective concern for humanity as a species.

DOI: 10.4324/9781003388081-19

Consideration of how to fully address the collective interest and collective rights – the spatial, planetary, dimension of the collective interest – requires urgent scrutiny in the Anthropocene. Spatial collective interests, insofar as they are addressed by current international law provisions, often fall between the two stools of mainstream human rights law provision and the fiction of state sovereignty. Neither is equal to the challenge. While international environmental law has engaged with global environmental concerns to a degree (Brunnée 2008), until quite recently there has been comparatively little consideration of the global societal dimensions involved. This is changing as international human rights law is increasingly interrogating the human implications of environmental crises but engagement with the collective dimensions involved at all scales (with the partial exception of Indigenous peoples, discussed below) remains underdeveloped. The strategies that have helped humanity to flourish thus far, notably the assumption of human supremacy over nature, the primacy of the individual and their human rights, and neo-Westphalian approaches to international interaction, may have enabled our species to shape the modern world to its own ends – but it is now evident that this has been to the peril of other forms of life and, ultimately, our own species.

The limits of our ability to fully predict, never mind remedy the impacts of the Anthropocene, render its recognition a call to correct, rather than continue on, our current course. At the very least, the fact that humanity as a whole now operates as a geological force, shaping the Earth system, must give us pause for thought. If we impact as a species, it behooves us to consider what it means to think and act purposely as a species. This chapter, therefore, contends that the responses prompted by the Anthropocene must include two entwined dimensions. First, revisiting both the relationship between humans now and in the future, addressing the collective, species-wide, human interest. Second, addressing the human relationship with the perivallon and the re-shaped world that we are creating. The ongoing rise to prominence of human rights talk, focused on individuals, *vis-à-vis* the environment, must be vigorously interrogated. In this, it is imperative to ensure that debate is neither narrowed to the exclusion of collective human concerns and the claims of future humans, nor allowed to perpetuate what has proved a disastrously narrow, instrumentalized view of the environment that has ill-served the perivallon and in the long run, most of humanity.

The Anthropocene is seeing human actions shift planetary systems away from the Holocene stability that has been conducive to humanity's flourishing, into uncertain and dangerous configurations, that operate to the detriment of many species, including, now, our own. Activity to address the crises of the Anthropocene has thus far been dominated by a plethora of, more-or-less technocratic, multinational environmental agreements, which have not delivered adequate progress (UNEP 2019b). As mentioned above, these have latterly been joined by a more obviously human/societal dimension, rooted in human rights, that focuses strongly on the dominant approach in this sector, founded on the individual. This chapter examines key aspects of the latter development and identifies areas of concern raised and potential means to address them.

While phenomena such as climate change and biodiversity loss point to long-term and accelerating manifestations of fundamental Anthropocene shifts, the Covid-19 pandemic shows that Anthropocene-induced change can also manifest with staggering speed. It also serves to reveal important ways in which modes of engagement with global predicaments are being found wanting. Covid-19 is thought by many to be rooted in increasing human reliance on bush meat (Vidal 2020), a quotidian example of broader human incursions into biodiversity, an already compromised planetary boundary (Vaughan 2020). Its origins notwithstanding, Covid's spread across the entire globe was, despite efforts to contain it, facilitated, and its impact amplified, by the intensely interactive and globally connected nature of human society. The questions raised in regard to societal impacts often involve the interface between individual and collective concerns and it is therefore unsurprising that, particularly in the Western world and within the UN, many criticisms of state handling of the Covid-19 crisis include a clear human rights dimension (Lebret 2020). The Covid-19 crisis has provided an exemplar of the importance of human rights questions in the broader context of negotiating a just approach to societal functioning within a safe operating space for humanity (Morrow 2021). Characterizing Covid-19 as an Anthropocene threat underlines that addressing it requires global action and the international community has conspicuously failed to deliver on this, augmenting the pandemic's impacts. Collective endeavors to engage with Covid-19 have fallen woefully short of the mark, at the cost of immense, preventable, human suffering, particularly among the poorest within and across nations. This is not only an enormous injustice in itself; it will ultimately work against the common global interest by prolonging the pandemic (Fallah 2021). The many emergent existential threats of the Anthropocene, require us to attend to systemic, planet-wide, issues that are collective concerns for humanity as a species and that relatedly shape human futures. We are however failing to grasp the need to adapt our perspectives, values, institutions, and behaviors to the fundamentally changed global context which we have wrought and continue to re-make, and in which our species must live now and in the future (Morrow 2017). The unavoidable challenge now is to do so, and swiftly.

## Framing Engagement with Collective Concerns

While collective interests may involve rights claims, collective rights are often viewed as a "human rights afterthought" (Mujkiv n.d.). In Vasak's influential generational account of rights, collective rights are referred to as third-generation/solidarity rights (Vasak 1977). They may be described as embracing:

> collective rights of society or peoples, such as the right to sustainable development, to peace or to a healthy environment … these rights would ensure the appropriate conditions for societies … to be able to provide the first and second generation rights that have already been recognised.
>
> *(Council of Europe, n.d.)*

It is therefore apparent that, although they currently function on the periphery of the human rights canon, collective rights are by no means a novel proposition in general and in environmentally related contexts in particular. Here, collective rights appear in a variety of international soft law instruments, including oblique reference to what "human beings" are "entitled" to in Principle 1 of the foundational Rio Declaration (UNGA 1992), raising an important precursor of what has subsequently been elaborated on, in the right to development. Likewise, the (collective) needs of future generations, are explicitly alluded to in Principle 3 of the Rio Declaration, the wording of which implies entitlement, if avoiding the explicit use of the language of rights (UNGA 1992).

However, broad coverage of collective rights and interests at a global level remains uncommon and, when it does exist, relatively underdeveloped. The most marked area of progress in respect of collective rights for the purposes of this chapter has been focused on groups deemed particularly vulnerable to environmental threats, notably in the United Nations Declaration on the Rights of Indigenous Peoples (UNGA 2007). Other instruments do however offer potentially useful coverage of cognate issues, notable the Declaration on the Right to Development (UNGA 1986), and the United Nations Educational, Scientific and Cultural Organization Declaration on the Responsibilities of the Present Generations Towards Future Generations (UNESCO 1997).

Each of the instruments identified raises issues that are germane to this chapter, and they will be considered below, but it is important to underline that they remain exceptions to the rule in international human rights law, which foregrounds individualism. There are several putative explanations for the continuing relatively tenuous status of collective rights at a global level, with some critics even going so far as to eschew their existence and/or status as human rights (Jones 1999). Given the instruments alluded to above, the latter view if it was ever tenable, no longer holds. However, it is true that engagement with collective human rights remains underdeveloped and that, given the global and long-term threats of the Anthropocene, they may have much to offer and thus merit urgent fuller consideration. Multiple dimensions of the collective human story are innate to the Anthropocene, and it is vital to consider how we might better incorporate them into our thinking. The Forum Social Mundial (FSM), a non-governmental space devoted to discussion on global solidarity, democracy, and fairness, has observed "the collective dimension of human rights to be of primary importance and an absolutely essential part of building another possible world." FSM noted that, notwithstanding, collective human rights issues are, at best, neglected by states and, at worst, regarded with outright hostility (Forum Social Mundial 2009). The advent of the Anthropocene and its expression in the multifarious and increasingly evident manifestations of human-driven impacts across the Earth system has necessary implications for effective governance at a planetary scale and in the long term.

## *Current Contexts (Individual) Human Rights and the Environment*

In order to consider the potential for collective rights in thought and practice relating to the environment, discussion must first be situated in the context of current debate. Widespread and intensifying concern about the environmental and societal impacts of the Anthropocene has naturally provoked enormous activism and activity and much of this has focused on matters of human rights. This is understandable, and attributable not only to the high profile enjoyed by human rights in international law but also to its relatively well-developed legal machinery (UNEP 2019a, 137–223 *passim*). In this, the existence of potential routes to a remedy for those whose human rights are adversely affected by environmental degradation, in particular, compares favorably to redress available in other areas, not least international environmental law, which is generally lacking in this regard. There are then certain advantages to pursuing a human rights approach in regard to environmental concerns, but it does come at a cost. In essence, the overtly anthropocentric stance involved reinforces human exceptionalism and risks further entrenching a damagingly myopic anthropocentrism. Moreover, the dominance of individualism in human rights law serves to narrow the ambit of coverage further still, neglecting full consideration of collective interests, and often limiting them to an oppositional framing when environment-based human rights claims are in play. A similarly constrained approach can be observed in the individualistic cast that has come to characterize the right to development. In effect, the collective interest tends to be rather simplistically equated with the state, law, and policy, and deemed to operate within states, where it is presented as infringing upon the human rights of the individual and justifiable only on carefully articulated principles.

External facing, global dimensions of collective concerns are for the most part left to statecraft, which, as currently oriented and operated, largely through the concept of sovereignty, is singularly ill-suited to engaging with the species-level interests that are evident in the Anthropocene (Matthews 2021). International environmental law has slowly come to challenge this parochial view of sovereignty, with innovation in treaties increasingly in evidence to give practical effect to engaging with global issues/matters of common concern (Brunnée 2008). That said, the approach is highly fragmented, with each and every issue seemingly requiring re-examination *ab initio*. What is required instead is a fundamental re-set of state sovereignty for the Anthropocene that situates it in a context delineated by a recognition that the common concerns of humanity be regarded as foundational and viewed first and always as operating within planetary boundaries. In short, legal fiction must defer to ecological facts.

As things stand, the relationship between individual and collective human rights and interests and the environment in the Anthropocene is a complex and shifting one. In some contexts, they may be viewed as mutually supportive, as for example, in the case of the right to education (Graham 2010), the right to health (Douwes et al. 2018), and in the context of sustainable development (Folkesson 2013). However, environment-based claims are one of the areas where the relationship between individual and collective rights may be viewed as capable of being antagonistic. It may also be argued that this is an area where states may "weaponize" solidarity rights and use collective rights justifications to curtail individual rights (Council of Europe, n.d.). This criticism is however overstated, as the vast majority of individual rights are already subject to limitations *vis-à-vis* the rights of others and in the broader public interest. Arguably well-crafted solidarity rights would offer a firmer, more fully thought-out basis upon which to delineate both the extent of individual rights and nature and the scope of justifiable constraints on them.

There are important practical questions attached to the idea of an environmental human right that suggest a poor fit for an individual rights focus. Environment-based human rights claims often involve hybrid concerns, encapsulating both individual and collective elements. While undoubtedly founded on environmental conditions, framing an individual environmental human right is inherently problematic. Take, for example, its application to air quality. Air quality considerations are collective, community, and/or population-based concerns and while certain individuals will be more adversely affected by poor air quality than the population at large, any redress available to them for infringements must also respect complex considerations of the public good. Conceptually, such claims may be less problematically located in more firmly established human rights contexts, such as the right to life and/or the right to health (Missone 2021).

Other environment-based claims can only be addressed (at best) partially by individual human rights and maybe even detrimentally affected by them. The interface between ecosystems and society is a case in point (Martin et al. 2016). While always growing, our scientific understanding of particular ecosystems is often wanting. Furthermore, human interests in ecosystem services do not necessarily sit well with one another and/or the viability of the perivallon (Birkhofer et al. 2015). That said, individually-focused human rights claims are capable of serving the collective good. Established civil and political rights such as freedom of expression, freedom of association, and even social and economic rights such as the right to development, for example, demonstrate inextricable links between individual and collective considerations, the complex interplay between them, and its implications. In the context of environment-based claims too, the interplay between the individual and collective requires full and careful attention. We may learn much from interrogating this dual-natured incarnation in other more established human rights – but it is also possible that there are novel factors in play here. It is certainly open to question if the environment is in fact an appropriate subject for human rights in any form, and if it is, can it be treated in the same way as other established rights topics. A good fit cannot and should not be assumed. In a given case, individual human rights-based claims may secure environmental protection at the same time as vindicating the interests of individual rights holders; but they may equally be used to advance individual human interests over aspects of the perivallon to its detriment and to that of broader collective interests in the short and/or long term. The actual position on the compatibility of individual and collective environmental rights and interests, therefore, lies somewhere between conflict and concord, and ultimately depends on the context and nature of the particular claims made.

It is also significant that a viable environment is foundational to supporting human life and flourishing and thus operates as the ultimate foundation of all extant human rights. This being the case, placing an environmental human right on a par with other rights does not necessarily sit well as a matter of principle. While a putative hierarchy of rights may appear to be a matter of solely academic interest (Müller 2019), in this context such considerations may have significant practical ramifications, signaling the relative positioning of the Anthropos and the perivallon, arguably augmenting anthropocentrism, and failing to engage with the realities of the Anthropocene.

While cogent criticisms of adopting an environmental human right have been with us for as long as this has been suggested (McGoldrick 1996, 111–112), nonetheless the idea has a broad appeal. In recent years momentum has been growing, perhaps unstoppably, behind calls for the adoption of a (predominantly individual-focused) right to the enjoyment of a safe, clean, healthy, and sustainable environment (UN Doc. 2018b, UNHRC 2021). This trend is typified by the recent overwhelming endorsement of this right by 43 to 0 (though with significant abstentions by China, India, Japan, and Russia) by a resolution of the UN Human Rights Council (Dewan et al. 2021) and a similarly strongly supported (albeit rather less detailed) General Assembly Resolution (UNGA 2022). The UNHRC resolution is the most fully developed incarnation of the new environmental right, strongly rooted in the high-profile work of the Office of the United Nations High Commissioner for Human Rights (UNOCHR) and its special rapporteurs on human rights and the environment. Over several years, the huge volume of research they have carried out has shaped international debate and built and sustained momentum behind the right to a safe, clean, and healthy environment. The work of the UNOCHR's special rapporteurs in particular has persistently underlined how human rights ultimately depend on viable biospheric conditions. In particular, the special rapporteur's introduction in 2018 of a set of framework principles on human rights and the environment has served to crystallize rapidly maturing debate in the area and provides a good example of the current trajectory of discussion (UN Doc. 2018a). However, for all of their many virtues, it will become apparent that framework principles' engagement with collective concerns remains selective – related primarily to vulnerable groups and Indigenous peoples – and very much supplementary to its chief focus on individual rights.

## The Framework Principles on Human Rights and the Environment

The general orientation of the current framework principles on human rights and the environment is broadly compatible with that exhibited in the innovative work carried out in the 1990s under the auspices of Fatma Zohra Ksentini, the special rapporteur to the UN Commission on Human Rights' Sub-Commission on Prevention of Discrimination and Protection of Minorities (Ksentini 1994). This work first broached the relationship between human rights and the environment in a UN institutional framing and produced a first set of draft principles for this area. The general stance they adopted is commensurate with that observed by McGoldrick as evident in the development of both human rights law and international environmental law more generally (McGoldrick 1996, 804). It is worth noting however that the line adopted by Ksentini, and later by Knox, and Boyd, tends to the idea that environmental vulnerability is the preserve of special groups, rather than merely being particularly evident and already manifest for them, but ultimately applicable to all people and peoples. In this regard, the current fairly limited engagement with collective interests and rights in environmental contexts is consistent with the historic framing of these issues in international law. In the most recent tranche of activity, it is also a product of the pragmatic approach adopted by the special rapporteurs to counter opposition on the part of some states to an environmental human right, by evidencing its presence in the operation of extant human rights law (UN Doc. 2018a, 4–5). Useful as this may be in strategic terms, it could also be said to undermine the case for a discrete human right to the enjoyment of a safe, clean, healthy, and sustainable environment referred to above, for if protection is already required in practice, what would a new right avail, beyond the symbolic? Additionally, adopting this type of incremental approach can mask the need for a deeper, revolutionary, change in how we regard the relationship between human rights and the environment in the Anthropocene (Morrow 2021).

While the main thrust of the coverage of the framework principles lies in individual rights, like its antecedents, it does contain some supplementary coverage of collective concerns. Framework Principle 14 on vulnerable groups (FP 14), and 15 on Indigenous peoples and traditional communities (FP 15) provide the most significant examples of the latter (UN Doc. 2018a, 16–20). Coverage in each instance is predicated on the interlinked nature of the exposure of the most vulnerable to environmental threats and total or partial inability to access human rights protection. While thus limited in application, there is much to admire in FP 14. Significantly, it adopts an intersectional approach in its view of vulnerable groups; acknowledges that they as suffer most acutely in this regard; and recognizes the dual individual and "community" (i.e. collective) nature of their experiences and rights. Additionally, the axes of vulnerability identified are broad, comprising gender, youth, old age, disability, indigeneity, traditional community membership, ethnic, racial, or other minority statuses, and displacement (UN Doc. 2018a, 16–17). A further important aspect of FP 14 is its focus on the practicalities of safeguarding the vulnerable, including the prioritizing of collecting disaggregated data to better identify the issues to be addressed and gauge progress (UN Doc. 2018a, 17–18).

While Indigenous peoples and traditional communities are addressed among the vulnerable groups identified in FP 14, as mentioned above, they are also dealt with discretely under FP15. In the case of the former group, this is attributable to pre-existing recognition of their particular situation and legal recognition for it in international human law, which is reinforced here and aspects of which will be discussed further below. With regard to the latter, inclusion here is significant, as it recognizes that they often enjoy a similar relationship with their lands to that of Indigenous peoples and experience similar vulnerabilities due to environmental degradation. Thus, there are arguments for the extension of some aspects of existing legal protection already in place for Indigenous peoples to traditional communities (UN Doc. 2018a, 19–20). This approach also implicitly signals acceptance of the idea that collective interests and rights is not, and should not be, regarded as a closed category.

## Climate Change – Examining an Anthropocene Phenomenon in a Human Rights Framing

The special rapporteur's 2019 report on human rights and the environment is focused on climate change and provides a characteristic example of the wider work of the mandate. It is of particular relevance to this chapter as it also maps the contours of current consideration of an archetypal Anthropocene issue in a human rights frame. The report's coverage centers on states' human rights obligations regarding climate change impacts and foregrounds the core requirements to respect, protect, and fulfill these in the face of the multiple and interrelated environmental threats involved (UN Doc. 2019, paras 63 and 70). As with the 2018 framework principles considered above, the 2019 report, while strongly focused on the human rights of individuals, also mentions collective concerns, including alluding in passing to inter-state and intergenerational issues (UN Doc. 2019, para 26). In addition, it too draws specific attention to the plight of groups deemed particularly vulnerable to climate change, and to state obligations toward them (UN Doc. 2019, 14, 22). The groups in question are deemed vulnerable by means of particular characteristics and/or positioning, including: "poverty, gender, age, disability, geography and cultural or ethnic background" (UN Doc. para 45). Furthermore, children are referred to specifically as vulnerable and discussed discretely (UN Doc. 2019, 13). The document goes on to focus on vulnerability based on gender, indigeneity, disability, and location (specifically in developing small island states) (UN Doc. 2019, 14). However, the coverage offered to collective concerns in the 2019 report is relatively brief and bypasses the core question about how best to address the inherently collective dimensions of human rights-based claims in the context of climate change. The approach of applying a standard human rights lens to climate change also evades the implications of the planetary nature of climate change as an expression of the Anthropocene, wherein an adequate response must reach beyond the limits of established state-based solutions.

In conclusion, both the framework principles on human rights and the environment and the climate change report do crucial work in drawing together an account of where we have been and where we are in their respective areas and, in this, they do consider collective concerns. That said, the nature and extent of coverage offered serve, in many ways, to amplify how limited our engagement with collective interests and rights is and underlines the fact that there is much further to go.

## *Existing International Law Instruments and Collective Interests*

As indicated above, the framework principles, in compiling an overview of provision at the nexus of human rights in the environment, provide important insights regarding the direction of travel of human rights provision in the Anthropocene, though they leave something to be desired with regard to collective concerns. However, there is existing international law provision in play in this regard that merits consideration and may offer further insights to assist in better addressing the particular spatial and temporal nature of the collective concerns of the Anthropocene. The United Nations Declarations on the Rights of Indigenous Peoples, and the Right to Development, and the UNESCO Declaration on the Responsibilities of the Present Generations Towards Future Generations offer approaches and elements that could be re-purposed to address at least some of the distinctive challenges of engaging with the planetary and epochal collective human concerns in the new epoch.

### The United Nations Declaration on the Rights of Indigenous Peoples (UNDRIP)

The recognition of collective rights has, at least in part, been shaped by questions centered on of protection of minorities within states and in particular Indigenous peoples (Freeman 1995). The issues arising with regard to the latter manifest in many ways, including inadequate legal protection, disparities in power and influence, and routine despoliation of tribal lands in the cause of economic development. These are pervasive matters of societal and legal conflict across the globe. Superficially, these issues can be framed around the need to address the consequences of incompatible world views and practices and thus addressed within fairly conventional human rights debates concerned with protecting minorities from oppression/exploitation by majorities (Grim 2001).

However, a conventional human rights treatment does not fully address the complexities involved, not least in conflicts focused on environment-based rights claims. The very lengthy gestation of UNDRIP, in which collective rights feature prominently, notably in regard to tribal lands and resources, (Morrow 2017) points to how highly contentious the issues are. UNDRIP is a carefully crafted compromise but it by no means fully diffuses the tensions that exist between states and Indigenous peoples (Engle 2011). The inherent nature of rights-based claims, deployed by individuals and (in this instance collectively) by minorities to counter the ill effects of law and policy favorable to the majority upon them, point to the more specific locus of tension here. The systemic failure of states, in pursuit of the interests of majority populations, to protect the collectively held homelands and environment and, by extension values, world views and life-ways of minority Indigenous populations makes full exercise of the right to self-determination an attractive proposition for many of the latter (Champagne 2013). However, UNDRIP offers only limited application of this central collective right. In so doing, it curtails potential challenges by Indigenous peoples to state sovereignty and control over territory and natural resources. Furthermore, the general framing adopted by UNDRIP, according to a degree of recognition of the collective interests of Indigenous peoples, has arguably siloed treatment of collective rights questions and deflected deeper and universal reflection in what it reveals about states and the collective interest. States are not (and in reality, never have been) in a position to claim a monopoly in representing collective interests in the environment, even within their territories, and while these issues are very obvious with regard to Indigenous peoples, they are by no means confined to them. This insight on the limits that apply to the horizons of states in engaging with collective concerns is arguably also applicable, though in a different guise, to matters of global/species-level import, which require a broader view of the collective than a purely state-centric approach can hope to offer.

Limitations aside, UNDRIP is of considerable interest for present purposes in the hybrid incarnation of individual and collective rights that permeates its approach. Article 1 states that:

> Indigenous peoples have the right to the full enjoyment, as a collective or as individuals, of all human rights and fundamental freedoms as recognized in the Charter of the United Nations, the Universal Declaration of Human Rights and international human rights law.
>
> *(UNGA 2007)*

Articles 26–29 of UNDRIP engage with a suite of rights relating to land, the defining and grounding core to much Indigenous epistemology and ontology. The coverage offered relates centrally to securing governance on Indigenous peoples' own terms in a particularized and partial form of self-determination (arts 26 and 27) and redress for infringement of land rights (art 28). Article 29, which deals with conservation and protection of the environment, is most pertinent to the present discussion. It shares the general emphasis of the approach taken to land issues, clearly foregrounding the collective interests of Indigenous peoples in ensuring environmental integrity in regard to hazardous substances (through provision for prior informed consent) and related protection for health. Such collective rights offer one of the few viable routes whereby Indigenous peoples may challenge the depredations of governments on their lands and lives. This type of approach it is also evident in regional human rights provision, most markedly in Africa and the Americas (Grant 2015).

The fusion of individual and collective interests in environmental viability, rooted in Indigenous cosmologies in UNDRIP and some regional human rights regimes could offer an important and ecologically literate corrective to dominant atomistic human rights thought. However, in attempting to address tensions between states and Indigenous minority populations, and collective and individual understandings of rights, UNDRIP represents an uneasy and unequal compromise between two very different value systems (Champagne 2013). In essentially grafting elements of Indigenous peoples' collective epistemology onto the dominant, individualistic, human rights framing, UNDRIP involves a forced fit, and a considerable degree of distortion, as Indigenous concepts are "translated" into the dominant regime. On the other hand, UNDRIP is ground-breaking in breaching the bulwarks of individualistic rights thought on the environment and in challenging the notion that states are the sole arbiters of the collective interest therein. These moves offer the potential for re-calibrating mainstream understanding of what it is to be human, characterizing us as relational beings, imbricated in discrete ecosystems, that may help speak to a renewed understanding of the place of our species in the biosphere.

### The United Nations Declaration on the Right to Development (UNDRD) and the Draft Convention on Right to Development (DCRD)

While UNDRIP represents the best-developed incarnation international law coverage for shared environmental concerns, it is not the only instrument that seeks to address collective issues. There have been a number of other soft law initiatives seeking to foster broader engagement with collective rights issues that may serve to further inform thinking on global, human species level, concerns in the Anthropocene. The UNDRD (UNGA 1986) is a case in point and there is much to be learned from its story (Arts and Tamo 2016, Schrijver 2020). Identifying the nature of the right to development, Schrijver 2020 terms it a "bridging right" in that it connects the rights of:

> individuals (citizens) with those of groups and peoples, including indigenous peoples. It is a fact of life that many human rights are mainly experienced in community, as part of a group or population, while they also have meaning for each individual.
>
> *(Schrijver 2020, 92)*

This makes for a particularly strong point of comparison with the dual or hybrid individual/collective nature of the environment-based human rights which we have been discussing. Originating under the auspices of the UNOHCHR, and subsequently adopted by a resolution of the General Assembly, the UNDRD is a short document, running to ten brief articles. As originally envisaged, the right to development would have been primarily collective in nature (Aarts and Tamo 2016, 224). However, the UNDRD as adopted indicates that it centrally concerns individuals (UNGA 1986 Art 2.1) but also applies to peoples, and even "the entire population" (UNGA 1986 preamble, para 2). Article 1 situates the right to development in support of other established human rights, a framing that has now become familiar in the context of human rights and the environment.

Article 3.1 of the UNDRD indicates extraterritorial spatial reach for state obligations, potentially extending to global responsibilities, stipulating that: "States have the primary responsibility for the creation of national and international conditions favourable to the realization of the right to development." Article 3 as a whole emphasizes the key role of inter-state cooperation in facilitating development. In short, the UNDRD characterized the right to development as encapsulating hybrid individual and collective elements, and identified the role of states in its realization as both inward (national) and outward (international/global) facing – approaches that would suit Anthropocene concerns.

Interesting and innovative as aspects of the UNDRD are, its contentious subject matter, centered on one of the most entrenched areas of North/South conflict in the international polis, has significantly constrained its implementation. The UNDRD did however put the right to development on the international legal agenda and has ensured that it has been a subject of fairly constant, if relatively low-key, engagement within the UN ever since (UN n.d.). The right to development has gained renewed prominence of late with the publication of a proposed Draft Convention on Right to Development (DCRD). The DCRD and its accompanying commentary, prepared by the latest UNOHCHR expert advice mechanism in this area, the working group on the right to development headed by Dr. Mihir Kanade, was published in 2020 (UN Doc. 2020).

In marked contrast to the 1986 declaration (and the other soft law instruments considered in this chapter, including the UNDRD), the DCRD seeks to push the treatment of the right to development into the realm of hard law. Whether this desire would in fact substantively progress the right to development remains to be seen (Schrijver 2020, 91), but past experience of difficulty in attempting to expand the human rights canon certainly signals that caution is in order (Morrow 2017). The practicalities of reaching agreement on a hard law provision aside, the content of the DCRD warrants consideration. The proposed draft declaration is considerably more substantial than its predecessor, currently running to 36, often quite lengthy, articles. Its substance, as one would expect, represents the substantial advances made in the area over the years, not least incorporating the now-core "respect, protect, fulfil" triad that is routinely applied to states' human rights obligations (UN Doc. 2020, para 6).

Tellingly, the strategic approach adopted in the Kanade report in some ways closely echoes that employed by Knox in the framework principles on human rights and the environment discussed above. Centrally it seeks to assuage state concerns about an expansionist human rights agenda by pointing to the presence of the right to development in extant legal provision. As alluded to above, this tactic, while intending to ensure states regard the prospect of action as appealing/unthreatening, by confirming the existence and clarifying the scope and content of the right in question, risks obviating the need for adopting further binding provision (Morrow 2021, and Schrijver 2020, 91).

These concerns aside, the proposed draft text contains much of interest. The draft preamble is, from its opening paragraph, considerably more forthright in stating the relevant context than its predecessor. Significantly, importing usage more common to international environmental law (Brunnée 2008), the draft text clearly identifies development as a common concern of humankind. In so doing, the DCRD underlines the global reach of the right to development, though it explicitly casts the approach to be adopted as remaining deferential to state sovereignty (UN Doc. 2020, 6). It is however unclear how state sovereignty, as currently understood, can be reconciled with an approach that requires planetary scale and species-level action. The current parlous state of nationally determined contributions for greenhouse gas emissions (UNFCCC 2015, Art 4 para 2) under the Paris Agreement, for example (UNFCCC 2021) strongly suggests that conferring primacy on sovereignty in this sort of context inevitably leads to strategic and systemic brinkmanship and results in action that falls far short of the mark. Thus, while the DCRD is shifting closer to an Anthropocene-appropriate planetary approach, it does not go far enough.

The opening words of article 4.1 of the draft Convention text state that: "Every human person and all peoples have the inalienable right to development" and the commentary underlines that the right to development, akin to the rights of Indigenous peoples discussed above, is now widely recognized as applicable to both individuals and collectively (UN Doc. 2020, 29). While space precludes full discussion here, it is salient to note that the commentary devotes considerable coverage to the various dimensions and implications of collective interests and rights as a recurrent theme. In this, the DCRD demonstrates an approach that has developed considerably since the UNDRD was adopted. A further hallmark of a maturing discourse also sees enhanced spatial framing for the right to development, focused on both internal and external dimensions. This is evident in the observation that:

> the duty to respect and protect the right to development is not restricted to territorial and extraterritorial obligations of States, but also [applies] when States act collectively at the international level.
>
> *(UN Doc. 2020, 56)*

This is precisely the sort of thinking on framing global perspectives that is required to deal with the planet and humanity-wide threats of the Anthropocene and it is a welcome addition to the toolbox that we urgently need to hand to scale up our responses to them.

## *The UNESCO Declaration on the Responsibilities of the Present Generations Towards Future Generations (DRPGFG)*

Global civil society initiatives at the interface between humanity and the environment often invoke the notion of responsibility, embracing individual and collective human obligations toward the planet and future generations (Morrow 2017). This spatially and temporally expansive bent is however seldom present as more than an aspiration in mainstream international law. It makes a rare appearance in the little-known, but interesting, DRPGFG (UNESCO 1997). This (again brief) soft law instrument runs to 12 concise articles and is expressly rooted in the then-emergent environmental and human rights law context. It addresses a broad range of cross-cutting concerns, including environmental issues (UNESCO 1997, Art 5). However, in focusing on the responsibilities of current generations to succeeding humans, and in referring to the "needs and interests" of the latter (UNESCO 1997, Art 1), the DRPGFG neatly side-steps engaging head-on with the contentious question of whether or not future generations can be said to hold rights. This is a strategy that may be usefully deployed in further treatment of the issue of future generations.

In the context of this chapter, the spatial reach of the DRPGFG is also of interest. UNESCO's aim of protecting the common (cultural) heritage (UNESCO 1997 Art 8) is of interest, raising a cognate notion to that of common concern, discussed above. At the same time, the DRPGFG's preamble explicitly acknowledges the concept of human, species-level concern stating that: "the very existence of humankind and its environment are threatened," and ties this to an extended temporal approach expressed in an avowed goal of "promoting inter-generational solidarity for the perpetuation of humankind" (UNESCO 1997). In so doing it is of great interest in the current context, prefiguring in many ways the type of multi-dimensional framing that engaging with the Anthropocene requires. Insofar as its substantive provisions are concerned, Article 3 of the DRPGFG also delivers an important insight in articulating the blending of collective and individual concerns that addressing the needs and interests of future generations requires:

> present generations should strive to ensure the maintenance and perpetuation of humankind with due respect for the dignity of the human person.

This brief clause, in attempting to engage more fully with how the present generation must address the needs and interests of future generations, and their implications for individual humans and our species, offers an approach that could usefully inform the development of a composite and hybrid (individual/collective), spatially, and temporally expansive approach to framing our priorities and actions necessitated by a growing awareness of the reach of the Anthropocene.

## Extending our Horizons: Adding Collective Global and Extended Temporal Dimensions to Frames of Reference

The Covid-19 pandemic is a harbinger of the changed context wrought by the Anthropocene; it reveals that states will not be able to meet their obligations to respect, protect, and fulfill the human rights of their people effectively when acting in isolation from one another (Fallah 2021). The collective concerns of the Anthropocene involved ultimately operate at a planetary (Steffen et al. 2015) and a species level (Horton 2021). Thus, the advent of the Anthropocene suggests that it is high time to revisit collective/third generation/solidarity rights and investigate what they may offer at multiple scales, up to and including at a global level, and to extend their temporal reach to embrace the future of the human species. Far from being an afterthought, in the context of the Anthropocene, the several dimensions of collective concern should be our first thought – and act as the foundation that informs and contextualizes individual environment-based human rights claims.

It is possible to adopt radical approaches to the horizons of what must be considered in this regard, as evidenced by the provisions of the Well Being of Future Generations (Wales) Act 2015 (WFGA). Set in a context that, under s79 of the Government of Wales Act 2006, requires the Welsh government to pursue sustainable development in the exercise of its functions, the WFGA extends this requirement to a broad range of public bodies in Wales. The approach adopted combines considerations of sustainability (ss 2 and 5), and a well-being duty applied to the activities of public bodies (s3), underpinned by seven well-being goals (s4). The latter are not only collective in nature in regard to Wales, but explicitly include a broader dimension, aiming to promote "A globally responsible Wales," requiring that action to pursue the sustainability of Wales "takes account of whether doing such a thing may make a positive contribution to global well-being" (WFGA s4). While not explicitly embracing species-level concerns, this acknowledgment of the salience of the global context to domestic activity is a good start. Furthermore, giving statutory effect to the classic/Brundtland formulation of sustainability (WCED 1987) in the sustainability principle under the WFGA, explicitly requiring that public bodies ensure that the ability of future generations to meet their needs is not compromised by current decisions, is a novel development, extending the temporal reach of what must be considered in arriving at decisions (Davidson 2020). While very much a work in progress (FGCW 2020), the WFGA seeks to change the horizons of public bodies in Wales by giving legal cognizance to expanded spatial and temporal frames of reference in decision-making. This is clearly a step in the right direction for engaging with the Anthropocene, and there will be much to learn from the successes and failures of this ambitious piece of legislation.

However, it is still the case that collective concerns and, in particular, as regards the emergent global threats of the Anthropocene are woefully under-interrogated. The nature of our present and rapidly unfolding predicament is such that revolutionary change is now required (Martin et al. 2016, 6105); evolutionary shifts cannot deliver the pace or extent of change required in our ways of being in the world (Morrow 2017). As a priority we must act on the recognition that the Anthropocene requires reframing the nexus between individual and collective rights issues, extending to the species and global level and on a vastly extended timescale.

There is, much as we might wish it otherwise, no silver bullet; no single solution, to the complex predicaments of the Anthropocene. Nor, if we are realistic, should there be. Complex problems rarely, if ever, have simple solutions. No one change will correct our present perilous course; rather many changes are required to achieve the necessary revolutionary shift in our view of the position of the Anthropos and the perivallon in response to the Anthropocene. The need to rapidly extend our frames of reference, taking a composite view of being human and human being in the world, embracing collective interests and rights, and adopting a global, long-term perspective is challenging but one of the necessary moves to ensure our flourishing, and ultimately survival, as a species. This chapter has shown that we already have many currently underused tools to hand that would assist us in this endeavor, and in the Anthropocene, we surely have the motivation to do so.

## References

Arts, Karin and Tamo, Atabongawung. 2016. "The Right to Development in International Law: New Momentum Thirty Years Down the Line?" *Netherlands International Law Review* 63(3), 221–249.

Brown Weiss, Edith. 1990. "Our Rights and Obligations to Future Generations for the Environment" *The American Journal of International Law* 84(1), 98–207.

Brunnée, Jutta. 2008. "Common Areas, Common Heritage, and Common Concern." In *The Oxford Handbook of International Environmental Law*, edited by Daniel Bodansky, Jutta Brunnée and Ellen Hey. Electronic Version 2012. https://doi.org/10.1093/oxfordhb/9780199552153.013.0023

Chakrabarty, Dipesh. 2018. "Planetary Crisis and the Difficulty of Being Modern." *Millennium: Journal of International Studies* 46(3), 259–282.

Champagne, Duane. 2013. "UNDRIP (United Nations Declaration on the Rights of Indigenous Peoples): Human, Civil, and Indigenous Rights." *Wicazo Sa Review* 28(1), 9–22.

Council of Europe. n.d. "The Evolution of Human Rights." Accessed November 30, 2020. https://www.coe.int/en/web/compass/the-evolution-of-human-rights

Davidson, Jane. 2020. *#futuregen: Lessons from a Small Country*. Vermont. Chelsea Green Publishing.

Dewan, Angela, Kennedy, Naimh and Said-Moorhouse, Lauran. 2021. "UN Says Access to a 'Clean, Healthy' Environment Is a Human Right." *CNN*, October 8, 2021. Accessed October 11, 2021. https://edition.cnn.com/2021/10/08/world/un-clean-environment-human-right-climate-intl/index.html

Douwes, Renate, Stuttaford, Maria and London, Leslie. 2018. "Social Solidarity, Human Rights, and Collective Action: Considerations in the Implementation of the National Health Insurance in South Africa." Accessed July 27, 2021 https://www.hhrjournal.org/2018/10/social-solidarity-human-rights-and-collective-action-considerations-in-the-implementation-of-the-national-health-insurance-in-south-africa/

Engel, Karen. 2011. "On Fragile Architecture: The UN Declaration on the Rights of Indigenous Peoples in the Context of Human Rights." *European Journal of International Law* 22(1), 141–163.

Fallah, Mosoka. 2021. "Remember Ebola: Stop Mass COVID Deaths in Africa." *Nature* 595(7869), 627.

Folkesson, Emelie. 2013. "Human Rights Courts Interpreting Sustainable Development: Balancing Individual Rights and the Collective Interest." *Erasmus Law Review* 6(2), 142.

Forum Social Mundial. 2009. "Respect for the Collective Rights of Peoples: One of the Cornerstones of Another Possible World." Accessed July 27, 2021. http://external.assaif.org/fsm2009/www.fsm2009amazonia.org.br/what-the-wsf-is.html

Freeman, Michael. 1995. "Are There Collective Human Rights?" *Political Studies*, XLIII, 25–40.

Future Generations Commissioner for Wales (FGCW). 2020. "The Future Generations Report 2020." Accessed August 8, 2021. https://www.futuregenerations.wales/wp-content/uploads/2020/05/FGC-Report-English.pdf

Government of Wales Act. 2006, 2006 c.32.

Graham, Lorie M. 2010. "Reconciling Collective and Individual Rights: Indigenous Education and International Human Rights Law." *UCLA Journal of International Law and Foreign Affairs* 15(1), 83–110.

Grant, Evadne. 2015. "International Human Rights Courts and Environmental Human Rights: Re-imagining Adjudicative Paradigms." *Journal of Human Rights and the Environment* 6(2), 156–176.

Grim, John A. 2001. *Indigenous Traditions and Ecology: The Interbeing of Cosmology and Community*. Cambridge, MA: Harvard University Press.

Hamilton, Clive. 2017. *Defiant Earth: The Fate of Humans in the Anthropocene*. Cambridge: Polity.

Horton, Richard C. 2021. *The COVID-19 Catastrophe: What's Gone Wrong and How to Stop It Happening Again*. Cambridge: Polity Press.

Jones, Peter 1999. "Human Rights, Group Rights and Peoples' Rights" *Human Rights Quarterly* Vol. 21, No. 1, 80–107.

Klaus, Birkhofer, Eva, Diehl, Jesper, Andersson, Johan, Ekroos, Andrea, Früh-Müller, Franziska, Machnikowski, Mader, Viktoria L., Lovisa, Nilsson, Keiko, Sasaki, Maj, Rundlöf, Volkmar, Wolters and Smith Henrik, G. 2015. "Ecosystem Services—Current Challenges and Opportunities for Ecological Research." *Frontiers in Ecology and Evolution*, 12 January https://doi.org/10.3389/fevo.2014.00087

Ksentini, Fatma, Zohra. 1994. "Human Rights and the Environment." Final Report, UN Doc.E.CN.4/Sub.2/1994/9.

Lade, Steven J., Steffen, Will, de Vries, Wim. et al. 2019. "Earth System Interactions Amplify Human Impacts on Planetary Boundaries." *Nature Sustainability* 3, 119–128.

Lebret, Audrey. 2020. "COVID-19 Pandemic and Derogation to Human Rights." *Journal of Law and the Biosciences*, 7(1) 1–15.
Litfin, Karen T. 2009. "Principles of Gaian Governance: A Rough Sketch." In Gaia in Turmoil*: Climate Change, Biodepletion, and Earth Ethics in an Age of Crisis*, edited by Eileen Crist and H. Bruce Rinker, 195–219. Cambridge, MA: MIT Press.
Martin, Jean-Louis, Maris, Virginie and Simberloff, Daniel S. 2016. "The Need to Respect Nature and Its Limits Challenges Society and Conservation Science." *PNAS* 113(22), 6105–6112.
Matthews, Daniel. 2021. "Reframing Sovereignty for the Anthropocene." *Transnational Legal Theory* 12(1), 44–77.
McGoldrick, Dominic. 1996. "Sustainable Development and Human Rights: An Integrated Conception." *International and Comparative Law Quarterly* 45(4), 796–818.
Misonne, Delphine. 2021. "The Emergence of a Right to Clean Air: Transforming European Union Law through Litigation and Citizen Science." *RECIEL* 30, 34–45.
Morrow, Karen. 2017. "Of Human Responsibility: Considering the Human/Environment Relationship and Ecosystems in the Anthropocene." In *Environmental Law and Governance for the Anthropocene*, edited by Louis Kotze, 269–287. Oxford: Hart Publishing.
Morrow, Karen. 2021. "Human Rights and the Environment: Substantive Rights'. In *Research Handbook on International Environmental Law*, edited by Malgosia Fitzmaurice, Marcel Brus and Panos Merkouris, 2nd edition, 353–376. Cheltenham: Edward Elgar.
Mujkiv, Dario. n.d. "Individual Rights and Solidarity." Accessed November 30, 2020. https://rightnow.org.au/opinion-3/individual-rights-and-solidarity/
Müller, Fernando Suárez. 2019. "The Hierarchy of Human Rights and the Transcendental System of Right." *Human Rights Review* 20(1), 47–66.
Potts, Rick. 2014. "The Moral Dilemma We Face in the Age of Humans." smithsonianmag.com, October 7, 2014. Accessed August 8, 2021. https://www.smithsonianmag.com/smithsonian-institution/moral-dilemma-we-face-age-of-humans-180952909/?no-ist
Schrijver, Nico. 2020. "A New Convention on the Human Right to Development: Putting the Cart Before the Horse?" *Netherlands Quarterly of Human Rights* 38(2), 84–93.
Steffen, Will et al. 2015. "Planetary Boundaries: Guiding Human Development on a Changing Planet." *Science* 347(6223), 1259855, 13 February 2015. Accessed November 12, 2020. https://science.sciencemag.org/content/347/6223/1259855.full
UN. n.d. "The Right to Development at a Glance." Accessed August 6, 2021. https://www.un.org/en/events/righttodevelopment/pdf/rtd_at_a_glance.pdf
UN Doc. 2018a. A/37/59 "Report of the Special Rapporteur on the Issue of Human Rights Obligations Relating to the Enjoyment of a Safe, Clean, Healthy and Sustainable Environment" Annex. Accessed July 28, 2021. https://undocs.org/en/A/HRC/37/59
UN Doc. 2018b. A/73/188 "Report of the Special Rapporteur on the Issue of Human Rights Obligations Relating to the Enjoyment of a Safe, Clean, Healthy and Sustainable Environment." Accessed July 28, 2021. https://undocs.org/a/73/188
UN Doc. 2019. A/74/161 "Report of the Special Rapporteur on the Issue of Human Rights Obligations Relating to the Enjoyment of a Safe, Clean, Healthy and Sustainable Environment." Accessed November 16, 2020. https://undocs.org/A/74/161
UN Doc. 2020. A/HRC/WG.2/21/2/Add.1 "Draft Convention on the Right to Development, With Commentaries." Accessed August 5, 2021. https://undocs.org/A/HRC/WG.2/21/2/Add.1
UNEP. 2019a. "Environmental Rule of Law: First Global Report." https://www.unenvironment.org/resources/assessment/environmental-rule-law-first-global-report
UNEP. 2019b. "Global Environment Outlook – GEO-6: Healthy Planet, Healthy People." *Nairobi*. https://www.unep.org/resources/global-environment-outlook-6
UNESCO. 1997. 29th General Conference, 29th, 1997. "Declaration on the Responsibilities of the Present Generations Towards Future Generations" 1069 Collation 12 November 1997. ITEM 44. 69–71. Accessed August 5, 2021. https://unesdoc.unesco.org/ark:/48223/pf0000110220
UNFCCC. 2015. "Paris Agreement." Accessed August 8, 2021. https://unfccc.int/files/meetings/paris_nov_2015/application/pdf/paris_agreement_english_.pdf
UNFCCC. 2021. "Climate Commitments Not on Track to Meet Paris Agreement Goals as NDC Synthesis Report Is Published." Accessed August 8, 2021. https://unfccc.int/news/climate-commitments-not-on-track-to-meet-paris-agreement-goals-as-ndc-synthesis-report-is-published

UNGA. 1986. "United Nations Declaration on the Right to Development: General Assembly Resolution 41/128 of 4 December 1986." Accessed January 12, 2021 https://www.ohchr.org/en/professionalinterest/pages/righttodevelopment/

UNGA. 1992. A/CONF.151/26 (Vol. I) "Report of the United Nations Conference on Environment and Development, Annex 1 Rio Declaration on the Environment and Development." http://www.un.org/documents/ga/conf151/aconf15126-1annex1.htm 1/5

UNGA. 2007. "Res 61/295 Declaration on the Rights of Indigenous Peoples." Accessed July 29, 2021. https://www.un.org/esa/socdev/unpfii/documents/DRIPS_en.pdf

UNGA. 2022. A/RES/76/300 'The human right to a clean, healthy and sustainable environment', 1 August 2022.

UNHRC. 2021. Res 46/l.6/REV.1 "Human Rights and the Environment." https://undocs.org/pdf?symbol=en/A/HRC/46/L.6/REV.1

Vasak, Karel. 1977. "Human Rights: A Thirty Year Struggle. The Sustained Efforts to Give Force of Law to the Universal Declaration of Human Rights." *Unesco Courier* 30(11), 29–32. Accessed July 20, 2021. http://unesdoc.unesco.org/images/0007/000748/074816eo.pdf

Vaughan, Adam. 2020. "Massive Failure: The World Has Missed All Its Biodiversity Targets." *New Scientist*, 15 September 2020. https://www.newscientist.com/article/2254460-massive-failure-the-world-has-missed-all-its-biodiversity-targets/

Vidal, John. 2020. "Tip of the Iceberg: Is Our Destruction of Nature Responsible for Covid-19?" *The Guardian*, March 18, 2020 https://www.theguardian.com/environment/2020/mar/18/tip-of-the-iceberg-is-our-destruction-of-nature-responsible-for-covid-19-aoe

Weisman, Alan. 2008. *The World Without Us*. London: Virgin Books.

Well-being of Future Generations (Wales) Act 2015, 2015 anaw 2.

World Commission on Environment and Development (WCED). 1987. *Our Common Future*. Oxford: Oxford University Press.

# 15
# DIGNITY IN THE ANTHROPOCENE

*Erin Daly and Dina Lupin*

The term "the Anthropocene" – from "anthro" for man and "cene" for new – is often used to describe a period or epoch in which human activity has been the major factor impacting Earth's biophysical systems, and specifically, in which human activities have caused significant impacts to those systems (Crutzen 2006). Since it was first coined, the concept of the "Anthropocene" has been contested and debated, and its meaning and import have continued to evolve as it has been adopted into new disciplines and policy-making arenas (Malhi 2017). Although it is often thought of as a geological idea proposed to describe a unit of geological time, it is in fact much more than that. It is both a normative and a descriptive concept, often associated with human-caused climate change, mass extinction, and the pollution of Earth's water, land, and air systems. It is a term used to encapsulate the worst excesses of human behavior and the most devastating of human impacts, deployed to highlight the need for far-reaching scientific, political, and social change (Crutzen 2002).

Embedded in the idea of the Anthropocene also is an assertion of an idea of the *anthropos*, the man or, perhaps, human, whose activities have defined and caused the excesses of this new epoch. Although rarely directly addressed, the idea of the Anthropocene seems to adopt a central conception of the human as a collective actor. Often obscured in uses of the concept of the Anthropocene is an approach to understanding our humanness at the level of species and in relation to the supposed collective action we have taken: our shared impact on the planet. As a collective actor, the Anthropocene asserts, we have a collective responsibility, and we face a common threat.

In this chapter, we examine the concept of the *anthropos* and critique the idea of collective human action and of universally shared responsibility that is implied in its use in defining the Anthropocene. In doing so, we join a growing number of critical, feminist, Third World, Indigenous, and Marxist scholars who challenge the account of *humanness* to which the Anthropocene seems to commit us.[1] These scholars have highlighted the ways in which the idea of the Anthropocene hides the power dynamics, racism, misogyny, and classism that have been intimately tied to and have enabled planetary-scale environmental destruction and the ongoing role of various modern forms of imperialism and colonialism in failures to address this destruction. Here, we adopt a perspective that highlights human dignity – the inherent equal worth of every person – to demonstrate how attention to each person's humanness can chal-

DOI: 10.4324/9781003388081-20

lenge the problematic assumptions of collectivism implicit in common uses of the concept of the Anthropocene.

In the context of human rights, human dignity is an idea that has been used to give expression to what it is to be human and to understand the role that legal rights play in protecting that humanness. Although human dignity is sometimes associated with accounts of thin and universal humanness in Western philosophical traditions, human rights law and rights adjudication have used human dignity to connect all humans in their humanity and at the same time to give expression to each person's unique, contextual, and relational human self. It is this aspect of humanness that is elided in the shorthand notion of the anthropos, contributing to a misguided understanding of both the causes and the solutions of the current "environmental apocalypse."[2]

A dignity lens reveals what the anthropos obscures, namely the diverse communities and individuals living their lives in their relationships with others and with the environments in which those lives unfold; changing and being changed by their contexts, in complex ways across time. A dignity lens, we argue, brings into relief the complex and constitutive relationships between human beings and the environment – relationships that are contextual and relational. Examining the Anthropocene through a dignity lens, we argue, allows for a more accurate and nuanced understanding of human responsibility for environmental conditions, and one that, through meaningful public participation and inclusion in environmental decision-making, allows for the possibility of human-centered solutions to our environmental crisis. A dignity lens is one that demands that we reconsider common understandings of the *anthropos* and examine whether the account of the human relationship to nature captured in the idea of the Anthropocene reflects the full diversity of stories that make up the many human/s relationships to and impacts on the environment.

This chapter begins with a discussion of an understanding of the place of the human being in the Anthropocene. It then suggests an alternative reading of humanity, one that is based on the dignity of every person. In the last part of the chapter, we consider how an approach to the conceptual disruption that is participatory and based on human dignity could produce a more accurate analysis and more human-centered and environmentally protective understanding of the Anthropocene and of our accountability for and relationships to the environment.

## The Misplaced Universality of the Anthropocene: A Common Responsibility and a Corporate Humanity

Much of the literature that investigates or deploys the concept of the Anthropocene does not directly engage with the idea of humanity that it implies, focusing instead on the impacts that humans as a species have had on the planet and what our species ought to do about them. Although the account of the relevant impacts (and the point at which they began) varies in uses of the Anthropocene in Earth systems sciences, ecological sciences, and geological sciences, references to "human domination," "human activities," and "human choice" are common to all three (Malhi 2017) – consistently describing the causes of current biodiversity and climatic conditions on a species-wide level.

The idea of an epoch defined by environmental degradation (of Earth's biology or on biogeochemical cycles, etc.) caused by human action and, even, "by human choice" implies a universal blameworthiness, bringing us to the point that "the dominant risk to our survival is ourselves." (UNDP Human Development Report 2020). But who are "ourselves"? In common uses of the term, the Anthropocene lays the responsibility for environmental harm at the feet of all humans, by virtue of their being humans, regardless of their context or contribution and regardless of the degree of choice they actually might have had (Davis and Todd 2017, 766). The idea of "human-caused" does not distinguish between the circumstances or decision-making authority of humans. The claim that this is an epoch defined by the activities of humans trades on the idea of the universal human; a humanity that is without specificity, context, and even time. It is, in this sense, a humanity that bears the collective responsibility for the current state of environmental crisis.

Accounts of a universal humanity in human rights law have been criticized for smuggling in Western conceptions of personhood that see our worth as connected to our capacity for reason and, in so doing, sever the mind from the body, and the human from the rest of nature.[3] While one finds versions of this universal humanity in accounts of the Anthropocene (most notably, Crutzen and Stoermer adopt the idea of the noösphere as a sphere of human consciousness that emerges out of the biosphere (Simpson 2018; Crutzen and Stoermer 2013)), the universal humanity of the Anthropocene usually binds humanity on an even narrower basis – we are bound, in the Anthropocene, in our culpability. In this sense, our common humanity is more corporate than transcendental.

## Humanity as a Corporate Entity

When we are told that we are living in a geological epoch of our own making – a period in which the greatest threat we face is a product of our own choices – who we are seems to be understood in light of the harm we have collectively caused: it is the "we" that is associated with "our" collective responsibility. As Birrell and Matthews point out, this account is consistent with "the universalist rendering of the human," (Birrell and Matthews 2020, 276), articulating a humanness that binds and elevates us. At the same time, it challenges idealist narratives of "progress" that have animated scholarship on law and rights in much of the modern era (Birrell and Matthews 2020). But in seeing us all simultaneously as blameworthy, the Anthropocene recognizes no one to hold to account (Grear 2015). In this respect, the humanity of the Anthropocene is corporate in nature – corporate in the sense that the grant of legal personhood to an aggregation of individuals makes it impossible for any individual person to be held accountable or to take responsibility for the actions of the group, or even for any individual to be distinguished from the corporate mass of personhood.

The corporation, in many legal jurisdictions, occupies an unusual position. Although it is made up of many individuals, from shareholders to directors to employees among other stakeholders, it enjoys in law a personality that is its own, designed to obscure the many individuals who constitute it.[4] In particular, corporate legal personality obscures from view the small group of individuals (usually the highest ranked and best paid) who make the key decisions. While providing for the opportunity of enormous individual enrichment, the corporate structure distributes the burdens of a failure to the whole, forcing all to share collectively in the burdens rather than falling on those who are responsible. What binds and defines those who bear the costs of corporate failure is their association with the corporation, not their degree of responsibility or complicity. Similarly, the anthropos offers us an account of humanity that obscures the individuals and communities collected into the category, hiding their individual blameworthiness, and making it harder to recognize the burdens that each of them bears.

## The Implicit Biases of Corporate Humanness

Just as the idea of the corporation might appear to be culturally neutral, the idea of a common humanity might seem, at first blush, to make only very minimal claims in regard to what it is to be human. However, the generality hides important assumptions and biases. For instance, the idea of the anthropos smuggles into our understanding of humanness a Western notion of personhood that claims neutrality, but in fact refers to the "rational," able-bodied, propertied, white man of the Global North that is separate, if not alienated, from context and surrounding (Malm and Hornborg 2014; Mirzoeff 2018). While this may be a better description of those actually responsible for the environmental harm we face today, it does not describe the vast majority of humanity. Indeed, by treating this undifferentiated humanity as the standard for personhood, it eliminates from view the half of all humans who are not gendered male, it ignores the fact that most of the human experience is situated within a particular social and natural environment, and it mis-distributes blame to all of humanity, ignoring the historical and ongoing contexts of colonialism, oppression, and violence in which most humans have lived and toiled (Kyle Powys Whyte 2017). Giovanna Di Chiro, for example, has argued:

> After extensive scientific assessments, the Anthropocene Working Group (82 per cent of whom are men, and the majority from Global North countries) concluded that Mankind has become such a dominant force of nature … that he has punted the planet out of the 10,000 years of relative climate stability recently enjoyed in the Holocene into a new eponymous epoch. … the Anthropocene retells the masculinist origin/self-birthing story that inevitably culminates in Man as the master creation, the Master of the Universe, and now its destroyer and, possibly, its saviour. […] the Anthropocene might more appropriately be coined the Manthropocene.[5]
>
> *(Di Chiro 2017, 488–489)*

The white (m)Anthropocene (as Di Chiro calls it) fails to take into account the racial and gendered hierarchies and practices of oppression that all too often determine who holds the decision-making power, as well as who benefits from or suffers the environmental harm (Davis and Todd 2017; Pulido 2018). The collective human responsibility narrative allows those who are actually responsible for the environmental and climate crisis to hide behind those who are its victims. Research suggests that more than a third of greenhouse gas emissions can be attributed to just 20 companies (Taylor and Watts 2019) and that the 22 richest men in the world have more wealth than all the women in Africa.[6] The extraordinary maldistribution of wealth and power in the world is obscured when we refer to the anthropos as the causal agent of the environmental failures of our era.

And yet, responsibility is laid at the feet of the multitudes of victims, not the elites who are responsible. Individuals are called on to change their lives to mitigate climate change. While major banks and other financial institutions have invested over $3.8 trillion in fossil fuels in the past five years,[7] individuals are encouraged to use their purchasing power for good, to buy less, or make green choices.[8] ("How Buying Stuff Drives Climate Change" 2020). Without distinguishing between the CEOs of Chevron and the children who walk to schools through trash dumps or study by candlelight in rural Limpopo[9] or urban Port au Prince,[10] the assertion that all of humanity is to blame says that all of us are equally, and individually, responsible for taking action to address the harm, improbable as that may be, while those who have had the opportunities to make decisions that could reduce climate change avoid accountability by hiding behind a veil of generality.

And it is not only a problem of naming rights but of internalized commitments about what kinds of behaviors are acceptable. The Western world has for centuries prioritized individualism, property, industrialization, and innovation that control and separate us from and extract resources from nature but don't enhance or protect it, with externalized costs, short-term gains with long-term expenses, entitlement to own and control, a concomitant failure to take responsibility, failure to develop restorative justice approaches, hence failure to manage problems, and so on. It values a certain form of expression, inculcated in the elite institutions of the Western world, comfortable in presentation-making if not in story-telling, and fluent in the languages of the world's dominant groups[11] but not in the forms of communication practiced by most of the world's people who lack access to the Western mold. The Anthropocene will be invariably defined by those who see themselves as a part of it.

## The Implications of Corporate Humanness

A corporate account of humanity has a number of implications for thinking about the Anthropocene and about what our collective or individual responsibility and obligations might be. Corporate humanness limits the ways in which the relationship between humans and their environments is accounted for, and this, in turn, shapes how people are allowed to relate to their environments in the future.

In sweeping all of humanity up into the idea of "human-caused harm," one account of the human relationship to nature has come to dominate the narrative in scholarship and policy. As a result, the Anthropocene seems to exclude the possibility of, and provide little platform for, very different accounts of human relationships with the environment. Virginia Marshall, for instance, has argued that the assertion that humans exploit and abuse the environment fails to "acknowledge or value the unique position of Indigenous peoples" (Marshall 2020, 13).[12] In the context of Aboriginal people in Australia, Marshall argues, this brand of universal responsibility ignores the history as well as the legal and cultural rights and duties Indigenous peoples have to care for their environment, just as it elides the infinitely varied ways in which the world's cultural communities care for and relate to their environments.

In corporate understandings of the human in the Anthropocene, to be a human is to be part of a phenomenon or a planetary force, like a glacial event (Chakrabarty 2009). However, in locating humans as *the cause* of epochal change, humans, unlike glaciers, seem to be located outside of nature. Their changes to the environment are thought to be unnatural, imposed, and fabricated as opposed to evolution within the natural order. However, most people live in complex and nuanced relationships with their environments, in which they both change their environments and are changed by their environments.

## The Complexity and Diversity of Human–Environmental Relationships and Histories

In generalizing and collectivizing human relationships to the environment in terms of harm, common uses of the notion of the Anthropocene overlook the ways in which most human relationships to the environment are formed through complex interactions and dependencies as well as long-standing practices and patterns. The people of Tsitas Nek village in Lesotho, for example, have practiced the same methods of farming and engaging with the land throughout their history. The methods for seed collection and planting, for land preparation and pest resistance, are handed down by word of mouth as are the ceremonies that must be practiced at each stage (Notsi 2012). The practices of the Tsitas Nek villagers have shaped their environment over generations and, at the same time, the environment has shaped the community. Their identity, and thus their human dignity, is bound up in and defined by the natural environment in which they have lived for generations, their ways of being with and on the land. Currently, the community faces high levels of poverty and food and water scarcity.

Some relationships of humans to their environments are new and emerge not from ancestral culture but affiliation; yet their members are also defined by and helping to define their natural environment. Bybi, a recently formed community of urban beekeepers in Oslo, Norway, for example, is working to build a bee highway through the city. In doing so, they are consciously trying to change their environment, creating "pollinator-friendly landscapes" within the urban limits.[13] Similar stories can be found among people in all parts of the world.

Whether old or new, most people's relationships with their environments are shaped by complex historical, social, political, economic, and environmental forces, too entangled to pull apart. For example, the Wataita people in Kenya are subsistence agriculturalists who, pre-colonization, negotiated claims to land through kinship ties and practiced seasonal grazing and hunting. With colonization, land in Kenya became "crown land," and the Wataita were evicted into "native reserves" while the land was given over to white-owned companies for coffee growing or set aside, eventually to be a large national park for the pleasure of colonial tourists. At independence, land redistribution programs created a series of ranches meant to protect the Wataita from incoming white settlers, but these ranches were registered in the names of a few community leaders, who have used their land rights to secure capital, leaving the community legally landless. Most recently, the area has become a REDD+ project site. While this has generated benefits for the elite landowners, the community can no longer engage in various income-generating activities and has seen very little of the financial benefits of the REDD+ scheme (Chomba et al. 2016).

In these three of many possible examples, there is no single way to account for the relationships that people develop with their environment or their practices of care or exploitation. This diversity points to the complex and important ways in which some humans make decisions while others bear the brunt. It thus renders absurd any effort to characterize environmental harm as the product of some universal human position in relation to the environment.

The failure to see human impacts on and relationships to the environment in all their complex diversity results in maladaptive responses to the environmental crisis that is constituted by climate change and biodiversity loss. Marshall, for example, argues that the failure to recognize Indigenous relationships to the environment has meant the adoption of policy approaches – including through the recognition of nature's rights – that risk severing the relationships of ownership and care that many Indigenous peoples have with their environments. In seeing the environment as simply needing protection from destructive humanity, Marshall argues, different kinds of relationships continue to be overlooked which reinforces the marginalization and feelings of powerlessness that so many of the world's peoples experience (Marshall 2020).

## Our Common Humanity in Our Contextualized and Relational Lives – A Human Dignity Approach

In the previous section, we argued that in identifying a universal humanity as the cause of this environmental harm, the Anthropocene obscures the agency of those actually responsible while invisibilizing the experiences, histories, and environmental relationships of everyone else.

Although corporate humanity seems to limit rather than broaden our understanding of the new epoch, not all attempts to account for our humanness point us in a hopelessly essentialist direction (Assiter 2021; Townsend 2020). While the anthropos suggests an account of humanness that leaves little space for meaningful engagement with the complex and changing relationships between humans and their environments or among humans, human dignity offers us an approach that centralizes those relationships by prioritizing the particularities of the human experience.

Human dignity was recognized as the foundation of international human rights law through its adoption in the Universal Declaration of Human Rights (UDHR). The twin revolutionary insights of the UDHR were, first, the universal application of individual human dignity – that is, the equal worth of every person, with no one having more or less than anyone else – and, second, that the recognition of inherent and universal human dignity gives rise to rights that have resonance in law.

The notion that every person (in present, past, and future generations as well)[14] partakes of equal human dignity suggests a universalist dimension: that human dignity is what distinguishes humanity, as a group, from other elements of worldly life. For instance, the idea of human dignity in ethical theory has classically been associated with universal accounts of a common humanness and an inherent human worth (Capps 2010). Perhaps the most influential account of human dignity in this line is that of Immanuel Kant who argued that we have, by virtue of the "humanity in our person" a value "above all price" – a non-comparative, inalienable, intrinsic value (Kant 1996). Kant wrote in the *Metaphysics of Morals*,

> as a person … he is not to be valued merely as a means to the ends of others or even to his own ends, but as an end in itself, that is, he possesses a dignity (an absolute inner worth) by which he exacts respect for himself from all other rational beings in the world.
>
> *(Kant 1996, 557)*

Insofar as Kant was interested in the distinctive qualities of humans as compared to other species, this account forms part of the basis of the modern conception of dignity implicit in the UDHR, which sought to reject the Nazi disdain for human life and to assure that human life would always be sacrosanct (Morsink 2010). Thus, after the UDHR, the universal application of equal worth could no longer be denied: systems of discrimination, oppression, slavery, supremacy, misogyny, etc. can no longer be countenanced in a world that recognizes universal equal dignity (Glendon 2002; Dicke 2002). In this limited sense, the essentialist account of dignity shares important features with the essentialist account of the anthropos in the Anthropocene.

But the UDHR said nothing about how to operationalize the recognition of human dignity or what that quality of dignity contained. Making sense of the quality and texture of dignity, and recognizing and responding to its demands has been the work of human rights courts, human rights scholars and practitioners, advocates and activists, international institutions, and community-based organizations (Daly 2013; Townsend 2020). And this is an ongoing task that is almost always worked out in a very specific context, mired in the details of a particular case, a particular community, or a particular individual (Townsend 2020, chap. 3). Josiah Ober's writing on dignity seeks to connect the universalist and the individualist conceptions of dignity:

> Human dignity as inherent worth is an inalienable right (or the foundational premise of rights), possessed by each individual as an irreducible aspect of his or her humanity. Universal human dignity … is equitably distributed among all beings possessed of reason. No one can possess more of it than anyone else, and so there is no competition over dignity. The concern for recognition in universal human dignity is omnidirectional: All persons, everywhere, must recognize everyone else's inherent worth, and therefore accord due respect to all others.
>
> *(Ober 2012, 832)*

The universalist account of dignity is therefore important not because it treats the human being as part of an undifferentiated mass of humanity but because it gives every person a claim to have their dignity respected by all others and to have the particularities of their personal circumstances recognized. It reinforces the idea that dignity applies to every person, in their contexts and in their time because it is inherent in the human person; it, therefore, demands attention and protection in all circumstances, regardless of jurisdiction or citizenship (Capps 2010; Addis 2013).

In the hands of courts around the world, human dignity reflects the equal and inherent worth of "all members of the human family."[15] While the phrase can be understood in both general (the human family) and particular (members) terms, the courts have focused on the particular circumstances of each person's situation. They have, for instance, required that governments provide individualized treatment and recognition to each person,[16] allowed people to express their religion or sexuality according to their own personal or social identity,[17] and denied states the authority to treat people in ways that are not based on their individual experience[18] or that lack empathy.[19] The implicit or explicit premise of these cases – as the core of the entire corpus of human rights law – is that each person has intrinsic and inalienable human value and that a person's story matters.

Thus, as the judicial conception of dignity has evolved, it is the equal value of the person (and of each person) that is paramount, and it is this attention to each person's unique needs, and points of view that poses a challenge to most accounts of the Anthropocene. Rather than treating humanity as an undifferentiated mass, the dignity lens sets the unit of value at the level of the person, in all their contextual, historical, and social specificity.

In working out the content and demands of dignity, and of dignity's universality, attention has to be paid to the embodied, emplaced, and context-specific nature of particular human lives. For this reason, a large number of cases that turn on human dignity, and on the protection of dignity rights, have been concerned with protecting that which is important to a person's self-understanding. This has often meant resisting efforts by states and others to wipe out, deny or criminalize aspects of a person's or a social group's identity, from gender expression and reproductive rights to religious and cultural rights. For this reason, dignity is associated with the interconnected ideas of self-actualization, individuation, and recognition (Daly 2013, chaps. 2, 4, 5; Rao 2011). This has been a critical understanding of dignity in cases on rights to marry;[20] rights to have a name;[21] to have one's official designation reflect one's gender identity;[22] to be recognized as an Indigenous community;[23] to be communicated with in one's own language;[24] among others.

The protection of dignity in these cases is not simply a protection of freedom of choice or personal autonomy (although it often includes aspects of both of those) but rather a protection of the person as profoundly relational. Courts have recognized dignity as bound up in practices of social recognition and have found that dignity both grounds obligations by society to individuals and by individuals to society (Townsend 2020, 146). Dignity is both "inward-looking and outward looking" (Daly 2013, 43). Dignity cases on prejudice, stereotyping, and hate speech have also recognized the ways in which our sense of self can be shaped and damaged by others.[25] But the understanding of dignity as relational extends beyond identity and recognition in case law, to the idea that dignity is a "public value"[26] – we all benefit when the dignity of any one of us is respected (Daly 2013, 121), and, equally, we are all demeaned when the dignity of any one of us is assailed.[27]

While dignity is both personal and relational, it is also emplaced. It is in dignity that human rights courts have recognized our environments as essential to and even constitutive of our humanness (Townsend 2016). In cases on rights to housing,[28] the choice of where to establish one's home[29] and in cases on the right to a healthy environment,[30] among others, human rights courts have recognized the importance of the places and spaces in which our lives unfold to the recognition and protection of dignity.

Each of these cases, in articulating an understanding of dignity that is meaningful and protects those whose rights and dignity have been assailed, has necessitated an intimate and detailed inquiry into the particular and the personal. It is only in the very detailed, intimate, and specific coming together of people with others, with their environments, with the law, and at the moment of their suffering or at the moment of their demand to be recognized, that dignity comes into its meaning and significance. That every person has dignity is guaranteed in its universality but what that means is profoundly personal and context-specific.

The idea of the Anthropocene all too often takes the idea of a decontextualized universalism as meaning no more than humanity as one undifferentiated mass – a mass which, in the context of what we have done to our planet, is worthy of quite of bit of blame and not much dignity or respect. This view deviates from the universality that we have argued is found in the idea of dignity. A dignity lens, by contrast, foregrounds the emplaced and embodied aspects of each person's humanness, that which makes us unique, whether in terms of our nationality, race, gender, sexuality, age, class, ethnicity, location, or any other social identity, distinguishing circumstance or feature of ourselves and our stories.

## A Dignity Response to the Anthropocene

In identifying humanity as responsible for the world's devastating environmental conditions, the idea of the Anthropocene fails to recognize that, given the variations in personal responsibility and burdens, the relevant unit of measure is not humanity as a whole undifferentiated mass, but rather the personal: the particular lived lives, identities, locally emplaced experiences, and relationships to the environment are lost in the Anthropocene's framing. Because dignity is both universally applicable and personal, each person's contributions to environmental degradation, as well as environmental understandings and solutions, matter. A dignity lens demands that individuals and their communities are given an opportunity to account for their own identity and humanness, for their own histories, understandings of their worth and, by extension, their own relationships to and responsibility for the current condition of the planet. It suggests that there is harm not only in relation to a failure to allocate blame where it is due but also in the failure to recognize and make space for individual and community accounts of personal histories and experiences in both understanding how humans have shaped our current epoch and in thinking about what this epoch requires of us going forward (Kyle P. Whyte 2018).

The individual quality of human dignity is now recognized in law as a fundamental value and actionable right in most international and regional human rights instruments, in most of the world's constitutions, and in laws and regulations throughout the world. Because of its widespread acceptance, its deep connections to fundamental human values, its status as the basis of global human rights, and its common recognition as a foundation of municipal constitutionalism, dignity provides a strong theoretical basis for both substantive and procedural human rights law as well (Daly 2013). That is – human dignity is the foundational justification not only for securing substantive rights to health, shelter, education, and a quality environment other things but also for securing rights to participation in environmental decision-making.[31] Thus, in the court process, law-making, policy-adoption, administrative decision-making, and many other areas of governance, the right to participate and to have a say in regard to matters that affect people has been recognized as a fundamental expression of human dignity[32] (Waldron 2012; Townsend 2019). It is a right to assert one's needs and interests but also a right to tell one's own story, to assert one's own identity, and account for one's history.

In this section, we argue for a dignity lens that ensures opportunities for each person to tell their story, and in doing so, to contribute to understandings of this epoch and the conceptual language of the Anthropocene in effective forms of participatory democratic decision-making regarding environmental matters.

## The Importance of Environmental Conditions to Human Dignity

Increasingly, philosophers, lawyers, and scholars are recognizing the environmental dimension of human identity and integrity and that failure to protect the environment will have damaging effects on the experience of human dignity for vulnerable populations around the world. It can no longer be denied that a degraded environment (not to mention climate change) has adverse effects on human beings: it can diminish their sense of place, it can make it harder to breathe, it can make it more likely that people will have diseases and less likely that they will have resilience.[33] Environmental threats relating to access to adequate water and sanitation and food insecurity are among the most obvious examples of the environmental threats to human dignity and these multiply when the environmental threats lead to war, displacement, interruptions in education and employment, and the destruction of the human, no less than the natural, habitat. And the concomitant loss of community, the loss of political structure, and the loss of civic space and opportunities for civic engagement are problematic as well and deserve attention.[34] Environmental integrity is therefore critical to protect the spectrum of interests necessary for a full experience of human dignity.

At the same time, the deprivation of dignity rights (including the right to shelter, to food, and to water) may burden environmental rights (where, for instance, people cut down trees for income or heating, or overfish because of other food scarcity) and so on. In short, human and environmental rights are inextricable; consequently, the need to have one's say about environmental matters derives not merely from the consensus of international or domestic positive law but from the very recognition of human dignity (Daly and May 2015).

## Rights to Environmental Participation

Participatory rights in environmental matters are among the clearest and most well-drawn instantiations of the state's obligation to establish processes and structures to advance human dignity. Participatory rights are generally understood to include rights to information, to participate in political decision-making, and to access justice,[35] although they can also involve freedom of speech, freedom of association, and voting rights, among others. In the environmental context, this set of rights may be especially important, given the profound, wide-ranging, and irreversible ways in which the environment affects the human experience and human dignity itself.

While many countries already provide for public participation in environmental decision-making – following Rio Principle 10, the Aarhus Convention for Europe and other countries, and the newly effective Escazú agreement for the Americas including the Caribbean – the touchstone for measuring the quality of such rights should be their protection and promotion of human dignity, not just compliance with positive binding law. Thus, a participatory process would be deemed to satisfy the human rights guarantee insofar as it respected and advanced the substantive quality of human dignity. Moreover, dignity can provide a framework for designing and implementing remedies when there are dignity-based breaches of political rights in environmental matters. Establishing dignity as the norm for procedural rights can also advance their adoption into constitutional and framework legislation and can galvanize judicial enforcement of dignity-based procedural rights, providing courts with a theoretical rationale for vindicating them and an interpretive tool for understanding and applying them, both of which will facilitate judicial engagement with them.

Public participation in environmental decision-making is an expression of human dignity because one aspect of human dignity is the capacity to claim and have rights. Public participation fulfills dignity both directly (people who participate in governance are more likely to feel and be recognized as having dignity) and indirectly (people who participate in governance are more likely to secure results that increase their environmental and social well-being). Collectively, this experience enhances community well-being as people, through self-governance, create and experience dignity in solidarity.[36]

Although rights to environmental participation are already well developed in legal systems throughout the world, they are agnostic as to what substantive rights or interests they protect (beyond matters relating to the environment). And yet they may encompass the full expanse of dignity's reach – implicating interests relating to identity, to material conditions of life, to the avoidance of humiliation, and so on, often in ways that demonstrate the indivisibility of procedural and substantive rights.

## Dignity Done Right

For rights to environmental participation to reflect and promote human dignity, they must satisfy certain conditions of both process and outcome. Josiah Ober notes four interlocking preconditions for dignity-promoting democracy: liberty, equality, information, and a certain level of material comfort that permits the exercise of participatory rights.

> Self-governance requires ready access to reliable information and stability over time. Dignity ensures that relevant information is made public. It stabilizes democracy by mediating between demands of liberty and equality, forbidding libertarian neglect of basic needs and egalitarian paternalism alike. Democracy without secure dignity is at best a fragile construct.
>
> *(Ober 2012, 828)*

Moreover, he says,

> Redistributive public welfare policies that ensure that all are provided with adequate food, shelter, security, education, and health care promote dignity by enhancing the opportunity for individuals to make meaningful personal choices, take calculated risks, and participate in the public domain.
>
> *(Ober 2012, 840)*

To these, of course, we would add that individuals must live in a stable and accommodating environment, with which they can form and continue their own relationships and that permits them to develop community, access and share information, and engage with one another in public decision-making.

Moreover, the structures of participation must ensure that each person has an equal opportunity to participate so that each voice is heard. The process must reflect the dignity of all, and that each person has the equal opportunity to express their dignity through participation. As Justice Harlan of the United States Supreme Court wrote, participatory democracy puts

> the decision as to what views shall be voiced largely into the hands of each of us, in the hope that use of such freedom will ultimately produce a more capable citizenry and more perfect polity and in the belief that no other approach would comport

> with the premise of individual dignity and choice upon which our political system rests.[37]

In addition to ensuring that decision-making is inclusive and representative of those affected, dignity-based participation is participation that gives those affected by a decision an opportunity to account for themselves, their identities, and their circumstances. There is a sense in which participation of this kind is not only concerned with looking forward – considering what comes next and what the outcomes of a decision might be – but also with looking back and with setting the record straight.

Often environmental decision-making – the decision to authorize a mining activity, for example – is accompanied by a narrative about the need for the activity and a description of the receiving environment. In the Endorois case heard by the African Commission of Human and Peoples' Rights, for example, the state of Kenya claimed to be forcibly moving the affected community to create protected areas.[38] The state asserted that the community was not a distinct people, had no claim to the land, and was harming the environment, and that their removal was just and fair. In finding that the community had a right to be consulted (a right denied to them), the Commission not only pointed to a procedural misstep by the state but recognized participation as essential to their very survival as a community through assimilation or extinction. The opportunity to participate is an opportunity to counter-balance the state's narrative with the community's own, to tell their story, to account for their history and for their relationship to the environment, and to articulate their aspirations for the future.

Participation must allow for these counter-narratives to not only play a role in decision-making about the environment but also to shape our understanding of our histories and our environments, as well as the best approaches to protecting that environment. It is only in this way that participation processes give expression to human dignity. It is also in this way that participation can allow for a more accurate understanding of how humans have shaped this planet and defined this epoch.

However, this is not something that will necessarily emerge from formal legal processes of participation. Formal, legally mandated participation processes are often designed to explicitly avoid the inclusion of counter-narratives, particularly those that resist development. In 2001, Cooke and Kothari famously argued that participation was a new form of tyranny (Cooke and Kothari 2001). In part, this was because they found that participation was often used to legitimize, rather than challenge, interrogate or problematize, the actions of developers and development agencies. In the context of consultation in Colombia, Garavito and Díaz have argued, in the context of consultation with Indigenous peoples, that "Along the way, indigenous political subjectivity is transformed. Rather than the characteristic protestor of the indigenous movements, the consultation requires a docile, conversational subject" (Garavito and Díaz 2018). In the context of REDD+ projects in Uganda, Mbeche has found that participation processes amount to little more than "'extractive' listening projects, as opposed to ongoing conversations" (Mbeche 2017, 429).

What dignity demands, however, is not the docile, conversational subject coerced into participation in a process that is premeditated and predetermined, replicating and reinforcing existing power structures and the narratives they choose. Instead, what should count as "participation" are those processes, engagements, and activities in which people are truly able to have their say and, in having their say, to tell their story and to account for their relationships with their environments, and for their say to be counted. This includes participation opportunities that people create for themselves, such as protest action. But it also demands that space is made for marginalized groups to tell their stories and to have a say, not only in relation to decisions that directly affect but also in the spaces where agendas are set and concepts are defined (Townsend 2021). This includes institutions like the Anthropocene Working Group but also academic spaces, creative spaces, policy-making spaces, and all the other places and spaces where concepts like "the Anthropocene" are thought up, defined, and applied (Todd 2015).

## Conclusion

In this chapter, we have argued for a dignity approach to understanding the epoch we currently live in – an epoch that is defined by human activity, decisions, and relationships to the environment. We have made this argument for two interconnected reasons. First, a dignity approach offers an understanding of what is problematic in uses of the anthropos to encompass all of humanity, across space and time. We have argued that the problem is not so much that the Anthropocene references a universal understanding of humanity, but that the Anthropocene's universality is a corporate humanity that hides the individuals responsible for environmental harm, holding the species instead collectively culpable. At the same time, this corporate humanity ignores and overlooks the rich, complex, and constitutive ways in which most people live in their environments. Second, in overlooking people and peoples in favor of a collective and corporate notion of humanness, the Anthropocene silences their voices and denies them the space with which to account for the ways in which they have shaped and are shaped by their environments.

A dignity approach, we have argued, means that all of these diverse voices and stories need to be included in the formulation and understanding of this epoch and this demands their participation. But participation cannot simply be another way to secure agreement with predetermined outcomes – it must be based on the recognition and assertion of human dignity which means not only inclusion but inclusion that allows people to assert their identities, to tell their histories, and to set the record straight. It is only when the idea of the "Anthropocene" accommodates and encapsulates this diversity of human stories and relationships to the environment that it can be said to describe an epoch shaped by humanity.

## Notes

1 See, among others, Birrell and Matthews 2020; Pulido 2018; Simpson 2018; Kyle P. Whyte 2018; Davis and Todd 2017; Di Chiro 2017; Haraway 2015; Grear 2015; Malm and Hornborg 2014.
2 Juliana v US, 9th Circuit (January 2020).
3 The UDHR's conception of dignity does not privilege any particular type of reasoning or reasoner but rather the human capacity to reason; it is neutral about whether we reason our way into or out of climate change. In this sense, it is anthropocentric, though not Anthropocentric.
4 Of course, this is a simplified account of the corporation and its relationship to the groups of individuals who constitute it. For a range of discussions on the theoretical, legal, and jurisdictional meanings of the corporation, see, generally, Tully 2005.
5 The Anthropocene Working Group is a research group established to study the Anthropocene as a geological time unit. It is part of the International Commission on Stratigraphy.
6 https://oxfamilibrary.openrepository.com/bitstream/handle/10546/620928/bp-time-to-care-inequality-200120-summ-en.pdf
7 See the report "Banking on Climate Chaos" published by the Rainforest Action Network and accessible at www.ran.org/bankingonclimatechaos2021/, accessed 3 February 2021.
8 See "How Buying Stuff Drives Climate Change." 2020. *State of the Planet* (blog). 16 December 2020. https://blogs.ei.columbia.edu/2020/12/16/buying-stuff-drives-climate-change/, accessed on 15 January 2021.
9 For an overview of civil society research and action on the right to education and sanitation in schools in Limpopo and South Africa, see https://section27.org.za/priority-work-areas/the-right-to-basic-education/school-sanitation/, accessed on 15 January 2021.

10 See e.g. United Nations Central Emergency Response Fund (UN CERF), Haiti: Executive Summary (19 July 2007), https://cerf.un.org/sites/default/files/resources/Haiti_2006_110308%20New%20Format.pdf; Milo Milfort, Who Benefits from the Poor Management of the Truitier Landfill?, Haiti Liberté (4 April 2018) https://haitiliberte.com/who-benefits-from-the-poor-management-of-the-truitier-landfill/; Dieu Nalio Chery, Haitians scour the country's largest trash dump, AP News (12 September 2018), https://apnews.com/50c5062763b64fe297b643815fbd6568. See also Petition And Request For Precautionary Measures (With Exhibits) To The Inter-American Commission On Human Rights on Behalf of Six Children Of Cité Soleil, Haiti And Sakala Community Center For Peaceful Alternatives, Concerning Violations Of The American Convention On Human Rights (filed 4 February 2021) available at https://delawarelaw.widener.edu/files/resources/sakalapetitioniachr4feb21.pdf.

11 In the context of climate change decision-making, Susan Buckingham argues that the women who are able to access and participate in decision-making processes and institutions are rarely those on the periphery, facing the struggles of impoverished, rural, working women. As a result, "Attending to numerical gender balance alone … is unlikely to significantly disrupt the system which has created the conditions for anthropogenic climate change, in order to create the structural social change that is needed" (Buckingham 2017, 394).

12 It is worth noting that Marshall's argument is rooted in the experience of First Nations in Australia and, in particular, the experiences of communities affected by rights of nature enterprises. Out of context, the quote from Marshall may seem to generalize across all Indigenous peoples, but that is not a reflection of Marshall's argument.

13 See the description of this project at https://bybi.no/, accessed on 15 February 2021.

14 For a discussion on inter-generational dignity, see Townsend 2020; Düwell 2016; Dupré 2016.

15 See the wording of the preamble to the UDHR, Preamble. See, generally, Daly and May 2020 and Daly 2013.

16 Lillu Rajesh v State of Haryana (2013), 14 SCC 643, 648 para. 13 (Supreme Court of India) (requiring sensitive treatment for survivors of rape); Port Elizabeth Municipality v Various Occupiers 2004 (12) BCLR 1268 (CC) (requiring individualized communications regarding housing options).

17 Sunil Babu Pant and Others v Nepal Government, Writ No. 917 of the Year 2064 (2007 AD) (Supreme Court of Nepal).

18 Judgment of 04 May 2011 – 2 BvR 2365/09, Constitutional Court of Germany (2011) (denying the power of preventive detention).

19 BVerfG, decision of the First Senate of 11 March 2003 – 1 BvR 426/02 –, Rn. 1-29 (Constitutional Court of Germany).

20 Obergefell et al. v Hodges, Director, Ohio Department of Health, 2015.

21 58/2001 (Name change case), Constitutional Court of Hungary, 2001.

22 Goodwin v United Kingdom. 1996, 22 EHRR 123. European Court of Human Rights.

23 The Yakye Axa Indigenous Community v Paraguay 2005; Centre for Minority Rights Development (Kenya) and Minority Rights Group (on behalf of Endorois Welfare Council) v Kenya 276/2003 2010.

24 López-Álvarez v Honduras 2006 IACHR Series C No 141.

25 Catherina Hendrika Myburgh v Commercial Bank of Namibia [2000] Case no SA 2/2000 (Supreme Court of Namibia); Ellwanger Case, Judgment of HC 82424 (Supreme Court of Brazil, 2003).

26 HCJ 7357/95 Berki Petta Humphries Ltd v State of Israel. 1996, 50(2) PD 769. The Supreme Court of Israel.

27 Port Elizabeth Municipality v Various Occupiers 2004 (12) BCLR 1268 (CC).

28 Ibid.

29 Godbout v Longueuil (City) 1997; R v Morgentaler 1988.

30 Zia v Water and Power Development Authority [1994] PLD 1994 SC 693 (Supreme Court of Pakistan); Center for Social Justice Studies et al. v Presidency of the Republic et al. Judgment T-622/16 Constitutional Court of Colombia (10 November 2016) (The Atrato River Case).

31 See e.g. American Bar Association Resolution 113B (August 2019), affirming that dignity rights are the foundation of a "just rule of law."

32 August and Another v Electoral Commission and Others (CCT8/99) [1999] ZACC 3; 1999 (3) SA 1; 1999 (4) BCLR 363 (1 April 1999) Arshad Mehmood vs Commissioner/Delimitation Authority, Gujranawala, 2014 Pld-Lahore-High-Court-Lahore 221 (2013).

33 See, generally, Townsend 2016; Daly and May 2016.

34 Queer and feminist scholars have highlighted how the loss of community and opportunities to engage are most keenly felt by those who are already marginalized and whose social structures and supports are unrecognized. See, for example, the discussion of LGBTIQA+ communities and the impacts of disasters and disaster-management responses in Dominey-Howes, Gorman-Murray, and McKinnon 2014; Townsend 2021.

35 Rio Principle 10.

36 As Arendt says, dignity gives people the right to have rights; the ability to claim those rights, then, reflects an acknowledgment of human dignity. At the same time, the purpose of claiming rights is to enhance human dignity in its individual, material, social, and political dimensions. Procedural rights are then both the reflection of human dignity and the avenue by which dignity is protected and promoted. See Arendt 1951, 296.

37 Cohen v California, 403 U.S. 15 (1971).

38 Centre for Minority Rights Development (Kenya) and Minority Rights Group (on behalf of Endorois Welfare Council) v Kenya 276/2003 2010 ACHPR.

## References

Addis, Adeno. 2013. "The Role of Human Dignity in a World of Plural Values and Ethical Commitments." *Netherlands Quarterly of Human Rights* 31(4): 403–444, https://doi.org/10.1177/016934411303100403.

Arendt, Hannah. 1951. *The Origins of Totalitarianism*. New York, NY: Shocken Books.

Assiter, Alison. 2021. *A New Theory of Human Rights: New Materialism and Zoroastrianism*. Lanham, Maryland, Rowman & Littlefield Publishers.

Birrell, Kathleen, and Daniel Matthews. 2020. "Re-storying Laws for the Anthropocene: Rights, Obligations and an Ethics of Encounter." *Law and Critique* 31(3): 275–92.

Capps, Patrick. 2010. *Human Dignity and the Foundations of International Law*. Reprint edition. Oxford, Portland, OR: Hart Publishing.

Chakrabarty, Dipesh. 2009. "The Climate of History: Four Theses." *Critical Inquiry* 35(2): 197–222.

Chomba, Susan, Juliet Kariuki, Jens Friis Lund, and Fergus Sinclair. 2016. "Roots of Inequity: How the Implementation of REDD+ Reinforces Past Injustices." *Land Use Policy* 50: 202–213.

Cooke, Bill, and Uma Kothari. 2001. "The Case for Participation as Tyranny." In *Participation: The New Tyranny?* edited by Bill Cooke, and Uma Kothari, 1–15. London: Zed Books.

Crutzen, Paul J. 2002. "Geology of Mankind." *Nature* 415(6867): 23.

———. 2006. *The "Anthropocene"*. Springer.

Crutzen, Paul J., and Eugene F. Stoermer. 2013. "The 'Anthropocene' (2000)." In *The Future of Nature*. Libby Robin, Sverker Sörlin and Paul Warde Eds., 479–90. New Haven, Connecticut: Yale University Press.

Daly, Erin. 2020. *Dignity Rights: Courts, Constitutions, and the Worth of the Human Person*. Democracy, Citizenship, and Constitutionalism. Philadelphia, PA: University of Pennsylvania Press.

Daly, Erin, and James R. May. 2015. "Robinson Township v. Pennsylvania: A Model for Environmental Constitutionalism Symposium: Global Environmental Constitutionalism." *Widener Law Review* 21: 151–70.

———. 2016. "Bridging Constitutional Dignity and Environmental Rights Jurisprudence." *Journal of Human Rights and the Environment* 7(2): 218–42.

———. 2020. *Dignity Law: Global Recognition, Cases, and Perspectives*. Getzville, New York, W.S. Hein.

Davis, Heather, and Zoe Todd. 2017. "On the Importance of a Date, or, Decolonizing the Anthropocene." *ACME: An International Journal for Critical Geographies* 16(4): 761–80.

Di Chiro, Giovanna. 2017. "Welcome to the White (m) Anthropocene? A Feminist-Environmentalist Critique." In *Routledge Handbook of Gender and Environment*, Sherilyn MacGregor ed. 487–505. Milton Park: Routledge.

Dicke, Klaus. 2002. "The Founding Function of Human Dignity in the Universal Declaration of Human Rights." In *The Concept of Human Dignity in Human Rights Discourse*, edited by David Kretzmer, and Eckart Klein, 111–20. The Hague: Kluwer Law International.

Dominey-Howes, Dale, Andrew Gorman-Murray, and Scott McKinnon. 2014. "Queering Disasters: On the Need to Account for LGBTI Experiences in Natural Disaster Contexts." *Gender, Place and Culture* 21(7): 905–18.

Dupré, Catherine. 2016. *The Age of Dignity: Human Rights and Constitutionalism in Europe*. London: Bloomsbury Publishing.

Düwell, Marcus. 2016. "Human Dignity and Intergenerational Human Rights." In *Human Rights and Sustainability: Moral Responsibilities for the Future*, edited by Marcus Düwell, and Gerhard Bos, 69. Milton Park, Abingdon-on-Thames, Oxfordshire, England, UK: Routledge.
Garavito, César Rodríguez, and Carlos Andrés Baquero Díaz. 2018. "The Right to Free, Prior, and Informed Consultation in Colombia: Advances and Setbacks." https://www.ohchr.org/Documents/Issues/IPeoples/EMRIP/FPIC/GaravitoAndDiaz.pdf.
Glendon, Mary Ann. 2002. *A World Made New: Eleanor Roosevelt and the Universal Declaration of Human Rights*. 1st edition. New York: Random House Trade Paperbacks.
Grear, Anna. 2015. "Deconstructing Anthropos: A Critical Legal Reflection on 'Anthropocentric' Law and Anthropocene 'Humanity'." *Law and Critique* 26(3): 225–49.
Haraway, Donna. 2015. "Anthropocene, Capitalocene, Plantationocene, Chthulucene: Making Kin." *Environmental Humanities* 6(1): 159–65.
Kant, Immanuel. 1996. *The Metaphysics of Morals*. Cambridge: Cambridge University Press.
Malhi, Yadvinder. 2017. "The Concept of the Anthropocene." *Annual Review of Environment and Resources* 42(1): 77–104.
Malm, Andreas, and Alf Hornborg. 2014. "The Geology of Mankind? A Critique of the Anthropocene Narrative." *The Anthropocene Review* 1(1): 62–9.
Marshall, Virginia. 2020. "Removing the Veil from the 'Rights of Nature': The Dichotomy between First Nations Customary Rights and Environmental Legal Personhood." *Australian Feminist Law Journal* 45(2): 1–16.
Mbeche, Robert. 2017. "Climbing the Ladder of Participation: Symbolic or Substantive Representation in Preparing Uganda for REDD+?" *Conservation and Society* 15(4): 426–38.
Mirzoeff, Nicholas. 2018. "It's Not the Anthropocene: It's the White Supremacy Scene; or, the Geological Color Line." *After Extinction*, 123–50. Richard Grusin, ed. Minneapolis, Minnesota: University of Minnesota Press.
Morsink, Johannes. 2010. *The Universal Declaration of Human Rights*. Philadelphia, Pennsylvania: University of Pennsylvania Press.
Notsi, L. 2012. "African Indigenous Farming Methods Used in the Cultivation of African Indigenous Vegetables: A Comparative Study of Tsitas Nek (Lesotho) and Mabeskraal Village (South Africa)." In *Conference on Strategies to Overcome Poverty and Inequality: Towards Carnegie III at University of Cape Town, South Africa*, 3–7.
Ober, Josiah. 2012. "Democracy's Dignity." *American Political Science Review* 106(4): 827–46.
Pulido, Laura. 2018. "Racism and the Anthropocene." In *Future Remains: A Cabinet of Curiosities for the Anthropocene*. Gregg Mitman, Marco Armiero Eds., Robert S. Emmett, 116–28. Chicago Illiniois: University of Chicago Press.
Rao, Neomi. 2011. "Three Concepts of Dignity in Constitutional Law." *Notre Dame Law Review* 86(1): 183.
Simpson, Michael. 2018. "The Anthropocene as Colonial Discourse." *Environment and Planning: Society and Space*, April.
Taylor, Matthew, and Jonathan Watts. 2019. "Revealed: The 20 Firms behind a Third of All Carbon Emissions." *The Guardian*, October 9, sec. Environment. https://www.theguardian.com/environment/2019/oct/09/revealed-20-firms-third-carbon-emissions.
Todd, Zoe. 2015. "Indigenizing the Anthropocene." In *Art in the Anthropocene: Encounters among Aesthetics, Politics, Environments and Epistemologies*, Heather Davis and Etienne Turpin Eds. 241–54, London: Open Humanities Press.
Townsend, Dina Lupin. 2016. "The Place of Human Dignity in Environmental Adjudication." *Oslo Law Review* 3(1): 27–50.
———. 2019. "Silencing, Consultation and Indigenous Descriptions of the World." *Journal of Human Rights and the Environment* 10(2): 193–214.
———. 2020. *Human Dignity and the Adjudication of Environmental Rights*. The Lypiatts, 15 Lansdown Road, Cheltenham, Gloucestershire, GL50 2JA: Edward Elgar Publishing Ltd.
———. 2021. *Exclusion, Objectification, Exploitation*. Pretoria: Centre for Sexualities, AIDS and Gender, University of Pretoria.
Tully, Stephen. 2005. *Research Handbook on Corporate Legal Responsibility*. The Lypiatts, 15 Lansdown Road, Cheltenham, Gloucestershire, GL50 2JA: Edward Elgar Publishing Ltd.
Waldron, Jeremy. 2012. "How Law Protects Dignity." *The Cambridge Law Journal* 71(1): 200–22.

Whyte, Kyle P. 2017. "Our Ancestors' Dystopia Now: Indigenous Conservation and the Anthropocene." In *The Routledge Companion to the Environmental Humanities*, Ursula K. Heise, Michelle Niemann, Jon Christensen Eds. 222–31. Milton Park, Abingdon, Oxfordshire: Routledge.
———. 2018. "Indigenous Science (Fiction) for the Anthropocene: Ancestral Dystopias and Fantasies of Climate Change Crises." *Environment and Planning E: Nature and Space* 1(1–2): 224–42.

# PART VI

# Regulating Nature and Nature Regulates

# 16

# REGULATING NATURE AND THE RULE OF LAW

*Han Somsen*

Environmental law scholars have been debating law's proper engagement with nature well before Paul Crutzen's moment of revelation, but since the Nobel Laureate's claim that the planet has entered the age of humans, this has become the debate defining our epoch (Crutzen, Steffen, and McNeill). The Anthropocene signifying one of only very few moments of collective reflexivity in humankind's history, it offers rare opportunities for profound change. Certainly, "reflexivity" is an ethos going well beyond what more conventionally and modestly drives "legal reform," as it amounts to:

> the capacity of structures, systems, and sets of ideas to question their own core commitments, and if necessary change themselves; to be something different, rather than just do different things.
>
> *(Dryzek and Pickering 2019, 17)*

As folk tales have it, Baron van Münchhausen managed single-handedly to rescue himself from a swamp by pulling himself to safety by his own hair, but for mere mortals, rescue would have required some external force (Raspe 2012). Likewise, external inputs offered by the full spectrum of (social) sciences are needed if law is to liberate itself from seemingly unassailable presuppositions that have shepherded the planet to this state. It doubtlessly is the case that the new geological era is triggering an avalanche of such multi-disciplinary inputs, infusing the adolescent epistemic space of environmental law with novel perspectives necessary to become "something different." However, if law is truly to rise to the ecological challenges of our time, the likely outcome of multi-disciplinary reflexivity is for law to transform not merely into something different but into something *uncomfortably* different. This is because there is no such thing as having cake and eating it and if, as looks inevitable, in a quest for human self-preservation the legal status of non-humans – which for the purpose of this chapter I shall stubbornly continue to refer to as "nature" – is to be enhanced, humans will have to forfeit precisely those legal privileges that formalize, legitimize, and perpetuate anthropo-exceptionalism.

At this juncture in Earth's history, when social and natural scientists concur that culture and nature have fused, this chapter starts by confronting understandings of "regulating nature" in natural sciences and law. The purpose of that exercise is to lay bare important conceptual, institutional and regulatory pain points in the relation between the rule of law and nature's

DOI: 10.4324/9781003388081-22

regulatory agency. In that vein, the next section departs conceptually from the notion of "regulation" arguing that, in the spirit of the natural sciences, "regulating nature" should not only be understood as "nature regulates," but in addition as "nature rules supreme." Hence, if nature is acknowledged as an autonomous source of regulation, that assertion is not merely empirical but instead is profoundly normative and constitutional, with nature becoming an essentially monist (as in "autonomous and supreme") regulatory order comprising humans. Law claiming *prima facie* supremacy over nature's regulatory agency then lacks legitimacy.

The third section explores the rule of law as an institution servicing and perpetuating human supremacist claims and speculates if its architecture allows for the kind of significant change that would be required for law to peacefully co-exist with nature's regulatory primacy. The fourth section then returns to the notion of regulation, this time from an instrumental rather than conceptual vantage point, and appreciates the rise of techno-regulation as a reassertion of human regulatory primacy over nature, whereby, with shallow legal endorsement, nature effectively becomes a technological artifact, thus bringing the project of anthropizing nature to its final conclusion. This chapter concludes with a call for law to recognize nature's universal regulatory autonomy and ultimate supremacy, with human dignity residing in the pursuit of its respect.

## Planetary Regulatory Monism

In collectivities subscribing to the rule of law, law claims precedence over alternative sources of regulation, in particular societies, markets, and technologies (Lessig 2006). Hence, in pursuit of the public good, it is law's prerogative to outlaw markets (e.g. in endangered species) or create them (e.g. in tradeable $CO_2$ permits), to mandate technologies (e.g. sewage treatment plants) or prohibit them (e.g. glue traps), and to criminalize societal agents of change (e.g. Extinction Rebellion) or mobilize them (e.g. the Forest Stewardship Council). The mere acknowledgment of nature's regulatory agency by itself would not affect this hierarchy: everything else being equal, environmental law would continue its job of subjugating or emancipating nature at the whim of democratically expressed collective human agency. Even if cognizant that "nature regulates," "regulating nature" within a rule-of-law framework is always understood one-dimensionally as the intentional *human* steering of *human* behavior through consensually promulgated legal rules, coaxing target regulatees (market participants, NGOs, tech industries, etc.) towards respecting, protecting, and improving nature. Nature consequently obtains legally protected status in so far as deemed appropriate and proportional, with due regard being afforded to individual fundamental rights such as property. Unlike humans, whose human dignity according to Article 1 of the Charter of Fundamental Rights of the European Union is "inviolable" and according to Article 5 of the Universal Declaration of Human Rights where humans should not arbitrarily be stripped of their citizenship, nature's protected status is always contingent and can be lost almost as easily as it was granted. It being law's preserve to decide which of nature's commands to heed and which to violate, in constitutional law parlance we would say that law's relationship with nature's regulatory agency is essentially "dualist."

EU environmental law is a case in point; serviced by the rule of law of Article 2 Treaty on European Union (TEU), it is as much a necessary precondition for exploitative market capitalism as a counterweight against it. The first EU environmental laws from the 1970s were internal market measures, and when 30 years after the signing of the Rome Treaty the word "environment" finally found its place in the EU treaties (in Article 130R through the so-called Single European Act), member states could veto acts that were not ancillary to market integration (adopted by a qualified majority under the then Article 100A). Today, Article 192 of the Treaty on the Functioning of the European Union (TFEU) provides ample powers to legislate for "the prudent and rational use of natural resources" and "protecting human health" while, paradoxically, the *lex specialis* provisions on energy (Huhta 2021) and health (De Ruijter 2019) provide the EU with much more limited powers to pursue discrete natural resource and human health policies.

In contrast to law, the natural sciences understand regulation monistically as any causal changes in systems, human or otherwise. Biologists, for example, think of regulation as the "adaptation of form or behavior of an organism to changed conditions" (biologyonline 2022). Whether changes to the Earth system are natural or anthropogenic, intentional or collateral, this has no scientific bearing on the fact that they invariably signal underlying regulatory "agents." Earth system scientists may refer to the role of the global carbonate cycle in the regulation and evolution of the Earth system (Ridgwell and Zeebe 2005) or the regulation of atmospheric $CO_2$ by deep-sea sediments (Ridgwell and Hargreaves 2007). From a natural science perspective, humans clearly do not hold a monopoly on regulation, but by virtue of their mere being are part of an essentially self-regulatory Earth system driven by biological, chemical, and physical regulatory agents.

"Regulating nature," in other words, means something very different to legal scholars and natural scientists. In fact, law is indifferent to the scientific notion that "nature regulates" because the rule of law is premised on the exclusive significance of *human* regulatory agency, so that regulating nature in rule-of-law collectivities can be but an anthropo-legal project. In Lon Fuller's words, "the view of man implicit in legal morality" is as "a self-determining agent" (Fuller, 1964, 162, 166).

Yet, as the consequences of the default supremacy of such anthropo-legalism over the regulatory agency of nature are revealing themselves as increasingly calamitous, the case for higher degrees of commensurability of legal and natural science understandings of "regulating nature" becomes compelling. Indeed, the draft Universal Declaration of the Rights of Mother Earth assigns constitutional significance to the reality that regulatory capacities of rule-of-law collectives are contingent on Earth systems autonomously regulating themselves in ways conducive to human life (Universal Declaration 2010). This then carries the radical but logical implication that the regulatory agency of Earth systems enjoys primacy over derived human regulatory ambitions.

Legal scholars might object that in the Earth regulatory order, humans, unlike daffodils, rocks, or street litter, simultaneously regulate as objects (in the same way daffodils, rocks, or street litter *do* regulate) and subjects (as agents of intentional change: diverting rivers, (re)introducing or exterminating species, discharging industrial waste, etc.). However, this does not undermine our understanding of the Earth's regulatory order as singular, universal, supreme, and hence essentially "monist." A monist perspective is also what Crutzen implies when he refers to humans interacting *as a geological force* with the other great forces of nature. Neither is it of particular concern or consequence to Earth regulatory systems whether humans so interact as object or subject, or even if they were to cease interacting altogether. Earth systems will regulate regardless of humans, while the reverse clearly does not hold.

As manifestly false as it obviously is, a dualist conception of "regulating nature" is a necessary precondition for collectivities subscribing to the rule of law legitimately to claim regulatory supremacy over nature. Such supremacy is exercised concretely each time such collectivities decide which of nature's regulatory commands to embrace, which to ignore, and which to fight.

Questions about supremacy, preemption, and fidelity *do* of course regularly occur also in monist regulatory landscapes, as the EU legal order illustrates, but as matter of constitutional principle must be settled by the autonomous authority from which derived powers flow (i.e. "nature"), and not by subordinate regulators (collectivities subscribing to the rule of law).

Current humanitarian crises, global warming, biodiversity loss, water shortages, etc. in essence are *ex-post* assertions of regulatory supremacy of an autonomous Earth regulator responding to systemic acts of disloyalty of subordinate human regulators. Environmental law, through this monist lens, on account of its disrespect for Earth system regulatory primacy lacks legitimacy, regardless of its rule-of-law pedigree in terms of democratic legitimacy, respect for human dignity, human rights, and solidarity.

## Rule-of-Law Regulatory Dualism

On a scale of deep time, the past 12,000 years may barely register, but that inter-glacial blip of stability allowed for the emergence and rise of human civilizations and institutions. Stability permitted institutions to emerge, and presumed background conditions of stability continue to inform their ethos and architecture. One such institution is the rule of law, promising human collectives social stability and deriving its legitimacy from the grant to citizens of procedural (consensus dictating substance), formal (governance by law), and substantive (human dignity, fundamental rights, solidarity, and justice) control over their futures. Although the rule of law does not necessarily imply a denial of regulatory pluralism, by dint of its pledge of governance through *law*, it claims supremacy over concurrent sources of regulatory agency, including nature, and does so regardless of consequence.

Yet, if collectivities subscribing to the rule of law entertain the ambition to extend their stay on Earth (maintain "a safe operating space for humanity") (Rockström, Steffen, and Noone 2009, 461), the Anthropocene forces them to come clean about the price they are prepared to pay for upholding their claim of regulatory supremacy. The choice faced by such collectivities could not be starker; either they capitulate and compromise on the most fundamental formal and substantive tenets of their constitutions, or persist in their defiance and pay the ultimate price. Not only is this a nigh impossible dilemma to resolve, but it is also questionable if the architecture of the rule of law is *prima facie* up to the task of resolving it. In particular, its insistence on law as the final instrument of governance, and collective (democracy) and individual (fundamental rights) vetoes against that kind of constitutional change amount to a pathological path dependency ruling out fundamental institutional transformation.

> What we will refer to as pathological path dependency decouples human institutions from the Earth system by embodying feedback mechanisms that systematically repress information about the condition of the Earth system, and systematically prioritize narrowly economic concerns. (…) Path dependency in dominant institutions is complicit in destabilizing the Earth system, and constrains what these institutions can do and how they can be changed in response to the emerging epoch of the Anthropocene.
>
> *(Dryzek and Pickering 2019).*

The pathological path dependency inherent in the rule of law, systematically suppressing nature's universal and autonomous regulatory agency, and prioritizing narrow economic (human) concerns, is located above all in the paramountcy it attaches to democracy and individual rights. Hence, rule-of-law collectivities would somehow collectively and individually need to agree or acquiesce to deep sacrifices over which they could exercise collective and individual veto rights. Evidence that they are capable or inclined to do so has thus far, unsurprisingly, been scarce.

Instead, throughout the world the Covid-19 pandemic set in motion transformations from governance by rule *of* law, marked by transparency, participation in rule-making, respect for fundamental rights, human dignity, non-discrimination, and solidarity, to governance through technologies legitimized *by* law. Under pressure to act quickly and decisively, executives and legislators employ law to respond to crises as best they can, and in doing so are systematically excused for rule-of-law shortcuts made in the process. Indeed, as the House of Commons Select Committees on Health and Social Care and Science and Technology in a report on the UK government's response to Covid-19 observed:

> The restrictions eventually imposed on the UK public because of the pandemic were unprecedented. Even in wartime there had been no equivalent of the order to make it a criminal offence for people to meet each other and to remain in their homes other than for specified reasons.
>
> *(HoC HSCST Committee. 2021, para 111)*

In sharp contrast to its scathing criticism of the government's initial conventional regulatory response aimed at dispersing crowds thus preventing the spread of infections, the report heaps praise on its role in promoting the development and deployment of vaccines. Where conventional public messaging through law aimed at prevention and control of the virus for numerous reasons had disastrously failed, the vaccines brought vital technological relief in an otherwise hopeless situation:

> The most successful component of the United Kingdom's response to the covid-19 pandemic has been the development and deployment of vaccines. Globally, it is one of the most stunning scientific achievements in history to have gone from having no protection against a devastating global virus, to deploying a range of effective vaccines in less than a year. In England alone it is estimated that more than 112,000 lives have already been saved by this extraordinary success, with tens of millions of infections being prevented.
>
> *(HoC HSCST Committee. 2021, para 343)*

What the UK government got right, according to the report, was its procurement policy, subsidizing a scaling-up of domestic manufacturing, and promoting agility in trials and regulatory approvals. These determinants of regulatory success or failure are strikingly shallow compared to the variables that make for rule-of-law governance, sitting uneasily with even its thinnest formal conceptions. A scrutiny committee designed to hold government publicly to account ends up praising it for, essentially, investing in the privatization of the public domain (public health regulation), removing standard-setting from the public realm, extinguishing avenues for public participation and accountability, and handsomely rewarding pharmaceutical moguls and shareholders for their efforts:

> In advance, it may not have been unreasonable to assume that the public would have a limited tolerance of such draconian restrictions. But that assumption turned out to be wrong.
>
> *(HoC HSCST Committee. 2021, para 111)*

Although the most eye-catching departures from the rule of law were situated in the realm of individual human rights, more profoundly what we are witnessing is a reassertion of human ambitions to exercise regulatory supremacy over nature, this time by technological means. Because, for reasons too obvious to recite, law is incapable of enforcing nature's subservience to human will, hopes are now firmly pinned on vaccines, genetic and climate engineering, and other technologies to achieve precisely that. Technologies have become the regulatory modality of choice, heralding the final completion of the human project to cultivate nature.

Indeed, the driving force behind the UK's vaccine success, again according to the report, was the Vaccine Taskforce (headed by the Life Science venture capitalist Kate Bingham) and its relative immunity from political oversight.

> The Taskforce was a team drawn of Life Sciences industry professionals, civil servants and scientists, and was based outside the Department of Health and Social Care physically and in reporting terms. The team was based in the Department for Business, Energy and Industrial Strategy and Kate Bingham reported directly to the Prime Minister.
>
> *(HoC HSCST Committee. 2021, para 351)*

For reasons explored next, this regulatory turn not only transforms nature into a technological artifact but also severely threatens human dignity.

## Techno Regulatory Monism

What few people realize is that Paul Crutzen did more than just point out that Earth has entered the geological epoch of humans. Intimidated by the forces nature was about to unleash on humankind, he stepped outside his comfort zone of atmospheric chemistry and articulated an exit strategy for the barrage of misery that would plague humans living on an angry planet:

> mankind will remain a major environmental force for many millennia. A daunting task lies ahead for scientists and engineers to guide society towards environmentally sustainable management during the era of the Anthropocene. This will require appropriate human behaviour at all scales, and may well involve internationally accepted, large-scale geo-engineering projects, for instance to "optimize" climate. At this stage, however, we are still largely treading on *terra incognita*.
>
> *(Crutzen 2002, 23)*

Crutzen in this quote distinguishes the two spheres that in the Anthropocene have fused into a toxic singularity, nature and culture, both of which he claims need to be regulated if Earth is to remain habitable. As regards the human world, he calls for "appropriate human behavior at all scales" and to move towards "environmentally sustainable management." Much more significant and controversial, however, is his emphasis on "scientists and engineers" as the drivers of those changes in human behavior, instead of parliaments and legislators (Somsen 2011).

Rather than rule of law, what Crutzen effectively proposes is rule by design. Nature, likewise, in Crutzen's mind no longer is salvageable conventionally, by merely legally persuading citizens to respect nature for future generations. What he proposes, in addition or perhaps even instead, is *large-scale geo-engineering*, involving carbon dioxide removal, increased reflexivity of the Earth's surface, injecting reflexive particles in the higher atmosphere, etc. (Reynolds 2021).

Whereas law's supremacist claim requires an ultimately untenable dualist approach towards nature's regulatory agency, technology can plausibly be thought of as the regulatory modality capable of crafting a monist anthropogenic regulatory space, encompassing both humans and other-than-humans. Crucially, unlike law, technologies hence offer a lifeline to struggling human ambitions to rule nature.

It would be too easy to dismiss such visions as products of narcissistic geniuses succumbing to hubris such as Paul Crutzen. Even geo-engineering techniques are now partly in use and have acquired a degree of implicit legal backing, for example in the Paris Agreement on Climate Change, that few would have believed possible only a decade ago. In addition, Crutzen acknowledges the uncertainty and risks that come with large-scale interventions into Earth's physical, chemical, and biological regulatory systems. However, he rates those risks as considerably inferior to the continued trust that ineffective, territorially fragmented consensual law will eventually realize to make the behavioral change so desperately needed. The dualist notion that law operates autonomously from and hence enjoys precedence over the regulatory agency of nature is, in his perspective, the epitome of hubris inevitably leading to nemesis.

What we must do now, he argues, is to interact with nature *directly*, despite all its associated risks, hence asserting human regulatory superiority through *technological* means. While (environmental) law is powerless to direct the planet to cool down, keep species within their historical ranges, have water purify itself, etc., technologies hold the promise of forcing both humans and nature into submission. In the Anthropocene, nature turns from legal object into technological artifact.

A sense of failure and shame should descend upon us if we pause and acknowledge that technologies are crowding out both law and nature. Law's operating system is normative, and its design is a product of public deliberative processes. It offers the opportunity to discuss the normative basis for a rule and the way in which that normativity is best articulated to become effective and fair. Laws can change, but this again requires public participation and consent, meaning that law offers certainty, transparency, and a degree of stability. Courts guard the proper application and interpretation of law and may invalidate laws that clash with norms featuring higher in the legal hierarchy (e.g. constitutional norms). The addressees of laws are always human, and although behavior prescribed by law affects the physical world, that final impact is contingent on compliance. Non-compliance is a serious weakness of the law but at the same time the ultimate safeguard of human autonomy and dignity. Unlike robots governed by operating systems, in expressing our human dignity we may decide not to obey the law and accept the possible consequences of our choice. Life under the rule of law, therefore, has been a precious good but a privilege doomed by its implied assertion that humans reign supreme over nature.

It is of some irony that humanity, rather than accepting nature's reign, for the sake of dominating nature is prepared to submit to technological rule and in so doing will sacrifice the core of what it means to be human. For, compared to the rule of law, rule by design makes for a very different living experience. Although law and public participation continue to have formal roles to play, much of what truly matters occurs not in houses of parliament but in laboratories and engineering plants of privately owned global firms yielding powers surpassing those of states. Global political leadership no longer is personified by charismatic visionaries as elected representatives but is claimed by self-absorbed tech entrepreneurs like Elon Musk, Richard Branson, and Bill Gates, who finance and implement their own space projects, climate technologies, and mass vaccination programs. Regardless of whether their work is profit-driven or not, this kind of global private techno-governance is not compatible with rule-of-law governance by any stretch of the imagination.

The products these global powerhouses produce say a great deal about what being human in the Anthropocene entails. Why bother breaking one's head about the trolley problem (a thought experiment in moral philosophy involving runaway illustrating that in moral decision-making negative duties appear to carry more weight than positive duties), if vehicles make autonomous split-second ethical decisions about if and how to avoid a collision? (Moolayil 2018). Likewise, computer programs respond to our private speech, store information, and suggest or decide what is best for us. The electrification of road transport pushed by Tesla and other car manufacturers dictates public energy, transport, and environmental policies, and not the other way around. Citizens have no role in influencing the profound normative impacts of these technological developments, and software updates quietly find their way into machines from which we have become inseparable without us even so much as noticing. Apathy, rather than conscious engagement, is the new default.

In a last resort response to runaway rates of extinction, habitat loss, atmospheric and aquatic pollution, etc., technologies in the Anthropocene also subjugate nature. Genetic modification of plants and animals is used to increase agricultural yields and progressively is becoming the primary tool to restore and enhance nature. Environmental law losing its primacy to such technologies, the political connection between collectivities subscribing to the rule of law and their natural surroundings becomes ever more tenuous and shallow. $CO_2$ reduction targets will have lost their political edge once large-scale carbon dioxide removal (CDR) and solar radiation management (SRM) technologies have been perfected, and nature conservation becomes an ethically sterile cost-benefit analysis once the benefits of economic development can be precisely weighed against the cost of technologically driven assisted migration and de-extinction programs.

Systemic recourse to technologies of course betrays massive present and past legal failure. The liming of Swedish rivers and lakes has been common practice for over 35 years after laws designed to prevent long-range atmospheric pollution had failed. Conservationists assist the migration of animals in trucks because area protection laws are failing. The Arctic is intentionally being covered in a white powder to slow down the melting of the ice after climate law has dramatically faltered. In all these examples, and there are many more, the deployment of technologies signifies that the point of legally *preventing* environmental destruction and harm by coaxing humans to respect nature has irreversibly passed. We are now having to pin our hopes on *rectifying* and *compensating* for damage done as well as we technologically can. As Crutzen acknowledges, such technology-driven remedial action is a high-risk operation, which would not have been necessary had humans understood and respected the regulatory primacy of nature.

Our environmental management options have essentially always consisted of three types: preventative, restorative, and what I shall call "palliative." The further we are forced to stray from preventative policies, the less law can mean and the more technologies occupy spaces long deemed exclusively legal. Conservation law still tries to stop the rot, of course, by preventing the extinction of species and preserving the biodiversity that still remains. But increasingly, we must conclude that it is too late, and our efforts must shift towards restoring and enhancing, by artificial means, "nature." Zoos have become indispensable depositories of biodiversity (Conde, Flesness, Colchero, Jones, and Scheurerlein 2011), breeding programs trumpet victory when species manage to reproduce in captivity, rewilding programs are taking off everywhere (Trouwborst 2021), and these days I am teaching my students the legal implications of "de-extinction" of animals through cloning and gene-editing techniques (Reynolds 2021).

The final phase we are now witnessing comes when we realize that Earth regulatory systems have become so erratic and unpredictable that nature has no time to adapt to the wide array of freak circumstances the planet throws at it. Forests can recover from a fire but not when forest fires have become endemic. Assisted migration policies, i.e. moving species north or to higher altitudes, at some point literally run out of road. No use, either, reviving species gone extinct if the conditions that led to their extinction have worsened. Once we have arrived at that point, conservation has become a palliative effort, reducing pain and discomfort to ourselves and other species as best as we can before silence descends upon our planet once again.

## Conclusion

Cruelly but unmistakably the Anthropocene exposes the rule of law's unconditional claim that law rules supreme as a major cause of the ecological and humanitarian crises defining our new epoch. Thus, the rule of law denies the monist nature of our planet's regulatory order, falsely but stubbornly asserting final authority over nature's autonomous and universal regulatory agency. That denial being glaringly self-destructive, this should be the obvious moment in human history constitutionally to recognize nature's regulatory supremacy to which rule-of-law collectives must yield. Certainly, that recognition would be nothing less than revolutionary, as it implies profound human sacrifice not just by the privileged few but by anyone endowed with fundamental rights including rights to property, and freedoms to choose an occupation, to conduct a business, of movement, etc.

Fundamentally, recognition of nature's regulatory primacy implies a radically different answer to the "why" question legal scholars spend too little time asking and answering: "why, in the final analysis, is law A or interpretation B *right*?" Law is right when it serves nature's universal regulatory authority, as a source of life and all good that is associated with it. Philosophers and legal scholars have of course in various ways proposed de-centering humans for the sake of establishing if laws are good or bad, and theologians have never wavered in their belief in a higher authority to which humans regardless of place and time are answerable (Jonas 1987; Serres 1995).

However, the rule of law was designed precisely to fend off assertions of universal regulatory authority: first, because law's authority and legitimacy are essentially local, i.e. territorially limited by the confines of jurisdictions in which laws are democratically promulgated; second, because within those jurisdictions law's authority and legitimacy are conditional upon respect for fundamental human rights. Combined, this results in a pathological path dependency by which law is destined forever to remain local, anthropocentric, and self-serving. A brilliant institutional architecture that took the best Greek brains to conceive and well over 2000 years further to evolve in its current forms obstructs universal respect for a non-human regulatory agent in ultimate command, even though the consequences of that systemic disloyalty are catastrophic.

At this time, when a wide array of anthropogenic disasters are proving the supremacy of law to be an untenable fiction, technologies reassert the dubious idea of the primacy of human regulatory agency. With merely the thinnest of legal backing and for all to see, technologies are transforming nature and humans into technological artifacts, bringing the fusion of nature and culture to its ultimate conclusion and hence closing the chapters of both nature and human dignity.

## References

"BiologyOnline." 2022. https://www.biologyonline.com/dictionary/regulation.

Conde, D., N. Flesness, F. Colchero, O. R. Jones and A. Scheuerlein. 2011. "An Emerging Role of Zoos to Conserve Biodiversity." *Science* 331: 390–391.

Crutzen, Paul. 2002. "Geology of Mankind." *Nature* 415(6867): 23.

Crutzen, Paul, Will Steffen and John McNeill. 2007. "The Anthropocene: Are Humans Now Overwhelming the Great Forces of Nature?" *AMBIO: A Journal of the Human Environment* 36: 614–621.

De Ruijter, Aniek. 2019. *EU Health Law and Policy*. Oxford: Oxford University Press.

Dryzek, John and Jonathan Pickering. 2019. *The Politics of the Anthropocene*. Oxford: Oxford University Press.

Fuller, Lon. 1964. *The Morality of Law*, revised. ed. New Haven, CT: Yale University Press.

"House of Commons Health and Social Care and Science and Technology Committees," *Coronavirus: Lessons Learned to Date*, Sixth Report of the Health and Social Care Committee and Third Report of the Science and Technology Committee of Session 2021–22, 22 October 2021.
Huhta, Kaisa. 2021. "The Scope of State Sovereignty under Article 194(2) and the Evolution of EU Competences in the Energy Sector." *International and Comparative Law Quarterly* 70(4): 991–1010.
Jonas, Hans. 1987. *Das Prinzip Verantwortung*. Frankfurt: Suhrkamp.
Lessig, Lawrence. 2006. *Code: And Other Laws of Cyberspace Version 2.0*. Cambridge: Basic Books.
Moolayil, Amar. 2018. "The Modern Trolley Problem: Ethical and Economically-Sound Liability Schemes for Autonomous Vehicles." *Case Western Reserve Journal of Law, Technology and the Internet* 9: 1–32.
Raspe, Rudolf Erich. 2012. *The Travels and Surprising Adventures of Baron Munchausen*. London: Melville House.
Reynolds, Jesse. 2021a. "Earth System Interventions as Technologies of the Anthropocene." *Environmental Innovation and Societal Transitions* 40: 132–146.
Reynolds, Jesse. 2021b. "Engineering Biological Diversity: The International Governance of Synthetic Biology, Gene Drives, and De-extinction for Conservation." *Current Opinion in Environmental Sustainability* 49: 1–6.
Ridgwell, Andy and Julia Hargreaves. 2007. "Regulation of Atmospheric $CO_2$ by Deep-Sea Sediments in an Earth System Model." *Global Biogeochemical Cycles* 21: 1–14.
Ridgwell, Andy and Richard Zeebe. 2005. "The Role of the Global Carbonate Cycle in the Regulation and Evolution of the Earth System." *Earth and Planetary Science Letters* Vol 234: 299–315.
Rockström, Johan, Will Steffen and Kevin Noone *et al*. 2009. "A Safe Operating Space for Humanity." *Nature* 461: 472–475.
Serres, Michel. 1995. *The Natural Contract*. Ann Arbor, MI: Michigan Publishing.
Somsen, Han. 2011. "When Regulators Mean Business." *Rechtsfilosofie & Rechtstheorie* 40: 47–57.
Trouwborst, Arie. 2021. "Megafauna Rewilding: Addressing Amnesia and Myopia in Biodiversity Law and Policy." *Journal of Environmental Law* 33(3): 639–667.
"Universal Declaration on the Rights of Mother Earth." 2010. https://celdf.org/wp-content/uploads/2016/03/UNIVERSAL-DECLARATION-OF-THE-RIGHTS-OF-MOTHER-EARTH-APRIL-22-2010.pdf.

# 17

# SOLAR GEOENGINEERING AND THE CHALLENGE OF GOVERNING MULTIPLE RISKS IN THE ANTHROPOCENE

*Kerryn Brent*

Solar geoengineering is intrinsically linked with the Anthropocene, the unofficial geological epoch in which humans have become the primary force of planetary change (Crutzen and Soemer 2002). Solar geoengineering proposals intend to *deliberately* manipulate the Earth's radiative balance to reduce temperatures at a global or regional scale as a response to climate change. Scientists suggest that this could be achieved by reflecting a small percentage of incoming solar radiation away from the Earth. A key proposal is stratospheric aerosol injection, which involves creating reflective particles in the stratosphere using sulfur dioxide or another precursor, essentially mimicking the cooling effect of a large volcanic eruption. Other proposals include enhancing the reflectivity of low-lying ocean clouds and placing reflective shields in space.

Proposals to develop solar geoengineering challenge the traditional environmentalist paradigm that privileges a "hands-off" approach to mother nature (Reynolds 2021, 137). This paradigm is characterized by willful restraint when it comes to interfering in ecological systems, primarily to respect the autonomy and/or integrity of nature (see Landres 2010, 91). Solar geoengineering challenges this paradigm because it would involve deliberate human manipulation of the Earth system, presenting new risks and uncertainties. Indeed, there has been considerable opposition to solar geoengineering on this basis. For example, 195 civil society organizations have signed the "Hands Off Mother Earth!" manifesto, calling for geoengineering to be banned, as it poses unacceptable risks and would violate the integrity of Mother Earth (Manifesto 2018). In June 2021, the Saami Council drafted a letter calling for Harvard researchers to cancel their solar geoengineering research program, stating that "Climate manipulation strongly contradicts our understanding and experience of how to respect and live in harmony with Mother Nature" (Sámiráđđi 2021b). This letter has been signed by approximately 30 Indigenous organizations (Doyle 2021). From these perspectives, geoengineering "represents the culmination of what climate change has begun: the elimination of an independent, wild nature and its replacement with a planet fully under the human thumb" (Thiele 2019, 464).

However, not developing solar geoengineering could have serious consequences. To be clear, scientists are not proposing solar geoengineering as a mitigation substitute but as an additional

DOI: 10.4324/9781003388081-23

tool to address climate change and prevent catastrophic impacts on human and Earth systems (NASEM 2021, 25–28). Humanity is now "perilously close" to exceeding the 1.5°C temperature target agreed to by states under the Paris Agreement (United Nations Secretary-General 2021) which will result in more extreme climate change impacts (Allen et al, 2018). As explained below, conventional mitigation strategies may not prevent temperatures from exceeding this threshold, or critical tipping points in the Earth system materializing. Despite presenting its own risks, solar geoengineering may nevertheless have an important role to play in addressing climate change, helping humanity achieve "effective planetary stewardship" in the Anthropocene (Asayama et al. 2019, 20). Adopting a "hands-off" approach to solar geoengineering would not, therefore, be risk-free.

These issues reflect broader questions as to how humanity should exercise power and influence over natural systems in the Anthropocene. Key issues associated with the Anthropocene, including climate change and biodiversity loss, are the result of humans misusing power over nature (Hamilton 2017). However, this does not mean that withdrawing power and adopting a "hands-off" approach is a suitable strategy for environmental management in the Anthropocene (see Hamilton 2017; Burdon 2020). Through past misuse of power, humans have arguably acquired responsibility for the Earth; withdrawing power could therefore be as problematic as continuing to use it recklessly (see Hamilton 2017, 35). In light of this view, Hamilton and Burdon propose that humanity must accept responsibility for the power and influence it exercises over nature, but use such power cautiously, with humility and restraint.

This raises a key question: could solar geoengineering be part of a "responsible" Anthropocene? Hamilton suggests that it could not; that solar geoengineering is, inherently, a technofix that would enable humanity to *avoid* responsibility and pursue mastery and control over nature (Hamilton 2017 21–23; 91–92). This chapter does not dispute that solar geoengineering, like any form of technological power, *could* be misused, but it questions whether this is inevitable. Can governance mechanisms promote a different outcome? There are emerging claims that the governance of solar geoengineering requires mechanisms that can weigh the risks associated with solar geoengineering research and/or deployment against the risks of *not* developing or using these technologies in light of worsening climate change. That is, we need to adopt a "risk tradeoff" approach to solar geoengineering governance. This chapter considers what such an approach might entail, and whether it might promote greater responsibility and humility regarding solar geoengineering while avoiding the pitfalls of outright prohibition.

The second section begins by providing an overview of solar geoengineering and considers arguments in favor of developing risk tradeoff mechanisms for future governance. The third section uses a framework called risk tradeoff analysis (Graham and Wiener 1997a) to provide a more nuanced understanding of what risk tradeoffs are and what this type of decision-making will likely entail in the context of solar geoengineering governance. The fourth section considers the extent to which this framework might promote a responsible approach to solar geoengineering. Risk tradeoff analysis may encourage a greater understanding of the consequences of decisions regarding solar geoengineering, but weighing up competing risks between solar geoengineering and climate change is likely to be significantly influenced by value judgments and other subjective considerations. Risk tradeoff analysis does not suggest what those values ought to be, or how they could be shaped to support greater responsibility for human power in the Anthropocene. The fifth section concludes by reflecting on the need to address value judgments alongside the development of objective risk assessment criteria in solar geoengineering governance.

## Solar Geoengineering Governance and the Need for a Risk Tradeoff Approach

The risks that anthropogenic climate change poses for human and natural systems are increasing. In August 2021, Working Group I (WGI) released its report as part of the Intergovernmental Panel on Climate Change's sixth assessment cycle. The report provides the latest scientific assessment of how the climate has changed and future climate pathways. The WGI report indicates that humans are causing the climate to warm at the fastest rate in over 2,000 years (Allan et al. 2021, 7). This is having further unprecedented effects on the climate system, including the fastest rates of sea level rise in 3,000 years and the highest rate of ocean warming in 11,000 years (Allan et al. 2021, 9). The report draws strong links between increases in the severity and frequency of extreme weather events, including heatwaves and droughts, and human influences (Allan et al. 2021, 10–11). Additionally, it notes that "[h]uman influence has *likely* increased the chance of compound extreme events since the 1950s," such as storm surges combined with extreme rainfall (Allan et al. 2021, 11, and fn 18). The report further signals that key tipping points, such as ice sheet collapse and abrupt ocean circulation changes, "cannot be ruled out" in emissions scenarios (Allan et al. 2021, 35). The report sets out five future climate scenarios (Allan et al. 2021, 41), only two of which have a "theoretical chance" of limiting global warming to 1.5–2°C (Rouse 2021). A key takeaway from the WGI report is that the window of opportunity to meet the Paris Agreement temperature targets and reduce the risk of catastrophic climate change impacts is rapidly closing.

Deep cuts to global greenhouse gas (GHG) emissions must be made immediately if we are to meet these targets (Allan et al. 2021, 36–38; United Nations Secretary-General 2021), but limiting future emissions may no longer be enough. Humanity must start "cleaning up its mess" by removing billions of tons of carbon dioxide directly from the atmosphere (Rouse 2021). Carbon dioxide removal (CDR) proposals are another suite of human interventions that are sometimes labeled as "geoengineering." CDR proposal range from nature-based/regenerative activities, such as reforestation/afforestation and blue carbon enhancement, to more technological land and marine-based proposals, including bioenergy with carbon capture and storage, direct air capture technologies, and ocean fertilization (see, e.g. Dooley, Harrould-Kolieb, and Talberg 2021, figure 2). However, there are numerous risks and side effects associated with CDR methods. There will be a lag in the climate's response to CDR, meaning that it will take several centuries for CDR to address key climate change issues, such as sea-level rise (Lee et al. 2021, 7, 83). Moreover, most CDR proposals are yet to be tested outside of laboratory settings or proven effective at the scale required by modeling scenarios (Andersen and Peters 2016). The extent to which CDR methods can be relied on to contribute to net zero emissions is therefore questionable. Further action will likely be needed to avoid overshooting the Paris Agreement temperature targets.

Solar geoengineering is being considered by scientists and policy-makers as an additional means to address climate change (e.g. Lee et al. 2021, 84; NASEM 2021, 25). As explained above, most solar geoengineering proposals aim to directly alter the Earth's radiative balance by reflecting a percentage of incoming solar radiation (sunlight).[1] The two most prominent proposals are stratospheric aerosol injection (SAI) and marine cloud brightening (MCB). Based on observations following large-scale volcanic eruptions, such as the 1991 eruption of Mt Pinatubo, scientists suggest that SAI could rapidly cool global temperatures if deployed on a large enough scale (Crutzen 2006). Preliminary cost estimates also indicate that a global SAI program could be achieved at a relatively affordable cost (Smith and Wagner 2018). On the other hand, MCB is largely being considered as a means of cooling temperatures at a local or regional scale to protect vulnerable ecosystems, such as the Great Barrier Reef, from climate change impacts (McDonald et al. 2019).

Scientific understanding of the potential climatic effects and negative impacts of solar geoengineering proposals remains limited. Current understanding is predominantly based on modeling and natural analogs (i.e. volcanic eruptions) (Lee 2021, 85). Research programs are now seeking to push beyond laboratory testing and modeling into outdoor experimentation. Researchers at Harvard University are seeking to test SAI delivery mechanisms and particle properties in the stratosphere (Keutsch Group, n.d.). In early 2021, the researchers had intended to conduct their first experiment in Sweden, but the experiment was canceled following a letter of complaint published by NGOs and the Indigenous Saami Council (Sámiráđđi 2021). In Australia, researchers are developing MCB as a regional form of solar geoengineering to prevent coral bleaching across large areas of the Great Barrier Reef. In March 2020, as part of the Reef Restoration and Adaptation Program, researchers conducted the first outdoor test of an apparatus designed to spray salt particles from seawater into clouds to enhance their reflectivity (Readfearn 2020).

In addition to these research programs, national and international scientific organizations have produced authoritative reports evaluating scientific and governance aspects of solar geoengineering (e.g. Shepherd 2009; NASEM 2021). Not only have these reports served to enhance scientific understanding, but they have also helped transform solar geoengineering from a taboo topic to a climate policy option that warrants further consideration. The WGI report is the latest such report. The IPCC is yet to include solar geoengineering in its climate modeling scenarios, but the WG I report contains the most extensive consideration of solar geoengineering by the IPCC to date. The report recognizes that, conceptually, solar geoengineering could be designed to help achieve "multiple climate policy goals" (Lee et al. 2021, 90). It nevertheless acknowledges that there are numerous uncertainties and risks associated with solar geoengineering. One issue is that solar geoengineering would merely "mask" the issues associated with climate change, as it does not address levels of GHGs in the atmosphere (Arias et al. 2021, 70). There are concerns that SAI could negatively impact the ozone layer and could significantly change monsoon and rainfall patterns in different regions (NASEM 2021, 52). MCB could also disproportionately impact regional precipitation patterns (NASEM 2021, 54). A further concern is the risk of rapid and severe warming if solar geoengineering activity is suddenly stopped (Arias et al. 2021, 70; NASEM 2021, 63). It may be possible to mitigate some of these risks through further research and project design (Grieger et al. 2019, 357). However, the scientific understanding of solar geoengineering and how the climate system will respond to it remains limited (Lee et al. 2021, 7). Some uncertainty concerning the magnitude and probability of negative impacts may nevertheless persist, despite further research.

In addition to environmental risks, solar geoengineering presents numerous social-political risks. Large-scale solar geoengineering could have transboundary impacts beyond the border of states who decide to use it (Brent, McGee, and Maguire 2015). Solar geoengineering by one state or a small group of states without wider consensus could lead to geopolitical disputes and inflame existing tensions between great powers (Lockyer and Symonds 2019). A further concern is that solar geoengineering could create a "moral hazard" in that research and/or successful deployment could detract from conventional mitigation efforts (Lin 2013). There is also concern that the implementation of solar geoengineering programs could lead to technological "lock-in," saddling future generations with the burden of maintaining such programs, especially if global GHG emissions are not significantly reduced (Cairns 2014).

Governance mechanisms must be developed across multiple scales to manage the risks presented by solar geoengineering. Early steps towards governing geoengineering at an international level (both CDR and solar geoengineering) have already been made under two international regimes: the *Convention on Biological Diversity* (Decision X/33) and *1996 Protocol to the Convention on the Prevention of Marine Pollution by Dumping of Wastes and other Matter,*

*1972* (Resolution LP.4(8)). However, these early efforts reflect a siloed and highly precautionary approach to the governance of geoengineering. They focus exclusively on the risks presented by geoengineering activities, including field testing, and not on the risks posed by climate change.

There is an emerging understanding that a more nuanced approach to risk management is needed for solar geoengineering. For example, Grieger et al. (2019, 375) acknowledge that the risks of deploying solar geoengineering "have to be compared to the consequences of unmitigated climate change" Jinnah et al. (2019, 3) similarly recognize that the risks associated with solar geoengineering research and deployment "need to be weighed against the grave environmental, social, ethical, and geopolitical risks arising from climate change." According to Nicholson (2020), governance discussions should be framed around the potential for solar geoengineering to address the risks associated with climate change, not the "worst-case scenario" that could result from solar geoengineering research or deployment. Focusing on the latter may result in rules that could unduly restrict responsible research and development, such as blanket moratoria (Nicholson 2020). These statements warn against taking a siloed approach to governing the risks of solar geoengineering. They emphasize that decisions to prevent or delay the development of solar geoengineering could also have serious environmental and socio-political consequences and that this needs to be accounted for in any future governance frameworks.

This process of weighing up competing risks in decision-making is commonly referred to as a "risk tradeoff." The following section uses a framework called risk tradeoff analysis to provide a more detailed understanding of what this type of decision-making might entail in the context of solar geoengineering.

## Understanding Risk Tradeoffs

Risk tradeoff analysis is a framework developed by Graham and Wiener in the mid-1990s in the context of long-standing efforts in the United States to identify and reduce risk across a wide range of sectors (1997b, 1–4, 6–8). Graham and Wiener were concerned that decision-makers were paying insufficient attention to the multitude of risks involved in decision-making, and that risk tradeoffs were taking place in a way that was not expressly acknowledged and/or were counterproductive to achieving an overall reduction in societal risk (1997b, 10). The purpose of risk tradeoff analysis is to help decision-makers comprehensively identify risk across a broad range of contexts, from medical treatments to environmental protection (1997b, 4). The framework also seeks to provide decision-makers with tools to weigh up different risks, with a view to minimizing the overall risk involved in decision-making (1997b, 4). In doing so, it provides a detailed explanation of what risk tradeoffs entail and the challenges they present for decision-makers and regulators. This section, therefore, examines risk tradeoff analysis to better understand what this type of decision-making will likely involve in the context of solar geoengineering governance.

Risk tradeoff analysis is underpinned by an understanding that we live in a "multirisk world" (Weiner 2020), in which actions taken to reduce one risk may have the "perverse effect" of promoting or creating other risks (Rascoff and Revesz 2002, 1765). Graham and Wiener describe the risk that is the object of intervention as the "target risk" (1997b, 23). Risks that flow from interventions to address the target risk are known as "countervailing risks" (1997b, 23). One of the many examples Graham and Wiener use to illustrate the relationship between target and countervailing risks is asbestos removal. The aim of asbestos removal is to protect occupants from the target risk of exposure, but removing the asbestos creates a countervailing risk of exposure to the removal workers (1997b, 16). Applying this logic to solar geoengineering, these proposals are best categorized as interventions to address climate change. The risks associated with climate change are target risks. The risks that solar geoengineering proposals themselves present are countervailing risks. When an intervention like asbestos removal or solar geoengineering generates a countervailing risk, it changes the overall "portfolio" or range of risks. This change is the "risk tradeoff" (Graham and Wiener 1997b, 23).

The first step in risk tradeoff analysis is to identify when tradeoffs are likely to occur and the implications they will have for the portfolio of risk. To help decision-makers better identify risk tradeoffs and the challenges they present, Graham and Wiener developed a typology of four different tradeoffs. This typology categorizes risk tradeoffs based on whether an intervention is likely to change the nature of the risk and/or who or what is affected by the risk (the "population"). First, interventions can offset a target risk by creating the same type of risk in a target population (e.g. phasing out coal-fired power stations and replacing them with gas) (Graham and Wiener 1997b, 25). Second, interventions may substitute one type of risk for another in the same population, (e.g. treating a headache with certain anti-inflammatory medication could cause nausea and digestive issues) (Graham and Wiener 1997b). Third, interventions can cause the same risk to be transferred to a different population (e.g. relocating a polluting industry offshore) (Graham and Wiener 1997b). Fourth, interventions can lead to risk transformation, creating new risks for a different population (e.g. policies that discourage the use of nuclear power, resulting in greater reliance on fossil fuels) (Graham and Wiener 1997b).

Categorizing risk tradeoffs in this manner helps highlight the different decision-making challenges that they are likely to present (Graham and Wiener 1997b, 25). For example, interventions that transfer or transform a risk to a different population arguably present more complex ethical challenges compared to interventions that will continue to affect the same population (35–36). One intervention may present multiple types of tradeoffs which will further compound these challenges. This is likely to be the case for solar geoengineering, which could substitute one type of climate risk for another. Solar geoengineering could also transfer or transform climate risks to other countries/regions and to future generations. A broad approach to risk identification for solar geoengineering is necessary to identify and contend with multiple types of risk tradeoffs.

After identifying countervailing risks and characterizing risk tradeoffs, the next challenge is deciding what action to take. Risk tradeoff analysis is a rational framework in that it assumes the overarching objective of decision-makers and regulators is to reduce overall exposure to risk (Graham and Wiener 1997b, 36–37). Graham and Wiener, therefore, recommend that the ideal course of action is to pursue "risk-superior moves." These are actions that address the target risk without introducing countervailing risks (1997b, 36–40) or convert countervailing harms into benefits (Weiner 2020, 2139). Risk-superior moves generally do not appear by happenchance and are usually the product of significant effort and innovation by scientists, experts, and entrepreneurs (Graham and Wiener 1997b, 40). When it comes to climate change and solar geoengineering, risk-superior moves will not be realized without significant research funding, incentives for innovation, and support for the exchange of ideas and information (see Graham and Wiener 1997b, 40).

While risk-superior moves are preferable, they are not always available, affordable or practical, and pursuing them could present significant opportunity costs (Graham and Wiener 1997b, 37–38). Where a risk-superior move is not possible, Graham and Weiner suggest that the following factors can help decision-makers evaluate target and countervailing risks: (1) the probability of risks materializing; (2) the size of the population that will be exposed to each risk; (3) the certainty of risks and gaps in scientific knowledge; (4) the type of adverse outcomes expected; (5) the extent to which tradeoffs will result in an uneven distribution of risk, especially among vulnerable populations; and (6) when the risks are likely to materialize (1997b, 29–36). These factors are grounded in a number of case studies that apply risk tradeoff analysis, including medical therapies and pollution control. In addition to these factors, decision-makers should also consider any "ancillary" benefits or "co-benefits" that might flow from the intervention (Rascoff and Revesz 2002, 1766–1767; Wiener 2020, 2139). Such factors could be incorporated into risk assessment frameworks for solar geoengineering to help develop a more holistic understanding of the nature of the target risks presented by climate change and how a solar geoengineering activity might affect those risks. The expertise of natural and social scientists will be essential to quantify these factors.

Quantifying each factor is one thing, but the process of weighing them up is undoubtedly more complex. Risk tradeoff analysis does not purport to provide decision-makers with an objective, mathematical formula to weigh up these factors and decide which risks to accept and which to avoid. Graham and Wiener acknowledge this limitation and indicate that subjective factors can play a significant role in this regard, such as the values of decision-makers and the subjective opinions of experts (1997b, 31). These subjective factors can shape risk tradeoffs from as early as the risk identification stage. For example, regulators and decision-makers may place different weight on different types of risk. Governance frameworks may therefore prioritize minimizing certain types of risks over others (i.e. risks to current, as opposed to future, generations) and, as a consequence, dedicate more resources to understanding the nature of such risks (Graham and Wiener 1997b, 21).

It may also be difficult for decision-makers to weigh up competing risk factors on purely objective grounds. One such instance is where there are significant degrees of scientific uncertainty regarding target and/or countervailing risks. It may be impossible to objectively quantify the degree of scientific uncertainty, leaving more room for subjective considerations to shape decision-making (Graham and Wiener 1997b, 31). According to Graham and Wiener (1997b, 34), decision-makers will likely exercise a value judgment if the types of risk are so widely dissimilar that they cannot be objectively compared. As noted above, transferring or transforming a risk to another population may present decision-makers with profound ethical dilemmas that cannot be resolved by comparing objective, quantifiable factors.

These issues are important to reflect on in relation to solar geoengineering and climate change. Both involve scientific uncertainty, and advancements in scientific understandings of climate change are not being matched for solar geoengineering (Harrison et al. 2021, 3). According to Harrison et al., there is an "information asymmetry rendering normative comparison of risks highly challenging." In other words, there is no objective scale against which different levels of uncertainty and risk can be compared. It is often said that solar geoengineering will produce "winners and losers" across the globe. The potential for solar geoengineering to disproportionately affect developing states and vulnerable populations raises ethical concerns that are unlikely to be resolved by utilitarian considerations. In this context, objective, quantifiable factors can help guide decision-making, but subjective factors are also likely to play a significant role.

Using risk tradeoff analysis, this section has provided a more detailed understanding of what risk tradeoffs are and what they might involve in the context of climate change and solar geoengineering. The next section considers the extent to which a risk tradeoff approach might promote solar geoengineering decision-making that aligns with greater human responsibility and judicious use of power over nature in the Anthropocene.

## Can Risk Tradeoff Analysis Promote a Responsible Approach to Solar Geoengineering?

A key step in promoting responsible use of human power in the Anthropocene is for humankind to recognize the nature and extent of its power and influence over the Earth. As explained by Hamilton (2017, 39), humans have radically and, in some cases irreversibly, changed Earth's processes. Humans had become "geological agents," with the population and technical capacity to cause planetary change (Chakrabarty, 206–207). At the same time, the Earth system has become more unstable, reacting to human influence in unpredictable ways (Hamilton, 15). In this new reality, holistic approaches are needed to better understand the likely consequences of human action and inaction. The research, development, and potential deployment of solar geoengineering are no exception.

Risk tradeoff analysis could encourage decision-makers to more holistically consider the implications of solar geoengineering research, development, and deployment. The underlying premise, that we live in a multirisk world in which human actions can have a plethora of consequences, is in keeping with the new reality of the Anthropocene, where humans have become active agents in the development of the Earth system. Compared to traditional, "siloed" approaches to risk assessment, risk tradeoff analysis recognizes that the "real world is not a series of separate risks, but a web of multiple causally interconnected risks and opportunities" (Wiener 2020, 2139). By encouraging a broader and more sophisticated approach to risk identification, risk tradeoff analysis could be a useful tool for developing a deeper appreciation of human influence in Earth systems.

From a practical perspective, adopting a broad approach to risk identification and assessment for solar geoengineering presents significant challenges. It will necessitate considering cumulative impacts from multiple activities by different actors across long timescales. This will be a time and resource-intensive process. It will require high levels of cooperation and coordination between state and non-state actors, and potentially also different international regimes. Limits will need to be set in order to keep such a process manageable and ensure that risk assessment does not unnecessarily delay action. The first "tough decision" that international policy-makers are likely to face in developing rules for solar geoengineering risk tradeoffs is to decide what the minimum scope of risk assessment for solar geoengineering ought to be, to strike a balance between breadth of assessment and practicability. Such decisions will limit the potential for a risk tradeoff approach to enhance our understanding of human power.

After identifying what the different tradeoffs are, decision-makers would then need to choose what action to take regarding solar geoengineering, assuming that risk-superior moves are unavailable. Risk tradeoff analysis provides objective factors that decision-makers can use in weighing up competing risks, but it does not tell decision-makers how to reach a decision. As explained above, subjective factors (i.e. value judgments) are likely to play a significant role in risk tradeoffs regarding solar geoengineering. The role of value judgments in risk assessment is a commonly recognized phenomenon (see Rozell 2020). For example, the IPCC in its guidance on risk for authors states that "balancing [risks] inevitably relies on individual or collective value judgments, including whether risks are viewed as manageable, intolerable or existential" (Reisinger et al. 2020). Subjective factors, assumptions, and judgments likely to affect solar geoengineering decision-making need to be accounted for, otherwise, they can "transform seemingly objective assessments into stealth policy advocacy" (Rozell 2020, 29).

Risk tradeoff analysis does not provide a framework for identifying what those values are likely to be or how to shape them. Adopting this approach in governance and risk assessment frameworks therefore will not provide a bulwark against ecomodernist or other values from influencing decision-making on solar geoengineering research development and deployment. At best, risk tradeoff analysis may provide a foundation for identifying when value judgments are likely to have greater influence in decision-making (i.e. where there are high levels of uncertainty, or where risks are so dissimilar that they cannot be objectively compared). On its own, this is unlikely to lead to greater humility and restraint concerning solar geoengineering. However, it may open up conversations about how to foster such values in environmental decision-making, not just for solar geoengineering but for other Earth system interventions in the Anthropocene. Such proposals include large-scale carbon dioxide removal, de-extinction, and high-tech ecosystem restoration (see Reynolds 2021).

## Conclusion

This chapter considered the potential of a risk tradeoff approach to contribute to solar geoengineering governance. It used Graham and Wiener's framework of risk tradeoff analysis to develop a better understanding of what risk tradeoffs are and how decision-makers can engage in this process. In addition to considering its merits in governing risk, this chapter considered whether this approach might promote greater responsibility and humility regarding solar geoengineering. Engaging in risk tradeoff analysis will encourage decision-makers to think holistically about the consequences of engaging or not engaging in solar geoengineering research, development, or deployment activities in light of the target risk of climate change. It can therefore enhance our understanding of the impacts human actions have on Earth systems. However, value judgments and other subjective factors are likely to play a significant role in weighing up competing risks. Risk tradeoff analysis recognizes this issue but provides no guidance on what values should underly risk tradeoffs or how values might be shaped.

This analysis highlights a broader issue for solar geoengineering law and governance. While it is important to develop quantifiable criteria for solar geoengineering risk assessment, law- and policy-makers should not assume that this will automatically result in objective decision-making. We need to carefully consider the values that decision-makers will bring to the table regarding solar geoengineering and climate change, and how these values are likely to influence their decision-making. Further research is needed on how value judgments can be accounted for in governance frameworks and how shared values might be developed for solar geoengineering and other interventions in the Anthropocene.

## Note

1 An exception is cirrus cloud thinning. While typically included in the category of solar geoengineering, cirrus cloud thinning aims to increase the amount of outgoing infrared radiation by thinning high-level cirrus clouds that otherwise trap heat in the atmosphere.

## References

Allan, Richard P. et al. 2021. "Summary for policymakers: Working group I contribution to the sixth assessment report of the intergovermenal panel on climate change." Intergovernmental Panel on Climate Change.

Allen, Myles et al, "Summary for policymakers" in Masson-Delmotte, V. et al *Global Warming of 1.5oC An IPCC Special Report on the impacts of global warming of 1.5oC above pre-industrial levels and related global greenhouse gas emission pathways, in the context of strengthening the global response to the threat of climate change, sustainable development and efforts to eradicate poverty*" Cambridge, UK and New York, USA: 2018 Intergovernmental Panel on Climate Change, Cambridge University Press, 3–24.

Andersen, Kevin and Glen Peters. 2016. "The trouble with negative emissions." *Science* 354(6309): 182–183.

Arias, Paola A. et al. 2021. "Technical summary: Working group I contribution to the sixth assessment report of the intergovernmental panel on climate change." Intergovernmental Panel on Climate Change.

Asayama, Shinichiro, Masahiro Sugiyama, Atsushi Ishii and Takanobu Kosugi. 2019. "Beyond solutionist science for the Anthropocene: To navigate the contentious atmosphere of solar geoengineering." *The Anthropocene Review* 6(1–2): 19–37.

Brent, K., J. McGee and A. Maguire. 2015. "Does the 'no-harm' rule have a role in preventing transboundary harm and harm to the global atmospheric commons from geoengineering?" *Climate Law* 5(1): 35–63.

Burdon, Peter D. 2020. "Ecological law in the Anthropocene" *Transnational Legal Theory* 11(1-2): 33–46.
Cairns, Rose C. 2014. "Climate geoengineering: Issues of path-dependence and socio-technical lock in." *Wiley Interdisciplinary Reviews: Climate Change* 5(5): 649–661.
Chakrabarty, Dipesh. 2009. "The climate of history: Four theses." *Critical Inquiry* 35(2): 197–222.
Crutzen, Paul J. 2006. "Albedo enhancement by stratospheric sulphur injections: A contribution to resolve a policy Dilemma?" *Climatic Change* 77(3–4): 211–219.
Crutzen, Paul J. and Eugene F. Soemer. 2002. "The Anthropocene." *Global Change Newsletter* 41: 17.
Decision adopted by the conference of the parties to the convention on biological diversity at its tenth meeting: X/33. Biodiversity and climate change, 10th mtg, Agenda Item 5.6, UNEP/CBD/COP/DEC/X/33 (29 October 2010) paragraph 8(w) ('Decision X/33').
Dooley, Kate, Ellycia Harrould-Kolieb and Anita Talberg. 2021. "Carbon-dioxide removal and biodiversity: A threat identification framework." *Global Policy* 12(1): 34–44.
Doyle, Alister, "Solar geoengineering? Not in our skies, say Indigenous groups" 10 June 2021 The Christian Science Monitor https://www.csmonitor.com/Environment/2021/0610/Solar-geoengineering-Not-in-our-skies-say-Indigenous-groups.
Graham, John D. and Jonathan Baert Wiener (eds.). 1997a. *Risk vs. Risk: Tradeoffs in Protecting Health and the Environment*. Cambridge, MA: Harvard University Press.
Graham, John D. and Jonathan Baert Wiener. 1997b. "Confronting risk tradeoffs." In John D. Graham and Jonathan Baert Wiener (eds.), *Risk vs. Risk: Tradeoffs in Protecting Health and the Environment*. Cambridge, MA: Harvard University Press, 1–41.
Grieger, Khara D., T. Felgenhauer, O. Renn, J. Wiener and M. Borsuk. 2019. "Emerging risk governance for stratospheric aerosol injection as a climate management technology." *Environment Systems and Decisions* 39(4): 371–382.
Hamilton, Clive. 2017. *Defiant earth*. Cambridge, England: Polity Press (ebook·edition).
"Hand off Mother Earth! Manifesto against geoengineering." October 2018 ("Manifesto"). https://www.geoengineeringmonitor.org/wp-content/uploads/2018/10/home-new-EN-feb6.pdf.
Harrison, Nicholas, Janos Pasztor and Kai-Uwe Barani Schmidt. 2021. "A risk assessment framework for solar radiation modification." International Risk Governance Center, 15 July 2021. https://www.epfl.ch/research/domains/irgc/spotlight-on-risk-series/a-risk-risk-assessment-framework-for-solar-radiation-modification/.
Jinnah, Sikina et al. 2019. "Governing climate engineering: A proposal for immediate governance of solar radiation management." *Sustainability* 11(14): 3954.
Keutsch Group at Harvard. n.d. "SCoPEx." Last accessed 22 October 2021. https://www.keutschgroup.com/scopex.
Landres, Peter. 2010. "Let it be: A hands-off approach to preserving wilderness in protected areas." In D. N. Cole and L. Yung (eds.), *Beyond naturalness: Rethinking park and wilderness stewardship in an era of rapid change*. Washington DC: Island Press, 88–105.
Lee, June-Yi et al. 2021. "Chapter 4: Future global climate: Scenario-based projections and near-term information. Working group I contribution to the sixth assessment report of the intergovernmental panel on climate change." Intergovernmental Panel on Climate Change.
Lin, Albert C. 2013. "Does geoengineering present a moral hazard?" *Ecology Law Quarterly* 40(3): 673–712.
Lockyer, Adam and Jonathan Symons. 2019. "The national security implications of solar geoengineering an Australian perspective." *Australian Journal of International Affairs* 73(5): 485–503.
McDonald, Jan, Jeffrey McGee, Kerryn Brent and Wil Burns. 2019. "Governing geoengineering research for the Great Barrier Reef." *Climate Policy* 19(7): 801–811.
National Academies of Sciences, Engineering, and Medicine. 2021. *Reflecting sunlight: Recommendations for solar geoengineering research and research governance*. Washington, DC: The National Academies Press. https://doi.org/10.17226/25762.
Nicholson, Simon. 2020. "Solar radiation management." Wilson Center, 30 September 2020. https://www.wilsoncenter.org/article/solar-radiation-management.
Rascoff, Samuel J. and Richard L. Revesz. 2002. "The biases of risk tradeoff analysis: Towards parity in environmental and health-and -Safety regulation." *The University of Chicago Law Review* 69(4): 1763–1836.
Readfearn, Graham. 2020. "Scientists trial Cloud brightening equipment to shade and cool the Great Barrier Reef." *The Guardian*, 17 April 2020. https://www.theguardian.com/environment/2020/apr/17/scientists-trial-cloud-brightening-equipment-to-shade-and-cool-great-barrier-reef.

Reisinger, Andy et al. "The concept of risk in the IPCC sixth assessment report: A summary of cross-working group discussions: Guidance of IPCC authors." 4 September 2020. https://www.ipcc.ch/site/assets/uploads/2021/02/Risk-guidance-FINAL_15Feb2021.pdf.

Resolution LP.4(8) on the amendment to the London protocol to regulate the placement of matter for ocean fertilization and other marine geoengineering activities (adopted on 18 October 2013), Report of the thirty-fifth consultative meeting and the eight meeting of contracting parties, 35$^{th}$ and 8$^{th}$ mtgs, Agenda Item 15, Annex 4, LC 35/15 (21 October 2013) ('LP.4(8)').

Reynolds, Jesse L. 2021. "Earth system interventions as technologies of the Anthropocene." *Environmental Innovation and Societal Transitions* 40: 132–146.

Rouse, Paul. 2021. "The new intergovernmental panel on climate change assessment report: A sobering read." C2G, 16 August 2021. https://www.c2g2.net/the-new-ipcc-assessment-report-a-sobering-read/.

Rozell, Daniel J. 2020. *Dangerous science: Science policy and risk analysis for scientists and engineers*. London Ubiquity Press.

Sámiráđđi. 2021a. "Open letter requesting cancellation of plans for geoengineering related test flights in Kiruna." 2 March 2021. https://www.saamicouncil.net/news-archive/open-letter-requesting-cancellation-of-plans-for-geoengineering.

Sámiráđđi. 2021b. "Indigenous Peoples call on Harvard to shut down the SCoPEx project." 4 June 2021. https://static1.squarespace.com/static/5dfb35a66f00d54ab0729b75/t/60c0a4bac8e3952583139537/1623237819160/Indigenous+Peoples+call+on+Harvard+to+shut+down+the+SCoPEx+project.pdf.

Shepherd, John et al. 2009. "Geoengineering the climate: Science, governance and uncertainty." Royal Society. https://royalsociety.org/-/media/Royal_Society_Content/policy/publications/2009/8693.pdf.

Smith, Wake and Gernot Wagner. 2018. "Straospheric aerosol injection tactics and costs in the first 15 years of deployment." *Environmental Research Letters* 13(12): 124001.

Thiele, Leslie Paul. 2019. "Geoengineering and sustainability." *Environmental Politics* 28(3): 460.

United Nations Secretary-General. 2021. "Secretary-general's statement on the IPCC working group 1 report on the physical science basis of the sixth assessment." 9 August 2021. https://www.un.org/sg/en/content/secretary-generals-statement-the-ipcc-working-group-1-report-the-physical-science-basis-of-the-sixth-assessment.

Wiener, Jonathan B. 2020. "Learning to manage the multirisk world." *Risk Analysis: An Official Publication of the Society for Risk Analysis* 40(1): 2137–2143.

# 18

# THE TRANSFORMATIVE POWER OF RECEPTIVITY

## Building a Smart Political Energy Grid in Response to Planetary Ecological Crisis

*Romand Coles and Lia Haro*

"Anthropocene" is a term in both scientific and popular discourse for the current epoch in which human beings are having a planetary-scale impact on Earth's geological and ecological systems. Etymologically, Anthropocene conjoins the Greek "anthropos" for human, with "cene" from the Greek "kainos," meaning new. "Cene" has been attached as a suffix to every geological epoch in the Cenozoic era – the era of a profusion of "new life" (from "kainos" and "zoon") that began to unfurl 66 million years ago after a meteor caused the fifth mass extinction. Yet, completely scrambling the resonances of new life, the "cene" of the human epoch is more associated with new death – a "sixth extinction" – that may bring the Cenozoic profusion to an end. Of course, as many have previously noted, the term Anthropocene lumps humanity in ways that conceal the enormously discrepant impacts that different human beings and human systems have had in relation to different modes of production, power relations of class, race, coloniality, etc. Terms such as Capitalocene, Plantationocene, and Eurocene have been offered to foreground such factors, as well as the exploitative-extractive character of the contemporary geo-ecological catastrophe.

In addition to these descriptive and analytic (mis)connotations, one might also strategically attach a more *prophetic* ring in the term Anthropocene, a call to new forms of human becoming and action in response to the planetary disaster. Responses to this call vary tremendously. To self-proclaimed "ecomodernists," the Anthropocene is heard as a call to secure human and planetary survival and well-being – a "great Anthropocene" – through hyper-intensification of technological developments such as nuclear fission, nuclear fusion, and genetically modified organisms to greatly increase agricultural and forest productivity. They claim that this will "decouple" human flourishing from environmental damage. Ecomodernist work contains almost no discussion of concentrated political power, economic inequality, or democracy, nor of the historically ongoing violence, exploitation, and extraction hazards associated with their own solutions, nor the strongly technocratic tendencies of their favored technologies (Asafu-Adjaye et al. 2015, 1–32).

More widespread responses to the Anthropocene tend toward reorienting liberal democracy and regulating capitalism in hopes of generating political, economic, technological, and social changes capable of mitigating ecological catastrophe to the extent possible and enhancing

 DOI: 10.4324/9781003388081-24

adaptive capacities in the face of changes we are unable to avert. Such efforts include calls for a Global Marshall Plan to combat climate change (Gore 1992, chapter 15) and various versions of a Green New Deal. These plans seek to foster substantial shifts away from fossil fuels toward ecologically sustainable economies that generate substantial redistributive effects, such as employment opportunities and income, and address long-standing issues of environmental injustice. While proponents of Green New Deals affirm rapid technological shifts, they tend to focus on renewables, efficiency, and innovations with far greater affinity with biological and ecological systems than the "ecomodernists" (Benyus 1997). The primary forms of agency and power in this paradigm continue to be liberal states (in collaboration with subnational governments and international regimes) and capitalist economies. It remains unclear whether and how these institutions and systems will be able to muster a steady stream of genuinely transformative political power that moves beyond the familiar patterns of offering "too little, too late," given the entrenched powers, binds, limits, and anti-democratic malignancies of neoliberalism. Typically, while proponents of these "solutions" make general references to the importance of "civil society," "deliberative planning," "stakeholders," etc., much too little attention is given to modes of democratic agency and power beyond states and corporations.

The pervasiveness of neoliberal political-economic blockages in combination with the increasing extremity of our ecological predicament, is leading growing numbers of people around the world toward more radical – and radically democratic – prophetic responses to the call for a new or renewed anthropos. Though Naomi Klein's major book on climate change, *This Changes Everything: Capitalism versus the Climate*, appeared in 2014 just prior to the widespread popular use of the term Anthropocene (and she has since been critical of it for reasons alluded to above), the radicality of the response she articulates – her own and those of movements she discusses – is apparent in her title (Klein 2014). Klein joins a critique of the catastrophic climate change wrought by capitalism with a searching, prophetic call to change *everything*, including, most importantly, *how* we strive to generate democratic change.

Beyond the systemic confines of states and capitalist corporations, Klein robustly locates the most hopeful power for generating transformation in growing networks of extremely diverse democratic social movements. From myriad Indigenous movements around the world to the so-called Cowboy-Indian alliance, to suburbanites resisting fracking, to the advocacy of environmental nonprofits, to local and regional publicly-owned and cooperative green initiatives, to the divestment movement, and more, Klein imagines political power for change being generated most significantly through a decentered network joining the agency of diverse constituencies. Beyond the gentler connotations of "civil society," she coins the term "Blockadia," both to name the "roving transnational conflict zone" (Klein 2014, chapter 9) where people are putting their bodies on the line to confront corporations and state power, and to make clear that powers of radical democratic mobilizing, organizing and contestation are crucial for creating urgent, necessary transformation. Insofar as states and some corporations continue to play important roles in this process (and they do), it is primarily insofar as they are transformed by being relocated in a different topography of powers – no longer at the commanding heights of sovereignty but rather situated within these imminently co-creative and conflictual networks of alternative agencies, in ways that alter major institutional operations and orientations: their purposes and limits, their leadership, system dynamics, incentives, and accountability.

Among the most promising aspects of the emergent social movements in Klein's account of what we might call Anthropocene democracy is how they are beginning to alter dominant understandings and practices of democratic capacities to create change. In widening catalytic margins, they are beginning to alter our sense of the character of new beginnings, or what Hannah Arendt calls natality, as such (Arendt 1958). They are shifting understandings of human agency away from notions of an exclusively human capacity of individual or collective subjects to spontaneously initiate action that stands apart from and over against the qualities, relationships, dynamics, and energies of the human and more-than-human world.

In marked contrast, the powers to generate newness that we increasingly discern in the emergent movements in Klein's narrative are generated precisely *in and through radically entangled, receptive and responsive relationships with the broader world of human and nonhumans – the perpetual birthing all around us* (Coles 2016 and 2018). Natality is itself born of intersections among widely distributed energies and agentic stirrings, and our powers of natality are enhanced as we pay attention and tend to this complex fabric. In multiple dimensions, the movements by which Klein is most taken are beginning to practice a notion of natality – and democracy – as *the power of receptive agency*. Their wager is that generating capacities to begin something new – new forms of becoming human in response to the Anthropocene – will require leading communities with our attentive ears, mustering up full-bodied receptivity to other constituencies across entrenched lines of historical conflict, acting receptively and responsively in relation to sentient nonhumans struggling to survive and thrive, cultivating attentive responsiveness to macro-ecological crises that manifest in heat waves, storms, droughts, fires, rising tides, and die-offs that are happening ever more frequently. The locus of our co-creative capacity for initiating change lies not in the subjective sovereignty of states, corporations, individuals, or even movements but in these myriad relational forms of profound attentiveness, responsiveness, and interweaving.

Yet we have so little time to veer away from the very worst scenarios of catastrophe, very little time to *change everything* that must shift if we are to do so. How could the profoundly slow work of careful, attentive, tending and weaving together of vastly distributed agencies stand a chance of coming together in swift collective action? And how could such a democratic assemblage possibly hope to muster enough political power not only to resist, displace, and transform states and economic organizations but simultaneously co-create alternative, ongoing patterns of providing right livelihood for people and ecosystems all across the planet? Do not the centrifugal, fissioning tendencies witnessed in Occupy gatherings debating pizza orders for hours, Monty-Pythonesque modes of identity politics, and regular feuding among environmental groups engaged in different modes of seeking change all seem to render these possibilities highly doubtful?

Nevertheless, there are reasons to be not unhopeful. Klein's call to change everything recalls Theodor Adorno's brilliant remark in *Negative Dialectics* that, "in the right condition, as in the Jewish *theologoumenon*, all things would differ only a little from the way they are, but not even the least can be conceived now as it would be then." This inconceivable radicality of the little differences of all things, he writes, is not some abstract idea hovering over the world. Rather, "we can talk of it only insofar as it keeps arising in reality, brought about by this context" (Adorno 1973, 299). In what sense is this hopeful? Amidst all the centrifugal, fissioning tendencies in our world today, Klein's account and others' bears witness to a receptive, responsive turning, among so many people who are stretching (often of necessity) beyond comfortable limits in ways that, through little practices of differing, begin form a network that might radically change everything. This, as we see it, would be the genuine newness of Anthropocene democracy.

To make this possibility plausible and to contribute to enhancing its probability, we provide the image of a smart political energy grid and discuss grassroots environmental politics in light of it. A smart political energy grid hinges on modes of receptivity that are radically nontechnocratic and emerging in environmental social movements. Nevertheless, the potential power of such a grid is dramatically illustrated and enhanced by the images of smart energy grids that are emerging at the cutting edges of technology.

Smart energy grids emerging today are built around tremendous receptivity and responsiveness among myriad modes of different energy production and use. Sensors along these grids enable different, highly distributed modes of energy production to modulate responsively in relation to each other's outputs and demand requirements. Sensors within many of the devices and appliances on the user end are similarly receptive and modulate in response to signals of aggregate energy supply and demand. In these ways, instead of centralized energy production conveyed through a relatively dumb grid to oblivious and statically operating appliances, a highly diverse, decentralized, and mutually modulating energy system can generate power more efficiently, cheaply, and usefully. The power of smart energy grids exceeds the energy production it enables insofar as its technological flexibility and techno-hospitality *foster* technological change toward renewable energy production and enable us to supplant the old grid and centralized production systems that have been rushing us headlong toward ecological collapse. It also enhances our potential to supplant the centralized and hierarchical modes of political power that correspond to centralized production and dumb grids – especially mega-states and mega-corporations that have long generated exploitation and extractive colonialism. The powers of smart energy grids are, then, manifold.

We believe that smart energy grids inspire a mode of responsive and receptive political engagement that would be necessary to transform the social and political landscapes of the Anthropocene as radically as smart energy grids transform the technological landscape. We would argue that such socio-political transformations are as urgent and necessary as the technological. Moreover, they are conditions of possibility for co-creating a smart energy grid quickly enough and with sufficient capacities to powerfully combat climate catastrophe and environmental injustice. We define a smart political energy grid as a dense network formed by highly receptive and responsive interconnections among different modes of environmental action – including broad-based community organizing, lobbying, and policy work of large environmental groups, environmental justice organizing in marginalized communities, nonviolent movements mobilizing direct action, environmentalism organized around the flows of everyday life, Blockadia, and more. A smart political energy grid begins to form as each of the different modes becomes more attentive to the capacities and limits of the others (and its own) and as they increasingly modulate in relation to each other through this growing receptivity and responsiveness. This enhances their capacities to collaborate and their collective powers to avert catastrophic climate injustice and generate democratic commonwealth and ecological sanity. Increasingly transformative actions generated through these collective powers could then form positive feedback loops in which increasing success bolsters organizational propensities toward further attentiveness and smart grid-like dynamic collaborations, in ways that, in turn, generate greater transformative power.

We begin with a discussion of smart energy grids in order to tap into a certain power of analogy, after which we again mark the important differences of a smart political energy grid so that this power may compound further and become useful.

## Imagining a Smart Political Energy Grid

As we seek to build new modes of resilient, expansive power in the face of ecological catastrophe, we find it useful to take some political cues from innovations in power generation in the technological sector. Generating the requisite and resilient power to alter today's political-economic systems hinges upon developing a smart *political* energy grid analogous to smart energy grid technologies that are currently emerging as an alternative to older grids associated with fossil fuel energy production.

Great leaps have been made in recent decades in the development of renewable energy. Indeed, experts in the technological aspects of renewable energy transition tell us that our biggest challenges in that domain do not concern *whether* sources of clean energy – such as solar, wind, geothermal, and hydroelectric – can fully power the world. The fast pace of renewable energy innovation makes it clear that they already can. Rather, they argue that the most needful innovations today involve creating a "smart grid" that can interweave these different sources of power quickly, and responsively to draw on the distinct proclivities of diverse sources and overcome their inherent limitations – like dependency on highly variable sources of sunshine, wind and water flows (Hawken 2017, 30–31).

Achieving a complete shift to renewable energy hinges upon creating a highly supple and responsive smart energy grid that can foster interconnections within and among several distinct forms of distributed renewable energy. This, in turn, must be linked with nimble interconnected modes of use and storage. Lacking this grid, energy production rises and plunges every day and night with a high degree of variability, insufficient reliability, and wasteful inefficiency. When the sun shines brightly or the wind blows strongly in one area, surges of energy production generate excess power that is evanescent and unusable in that particular location while much needed elsewhere or at another time. The different supply sources do not combine into an energy generation system that can respond flexibly to the changing needs of the whole and its diverse parts. Overproduction and shortfalls oscillate in chaotic ways. The system thus lacks the resilient capacities to successfully power modern societies in a transition toward zero carbon energy emissions. The variability and distributed quality of renewable energy make it less predictable and reliable than fossil fuel energy, which slows the transition.

To move beyond the impasse, new smart grids must create nimble, highly adaptive networks capable of multi-directional communication across many different, inter-articulated sources that can rapidly modulate flows in response to shifts in supply source, demand, and storage. A smart energy grid teems with myriad highly adaptive supply and storage capacities, finely tuned sensors along the powerlines that capture and report real-time information on multi-directional flows (sometimes at intervals of over 50,000 per second), advanced meters, as well as receptive home appliances, thermostats, and plugs that are connected to the internet and sensitively respond to real-time modulations in overall supply and demand. Such grids function more like *neurological systems* than the comparatively one-directional systems of centralized grids. They also create favorable conditions that invite and stimulate further innovations in these modes of production and use (Momoh 2012). The image of a smart grid is pivotal, Rifken argues, not only for energy transition, but for a "third industrial revolution" more generally – involving water, transportation, food, materials, information, and more (Rifkin 2011).

While the technological development of smart grids is a crucial hinge for a sustainable ecological future, the cultivation of a smart *political* energy grid may be even more important. This is so, in no small part, precisely because smart energy grids will almost certainly not be constructed in time to avert ecological collapse without the powers of a smart political energy grid to overpower the intransigence of centralized fossil fuel political-economic powers. Analogous to smart grids in the energy sector, a smart political energy grid can responsively interweave myriad modes of *political* and *social* energy production – each with its own proclivities and variabilities – to build an extremely powerful, flexible assemblage of transformation. In other words, creating transformation in our times requires cultivating mutually receptive, responsive political and social energies, and interweaving them into a powerful political energy smart grid with the capacities to resiliently and reliably displace the older grid of corporatized state and global powers that fuel the inferno. A smart political energy grid would flexibly interconnect these social and political configurations together in new, more responsive, and complementary – mutually amplifying – relationships so that they form a political energy system that is sufficient to power the urgent transformative work and action we need. At the same time, a smart political energy grid can ensure that the potential new technologies bring for political and economic decentralization and myriad forms of public ownership is realized.

Of course, this analogy has important limits. Smart energy grids operate through fine-tuned sensors that measure *quantitative* flows. Moreover, pricing and marketized exchange value play an integral role in modulating diverse supplies and myriad demands. These operate according to highly presentist temporalities that devalue deep-time inheritances from the past in relation to climate and ecosystems, and discount futures that exceed several years to nearly zero.

In contrast, the sensors of different modes of political energy production and use must be *qualitatively* tuned and form patterns of highly responsive collaboration based on difficult, discerning dialogues and judgments among different groups seeking to generate powerful, multifaceted contestation and resilient forms of transformative Anthropocene democracy. The sensors of smart political energy grids must be multi-temporal. They must be tuned to histories of colonialism, white supremacy and class exploitation, and deep-time geo-ecological inheritances, as well as future precarities and emergent possibilities of myriad interconnected systems. They must negotiate powerful connections between what Adrienne Rich called forms of "wild patience" (Rich 1981) that can birth unexpectedly rapid forms of change and the growing weight of what Martin Luther King Jr. frequently called the "fierce urgency of now" in his later speeches and sermons. Thus grid-like networked relationality is, paradoxically, constructed in the dialogical interplay among many forms of receptivity and responsiveness (including those of nonhuman beings and systems) that are, in an important sense, "ungrid-able" (Meyers 2017). By ungridable, we have in mind mutual receptivities and modulating modes of interactive responses that are irreducible to one hegemonic mode or logic of sensing.

These characteristics make forming a smart political energy grid more challenging than creating the technologically governed smart energy grids that are emerging today. At the same time, however, as our lives become more plugged into smart energy grids we may become informed and energized in ways that increase our propensities to lend ourselves more fully to negotiating these challenges in generative ways. The present especially calls us to this work insofar as relatively separated modes of political action repeatedly show their futility in the face of dominant contemporary powers and pending catastrophe. Moreover, the paradoxical project of building a smart political energy grid through relationships that hinge on each of the different nodes cultivating a reflexive awareness of the "ungrid-able" dimensions of the others, would infuse this new grid-like politics with energies that persistently escape the neoliberal marketizing tendencies of technological smart energy grids – and proliferate possibilities beyond the imagination of the latter.

Thus, we think the contemporary political project is to create qualitative receptors tuned to the capacities, needs, and limits of different modes of action, and mutually supportive responsiveness in and across countless forms of endeavor. These manifold receptors would be based on an increasingly confirmed sense that complex, integrated work and action are usually far superior to the efforts of a single mode. Becoming receptive in this context requires both knowledge of the typicalities and histories of mutually supportive interrelationships, as well as a sensitivity to emergent communication in relation to new situations. Becoming responsive requires a capacious sense of how the power of several different smartly interrelated modes usually far exceeds any one of them, and how these relations are often difficult, full of tensions, and in need of frequent readjustment – yet well worth the effort of "staying with the trouble" (Coles 2016; Haraway 2016).

As we suggested, smart political energy grids are likely a condition of possibility for building techno-smart energy grids rapidly enough to avert the worst of climate catastrophe. Moreover, just as techno-energy grids may help inspire and inform the political energy grids that enable them, the reverse is also true. Where the dominant powers today are pushed and pulled to veer away from ecological disaster, they typically seek to shape any future smart energy grids in ways that continue to enhance their own hegemony. By contrast, a smart political energy grid might not only thwart capitalist colonization of emergent grids but also – in a dialectical twist – alter some of the technological aspects of smart energy grids themselves so they might incorporate qualitative receptivities and values into their transmissions in ways we cannot yet imagine.

If we fail to co-create a highly responsive, multi-directional political energy smart grid, dominant forces – centralized, hierarchical, and extremely unequal forms of political and economic power formed in relation to extractive power generation and dumb grids – will likely succeed in impeding transition. We will be unable to form a robust, resilient, and systemically powerful alternative. This will not only mean too little too late; it will also foment waves of increasingly authoritarian responses to severe disruptions, displacements, and shortages that are certain to otherwise occur. But, by orienting toward building a smart political energy grid, the diverse resources and powers of different movements, communities, and individuals can come together to create and sustain mutually nurturing currents of electricity – currents that can change everything. In that process, they can scramble and overwhelm the defenses of corporate governance while creating a smart-flexible platform for an ecologically resilient democratic world.

## Power Potentials and Failures in Environmental Politics

Several modes of promising change have emerged in the last 50 years, each with many valuable characteristics necessary for altering the present catastrophe. Many of the power shortcomings of the various, valuable approaches to environmental change reflect a disarticulated system of variable energies and powers similar to current renewable energy technologies. At present, these different modes of democratic response to the ecological crisis are often isolated or even at odds with each other rather than interconnected in mutually receptive and evolving ways. The limitations and disconnections of today's efforts to foster environmental political change reflect their historical evolution in relation to each other and to the dominant order.

A brief historical sketch of three major modes of environmental politics can help identify distinct powers that are indispensable for creating a smart political energy grid, as well as ways to modulate and connect them to address the current political power failures of which growing numbers involved are becoming aware.

### *The Big Ten*

In the decade following the historic Earth Day rallies and teach-ins of April 1970, several large environmental organizations grew in strength and power with others emerging on the stage. These included organizations like Natural Resources Defense Council, Environmental Defense Fund, World Wildlife Fund, Sierra Club, and Greenpeace. Together, these organizations have historically focused primarily on reforming national policy.

As they evolved in the 1970s, these larger environmental organizations almost entirely disregarded or marginalized the energetic and imaginative modes of grassroots participation and radical vision that characterized many social movements of the 1960s. Instead, they focused on accruing multi-million-dollar budgets that enabled them to operate with high-salaried executive directors and expert staff of analysts, lobbyists, and marketers. Many of them accepted funding from major corporations, made corporate partnerships central to their strategy, and have corporate representatives on their governing boards. With the notable exception of the Sierra Club, most have lacked serious accountability to their members, beyond communications sufficient for membership renewal.

Although important capacities in relation to lobbying, policy, and legislating have emerged in these large organizations, and some admirable victories have been won, their political-economic approach has demonstrated only weak capacities for addressing major problems and attenuating malignant power dynamics. Several decades of this approach (in isolation) have proven to be woefully inadequate in relation to climate change, the sixth extinction, and incredibly severe patterns of environmental injustice associated with continuously expanding, extractive, exploitative, and excremental circulations of global capitalism.

The heart of the problem is that these organizations lack "people power" – which comes from cultivating connective "resonance" with the public and organizing a broad base of members around environmental transformation. This leads them to seek to advance their goals by pursuing an insiders game (and becoming insiders), narrowing their relational networks, working comfortably within the dominant framework of current systems, hardening their sense of limits in relation to the interests of those in power, and becoming inattentive to issues of resonance with peoples everyday lives, and so forth (Gottlieb 2005, chapter 4; Meyer 2015). This strategy limits their interventions to very modest, incremental policy shifts – interspersed with backlash in some countries. At the same time, they often much too cheaply enhance the credibility of state and corporate institutions.

The Group of Ten environmental organizations operate with a political-economic imaginary analogous to the older centralized fossil fuel energy grid. Their modes of one-directional communication with membership, corporate governance, and state-focused campaigns reinforce the central towers of power while suppressing innovative growth of distributed renewable political energy and transformative power generated by grassroots democratic responsive organizing and action. This problem of unreceptive disconnection manifests externally, as well, when organizations seek to gain credibility in the halls of power by branding themselves in sharp opposition to the unprofessional, unruly character of more radical grassroots organizations, foreclosing coalitional, network possibilities for creating a smart political energy grid.

## The Environmentalism of Everyday Life

In response to the repeated disappointments of this approach, many of those hungering for radical change have shifted their energies toward withdrawing from the massive circulations through which so much political-economic power is entrenched – industrially produced food, energy, clothing, mega-finance, transport, water and so on. These modes of *resistance* simultaneously create *alternative* flows of things, beings, and money that are becoming much more responsive to challenges of local and planetary ecological resilience, and advance more egalitarian, democratic, and inclusive forms of community and political economy (Coles 2016; Schlosberg and Coles 2016).

These experimental rearticulations of a new sustainable, ethical materialism are visible in local organic farming networks, farmers' markets, community and school gardens, community-based alternative energy processes, alternative water practices and governance, more just and sustainable forms of growing, making and distributing clothing and other goods, community-based finance and economic development, and more.

Beginning in the margins, these modes of political transformation generate deep resonances in people's everyday practices, homes, community lifeworlds, and bodies in ways that tend to proliferate *regenerative* political energy for further action. The practices associated with these environmental social movements of everyday life tend to tangibly improve health and generate pleasures, conviviality, solidarities, colorful community spaces, and patterns of mutuality. In these ways, they generate remarkably renewable forms of political energy fueled by enlivened senses of taste, sight, smell, hearing, feel, vitality, and so forth. These highly renewable and interconnected forms of political energy, in turn, create positive feedback dynamics for deepening change.

For many years these were not recognized as social movements – nor did they necessarily consider themselves as such – because their primary modes of action were not focused on protest, political advocacy, or altering national politics. The initiatives sprung forth through highly distributed, often separate, efforts that reflected a wide range of diverse aspirations. In the past decade, we see a great increase in organization, both across different initiatives within localities and among different places. The movements of everyday environmental justice work below the traditional political radars directly on the material and ethical conditions of our lives, our relationships with each other, and with the nonhuman world in which we are embedded. They are profoundly political insofar as they constitute collective democratic modes of power for addressing how we govern our co-existence.

These movements are also political insofar as they aspire to generate broader patterns of change beyond the specific places in which they tend to be rooted. They seek to do this more by replicating successful initiatives across different localities – scaling *out* alternative political initiatives, actions, energies, more than scaling *up* – and have created institutions across multiple scales, from local to national, that advance these purposes. In this way, these modes prefigure alternative distributed energy grids and patterns of responsive, rapidly evolving, localized circulation (Schlosberg and Craven 2019).

One example of this is seen in the growth of farmers' markets in the United States from about 2,000 in 1994 to 8,600 registered today, including many in impoverished urban communities of color that tend explicitly to questions of social and environmental justice. The broad and deep transformative potentials of such new materialist social movements are striking in terms of their rapid growth in the past couple of decades and their potential to create more radical political and economic change over the long haul (Coles 2016).

However, as more than a few proponents have worried, these efforts are currently somewhat analogous to a peloton of fast bicycles heading toward promising horizons at the same time that huge fleets of semi-trucks are surging in the opposite direction toward the abyss. Even as the alternative flows are developing at impressive rates, the mega-circulations that are devastating people and the planet continue to intensify even more quickly.

Unlike the environmental politics of the Big Ten organizations, these environmental movements are resonant, responsively interwoven with the materiality of people's everyday lives and with the nonhuman world, and they generate renewable political energy. Yet advancing their scope and pace to sufficiently respond to the escalating ecological catastrophe would require participants in everyday environmental movements to supplement their creative engagements with contestational politics against disastrous mega-circulations. Building the power necessary for serious contestation, in turn, would require that they collaborate extensively to create an ever-more expansive network of diverse peoples and political modes.

Movements for everyday sustainability presently have an uneven track record in the face of these two challenges. Many engaged in everyday environmental politics do become involved in new relationships, experiences, modes of knowledge, and emergent aspirations that draw them powerfully into broader organizing projects as well as feisty struggles for systemic change (Gottlieb and Joshi 2010).

Yet the situation is complicated. While there are many examples of alternative practices such as farmers' markets and urban agricultural spaces where people form relationships and greater justice across differences, there are also many cases in which people gather in ways that are quite segregated by culture, race, and class.

Moreover, for many, the emphasis on caring well for one's immediate community and context can lead to forms of engagement that remain both too exclusively local and too homogenous. The solace found in this work may amplify energies of withdrawal associated with the disappointments of frequent defeats at the hands of mega-powers. Some of these dynamics may inadvertently impede the advance of transformative everyday politics insofar as they unplug broader and more intense challenges to subjugative and ecologically catastrophic aspects of the order, as well as macropolitical work to create political-economic regulatory environments more favorable to their endeavors.

Thus, while this politics is extremely promising, it also sometimes harbors trajectories of disconnection that could potentially undermine its capacities to generate resilient, large-scale change.

## Direct Action

During the past dozen years, growing numbers of people around the world have begun sensing the insufficiency of lower-voltage action repertoires of everyday environmentalism, nonprofits, formulaic protests, and corporatized representative politics in the face of the unfurling climate inferno. As mentioned above, the need to disrupt extraction, stop carbon overload, and halt pipelines has led to the development of the diffuse transnational conflict zone of blockades and occupations that Klein calls Blockadia. Simultaneously, 350.org's Fossil Free Divestment campaign (350.org, n.d.) has utilized nonviolent direct action – particularly in the form of campus sit-ins – in an effort to politicize and halt higher education investments in the fossil fuel industry. New coalitions *across differences* have also begun to develop along with the more disruptive grassroots action repertoire, including the Green-Brown alliance of Lock the Gate in Australia, the Cowboy-Indian alliance in North America, and Indigenous networks around the world.

Since 2018, Extinction Rebellion (XR) and the global school strikes have sent important, much needed, jolts of energy into climate politics and provoked increasing attention to the climate emergency in myriad communities, mainstream media, and within some representative political bodies (Extinction Rebellion 2019; Hallam 2019; Read 2020). With a shock doctrine of the left, these new movements seek to deploy higher voltage jolts to the system as part of a broader proactive effort to pull the emergency brake on carbon-extractive civilization altogether (Coles 2016, chapter 4; Jones 2018).

Entirely rejecting a politics of compromise, XR demands that nations declare a climate emergency, commit to zero carbon emissions by 2025 and establish assemblies of people selected by lot to deliberate and decide upon policies that will achieve these goals. At the same time, around the world, school climate strikers have staged walkouts in which millions of youth and their allies around the world refuse to participate in "business as usual." Their street actions take the form of protests. However, both their youth leadership and their calls for increasingly general strikes for climate action raise the specter of a form of *mass resistance* that could become more powerful than any seen thus far.

Emblematic of broader trends in emergent direct-action politics, XR has deployed a strategy of dramatic disruption in the hopes of provoking mass arrests in major cities to rapidly increase attention to the climate emergency and trigger active support from a small but crucial percentage of the population. Typically, their actions involve street theatre and the disruption of traffic on highways, in train stations and airports, and so on. XR strategists believe that this approach can create quick change, wagering that if actions succeed in one country they can become globally contagious. While surges of "wake up" energies are indispensable for creating systemic change in the face of invested political and economic interests driving ecological crisis, the extent to which XR will be able to escalate further and cultivate resilient transformative power remains in question. As serious limitations in their strategy are generally characteristic of many campaigns that focus on mobilizing intense evanescent disruptive action, it is important to consider them here.

XR has been significantly inattentive to the way their actions actually resonate in the everyday lives of those whom they disrupt. They have been formed without dialogue among diverse communities. Challenges of receptive and resonant connectivity have appeared repeatedly in the criticisms levied by many people of color about how XR's overwhelmingly white middle-class composition is undermining its goals, strategies, and tactics (Wretched of the Earth 2019). Their dramatic actions are one-directionally focused on projecting a message, while ignoring receptive engagements with the broader publics whom they are disrupting. Images of traumatized people in blocked traffic and commuters furiously attacking XR protesters in a train station in working-class London disclose a *resonance problem* that has manifested repeatedly.. After conducting such actions for a few years (not including the pandemic pause), repeated public opinion polls in many countries suggest that the predominant result has been widespread alienation, significant anger at activists, as well as minimal and declining support even among those for whom climate change is the most important issue we face.

Perhaps predictably, on December 31, 2022, XR released a public announcement entitled "We Quit", calling for an indeterminate pause on direct action and a rethinking of strategy, the need for coalitions with diverse communities, etc. (XR, 2022). Their announcement was hauntingly like one released a decade earlier by the group, Rise Up!, after a few years of their own noble efforts at direct action petered out in the face of similar resonance problem. Meanwhile, a set of recent XR spin-off groups in several countries have conducted direct actions in museums – tossing tomato soup and super gluing themselves to great works of art in public museums. Given the ongoing unpopularity of these actions, it appears they are largely dramatizing impotence, desperate isolation, and a paucity of political imagination, rather than generating resonant calls concerning climate catastrophe and the mode of action they seek to advance.

One central problem is that this common direct action paradigm continually relies on magical thinking: Dramatic actions will magnetically increase participation and numbers of arrests. Intention statements about diverse coalitions can substitute for the painstaking hard work of learning with diverse groups about how this might be advanced in contexts of racism and colonialism. The 3.5% participation rate that some scholars claim can lead to the nonviolent overthrow of a dictator that will be equally effective against a democratically elected government, a dense system of powers, and a circulatory apparatus that runs through our lives. Regime change will rapidly lead to citizens' assemblies and a successful five-year pathway to net-zero. Revolution in one country will spread like a virus around the globe.

Yet these paradigmatic assumptions about whirlwind-like temporal and spatial acceleration are not merely wrong. In every instance they serve to divert adherents from staying with difficult questions, searching reflection, and efforts toward creative innovation. They divert people from the hard work and actions that would be required to accomplish anything close to what is prophesied in the short term, let alone to generate the renewable social and political energy required to advance transformation over the longer term. Ironically, this paradigm for direct action relies on a vision of political transformation as energized from relatively centralized power generators (i.e., brief direct action and arrests, combined with dramatic messaging) that produce shocks and surges through an old political energy grid to bring down the system.

We think that political modes that can generate intense shocks and disruptive energies are indispensable to any smart political energy grid that could create systemic change in the face of the political economic system that is driving catastrophic climate change and injustice. Our questions concern: First, what sort of shocks and disruptions might be far more powerful and resilient? As we discuss below, direct action groups would do well to experiment with *mass receptivity shocks* as an integral to their actions. Second, how might these reimagined high voltage actions be rearticulated so that they are immanently interconnected with other political modes, both energized by and energizing a broader smart political energy grid?

## Receptive Relationality and Arts of Broad-Based Organizing

Largely underplayed in the manifold politics of environmental justice are practices that might organize a web of interconnected energies that each contribute vital powers for broad systemic change. The relational practices of building power through broad-based organizing would be necessary for creating the connections so vital for a smart political energy grid. Even if movements do not ultimately succeed in turning the tides of climate change, such practices would be invaluable for surviving the catastrophic elements that may already be "locked in," as well as crafting new forms of commonwealth in their wake.

Broad-based community organizing focuses on deepening and expanding *relational* cultures, as the wellsprings of renewable grassroots political power. In every case, these initiatives give rise to an "organization of organizations" – a network of diverse congregations, community centers, nonprofits, neighborhood associations, unions, and schools. These processes often last for decades and serve as powerful venues through which thousands of people become regularly active democratic citizens, regardless of legal status. They form extensive political relationships across differences that are rarely bridged, in order to work on common challenges and build commonwealth through organized people power. This type of organization is practiced in several large grassroots democracy networks – most prominently the Industrial Areas Foundation (IAF), but also Faith in Action, Direct Action Research and Training Center (DART), and Gamaliel – that are engaged in scores of cities across the United States, as well as newer efforts in the UK, Australia, New Zealand, Germany, and elsewhere.

Unlike large environmental organizations, broad-based community organizing efforts, when they are working well, engage large numbers of their members on a regular basis. They generate quotidian relational political power in several important ways. They organize *within* member organizations to deepen the relational networks and democratic capacities internally, so the agency of each organization increases with more active and connected members. They also focus on proliferating a web of responsive relationships *among* the different organizations – a smart political energy and action grid, if you will – that generates substantial collective powers that were usually nonexistent before (Warren 2001; Wood 2002).

One of the most vital practices in this mode of organizing is the one-on-one relational meeting. In these one-on-one meetings, people sit down together and listen deeply to each other as they share stories of how they – and their families, neighborhoods, organizations, and communities – are personally experiencing the challenges created by the dominant political-economic order. The aim of a good one-on-one dialogue is to discover the relationships that connect one to broader communities and engage in mutual discernment about why these relationships are important to the other, as well as how they are motivated in relation to public matters. As organizers coach people who are new to the art of engaging in one-on-ones, they emphasize that people are not isolated individuals with separate interests. Rather we are profoundly relational and our interests are formed and met in these relationships, an idea often articulated with Hannah Arendt's illuminating etymological reflections on interest as rooted in the Latin *interesse*, or *between being*. The practice of having people draw stick figures with their myriad mutually constitutive connections with others, groups, institutions, and the material world is frequently used to explore this idea.

In a one-on-one, each person listens to and shares the ethical sources and textures of life that orient and inspire their dreams, fears, anger, and engagement for a better future. Through these meetings, people "get real" with each other and connect in ways that we so often otherwise avoid. When done well, they are practices that revivify the cultures within organizations and, even more importantly, cultivate relationships that bridge and erode the stratifications, prejudice, separations, and indifference that are so much a feature of our world.

In these processes, participants begin not only to *understand* others. They gain a sense of how others *sense* and *feel* the world. The emergence of more full-bodied senses across differences is enhanced because community organizing processes intentionally shift locations of meetings so that people find themselves moving beyond comfort zones in places they have not typically frequented with care, attention, and dialogue. As the broader organization moves meeting locations to the tables in diverse organizational spaces, our embodied imaginations of where democracy happens expand and become more mobile so that no place, institution, mode of interaction, or group of people is insinuated to be the privileged site of democracy.

Democracy moves. As it does, we begin to understand a bit more about life in different ways, with diverse people, according to different traditions. Something utterly powerful and energizing often happens in this process – a new awareness of differences and commonalities arises, a widening sense of different ways of working together. Enthusiastic feelings of political possibility rattle the cages of long-embodied cynicism. As we move beyond our comfort zones, creative strategic paths and actions are spurred beyond the invariant rutted highways so often taken by the "usual suspects." (Coles 2005)

In all these ways, such organizing processes generate renewable, distributed political energy. An enormous quantum of human energy is required to sustain the oblivion, defensiveness, and hostilities lodged in so many aspects of contemporary life. When we connect in ways that are deep, and deeply political, these exhausting patterns begin to dissipate and renewed vitality is freed for other purposes. *Relational political engagement* is often highly energizing because connecting deeply with each other's sorrows, frustrations, anger, aspirations and emerging common dreams creates electrical charges of emotion between people. Currents of possibility begin to flow between people and as they do we begin to forge new powers more capable of gaining political ground. When this work is carefully cultivated, richer forms of political symbiosis can be co-created (Coles 2016, chapter 1).

Even though such organizing involves hard work and no effort can overcome the precariousness of democracy in highly anti-democratic orders, the track record of relational organizing – in terms of levels of resilient dialogical engagement, powerful action, and significant-if-modest change – is remarkable in many places.

Yet, this political mode also has some serious limitations that must be critically questioned. A large part of their resonant power and resilience stems from their persistent, receptive connections with concerns voiced by people in relation to their everyday lives. Wary of how abstract ideologies often fail to connect with people to create genuinely democratic change, broad-based organizing models typically frame their approach by focusing on very specific "issues" understood in polemical opposition to "problems" that are abstract and deemed to be "unwinnable." While this is a good starting point, creating a stark divide between *issues* and *problems* cuts broad-based organizations off from addressing larger patterns of injustice, ecocide, and suffering. It also stymies reflection on larger systems of power that create problems on a planetary scale (Coles 2016, chapter 3).

For example, while they may organize around issues like lead toxicity in poor neighborhoods, they tend to greatly minimize discussion of broader patterns of environmental injustice linked to racism and capitalism along with the need for broad political-economic transformation. Bracketing attention to more systemic problems, they also marginalize attention to the myriad modes of organizing that would be required to address them. Thus, the very way in which they *generate* political energy also tends to *limit* it and impedes their capacity to form responsive relationships with organizations who don't fall under their umbrella, as well as movements working to address "problems" in a variety of ways – like climate emergency and direct-action responses.

This effectively unplugs the otherwise quite brilliant connective capacities of broad-based organizing, so that too often they fail to co-create relationships that could nurture precisely the sorts of more diverse multi-modal political networks we need today.

## Building a Smart Political Energy Grid

Each of the political modes discussed produces vital political energies needed for genuine ecological transformation. Amplifying the collective transformative capacities of radical and ecological democracy now requires powerfully bringing them together in unprecedented ways.

There are good reasons for each of these modes to maintain their differences, insofar as each has vital, specific capacities that might be diminished if collapsed into other approaches. The question is not one of creating a homogenous unity. The manifold dynamics of the present catastrophe demand something far more sophisticated: generating explicitly imagined and carefully crafted system dynamics among variegated powers that remain distinct while also sufficiently collaborative to drive the broad, deep, and rapid changes that must be made.

All modes can benefit greatly if they learn ways both to selectively incorporate important elements from the others and to intentionally collaborate. To do this, each mode needs to develop receptors that, like smart energy grid components, enable two-way and multi-directional communications constitutive of more supple interaction. *Relational arts* involving listening, patience, tarrying with ambiguity, embracing tensions, becoming familiar with different lifeworlds, and co-creative imagination will clearly be crucial for this.

Broad-based community organizing can contribute greatly to forming receptors and connectors in the smart energy grid of environmental politics. However, to do so will require changing the dichotomous issue-problem relationship so that the two are brought into an open-ended, democratically negotiated dialectic that expands a sense of the range of political actions that may be acceptable and desirable. Dialogical learning oriented in this way reflects among multiple instances of the most specific aspects of our lives – for instance, the unliveableness of particular buildings during heat waves, the lack of access to energy efficiency and renewables in poor neighborhoods, the unresponsiveness of political representatives to people deeply concerned about these things – to generate expansive insights into increasingly systemic patterns of power, suffering, aspiration, and action.

This sort of democratic inquiry cultivates forms of organizing that, while imminently rooted in the knowledge that people draw from their everyday lives, generate broader critical analysis that newly illuminates problems, strategies, and visions of change. Relatedly, deeper understandings of systemically entrenched power relations tend to open reflection upon a broad range of action modalities that may be required for meaningful transformation. All of this opens significant pathways for expansive dialogue among groups that act in different ways and thereby fosters previously tabooed coalitional possibilities.

This small shift could create vital receptors where we currently find a dulled apparatus, blocked lines, and impeded connections. While the focus of broad-based democracy groups would remain upon generating relational organizing for grassroots power, this modulation would enable them to better utilize the expertise of groups (such as nonprofits) more singularly focused on a single-issue-problem domain (like climate justice). In turn, broad-based organizations could lend the more energetic engagement of their diverse members to key events in which single-issue organizations would benefit from people power they cannot muster as well on their own (for example, at public meetings of governments, with representatives and administrators). There are numerous examples where such relationships are forming. The key is to cultivate them more intentionally to rapidly generate thicker and more powerful webs of cooperation.

If we turn our attention to the challenges and opportunities facing environmental movements reshaping the material flow and conditions of everyday life, further possibilities for generating receptors and connectors come to light. As we have suggested, the work of these movements is indispensable for vivifying change in the present and modeling sustainable ecological practices that can be scaled out. Yet these modes of engagement sometimes replicate broader societal patterns of inequality, indifference, and minimal relationships across diverse groups.

Here, too, we think inviting people to engage in discussions (for instance, at farmers' markets, community gardens, or wherever) through which challenges across communities and groups can be linked to analyses of broader systemic problems and more transformative horizons could be helpful. This would foster perspectives that are more energetically *charged* with felt needs for greater collaboration across differences and places.

The idea is not that most sustainability movements should become broad-based relational organizing initiatives. Rather, they might employ some of these relational arts selectively, where bridging divides seems most pressing and the transformative opportunities are deemed to be greatest. Just as importantly, they might seek connections with broad-based community organizing initiatives in ways that enable environmental movements to tap into relational networks that have already bridged important divides. This would enable everyday environmental movements to more easily and responsively proliferate initiatives to different communities. It would enable broad-based community organizations to become more involved in projects that tangibly improve the well-being of their members – and join in advocating for such projects.

How might forms of direct action and dramatic street politics develop receptors and connectors that would enhance their capacities as well as help compose a broader smart political energy grid? Imagine if such receptors were *built into* the very drama of these actions. Instead of being guided so thoroughly by the image of a bullhorn, we might also imagine our actions together as collectively manifesting large, powerful *ears*, as well. The substantial power of many movements has come in large part from *listening attentively to others*, as well as from *loud dramatic expression* (Coles and Hauerwas 2008). Imagine if, in addition to shouting slogans and "speaking truth to power," activists sought to create potent performances that engage bystanders, not as a passive audience, but as fellow citizen-participants to be invited, welcomed, and curiously engaged in intense – but open-ended and dialogical – dramas around, for example, climate emergency:

- How is it affecting our lives, the places we love, the futures of our children?
- How is this making people *feel*?
- What are your fears about a transition toward ecological sustainability?
- How might we stop the madness and create a better world together?

Imagine, too, large actions that frequently fanned out into neighborhoods to creatively solicit receptive dialogue with a broad range of people. Not only would actions that involved such full-bodied receptivity prefigure a politics of democratic solidarity, but they would also likely muster remarkably magnetic powers capable of unplugging much of the defensiveness of many people otherwise too ready to ignore usual forms of protest. Such actions would likely powerfully engage a much wider range of the political spectrum to draw forth people's creative involvement and energies.

A lot of learning can happen when we begin to engage in dialogue with those beyond our comfort zones. One thing we suspect rebellious groups might quickly come to realize is that building power requires engaging in regular dialogues in diverse communities to build a wider network of relationships, foster understanding, and generate political energy. In contrast to the need among community organizing groups to devote more energy to reflection ascending from issues to broader patterns of power and transformation, groups like XR would do well to devote more energy in the opposite direction. They may generate many more connections by shifting beyond their nearly exclusive focus on the broadest problems (climate emergency) to include specific issues that are making people's everyday lives unlivable *now* – like buildings that bake people in heat waves, fires that threaten communities, poorer neighborhoods consistently located in flood zones, myriad aspects of food insecurity, and so on.

Connections between direct-action organizations and broad-based organizing initiatives that already excel in this political modality could be mutually beneficial here. The deeper and more continuous organizing efforts of broad-based groups constitute relational networks, substantive insights, and political energies that could be drawn into more complementary relationships with punctuated periods of direct action.

Imagine, for example, how much more powerful a period of nonviolent direct action would be if coordinated broad-based organizing involving hundreds of small group discussions on issues *and* problems of climate change in diverse organizations and communities. Imagine too, how carefully crafted disruptions of direct-action groups might enhance the public resonance and power dynamics in well-timed broad-based organizing meetings on specific issues with political representatives.

Of course, it is probable that the radical militancy of even more receptively and relationally oriented, nonviolent direct-action organizations would create substantial challenges for broad-based organizing efforts seeking to build collaborative relationships across a much wider political spectrum. And many communities are far too vulnerable, or for other reasons not favorably disposed, to risk arrest. Thus, though the relationship between these two modes of energetic engagement might be carefully crafted for complementarity, it is likely that strong distinctions, certain respectful distances, and some tensions would likely remain.

For one more example of how smart-grid receptors and connectors might develop among different modes, consider what might happen if the large environmental nonprofits selectively adopted lessons from broad-based organizing, so that they enhanced their capacities to draw more upon the energetic engagement and insights of more diverse memberships. This would increase their "people power" in ways that would allow them to move beyond the limits that accompany their heavy reliance upon corporate money and relationships, and their too-heavy accent on playing an insider game with high-level state actors. This democratization would expand their freedom to enter into relationships with groups organized according to other political modalities in ways that would, in turn, likely magnify their own powers and the collective powers of an emergent smart political energy grid – especially if the other modalities were to embark upon analogous journeys of learning and selective modulation as well.

The large environmental organizations would continue to focus on employing their knowledge, experience, and elite relationships to advocate for policy changes in large systems of power. Their engagements in relational organizing would be significantly less deep than those of broad-based community organizing groups. Yet significant, if more modest efforts to enhance democratic engagement among their members would increase their power, this power would be further enhanced through collaborations with, say, broad-based organizing efforts working on related issues and environmental movements of everyday life generating change that make aspirations for a better future tangible, enjoyable, and energizing right now. They would also benefit from shifting power dynamics that could be co-created in collaboration with groups oriented toward creating intense contestation by means of large, dramatic, and disruptive actions.

We emphasize again that the idea is not to blend modalities into a homogenized mix. The goal is to create a responsive smart grid that cultivates alternating energy currents to and fro among them. The brief examples we've sketched out are intended merely to illuminate a few possibilities of what this might look like. We suspect that they are just the tip of the proverbial iceberg. Many others would emerge in the process of co-imagining and bringing to life a smart grid for democratic and ecological transformation, including those that reshape and resituate electoral politics and representative governments in ways that render them more responsive to communities, ecosystems, and commonwealth rather than corporate fossil fuel capitalism.

Benefits in each case of responsive interconnection would likely enhance the magnetism of a smart political energy grid horizon and energize further efforts to build receptors and connectors in ways that just might generate a cascading evolutionary democratic process that could begin to address the tremendous challenges of cascading extinction. While such a radical shift may seem far-fetched, the more responsive relationships emerging across diverse constituencies and social movements, along with the searching questions that accompany such relationships, give us reason to hope that diverse *modes* of political engagement may become more receptive, responsive, and interconnected. In such a reorientation, echoing Adorno, these modes would in important ways differ only a little from how they are now and bring their diverse, substantial powers into the composition of a smart political energy grid. Yet in so doing, they would become nearly unrecognizable themselves and create a constellation that would change everything. This, it seems to us, would be the shape of a powerful response to the call for Anthropocene democracy.

## References


350.org, n.d. "350 Celebrates a Decade of Action." Accessed May 12, 2021. https://350.org/350-campaign-update-divestment/.

Adorno, Theodor. 1973. *Negative Dialectics*. New York: Continuum.

Ahmed, Nafeez. 2019. "The Flawed Social Science Behind Extinction Rebellion's Change Strategy." *Resilience*. Accessed May 12, 2021. https://www.resilience.org/stories/2019-10-31/the-flawed-social-science-behind-extinction-rebellions-change-strategy/.

Al Gore. 1992. *Earth in the Balance: Forging a New Common Purpose*. New York: Taylor & Francis.

Arendt, Hannah. 1958. *The Human Condition*. Chicago, IL: University of Chicago Press.

Asafu-Adjaye, John et al. 2015. "An Ecomodernist Manifesto." Accessed May 1, 2021. http://www.ecomodernism.org/.

Benyus, Janine. 1997. *Biomimicry: Innovation Inspired by Nature*. New York: William Morrow & Company.

Coles, Romand. 2005. "Moving Democracy: Industrial Areas Foundations Social Movements and the Political Arts of Listening, Traveling and Tabling." *Political Theory* 32(5 October): 678–705.

Coles, Romand and Hauerwas, Stanely. 2008. *Christianity, Democracy and the Radical Ordinary: Conversations between a Radical Democrat and a Christian*. Eugene, OR: Wipf and Stock Press.

Coles, Romand. 2016. *Visionary Pragmatism: Radical and Ecological Democracy in Neoliberal Times*. Durham, NC: Duke University Press.

Coles, Romand. 2018. "Biocultural Polymorphic Fields, Receptive Agency and Symbiotic Evolution beyond the Anthropocentric Wave." *Theory & Event* 21(2 April): 495–507.

Extinction Rebellion. 2019. *This is Not a Drill: An Extinction Rebellion Handbook.* New York: Penguin Press.
Extinction Rebellion. 2022. "*We Quit*". Accessed January 2, 2023. https//extinctionrebellion.uk/2022/12/31/we-quit/.
Gottlieb, Robert. 2005. *Forcing the Spring: The Transformation of the American Environmental Movement.* Washington, DC: Island Press.
Gottlieb, Robert and Joshi, Anupama. 2010. *Food Justice.* Cambridge, MA: Massachusetts Institute of Technology Press.
Hallam, Roger. 2019. *Common Sense for the 21st Century: Only Nonviolent Rebellion Can Now Stop Climate Breakdown and Social Collapse.* Self-published. Accessed May 12, 2021. https://www.rogerhallam.com/wp-content/uploads/2019/08/Common-Sense-for-the-21st-Century_by-Roger-Hallam-Download-version.pdf.
Haraway, Donna. 2016. *Staying with the Trouble: Making Kin in the Chthulucene.* Durham, NC: Duke University Press.
Hawken, Paul, ed. 2017. *Drawdown: The Most Comprehensive Plan Ever Proposed to Reverse Global Warming.* New York: Penguin Press.
Jones, Graham. 2018. *The Shock Doctrine of the Left.* Oxford: Polity Press.
Klein, Naomi. 2014. *This Changes Everything: Capitalism Versus the Climate.* New York: Simon and Schuster.
Meyer, John. 2015. *Engaging the Everyday: Environmental Social Criticism and the Resonance Dilemma.* Cambridge, MA: Massachusetts Institute of Technology Press.
Meyers, Nicole. 2017. "Ungrid-Able Ecologies: Decolonizing the Ecological Sensorium in a 10,000 Year-Old NaturalCultural Happening." *Catalyst: Feminism, Theory, Technoscience* 3(2): 1–24.
Momoh, James. 2012. *Smart Grid: Fundamentals of Design and Analysis.* Hoboken, NJ: John Wiley and Sons.
Read, Rupert. 2020. *Extinction Rebellion: Insights from the Inside.* Westerville, Ohio: Simplicity Institute.
Rich, Adrienne. 1981. *A Wild Patience Has Taken Me Thus Far: Poems 1978–1981.* New York: W.W. Norton and Company.
Rifkin, Jeremy. 2011. *The Third Industrial Revolution: How Lateral Power Is Transforming Energy, the Economy, and the World.* Adelaide: Griffin Press.
Schlosberg, David and Coles, Romand. 2016. "The New Environmentalism of Everyday Life: Sustainability, Material Flows, and Movements." *Contemporary Political Theory* 15(2): 160–181.
Schlosberg, David and Craven, Luke. 2019. *Sustainable Materialism: Environmental Movements and the Politics of Everyday Life.* Oxford: Oxford University Press.
Warren, Mark. 2001. *Dry Bones Rattling: Community Building to Rebuild American Democracy.* Princeton, NJ: Princeton University Press.
Wood, Richard. 2002. *Faith in Action: Religion, Race and Democratic Organizing in America.* Chicago, IL: University of Chicago Press.
Wretched of the Earth. 2019. "An Open Letter to Extinction Rebellion." *Common Dreams.* Accessed May 12, 2021. https://www.commondreams.org/views/2019/05/04/open-letter-extinction-rebellion.

# PART VII

# Imagination and Utopia

# 19
# IMAGINED UTOPIAS

*Benjamin J. Richardson*

Overcoming the environmental vicissitudes of the Anthropocene requires imagining both the future we desire and divesting our lives of the world we abhor. The latter are the fragments of an incipient dystopia already encountered, associated with climate breakdown, mass extinctions, and other cataclysmic upheavals. Identifying from our lives the activities that threaten to unleash this dystopia – like fossil fuel industries, throw-away consumerism, and deforestation – is just part of forging radical change in the Anthropocene. Equally important, societies must conjure empowering ideas of the world they desire: a planet in which humankind co-exists with rather than dominates other biota (Gillespie 2019).

Imagination is indispensable to directed societal change, generating beacons of hope that can motivate and guide positive action (Sheppard et al. 2011, 400). Utopian imagination may range from the fantastical, out-of-this-world, to more realistic or plausible scenarios of a future we earnestly believe is attainable. The most pessimistic, beset by climate grief, may aspire pragmatically to achieve merely the least-worst outcome in an increasingly dystopian world, an outcome some may associate with "adaptation" to climate change and other environmental adversities. Others may dream of revolutionary change to be forged out of the looming environmental emergency.

Human imagination, believe some critics, has yet to play these empowering roles in navigating through the planetary crisis. Political scientist Manjana Milkoreit (2017, 62) identifies "a failure of imagination concerning the reality and severity of the risks of climate change" and "a failure to imagine solution pathways and visions of possible and sustainable futures" as relevant to the "lackluster response" of societies to contemporary environmental problems. Others apparently more familiar with the history of environmental thought will appreciate that there has been some progress in utopian imagination, such as in deep ecology and eco-feminism, in addition to experiments to create green utopias today.

Utopian imagination is not just about individuals' personal ruminations, even though they can be the wellspring of important ideas. Imagination needs to be embedded in a collective process by which ideas for a better future are shared and debated because at stake is the creation of a desirable future for whole societies and the biosphere at large rather than merely any personal nirvana. The mechanisms to facilitate such collective imagining are diverse. The arts and literature can help us to conceive of a future beyond people's immediate sensory perception and experience (Richardson 2019). The legal and political systems can also contribute, such as through official forums by which citizens can deliberate on environmental policy options. Such

DOI: 10.4324/9781003388081-26

deliberation may also occur outside of or in defiance of officialdom, such as associated with environmental protest activism.

Investigating how green utopian imagination may support radical social change out of the destructive Anthropocene, this chapter makes five contributions to the field. First, I examine notions of "imagination" and "utopia" in their foundational senses in order to understand how they may underpin aspirational environmental thinking. Second, I identify the relevance of the law to green utopians, and in particular its role in nurturing the imagination processes for social change. Third, I explain how green utopian imagination is never far from its alter ego – the looming dystopian world. Fourth, responses to apocalyptic scenarios are examined to show the risks and opportunities posed by dystopian thinking for progressive change. Finally, I identify some contemporary efforts to establish elements of green utopianism, from the creation of eco-communes to the restoration of degraded landscapes.

Before proceeding with these issues, I wish to acknowledge one future scenario – an imagined utopia without humankind. An environmental nirvana may be realizable without nothing more than simply waiting for humankind to disappear, to become extinct, as is the fate of all species eventually. In his best-seller, Alan Weisman (2007) predicts that, liberated from humankind's environmentally poisonous burden, the planet would quickly recover within a few thousand years, and within a few million years only the most virtually indestructible plastics and radioactive materials would linger, likely buried out of harm's way. The ability of nature to rebound from the worst assaults is already evident; at Chernobyl, in the former Soviet Union, animal life has blossomed since the 1986 deadly radiation leak, and on the Korean peninsula, the unoccupied demilitarized zone has become a haven for wildlife. In his imaginary future, Weisman predicts traces of humankind would persist in just a few places, such as Moscow's deep underground subway and Mount Rushmore's carvings of American presidents. However, as the disappearance of humanity is not something most will contemplate – though in 1991 some activists launched a Voluntary Human Extinction Movement, which calls for all people to abstain from reproduction (The Voluntary Human Extinction Movement n.d.) – this chapter will focus on imaginary utopias that include *Homo sapiens*.

## Imagination and the Imaginary

"To know is nothing at all; to imagine is everything," so said novelist Anatole France (1844–1924), a Nobel laureate. Imagination can spawn manifold perspectives and possibilities about our understanding of the world, leaping infinitely beyond what one directly experiences or knows first-hand (Brann 1991). Imagination enlivens our understanding of the future, endowing us with the capacity to envision and cultivate the meaning of alternate states for the outlook of Earth and humankind. Scientists can provide data that postulate future scenarios, from a planetary hothouse to a rewilded nature, but we need imagination to render such knowledge more meaningful in terms of goals, hopes, and options. Without imagination, we would be stubbornly tethered to the present, struggling to contemplate a different future. Given the distended and complex timescales of the natural world and anthropogenic impacts on it, which dwarf the fleeting lives of individual persons, imagination is indispensable to appreciating the Anthropocene and our hopes for a safe and sustainable future (Richardson 2017). Although imagination begins with thinking individuals' minds, rather than institutions such as business corporations or nation-states, the individual faculty of imagination impregnates the institutional life of modern society through the roles individuals hold, whether as judges or legislators, and in the forums and processes by which citizens come together to debate and forge their future.

Related to imagination, as a thought process, is the concept of the "imaginary," as a point of reference whether descriptive of current conditions or aspirational in character. For Cornelius Castoriadis (1997, 145), the social imaginary is a society's ability to create for itself "its singular way of living, seeing and making its own existence." Often only vaguely sensed or articulated, the social imaginary, suggests Charles Taylor, refers to "ways people imagine their social existence, [...] the expectations that are normally met, and the deeper normative notions and images that underline these expectations" (2004, 23). Manfred Steger and Paul James depict the imaginary as those "deep-seated modes of understanding [that] provide largely pre-reflexive parameters within which people imagine their social existence" (2013, 17, 23). Unlike these understandings of the imaginary, Sheila Jasanoff and Sang Hyun Kim (2015) see imaginaries as also future-oriented and normative, expressing futures that a society hopes to attain.

Whether understood as a collective process of making meaning of the world or a desired future, the social imaginary tends to assume some underlying, shared values in society. Those values are often missing from contemporary environmental policy in our heterogeneous and discordant societies. While there is some congruence of opinion about the desirability of avoiding climate change that harms humanity itself, many people would disagree with any suggestion that the environmental changes associated with the Anthropocene are wholly negative, especially given the perception that exploitation of natural resources generally contributes to human prosperity (Lucas and Warman 2018, 987). Thus, the social imaginary of contemporary life can generate a multiplicity of utopias in which any elements in common relating to environmental and social well-being diminish once specific details are considered beyond vague generalities such as human flourishing and well-being. A further limitation of some understandings of the prescriptive or aspirational social imaginary is they ignore the looming dystopian shadows of an undesirable future, which may be just as important in motivating societal change as utopian dreams – an issue I will return to shortly.

Some scholars are starting to use the imaginary to understand societal expectations and hopes in relation to environmental adversity, particularly climate change (Wright et al. 2013, 647; Levy and Spicer 2013, 659). The latter has become the masthead of a planet in distress, with the public lexicon increasingly acknowledging "climate grief," a phrase coined to capture the anxious, helpless feelings in response to overwhelming environmental degradation (Pikhala 2020). Greenhouse gas emissions have soared to levels unprecedented for eons, and some of the hottest years on record have been endured in the early twenty-first century, associated with forest fires, mass coral-reef bleaching, and melting glaciers (World Meteorological Organization 2020). Climate change is intertwined with other upheavals including loss of wildlife, oceans contaminated with plastics, and other accounts of the Anthropocene familiar to readers that do not need to be repeated here. The Covid-19 pandemic has added another layer of adversity, stoking fears of further uncontrollable pandemics. A nuclear holocaust remains, however, as it has for the past 75 years, the most (un)imaginable horror.

Conversely, we can imagine brighter prospects enlivened by sustainable development policies, local community organization, and democratic renewal. Imagination in this context is closely related to *hope*, the expectation or desire of something eventuating, and its importance to enable surviving the Anthropocene is recognized by many scholars (Muir, Newell, and Wehner 2020). Hope for a better future may simply reflect an optimism that the direst environmental forecasts, from severe climate change to mass species extinction, will not materialize because of advances in technology or better laws. Or the hope may hinge on a spiritual turn toward a more enlightened environmental ethic. Hope can also be passive, a mere expectation without overt creative thinking directed toward devising concrete solutions.

While the foregoing observations speak to how imagination orients people with their future, imagination can also temporally connect us to the *past*. Environmental and human history can never be fully understood as an objective reality; rather, our memories are shaped by the histories curated via monuments, museums, memoirs, and other mediums that are never a perfect facsimile of the past (Groes 2016; Lowenthal 2015). This imagined past can be sanitized to erase history's "losers" – the colonized and vanquished, such as settler society narratives that celebrate the taming of wilderness or the "civilizing" of Indigenous peoples (Mar and Edwards 2010). People may also lack the capacity to imagine the past because of the assumption that current environmental conditions, from the plants and animals they observe to the climate they experience, have existed since immemorial. This amnesia, explains Canadian ecologist Daniel Pauly, leads to "shifting environmental baselines," in which successive human generations fail to discern the incremental attrition in the ecological richness and diversity of nature (1995, 430). The past is thus not simply "the past" but rather inhabits the present that will inform societies' reflections on their current condition and hopes for a better future. More critical imagination can help to reflect on nature's former glories and losses as motivation for progressive social change.

## Green Utopianism

If imagination is the faculty to think about something different from our present reality, utopia is to identify with a particular vision of this alternate reality. The word "utopia" generically means an imagined society or state of affairs idealized for its perfect qualities, though sometimes it refers to a place already encountered. Australia's outback has a place called Utopia, which I visited many years ago during its emergence as a mecca for Aboriginal artists. It was named so in the 1920s by arriving white pastoralists because it was then so lush and populated by numerous kinds of game that could be easily caught – desert landscapes can be misleading to the unfamiliar after unseasonal heavy rains. The term utopia has a much older history than this example, however, having been introduced into our lexicon by English philosopher and lawyer Thomas More in his book *Utopia or the Treaty on the Best Form of Government*, published in 1516, where he contrasted the difficult life of European societies with that of an exemplary society governed entirely by reason on an imaginary island faraway. Around 1595, the famous Flanders cartographer Abraham Ortelius, who lived in Antwerp where More also wrote much of *Utopia*, conjured a map of the fictional ideal that More described (see Figure 19.1). Ortelius' rendering was not random but rather reflected his detailed study of More's book.

Utopian visions have filled literature, art, religion, politics, law, and other domains over the centuries (Levitas 2013). They have idolized a variety of subjects, including futuristic technologies, new socio-political orders, and pristine natural environments. Such visions are not potentially unproblematic, however, for some may become totalitarian master plans or technocentric blueprints, or impossible and impractical ideals. Moreover, the underlying assumption of a perfect society may itself be problematic in its denial of aspects of the human condition, such as fallibility, and the need to accept that every society should be able to democratically evolve and respond to ongoing changes in its cultural and ecological context (Popper 1945). Thus, utopian desires may be most helpful for surviving the Anthropocene when developed as provisional ideas, open to critical and creative development and revision.

Thinking about green utopias has intensified over the past half-century, coinciding with the intensification of the Anthropocene. The utopians may range from detailed green blueprints to vague visions of societies simply co-existing sustainably with their natural surroundings (Garforth 2018).

*Figure 19.1* Map of Utopia, by cartographer Abraham Ortelius, c. 1595.

One strand of green utopianism aspires to build new economic models, aiming to serve people's core needs rather than that of the economic system (capitalism) itself. In *Small Is Beautiful*, Ernst Schumacher (1973) called for decentralizing and collectivizing economic activity under the auspices of local communities. Of similar vintage, The Ecologist magazine's *A Blueprint for Survival*, issued in 1972, outlined the building blocks of an ecologically and economically enduring society (Goldsmith et al. 1972). In recent years, proposals for a Green New Deal, involving top-down, state-led transformation to a post-carbon future, have begun to gain traction with the backing of prominent environmental writers such as Naomi Klein (2019). The Green New Deal feeds off the discourse of sustainable development that emerged in the 1980s, yet emphasizes the visible support of the state over the invisible hand of the market. As a utopian vision reformist, the pragmatic agenda of sustainability has remained problematic for many as it remains embedded in the same institutions and processes of global capitalism that have intensified the Anthropocene (Kenis and Lievens 2015).

Another version of green utopia has been cultivated by deep ecologists, who challenge Western culture's assumption of the ontological divide between humans and nature, and the collusive anthropocentrism in such dualism. Unlike the earlier focus on the limits to growth, which saw humankind as constrained by and dependent on a finite natural environment, but not inherently part of it, deep ecologists, such as Arne Naess (2016) and Bill Devall (1985), start from the interconnectedness of the entire biosphere including human beings. A central element of its ecocentric cosmology is wilderness – an unadulterated place for spiritual and ethical immersion into the natural world. A green utopia comes not merely from better husbandry of natural resources through environmental laws or technological innovations but via a fundamental, grass-roots transformation in our environmental consciousness. Deep ecology is not however a homogenous philosophy: it includes a more politically charged stand of green resistance, as epitomized by Derrick Jensen's call to revolt against human civilization, which he sees as fundamentally incompatible with anything environmentally sustainable (Jensen 2006).

While the deep ecology impulse grapples with what some environmental law scholars see as ethical transformation essential for overcoming the environmental crisis (Bosselmann 1995), the ecocentric utopianism may be too nostalgic for some, and unviable in its implicit yearning for a pre-modern human society such as that associated with Indigenous peoples or pre-industrial agriculture. Moreover, the spiritual strand of deep ecology lacks details on the process of social change to realize its utopian vision (Dobson 1995, 23). Attempts to address this deficit include legal scholars exploring how constitutional law reform could enshrine fundamental pro-environmental values as governing considerations in national and international decision-making (Kotze 2016). Another legal model, also already adopted in a few jurisdictions including Ecuador and New Zealand, endows natural areas such as rivers and mountains with a legal personality, thereby "transform[ing] the status of nature from being regarded as property" to having rights "to exist, thrive and evolve" (Australian Earth Laws Alliance n.d.).

Eco-feminist utopianism is another beacon of hope for some (Mies and Shiva 1993). One of the several strands of eco-feminism postulates that women and the natural environment are exploited in the same, interwoven way by dominating, patriarchal forces, which treat women as a resource to be exploited or plundered. Alternatively, the cultural eco-feminism strand celebrates an empowering affinity between nature and women, picturing the female gender as uniquely affiliated to natural processes through biological experiences, such as childbirth and menstruation, which supposedly render women more sensitive to environmental harm and willing to play a nurturing role in caring for the natural world.

Another utopian future is tied to Indigenous livelihoods, especially in countries such as Australia and Canada with Indigenous First Nations. Some environmentalists believe the path to a greener future lies in adopting or respecting Indigenous cultural practices associated with environmental stewardship (Grim 1997, 139). Australia's Matthew Colloff has extolled the value of Indigenous practices in offering a path to reconciliation for all Australians with their degraded environment (Colloff 2000). In New Zealand, the Maori concept of "kaitiakitanga," meaning the exercise of guardianship over an area, is already enshrined in section 7(a) of the country's Resource Management Act as a guiding principle for environmental managers to follow (New Zealand, Resource Management Act 1991).

The abstract character of some green utopianism, having little traction in mass society outside of academic and legal circles, has led some to look to utopian imaginations found in more accessible sources such as popular literature. Lisa Garforth has identified a number of fiction novels, such as Kim Stanley Robinson's *Pacific Edge* (1995) and Ursula K. Le Guin's *Always Coming Home* (1985), as useful, as "they flesh out and bring to life the proposals of deep ecology" and "invite identification with and empathy for the particularities and contingencies of daily life in an imagined green world" (Garforth 2018, 93). In other words, eco-utopian fiction can help bridge fantasy and reality. This may be particularly useful given many people can easily profess a desire for a green utopia but in practice be unwilling to make personal sacrifices to their own materialistic and consumerist lifestyles. Utopian imagination risks becoming a dangerous flight from reality in which people have an excuse to overlook their own current profligacy or carelessness. Hence, legal and institutional processes remain important to minimize such temptations or insouciance.

## Law and Green Utopias

Law matters both for the journey to reach a green utopia and the arrangements to implement it. The original conception of a utopia, in Thomas More's 1516 eponymous work, centered on a perfect legal and political system. Some scholars have asked whether a perfect society in fact would need laws if law implies limitations on human activities (Eliav-Feldon 1982). One might assume that as law serves to correct social imperfections, it should be redundant in an ideal society that is peaceful and ordered. Miriam Eliav-Feldon (1982, 107–108) identifies in Western thinking three types of ideal society without laws, such as a "paradise for the individual who seeks total freedom from restraint, obligation, and hardship" or "a community of people so learned or so pious by nature that they require no external rules of conduct – instinctively all their actions would be moral." Other legal commentators on this subject, such as Miguel Angel Ramiro Avilés, caution however that the absence of law, and specifically governments to make laws, would make it easy for the weak to be exploited by the strong, and that the pre-conditions for any of the above models of an anomic society could only come about by creating a new human nature that could allow people to co-exist without rules (Avilés 2000, 225, 233).

Thus, a role for law in a utopian society is plausible for undertaking social reform and creating institutions for prosperity and peace More's original conception of a utopia considered law as a fundamental mechanism for its creation and maintenance, serving to address the problems of scarcity of resources and limits to human altruism. Law itself can be an idealized instrument for creating and maintaining social perfection to compensate for the inherent imperfections in nature: "laws were not to be moulded to men but men to be moulded by and to the laws" (Davis 1991, 329, 342). Law thus can underpin utopia rather than be viewed as a sign of its absence.

The important question that follows here is what kind of law does a green utopia need? Scholarship on environmental law has given a plethora of answers that invariably feed off the underlying policies needed to curb environmental degradation, including that natural resources are used sustainably, energy flows from clean renewable sources, and biodiversity is protected and restored (Richardson and Wood 2006). Scholars have also identified legal instruments to implement such policies, many well established, such as environmental impact assessment procedures, land use planning, pollution licensing, and, from the most recent legal innovations, rights of nature. There is no shortage of legal ideas for a green future; the problem is political and institutional – the resistance to undertaking deep reform and the institutional fallibilities that result in ineffective or incomplete implementation of adopted laws. The ambitiousness and efficacy of the law will be shaped by how committed lawmakers are to serious action.

Already, a number of international governance statements, albeit in the realm of "soft law," envision the need for such a fundamental shift. The World Charter of Nature, adopted in 1982 by the United Nations General Assembly, opens with the declaration that "Civilization is rooted in nature, […] and living in harmony with nature gives man the best opportunities for the development of his creativity, and for rest and recreation" (United Nations 1982, preamble). The Charter's substantive provisions would surely be part of an environmental utopia, such as principles that "nature shall be respected and its essential processes shall not be impaired" (Article 1), "the genetic viability on the earth shall not be compromised" (Article 2); "living resources shall not be utilized in excess of their natural capacity for regeneration" (Article 10(a)); and "each person […] shall strive to ensure that the objectives and requirements of the present Charter are met" (Article 24) (United Nations 1982).

Of similar spirit is the Earth Charter, drafted in 2000 after a decade-long dialogue among environmental organizations, that "envisions and builds a shared common idea of what 'ethics for sustainability' could be" (Contini and Pascual 2010, 27; Taylor 2022). Its opening four guiding norms are "respect Earth and life in all its diversity"; "care for the community of life with understanding, compassion, and love"; "build democratic societies that are just, participatory, sustainable and peaceful"; and "secure the Earth's bounty and beauty for present and future generations" (Earth Charter Commission 2000). The remaining sections of the Charter, numbering 16 in total, deal with protecting "ecological integrity," "social and economic justice," and "democracy, nonviolence and peace." Some 50,000 organizations including some governments have endorsed the Earth Charter as of 2021 thus committing themselves "to adopt and promote the values and objectives of the Charter" (Earth Charter Commission 2000). Such international statements are not legally binding and offer little guidance on how to regulate specific activities but may help shift the legal and political culture to spur the progressive development of environmental law.

Law can also assist with the journey of utopian imagination by enabling creative and collective processes to flourish. Democratic processes are one arena, though their susceptibility to short-term thinking and party politics means other institutions and forums are vital for critical imagination. Environmental law itself provides some, such as public inquiries and public consultation processes, in a variety of environmental decision-making. The right to protest and challenge deficient environmental laws and policies is also vitally necessary, which takes us into civil liberties and human rights as buttresses of free association and speech. In some cases, environmental activists may also resort to defying the law through civil disobedience, as exemplified recently by the Extinction Rebellion movement, whose role this chapter will return to later.

## Dystopian Imaginaries

Much thinking about a greener future involves imagining the world we wish to avoid. Pandemics, famines, wars, authoritarianism, mass species extinctions, and other dystopian futures often come to mind in a turbulent, out-of-control Anthropocene. The specter of environmental disaster confronting humankind a generation ago, during the Cold War, was most commonly associated with nuclear war. Today it is climate breakdown, and since Covid-19, pandemics as well. Dystopian fictions often emanate from contemporary socio-political experiences from which we extrapolate possible graver scenarios, as though providing a warning to current generations of the risks they are fomenting. Indeed, in the midst of resource-hungry capitalism and a destructive global pandemic rooted in trespassing on nature's domain, it seems difficult to imagine anything other than humanity's ecological doom (Milkoreit 2017, 62). Dystopian thinking, increasingly felt rather than merely imagined, risks sapping the creative hope needed to imagine and create a green utopia.

In the early 1970s, the first wave of environmental-related apocalyptic futures began to emerge from academic and scientific circles, such as Paul Ehrlich's (1971) warnings about the "population bomb," The Club of Rome's forecasts about the impossibility of exponential economic growth in its seminal report *The Limits to Growth* (Meadows et al. 1972), and the notion of finite natural resources captured by the popular metaphor of "spaceship earth" (Boulding 1966, 3). Such Malthusian gloom of impending overshoot moderated in the 1980s and 1990s as the ebullient discourse of sustainable development took hold, promising a feasible way to overcome the tensions between economic expansion and environmental constraint (World Commission on Environment and Development 1987). Although the sustainability ideal continues to hold sway among policy-makers, as evident in the United Nations' adoption in 2015 of an elaborate set of Sustainable Development Goals (United Nations n.d.), it has not held back increasing public anxiety about deteriorating environmental conditions as scientific evidence is reported in the mass media.

*Figure 19.2* "Blue Marble," Apollo 17 crew, NASA, December 1972.

Also important to shifting environmental consciousness and imagination was the availability of new aesthetics of Earth. With the expanding spatial and temporal scales of anthropogenic impacts, from global warming to marine plastic debris, far from the environs we inhabit, the availability of new aesthetics was important to help raise awareness of environmental change. Some of NASA's earliest photographs of Earth – most famously, the iconic *Earthrise*, taken in December 1968 by the Apollo 8 crew, and the *Blue Marble*, captured in December 1972 by the Apollo 17 crew – were formative such influences (Kelsey 2011, 10, 12; see Figure 19.2). Their social importance was foreshadowed in 1948 by astronomer Fred Hoyle, who remarked:

> once a photograph is taken of Earth taken from outside, is available, we shall, in an emotional sense, acquire an additional dimension … once let the sheer isolation of the Earth become plain to every man, whatever his nationality or creed, and a new idea as powerful as any in history will be let loose.
>
> *(Goldberg 1991, 52)*

The plethora of science fiction literature and films devoted to some variant of global cataclysm has also made it easier for the general public to appreciate possible dystopian futures (Hughes and Wheeler 2013, 1). Hollywood disaster movies like the blockbuster *The Day After Tomorrow* (2004) depict world-altering climate breakdown. In Cormac McCarthy's novel *The Road* (2006), the unnamed protagonist wanders with his son through a bleak, devastated landscape, where social norms have disintegrated alongside ecosystems. Cannibalism, for instance, is rampant in the struggle to survive. Earlier pioneering fictional tales about dystopian futures are Aldous Huxley's *Brave New World* (1932), George Orwell's *Nineteen Eighty-Four* (1949), and John Wyndham's *The Chrysalids* (1955).

Terrifying dystopia is no longer confined to science fiction books or movies. Destructive mega bushfires in Australia and California, the devastating Covid-19 pandemic, and the rise of authoritarian populism in some nation have all been part of our lives in recent times, coupled with growing numbers of governments and legislatures declaring a "climate emergency" (Cockburn 2020) and, with Covid-19, initiating draconian emergency measures to control the pandemic. The future has arrived, marking a decisive shift from thinking just a few decades ago when environmental scholars habitually spoke about the importance of "intergenerational equity" to respect the interests of future generations, as though serious environmental harm including climate breakdown only threatened posterity (Weiss 1989).

## Responding to an Apocalyptic Future

Apocalyptic *imagination* may no longer be necessary, but publicizing it to galvanize governments to take urgent action also risks shocking the public such that hopeful utopian imagination is lost. To a fearful public, climate change may simply become an insurmountable, "wicked" problem, too late to intervene. The language of climate grief and environmental despair has become increasingly prevalent, acknowledging feelings of apathy, helplessness, or anxiety in anticipation of massive environmental upheaval and loss (Head 2016).

Some environmental thinkers believe the natural world is already so degraded and damaged by humankind that it cannot be a source of hope for a better future. Bill McKibben (1989) wrote of the "end of nature" in the Anthropocene, which had consumed the last wilderness refuges and marinated the planet in chemical pollution, even before taking into account runaway climate change. As McKibben explains, "by changing the weather we are making every spot on earth man-made and artificial. We have deprived nature of its independence … without it there is nothing but us" (ibid., 60–61). With most environmental quality indices worsening in the three decades since McKibben's eulogy for nature, his grim conclusion that we have entered a "post-natural" era would seem even more compelling (ibid., 64). On the other hand, McKibben's romantic ideal of an untrammeled pre-Anthropocene world is implausible given evidence of significant anthropogenic environmental change over many millennia before the Industrial Revolution and indeed even before the advent of agriculture (Flannery 1994). Conversely, it is also highly questionable to conclude that nature has ended or ceased – human agency has certainly not become so omnipresent as to neuter all or even most fundamental ecological and biological processes. Indeed, to return to Weisman's thesis in *The World Without Us*, even the direst environmental forecasts may in the very long term be immaterial.

Another perspective, associated with philosopher Timothy Morton (2007), postulates that nature as an ontological category is just a fiction of our imagination, which harmfully separates humankind from its ecological context. Thus, any utopian imagination of getting back into nature, a supposed unadulterated realm outside of our socialized environments, is problematic for perpetuating that dualism. In a similar vein, Bruno Latour (2004, 276) argues that we abandon our fixation on nature as an object of green hope and instead cultivate a view of a more nuanced and interconnected relationship of humankind in the natural world. For utopian imagination, these perspectives challenge the deep ecologists' adoration of nature, rejecting that nature has intrinsic value and spiritual significance. The risk of embracing "ecology without nature," to borrow Morton's words, is that the natural world is rendered even less important in anthropocentric decision-making. A green utopia forged on this premise might celebrate the monetized value of essential ecological "services" and "resources," promote climate engineering, and open wilderness areas to more recreation and tourism – a world that many environmentalists would reject.

Another response to the specter of an apocalyptic future is rebellion. Environmental activism is surging as concerned people shift their attention from utopian imagination to practical action. The most radical of the new wave of grass-roots activism is Extinction Rebellion (XR), a global movement launched in the United Kingdom in April 2018 with a strategy of mass civil disobedience to compel authorities to take action in the climate "emergency." XR aims to compel governments to meet its demands to tell the truth about the climate emergency, to dramatically cut carbon emissions, and to convene citizen assemblies to debate new policies for social and environmental well-being (Richardson 2020, 1, 5; see Figure 19.3). Another strand of the new activism also associated with the narrative of environmental emergency is the youth-led climate strikes associated with Greta Thunberg (2019), in which school students skip Friday classes to participate in protests against climate inaction. Discrete protests targeting specific grievances also occur, such as Indigenous First Nations blockading oil pipelines or coal mines imposed on their traditional homelands that threaten to create their own local dystopia (Lindeman 2020).

*Figure 19.3* XR's "Dead Sea March," 3 October 2020, Hobart, Australia; photograph by Benjamin J. Richardson.

The XR vision is premised on a theory of change that reformist politics have failed but rebellion can succeed when the critical threshold of 3.5 percent of the population revolts. That number comes from the conclusions of social movement researchers such as Erica Chenoweth and Maria Stephan (2011), whose analysis of past social uprisings found that when at least 3.5 percent of the population mobilized non-violently, the campaign's demands were met approximately 50 percent of the time and were successful more often compared to violent dissent.

In contrast to challenging business as usual, another path pursued is faith in incremental adaptation to global warming and other adversities, a prevalent position among contemporary environmental thinkers and policy-makers. It recognizes impending adversity but that it can be navigated through reformist solutions engineered through liberal democratic systems. The underlying assumption is that a green utopia is not radically different from current conditions, and can be achieved without major social upheaval. Adaptation may ensue through smart decarbonization strategies such as investment in renewable energy and green retrofitting infrastructure and cities and green tech innovations (Lorenzoni, O'Brien, and Adger 2009; Australian Panel of Experts on Environmental Law 2017). The ecological modernization paradigm is one prominent strand of this reformist utopianism, deftly reframing the ethical and political dilemmas of the Anthropocene as manageable technical and economic challenges, harnessing new technologies, business acumen, and managerial creativity (Gouldson and Murphy 1996, 11; Hajer 1995). The adequacy of the reformist approach to a greener future has, however, become increasingly incredulous in recent years as projections of climate change and environmental breakdown have become more ominous.

## Realizing Green Utopias Today

A range of green utopians ideals has been implemented already: small-scale eco-communities, smart cities, co-operative housing, nature rewilding, ecological restoration, slow food, socially responsible finance, and post-carbon lifestyles. These experiments have been initiated by civil society and business groups in some cases or directed by governments.

For many nature enthusiasts, wilderness is the epitome of an environmental utopia – areas of the planet where unadulterated, wild natural processes continue to flourish without any appreciable human interference. As the world's wild areas have shrunk in recent decades, wilderness has correspondingly become an even more precious realm. The world's first explicit wilderness protection law, the United States' Wilderness Act 1964, sought to secure areas to remain untouched by humankind for generations to come. Efforts to conserve wilderness have been stepped up in a number of countries through new legislation, although a green utopia, even with the best legislation, is still imperiled as global climate change reaches every corner of the planet (Takacs et al. 2021).

A different green archetype for some environmentalists is the bucolic and picturesque landscape, gently socialized by humankind with manicured gardens and peaceful rural vistas of serpentine paths and rolling hills adorned with shepherds and flocks of sheep (see Figure 19.4). The idolization of rural life was one way that Romantic artists and writers of the eighteenth and nineteenth centuries sought to distance themselves from the corrosive urban-industrial culture emerging in that era. Instead of viewing nature as a foreign presence that they toiled against, the Romantics saw nature as a moralizing and rejuvenating entity that people could emotionally connect with (Bermingham 1986). This sentimentalization of nature and small-scale farming initiatives that embrace slow food, permaculture, and other eco-friendly agricultural practices remain a potent force for many environmentalists (Rosin, Carolan, and Stock 2015).

*Figure 19.4* John Constable, "Wivenhoe Park, Essex," oil painting (1816), National Gallery of Art.

A third eco-utopian vision seeks to bring nature into the places most intensely occupied by people. An important shift in the philosophy of Western town planning and architecture in the late nineteenth century emphasized improving the health and convenience of city denizens. The "garden city" movement extolled the benefits of public amenities associated with access to open space and greenery – a reaction against the squalor and stench created by the Industrial Revolution. British planner Ebenezer Howard's promotion of garden cities was influential in this shift. His legacy continues today in the practices of urban planning and interest in the design of futurist eco-cities (Schuyler and Parsons 2002). The Ecotopia 2121 project is one creative effort to envision how different cities from the world, from London to New York, might be transformed over the next century into green utopias. For Budapest, it envisions roadside horticulture, community solar energy schemes, and urban reforestation (Marshall n.d.).

Another effort to realize eco-utopia today is through the network of eco-villages. They are human settlements that aim not only to reduce ecological footprint but to regenerate social and economic systems such as through an emphasis on locally owned, participatory decision-making. One pioneer is the community in Findhorn, northeast Scotland, whose 450 permanent residents implement many tenets of sustainable living including eco-friendly farming, eco-designed housing, and renewable energy sourcing, and numerous international visitors swarm to Findhorn during the summer for its spiritual and environmental enlightenment programs (Findhorn Community 1975). In 1998, Findhorn was awarded a UN Habitat Best Practice designation from the UN Centre for Human Habitats, and in 2005 it was measured as having the lowest ecological footprint of any community in the developed world, and half that of Britain's average (Tinsey n.d.). Other famous eco-villages around the world recognized for their trail-blazing efforts include Gaia (Argentina), Crystal Waters (Australia), Ithaca (United States), and Tamera (Portugal).

Another attempt to create a green utopia today is the global rewilding movement. This arose in the 1980s through collaborations between North American environmentalists seeking scientific and policy support for enlarged networks of wilderness, although today the goal is generally to make nature "wild" again as against pristine wilderness, and it is being adopted as a strategy even in densely populated countries (Fraser 2009). Rewilding emphasizes the reestablishment of keystone species, particularly apex carnivores, extensive afforestation, and removal of intrusive human infrastructure such as roads and dams (Foreman 1998; Monbiot 2013; O'Connor 2015). Thus far, most rewilding has taken the form of ecological restoration projects, such as revegetating landscapes, replenishing wetlands, removing pests and weeds, and other interventions, with important benefits for biodiversity and ecological systems but also incorporating social and economic gains for human communities (Richardson 2016, 277). The United Nation's Decade of Ecosystem Restoration for 2021–2030 signals the international significance of this trend (United Nations Environment Program).

## Conclusion

There is no one green utopia to imagine. A variety of environmental futures have been proposed and debated among scholars and activists over at least the past half-century, as shaped by perceptions of current problems and available solutions. In the 1970s, environmentalism focused on Malthusian resource limits and impending overshoot. In the 1980s and 1990s, optimism emerged that environmental constraints could be indefinitely overcome by following a sustainable development path, and since 2000, "adaptation" to climate breakdown has gained ascendancy. None of these narratives had much to say about past or current environmental losses. In recent decades as the specter of climate breakdown grows, such losses have started to become more extensive and visible for the present generation and, with that, a growing sense of urgency that reformist strategies are insufficient. These losses have also fueled increasing grief and fear that humankind is incapable of solving wicked problems that stand in the way of a post-carbon future. For some, a green utopia will only ever be a fiction of their imagination, as they mourn the end of nature and simply rely on an image of a past nature, one that was alive and thriving, for solace.

Rather than thinking of a green utopia as a destination, it could be imagined as a journey, with a focus on the *means* to achieve the desired change. Such a view of utopianism may celebrate the value of the process of transformative change, such as participating in the climate justice street marches or the disruptive protest activism of Earth First or XR. The utopian oeuvre centers on finding empowering solidarity with like-minded people to take action that leverages real change, such as mass civil disobedience that forces concessions from political and economic elites. The XR movement itself explicitly disavows prescribing any utopian futures or solutions, instead focusing on the means of bringing change, such as civil disobedience and convening citizen assemblies to deliberate on future environmental policies.

Once we think of green utopias as less a destination and more a journey, the emphasis shifts to critical thinking and activism to challenge environmentally destructive norms and practices. The prevailing sustainable development agenda in environmental policy-making has failed to provide the political and social space for critical thinking about environmental futures necessary for utopian imagination (Garforth 2018, 47). The radical activism of XR and other environmental protest groups taking to the streets is helpful in injecting a more critical perspective but also deficient to the extent that it focuses on the future we wish to avoid rather than the future we desire. Some groups are attempting to realize a green utopia today, in small, incremental experiments from eco-restoration to eco-friendly rural livelihoods which, although insufficient to respond to the Anthropocene, can give us hope and tools to build a larger green utopia.

## References


Australian Earth Laws Alliance. (n.d.) *Rights of nature*. Available at: www.earthlaws.org.au/what-we-do-international (Accessed 15 May 2022).

Australian Panel of Experts on Environmental Law. (2017) *Blueprint for the next generation of Australian environmental law*. Melbourne: APEEL.

Avilés, M.A.R. (2000) 'The law-based Utopia', *Critical Review of International Social and Political Philosophy*, 3(2–3), pp. 225–248.

Bermingham, A. (1986) *Landscape and ideology: The English rustic tradition, 1740–1860*. Oakland: University of California Press.

Bosselmann, K. (1995) *When two worlds collide: Society and ecology*. Waiheke Island: RSVP Publishing.

Boulding, K. (1966) 'The economics of the coming spaceship earth', in H. Jarrett (ed.), *Environmental quality in a growing Economy*. New York: Johns Hopkins University Press, pp. 1–17.

Brann, E. (1991) *The world of the imagination*. Maryland: Rowman & Littlefield.

Castoriadis, C. (1997) *The imaginary institution of society*. Translated by K. Blamey. Cambridge: MIT Press.

Chenoweth, E. and Stephan, M. (2011) *Why civil resistance works: The strategic logic of nonviolent conflict*. New York: Columbia University Press.

Colloff, M. (2000) *Landscapes of our hearts: Reconciling people and environment*. London: Thames & Hudson.

Contini, V. and Pascual, E.G. (2010) 'The Earth Charter: An ethical framework for a feasible utopia', *Discourse and Communication for Sustainable Education*, 1(2), pp. 25–33.

Davis, C. (1991) 'Utopianism', in J.H. Burns and M. Goldie (eds.), *The Cambridge history of political thought 1450–1700*. Cambridge: Cambridge University Press.

Devall, B. and Sessions, G. (1985) *Deep ecology*. Ann Arbor: University of Michigan Press.

Dobson, A. (1995) *Green political thought*. Abingdon: Routledge.

Earth Charter Commission. (2000) *The Earth Charter*. Available at: https://earthcharter.org/wp-content/uploads/2020/03/echarter_english.pdf?x79755 (Accessed 15 May 2022).

Ehrlich, P. (1971) *The population bomb*. New York: Ballantine Books.

Eliav-Feldon, M. (1982) *Realistic Utopias: The ideal imaginary societies of the renaissance, 1516–1630*. Oxford: Clarendon Press.

Findhorn Community. (1975) *The Findhorn garden story*. Rochester: Findhorn Press.

Flannery, T. (1994) *The future eaters*. Sydney: New Holland Publishers.

Foreman, D. (1998) 'The Wildlands Project and the rewilding of North America', *Denver University Law Review*, 76, pp. 535–553.

Fraser, C. (2009) *Rewilding the world: Dispatches from the conservation revolution*. London: Picador.

Garforth, L. (2018) *Green Utopias: Environmental hope before and after nature*. Cambridge: Polity Press.

Gillespie, S. (2019) *Climate crisis and consciousness: Re-imagining our world and ourselves*. Abingdon: Routledge.

Goldberg, V. (1991) *The power of photography: How photographs changed our lives*. New York: Abbeville Press.

Goldsmith, E. *et al.* (1972) 'Blueprint for survival', *The Ecologist*, 2(1), pp.136–139.

Gouldson, A. and Murphy, J. (1996) 'Ecological modernization and the European Union', *Geoforum*, 27(1), pp. 11–21.

Grim, J.A. (1997) 'Indigenous traditions and ecological ethics in earth's insights', *Worldviews: Global Religions, Culture, and Ecology*, 1(2), pp. 139–149.

Groes, S. ed. (2016) *Memory in the twenty-first century: New critical perspectives from the arts, humanities, and sciences*. London: Palgrave Macmillan.

Hajer, M. (1995) *The politics of environmental discourse: Ecological modernisation and the policy process*. Oxford University Press.

Half-Earth Project. *Half the earth for the rest of life*. Available at: https://www.half-earthproject.org (Accessed 15 May 2021).

Head, L. (2016) *Hope and grief in the Anthropocene: Re-conceptualising human-nature relations*. Abingdon: Routledge.

Hughes, R. and Wheeler, P. (2013) 'Introduction: Eco-dystopias – nature and the dystopian imagination', *Critical Survey*, 25(2), pp. 1–6.

Huxley, A. (1932) *Brave new world*. London: Chatto and Windus.

Jasanoff, S. and Kim, S.H. (2015) *Dreamscapes of modernity: Sociotechnical imaginaries and the fabrication of power*. Chicago: University of Chicago Press.

Jensen, D. (2006) *End game*. New York: Seven Stories Press.

Kelsey, R. (2011) 'Reverse shot: Earthrise and blue marble in the American imagination', in E.H. Jazairy (ed.), *Scales of the earth*. Cambridge: Harvard University Press, pp. 10–16.

Kenis, A. and Lievens, M. (2015) *The limits of the green economy: From re-inventing capitalism to re-politicising the present*. Abingdon: Taylor & Francis.

Klein, N. (2019) *On fire: The (burning) case for a green new deal*. London: Penguin.

Kotze, L. (2016) *Global environmental constitutionalism in the Anthropocene*. London: Bloomsbury.

Latour, B. (2004) *Politics of nature: How to bring the sciences into democracy*. Cambridge: Harvard University Press.

Le Guin, U.K. (1985) *Always coming home*. New York: Harper and Row.

Levitas, R. (2013) *Utopia as method: The imaginary reconstitution of society*. London: Palgrave Macmillan.

Levy, D.L. and Spicer, A. (2013) 'Contested imaginaries and the cultural political economy of climate change', *Organization*, 20(5), pp. 659–678.

Lindeman, T. (2020) '"Revolution is alive": Canada protests spawn climate and indigenous rights movement', *The Guardian*, February 28, 2020. Available at: https://www.theguardian.com/world/2020/feb/28/canada-pipeline-protests-climate-indigenous-rights (Accessed 1 May 2021).

Lorenzoni, I., O'Brien, K.L. and Adger, W.N. (2009) *Adapting to climate change: Thresholds, values, governance*. Cambridge: Cambridge University Press.

Lowenthal, D. (2015) *The past is a foreign country – revisited*. Cambridge: Cambridge University Press.

Lucas, C. and Warman, R. (2018) 'Disrupting polarized discourses: Can we get out of the ruts of environmental conflicts?', *Environment and Planning C: Politics and Space*, 36(6), pp. 987–1005.

Mar, T. and Edwards, P. (2010) *Making settler colonial space: Perspectives on race, place and identity*. New York: Springer.

Marshall, A. (n.d.) '100 cities of the future', *Ecotopia 2121: A vision for our future green Utopia – in 100 cities*. Available at: https://www.ecotopia2121.com (Accessed 12 June 2021).

McCarthy, C. (2006) *The road*. London: Picador.

McKibben, B. (1989) *The end of nature: Humanity, climate change and the natural world*. New York: Anchor.

Meadows, D.H., Meadows, D.L., Randers, J. and Behrens III, W.W. (1972) *The limits to growth: A report for the club of Rome's project on the predicament of mankind*. East Sussex: Earth Island.

Mies, M. and Shiva, V. eds. (1993) *Ecofeminism*. London: Zed Books.

Milkoreit, M., Kapuscinski, A.R., Locke, K. and Iles, A. (2017) 'Imaginary politics: Climate change and making the future', *Elementa: Science of the Anthropocene*, 5, pp. 62–75.

Monbiot, G. (2013) *Feral: Searching for enchantment on the frontiers of rewilding*. London: Penguin.

Morton, T. (2007) *Ecology without nature: Rethinking environmental aesthetics*. Cambridge: Harvard University Press.

Muir, C., Wehner, K. and Newell, J. (2020) *Living with the Anthropocene: Love, loss and hope in the face of environmental crisis*. Sydney: NewSouth Publishing.

Naess, A. *The ecology of wisdom*. London: Penguin.

'New Zealand, resource management act 1991, version as at 12 April 2022'. Available at: https://www.legislation.govt.nz/act/public/1991/0069/latest/DLM230265.html (Accessed 12 April 2022).

O'Connor, M.R. (2015) *Resurrection science: Conservation, de-extinction and the precarious future of wild things*. New York: St Martin's Press.

Orwell, G.. (1949) *Nineteen eighty-four*. London: Decker and Warburg.

Pauly, D. (1995) 'Anecdotes and the shifting baseline syndrome of fisheries', *Trends in Ecology and Evolution*, 10(10), p. 430.

Pihkala, P. (2020) 'Climate grief: How we mourn a changing planet', *BBC Future*, 3 April 2020. Available at: https://www.bbc.com/future/article/20200402-climate-grief-mourning-loss-due-to-climate-change (Accessed 5 May 2021).

Popper, K.R. (1945) *The open society and its enemies*. Princeton: Princeton University Press.

Richardson, B.J. (2016) 'The emerging age of ecological restoration law', *Review of European, Comparative and International Environmental Law*, 25(3), pp. 277–290.

———. (2017) *Time and environmental law: Telling nature's time*. Cambridge: Cambridge University Press.

———. (2019) *The art of environmental law: Governing with aesthetics*. London: Hart/Bloomsbury.

———. (2020) 'Climate strikes to extinction rebellion: Environmental activism shaping our future', *Journal of Human Rights and the Environment*, 11(3), pp. 1–9.

Richardson, B.J. and Wood, S. eds. (2006) *Environmental law for sustainability*. Oxford: Hart Publishing.

Robinson, K.S. (1995) *Pacific edge*. New York: Orb Books.

Rosin, C., Carolan, M. and Stock, P.V. eds. (2015) *Food Utopias: Reimagining citizenship, ethics and community*. Abingdon: Taylor & Francis.

Schumacher, E.F. (1973) *Small is beautiful: A study of economics as if people mattered*. London: Vintage.

Schuyler, D. and Parsons, K.C. (2002) *From garden city to green city: The legacy of Ebenezer Howard*. Baltimore: Johns Hopkins University Press.
Sheppard, S.R.J., Shaw, A., Flanders, D., Burch, S., Wiek, A., Carmichael, J., Robinson, J. and Cohen, S. (2011) 'Future visioning of local climate change: A framework for community engagement and planning with scenarios and visualisation', *Futures*, 43(4), pp. 400–412.
Steger, M.B. and James, P. (2013) 'Levels of subjective globalization: Ideologies, imaginaries, ontologies', *Perspectives on Global Development and Technology*, 12(1–2), pp. 17–40.
Takacs, D., Bastmeijer,, K., McCormack, P. and Richardson, B.J. (2021) 'Wilderness law in the Anthropocene: Pragmatism and purism', *Environmental Law*, 51(2), pp. 383–435.
Taylor, C. (2004) *Modern social imaginaries*. Durham: Duke University Press.
——— (2022) *The way forward*. Available at: https://earthcharter.org/read-the-earth-charter/the-way-forward (Accessed 15 May 2022).
The Voluntary Human Extinction Movement. (n.d.) *The voluntary human extinction movement*. Available at: https://www.vhemt.org/ (Accessed 1 June 2021).
Thunberg, G. (2019) *No one is too small to make a difference*. London: Penguin.
Tinsey, S. (n.d.) *Ecological footprint of the findhorn foundation and community*. Available at: www.ecovillagefindhorn.com/docs/FF%20Footprint.pdf&gt (Accessed 4 June 2021).
United Nations. (1982) 'World Charter for nature, general assembly resolution, 37/7', 28 October 1982.
United Nations. (n.d.) *Sustainable development goals*. Department of Economic and Social Affairs: Sustainable Development. Available at: https://sdgs.un.org/goals (Accessed 28 May 2021).
United Nations Environment Program. (n.d.) *Preventing, halting and reversing the degradation of ecosystems worldwide*. United Nations decade on ecosystem restoration 2021–2030. Available at: https://www.decadeonrestoration.org (Accessed 14 June 2021).
United States. (1964) 'Wilderness Act, Public Law 88-57716 U.S.C. 1131-1136'.
Weisman, A. (2007) *The world without us*. New York: Thomas Dunne Books/St. Martin's Press.
Weiss, E.H.B. (1989) *In fairness to future generations: International law, common patrimony and intergenerational equity*. New York: Transnational Publishers.
World Commission on Environment and Development. (1987) *Our common future*. New York: Oxford University Press.
World Meteorological Organization. (2020) *Australia suffers devastating fires after hottest, driest year on record*. Available at: https://public.wmo.int/en/media/news/australia-suffers-devastating-fires-after-hottest-driest-year-record (Accessed 3 July 2021).
Wright, C., Nyberg, D., De Cock, C. and Whiteman, G. (2013) 'Future imaginings: Organizing in response to climate change', *Organization*, 20(5), pp. 647–658.
Wyndam, J. (1955) *The chrysalids*, London: Penguin.

# 20
# MYTH FOR THE ANTHROPOCENE

*Peter D. Burdon and James Martel*

When considering a subject as massive as the question of human beings and their place in, connection to, and effect on the environment, it seems that we must make recourse to mythology. Earlier times had myths of their own, myths that explained how to engage with nature, how it might be appeased, and what parts of nature must simply be accepted. Our own time is no less mythological for all of our senses that modernity is disenchanted (one of our writers, Kirsten Anker said in this regard that "we have never been disenchanted.") If anything, it may be *more* mythological. This is certainly the position of Walter Benjamin (2002), who, in his great study of nineteenth-century France and the dawn of the modern capitalist age, showed how myth as well as what he called the "phantasmagoria"[1] helped not only to explain the modern condition but also to determine and bind it. Myth, for Benjamin, can be either depoliticized, in which case we become wholly dependent upon the mythmakers, or it can be understood in an explicitly political sense. Yet, even the latter, more radical (and, we would add, anarchist) understanding of myth is subject to obfuscation and unintended consequences. Myth by its nature is never entirely direct. William E. Connolly (2017) considers the extent to which myth operates below the level of official expression – a wild dream when things are going well or a portent during times of crisis or pain. Underpinning this analysis is Connolly's insistency that "some old myths now feel revelatory" and that the "turn to myth is a turn toward an insurrection of voices straining to be heard beneath the clamor of dominant stories" (2017, 1).

In this volume, the authors that we have invited to comment upon the Anthropocene are themselves dealing with various sorts of myths. Myths of human omnipotence as well as of human vulnerability, myths of savage nature, and nature as the balm of all ills. These scholars come from a vast number of different fields; they come from the study of law, politics, philosophy, Indigenous traditions and contemporary modes of being, political theology, Earth science, environmental studies, and many more. In all cases, the act of writing about the Anthropocene reproduces a basic paradox about this question. On the one hand, the Anthropocene is a moment when humanity's power over the world seems absolute. While all creatures affect the environment just as it affects them, the Anthropocene is the first time that one species has altered the world on a planetary scale. Yet, even as this power may give human beings both a sense of hubris or despair, it is equally true that the Anthropocene has shown the limits of human power; the inadvertent and perilous effects of global warming, rising sea levels, plastic in the ocean, and


DOI: 10.4324/9781003388081-27

junk in outer space all spell out a way that we are not in control of the environment (and never were), even when we are tangibly and unmistakably causing it to change.

In this regard, a turn to mythology[2] may be a way to try to understand or at least speak about our condition because in myth too, an apparently tangible power (the power to make myths to explain the world to ourselves) is also a power over us as much as it is in our hands. The myth-maker, like the subject of the global environment, can use her power to change the world, but she can also be changed by that world. She can assert her control, but she is as much controlled by what she regards as her instrument, effectively becoming an instrument herself.

Bearing this in mind, we begin this chapter by describing how advances in Earth systems science have disturbed standard assumptions in ethics in law – such as the idea that agency is limited to human beings. The Anthropocene describes a rupture in the Earth system that has awakened the slumbering behemoth beneath our feet and given rise to new and unpredictable forms of power. To comprehend these changes, we examine two kinds of myth. The first batch contains Ovid's Phaethon in "Metamorphoses" and Goethe's "The Sorcerer's Apprentice." These are pre-ethical stories that warn of the risk that comes when humans transcend physical and moral laws. As Hegel noted: "Man uses nature for his own ends; but where nature is too powerful, it does not allow itself to be used as means" (quoted in Gregory 2001, 89). In this sense, our first two myths are descriptive of our current predicament and a further warning to those who seek more power (ecomodernists) or argue that human ingenuity can be put in service of a "good Anthropocene." Following this, our final story is a contemporary myth from Octavia Butler's *Parable* series. These stories speak to that other side of the Anthropocene, the one where we seem to have no control, the one which seems to doom us (and by our own hand). In these latter myths, we see however that just as the earlier myths warned us not to treat nature as a commodity, in Butler's novels we see a corollary idea that human agency need not be swallowed up by the vastness of the world but can instead remain a source of agency and change so long as we realize that we are part of and not merely authors of that change. Finally, in the last part of the chapter, we draw out lessons from these myths.

## Mythology for the Anthropocene

Earth systems science provides a succinct definition of the Anthropocene: a "recent rupture in Earth history arising from the impact of human activity on the Earth System as a whole" (Hamilton 2017, 9). There is a lot to unpack in this statement, but we first want to underline that the Anthropocene is fundamentally about changes to the Earth system. It is not about isolated environmental impacts or a term to describe the deepening environmental crisis.[3] It is a rupture that is so significant that the Earth may have entered a new geological epoch.

A lot follows from this, and some of those issues are explored in this volume. In this chapter, we dwell on how the Anthropocene provides an opportunity for rethinking fundamental assumptions that have shaped Western ethics[4] and law. To date, all ethics have been written with certain assumptions in mind – including the idea that humans alone are moral subjects, that the environment is an object, and that there is a one-way dynamic of power/agency between humans and the Earth. As a result of these presumptions, ethics has found itself ill-equipped to grapple with the enormity of the Anthropocene. What utilitarian calculus could comprehend the changes we are making to Earth's geological history? From a different perspective, what can notions of intrinsic value or rights mean in the context of an Earth system that is increasingly volatile and unpredictable? As Isabelle Stengers (2015, 47) has argued: "We will have to go on answering for what we are undertaking in the face of an implacable being who is deaf to our justifications." In Western thought at least, there is a significant gap between our current situation and the intellectual tools that were developed in the Holocene.

In the Anthropocene, human power[5] is in tension with a concomitant increased power in the Earth system. "Taken together" Hamilton (2017, 45) observes, "there is more power at work on Earth." To comprehend this change some authors use metaphor and describe the Earth as "Gaia" (Stengers 2015; Latour 2017) or argue that the Earth has "awakened" (Hamilton 2017, 47). This is not a system that humans can dominate like Francis Bacon wished: "putting [nature] on the rack and extracting her secrets … storming her strongholds and castles" (Farrington 1949, 62). Redundant also are passive descriptions of nature as a "sister with whom we share our life and a beautiful mother who opens her arms to embrace us" (Francis 2015). These are Holocene ideas and are imbued with the dying remnants of romanticism and wilderness ethics. Hamilton (2015) describes the convergence of human and Earth system power:

> Against the foundation of modern law and ethics in the moral autonomy of the subject we find ourselves in an increasingly heteronomous world. We no longer have a monopoly on agency. We have assumed that the only kind of willing in the world lies in the consciousness of human beings; yet in the Anthropocene we must confront the possibility of a "will" beyond our own, that which we can only gesture at with metaphors like "the awakened beast."

As we grapple to come to terms with the Anthropocene, we might – paradoxically – find it profitable to look back and examine Western mythology from a time when people did view themselves as in relationship with an animate Earth. Frequently in these stories, when conflict does arise between humans and nature, it is because of human arrogance or hubris. Thus the stories served a didactic purpose. It is not our intention here to repurpose the stories for that function – we are too late to prevent changes to the Earth system. But we argue that the stories are useful as we grapple with events that, while they seem unprecedented, are actually the logical conclusion of many belief structures and actions that have led to the Anthropocene in the first place. They also provide instruction for how we might continue to live within an Earth system that is undergoing irreversible changes. There is no returning to the Holocene, and we must find guardrails to guide us nevertheless (an idea we will return to in our reading of Butler's novels as well).

Phaethon

In his "Metamorphoses," the poet Ovid presented a vision of the universe that was embedded in flux and change (2004, 602). One tale that he weaves early in his text is the story of Phaethon. Phaethon was the son of Clymene and the sun God, Apollo.[6] More than anything, Phaethon sought proof that Apollo was his father, and so one day he confronted him in the dawn palace. After some initial awkwardness, Apollo swore a binding oath that he would grant his son anything he wished. Apollo had barely finished speaking when Phaethon asked if he could drive his father's mighty horses and pull the sun up into the sky. Apollo became immediately frightened. He understood that Phaethon did not have the strength or the skill to ascend to the seat of the Gods. And so Apollo issued these words of caution:

> Be persuaded
> The danger of what you ask is infinite –
> To yourself, to the whole Creation.
> The forces, the materials, the laws
> Of all Creation are balanced.
> …
> Only see how foolish you are.

The most conceited of the gods
Knows better
Than to dream he could survive
One day riding the burning axle-tree.

(Hughes 2007, 26)[7]

Here we see a warning that could very well be applied to our own time and our own (Anthropocenic) age. Despite this warning, Phaethon is intoxicated by the prospect of power. He is deaf to Apollo's pleas and mounts the chariot of the sun with no sense of responsibility or obligation to Gaia. With arrogance and hubris, Phaethon strikes the horses and the chariot sets off. The consequences are predictable and the sun veers out of control. In language, that mirrors how many Australians or residents of California felt after the 2019–2020 bushfires, Ovid reports:

Earth began to burn, the summits first.
Baked, the cracks gaped. All fields, all thickets,
All crops were instant fuel –
The land blazed briefly.
In the one flare noble cities
Were rendered
To black stumps or burnt stone.
...
Now Phaethon saw the whole world
Mapped with fire. He looked through the flames
And he breathed flames.
Flame in and flame out, like a fire-eater.
As the chariot sparked white-hot
He cowered from the showering cinders
His eyes streamed in the fire-smoke.
And in the boiling darkness
He no longer knew where he was
Or where he was going.

(Hughes 1997, 35)

In this poem, even Gaia calls out in pain and prays to be put out of her misery:

You God of the Gods,
If my annihilation has been decided, why drag it out?
Where are your thunderbolts
To finish the whole thing quickly?
If I am to end in fire
Let it be your fire, O God,
That would redeem it a little.
I can hardly speak.

(Hughes 1997, 37)

By having nature itself personified as Gaia, Ovid (and the authors of the myth that he drew upon) make(s) it possible for human beings to understand what is otherwise very difficult to conceptualize. If nature is just a vast environment around us, it is difficult to think about how it could be "hurt" or even destroyed. Gaia articulates the damage that human beings can cause in and to the world, including the damage that they bring onto themselves (since we too are part of, subject to, nature/Gaia). In this story, Zeus destroys Phaethon with his thunderbolt and prevents the Earth goddess from burning. Nymphs find his remains, bury the body, and place an inscription over his grave that reads:

> Here lies Phoebus' boy who died
> In the sun's chariot
> His strength too human, and too hot
> His courage and his pride.
>
> (Hughes 1997, 40)

As this poem exemplifies, the consequences of hubris are well-known and long-attested. But the situation will be quite different for us in our own modern dilemmas. This time there will be no divine intervention to prevent us from burning the Earth and nobody to record the cause of our self-destruction. Unless we learn to temper our power with humility, responsibility, and obligations for others, we may also fall prey to our newfound power as weather makers. This is not to say that this myth only serves as a warning for what will inevitably happen to us. Once again, by personifying both nature (as Gaia) and the force of destruction (as the sun, Zeus, and Apollo), these things become comprehensible on a human scale. While anthropomorphism has long been a way to make nature subject to human agency, it also makes natural agency legible to us. The concept that there is a thing called "nature" and that we are part of it even as we seek to shape it helps us to see that there are options between total acquiescence to global catastrophe and total disregard. Nature can become a legible part of the human world and, in so doing, can be contended with in ways that do not simply replicate the binarism of mastery and non-mastery that dominates in modernity.

## Goethe: "The Sorcerer's Apprentice"[8]

If Ovid's telling of the Phaethon speaks to hubris, Goethe captured the serialism of living in a world that has become animated and courses with newfound power. Here, the vast changes in relation to nature and the environment afforded by the age of imperialism and the nascent industrial revolution require a different sort of personification of nature, one that Goethe ably provides us. Prior to the time of techno-industrialism, respect for the forces of nature was embedded into folk wisdom. In some sense, Goethe is reviving that wisdom by repurposing it for a new age. "The Sorcerer's Apprentice" is an ancient story – it had the function of myth for many people. Goethe rendered it as a 14-stanza poem in 1797.

In the poem, a powerful sorcerer departs his sanctuary and leaves his apprentice to study. The apprentice is filled with youthful conviction of his own power and mastery over the elements. He is impatient to feel power and believes that he can activate and control his master's magic:

> I'm now master,
> I'm tactician,
> All his ghosts must do my bidding.
> Know his incantation,
> Spell and gestures too;
> By my mind's creation
> Wonders shall I do.
>
> (Goethe 1779)

Those who have watched Disney's 1940 adaptation will be familiar with the next part of the story. The apprentice commands a broom and basin of water to clean:

> Like a whirlwind he is going
> To the stream, and then in
> Like an engine he is throwing
> Water for my use; with flurry
> Do I watch the steady;
> Not a drop is spilled,
> Basin, bowls already
> Are with water filled.
>
> (Goethe 1779)

The apprentice, however, is unable to control the power he has unleashed. He reacts with anger and perhaps a touch of shame: "Be a broom! Be not renewing." The broom pays no heed to his command but rather than ask for help or show humility, the apprentice doubles down and tries to tap into more powerful magic:

> No, no longer
> Shall I *suffer*
> You to offer
> Bold defiance.
> I have brains,
> I am the stronger
> And I shall enforce compliance.
>
> (Goethe 1779)

But in a twist that ought to give ecomodernists pause, we learn that bravado is no substitute for true mastery. The broom is deaf to the commands of the apprentice, and as things spiral out of control he takes increasingly desperate action. First, he dares to pick up his master's wand, but he cannot command it. Then the apprentice abandons magic and tries to restore order with brute force. He reaches for the closest weapon – an axe – and chops the broom in two. But there is so much that the apprentice does not know or understand about the magic he has unleashed. The broom does not fall to the floor but instead, it resurrects in two halves and both pieces continue with their work. The apprentice chops again but he finds that the inanimate thing is infused with life, agency, and powers that he cannot control. Eventually, the apprentice cries out in distress:

> You, hell's miscreate abortion,
> Is this house doomed to perdition?
> Signs I see in every portion
> Of impending demolition.
> …
> Both are running, both are plodding
> And with still increased persistence
> Hall and work-shop they are flooding.
>
> (Goethe 1779)

But just like the tale of Phaethon, there is a higher power in this story that can save the day. The sorcerer returns to his house and restores order with the slightest gesture. The sorcerer commands the broom:

> Be obedient
> Broom, be hiding
> And subsiding!
> None should ever
> But the master, when expedient,
> Call you as a ghostly lever!
>
> (Goethe 1779)

Here, we see several critical elements. Nature is again personified but this time in the form of an animated broom rather than a human-appearing goddess. This suggests that the relationship to nature has been altered, and a more instrumental approach is at work in this story. But the instrument has not lost its human-like and independent character. The brooms betray the apprentice by asserting their own power precisely by refusing to do anything but what they were built to do: sweep. This shows that instrumentality can backfire and that at times it can be difficult to discern who is instrumentalizing whom. The danger of nature acting back onto the very humans who seem to control it is a fitting anticipation of the Anthropocene age but in Goethe's case, that danger is cut short by the reappearance of the sorcerer, a deus ex machina who restores the order of human supremacy.

This resolution may help to explain many current approaches to the Anthropocene whereby science and technology are seen as the cures for the very problems that such systems have generated in the first place. This may well be a misplaced hope. Perhaps Goethe, at a time when the Anthropocene was not yet in evidence, felt that the danger, however real and imminent, could be contained. It therefore might require a very different form of myth to confront our own modern time.

## *The Parable of the Sower* and *The Parable of the Talents*[9]

In Octavia Butler's two-part *Parable* series, we see a myth that is perhaps better suited for the paradoxes and ambiguities of the Anthropocenic age. These books were written in the early 1990s but are amazingly prescient about the nature of the threat we face today as well as suggested ways to engage with that threat. Far from the deus ex machina which resolves both Ovid's story of Phaethon and Goethe's "The Sorcerer's Apprentice," in the *Parable* series, Butler presents us with a world that seems to have been abandoned by God(s) altogether. The sequential novels are set in the near future in a California that has been wracked by a combination of environmental destruction and nascent political fascism that has brought society very low. The heroine of the novel, Lauren Olamina, lives in a compound in suburban Los Angeles that survives by putting up walls around the community and growing food in what was once a cul-de-sac. Eventually, that compound is overrun by a mob, and Lauren barely gets out alive, her family all murdered or missing. As she heads north toward Oregon, Lauren encounters the effects of environmental devastation. Food is scarce, and there are huge dangers posed by other people in this deeply stressed context.

However, Lauren is not helpless in her experience of this ongoing catastrophe. As it happens, she is a prophet and has created (or as she puts it "discovered") a new religion called Earthseed. Earthseed is a doctrine that does not seek to control or dominate a world that clearly has bucked human determination (even though the increasingly fascist nature of the society in a postapocalyptic USA is an attempt to restore that control). Lauren's religion is based on the idea that "God is Change." The central doctrine of Earthseed is as follows:

All that you touch
You Change.
All that you Change
Changes you.
The only lasting truth is Change
God is Change.

(Butler 1993, 3)

These tenets seem quite simple but represent a sophisticated theology for an age marked by loss and intense contingency. When she writes, "all that you touch/You Change," Lauren is indicating the Midas-like nature of human actors. Whatever they encounter they alter, irrevocably and irreversibly. This so far is consistent with the doctrines of Lockean capitalism but the next stanza reverses this relationship (without however displacing it). "All that you Change/Changes you" is not supposed to happen in the enlightenment image of the human actor amidst nature (as well as amidst other, inferior human subjects). But Lauren recognizes and accepts this basic fact about the universe. When she says, "The only lasting truth is Change," she is in fact acknowledging that truth itself is not a constant and that contingency, rather than being something for human beings to conquer and control, is the basis of the universe. Finally, saying that "God is Change," takes the figure that human actors ascribe as the origin of all of their power and motivation and changes the deity from the source of human power to an ongoing and permanent source of flux and lack of control. Instead of control, Lauren's religion seeks adaptation and also a certain degree of humility given that we human beings are never as powerful or autonomous as we think we are.

In some ways, Octavia Butler's *Parable* series, like her other writings, reflects her own experience as a Black woman in the contemporary USA. From her position, the disasters that she depicts in these and other novels are not science fiction but conditions that are already here. The brutalities visited upon the characters in the *Parable* series – murder, rape, genocide, slavery – have always been part of the Black American experience. By writing science fiction, Butler is extending that perspective to other communities, including the dominant white community, to show how another way to be in and with the world is both possible and necessary.

Through her character of Lauren Olamina, Butler acknowledges the difficulties of this other way of being in the world. Lauren's life is marked by repeated trauma and violation. In a poem from her scripture, *Earthseed: The Book of the Living*, Lauren writes:

Beware:
All too often,
We say
What we hear others say.
We think
What we're told that we think.
We see
What we're permitted to see.
Worse!
We see what we're told that we see.
Repetition and pride are the keys to this.
To hear and to see

Even an obvious lie
Again
And again and again
May be to say it,
Almost by reflex
Then to defend it
Because we've said it
And at last to embrace it
Because we've defended it
And because we cannot admit
That we've embraced and defended
An obvious lie,
Thus, without thought,
Without intent.
We make
Mere echoes
Of ourselves—
And we say
What we hear others say.

(Butler 2000, 308)

This anticipates the age of Trump and Bolsonaro, a turn toward authoritarianism as the consequences of environmental devastation plays itself out, but it also speaks to the fact, consistent with the doctrine of Earthseed, that truth itself is, as she tells us, always in flux. This makes us vulnerable to the lies and deceptions of others, to lies that are repeated so often that they "become" true.

Yet for all of this danger and for all of the miseries of the world that Lauren lives in (a world that is in fact already here), her creed sustains her, and, in the end, Earthseed itself becomes a widespread belief. The novels end with the fulfillment of what Lauren calls "the Destiny" which is to have human beings go out into the universe to settle other planets. While this might seem redolent of the very colonizing principles that brought Earth to the condition that Lauren finds it in in the first place, it becomes clear in the novel that the purpose of the Destiny is to actively engage with the universe and, in so doing, to remove this concept from the liberal/capitalist/white supremacist uses that it has long been employed for. The universe has long served as a site that was transcendent and superior to the world. It was a site that Western thinkers would draw upon to render the material world inferior and subject to human (that is to say white, male, affluent) power. By turning the universe from a shadowy abstraction into a home for humanity, the Destiny removes this notion, just as Earthseed removes God, as a bedrock for the instrumentalism and domination of Western thought and practices. In this way, Butler has given us a series of parables for how to think about, live in and be both changing of and changed by the world and one another.

## Lessons from Myth

In looking at our three myths, one from antiquity, one at the dawn of the industrial era, and one from our own times, we can begin to make some distinctions. The first two myths, for all of their differences from one another, could be described as pre-ethical. The actions of Phaethon or the apprentice are more foolish, risky, and hubristic than they are unethical. Both stories capture the experience of young people that aspire to rise above their station and transcend moral laws. They aspire to be like gods themselves. They are stories about what happens when we try to rise above the proper bounds of human agency – when divinity or magic confers too much agency and which leads us to believe that we are above ethical implications. Although these myths are both from long ago and largely pre-industrial, they speak directly to our contemporary condition. And the impulse that they warn us against is far from gone; some celebrate this newfound power and seek to construct a "good Anthropocene" where human intervention and technology can keep at bay the forces of nature we have awakened. This can be seen in geoengineering schemes aimed at regulating the extent to which solar energy reaches the planet. Yet, at the same time, the resolution of these two myths is no longer available to us. Human beings stand in the shoes of Phaethon or the apprentice. Our world is spiraling, but there is now no higher power to save us or assist in our dying.

These myths get us to ask fundamental questions about ourselves and our relationship with the world, nature, and the universe. What is the essential flaw in the human being, the being that can spread across the entire surface of the Earth and create fantastically elaborate social structures, including systems of law to govern its behavior, and yet send the planet careening off onto a new and dangerous trajectory that jeopardizes all forms of life? Although they predate the full flowering of contemporary subjectivity and to some extent the revelation of the Anthropocene itself, these myths already call into question the hubris and danger of the modern condition. Through them, we can already begin to see how Western modernity's greatest philosophical invention, the autonomous subject, now stands on shaky ground, the trembling of "the giant beneath our feet" (Hamilton 2015).

The myths presented to us by Octavia Butler are somewhat different. Written in the face of the Anthropocene, they have, as we've already seen, no recourse to a saving deity. The deity herself has become a source of danger but also of promise and possibility. Here the paradox and ambivalence of the Anthropocene become, not things to game and control, but a way of life, an endless navigation and entanglement between human changers (the clergy of Earthseed come to be called "Shapers") and the world that changes us in turn.

If the myths of Phaethon and "The Sorcerer's Apprentice" are pre-ethical, you could say that the *Parable* series is itself post-ethical. That is to say, rather than anticipating an ethics based on the liberal autonomous subject, the controller of themselves, and the world around them, as the first two myths do, we have here a story of the self after the collapse of that ethical system (if it ever actually existed). In the early parts of *Parable of the Sower*, Lauren has a conversation with her father, who is a Christian preacher. He urges Lauren to stop scaring the members of their community with tales of destruction. This is part of that conversation:

> "It's better to teach people than to scare them, Lauren. If you scare them and nothing happens, they lose their fear and you lose some of your authority with them. It's harder to scare them a second time, harder to teach them harder to win back their trust … If you can think of ways to entertain them and teach them at the same time, you'll get your information out. And all without making anyone look down."
>
> "Look down …?"
>
> "Into the abyss, Daughter … You've just noticed the abyss," he continued. "The adults in this community have been balancing at the edge of it for more years than you've been alive."
>
> I got up, went over to him and took his hand. "It's getting worse, Dad."
>
> "I know."
>
> "Maybe it's time to look down. Time for some hand and foot holds before we just get pushed in."
>
> *(Butler 1993, 65–66)*

When the abyss ceases to be a place to be avoided at all costs, when the desire to control and guarantee the world according to set and unchanging principles becomes impossible, Lauren's philosophy supersedes that of her father's. What was once an abyss, a site of contingency and indeterminacy now becomes a home, a world in which Lauren means to make her own life. Now that the old ethics no longer apply (insofar as they serve a universe in which human beings are the absolute master and nature itself is passive and receptive to that mastery), a new way of life must be created. Butler shows us that such a task is not only possible but can be (must be) done in the face of the catastrophe that we have brought onto ourselves.[10] If God is not going to save us this time, if God is Change, then it is our responsibility to learn how to navigate a world that we have created. In this way, Butler's *Parable of the Sower* may be the correct myth for our own beleaguered and perilous time.

To end with one final, brief myth, perhaps the most appropriate myth of all for the Anthropocene era is that of King Midas. King Midas famously turned everything that he touched into gold. Unfortunately for him that meant that his touch killed everyone that he knew and loved. He ended up alone in a palace where everything was gold. He was unable to enjoy his untold wealth because he could not eat, drink, or touch another human being. King Midas, we think, is akin to the state and the market and their attempts to "solve" the Anthropocene. They may have the best of intentions whether via state-negotiated limitations on greenhouse gases or market-oriented logics like cap and trade, but they cannot not destroy what they touch. Very much like King Midas himself, everything the state and the market touches turns into a commodity, a source of profit. Such hands are not made for healing and nurturing, only for exploiting and dominating. We cannot look to these sources for solutions. They must come from the community itself, a community which, via its ongoing forms of mythmaking is always creating new ways to conceptualize and engage with the world around us. The stories that we tell help us to find our way, to resist the blandishments of state and market, and think and act in ways that are not predetermined by the capitalist and statist logics that got us into this mess in the first place. As we move forward into the Anthropocene, these stories are and will be desperately needed to counteract, redirect, and reconsider the way we think about and act within the world itself.

## Notes

1 Benjamin took this term from Marx. For a discussion, see Cohen (1989).
2 We follow Midgley (2004) in interpreting mythology as encompassing cultural stories that shape our thoughts in conscious and unconscious ways.
3 For an excellent summary of the science, see Angus (2016, 25–106).
4 From hereon, we just use the term "ethics" when talking about Western ethics.
5 For an overview on debates about the term Anthropocene, see Kunkel (2017). The authors accept the well-made critique that the term "Anthropocene" disguises the fact that only a very small part of humanity have caused changes to the Anthropocene and that those who have contributed least to the problem are the first to suffer from it.
6 For commentary on this poem, see Brown (1987).
7 See also Ovid (2004, 47–66)
8 Hamilton (2015) also unpacks this tale in the context of the Anthropocene.
9 Another example from contemporary literature is Robinson (2009). For a discussion of this in the context of the Anthropocene, see Wark (2016).
10 A very similar momentum drives Kim Stanley Robinson's (2020) latest attempt to grapple with the Anthropocene.

## References

Angus, I. (2016). *Facing the Anthropocene*. Monthly Review Press.
Benjamin, W. (2002) *The Arcades Project*. Harvard University Press.
Brown, R. (1987) 'The Palace of the Sun in Ovid's Metamorphoses', in M. Whitby, P. Hardie and M. Whitby (eds.), *Homo Viator: Classical Essays for John Bramble*. 211–220, Bristol Classical Press.
Butler, O. (1993) *Parable of the Sower*. Grand Central Publishing.
———. (2000) *Parable of the Talents*. Grand Central Publishing.
Cohen, M. (1989) 'Walter Benjamin's Phantasmagoria', *New German Critique*, 48, p. 87.
Connolly, W.E. (2017) *Facing the Planetary: Entangled Humanism and the Politics of Swarming*. Duke University Press.
Farrington, B. (1949) *Francis Bacon: Philosopher of Industrial Science*. Schumann.
Goethe, J.W. (1779) *The Sorcerer's Apprentice*. Translated by Paul Dyrsen (1878). Available at: https://german-stories.vcu.edu/goethe/zauber_e4.html.
Gregory, D. (2001) 'Post (Colonialism) and the Production of Nature', in N. Castree and B. Barun (eds.), *Social Nature: Theory, Practice, and Politics*. 84–111, Blackwell.
Hamilton, C. (2015) 'The Banality of Ethics in the Anthropocene, Part 2', *The Conversation*, 14 July 2015. Available at: https://theconversation.com/the-banality-of-ethics-in-the-anthropocene-part-2-44647 (Accessed: 20 September 2021).
Hamilton, C. (2017) *Defiant Earth: The Fate of Humans in the Anthropocene*. Allen & Unwin.
Hughes, T. (2007). *Tales from Ovid*. Faber Poetry.
Kunkel, B. (2017) 'The Capitalocene', *London Review of Books*, 39(5). Available at: https://www.lrb.co.uk/the-paper/v39/n05/benjamin-kunkel/the-capitalocene.
Latour, B. (2017) *Facing Gaia: Eight Lectures on the New Climatic Regime*. Polity.
Midgley, M. (2004) *The Myths We Live By*. Routledge.
Ovid. (2004) *Metamorphoses*. Penguin.
Pope, Francis (2015) *Laudato Si: On Care for Our Common Home*. Our Sunday Visitor.
Robinson, K.S. (2009) *Red Mars*. Voyager.
———. (2020) *The Ministry for the Future*. Orbit.
Stengers, I. (2015) *In Catastrophic Times: Resisting the Coming Barbarism*. Open Humanities Press.
Wark, M. (2016) *Molecular Red: Theory for the Anthropocene*. Verso.

# 21
# THE NOMOS OF CREATIVITY IN THE ANTHROPOCENE

*Afshin Akhtar-Khavari and Lachlan Hoy*

In *Malfeasance*, Michel Serres starts his book with a provocative description of how it's not just humans that appropriate. He writes:

> TIGERS PISS ON THE EDGE OF THEIR LAIR. And so do lions and dogs. Like those carnivorous mammals, many animals, our cousins, *mark* their territory with their harsh, stinking urine or with their howling, while other such as finches and nightingales use sweet songs.
>
> (*Serres 2011, 1, emphasis in the original*)

While Serres doesn't do this himself, we think that these comments and the book as a whole are a direct contrast to and comment on the well-known work of Carl Schmitt in *The Nomos of Earth in the International Law of the Jus Publicum Europaeum* (2003), where he argued that nomos should be understood as a taking of land formalized through the naming of the land by its ruler. Since the *Peace of Westphalia* sovereigns have been "*marking*" land on Earth using the law, and in that process also appropriating and directing nonhuman creativity.

The order that Schmitt's nomos seeks to control and regulate is the *physis* or the natural world. Ecomodernists increasingly speculate that technology, and not rulers and kings, determine how we will "mark" land and life on Earth. The authors of *The Ecomodernist Manifesto* take great pains for instance to stress that they do not see the limits to the growth of production as finite (Asafu-Adjaye 2015). Citing a lack of scientific consensus, they posit that all material limits could be functionally overcome by technological innovations, such as overcoming ecological crises led by fossil fuels by recourse to nuclear technologies. Even critics of an ecomodernist ethos, humanist scholars such as Hamilton, argue that this could be an appropriate response to ruptures in Earth systems which define the Anthropocene (Hamilton 2017), thus placing them into the same ecomodernist camp as the subjects of their criticism. While acknowledging the impact of technology on nature, ecomodernists refuse to accept that this is the inevitable result of technology existing within nature and therefore necessarily changing its environment as it appropriates and operationalizes it. As such, the ecomodernist position is unable to accept nature's reciprocal influence on technology, instead seeming to mis-identify technic as altogether outside of nature and capable of imposing order on an otherwise unruly world. In doing


DOI: 10.4324/9781003388081-28

so, we argue that the ecomodernist position can be taken as an extension, or rehabilitation, of Schmitt's nomos, and brings with it all the limitations of its predecessor.

In this chapter, we explain what we see as the creativity that's deeply inherent and central to the natural world. While human beings are critically responsible for the ruptures of the Anthropocene, the natural world also works to a nomos. Our discussion of creativity and ingenuity in the natural world is aimed at helping us understand, and ultimately mediate, the relations between all things in the broader environment, by looking to the underlying creativity of the way all things negotiate space and relations. Our approach follows post-humanist thinkers such as Serres and Whitehead, whose works demonstrate the great influence of the nonhuman world on the development of our own world and jurisprudence, highlighting the necessity of engaging with this broader milieux in order to better understand our own position within it (Serres 1990; Whitehead 1978). Scholars like Hamilton will argue that the Earth's response to these ruptures will be one of "defiance" (Hamilton 2017), suggesting that our volition marks us out as the dominant actors on the geological stage. Without an ontology that explains why the Earth is defiant, he resorts to a common-sense position that dilutes the deep influence that the nonhuman has on its environment, his argument ultimately resembling that of the ecomodernists he tries to resist. The ecomodernist is thus unable to recognize that in the face of the Anthropocene, our environment is as likely to overcome us as we are to overcome it, hardly restricted to simple subservience or passive resistance.

The key question of the Anthropocene is the extent and manner to which these ruptures in Earth systems will disrupt nature's *omnia* (Greek for the ability to respond to anything) or its ability to creatively adapt and draw upon its inherent capacity for ingenuity to solve its own problems in ways that do not account for human need. What we argue is that the nomos, the underlying spirit and ethos, of our adaptive response to the Anthropocene has to recognize the capacity for ordering that exists from within the natural world. Whitehead's work as we discuss below enables us to see a nomos and a reality beyond the traditional role we see as being played by the sovereign or humans. We argue that the wider and more inclusive view of reality encouraged by reading Whitehead allows us to see the natural world in the very foundations of what we come to view as the basis for creating an ordered life, that is, the nomos of the Anthropocene.

Below, we will first discuss the idea of the nomos and why – given what scholars see as its role in shaping our law, seeking to uncover and change – it must be part of our efforts to face the Anthropocene. In the second part, we discuss the idea of creativity and ingenuity in the natural world as having a foundation not in causality but in an alternative ontology that explains the processes of change in the natural world. We use this to conclude that the new nomos for the Anthropocene must deeply account for this nonhuman world-making potential if it is to orient us in this age of rupture. Such a nomos should encourage the sort of pragmatic uncertainty that we, following Whitehead, suggest is needed for human beings to engage symbiotically with the natural world. If law is a cultural institution, then a nomos that accounts for creativity will increasingly adapt to include the nonhuman as central to its evolution rather than as a governance tool for managing human needs and technological change.

## Nomos

It is perhaps impossible to definitively form a definition of *nomos*, given its millennia of (largely oral and thus unrecorded) history, stretching back at least to ancient Greece. Zartaloudis makes the point that the word, in its original context, was polyvalent; it has several recorded uses, and these can even seem contradictory (Zartaloudis 2018, 387). In contrast, Carl Schmitt famously argued in his book *The Nomos of Earth* (as well as its subsequent addendums) that nomos should be understood as a taking of land formalized through the naming of the land by its ruler (Schmitt 2006, 349). Schmitt's nomos is therefore an immediate act of violence, a taking of land in the name of a ruler, that is the constitutive ground of their sovereign right (Stergiopoulou 2014, 117). Contrast this with the nomos of Agamben, who, obviously sympathetic to Schmitt's efforts but evidently disagreeing with his conclusions, prefers to cast nomos as a sort of "spatial order," drawing on Schmitt's understanding of spaces that mark the inside and the outside of the law in the development of his theory of sovereignty and distribution (Agamben 1998, 18–19). It is this sovereign power to exclude territory from the legal order, and the exteriority that it creates, that comes to define Agamben's nomos and enables his "state of exception," which, following Schmitt, he sees as defining the very substance of sovereignty (Agamben 1998, 25–27). The sovereign is therefore, according to Agamben, defined as the one who can suspend the legal order, and it is the right to designate what is outside the normative juridical order (and the exercise of this right by way of this legal order) that comprises the nomos of the sovereign (Agamben 1998, 28–29). More specifically, Agamben argues along these lines that it is the ability to exclude some from the protections of the legal order, to reduce them to bare life as part of the exception to legal order, which is the "originary act of sovereignty" (Agamben 1998, 83), so defining the nomos of the modern day (Deuber-Mankowsky 2015, 59).

The work of Schmitt, influential as it has been on our conception of nomos, has been called into question, however, especially by authors of more robust etymological and philological explorations of the classical terms Schmitt relies upon. Stergiopoulou notes that Schmitt's analysis of the term nomos is largely a poetic one, rather than a juridical one, which rejects etymological evidence in favor of tying nomos to the appropriation of land, clearly influenced by the German expansionist thought of his day (Stergiopoulou 2014, 121–122). She notes his unjustified modification of the etymological record goes so far as to come off as more artistic than philological, expressly ignoring any evidence that might threaten his association of legal legitimacy with an instantiating and immediate act of violent appropriation (Stergiopoulou 2014, 111). Some historians take this critique a step further, arguing that Schmitt's conception of nomos is explicitly underpinned by his antisemitism and association with the Nazi party after 1933 (Gross 2017, 4). This influence is demonstrated, for instance, by his resistance to both the "universal norms" of "Jewish liberalism," as well as his explicit affirmations of Jewish people as an "enemy" to be feared (Deuber-Mankowsky 2015, 55). Given this history, we stress that any strict association between nomos and positive law, in the sense that the two are seen as co-emergent, must be resisted: the term, in its polyvalence, properly refers to a highly contingent and creative form of rules and principles and must remain theoretically distinct from the law of the sovereign.

Thus, we reject the rebranding of nomos by Schmitt, preferring a more historical understanding of the term. Schmitt was correct in asserting that nomos is more embedded than the universal laws of, for example, liberalism; he fails to acknowledge, however, its plurality (including its rejection of the nonhuman), blinded as he is by the ideological preoccupations of his contemporaries, including and especially antisemitism. We prefer to adopt a definition of nomos closer to that forwarded by Zartaloudis (Zartaloudis 2018), one which, as Stergiopoulou highlights through historical evidence (Stergiopoulou 2014, 113), Schmitt railed against in his criticisms of Hölderlin. Both scholars relying on passages from Pindar to interpret "nomos," Schmitt argues that Hölderlin has fallen into the classic trap of reducing nomos to law as it exists, where he would prefer to see it understood as the "immediate form in which the political and social order of a people is revealed" (Schmitt 2006, 70). This immediate act through which nomos is revealed is specifically constituted through the naming of land by the sovereign, formally enfolding it into the legal order. What he misses, however, is that Hölderlin recognizes the impossibility of understanding nomos through the analysis of things in their immediate form, noting that nomos necessarily emerges through a process of mediation and negotiation (Hölderlin 2004, 229–230, cited Zaratalоudis (2020); Stergiopoulou 2014, 113–114).

This contingent and exploratory conception of nomos is clarified in the work of new materialists who, by way of Delueze and Guattari, expressly connect the concept of nomos to the creative emergence of rules or laws through discovery (e.g. Phillipopoulos-Mihalopoulos 2015, 67 and 225). Given his foundational role in the work of Deleuze and Guattari, it should be stressed here that the creativity underlying this emergence is the same sort to which Whitehead attributes metaphysical primacy, arguing that it is creativity (rather than a transcendental essence) to which we owe credit for the ordering of beings in the universe (Whitehead 1978, 20). On this understanding, nomos is framed as an innate, creative potential – a discoverable, normative line of flight for a collective body – that precedes and undergirds the sovereign law Schmitt discusses, which we might instead call logos (Phillipopoulos-Mihalopoulos 2015, 56).

Put simply, nomos is the normative content of rules or customs that precede and justify their enactment. According to the Hellenistic tradition on which scholars such as Schmitt rely, it is necessarily uncovered, and never wholly, through active discovery (Plato 1927, 395–397; Zartaloudis 2018, xv). It might be understood then as natural law, a customary order such as that which motivates Antigone when she sees refusing the burial of a son of Athens as a disgrace to the gods themselves (Sophocles 2003, 73). Nomos is the source of that which "moral and religious consciousness knows to be right and necessary" (Kirkwood 1947, 64); that is, nomos should be understood as normative and best discovered through a process of discovery and consideration but not, as we will argue, determined by only humans. Through this broad and active consideration of processes of adaptation, nomos can be understood as the rules for discovering a truly unifying mode of being, a customary way of living and ordering things, including resources and political power, that fully accounts for the context of its particular *milieu*. As Zartaloudis makes clear in his extensive study of the word's etymology, nomos, in its ancient Greek context, can be understood as a customary way of ordering life that all things, including the divine itself, are subject to (Zartaloudis 2018, 322). However, this ordering has to be seen as more encompassing of the nonhuman and its potential role in determining the cultural life of humans. For the order we draw from nomos to fully reflect the collective, the milieu, in which we are submerged, it must account for the essential ways in which the nonhuman actively participates in, and even facilitates, that emergent ordering of things.

There is significant overlap here between concepts that we would consider religious, legal, scientific, and political, primarily because these ideas were not distinct to the people of the Archaic era to which we owe the term nomos (Zartaloudis 2018, xxxviii–xxxix). This way of being is necessarily emergent, only able to be discovered through experience. It "permeates the metaphysical cosmos" flowing from all agents regardless of status (Zartaloudis 2018, 320). This is not the static law of Schmitt, of logos, and must be progressively discovered (Zartaloudis 2018, xxx). This terminological indeterminacy also highlights the source of some of the difficulty in directly translating these ancient terms to modern contexts, suggesting that we would be better served by theoretical signposts than strict definitions.

Therefore, since nomos comprises emergent and uncovered norms that underlie, but are not irreducible to, immediate distributions of power, it must be understood as subject to negotiation that is heavily dependent on the climate and relations of the relevant age. For our purposes, then, it can then be tentatively argued that nomos is: (1) custom; (2) collectively felt and discovered (it flows between all bodies, to borrow terms from affect theorists); and (3) thus dependent on (as it is situated in) the milieu in which it is discovered. Nomos, and the laws and norms we derive therefrom, has scope to adapt and encompass new subjects, including nonhuman beings, which might provide us with new avenues for collectively negotiating our position within the unprecedented age of the Anthropocene. Such a break with precedent, we argue, calls for a return to the law's wellspring: nomos.

## Creativity

Given the importance of finding a nomos that can "permeate the metaphysical cosmos" and mediate and shape (the relations of) our emergent spatial order, we turn our gaze in this section to an ontology that can meaningfully describe the nonhuman's role in responding to the ruptures defining the Anthropocene. This should not be taken to mean that evolution itself is a conscious or intentional process of adaptation, as if guided by a higher power, nor as taking a position on evolutionary debates about the nature and gradations of consciousness. Rather, the creative agents we imagine are the pluralistic assemblages of Deleuze and Guatarri, a web of bodies and relations united not by common will but by interrelation (Deleuze and Guattari 2013, 24). We draw on Whitehead's work in this part to provide us with the foundations for recasting creativity as the nomos for ordering life.

## The Loss of Objectivity

Modern science's central claim to objectivity, and thus its methods of knowledge-creation, are all founded on a simple truth – "simple location" (Whitehead 1978, 137; Sehgal 2014, 190). Responding to the demands of Nietzsche's (1974, 181-2) madman with an almost paranoid pragmatism, "scientific materialism" begins from the Cartesian position that the mind, through reflection upon the information of the senses, is the only source of objective truth about the world (Descartes 2008, 11). The empirical sciences have thus proceeded from the premise that only by measuring and verifying the so-called objective properties of matter can we approach an objective understanding of its nature. Put simply, modern physics is thus built on the idea that, by observing patterns of changes to these objective traits (simple location, shape, chemical construction, etc.), we can understand it in totality.

Matter is thus bifurcated, fundamentally split into its primary (objectively measurable) properties, and secondary qualities, or *qualia* (Godfrey-Smith 2020, 83). These qualitative aspects of perception, things such as color, taste, affect, and the like, were relegated to speculative phenomenology and, more recently, a strictly mechanistic neuroscience, under the belief that they were simple "psychic additions" – the inevitable and deterministic result of our brains interpreting this objective sense data (Whitehead 1964, 29; Locke 2004, ch 8 [13]). Thus, through Enlightenment thinkers, epistemology and ontology became thoroughly fused in one "substance ontology," which supposes that all of the universe is comprised of bare matter subjected to random natural forces, all acting according to strictly observable, mechanistic rules (Debaise 2017, 7). By the turn of the twentieth century, however, science's own methods began to call this faith in simple location into question, and the resulting loss of certainty posed a threat to the very objectivity on which the Scientific Revolution was premised (Whitehead 1978, 264; Nicholson 2019, 108).

Working in the first half of the twentieth century as a mathematician, Whitehead and his contemporaries witnessed firsthand the clear deficiencies of scientific materialism (along with its mechanistic model of nature), particularly when tasked with explaining the findings of emerging fields such as quantum physics (Rescher 1996, 17; Nicholson 2019, 109–110). In the face of this loss of certainty, Whitehead began to find himself increasingly drawn away from substance ontology and toward what he would come to describe as a speculative "philosophy of organism" (Whitehead 1978, xi). Much like the limited nomos of Schmitt, the laws of Newtonian physics could provide only a snapshot of the spatial order as seen from a particular perspective. Just as the Anthropocene unsettles all prior norms, this era of quantum physics signaled a break with the assumptions that had thus far guided the field. Faced with this break from precedent, Whitehead's cosmology had to return to the fundamentals; where for law this is nomos, for physics this required a return to metaphysics.

Where Schmitt is focused on the perspective of the sovereign, Newton's laws derive from the observations of a theoretical outside observer, giving rise to contemporary science's "view from Sirius," which, like the arbitrary and externally imposed spatial order of the sovereign's law, takes context to be of secondary importance to generalizable rules (Latour 2018, 68). Whitehead's resulting theory, the philosophy of "organicism," attempts to overcome what he saw as the fundamental misconception of scientific materialism – the bifurcation of nature – by way of a reflexive metaphysics that could underpin the development of a truly coherent, logical, and adequate cosmology (Whitehead 1978, 3–4).

## Creativity and Organicism

For Whitehead, speculative philosophy should remain suspicious of simple answers. As such, organicism had to replace the intuitive principles of scientific materialism with metaphysical principles that were aimed at explaining, rather than denying, the variability of all things in nature. In contrast, the traditional scientific materialist belief was in the "mechanical" model of nature, which has come to dominate both our understanding of human and nonhuman nature, and sees all of the universe as a great machine, albeit one that far outstrips any human invention (Nicholson 2019, 109). This complexity derives from the fact that each part in this grand machine is a complex machine in itself, each also made up of similarly complex machines, "*ad infinitum*" (Leibniz 1898, 254). Life itself is therefore reduced to natural laws that determine the nature and function of these machines, all turning in harmony like the inner workings of a grand clock.

The nomos of such a universe is thus written in its history, in the patterns that have come to dictate this history, patterns which come to serve as almost a pre-determined blueprint for the endless generation of these self-assembling, self-replicating machines (Nicholson 2019, 109; Merrell 2006, 121). Unfortunately, this overly mechanistic model of nature has remained dominant, and the dichotomies flowing from the strict bifurcation of the Cartesian sciences haunt all corners of modern scholarship. In the face of this, it will not do to simply reformulate the strict dichotomy between humanity and its natural environment that has proliferated since the Enlightenment (Whitehead 1978, 10–11).

If, as Whitehead (1925, 22) suggested, these bifurcations were unsuitable for the scientific situation of the previous century, then they are certainly anachronistic in the present day. Just as simple location was being debunked by the early findings of quantum physics, as expressed by theories such as Heisenberg's uncertainty principle (Sehgal 2014, 189), contemporary evidence from fields such as molecular and evolutionary biology, and, as we suggest, geological evidence such as that of the emerging Anthropocene, continue to demonstrate the need to reimagine nomos as something other than the pre-determined mechanics of an endless assembly line (e.g. Godfrey-Smith 2020; Debaise 2017; Nicholson 2019). In its place, Whitehead's organicism gives metaphysical primacy to creativity providing us a foundation for the elucidation of a nomos rooted in creativity rather than mechanicism.

To demonstrate this point, in these final pages we offer a paradigmatic summary of Whitehead's cosmology and consider its relevance in light of modern scientific evidence. It should be noted that in outlining the innate "multiplicity" of his metaphysical concepts, organicism can sometimes be difficult to understand in its own terms. To aid our discussion, and to more clearly demonstrate its relevance to the discovery of nomos in the face of such immense ruptures to the Earth system, we will also refer to those contemporary trends in post-humanist scholarship that have built upon the legacy of Whitehead's cosmology.

If creativity is the primary metaphysical principle of organicism, then its speculative ontology must be understood as an ontology entirely comprised of creative agents, which Whitehead describes simply as "actual entities" or "actual occasions," which account for all those Cartesian objects of modern epistemology, those objects that comprise the world which we experience. Rather than separating these objects into types or assigning a hierarchy to these actual entities, Whitehead conceives of these entities as infinitely divisible, analyzable as *societies, propositions, or eternal objects*. Societies might be understood as "assemblages" of objects, referring to the way entities are made up of a complex interrelated series of parts (each themselves an assemblage in turn), while nonetheless maintaining a common form (Deleuze and Guattari 2013, 385–389; Whitehead 1978, 34). Eternal objects are those phenomenological aspects within an actual entity that renders it recognizable through time, even as it is subject to endless, creative flux (Whitehead 1978, 23). Finally, propositions are those dimensions of entities that are taken up by others, influencing the broader world and its unfolding. To grasp the difference, we might look to Heraclitus, whom Whitehead cites with approval, and his belief that it is impossible, given the inherent flux of all things, to ever step in the same river twice, given that the flow of water will inevitably lead to the replacement and renewal of the river through time (Whitehead 1978, 309). In this instance, the river's form, the riverbed, the water, and all other objects involved in the assemblage that comprise a river are the actual entities of Whitehead's cosmology. The society is the river, understood as a totality, all maintaining a unified form and purpose. The proposition is the way the river invites you to cross, the way its water soaks through your shoes, and the way it indelibly marks the crossing on your personal history. Finally, the river you recognize, despite its changes, on returning to the site, is the eternal object – the result of a phenomenological recognition of an ultimately different entity.

It is important to understand though, that while this philosophy is speculative in a literal sense, he has no interest in the transcendental. Rather, Whitehead is concerned with critiquing the underlying cosmology of the mechanical model of nature and replacing it with a cosmology that is logical, coherent, and practically applicable. In this endeavor, he develops a sort of phenomenology that rejects any bifurcation of nature into primary and secondary attributes in the Lockean sense and seeks to place these all within the phenomenological entities of our experience.

To do so, Whitehead splits these objects of our experience into different types of societies, dividing them along the lines of living societies (such as animals and ecosystems) and structured societies (such as rocks, the atmosphere, and other "non-living" things) (Whitehead 1978, 99–100). There is, however, no clear distinction between living and structured societies, as all animals are made up of bundles of raw molecules that could be considered physical and non-living seen on their own. Rather, Whitehead's philosophy rejects Cartesian dualism in favor of a dipolar monism, wherein all societies exhibit varying levels of activity along mental and physical poles (Whitehead 1978, 239) As such, individual societies contain two identities within themselves: the striated, disjunctive universe comprised of individuated societies, and as parts of the concurrent universe, the broad society that makes up all of nature and existence.

Other organicist and post-human scholars have set out to clarify Whitehead's cosmology, seeking to understand the multiplicity of his metaphysical scheme. Deleuze and Guattari (2013, 2, 46) describe assemblages developing through the emergence of a new expression of identity in matter, such as the sedimentary rock that forms from the eventual intensification of the entanglement of once-loose sediment. In this sense, their assemblages are the outcome of the interrelation of Whitehead's societies to the point that they are recognized as having formed something new, both a new structured society and, if some entity comes to recognize it, an eternal object (Whitehead 1978, 43–44).

This is not to say that Whitehead rejects any bifurcation, but he recognizes this as fundamental to *all* creativity, not just to that of human beings. He points to it as the ultimate matter of fact, the underlying principle that enables the novelty by which individual societies come to be. This speaks to the primacy of affects, or feelings, in Whitehead's cosmology, as it is the *feeling* of self that creates the self, not the other way around (Whitehead 1978, 179). For Whitehead (1978, 66), there is no firm boundary between societies – every society is an embedded assemblage of societies, *ad infinitum*, made whole only through the collation of various feelings and sensory inputs into one unitary experience. This is not to say that the societies within societies are not free themselves, of course; it is important to note that the cells in your body live for themselves, not for the greater *You* that they comprise (Smith 2020, 30). This forms a sort of reciprocal relationship between the societies at various levels of each larger society, all the way up to the entire universe as a whole. Thus, it is the experience of self, as each society in the greater body feeds into this coalescence of experience that allows for the enjoyment of the self and creates individuals. This cosmology potentially renders all of Schmitt's ideas of nomos fairly pointless.

This internal reciprocity can be understood in the context of what Deleuze and Guattari (2013, 5) would dub "a rhizomatic structure." Rhizomes are the structure of their "body without organs" or "BwO," the form of the greater "plane of consistency" (Deleuze and Guattari 2013, 84). A rhizome is primarily understood through the reciprocity of flows throughout the structure, where flows travel through and between each point in the structure rather than along specific lines (Deleuze and Guattari 2013, 6–7). Thus, the rhizome rejects a hierarchy of parts and is a fundamentally interconnected and situated structure. Ever changing and permeable, the structure of a rhizome expands through the selective inclusion of material from its plane of consistency or milieu (or antecedent environment, to borrow from Whitehead (1978, 67–68)). This is the *extensive* nature of the rhizome, its proliferation through space and through other rhizomatic structures (Deleuze and Guattari 2013, 590; Whitehead 1978, 69).

Take the example of a flock of sheep traveling with, and not necessarily guided by, their nomadic shepherd: as Philippopoulos-Mihalopoulos (2015, 153–154) notes, they form a single, interfolded multiplicity, coordinating along a single line of flight by the flow of affect between and among all the actual objects of its structure. This society, or assemblage, can survive the subtraction or addition of other parts that aid in its line of flight, be that through the loss of a sheep or the inclusion of grass for grazing into the assemblage. Similarly, it can pass through and fuse with other rhizomatic assemblages, such as forests and planes and urban environments that interrupt, or rupture, these landscapes. This emergence as a nomadic flock along a line of flight is therefore stable, but only to a point: to lose all the sheep or to lose the shepherd, for example, would take this society along a line of flight that leads it to exceed its *intensive* expression, creating a new emergent assemblage that proposes a new eternal object and takes on a new expressive identity (Whitehead 1978, 240).

The focus of each society is therefore on the perpetuation of its own modes of living, of its "historic route" that has allowed general stability, and the varying levels of polar activity determine *how* this is done (Whitehead 1978, 56). Structured societies, on the one hand, diffuse and generalize external pressures by limiting the ways in which the societies around them can affect them (Whitehead 1978, 101–102). Living societies, on the other hand, transform and morph in the face of pressures, changing in order to maintain an identity in the face of a changing environment by engaging in activity along the mental pole (Whitehead 1978, 103). Greater mental activity allows for a wider variety of nuanced responses to pressures (Whitehead 1978, 277), but, as noted, it is impossible to reduce even the most physical of societies to a deterministic mechanism – choices must always be made. These choices are creativity made manifest, as each choice is rooted in the antecedent environment, but what will be done with the data gathered from this environment is up to the individual assemblages – societies – involved.

To demonstrate the mental activity of physical societies, we should look for a moment to the work of Jane Bennet in her book, *Vibrant Matter* (2010). Bennet notes that even a hunk of metal is better defined by its vibration than by its static structure. Looking to the microscopic structure of the atoms (actual objects) in a hunk of metal (a non-living society), Bennet, drawing upon the work of Cyril Smith, notes that while much of the objects of its composition are in a predictable, lattice-like structure, it is full of tiny crystalline structures, inconsistencies proliferate at the edges and between these structures (Bennett 2010, 52). It is here that the interrelation of the objects in this metal society occurs, where atomic particles are shared between the "grains" of the structure while belonging to none – this determines the shape of the grains more than the structure of the whole and is what allows the interplay of atomic charges that allows the society to hold together. Bennett (2010, 62) calls this flux or "quivering" movement of the free atoms in the lattice an example of a metal's "vitality." In large part, this vitality holds the society together in the face of external pressure, creating a (perhaps even imperceptibly) novel structure or emergence (Whitehead 1978, 35).

This is what Whitehead (1978, 34) means when he refers to the creative ignorance of external pressures that physical societies exhibit, in contrast to the adaptation of living ones. This can also be seen in the way that cracks in a metal lattice spread by way of the creative contingency of the society, forming as a consequence of the idiosyncratic movement of all the pieces, all responding to each other in a cascade (Bennett 2010, 94; De Landa 1995). Finally, this idea of cracking metal as a manifestation of creative potential is demonstrative of the way that stability can be compromised by creativity in physical structures more easily, as the cracking may eventually lead to a complete splitting of the lattice into two, new, separate objects; it continues on this "cracking" line of flight until it exceeds its original intensity and forms new assemblages.

Whitehead (1978, 88 and 345) takes this idea a step further, however, and identifies creativity as derived from God. This may seem an exaggeration, but it is vital to understand that Whitehead's God is not supernatural: as Mesle (2008, 85) notes, in Whitehead's cosmology "there is to be no metaphysical cheating." He sees this as necessary, an extension of the principle that nothing can be created from nothing. As such, Whitehead's God is understood as the source of novelty, equally interested in all perspectives and suffering with us in all things (Whitehead 1978, 346; Pandiyath 2014, 130–131). Recall that Whitehead's organicism seeks to elevate the phenomenological to the level of ontology (and can thus be called onto-phenomenological by nature), so creativity's primacy being rooted in the perpetuation of *all* experiences can be seen as the source of radical moral obligations (Sehgal 2014, 193). It also means that, if creativity is a matter of fact, it must have a source.

God, now stripped of supernatural power and any unequal bias, is something of a symbolic entity, possibly influenced by Whitehead's prior religious beliefs, before coming to identify as an atheist (Mesle 2008, 83). For whatever reason, he felt the need to draw on this notion of God, seeing it as the most reasonable explanation for the creation of creativity in a universe that once did not have it prior. God might then be understood in the same way as Neptune was seen by classical astronomers who knew that a planet of that size, mass, and orbit *must* be affecting the orbits of other planets, which ultimately led to the discovery of the planet itself (Mesle 2008, 83–84). Coupled with his statements that the "universe is a creative advance into novelty" (Whitehead 1978, 222), his concept of God could be better understood as the conjunctive universe itself, embedded in and comprised of all the other societies of existence and thus equally invested in all of them. It is a useful analogy, therefore, for understanding the vastness of an interconnected universe we do not understand well enough to conceive of more fully.

If creativity is understood then as the march into novelty of the conjunctive universe, it can be seen how this creativity can be found in the decisions of its individual parts in their emergence into novelty as well. It is this creative drive, deriving from the differing ways that each society experiences and thus feels their antecedent conditions and the decisions they make in response to these feelings, that underpins this evolution. Decisions are therefore reduced to their technical sense – the canalizing of potentials into a specific path, by picking one set of possible outcomes and shutting off another (Debaise 2017, 66). Novelty naturally emerges from this process, as the constant creativity of all societies leads to them absorbing and rejecting various parts of their environment in an unpredictable way. As all societies are part of the greater plane of nature, this immutable, creative flux ensures that the antecedent environment is never identical to any environment past.

Therefore, we do not need to reject Whitehead's claim that all societies follow a "historic route" based on an understanding of the potentials chosen and rejected in the past, as no choice can ever result in the same outcome in a changing environment (Whitehead 1978, 22–23). These routes can be seen then as guides, to be interpreted as the societies who encounter them see fit. This fits with emerging ideas of nature as self-organizing where this route might be understood as less of a blueprint and more like an elucidation of lessons learned in the search for stability in the past. As such, Whitehead's natural God is thoroughly secularized, and the role of creativity in the creation of novelty, and nature itself, is secured. It is this creative force then, this apparent mutual emergence toward creative novelty, that forces us to recognize our ultimate interdependence with the nonhuman, deeply embedded in this process with them as we are. Like our nomos, Whitehead's God is the source of collective action, the wellspring of normativity and thus of law.

This creativity is not deterministic, and indeed its primacy is emblematic of the limitations of determinism. It also does not require, as it might seem, a strange extension of dualism to the rest of nature – to simply allow for a Cartesian "mind," outside of matter, that is not exclusive to *Homo sapiens*. This would be to anthropomorphize nature, to give it traits that are considered human, and for Whitehead's ontology, there cannot be any such transcendental traits. It is important to understand that the inherent contingency of matter on a quantum scale, as it has led to the increased understanding of nature as self-organizing, is able to create novelty and resist determination without importing humanized agency or intention into it. This is demonstrated quite effectively by the work of Peter Godfrey-Smith (2020, 203–207), who argues that if we are able to accept evolution on Earth as beginning with single-celled organisms slowly changing over generations, we can accept that it is not so strange for a mind to evolve in this process – the necessary result of bodies that require coordinated movement and the interpretation of increasingly complex sensory data to ensure survival.

This fuzziness is uncomfortable, perhaps, but Morton (2021, 72) argues we would do well to embrace this discomfort. It is this discomfort that allows for the experience of beauty, or perhaps more accurately it is beauty. Morton (2021, 81) puts this in the context of art, arguing that to appreciate art requires a tacit recognition that we have "psychically melded" with the nonhuman in a way that is inherently uncomfortable (Morton 2021, 54). It reminds us of the blurred distinction between us and the nonhuman, or in Whitehead's terms, that we are part of one society, both in the room and as a part of a broader universe. As Keller (2019, 53–54) notes, Whitehead's "advance into novelty" is equivalent to the creation of beauty, a *kalogenesis*. In allowing for the formation of a new assemblage between one's self and a piece of art, Morton (2021, 81) suggests, we can experience this beauty directly as affect, through the novel assemblage of self and art that this creates.

This blurriness, this vibratory nature of the concurrent universe, is seen in much contemporary ecological thought, including the post-human insistence that we are all ecological units in themselves, tiny ecosystems made up as much of other nonhuman living things (and non-living matter) as we are of things recognizably human (Derossi 2020, 15). In other words, we recognize the historic route of both ourselves and the art we appreciate (which, in truth, is the same route), which requires acknowledging that we were just as likely to become that art as this human, for example. The historic route, as Whitehead (1978, 187) notes, recalls not just the choices made, but those rejected. This is Deleuze's true creativity made real: the inclusion of all possibilities excluded as well as those included. Phillipopoulos-Mihalopoulos (2015, 93) takes care to note that this carving of the past is literal, pointing to the way that these choices all affect the form of the bodies, carving their lines of flight into their skin in this vibrating plane of consistency, or lawscape as he would refer to it.

## Conclusion

In this chapter, we have attempted to navigate debates around the definition of nomos, arguing that a more historically accurate, not to mention more analytically valuable, understanding of the term is of a natural creative tendency to adaptation, best understood through a process of discovery rather than through the immediate appearance of the (contingent) social order as it exists in any instant. Understanding this creativity can allow us to better expose the limitations of the ecomodernist agenda, which remains rooted in the belief that human intervention could supersede the will of a broader, nonhuman nature. Even supposed critics of the ecomodernist agenda cede that humans mark the single volitional world-making agents, suggesting that technology derives its destructive force from somewhere outside of the natural order. What advocates of such an anthropocentric cosmology cannot grasp is that far from originating outside of the broader natural environment, our "world-making" potential comes from our position *within* a constantly (re) negotiated spatial order. While this may seem a petty distinction, it is essential to understand how we have found ourselves here if we are to appropriately face the crises that have begun to emerge from the ruptures of the Anthropocene. By resituating nomos in a greater processual cosmology, rather than in human legal orders, we can recognize that the Earth is not showing "defiance" in the face of human will, it is simply exhibiting its creative potential under a wildly altered set of circumstances. Without the humility to recognize the creativity of nature, we will be stuck trying to search for tricks to dominate its otherwise random forces, tilting at windmills all the while. Respecting a nomos that goes beyond our own limited desires and perspectives is the first step toward a holistic symbiosis between the human and nonhuman world, which recognizes our interdependence and does not jeopardize it with doomed attempts at total appropriation.

## References

Asafu-Adjaya, J. *et al.* (2015) *An EcoModernist Manifesto*. Available at: www.ecomodernism.org (Accessed: 29 January 2022).

Bennett, J. (2010) *Vibrant Matter: A Political Ecology of Things*. Duke University Press.

Debaise, D. (2017) *Nature as Event: The Lure of the Possible*. Translated by M. Halewood. Duke University Press.

G. Deleuze and Guattari, F. (2013) *A Thousand Plateaus*. Bloomsbury.

Derossi, N. (2020) 'Rethinking Whitehead's Influence and Rethinking Scientific Practices', *Erasmus Student Journal of Philosophy*, 18, p. 8.

Descartes, R. (2008) *Meditations on First Philosophy*. Oxford University Press.

Deuber-Mankowsky, A. (2015) 'Cutting off mediation: Agamben as a master thinker.', *Acta Poética*, 36(1).

De Landa, M. (1995) 'Uniformity and Variability: An Essay on the Philosophy of Matter.' Presented at Doors of Perception 3: On Matter Conference, Netherlands Design Institute.
Godfrey-Smith, P. (2020) *Metazoa: Animal Life and the Birth of the Mind*. Farrar, Straus and Giroux.
Gross, R. (2017), *Carl Schmitt and the Jews*. University of Wisconsin Press.
Hamilton, C. (2017) *The Defiant Earth: The Fate of Humans in the Anthropocene*. Allen & Unwin.
Hölderlin, F. (2004) *Sämtliche Werke*. WBG.
Keller, D.R. (2019) *Ecology and Justice: Citizenship in Biotic Communities*. Springer.
Kirkwood, G. (1947) 'Hecuba and nomos.' *Transactions of the American Philological Association*, 78. p. 61.
Latour, B. (2018) *Down to Earth: Politics in the New Climatic Regime*. John Wiley & Sons.
Leibniz, GW. (1898) *The Monadology and Other Philosophical Writings*. Clarendon Press.
Locke, J. (2004) *An Essay Concerning Human Understanding*. Project Gutenberg.
Merrell, F. (2006) 'Creation: Algorithmic, Organicist, or Emergent Metaphorical Process?', *Semiotica*, 161(1), p. 119.
Mesle, C.R. (2008) *Process-Relational Philosophy: An Introduction to Alfred North Whitehead*. Templeton Foundation Press.
Morton, T. (2021) *All Art Is Ecological*. Penguin Books.
Nicholson, D. (2019) 'Is the Cell Really a Machine?', *Journal of Theoretical Biology*, 477, p. 108.
Nietzsche, F. (1974) *The Gay Science*. Vintage Books.
Padiyath, T. (2014) *The Metaphysics of Becoming: On the Relationship between Creativity and God in Whitehead and Supermind and Sachchidananda in Aurobindo*. Walter de Gruyter.
Philippopoulos-Mihalopoulos, A. (2015) *Spatial Justice: Body, Lawscape, Atmosphere*. Routledge.
Plato. (1927) *Plato with an English Translation, volume VIII*. William Heineman Ltd.
Rescher, N. (1996) *Process Metaphysics: An Introduction to Process Philosophy*. State University of New York Press.
Schmitt, C. (2006) *The Nomos of the Earth in the International Law of the Jus Publicum Europaeum*. Telos.
Sehgal, M. (2014) 'Diffractive Propositions: Reading Alfred North Whitehead with Donna Haraway and Karen Barad', *Parallax*, 20(3), p. 188.
Serres, M. (1990) *The Natural Contract*. Michigan University Press.
Serres, M. (2011) *Malfeasance: Appropriation Through Pollution?* Stanford University Press.
Stergiopoulou, K. (2014) '*Taking Nomos: Carl Schmitt's Philology Unbound*', *October*, 149, p. 95.
Sophocles. (2003) *Sophocles: Antigone*. Oxford University Press.
Whitehead, AN. (1925), *Science and the Modern World: Lowell Lectures 1925*. Cambridge University Press.
Whitehead, A.N. (1964) *The Concept of Nature*. Cambridge University Press.
Whitehead, A.N. (1978) *Process and Reality: An Essay in Cosmology*. The Free Press.
Zarataloudis, T. (2020) *The Birth of Nomos*. Edinburgh University Press.

# 22

# LEARNING ECOLOGICAL LAW

## Innovating Legal Curriculum and Pedagogy

*Kate Galloway and Nicole Graham*

As Australia burned during the Black Summer of 2019–2020 (Rogers 2019; Celermajer 2021), the impoverished nature of the legal discourse adopted by Australian lawmakers became clear. Having denied the effects of climate change for at least a decade (Stoianoff and Guglyuvatyy 2020), lawmakers demonstrated their limited capacity to comprehend the enormity of the tragedy. By prioritizing the catastrophe's economic consequences, they revealed their complicity in its genesis (Kelman 2019). As the fires grew and merged across vast territories, it became increasingly clear that governments at all levels needed the capacity to think strategically beyond local, regional, state, and national economic concerns. The scale of the damage and its impacts extended to entire ecologies, whole communities, and the planet itself.[1]

The challenge of dealing with the aftermath of the bushfires – and preparing for the inevitable next conflagration – is not limited to the siloes of government administration. The law as it is currently oriented is inadequate to facilitate the responsibilities of governments and, indeed, citizens to serve and protect the more-than-human world. Before the flames had been extinguished, ordinary people were already seeking to understand where responsibility lay (Galloway 2020). The strictures of the law, however, appear unsuited to translating or accommodating the nature of the problem, including its scale and complexity, into readily available rights and remedies.

Environmental law would seem to provide a logical starting point for environmental protection and for the redress of environmental damage. The Black Summer bushfires, for example, highlighted the complex interrelationship between different legal obligations and remedies: state-commonwealth constitutional arrangements, tortious duties, public law principles, private property, financial industry regulation, and so on. The massive event demonstrated that although environmental law is necessary, it is insufficient as a legal foundation from which to protect the more-than-human. While law is necessarily concerned with the human, it seems to be exclusively concerned with the human sphere – as if humans are separable from the rest of the world. But the law is not only anthropocentric (it prioritizes human interests, narrowly conceived); it is also anthroparchic, meaning that it satisfies human interests by legitimating the exploitation of the more-than-human (Graham 2011a).

In this chapter, we consider the role of law's actors – lawyers – and the ways in which they are inculcated into the anthroparchism of the discipline. The premise of the chapter is that to address the existential challenge of the Anthropocene, it is necessary to alter the trajectory of the law by


DOI: 10.4324/9781003388081-29

changing the way in which law's new recruits – graduate lawyers – perceive and construe the human–Earth relationship that is manifest in legal discourse and practice. Recognizing that the dominant modes of law are inherently anthroparchic, the next part of the chapter analyses the role of legal education in reproducing those norms through a critical account of its pedagogy and core curriculum. The following part encourages an optimistic consideration of the ways in which legal education might challenge the status quo and innovate professional knowledge, skills, and dispositions that adapt to and redress the catastrophic problems and disputes that beset the Anthropocene.

## The Role of Legal Education in Reproducing Anthroparchic Norms

The goal of professional education is to instill in its apprentices the norms of the profession. Law is no exception (Flood 2019; Galloway et al. 2019). The standards of admission to a given profession are determined by its accrediting bodies, which often prescribe the program of education and associated training.[2] The priorities for admission will therefore inevitably reflect the priorities of the profession itself.[3] For legal professional accreditation frameworks, there are two significant features of the curriculum – by which we mean, in the narrow sense,[4] consciously designed, aligned, and sequenced subjects, learning activities, teaching modes, and assessment items. First, the frameworks reflect the capitalistic purpose of law's taxonomy (Graham 2014). Second, they emphasize content (principles and doctrines) over skills. Together, these two features underpin legal pedagogy and the authority of legal education to instill particular conceptualizations of law and human–Earth relations. This, combined with the fact of professional accreditation, constrains the capacity of law graduates to critique, adapt, and innovate law.

> Students accept theories on the authority of teacher and text, not because of evidence. What alternatives have they, or what competence? The applications given in texts are not there as evidence but because learning them is part of learning the paradigm at the base of current practice.
>
> *(Kuhn 1996, 88)*

In the following two sections, we discuss key features of the conventional curriculum of law and the dominant pedagogical modes that together inhibit the learning necessary for emergent legal professionals to challenge the law's existing paradigm.

### *The Curriculum and Taxonomy of Law*

Exploring the anthroparchic nature of the law curriculum requires an understanding of the common law's history and philosophical foundations. These foundations are constantly reinforced through the development of professional identities that, when calcified, become obstacles to change (Galloway et al. 2019, 31). The rise of what Sugarman refers to as the "textbook tradition" of law – whereby law became a coherent and unified body of rules (Sugarman 1986, 26) – coincided with Enlightenment thought and the Industrial Revolution. These co-constructed epistemological and economic changes (Mokyr 2011), together with the rise of legal positivism, produced a powerful discourse of cultural progress, economic growth, and legal entitlement that was supported through the institutions of the modern contract, private property, and the corporation (Atiyah 1979; Graham 2011a; Pahuja 2011; Wheeler 2017). These institutions provided the academic foundation of the law textbook, whereby complex human–Earth relations were abstracted into transactional mechanisms manifest as separate and distinctive sub-disciplinary components. The taxonomy of law facilitated by the textbook tradition of discrete juristic categories also fortified the conceptual separation of the world into public and private spheres (Graham 2014). As with the categories themselves, the public/private divide serves to legitimate and protect individual wealth and shield it from collective interests (Priel 2013, 504–505) on Earth, its people, and the resources from which wealth derives.

Following John Locke's seventeenth-century justification of an individualistic model of private property (Locke 1689), land became increasingly commodified. Like other non-specific economic "things," land was recognized as an object of property and was subject to market forces (Graham 2011a). The state played a critical role in the development of private property on land by guaranteeing the individual's legal right to the "disposal as well as the use of things" (Locke 1689, 111). These foundational tenets of liberal capitalism underpinned colonization and were profoundly instrumental in the dehumanization and dispossession of peoples all over the world (Williams 1994; Draper 2010; Levien 2013; Watson 2015; Greer 2018). Genocidal processes were often enforced by state-protected corporations that aimed to exploit the resources of lands and peoples in order to maximize profit for shareholders (Dalrymple 2019; Birchall 2020; Vermeulen and van Lint 2020).

In England, capitalist relations borne of the Industrial Revolution required the legal recognition of men as free to contract their labor in the market (Macpherson 1975, 112; Atiyah 1979; D. Kennedy 1998). "All legal rules were more and more cast in terms of areas of autonomy for the wills of legal actors, whether those were private individuals, state legislatures or the federal Congress" (D. Kennedy 1998, 248). Contractarianism is of increasing legal significance, even in the administration of public law, with governments at all levels now contracting out their responsibilities (Loewenstein 2013). Matters that may once have been regarded as properly situated within the realm of public law as a concern of the state are often now subsumed within private law and subject to commercial-in-confidence provisions. Furthermore, as Braithwaite points out, markets themselves are now "important national, regional and global regulators" (Braithwaite 2008, 29). Today, the market supplements and even replaces the role of government. The corporation, contract law, and private property provide, in concert, the central organizing structure of law.

The political and economic centrality of private law is reflected in the commercial orientation of the legal profession (Garth and Dezalay 2011; Flood and Lederer 2012) and embedded in the core curriculum of law degree programs. In Australia, for example, although the threshold learning outcomes for law seek to embrace the "broader contexts of the law" (Kift et al. 2010) within the remit of threshold graduate competencies, the omission of Indigenous cultural competency and knowledges, along with issues of environment and ecology, reflects the reticence of the legal profession to question its commercial orientation. The absence of Indigenous perspectives prompted Watson and Burns to describe the threshold learning outcomes as a "virtual terra nullius" (Watson and Burns 2015, 44).

The structure and content of the law curriculum reflect the priority of private interests in the law and their protection via the legal profession, which is responsible for accrediting the law degree as a requirement of admission to practice. Thornton argues that this shows how "dominant interests are served by sites and techniques within both legal education and legal practice, together with the way in which they are imbricated with each other" (Thornton 1998, 371). More recently, Thornton has observed the neoliberal university's jettison of critical analysis, preferring doctrinal knowledge that is ostensibly practical (Thornton 2012, 59–109). Although critique may not be sufficient to re-orient law's anthropocentrism, it is at least necessary. The consequences of what Thornton observes are an implicitly commercial orientation of the accredited law degree. This is inherent also in the public/private taxonomy of law that elevates the human and the corporation to the role of legal actor while all else – including non-human living creatures and the more-than-human world – remain mere objects of the law. While this is apparent from the structure and organization of the law and legal education, it is reinforced by a dominant pedagogy.

## The Pedagogy of Law

While curriculum establishes the content of a law degree, pedagogy informs how that content is taught. Watkins and Mortimore observe that pedagogy is "any conscious activity by one person designed to enhance learning in another" (Watkins and Mortimore 1999, 3), suggesting that curriculum is nested within it. Pedagogy speaks to the decisions that are made to promote learning and, implicitly, what that learning will comprise. On this understanding, pedagogy inevitably emerges from the particular philosophical standpoint of the teacher and, specifically, whether their pedagogy hinges on the activity of teaching or learning (Samuelowicz and Bain 2001). We suggest that the dominant pedagogy in legal education emerges from conventional notions of the authority and taxonomy of law that foreground the teaching of content.

Scholarly literature on pedagogy is mostly concerned with two major themes. One is the theorization of pedagogy; the other is the practice of pedagogy and teachers' perceptions of their own pedagogies. The latter theme encompasses five general topics: "[g]etting more knowledge," "[m]emorizing and reproducing," "[a]cquiring and applying procedures," "[m]aking sense or meaning," and "[p]ersonal change" (Watkins and Mortimore 1999). As evidenced by accredited law curricula, gaining knowledge and memorizing are arguably the curricular goals of legal education – articulated as "knowing the law." Teaching legal doctrine is often based on the metaphor of "filling the empty vessel," with students arriving in law school not knowing law and leaving with a "coherent body of knowledge that includes … the fundamental areas of legal knowledge" (Kift et al. 2010, 9). The dominant pedagogy of legal education thus preserves the status quo by reproducing the norms of the legal profession (Galloway et al. 2019), rather than encouraging law students to develop the skills to work within an increasingly complex and uncertain future (see generally Barnett and Hallam 1999; Barnett 2000; Barnett 2012).

Any discipline, including law, is populated by academics who were once, as students, inculcated into the norms and conventions of that discipline (Jones and Galloway 2012; Galloway and Jones 2014; Jones and Galloway 2015). As is the case for other disciplines, law teachers are likely to form their ideas about the nature of law and legal education through their own experience as law students (Ramsden 2003, 12–16) and, perhaps, also as legal practitioners (Jones and Galloway 2015). This increases the likelihood of reproducing the curriculum across generations. It also accounts for the persistent predominance of a particular kind of pedagogy in legal education. The foundations of this pedagogy stretch back to the Industrial Revolution (Jessup and Carroll 2017) and perpetuate anthroparchic ways of living in a dematerialized world (Graham 2021a).

For example, a key feature of the pedagogy of legal education is the methodological conceit of abstraction that is intrinsic to legal reasoning (Finley 1989, 905; Lucy 2009). In this method, knowledge is imparted through engagement with abstract concepts of the law in the absence of an examination of their effect on the material world (Graham 2014). The focus of legal reasoning is on the "correct" apportionment of rights as between parties through adversarial means. Thus, the destruction of the Juukan Gorge caves in Western Australia by mining giant Rio Tinto in 2020 is not significant in terms of the relevant legal reasoning, as there was no competition of legal rights. The miner had obtained the necessary permissions under section 18 of the *Aboriginal Heritage Act 1972* (WA), enabling it to destroy the culturally significant site. This calamitous event has attracted substantial attention and legal analysis in terms of potential law reform, but an analysis of the parties' respective rights affords no insights into the material damage done to the land – or to the harms meted out to the Puutu Kunti Kurrama and Pinikura, the traditional owners of the site. These harms are collateral to law.

The problem with teaching law through legal reasoning is that it decouples doctrine from its social, cultural, and ecological contexts. Learning the law as a series of abstract doctrines worked through a process of legal reasoning detaches the learner from law's agency in the world and its facilitation of the Anthropocene (Graham 2021b). It is precisely in this way that colonial legal systems developed without regard for First Nations peoples and their place-based laws (Graham 2009). Contract law is emblematic of free will but conceals corollary structural and material inequities, including the global labor market. Property law is emblematic of the free alienation of legally protected rights over any "valuable subject matters of possession" (Postema 1986, 174), but it conceals corollary anthropogenic environmental change arising from rights to exhaust and waste such property (Graham 2012). Even environmental law itself is concerned less with the more-than-human than with decisions of the executive arms of government according to the principles of administrative law (Galloway 2017).

Increasingly, legal education has incorporated critical approaches to learning and analyzing the law, representing an important shift in pedagogy. Certainly, socio-legal approaches to legal inquiry (Parker and Goldsmith 1998; Collier 2004), the contemporary move toward "Indigenizing" curriculum (Graham 2009; Wood 2013; Burns 2014; Burns 2018; Galloway 2018), sustainability education (Galloway et al. 2012; Galloway 2015), and place-based approaches (A. Kennedy et al. 2014; A. Kennedy et al. 2016; Van Wagner 2017) are examples of a commitment to the reorientation of legal education and a conscious challenge to the myth of its liberal promise (see, e.g., Thornton 1991). But a critical or contextual pedagogy in legal education is not enough on its own to facilitate the change required to redress the legal conditions of the Anthropocene. Despite decades of critical progress in Australian legal education (Thornton 1998; Thornton 2008; Carrigan 2013; Ardill 2016), the inertia wrought by the law's own structures, reflected within and reproduced by legal education and the academy itself (Thornton 2012), remains a major challenge. To equip law graduates of the twenty-first century to break down the structures that contribute to climate change requires more than a reorientation of curriculum, or a critical mindset. It requires us to help law students unlearn the model of the human–Earth relationship underpinning the paradigm of modern law that we must teach while we also foreground the agency of law in the more-than-human world and the dependence of humans on that world. A fundamental pivot from the Industrial Revolution foundations of legal education to a reimagined curriculum embracing an unfamiliar pedagogy must occur.

## A Pivot in Legal Education

The first step in changing the role of legal education in reproducing the legal conditions of the Anthropocene is recognizing that this role exists. "Transcending the common law mind requires that we become conscious of the choices that are made for us by its reified logic and categories" (Sugarman 1986, 28). Legal educators and students must develop a contextual view of law so that they are able to recognize the ways in which its categories and logic facilitate the conditions of the Anthropocene. In this part of the chapter, we first reimagine the law curriculum and the taxonomy on which it depends through a consideration of three curricular possibilities that we describe as material, lexically reordered, and divergent. We then connect these curricular possibilities with three alternative pedagogies that we describe as integrative, ecological, and place-based. The objective is to develop and deliver legal education to better equip graduates with the knowledge, skills, and attributes that can redress the complex problems of the Anthropocene.

## New Curriculum

The first possibility is a material curriculum that would be concerned with the material agency of law on lands and waters, as well as with the agency of lands and waters in and on laws. Even within the Priestley 11 constraints of doctrinal focus, the orientation of the curriculum might be designed through the framework of Earth jurisprudence[5] and/or of a legal geographical (Bartel et al. 2013) approach. Earth jurisprudence is a legal philosophy that positions Earth at the center of the moral community (Koons 2008). Against the dominance of the anthropocentric notion that human beings can and should hold legal rights at the expense of the more-than-human world, this philosophy positions the Earth itself as a moral and legal rights-bearing subject of law. The approach conceptualizes human beings and their laws within the interconnected community of relations of life on Earth and is consistent with an ecological, rather than anthroparchic, worldview. A material curriculum would be underpinned by a commitment to the flourishing of all life on Earth and to preserving the integrity of Earth systems. Importantly, a material curriculum would empower the climate-striking generation with the knowledge of the emancipatory capacity of law to effect social and ecological changes.

A material curriculum could also be designed using legal geography, which is a methodology used to "include what has traditionally lain beyond the scope of the discipline of law" and addresses "the solipsistic claim the law makes for its separateness and supremacy, in order to understand laws as embedded … [and] emplaced" (Bartel et al. 2013, 340). In this way, a material curriculum is fundamentally interdisciplinary because it incorporates perspectives and skills from non-law disciplines – including the sciences, geography, history, and Indigenous knowledges – that are relevant to questions arising in legal disputes. This is critical to the ability of law students to develop climate change literacy irrespective of approach (adversarial, negotiation, or law reform). As Finley observes, "[a]nalysis of the way the law structures thought and talk about social problems is necessary to understand how the law can limit our understandings of the nature of problems and can confine our visions for change" (Finley 1989, 895). A material curriculum moves beyond those limited understandings to liberate the intellect and imagination in preparation for dealing with the complex problems of the Anthropocene.

A second curricular possibility is a lexically reordered curriculum that adopts the taxonomic structure of the current dominant law curriculum but reframes it to afford lexical priority to the more-than-human. This approach centers that which is "null" in the current curriculum (Flinders et al. 1986) – that is, "the options students are not afforded, the perspectives they may never know about, much less be able to use, the concepts and skills that are not part of their intellectual repertoire" (Eisner 1985, 107). Even though the list of headline topics in such a curriculum might reflect the status quo, the content and presentation of each topic would explicitly engage first with the more-than-human, providing a foundation from which to critique the assumptions inherent in the doctrine that follows.

In our experience as law teachers, students might enroll in "land law" expecting that the unit involves the subject matter of actual land, environments, or ecologies – only to be disappointed to learn that it is concerned principally with the abstraction of land into various forms of legal estates and interests with attendant rights (Graham 2011b). Using lands, environments, or ecologies as a starting point to teach land law (now referred to almost uniformly as property law) offers the basis from which to highlight the absence of environmental and ecological concerns in English land law, as would an emphasis on First Nations' conceptions of country within Indigenous legal systems (Graham 2009; Watson 2015). The various facets of the subject – the meaning of land, the nature of the estate, the role of rights within broader and more-than-human contexts, and the derivation of land law itself through the smoke and mirrors (Keenan

2017) of colonial doctrine, the international law of empire, and registration – all work together to elucidate the law's own priorities and the harms that ensue.

The third possibility, a "divergent" curriculum, would identify socio-legal and scientific concepts such as land rights and ecology, and would structure the curriculum around these issues, using the law to illustrate their contingency in our world. In such a curriculum, there is room to generate new thinking around core features of the law – such as rights, duties, and remedies – as a means of solving complex problems. Adopting this approach might involve arranging the units within a core curriculum thematically as a strategy by which students could learn and evaluate laws through their interaction with the material world. Property law would be renamed land law[6] and could include questions of ownership in relation also to water and other biological and geological features of the more-than-human world. Environmental law would embrace the breadth of opportunities to protect ecological systems, rather than being constrained to environmental decision-making through the lens of administrative law per se.[7] Climate change offers the thematic opportunity to explore almost all domains of the law, their culpability and promise, and their limitations and scope (see, e.g., Preston 2009; Peel et al. 2017; Ganguly et al. 2018; Avgoustinos 2020; Graham 2021c). Animals (Brooman 2017; Deckha 2017), shelter, and food (A. Kennedy and Liljeblad 2016) all offer the thematic framing for an intellectual examination of the world, both human and more-than-human. To the extent that these themes concern the material world, rather than abstractions in the form of "rights" alone, the divergent curriculum intersects with the material curriculum.

## New Pedagogies

A re-oriented curriculum is necessary but is not sufficient to confront the challenges of the Anthropocene. The shift in curriculum must be accompanied by new pedagogies in order for the change to manifest – both as a precursor to designing the curriculum itself and to inform the way in which it is taught. We suggest three approaches to pedagogy that align with the intersections between the curriculum approaches in the previous section: an integrative pedagogy, an ecological pedagogy, and place-based learning.

As a starting point, the conventional and didactic approach of filling the empty vessel of a law student's mind with context-free doctrine using the authoritative disciplinary voice of the educator is problematic for several reasons. First, and contrary to the recognized benefits of active engagement for student learning (Ramsden 2003, 86), it constructs learning as passive. Additionally, the passive learning experience contradicts the imperative of *active*, rather than passive, lawyering in – and in response to – the Anthropocene, evidenced recently in matters such as *Sharma v Minister for Environment* (2021), the climate change action brought by the so-called Torres Strait 8 before the UN Human Rights Committee in 2019 (Marjanac and Hunter Jones 2020), and *AGL Energy Limited v Greenpeace Australia Pacific Limited* (2021).

Second, it confines the student experience to inculcation in the hierarchy of law, rather than empowering students to interrogate that hierarchy. Third, it artificially disconnects law students' knowledge of non-law disciplines and of other legal regimes from the law that is poured into the vessel, rather than enabling students to situate law in myriad contexts – such as history, economy, ecology, and culture. Rejecting this approach requires a pedagogy that considers law in relation to "diverse cultures, classes, races, genders and generations" (Graham 2021b, 217).

To address the complex problems of the Anthropocene, legal education could adopt an "integrative pedagogy": one that brings together four "tightly integrated" elements of "theoretical, practical, self-regulative and sociocultural knowledge" to develop "deep expertise" (Tynjälä and Gijbels 2012, 209) in students. The first three of these elements are brought together through problem-solving – but, within integrative pedagogy, the learner employs "integrative thinking" that demands that they "unite different, sometimes even conflicting, elements into an integrated whole" (Tynjälä et al. 2016, 371). Furthermore, this must necessarily occur within a particular sociocultural context that is reflective of the communication practices within a given environment (Tynjälä and Gijbels 2012, 208).

An integrative pedagogy works to promote graduates who have "professional expertise" rather than producing new lawyers as such. Tynjälä and Gijbels observe that this involves progressive problem-solving and work that is "highly collaborative and transformative in nature" (2012, 208). Their contention is that within a multi-professional team, the professional of the future is an agent of change (ibid.), "bringing about transformation in [their] work" (ibid., citing Engeström 2004, 145). It is therefore our responsibility as educators to enable our students to develop new ways of working, bringing their legal knowledge and skills to the table together with diverse professional orientations to collaboratively address the complex problems of the Anthropocene.

Skills of collaboration are critical to anthropocentric professionals. Collaboration gathers up both the multidisciplinary approach to learning and the skills of engaging with others and communicating effectively, along with the disposition of embracing cooperative and creative endeavors. This necessitates a movement away from law as an exclusive domain and toward a partnership of co-produced multidisciplinary knowledge (Robinson 2008; Leinfelder 2013; Graham 2014; Matsuda 2014; Brown and Erickson 2016; Rousell 2016) that is responsive to the learner's own conceptualization of the elements of the problem to be solved. All partners require a baseline comprehension of the cultural, economic, ecological, and social contexts within which challenges of the Anthropocene arise, as well as the skills to identify both component problems and their interrelationships. An integrative pedagogy that emphasizes collaborative skills will facilitate the interaction of knowledges, skills, and experiences to generate a holistic and more effective analysis of climate change problems. In contrast to the dominant pedagogy, which tends to constrain the analysis of problems to disciplinary limits, the impact of the aggregation of disciplines, skills, and collaborators is greater than the sum of its separate discipline-based parts (Ong 2016; MacLean 2020).

The "integral theory" of Esbjörn-Hargens offers a segue from integrative education to ecological thinking. He describes the practice of integral theory as a "widening of identity" and a "creative expansion" from me to my group, to my country, to "all of us," to all beings, and, finally, to "all of reality" (Esbjörn-Hargens 2010, 42). Du Plessis and Branden describe such a shift in ecological terms, "from a mechanistic to an ecological/living systems worldview" (Du Plessis and Brandon 2015, 53). Importantly, their claim is not to reject a mechanistic worldview but rather to recognize its evolution toward a more comprehensive and holistic comprehension of our place in the world. An ecological consciousness rejects an oppositional binary of humans as subject and "nature" as object, altering one's epistemological standpoint to generate an "alternative way of thinking, which implements the 'man [sic] as the subject of the planet (the noosphere) – the planet as a subject of natural development'" (Panov 2013, 380).

Ecological pedagogy would challenge legal educators to develop an ecological consciousness in the conceptualization and norms of their discipline and to teach accordingly. The approach is reformist in nature. It operates at the level of the Earth's systems, rather than at the level of human jurisdictions abstracted from those systems. Rejecting the artificial boundaries imposed by law on the material world, it would require the law to engage with geography, geology, and ecological processes and would encourage engagement with the legal regimes of First Nations that seek to align human laws with Earth's laws. Ecological pedagogy could function at the "cultural interface" (Nakata 2007), providing a more powerful learning experience than that of the dominant pedagogy.

Engaging with non-Western legal regimes introduces students to considerations of place-based laws (Watson 2008; Watson 2009). Place-based pedagogies (Van Wagner 2017), as with a material curriculum, help law students to situate law as being capable of shaping, and being shaped by, the physical world. The connection between teacher, learner, law, and place can reveal the impacts of the Anthropocene not merely as an intellectual construct but in material and experiential terms (Schlosberg 2016).

## Conclusion

The dominant Western legal regime developed to facilitate global capitalism and colonization. Legal education continues to teach law students the doctrines, cases, and legislation that define these ongoing conditions of the Anthropocene. While the law itself must change, so too must its disciplinary processes, curriculum, and pedagogy. Law teachers can change the way we teach to graduate a new generation of lawyers who are literate in the supercomplexity of climate change and climate justice. The disciplinary expertise that we hold and reproduce is inadequate to meet the needs of today's law students and society. It is time for us to direct our expertise toward developing new and collaborative methods of teaching and curriculum design that reflect the urgent need for integrative ecological thinking. The Anthropocene demands immediate attention (Slaughter 2012; Biber 2017) for a radical reconsideration of legal pedagogy and curriculum.

## Notes

1 The smoke drifted three times around the globe (Rogers 2019; Verlie 2021).
2 Admission to practice law requires an accredited degree. In Australia, law degrees should meet the so-called Priestley 11 subject areas, with training covering an additional suite of subject areas. Both standards are embodied in legislation in all Australian states and territories.
3 Though see the discussion in Galloway et al. (forthcoming).
4 For a comparison of broad and narrow curricula, see, e.g., Bagilhole and Goode 1998.
5 For an overview of Earth jurisprudence, see, e.g., Cullinan 2002; Rogers and Maloney 2017.
6 For how this might be applied, see Galloway 2012; Graham 2009.
7 The relevant law might involve transnational torts; see Enneking 2019.

## References

*AGL Energy Limited v Greenpeace Australia Pacific Limited* [2021] FCA 625.

Ardill, A. (2016) 'Critique in legal education: Another journey', *Legal Education Review*, 26(1), pp. 137–160.

Atiyah, P. (1979) *The Rise and Fall of Freedom of Contract*. Oxford: Oxford University Press.

Avgoustinos, C. (2020) 'Climate change and the Australian constitution: The case for the ecological limitation', PhD thesis, University of New South Wales, Australia.

Bagilhole, B. and Goode, J. (1998) 'The "gender dimension" of both the "narrow" and "broad" curriculum in UK higher education: Do women lose out in both?', *Gender and Education*, 10(4), pp. 445–458.

Barnett, R. (2000) *Realizing the University in an Age of Supercomplexity*. Buckingham: Open University Press.

Barnett, R. (2012) 'Learning for an unknown future', *Higher Education Research and Development*, 31(1), pp. 65–77.

Barnett, R. and Hallam, S. (1999) 'Teaching for supercomplexity: A pedagogy for higher education', in P. Mortimore (ed.), *Understanding Pedagogy and Its Impact on Learning*. pp.137–154, London: SAGE.

Bartel, R. *et al.* (2013) 'Legal geography: An Australian perspective', *Geographical Research*, 51(4), pp. 339–353.

Biber, E. (2017) 'Law in the Anthropocene epoch', *Georgetown Law Journal*, 106(1), pp. 1–68.

Birchall, M. (2020) 'History, sovereignty, capital: Company colonization in South Australia and New Zealand', *Journal of Global History*, 16(1), pp. 1–17.

Braithwaite, J. (2008) *Regulatory Capitalism: How It Works, Ideas for Making It Work Better*. Cheltenham: Edward Elgar.

Brooman, S. (2017) 'Creatures, the academic lawyer and a socio-legal approach: Introducing animal law into the legal education curriculum', *Liverpool Law Review*, 38(3), pp. 243–257.

Brown, P. G. and Erickson, J. D. (2016) 'How higher education imperils the future: An urgent call for action', *Balance*, 1(2), pp. 42–48.

Burns, M. (2014) 'Towards growing Indigenous culturally competent legal professionals in Australia'. *International education Journal: Comparative Perspectives*, 12(1), pp. 226–248.

Burns, M. (2018) 'Are we there yet?: Indigenous cultural competency in legal education', *Legal Education Review*, 28(2), pp. 1–30.

Carrigan, F. (2013) 'They make a desert and call it peace', *Legal Education Review*, 23(2), pp. 313–343.

Celermajer, D. (2021) *Summertime: Reflections on a Vanishing Future*. North Sydney: Penguin.

Collier, R. (2004) 'We're all socio-legal now? Legal education, scholarship and the "global knowledge economy" – Reflections on the UK experience', *Sydney Law Review*, 26(4), pp. 503–536.

Cullinan, C. (2002) *Wild Law*. Claremont: Siber Ink.

Dalrymple, W. (2019) *The Anarchy: The Relentless Rise of the East India Company*. London: Bloomsbury.

Deckha, M. (2017) 'Critical animal studies and animal law', *Animal Law*, 18(2), pp. 207–236.

Draper, N. (2010) *The Price of Emancipation, Slave-Ownership, Compensation and British Society at the End of Slavery*. Cambridge: Cambridge University Press.

Du Plessis, C. and Brandon, P. S. (2015) 'An ecological worldview as basis for a regenerative sustainability paradigm for the built environment', *Journal of Cleaner Production*, 53(109), pp. 53–61.

Eisner, E. W. (1985) *The Educational Imagination: On the Design and Evaluation of School Programs*. 2nd ed. New York: Macmillan.

Engeström, Y. (2004) 'The new generation of expertise: Seven theses', in A. Fuller et al. (eds.), *Workplace Learning in Context*. pp. 145–165, London: Routledge.

Enneking, L. F. H. (2019) 'Transnational human rights and environmental litigation: A study of case law relating to Shell in Nigeria', in I. Feichtner et al. (eds.), *Human Rights in the Extractive Industries*. pp. 511–551, Cham: Springer.

Esbjörn-Hargens, S. (2010) 'An overview of integral theory: An all-inclusive framework for the twenty-first century', in S. Esbjörn-Hargens (ed.), *Integral Theory in Action, Applied, Theoretical, and Constructive Perspectives on the AQAL Model*. pp. 33–62, New York: SUNY Press.

Finley, L. M. (1989) 'Breaking women's silence in law: The dilemma of the gendered nature of legal reasoning', *Notre Dame Law Review*, 64(5), pp. 886–910.

Flinders, D. J. *et al.* (1986) 'The null curriculum: Its theoretical basis and practical implications', *Curriculum Inquiry*, 16(1), pp. 33–42.

Flood, J. (2019) 'Legal professionals of the future: Their ethos, role and skills', in M. DeStefano and G. Dobrauz-Saldapenna (eds.), *New Suits: Appetite for Disruption in the Legal World*. pp. 115–129, Bern: Stämpfli Verlag.

Flood, J. and Lederer, P. D. (2012) 'Becoming a cosmopolitan lawyer', *Fordham Law Review*, 80(6), pp. 2513–2539.

Galloway, K. (2012) 'Landowners' vs miners' property interests: The unsustainability of property as dominion', *Alternative Law Journal*, 37(2), pp. 77–81.

Galloway, K. (2015) 'Sustainability in the real property law curriculum: Why and how', *Journal of Learning Design*, 8(2), pp. 31–42.

Galloway, K. (2017) 'Big data: A case study of disruption and government power', *Alternative Law Journal*, 42(2), pp. 89–95.

Galloway, K. (2018) 'Indigenous contexts in the law curriculum: Process and structure', *Legal Education Review*, 28(2), pp. 1–24.

Galloway, K. (2020) *Analysis: Holding Government to Account*. Environmental Defenders Office. Available at: www.edo.org.au/2020/01/24/holding-govt-to-account/ (Accessed: 7 November 2021).

Galloway, K. and Jones, P. (2014) 'Guarding our identities: The dilemma of transformation in the legal academy', *QUT Law Review*, 14(1), pp. 15–26.

Galloway, K., Shircore, M. and Bradshaw, R. (2012) 'Using sustainability to inform renewal of the LLB foundation curriculum: Knowledge skills and attitudes for the future', *QUT Law Review*, 12(1), pp. 1–20.

Galloway, K. *et al.* (2019) 'The legal academy's engagements with lawtech: Technology narratives and archetypes as drivers of change', *Law, Technology and Humans*, 1(1), pp. 27–45.
Galloway, K. *et al.* (forthcoming) 'Hacking the Priestleys', in H. Gibbon et al. (eds.), *Critical Legal Education as a Subversive Activity*. pp. 127–146, London: Routledge.
Ganguly, G., Setzer, J. and Heyvaert, V. (2018) 'If at first you don't succeed: Suing corporations for climate change', *Oxford Journal of Legal Studies*, 38(4), pp. 841–868.
Garth, B. G. and Dezalay, Y. (2011) 'Introduction: Lawyers, law, and society', in Y. Dezalay and B. G. Garth (eds.), *Lawyers and the Rule of Law in an Era of Globalization*. pp. 1–16, London: Routledge.
Graham, N. (2009) 'Indigenous property matters in real property courses at Australian universities', *Legal Education Review*, 19(1–2), pp. 289–304.
Graham, N. (2011a) *Lawscape: Property, Environment, Law*. London: Routledge.
Graham, N. (2011b) 'Owning the Earth', in P. Burdon (ed.), *Exploring Wild Law: The Philosophy of Earth Jurisprudence*. pp. 259–269, Kent Town: Wakefield Press.
Graham, N. (2012) 'Dephysicalisation and entitlement: Legal and cultural discourses of place as property', in B. Jessup and K. Rubenstein (eds.), *Environmental Discourses in Public and International Law*. pp. 96–120, New York: Cambridge University Press.
Graham, N. (2014) 'This is not a thing: Land, sustainability and legal education', *Journal of Environmental Law*, 26(3), pp. 395–422.
Graham, N. (2021a) 'Dephysicalised property and shadow lands', in R. Bartel and J. Carter (eds.), *Handbook of Law, Space and Place*. 281–291, Cheltenham: Edward Elgar.
Graham, N. (2021b) 'Learning sacrifice: Legal education in the Anthropocene', in K. Anker et al. (eds.), *From Environmental to Ecological Law*. pp. 209–222 London: Routledge.
Graham, N. (2021c) 'Teaching private law in a climate crisis', *University of Queensland Law Journal*, 40(3), pp. 403–419.
Greer, A. (2018) *Property and Dispossession: Natives, Empires and Land in Early Modern North America*. Cambridge: Cambridge University Press.
Jessup, B. and Carroll, C. (2017) 'The sustainability business clinic – Australian clinical legal education for a "new environmentalism" and new environmental law', *Environmental and Planning Law Journal*, 34(6), pp. 542–559.
Jones, P. and Galloway, K. (2012) 'Professional transitions in the academy: A conversation', *Journal of Transformative Education*, 10(2), pp. 90–107.
Jones, P. and Galloway, K. (2015) 'Why so slow? Academic and discipline identities as obstacles to engaging with education for sustainability: Lessons from law and social work', *International Journal of Sustainability Education*, 11(2), pp. 1–10.
Keenan, S. (2017) 'Smoke, curtains and mirrors: The production of race through time and time registration', *Law and Critique*, 28(1), pp. 87–108.
Kelman, I. (2019) *Disaster by Choice: How Our Actions Turn Natural Hazards into Catastrophes*. Oxford: Oxford University Press.
Kennedy, A. and Liljeblad, J. (eds.). (2016) *Food Systems Governance: Challenges for Justice, Equality and Human Rights*. London: Routledge.
Kennedy, A., Mundy, T. and Nielsen, J. M. (2016) '"Bush Law 101": Realising place and conscious pedagogy in the law curriculum', *Journal of University Teaching and Learning Practice*, 13(1), pp. 10–19.
Kennedy, A. *et al.* (2014) 'Educating law students for rural and regional legal practice; Embedding place consciousness in law curricula', *Legal Education Review*, 24(1), pp. 6–27.
Kennedy, D. (1998) *The Rise and Fall of Classical Legal Thought*. 2nd ed. Cambridge: Afar.
Kift, S. *et al.* (2010) *Bachelor of Laws Learning and Teaching Academic Standards Statement*. Strawberry Hills: Australian Learning and Teaching Council.
Koons, J. E. (2008) 'Earth jurisprudence: The moral value of nature', *Pace Environmental Law Review*, 25(2), pp. 263–339.
Kuhn, T. (1996) *The Structure of Scientific Revolutions*. 3rd ed. Chicago: Chicago University Press.
Leinfelder, R. (2013) 'Assuming responsibility for the Anthropocene: Challenges and opportunities in education', in H. Trischler (ed.), *Anthropocene: Envisioning the Future of the Age of Humans, RCC Perspectives*. Munich: Rachel Carson Centre, pp. 9–18.
Levien, M. (2013) *Regimes of Dispossession*. Berkeley: University of California Press.
Locke, J. (1689) *Two Treatises on Government*. Reprint (1960), P. Laslett (ed.). Cambridge: Cambridge University Press.

Loewenstein, A. (2013) *Profits of Doom: How Vulture Capitalism Is Swallowing the World*. Melbourne: Melbourne University Press.

Lucy, W. (2009) 'Abstraction and the rule of law', *Oxford Journal of Legal Studies*, 29(3), pp. 481–509.

MacLean, J. (2020) 'Curriculum design for the Anthropocene: Review of Meinhard Doelle & Chris Tollefson, Environmental Law: Cases and Materials, third edition', *McGill Journal of Sustainable Development Law*, 16(1), pp. 4–36.

Macpherson, C. B. (1975) 'Capitalism and the changing concept of property', in E. Kamenka and R. S. Neal (eds.), *Feudalism, Capitalism and Beyond*. pp. 104–124, Canberra: ANU Press.

Marjanac, S. and Hunter Jones, S. (2020) 'Are matters of national survival related to climate change really beyond a court's power?', *Open Global Rights*. Available at: https://www.openglobalrights.org/matters-of-national-survival-climate-change-beyond-courts/ (Accessed: 28 June 2020).

Matsuda, M. J. (2014) 'Admit that the waters around you have grown: Change and legal education', *Indiana Law Journal*, 89(4), pp. 1381–1400.

Mokyr, J. (2011) 'The European Enlightenment, the industrial revolution, and modern economic growth', in P. Zumbansen and G.-P. Calliess (eds.), *Law, Economics and Evolutionary Theory*. pp. 33–53, Cheltenham: Edward Elgar.

Nakata, M. (2007) 'The cultural interface', *Australian Journal of Indigenous Education*, 36(S1), pp. 7–14.

Ong, D. M. (2016) 'Prospects for integrating an environmental sustainability perspective within the university law curriculum in England', *Law Teacher*, 50(3), pp. 276–299.

Pahuja, S. (2011) *Decolonising International Law: Development, Economic Growth and the Politics of Universality*. Cambridge: Cambridge University Press.

Panov, V. I. (2013) 'Ecological thinking, consciousness, responsibility', *Procedia-Social and Behavioral Sciences*, 86, pp. 379–383.

Parker, C. and Goldsmith, A. (1998) '"Failed sociologists" in the market place: Law schools in Australia', *Journal of Law and in Society*, 25(1), pp. 33–50.

Peel, J. *et al.* (2017) 'Shaping the next generation of climate change litigation in Australia', *Melbourne University Law Review*, 41(2), pp. 793–844.

Postema, G. (1986) *Bentham and the Common Law Tradition*. Oxford: Clarendon Press.

Preston, B. (2009) 'Climate change litigation', *Judicial Review*, 9(2), pp. 205–236.

Priel, D. (2013) 'The political origins of English private law', *Journal of Law and in Society*, 40(4), pp. 481–508.

Ramsden, P. (2003) *Learning to Teach in Higher Education*. London: Routledge.

Robinson, J. (2008) 'Being undisciplined: Transgressions and intersections in academia and beyond', *Futures*, 40(1), pp. 70–86.

Rogers, N. (2019) *Law, Fiction and Activism in a Time of Climate Change*. London: Routledge.

Rogers, N. and Maloney, M. (eds.). (2017) *Law as If Earth Really Mattered: The Wild Law Judgment Project*. London: Routledge.

Rousell, D. (2016) 'Dwelling in the Anthropocene: Reimagining university learning environments in response to social and ecological change', *Australian Journal of Environmental Education*, 32(2), pp. 137–153.

Samuelowicz, K. and Bain, J. D. (2001) 'Revisiting academics' beliefs about teaching and learning', *Higher Education*, 41(3), pp. 299–325.

Schlosberg, D. (2016) 'Environmental management in the Anthropocene', in T. Gabrielson et al. (eds.), *Oxford Handbook of Environmental Political Theory*. pp. 193–208, Oxford: Oxford University Press.

*Sharma by her litigation representative Sister Marie Brigid Arthur v Minister for the Environment* (2021) FCA 560.

Slaughter, R. (2012) 'Welcome to the Anthropocene', *Futures*, 44(2), pp. 119–126.

Stoianoff, N. and Guglyuvatyy, E. (2020) 'Australian carbon policy: Two steps forward, one step backwards?', in: T. Zachariadis et al. (eds.), *Economic Instruments for a Low-Carbon Future*. pp. 82–97, Cheltenham: Edward Elgar.

Sugarman, D. (1986) 'Legal theory, the common law mind and the making of textbook tradition', in W. Twining (ed.), *Legal Theory and Common Law*. pp. 26–62, Oxford: Basil Blackwell

Thornton, M. (1991) *The Liberal Promise: Anti-discrimination Legislation in Australia*. Melbourne: Oxford University Press.

Thornton, M. (1998) 'Technocentrism in the law school: Why the gender and colour of law remain the same', *Osgoode Hall Law Journal*, 36(2), pp. 369–398.

Thornton, M. (2008) 'The retreat from the critical: Social science research in the corporatised university', *Australian Universities Review*, 50(1), pp. 5–10.

Thornton, M. (2012) *Privatising the Public University*. Oxford: Routledge.

Tynjälä, P. and Gijbels, D. (2012) 'Changing the world: Changing pedagogy', in P. Tynjälä et al. (eds.), *Transitions and Transformations in Learning and Education*. pp. 205–222, Dordrecht: Springer.

Tynjälä, P. *et al.* (2016) 'Developing social competence and other generic skills in teacher education: Applying the model of integrative pedagogy', *European Journal of Teacher Education*, 39(3), pp. 368–387.

Van Wagner, E. (2017) '"Seeing the place makes it real": Place-based teaching in the environmental and planning law classroom', *Environmental and Planning Law Journal*, 34(6), pp. 522–541.

Verlie, B. (2021) *Learning to Live with Climate Change: From Anxiety to Transformation*. London: Routledge.

Vermeulen, P. A. M. and van Lint, A. C. (2020) 'The rise of the Dutch East India Company', in D. Billis and C. Rochester (eds.), *Handbook on Hybrid Organisations*. pp. 106–205 Cheltenham: Edward Elgar.

Watkins, C. and Mortimore, P. (1999) 'Pedagogy: What do we know?', in P. Mortimore (ed.), *Understanding Pedagogy and Its Impact on Learning*. pp. 1–19, London: SAGE

Watson, I. (2008) 'De-colonising the space: Dreaming back to country', in S. Morgan et al. (eds.), *Heartsick for Country: 52 Stories of Love, Spirit and Creation*. pp. 82–100, Fremantle: Fremantle Press.

Watson, I. (2009) 'Sovereign spaces, caring for country, and the homeless position of Aboriginal peoples', *South Atlantic Quarterly*, 108(1), pp. 27–51.

Watson, I. (2015) *Aboriginal Peoples, Colonialism and International Law: Raw Law*. London: Routledge.

Watson, I. and Burns, M. (2015) 'Indigenous knowledges: A strategy for first nations peoples engagement in higher education', in S. Varnham et al. (eds.), *Higher Education and the Law*. pp. 41–52, Annandale: Federation Press.

Wheeler, S. (2017) 'The corporation and the Anthropocene', in L. J. Kotzé (ed.), *Reimagining Environmental Law and Governance for the Anthropocene*. London: Bloomsbury.

Williams, E. (1994) *Capitalism and Slavery*. Chapel Hill: University of North Carolina Press.

Wood, A. J. (2013) 'Incorporating Indigenous cultural competency through the broader law curriculum', *Legal Education Review*, 23(1), pp. 57–81.

# PART VIII

# Post-Script

# 23

# LAW, RESPONSIBILITY, AND THE CAPITALOCENE

## In Search of New Arts of Living

*Sally Wheeler and Anna Grear in Conversation with Peter Burdon*[1]

**Peter Burdon**: I want to begin with a broad question that gives you both some space to develop some themes that we can return to. Sally beginning with you, what do you think legal scholars should know about the Anthropocene?**Sally Wheeler**: They should know that it is an interdisciplinary concept that spans across a wide range of things. They should know something about the various different possible layers of intervention. Is that through the power of the state? Is it through NGOs and Quangos? At a global, national, or local level? Is it through the corporate sector? And if it is, what that means. I guess they should have some understanding of what Anthropocene stands in opposition to – that there are other ways of constructing what we see as "our epoch" if you like.

*It fascinates me that the whole idea of the Anthropocene is based on a one-page piece in Nature (Crutzen 2002). That goes to my worldview about how publications and impact works, in the context of scholarly work, and the things that I think are terribly important; understanding the intellectual heritage and pedigree of your ideas, tracking down the single last reference to that, and really interrogating it.*

**Peter Burdon**: Anna?

**Anna Grear**: Picking up on what Sally's saying there about the naming of the epoch, obviously that's a highly contestable issue, and there are a multiplicity of alternative namings, so much so that I think one scholar called it the "Neologismcene" (Mentz 2017) because naming has gone completely nuts (Ford 2018, 1).

*I think the Anthropocene radically throws into question most of liberal Western law's fundamental "taken for granted." The Anthropocene and obviously other social and philosophical movements too, throw into question the whole issue of law's subject–object relations; law's assumptions concerning human centrality and the nature of human agency, and the predominantly unquestioned – I would say – structural centrality to the international legal order of fundamentally appropriative dynamics and the avatar of the colonial Eurocentric actor in the transnational corporate form and its dominance. And the Anthropocene's fallouts, its material injuries, also challenge law's construction of law's relatively disembodied form of rationality and all that that rationality tends to smuggle in, in terms of hierarchical dynamics and civilizational assumptions.*

DOI: 10.4324/9781003388081-31

*So, I think that legal scholars need to realize that in a sense the Anthropocene is the mess we're all in, and that this mess confronts law with some very profound questions concerning the ideological constructions that tend to operate in it. The notion of the person, for example, is being exploded into a much more dynamic, plastic response to a range of different challenges and vulnerabilities.*

*The person-property division might need its sacred mythic status questioning – and persons and property both need reimagining in order that law can operate normatively in the world in ways that are less oppressive than the kind of oppressions that have rolled out under the discourse of private property, and what that has facilitated.*

*And I think most of all, that the Anthropocene predicament challenges law's most fundamental onto-epistemic commitments and ethical priorities, all the way up and down.*

*So, I think this convergence of impacts calls legal scholarship into a critical-creative, hardworking set of engagements with a vitally necessary project, which is the reimagination and evolution of law itself in newly responsibilized, humbled ways that have to be freshly open to multiple ways of being and to multiple ways of knowing – to a world of multiple worlds, including Indigenous life-worlds – which have been for so long marginalized and plundered by the appropriative predatory dynamics of anthropocentric law, by colonial law. The Anthropocene and colonial/neo-colonial practices overlap quite strongly.*

*That's it really.*

**Peter Burdon**: Sally, my next few questions are directed specifically to you. You've written that "the ecological time bomb, that is the Anthropocene, has corporate activity at its centre" (Wheeler 2017). Could you talk about how the corporate form has empowered a small group of people to cause a rupture in the earth system?

**Sally Wheeler**: Well, I think, for me, a lot of that is about the role of the State and the way in which the State has facilitated corporations to perform functions that it doesn't want to do. You can see a lot of that in the post-GFC austerity measures taken by states. Political regimes around the world were only too happy to divest themselves of a large range of services that they would have offered otherwise by pushing them into the corporate structure. I think here of the financing of infrastructure such as housing and outsourcing of basic utilities such as water (Cowan and Wheeler 2015).

*Individuals have been encouraged within the logics of neoliberalism to plan for their own retirement, for their own well-being, and that means essentially becoming the holders of 401k plans in the US, Superann in Australia, defined contribution pensions in the UK, so they are locked into the profits that corporates are making. They have I suppose, in corporate law terms, an indirect investment interest, but I would have thought in policy terms a direct interest in what those corporations are doing. Previously this financing of retirement would have been undertaken by the state with potential income guarantees coming from the corporate sector in the form of employment-driven defined benefit pensions (Langley and Leaver 2012).*

*The sorts of things that have encouraged the corporate sector to take on these activities, and I think about Rio Tinto, for example, which is particularly topical here in Australia at the moment – what caused Rio Tinto to move from being a so-called leader in sustainability around mining (leaving aside that that is obviously a total oxymoron, but they were considered to be best in class, if you like) to blow up Juukan Gorge in pursuit of iron ore?*

*Well, it's essentially the pull of shareholder value. And who are shareholders? Well, they are the asset managers of large investment funds. And who puts asset managers under pressure to invest in high-yield stock? It's indirect investors.*

*There is a whole group of people who are pulled into willing the corporation to succeed at all costs because their mortgage or their pension depends on share market performance. And When they say "oh, you know USS (the pension fund in the UK that many academics are members of) doesn't invest in this," or "Fidelity doesn't invest in that," the answer is actually it probably does through the use of an index tracker investment or investment in a large conglomerate that has an enormous range of industries and activities as part of its business.*

*There's an awful lot that we can say about so-called ESG investments; many funds draw on activities that are a long way from things people might naturally think goes into the ESG basket (Berg, Koelbel, and Rigobon 2020). Once you take out obvious things like arms and tobacco that are socially undesirable, there are an awful lot of business processes that involve fossil fuel. A lot of what appears to be ESG-suitable activities are in fact high pollution businesses: dyes in fabric production, fertilizer and energy in natural fibers for clothing, and crops for cheap and fast-food production (Bick, Halsey, and Ekenga 2018). Those things, I think, make a huge number of people complicit in what is going on in the corporate space.*

**Peter Burdon***:* At the same time, we are often encouraged to take individual action in response to climate change and the kinds of activity that are giving rise to the Anthropocene. What you're describing is a complex web where it's not easy to make sure that what we're doing is good for the environment.

**Sally Wheeler***:* I'm quite taken with Iris Marion Young's work where she's focusing on a form of localism on which to found responsibility or, as she terms it, *political responsibility* (Young 2006). There is an argument that says, well I'm never, for example, going to wear leather shoes because of what is involved in the production of them; animal cruelty and environmental damage through animal-related methane gas release. But if one wears shoes at all, what are they going to be made of? Because just about all natural fiber or man-made material in the situation that we are in now has a climate impact. So, how do you start to untangle that web of responsibility?

*Iris Marion Young had a way of talking about how structural social injustice or vulnerability should be addressed by political action that was underpinned by responsibility. She stressed that responsibility came not from liability but from social connection. This social connection comes not simply from co-existence but from our taking a place within the web of processes and dynamics that combine together to produce unavoidable structural injustices (Young 2011).*

*When people talk about a post-Covid economy being one that might be embedded in the local, that gives us an opportunity to push back on some obvious harms and inequalities. We could start with what are the most egregious climate harms – one of those has to be around many Western forms of farming and another the idea of fast clothing. More clothing of mixed fibers construction is thrown away than ever before, and clothing is one of the things that has actually seen its retail price to the consumer reduce over the last ten years rather than increase (Niinimäki et al. 2020).*

*What I'm saying is that if we want to be activists, then one of the things we can focus on is what goes on immediately around us. Those of us who are in the game for private pensions – a certain sort of middle-class existence or better – should think realistically about the sort of return on investment we demand, and how we think those returns are assembled.*

**Peter Burdon***:* Your writing has also investigated mechanisms for changing corporate behavior so that it has a sensibility for interests that are prior to or different than the corporation, and in particular you've drawn on Levinas in this work. What resources do you think Levinas gives us to help us think about the responsibility we have for other things or interests prior to the corporation?

**Sally Wheeler***:* That's a really interesting question because I suspect that many Levinas scholars would say that Levinas' work is not a suitable starting point for the corporation but rather individual managerial ethics. That might be something that we need to come back to.

*At heart what Levinas is giving us is a language to talk about the corporation being in and of itself a responsible subject, and my point has always been that if we don't see the corporation as a subject in some way, what do we see it as?*

*We have to have something that we can anchor the corporation to. Levinas is talking about an ethical connection between responsible subjects that enjoy an equality of rights of sorts in that the "Other" is neither subjected nor dominated (Levinas 1985, 96–99). If we are to take corporate power seriously then this is a key issue. If we maintain the other is a subject which enjoys a certain sort of equality of rights, the corporation is not subjected to anything, it's not dominated. On that scale, we also have to be able to see where the corporation fits if we are to take corporate power seriously and think about being able to do anything about corporate power (Karamali 2007).*

*We have to see the corporation, first and foremost, as potentially a responsible subject, then we are talking about, an ethically grounded commitment that is just not reducible to contract. It is a commitment that is absolute and universal. It is compassionate, but it is not about moral norms and it is not about adaption. This is our starting point for that sort of aggregation of power, I think (Shapiro 2018).*

**Peter Burdon***:* I want to come back to then something you mentioned at the beginning of those remarks. For some scholars, Levinas is not necessarily someone that they would associate with an environmental sensibility. Following Judith Butler (2021), do you think we need to read Levinas against himself or appropriate his ethics for situations that he did not foresee or intend? Or are you finding an ecological sensibility within his work?

**Sally Wheeler***:* I think I managed to come up with a construction of his work that lets me feel that he's not excluding the environment. I am thinking of a piece that I wrote in a collection which Louis Kotzé edited where I found a way through Levinas which allowed the environment to be included (Wheeler 2017). I suspect more difficult is the inclusion of the corporation into a Levinasian schema. If you think about the people that I see as the leading Levinas scholars in this area: Campbell Jones, who is at Auckland now, Martin Parker who, I think, is at Bristol and John Roberts from Sydney (Jones, Parker, and Ten Bos 2005, 73–79), they would say that Levinas offers a condemnation of managerial derived business ethics. For them, most forms of corporate business ethics are a narcissistic ethics concerned with corporate self-presentation (Roberts 2003).

*In many ways, I agree with their position, but I do think it is possible to use Levinas for a recreation of a corporate ethics. And you do have to read Levinas against himself, I suspect, because, if the corporation is not a "true" person, and I have difficulties with some of corporate law scholarship around corporate personhood that ignores the significance of the state (Watson 2019), you might see the corporation as a type of social system; it doesn't have a body, doesn't have a face, it doesn't have feelings but it has assets.*

*What a corporation does have is history, it has actions, it has a presence. Whether we think of that as being personhood or not, I think Levinas does allow us to look at abstract entities. I don't think an encounter in Levinasian terms necessarily has to be an encounter between living beings as we might understand that. I think we can extend this to the corporation, and we have to because we need something that pushes us back beyond the start of the aggregation of corporate power. Levinas' work is the only way to do this.*

*My problem with saying, "the corporation is an abstraction," it can't become a "hostage of the other," is that you are ignoring the realities of power and aggregation of power. You are then just looking at corporate managers without understanding that actually the most significant people within the corporation are its shareholders. It is the relationship with shareholders and reshaping and reinvigorating of shareholder responsibility we should be looking at (Bottomley 2021). We need to see the corporation in those terms in order to be able to tackle it in any meaningful sense.*

**Peter Burdon**: In putting that argument forward are you also asking a corporation who wants to have this identity as a legal person and the benefits that come with that to take that responsibility seriously? Or do you think that affirms the notion of personhood too much?

**Sally Wheeler**: So, one of the things I find fascinating about corporations at the moment is the move away from being corporations listed on exchanges (Edinburgh 2020).

*One of the things that all states do, because shareholders have petitioned for and pushed for it throughout the evolution of corporate law, is offer a system of rules and regulations around public companies that includes things such as the disclosure of major shareholdings and related party transactions and the preparation and publication of accounts. The argument has always been that if you want the benefit of being able to raise capital publicly then you have to be prepared to undergo this amount of scrutiny. You need to be prepared to declare these transactions, to present an account of yourself.*

*What we see now, globally are fewer and fewer corporations going for initial public offerings (IPOs). Fewer corporations seem to want to raise capital in this way. We are also seeing existing corporations moving off the exchange and go dark (into private company mode), as it were, so that they can have the benefits of corporate personhood, without needing to fulfill the regulatory demands placed on public companies (Fidanza, Morresi, and Pezzi 2108).*

*Yesterday (5 July 2021) there was a takeover bid for Sydney airport (Wiggins 2021). Who would have thought that the share price of an airport during a pandemic in a state with closed external borders would rocket up. And one of the things that it is rumored will happen if the bid is accepted is that Sydney airport will cease to be a listed company and will immediately go dark. And the reason for that is that it will allow particular transactions to be done which the regulatory framework for public companies will not permit. I find this whole notion of personhood, its negotiation, its changing dynamics, and its gaming of public scrutiny fascinating.*

**Peter Burdon**: I want to return to your comments about indirect investors. One of the things you have explored is the possibility for indirect investors to put pressure on corporations to change their policies. This work draws Hans Jonas and deep notions of responsibility. How have you evaluated the recent wave of shareholder activism? Does it give you optimism that investors might recognize and accept responsibility for the incredible power that we have to alter, change, or to rupture the Earth system?

**Sally Wheeler**: So, I think there are two things there. There is shareholder activism around corporate profit and performance, and there is shareholder activism around recognizing our responsibility for the state of the earth (issue activism, if you like). I think these are two very different things.

*I suspect for a lot of shareholders what they worry about are risks to the value of their investment caused by shocks to the business model of their investment vehicle. What worries them is new government regulation that is going to impose costs on the company they have invested in.*

*So, for example, if the Australian Government suddenly indicated that it was considering no longer allowing fossil fuel extraction, shareholders with large exposure in those industries would become activist investors worried about falling share prices. They would start to demand that the corporations they were invested in explored a new business model ahead of that regulation – not because they have suddenly become conscious of the environmental damage caused but because they are worried about the value of their investment.*

*There are activist pension funds that adopt a position of socially responsible investment. There are others that go even further and decide to disinvest entirely in what they term "sin stocks." It is possible for activist shareholders to send messages to corporations and their executives about conduct and culture. The contours of share ownership have changed a lot over the years and despite the surface similarities of the US, UK, and Australian share markets, they are quite different (Davies 2015). The shape of the market: prevalence of block holding, prevalence of block management, and the popularity or not of investment vehicles like index tracker funds dictate how much issue activism there will be. Putting pressure on investment managers to get them to exercise proper stewardship is difficult at a time when corporate profits are supporting pension accumulation rather than state-based guarantees of retirement income.*

**Peter Burdon**: In reading your work I could not help but wonder what you think of the term "Anthropocene" as opposed to alternative names such as "Capitalocene." Does that debate have meaning for you and the work you do in this area?

**Sally Wheeler**: Framed as the "Capitalocene," it is easier to be clearer about whose responsibility this is. It is not everyone's. I think you have to recognize yawning inequalities as well. There are large numbers of people for whom the sorts of issues that we've just been talking about, activist investors, pension plans, all of those sorts of things, that is not part of their world.

*And so, while the constellation of who is in the "Capitalocene" changes all the time, I do think we have to recognize that it is fundamentally, it's a class issue for me, it is a class of people whose living, whose future living, is derived from the activities of corporations in more than simply an employment sense. Employees who have no stake other than their wage have, I think, a right to earn a living. Where else are you going to get that? You have less choice. It's about those of us who have choices. Maybe we don't realize we have choices within the "Capitalocene," but we do (Moore 2018).*

**Peter Burdon**: Can a corporation open itself to the kind of responsibility and ethics that you've been describing under the conditions of industrial capitalism? How does that conflict with the structural and legal pressures for continuous growth?

**Sally Wheeler**: I think it can. There's a movement called B Corps which I haven't really explored very much but that seems to have a potential to be something else. My economics is not good enough to work out the extent to which you can plan for constrained growth, as it were, and the extent to which you have to have growth, but I certainly think it is possible. Once you move away from saying shareholder value is all we care about, it is certainly possible to have either a cooperative form like the Mondragon system (Bamburg 2017) or a B form company that embraces much broader interests (Marquis 2020).

**Peter Burdon**: Thank you, Sally. However, we think about getting out (or living with) this mess, the corporation and the corporate form are going to be topics we are going to have to think about. Anna, you've had some time to listen to Sally, is there anything you would like to say in response or a question you'd like to pose?

**Anna Grear**: I think Sally's absolutely right to emphasize the "Capitalocene." I think there's quite a lot of convincing analysis of the Anthropocene that really does demonstrate the disproportionate effect of small classes of people and corporate actors (Moore 2016; Malm 2016).

*And I think some of the statistics about climate change entirely back up what Sally's saying here about the disproportionate nature of corporate impact, and I guess also it's important to think of corporations, in a sense, as cloaking devices: Sally's language of "going dark" fits with a broader reading of the corporate form as a cloaking device for the acquisition of power by certain groups of people – which has always been the case (Grear 2015).*

*And if you think about the role of early transnational corporations in the colonial imperial endeavors of the European powers (McLean 2004), and you think about the actions of the British East India Company in India, and things like that, the corporation in a sense has always been a cloaking device for the accumulation of largely, let's call it Global North now (in the conditions of neoliberalism/advanced capitalism), but Global North power over resources: the power to collect and accumulate massive amounts of economic and material power at the expense of a whole series of groups of people who are constructed as somehow being "other" or marginal. And that operation of predatory power is justified by certain legal doctrines and discourses that imply a kind of neutrality, a kind of legitimacy (Gill 2002).*

*So, I think what Sally saying is absolutely spot on actually, though I'm not an expert in corporate law.*

*I'm just wondering, Sally, whether you think there's any mileage in thinking of the corporation as an assemblage. We were talking there about problems with personating them, and how we want to think of corporate persons as a subject for certain purposes, particularly for the purpose of responsibilization – but we were also talking about structural logics, structural complexities, individual motivations, class motivations, material arrangements of power, and so on. I'm just wondering if it helps if we think of a corporation as fundamentally non-unitary – even the simplest form of corporation as being a fundamentally non-unitary thing, as being something more dynamic, more assemblage-like with, you know, different energies and different flows and blockages and assumptions and contestations going on.*

*Do you think that would be useful, Sally?*

**Sally Wheeler**: Yeah, you know I think that is really useful. I've often thought of them in the past as kind of vehicular ideal, you know, they're an object for us to be able to sort of go around and pick up this and pick up that, and you know I mean these days it's not only assets, it's IP as well. We constantly register patents that might actually be green, for example, to stop other people from using them.

*But I like that idea of an assemblage because I do see them as sort of porous networks, and people move in and out, resources move in and out, they constantly sort of change shape.*

*The whole idea of capital to me is quite like water, you know, it's if you have an old house then you'll know what I mean, you know sort of it pours with rain and water will flow in the strangest places, but it always finds its way in and it always merges down to the lowest possible level and the easiest pathway through.*

*And I think of sort of corporations as sort of molding and weaving even. They're sort of constantly switching between sort of probing privately held, publicly held, back to being privately held again, that just constant changing in form.*

**Anna Grear**: Absolutely. They have this kind of morphogenic capacity don't they – that individual embodied human beings don't have. One of the things that I was struck by is the way in which corporations can effortlessly relocate themselves across jurisdictional boundaries by the trick of law, leaving behind the infrastructure, and whatever it is that they don't need or want or are driven away from. Whereas, at the same time, we're seeing an age of climate crisis with mass movements of people whose bodies are pressed against fences and borders and walls (Marshall 2018; Brown 2010; Sassen 2014). The contrast between those two forms of embodiment, corporate and human to me is really stark and problematic, and for me, there's something about that contrast that really brings to a head the advantages of the corporation and the fact that we absolutely do need to reimagine it. We do need to find ways to respond to its complexity and to respond to it's "slipperiness" (Grear 2014; Blanco and Grear 2019).

**Sally Wheeler**: I really like your contrast of people pressed up against fences and physical boundaries, but also, you know electronic boundaries as well, and yet the corporation can sort of slip and slide and just overcome, roll over all of those.

**Anna Grear**: It's very problematic.

**Peter Burdon**: Anna we've already been discussing the possibility of reading thinkers like Levinas against himself to bring nature and matter into focus, but your writing on the Anthropocene engages a different set of conversation partners, so perhaps for someone who's unfamiliar, what is new materialism?

**Anna Grear**: It kind of depends who you ask in one sense, because it's best, I think, to think of new materialisms in the plural, and to recognize that the field is incredibly lively, heterogeneous, and unsettled (Quiroga-Villamarín 2020). I actually really welcome that, because I think that it is dynamic. It's productively open. I love the energy and the lack of settlement. I love the lack of orthodoxy.

*That said, I think there are some broad generalizations that give a kind of broad brush understanding of the inflections, if you like, of new materialist thinking, and central to it, I would say (and forgive me any new materialists reading this who would disagree), is an attentiveness to matter and to processes of materialization. New materialisms are both post-humanist and post-anthropocentric, but I think there are some new materialist thinkers that would really resist the label "post-humanist" precisely because it still has the human-humanist center as a kind of implied referent, even though it's a "post-relation." I've heard Donna Haraway say something similar on this point.*

*So, I think the most telling inflection of the new materialisms is this passionate attention to matter itself, and to these processes of materialization (Coole and Frost 2010), and to questions of how matter itself, as forms of liveliness that are meaning-generating entanglements that have, as Jane Bennett might put it, "an intransigence of their own," come to matter (Bennett 2010). These processes are not reducible to a blank inert field upon which human activity and the action of humans will takes place. I guess one natural question to ask of new materialisms would be, "well okay so what's new about new materialisms? What's their relationship with the older materialisms, for example, such as Marxism?"*

*Jane Bennett, for example, doesn't reject the older materialisms, but she argues that they neglected attentiveness to the agentic significance of matter itself. So, Bennett is bringing in a post-anthropocentric supplement to the older materialisms. Karen Barad goes a bit further because she points to an important difference in their ontology of matter. It's probably best to quote her. She says in her book Meeting the Universe Halfway that "matter is not little bits of nature or a blank slate surface or site passively awaiting significations, nor is it an uncontested ground for scientific feminist or Marxist theories. Matter is not immutable or passive, nor is it a fixed support, location, referent or source of sustainability for discourse" (Barad 2006, 25).*

*So, Barad's driving there at an ontological significance of matter, a matter that is irreducible. It's not just this inert Cartesian slate as is so often assumed by various discourses. She's driving at the way in which many critical theories have not engaged seriously with the significance of matter itself. They've rightly criticized naive or representationalistic accounts of matters that operate as if power didn't matter, and that, of course, is a hugely significant contribution. New materialism doesn't reject that contribution, but it's just saying "hey, we've missed something." We need to re-attend to the liveliness and the significance of what's here.*

*And the other thing that's new about new materialist thought, I think, is its science-inspired energy, the aspects of new materialisms that draw on new insights in biology and in quantum physics. For example, Barad's work draws strongly on quantum physics. And so, in a way, new materialism a contemporary science-informed, highly reflective, energetic, passionate engagement with why, where, and how matter materializes, comes to matter, and matters for questions right across the disciplines concerning the most fundamental questions of how we live together on this planet – in the mess "we" are all in as what Haraway might call "kin" (Haraway 2015).*

*And I think that new materialist thinking ties in strongly in a sense with what Sally was saying about the environmental questions that hang around the dominance of corporate form:* if we're going to get this kind of shift that Sally's talking about and drawing on Levinas and Jonas for, I would argue that one fundamental thing we need to do is to reimagine the material itself. We actually have to reconsider the whole question of what it means to be a human being as a material being in a material world.

**Peter Burdon**: In contrast to older forms of materialism, are you highlighting the agency of matter and the decentering of human subject?

**Anna Grear**: Yes, I think new materialism gives materiality a far greater liveliness of its own, and one of the most important insights I think is the meaning-making capacity of matter, what Donna Haraway calls, I think she calls it, materio-semiotics, or the other way around – I can't quite remember now (Haraway 2016a).

*But new materialist thinking definitely moves away from the idea of the human as central, so the human is not the sole beneficiary. The notion of "the environment" (and we are using it here quite loosely in this conversation) but it's a problematic term for me, because to think in terms of "the environment" is inherently to objectify and reduce to an environ, a surround, something far more lively – to think as if there's a separate human at the center and that there is also that which circles around the human. Timothy Luke wrote a piece where he did a Foucauldian genealogical analysis of the term "environment," where he argues that "to environ" is to surround: it's a circular policing move, a kind of an embattling move where you encircle a ground for governance, where you bring discourses of power and control to bear on something (Luke 1995). I think the really important insight here from the new materialisms is that they explode that subject–object relationality, and change subject–object relations into contingent relations that are drawn in particular circumstances for particular reasons but do not imply some prior ontological hierarchy or priority between that thing that's designated as a subject and that which is designated as an object. In contrast, in environmental law and environmental approaches generally, as you rightly say, the human is still assumed to be a certain thing and the environment is still assumed kind of to be "out there" – that which is merely the objectified context for the subject.*

**Sally Wheeler**: You kind of have to do that in order to be able to exert any sort of influence over the corporate and any sort of influence over those actors that are operating within and around the corporate because you have to sort of see, I suppose, the environment as a commons, you have to see it as something that everybody needs, everybody shares, that is something that cannot be captured by the corporation so it's more of, it's operating in opposition, if you like, to the corporation, which is why I kind of see it in that sort of surrounded flat sense.

**Anna Grear**: Yeah, I think, often in law, we do need to construct those kind of relations in order to get at things normatively. And I think the problem though is with the ontology. The environment is construed as being just a screen or an object. I think it's quite possible to build a notion of corporate responsibility toward the environment as lively sites of agency, as lively sites of different kinds of subjectivity: animals' subjectivity – and other different forms of liveliness. And I think this challenge comes down to this fundamental question of ontology and how we construct even the term "environment." We could spend three hours discussing what that means: deconstructing it, pulling out different dimensions and elements of it. So, I think, yes, we do have to simplify and we do have to categorize in order to have meaningful juridical ways of dealing with things, and Sally you're implying that in a sense, the environment's being used as a force that pushes back to press limits on corporate activity, by saying the environment is something we value. And you know that's one powerful political discursive and potentially legal move, but it doesn't catch fully what we refer to when we talk about the environment, and it doesn't exhaust meanings of that liveliness. It's purely strategic and I think you're absolutely right: we do need these strategic choices, and I think that Barad's work also implies that those choices (including the identification of subject and object) are strategic: they're not ontologically final. Such approaches don't posit an ultimate separation between the corporation and its environment. There is a sense in which the environment is also agentic for the corporation: for example, the material conditions in which people work have influences on their bodies, perhaps then influencing local corporate policy, for example.

*It comes back to what you were saying when you asked the question: how do you build this responsibility and said "you look at the local." To me, that's speaking the language of the emergent. That's the language of encounter with what's on the ground, and it demands a closer attention to who and what is there and in which ways it matters and/or comes to matter.*

*And so, this question of responsibility has this lively entangled assemblage-like quality that needs to be engaged with, picked apart, understood, but from a very respectful on-the-ground kind of position, where one is learning from materiality itself rather than simply imposing human concepts and constructs on it. To me, this is a very important part of the whole picture, alongside Indigenous cosmovisions, which I think Western law really, really needs to take seriously and to learn from.*

**Peter Burdon**: When you were describing new materialism, you noted a critique of various kinds of splits which are deep in our culture and are embedded in our law such as subject/object, nature/culture, and obviously I think feminist theory and feminist legal theory has done that kind of splitting down of those dualisms for a very long time. Do you want to talk about the relationship between new materialism and feminist theory as well?

**Anna Grear**: Well, yeah, obviously feminist theory pays great attention to embodiment, materiality, and so on. I think there are some new materialists that might feel that some feminist theory still sticks with quite a discursive reading of things like embodiment and that that approach is too constructivist, and isn't adequately attentive to materiality itself, but rather as a field for significations of political critique, which I think is partly what that quote from Barad was driving at.

*But what's interesting is that a lot of new materialists (the leading ones) are women. I hope I'm not doing the "canon" an injustice! I know there's Manuel DeLanda, a powerful new materialist thinker, but a lot of the leading figures are women, which I find really interesting and actually, not only are they women, they're feminist women.*

*In a sense, I guess you could see new materialism in their hands as a more radical development of materialist feminism. It's a post-anthropocentric feminist move, in a sense. That might sound overly reductive to some, but I think it's not an illegitimate inflection to bring when you actually examine some of the theories. For example, Stacey Alaimo's work is overtly feminist. She criticizes what she calls toxic masculinity in relation to climate toxicity, and draws very clear links between those dynamics (Alaimo 2010). And I think it's very hard to read Donna Haraway without understanding that she is a passionate feminist, for example.*

**Peter Burdon**: Completely agree. On a different topic, you have written about law having an imaginary or set of dominant ideas. What does it mean to say that law's imaginary is disembodied or to borrow a phrase from Nicole Graham (2011), physicalized?

**Anna Grear**: For me, that has hinged on the kind of centrality to law of a certain kind of rationality that has been assumed, which broadly draws from Descartes and then on Kantian approaches to the idea of the disembodied human moral subject, the moral reasoner (Halewood 1996).

*Obviously, we can link those philosophical positions to things like the rational contractor, or the paradigmatic rational landowning citizen-subject and so on and so forth. So, for a long time, I think, in law there's been this assumed central subject, which is identifiable by its exclusions and marginalizations:* this subject at the center is a bit like a photographic negative, and the more that you peel away its "others" (women, people of color, nomads, etc., etc.), the more you peel away all those "others" who throughout social history have fought for their rights and resisted their sense of marginalization, of being controlled by particular elite class, the more you press at that, the more that what emerges in the center – and which is clearly privileged – is a construct of a white European, masculinist, property-owning, rational, civilized subject.

*This is the master knower with the view from nowhere, disembodied in the Cartesian sense – separated even from its own body. The mind, the thinking thing (res cogitans) is sheared off from res extensa. We know that the body is part of res extensa, and this separation produces this panoptic, all-knowing subject. This subject is not unique to law. It has existed for a long time in science too, and in politics and economics. There has been a lot of contestation in critical theory of that subject, and of its limitations and its implications for the structuration and mediation of power. I read the corporation as its apotheosis (Grear 2015). I think that the corporation is the perfect instantiation of law's disembodied subject: it has qualities that align with law's central subject in a way that human beings simply can't. Corporations to me are the paradigmatic legal actor. And so that's what I'm driving at when I talk about the disembodied imaginary of law.*

*And, of course, to separate the mind from the body and to separate mind from everything else is in a sense to produce materiality as a surface laid bare to the rational operation of this thinking and acting thing. I think law selectively uses dematerialization and disembodiment. I mean one of the problems of controlling the corporate form is that there is a sense in which juridically, it is also disembodied. It has a capacity to dematerialize and rematerialize in ways that corporeal individual human bodies simply do not possess and never have possessed. And so, for me, that's the problematic. And given the centrality of that subject to law's imaginary, I honestly think that we cannot move law into a more life-giving direction without de-centering that subject and re-inhabiting law's imaginary with multiple forms of liveliness and with questions about equalities and diversities and multiplicity, including the idea of embracing multiple ontologies and multiple epistemologies in a way that shifts away from any kind of center to a much more a-centric conversation (Grear 2020). This is not to deny what Sally is saying about the need to keep searching for forms and theories of responsibility and responsibilization and accountability. We have to do that, and we have to do it more realistically. If science is showing us that matter is not what law has assumed it is, and if agency is not what law assumes it is in relation to matter, then it's an injustice not to attend – to the best of our knowledge – to what's really there and how things really interact to produce outcomes (or what we think of as outcomes) because an outcome is really just a temporal lock, isn't it? It's a moment where we say "that's an outcome." But unless we can attend to those things more astutely, more closely – to attend to the ways in which our practices matter in every sense of that word – then I think that law's imaginary will continue to produce radical injustice on a colossal scale as it currently does, particularly in the conditions of late capitalism, advanced capitalism, neoliberalism, whatever you want to call it.*

**Peter Burdon**: Sally is there anything you would like to add here?

**Sally Wheeler**: I suppose I kind of find it difficult to divorce myself from the sort of very embedded interests that you get within the corporation, and also, you know, there are plenty of things that a corporation is and can do that, obviously no form of matter can have, and a person can't have, I mean this whole notion of perpetual succession. And you know we're supposed to sort of think of the corporation as being as having perpetual succession, the same time as we think of it as a person, but you know nothing has immortality so that, I think, is quite interesting when we set those two things alongside each other.

*In many ways, I think our analysis, what we can do with the corporation, or the corporate form, are hamstrung by those very early analyses which tried to find some sort of place for it. We tried to find a way of cloaking that power and put it in the form of personhood. I think has stood in the way of so many meaningful analyses of what it is the corporation is, and how we approach it, and what we can do with it.*

**Anna Grear**: Absolutely.

**Peter Burdon**: Anna you've just given us a really clear description of our current legal imaginary, and you started talking as well about how it might change. You've written about how it's not just a cognitive argument you're trying to make. The shift in the legal imaginary requires openness as well. Do you want to talk about the role of emotion and how you, how we, change legal imaginary at an effective level?

**Anna Grear**: I think that's a really interesting question that raises lots of complexities, and I'm not sure I really have an answer to it at this point, Pete. It's something that I'm thinking through. When I talk about affect, I don't just mean the emotional. I think I mean something a little bit broader, but I think one way that we can do this is by moving in a trans-disciplinary direction as scholars. I think trans-disciplinarity is going to be hugely important and that there is a whole world of "law-and" conversations. I don't know if you've seen that *Routledge Handbook of Law and Theory* (Philippopoulos-Mihalopoulos 2019) that Andreas Philippopoulos-Mihalopoulos has recently edited that shows how legal theorists are getting to grips with such a wide range of imaginative ideas. I'm particularly excited by the idea of the arts in relation to law, there are artists who are beginning to explore law through forms of art. I also know lawyers who are beginning to work in the arts: Andreas, for example, as a standout case of someone who's moving into a performative arts practice alongside his legal theorization. I think what that cross-engagement does is to allow for unpredictable intuition-led sparks of theoretical insight to arise. I can't remember it now, but I recently wrote an article about – you might remember better than me – about sympoietic normativities, which is something I drew from Haraway's notion of sympoiesis (Grear 2020). I started to think very briefly – and it's work I want to do – I haven't really even started it properly – about how normativity might be sympoietic. Normativity could be co-produced on the ground in commons collectives and other forms of community, which would involve a multiplicity of different forms of practice, including potentially arts-based practices. In Bristol, for example, there's a group of people who are using arts-based practice to engage in a ritual of climate mourning. Now these things open up people's imaginations. And it seems to me that when we're talking about reimagining the corporate form and we're talking about reimagining how law sets up "reality", imaginative breakthroughs can give people the "aha" moment that allows for that intuitive shift that enables them to move from the cognitive structures that they've always assumed are somehow immutable into different possibilities. Yes, it can be intrinsically destabilizing but it's also a wonderful thing, because it actually opens up the possibility for much, much more exciting, unexpected discoveries.

*So, for me, I would say that, yes, it's vitally important to move away from this disembodied rationalistic conception of the human and to think of the human as an embodied assemblage full of complex communities. I mean, we're full of microbiota and viruses and bacteria:* even the thing we take to be the human is not what we have taken it to be. We are porously open. We are a multiplicity. We are a multiplicity psychically, let alone physiologically: the sense of self is really an illusion produced by the brain in little instances over time. There isn't this thing called "I" that is as stable as we have taken ourselves to be. Now, somehow, we need to learn to come into contact with these actualities and live with them in ways that are intrinsically open, intrinsically humble, and that build the capacity to be an unthreatened self. We have to learn to confront what we think of as difference and to be unfazed by it, to be able to stay in the space, to "stay with the trouble," too, as Haraway puts it, and to see others, including non-human others, as "kin" (Haraway 2016b).

*Beginning new practices of kin-making to me seems an important direction for legal theorists to be thinking in. I don't yet know what that would mean in juridical practice. I don't have a formed sense of that. What I do have a sense of I think, is that this kind of approach would absolutely dethrone the idea of any Promethean top-down global aspirations for control. This kind of sympoietic formation and re-formation enables the idea of law as a generative form – or forms – of facilitation of multiple, grounded communities, which don't have to be the same, which don't have to have the same values, but which would, I suspect, need to live their respect for their material world in ways that would in the end, allow that world to flourish, not least because their own self-interest would be entirely wrapped up with that flourishing – including flourishing set down at that local level (bearing in mind that the local is never separate from the "non-local" in any ontological sense).*

*So, I think we have to get to grips with complexity. We have to analyze at meta-, meso-, and micro-levels. We have to find new forms of practice that allow humans to actually experience and inhabit different ways of being and living that then feed back into governance structures, and feed back into the kinds of aspirations we have for law and for politics. So that's my best answer. It's probably just ramblings.*

**Peter Burdon**: I love that. You develop this line of argument through an idea called "sympoietic normativities." Here is a quote from a recent article of yours: "These normativities can arise out of non-human working groups in a wide range of situated endeavours in commons based grassroots initiative expanded to embrace commoners who are more than simply human" (Grear 2020). Part of what I'm hearing from you is the possibilities that emerge from different material contexts. This is a theme on old materialism, and it strikes me as relevant to current attempts to break down the kinds of dualism and dichotomies that law currently holds as being so sacred.

**Anna Grear**: Yeah. I think it also makes room for the unexpected, which I think is a great thing. I think law's interesting in this respect because it's got to have – you know I can only speak as a common lawyer – an interest in holding onto the past because of the need for settled principles and consistency, some notion of predictability and fairness. You can't just switch out expectations on people, so there has to be some systemic sense of faithfulness to what's gone before, and a reasonable way of allowing for change in a way that allows people to govern their behaviors and to predict legal outcomes. Yet, law is also future-facing, in the sense that it does attempt to respond to social change: it has an evolutive character, mediated through judicial reasoning and legislatures attempting to grapple with new problems. And, in fact, law's got the tools for sometimes surprisingly rapid evolution: a brand-new precedent can overturn a whole line of doctrine, which sometimes happens, and then you get surprising shifts. So law's got the capacity for adaptive change.

*The problem, I think – or some of the problems – lie in the consolidation of power, the question of who has access to control the legal system. And there is the related problem of the ontological and epistemic closure of the system in the sense that the liberal legal system very much relies on Eurocentric assumptions about the world. On that framing, to think about Indigenous law is to make a merely cultural concession rather than to acknowledge that here is an equal ontology and an epistemology and rationality that we need to respect as another rationality. And that's not good enough. I think we actually need to move to a multiple-world notion away from a "one world" notion (Escobar 2015), and I think law has the capacity to mediate that intelligently, provided that we explode assumptions about privilege, power, and the class interests that law in the West at least, and in neoliberalism, predominantly exists to serve. And this point brings us right back to what Sally was saying, that the questions of corporate parent and everything else are fundamentally protecting class-based interests.*

**Peter Burdon**: When you started talking, you said one of the things that attracts you to new materialism is its lack of settlement and its lack of orthodoxy. And yet, as Sally has also noted, when we are talking about law there is pressure to stay with the fixed, stable, and certain. As humans better understand our status as subjects and place alongside matter, does the role of law also change?

**Anna Grear**: I think it inevitably would. This is not a subject I've got so far along the line with thinking through at the moment, but you would still need a responsibility-constructing legal capacity, because you can't be naive about the world. The "trouble" is here to stay. There will always be people with motivations that are destructive. There will always be people who are appropriative and predatory and so on – and systems and structures that are appropriative and potentially predatory would need engaging with. So it's not as if you're saying, "oh look we're all holding hands in the field: law is going to emerge from some pretty little game of agreement that we have." It's far removed from that. However, I think for me one shift would be toward a more facilitative concept whereby local communities and initiatives are given more autonomy or given (perhaps autonomy is the wrong word) space in which to explore what they can become. Those spaces, need to be legally protected from authoritarian controls that might otherwise seek to subvert their energies back into the priorities of the existing dominant system. At one level, this aspiration seems naive, because capitalism (and neoliberalism in particular) always manages to reinvent itself in the guise of its critiques and always manages to, as Sally said, seep through into the lowest basement levels. So, you would need some ongoing critical engagement and you would need some ongoing awareness, but I think it is important to at least *think* about these questions, and to start engaging in this way. I also think that if you've got more facilitated space for autonomous communities, you would need a more conversational mediative structure whereby these communities could also cross-engage. That might be digital, it might be achieved in another way. I don't know. I don't really have the answers at this point. These are kind of questions that I would want to press in on and I'm very excited to see how many younger legal scholars are really running with post-humanist legal theory and new materialist legal theory now. It's very exciting. There's an explosion of it – and it's really necessary. I think it's a moment when we absolutely have to think much, much more imaginatively.

**Peter Burdon**: I also hear you extending an invitation for people to think along these lines as well.

**Anna Grear**: Oh totally. I think not just an invitation. I actually think it is crucial that we start thinking along these lines.

**Peter Burdon**: One last question Anna. In the literature on the Anthropocene, there is a subset of writers who present a very masculine response to new materialism (Hamilton 2017). This response underlines centrality of human beings to ethics and law. It also argues that new materialism deflates human power, inflates the agency of non-human matter, and/or denies that matter has subjectivity of agency. What do you make of those critiques?

**Anna Grear**: What do I make of them? Well, I first want to say "Covid-19" to all those who think that the non-human has no ability to control humans to a significant extent. I know that's a cheap point. I think it's a misunderstanding of new materialism to think that it can't account for the power of human action, or for the history of human action. I think that's a misreading of the flat ontology of new materialism.

*New materialism distributes agency. It doesn't reduce agency all to one and the same thing, and it doesn't, by decentering the human, ignore the fact that humans also have specific endowments that may or may not coincide with specific endowments of non-human animals, or of other forms of materiality. New materialism just challenges this latent need to keep banging on about the uniqueness, the specialness, the hierarchical superiority of the human.*

*That position doesn't make questions of responsibility impossible; it makes them more complex, and is also more empirically faithful to the complexity of what's there. New materialism moves away from reductionist characterizations and it problematizes notions of Promethean human agency, the Zeus-like figure (as Bennett has recently described it) at the center and which "controls" the world. The Anthropocene can't entirely be read as a demonstration of human centrality either, because the Anthropocene can also be read as the planet pushing back. There's an agentic force in the planetary itself which we can't afford to overlook. We can't afford to assume that the planet is this inert thing that humans came in and messed up and now we've got ourselves in a bit of a tangle. We actually have to think about the forces of the planetary itself and their significance, their agentic significance for how we need to think (Connolly 2017). And if we think we can control the planet in this Anthropocene moment, I think that's an old masculinist fantasy. New materialism isn't really about control, and control is not an obsession within new materialism. Control, to me, is an inherently masculinist obsession. New materialism is more interested in how we account for the ways in which our practices matter and come to matter in the light of these new insights that we have about the nature of matter and processes of materialization, in full understanding of older materialisms, critical theories, and so on. A central question is: how do we face the uniquely challenging moment that we're in together, not just the human species, but as the whole planetary community? How do we face this challenging predicament as kin, in ways that roll back the destructive material implications and outworkings of those tired old masculinist assumptions of human centrality and agency?*

*This is not to call for a naive return to everyone sitting in circles in fields. Alaimo is very clear that we need science as a kind of prosthesis even adequately to understand the self in this new configuration of forces (Alaimo 2010). It is a call for a thoroughly future-facing, complexity-embracing new level of human humility and for an engagement with systemic complexity at all levels up and down.*

*And it really does push away the old fantasy, the old egoic fantasy of human exceptionalism and that, to me, is the central point in response to those arguments. The only one that I'm even vaguely familiar with, Peter, is Hamilton, and I think this language that he uses of control is really interesting because in the end it's not about purely human control:* we have to enter into responsibilized partnerships – into human-non-human working groups characterized by wisdom, not by hubris.

**Peter Burdon***:* Humility is a word you've used a few times already. That's not a bad trait Sally, I'll give you the same invitation provided to Anna. Is there anything you'd like to say, or a question you'd like to pose?

**Sally Wheeler***:* This has been a valuable talk, because it has made me reflect on some of my assumptions about law, about what law can do, about what law will do, and the whole relation in which we stand. And around a sort of the values framework that we put around are the demands we make of law, so it made me reflect on all of those.

## Note

1 Thank you to Lilly Deluca for transcribing this interview.

## References


Alaimo, S. 2010. *Bodily Natures: Science, Environment and the Material Self.* Bloomington, IN: Indiana University Press.

Bamburg, Jill. 2017. "Mondragon through a Critical Lens," *Employee Ownership News*. https://medium.com/fifty-by-fifty/mondragon-through-a-critical-lens-b29de8c6049.

Barad, K. 2006. "Posthuman Performativity: Towards an Understanding of How Matter Comes to Matter," in *Belief, Bodies and Being: Feminist Reflections on Embodiment*, edited by D. Orr, L. López McAllister, E. Karl and K. Earle, 11–36. New York: Rowman and Littlefield.

Bennett, J. 2010. *Vibrant Matter: A Political Ecology of Things*. Durham, NC: Duke University Press.

Berg, Florian, Koelbel, Julian, and Rigobon, Roberto. 2020. "Aggregate Confusion: The Divergence of ESG Ratings." http://dx.doi.org/10.2139/ssrn.3438533.

Bick, Rachel, Halsey, Erika, and Ekenga, Christine. 2018. "The Global Injustice of Fast Fashion," *Environmental Health: A Global Access Science Source* 17(1): 92–96.

Blanco, E. and Grear, A. 2019. "Personhood, Jurisdiction and Injustice: Law, Colonialities and the Global Order," *Journal of Human Rights and the Environment* 10(1): 86–117.

Bottomley, Stephen. 2021. *The Responsible Shareholder*. Cheltenham: Edward Elgar.

Brown, W. 2010. *Walled States, Waning Sovereignty*. New York: Zone Books.

Buttler, J. 2021. *The Force of Nonviolence: An Ethico-Political Bind*. New York: Verso.

Connolly, W. 2017. *Facing the Planetary: Entangled Humanism and the Politics of Swarming*. Durham, NC: Duke University Press.

Coole, D. and Frost, S. 2010. *New Materialisms: Agency, Ontology, Politics*. Durham, NC: Duke University Press.

Cowan, Dave and Wheeler, Sally. 2015. "The Reach of Human Rights," in *Property and Human Rights in a Global Context*, edited by Jean Allain and Ting Xu, 197–221. Oxford: Hart Publishing.

Crutzen, Paul J. 2002. "Geology of Mankind," *Nature* 415(6867): 23.

Davies, Paul. 2015. "Shareholders in the United Kingdom," in *Research Handbook on Shareholder Power*, edited by Randall Thomas and Jennifer Hill, 355–382. Cheltenham: Edward Elgar.

Edinburgh Business School. 2020. "Factors Influencing the Decline in the Number of Public Companies in the UK." Accessible at https://www.appcgg.co.uk/wp-content/uploads/2020/12/APPCGG-202-report-Edinburgh.pdf.

Escobar, A. 2015. "Commons in the Pluriverse," in *Patterns of Commoning*, edited by D. Bollier and S. Helfrich, 348–360. Amherst, MA: The Commons Strategies Group.

Fidanza, Barbara, Morresi, Ottorino, and Pezzi, Alberto. 2018. *The Decision to Delist from the Stock Market*. Switzerland: Springer Nature.

Ford, T. H. 2018. "The Romanthropocene," *Literature Compass* 15(5): 1–13.

Gill, S. 2002. "Constitutionalizing Inequality and the Clash of Globalizations," *International Studies Review* 4(2): 47–65.

Graham, N. 2011. *Lawscape Property, Environment, Law*. London: Routledge.

Grear, A. 2014. "Towards 'Climate Justice'? A Critical Reflection on Legal Subjectivity and Climate Injustice: Warning Signals, Patterned Hierarchies, Directions for Future Law and Policy," *Journal of Human Rights and the Environment*: 103–133 https://doi.org/10.4337/jhre.2014.02.08.

Grear, A. 2015. "Deconstructing *Anthropos*: A Critical Legal Reflection on 'Anthropocentric' Law and Anthropocene 'Humanity'," *Law and Critique* 26(3): 225–249.

Grear, A. 2020. "Legal Imaginaries and the Anthropocene: 'Of' and 'For'," *Law and Critique* Special Issue: 'Laws for the Anthropocene' 31(3): 351–366.

Halewood, P. 1996. "Law's Bodies: Disembodiment and the Structure of Liberal Property Rights," *Iowa Law Review* 81: 1331–1393.

Hamilton, C. 2017. *Defiant Earth: The Fate of Humans in the Anthropocene*. Sydney: Allen & Unwin.

Haraway, D. J. 2015. "Anthropocene, Capitalocene, Plantationocene, Chthulucene: Making Kin," *Environmental Humanities* 6(1): 159–165.

Haraway, D. J. 2016a. *Manifestly Haraway*. Minneapolis, MN: University of Minnesota Press.

Haraway, D. J. 2016b. *Staying with the Trouble: Making Kin in the Chthulucene*. Durham, NC and London: Duke University Press.

Jones, Campbell, Parker, Martin, and Ten Bos, Rene. 2005. *For Business Ethics*. Abingdon: Routledge.

Karamali, Eleni. 2007. "Has the Guest Arrived Yet? Emmanuel Levinas, a Stranger in Business Ethics," *Business Ethics: A European Review* 16(3): 313–321.

Langley, Paul and Leaver, Adam. 2012. "Remaking Retirement Investors," *Journal of Cultural Economy* 5(4): 473–488.

Levinas, Emmanuel. 1985. *Ethics and Infinity – Conversations with Philippe Nemo*. Pittsburgh, PA: Duquense University Press.

Luke, T.W. 1995. "On Environmentality: Geopower and Eco-knowledge in the Discourse of Contemporary Environmentalism," *Cultural Critique* 31: 57–81.

Malm, A. 2016. *Fossil Capital: The Rise of Steam Power and the Roots of Global Warming*. London: Verso.

Marquis, Christopher. 2020. *How the B Corp Movement Is Remaking Capitalism*. New Haven, CT: Yale University Press.

Marshall, T. 2018. *The Age of Walls: How Barriers Between Nations Are Changing Our World*. New York: Scribner.

McLean, J. 2004. "The Transnational Corporation in History: Lessons for Today?" *Indiana Law Journal* 79: 363–377.

Mentz, S. 2017. "The Neologismcene" [Blog post]. Available at http://arcade.stanford.edu/blogs/neologismcene (Date of Last Access. 1st September 2021).

Moore, Jason. 2018. "The Capitalocene Part II: Accumulation by Appropriation and the Centrality of Unpaid Work/Energy," *The Journal of Peasant Studies* 44(3): 594–630.

Moore, J. W. 2016. *Anthropocene or Capitalocene? Nature, History, and the Crisis of Capitalism*. Oakland, CA: PM Press.

Niinimäki, Kirsi, Peters, Greg, Dahlbo, Helena, Perry, Patsy, Rissanen, Timo and Gwilt, Alison. 2020. "The Environmental Price of Fast Fashion," *Nature Reviews* 1: 189–200.

Philippopoulos-Mihalopoulos, A. 2019. *Routledge Handbook of Law and Theory*. Abingdon: Routledge.

Quiroga-Villamarín, D. R. 2020. "Domains of Objects, Rituals of Truth: Mapping Intersections between International Legal History and the New Materialisms," *International Politics Reviews* 8(2): 129–151.

Roberts, John. 2003. "The Manufacture of Corporate Social Responsibility: Constructing Corporate Sensibility," *Organization* 10(2): 249–265.

Sassen, S. 2014. *Expulsions: Brutality and Complexity in the Global Economy*. Cambridge, MA: Harvard University Press.

Shapiro, Alex. 2018. "Toward a Stewardship Framework of CSR: Levinas and Multinational Responses to Climate Change," in *CSR and Climate Change Implications for Multinational Enterprise*, edited by John R. McIntyre, Silvester Ivanaj and Vera Ivanaj, 96–118. Cheltenham: Edward Elgar.

Watson, Susan. 2019. "The Corporate Legal Person," *Journal of Corporate Law Studies* 19(1): 137–166.

Wheeler, Sally. 2017. "The Corporation and the Anthropocene," in *Law and the Anthropocene*, edited by Louis Kotze, 289–307. Oxford: Hart Publishing.

Wiggins, Jenny. 2021. "Big Super Lobs $22b for Nation's Biggest Airport," *Australian Financial Review*, July 5, 2021. https://www.afr.com/companies/infrastructure/sydney-airport-caught-up-in-global-m-and-a-boom-20210705-p586v6.

Young, Iris Marion. 2006. "Responsibility and Global Justice: A Social Connection Model," *Social Philosophy and Policy* 23(1): 102–130.

Young, Iris Marion. 2011. *Responsibility for Justice*. Oxford: Oxford University Press.

# INDEX

**Page numbers in **bold** reference tables.

Kolibri 360 GmbH
Ferdinand-Jühlke-Straße 7
99095 Erfurt, Deutschland
produktsicherheit@kolibri360.de